W9-CJD-066

Chief Modern Poets of England and America

THE MACMILLAN COMPANY
NEW YORK · BOSTON · CHICAGO · DALLAS
ATLANTA · SAN FRANCISCO
MACMILLAN AND CO., Limited
LONDON · BOMBAY · CALCUTTA · MADRAS
MELBOURNE
THE MACMILLAN COMPANY
OF CANADA, Limited
TORONTO

CHIEF MODERN POETS

OF ENGLAND & AMERICA

SELECTED AND EDITED BY

Gerald DeWitt Sanders and John Herbert Nelson

THIRD EDITION

New York · The Macmillan Company

1944

Published January, 1943
Reprinted January, 1944

PRINTED IN THE UNITED STATES OF AMERICA

Preface

According to an old anecdote, Charles Lamb, speaking of someone to a friend, once said: "I hate that man." "Why, I didn't think you knew him," his friend replied. "I don't," said Lamb; "I never hate anyone I know." The primary aim of this book is to present, in such a way that students may come to know and like them, the chief poets writing in English in this century. To this end, each is represented by a sufficient proportion of his work to permit a reader to gain an intelligent understanding of his ideas and methods and to make a just estimate of his achievement. To give a comprehensive idea of the period, moreover, a few others are included who, although of somewhat less significance, require consideration because of their influence or of their position in some important movement; and one poet is added who though of a former time belongs to this age because of the exigency of late publication and his contemporary influence. For each poet a biographical sketch, giving all pertinent available information about him, is included; the date of first book publication of each poem is noted at the end of the poem (when two dates occur, the first is that of composition); and, at the end of the book, a complete list of his poetical works is given, as well as a selected list of critical references.

The British and American authors are grouped separately; in each main division the poets are presented in the order of their birth, and the poems of each author are arranged in the order of publication. In the very few instances when an excerpt from a long poem is given, the fact is noted, and no excerpt is included which is not complete in itself. When an author has not supplied a title for a poem, the editors have used the first line as the title and have placed it in square brackets. When an author himself uses the first line as a title, his practice in the use of quotation marks is followed. The text in general is that of the latest edition of a poet's work, although in a few instances, when an earlier version seems superior, the original version is retained.

G. D. S.
J. H. N.

December, 1942

Acknowledgments

The appreciative thanks of the editors are tendered to the following publishers and individuals, who have generously consented to the reprinting of the material indicated, which they control as holders of the copyright, as authorized publishers, or both:

D. Appleton and Company, New York: For "The Comet of Going-to-the-Sun" from *Going-to-the-Sun* (copyright 1923), and "Rain" and "Nancy Hanks, Mother of Abraham Lincoln" from *Going-to-the-Stars* (copyright 1926) by Vachel Lindsay.

Jonathan Cape, Ltd., London: For "The Worms' Contempt" and "Life" from *The Loneliest Mountain and Other Poems* by W. H. Davies.

Chatto and Windus, London: For selections from *The Earth for Sale* by Harold Monro.

The Clarendon Press, Oxford: For "I Never Shall Love the Snow Again" from *The Shorter Poems of Robert Bridges*, 1931.

Walter de la Mare, Esq.: "Forests," "Lucy," and "A Robin" from *The Fleeting* (copyright 1933) by Walter de la Mare are reprinted by permission of the author and with the consent of the publisher, Alfred A. Knopf, Inc., New York.

Doubleday, Doran & Company, Inc., New York: "The Last Chantey" from *Collected Verse of Rudyard Kipling* (copyright 1907, 1935); "When Earth's Last Picture Is Painted" from *The Seven Seas*, by Rudyard Kipling (copyright 1892, 1920); "The Ballad of East and West," "Tomlinson," "Danny Deever," "Gunga Din," and "Mandalay" from *Departmental Ditties and Barrack-Room Ballads*, by Rudyard Kipling (copyright 1892, 1893, 1899, 1927); "The Dykes" and "Recessional" from *The Five Nations*, by Rudyard Kipling, (copyright 1903, 1931); and "If" from *Rewards and Fairies*, by Rudyard Kipling (copyright 1910, 1938), are reprinted by permission of Doubleday, Doran and Company, Inc.

Duell, Sloan & Pearce, Inc., New York: Sonnets I and XV from *And in the Human Heart* by Conrad Aiken; "if you can't eat you got to," "a pretty a day," "as freedom is a breakfastfood," "anyone lived in a pretty how town," "my father moved through dooms of love," "love is the every only god," and "i am so glad and very" from 50 *Poems* by E. E. Cummings; and "America Was Promises" from *America Was Promises* by Archibald MacLeish are reprinted by permission of the publishers, Duell, Sloan & Pearce, Inc.

E. P. Dutton and Company, Inc., New York: The selections from *The Old Huntsman, Counter-Attack*, and *Picture-Show* by Siegfried Sassoon, and the sentence from Axel Munthe's *Story of San Michele*, quoted in the footnote on page 23, are used by permission of E. P. Dutton and Co., Inc., New York.

T. S. Eliot, Esq.: The poems of T. S. Eliot, from *Collected Poems: 1909-1935*, are reprinted by permission of the author.

Farrar & Rinehart, Inc., New York: "Canto XXI" from *A Draft of XXX Cantos* by Ezra Pound is reprinted by permission of Farrar & Rinehart, Inc., Publishers.

John Gould Fletcher, Esq.: For "The Caged Eagle" from *Visions of the Evening* (copyright 1913), "A Woman in Winter Costume," "Changing Love," and "Evening Sky" from *Japanese Prints* (copyright 1918), "Down the Mississippi" from *Breakers and Granite* (copyright 1921), and "Lost Corner," and the footnote on p. 697 by John Gould Fletcher.

The Four Seas Company, Boston: For "Morning Song of Senlin" and "Wind in the Old Trees" from *The Charnel Rose* (copyright 1918) and "Portrait of One Dead" and "Palimpsest" from *The House of Dust* (copyright 1920) by Conrad Aiken; and "A Woman Standing by a Gate with an Umbrella," "A Life," "Mutability," and "Fugitive Beauty" from *Japanese Prints* (copyright 1918) by John Gould Fletcher.

Harcourt, Brace and Company, Inc., New York: "All in Green Went My Love Riding," "The Hours Rise Up," "When God Lets My Body Be," and "In Just-Spring When" from *Collected Poems* by E. E. Cummings (copyright 1923, 1925, 1931, 1935, 1938, by E. E. Cummings); selections from *Secrets* by W. H. Davies; selections from *Poems 1909-1925* by T. S. Eliot and *Collected Poems of T. S. Eliot* (copyright 1936, by Harcourt, Brace and Co., Inc.); selections from *Poems: 1930-1940* by Horace Gregory (copyright 1941, by Horace Gregory); and selections from *Smoke and Steel* (copyright 1920, by Harcourt, Brace and Howe), *Slabs of the Sunburnt West* (copyright 1922, by Harcourt, Brace and Co., Inc.), *Good Morning, America* (copyright 1928, by Carl Sandburg), and *The People, Yes* (copyright 1936, by Harcourt, Brace and Co., Inc.) by Carl Sandburg are reprinted by permission of Harcourt, Brace and Company, Inc.

HARPER AND BROTHERS, New York: For the selections from *Collected Poems, Second Series* by W. H. Davies; for "Renascence," "God's World," and "Thou Art Not Lovelier Than Lilacs" from *Renascence and Other Poems*, published by Harper & Brothers (copyright 1917 by Edna St. Vincent Millay), "The Philosopher" and "Oh, Think Not I am Faithful to a Vow" from *A Few Figs from Thistles*, published by Harper & Brothers (copyright 1922 by Edna St. Vincent Millay), "Elegy Before Death" and "Song of a Second April" from *Second April*, published by Harper & Brothers (copyright 1921 by Edna St. Vincent Millay), "I Know I Am but Summer to Your Heart" and "Euclid Alone Has Looked on Beauty Bare" from *The Harp Weaver and Other Poems*, published by Harper & Brothers (copyright 1920, 1921, 1922, 1923 by Edna St. Vincent Millay), "The Anguish" and "To Jesus on His Birthday" from *The Buck in the Snow*, published by Harper & Brothers (copyright 1928 by Edna St. Vincent Millay), "On the Wide Heath" and "My Spirit Sore from Marching" from *Wine from These Grapes*, published by Harper & Brothers (copyright 1934 by Edna St. Vincent Millay), and Sonnets XI and XXX from *Fatal Interview*, published by Harper & Brothers (copyright 1931 by Edna St. Vincent Millay), by Edna St. Vincent Millay; and for the selections from *The Heart's Journey* by Siegfried Sassoon.

HENRY HOLT AND COMPANY, New York: For selections from *Collected Poems, Down-adown-Derry, Memory and Other Poems, Motley and Other Poems, The Veil and Other Poems, Peacock Pie,* and *Poems for Children* by Walter de la Mare; from *A Boy's Will, North of Boston, Mountain Interval, New Hampshire, West-Running Brook,* and *A Further Range* by Robert Frost; from *Last Poems* by A. E. Housman; and from *Chicago Poems* and *Cornhuskers* by Carl Sandburg.

HOUGHTON MIFFLIN COMPANY, Boston: The selections from *Irradiations—Sand and Spray* and *Goblins and Pagodas* by John Gould Fletcher; from *Sword Blades and Poppy Seeds, Men, Women and Ghosts, Pictures of the Floating World, Legends, What's O'Clock, East Wind,* and *Ballads for Sale* by Amy Lowell; and from *Poems 1924-1933* by Archibald MacLeish are used by permission of, and by arrangement with, Houghton Mifflin Company.

A. E. HOUSMAN: "Ho, Everyone That Thirsteth" and "For my Funeral" are used by permission of the estate of the late A. E. Housman.

RUDYARD KIPLING: For "The Dykes" and "Recessional" from *The Five Nations*; "The Last Chantey" and "When Earth's Last Picture Is Painted" from *The Seven Seas*; "The Ballad of East and West," "Danny Deever," "Gunga Din," "Mandalay," and "Tomlinson" from *Barrack Room Ballads*; and "If" from *Rewards and*

Fairies by Rudyard Kipling, to the executrix of the estate of Rudyard Kipling.

ALFRED A. KNOPF, INC., New York: Selections from *October and Other Poems* by Robert Bridges; *Collected Poems, First Series*, by W. H. Davies; *The Fleeting* by Walter de la Mare; *More Poems* by A. E. Housman; *Collected Poems* by Elinor Wylie; and *Chills and Fever* and *Two Gentlemen in Bonds* by John Crowe Ransom are reprinted by permission of and special arrangement with Alfred A. Knopf, Inc., authorized publishers.

HORACE LIVERIGHT, INC., New York: For selections from *Priapus and the Pool and Other Poems* by Conrad Aiken; from *Collected Poems* by H. D.; and from *Personae* by Ezra Pound.

LIVERIGHT PUBLISHING CORPORATION, New York: For "Nobody Loses All the Time," "It is So Long Since," and "If I Have Made, My Lady" from *Is Five* by E. E. Cummings; and the selections from *Collected Poems* by Hart Crane.

THE MACMILLAN COMPANY, New York: For selections from *The Tree of Life* (copyright 1918) and *Breakers and Granite* (copyright 1921) by John Gould Fletcher; from *The Stonefolds* (copyright 1907), *Daily Bread* (copyright 1912), *Fires* (copyright 1912), *Borderlands and Thoroughfares* (copyright 1914), *Battle* (copyright 1915), *Livelihood* (copyright 1917), *Hill-Tracks* (copyright 1918), *Neighbors* (copyright 1920), *I Heard a Sailor* (copyright 1925), *Hazards* (copyright 1930), and *Islands* (copyright 1932) by Wilfrid Gibson; from *Wessex Poems* (copyright 1898), *Poems of the Past and Present* (copyright 1902), *Time's Laughingstocks* (copyright 1909), *Satires of Circumstance* (copyright 1914), *Moments of Vision* (copyright 1917), *Late Lyrics and Earlier* (copyright 1922), *Human Shows—Far Phantasies* (copyright 1925), and *Winter Words in Various Moods and Metres* (copyright 1928 by Florence E. Hardy and Sydney E. Cockerell) by Thomas Hardy; from *The Last Blackbird* (copyright 1907) and *Poems* (copyright 1917) by Ralph Hodgson; from *General William Booth Enters into Heaven* (copyright 1913), *The Congo* (copyright 1914), *The Chinese Nightingale* (copyright 1917), *The Golden Whales of California* (copyright 1920), and *Collected Poems* (copyright 1913, 1914, 1916, 1917, 1919, 1920, 1923, 1925) by Vachel Lindsay; from *Salt Water Ballads* (copyright 1902), *The Story of a Roundhouse and Other Poems* (copyright 1912), *Dauber* (copyright 1913), *Reynard the Fox* (copyright 1919), *Enslaved and Other Poems* (copyright 1920), and *Collected Poems* (copyright 1912, 1913, and 1914 by The Macmillan Company, and 1916, 1919, 1920, 1921, 1922, 1923, and 1925 by John Masefield) by John Masefield; from *Spoon River Anthology* (copyright 1915, 1916), *Songs and Satires* (copyright 1916), *The Great Valley* (copyright 1916), *Toward the Gulf* (copyright 1918), *Starved*

Rock (copyright 1919), *Lee: A Dramatic Poem* (copyright 1926), and *Invisible Landscapes* (copyright 1935) by Edgar Lee Masters; from *Real Property* (copyright 1922) by Harold Monro; from *Captain Craig* (copyright 1902) *The Man Against the Sky* (copyright 1916), *The Three Taverns* (copyright 1920), *Avon's Harvest* (copyright 1921), *Dionysus in Doubt* (copyright 1925), and *Collected Poems* (copyright 1916, 1917, 1920, 1921) by Edwin Arlington Robinson; from *Homeward, Songs by the Way* (copyright 1894), *The Earth Breath* (copyright 1897), *The Divine Vision* (copyright 1904), *Voices of the Stones* (copyright 1925), *Collected Poems* (copyright 1913, 1919, 1926), *Vale and Other Poems* (copyright 1931), and *The House of the Titans* and Other Poems (copyright 1934), by A. E. (G. W. Russell); from *Insurrections* (copyright 1909), *The Hill of Vision* (copyright 1912), *The Rocky Road to Dublin* (copyright 1915), *Songs from the Clay* (copyright 1915), *Reincarnations* (copyright 1918), and *Collected Poems* (copyright 1909, 1912, 1915, 1918, 1925, 1926) by James Stephens; from *Helen of Troy* (copyright 1911), *Rivers to the Sea* (copyright 1915), *Love Songs* (copyright 1917), *Flame and Shadow* (copyright 1920), *Dark of the Moon* (copyright 1926), and *Strange Victory* (copyright 1933) by Sara Teasdale; from *In the Seven Woods* (copyright 1903), *The Green Helmet and Other Poems* (copyright 1912), *Responsibilities and Other Poems* (copyright 1916), *Lyric Poems* (copyright 1916), *The Wild Swans at Coole* (copyright 1917), *Later Poems* (copyright 1922), *Early Poems and Stories* (copyright 1925), *The Tower* (copyright 1928), *The Winding Stair and Other Poems* (copyright 1933), *Collected Poems* (copyright 1933), and *Last Poems and Plays* (copyright 1940) by W. B. Yeats; and for quotations used in the biographical sketches of W. B. Yeats and A. E., and in footnotes quoted from *Autobiographies* (copyright 1916) and *The Tower* (copyright 1928), by W. B. Yeats, *Collected Poems* (copyright 1926) by A. E., and *Song and Its Fountains* (copyright 1932) by A. E.

EDGAR LEE MASTERS, ESQ., For the selections from *Songs and Satires*, *Spoon River Anthology*, *The Great Valley*, *Toward the Gulf*, *Starved Rock*, *New Spoon River*, *Lee: A Dramatic Poem*, *Gettysburg Manila Acoma*, and *Invisible Landscapes*.

MRS. HAROLD MONRO: For selections from *Collected Poems* by Harold Monro.

JOHN MURRAY, London: For selections from *Poetical Works* by Robert Bridges.

OXFORD UNIVERSITY PRESS, New York: The selections from *Poems of Gerard Manley Hopkins* by Gerard Manley Hopkins are used by permission of Oxford University Press, New York.

THE POETRY BOOKSHOP, London: For selections from *Children of Love* and *Strange Meetings* by Harold Monro.

RANDOM HOUSE, New York: Selections from *Poems, On This Island, Journey to a War, Letters from Iceland, Another Time,* and *The Double Man* by W. H. Auden; *Collected Poems of Kenneth Fearing* by Kenneth Fearing; *Roan Stallion, Tamar and Other Poems, Cawdor and Other Poems, Thurso's Landing and Other Poems, Give Your Heart to the Hawks, Solstice, Such Counsels You Gave to Me,* and *Be Angry at the Sun* by Robinson Jeffers; *Poems* and *Overtures to Death* by C. Day Lewis; *Poems 1925-1940* by Louis MacNeice; and *Poems* and *The Still Centre* by Stephen Spender are reprinted by permission of Random House, Inc.

SIEGFRIED SASSOON, ESQ.: For selections from *The Road to Ruin* and *Vigils* by Siegfried Sassoon.

CHARLES SCRIBNER'S SONS, New York: For selections from *Selected Poems* and *Preludes for Memnon* by Conrad Aiken; and from *The Children of the Night* and *The Town Down the River* by E. A. Robinson.

FREDERICK A. STOKES COMPANY, New York: For "The Barrel-Organ" (copyright 1906), "Forty Singing Seamen" (copyright 1906), "The Highwayman" (copyright 1906), and "Song—Let Not Love Go Too" from *Drake* (copyright 1909), from *Collected Poems,* Volume I; "Seven Wise Men" from *A Coiner of Angels* (copyright 1913), from *Collected Poems,* Volume II; and "The Silver Crook" (copyright 1920), from *Collected Poems,* Volume III, by Alfred Noyes.

THE VIKING PRESS, INC., New York: For "On Reading the War Diary of a Defunct Ambassador" and "An Old World Effect" from *Satirical Poems* (copyright 1926) and "It Was the Love of Life," "December Stillness," and "Vigils" from *Vigils* (copyright 1936) by Siegfried Sassoon.

For counsel, advice, information, and aid of other kinds we are indebted to many different persons, but we should like especially to record our thanks to the following: Professors Philo Buck of the University of Wisconsin, Oscar Cargill of New York University, Charles W. Everett of Columbia University, Walter H. French of Cornell University, Millett Henshaw of St. Louis University, Glenn Hughes of the University of Washington, William S. Johnson of the University of Kansas, John Francis McDermott of Washington University, A. M. Mizener of Wells College, John Henry Owens of the Michigan State Normal College, Sidney F. Pattison of the University of Arizona, the late Martin W. Sampson of Cornell University, Kendall B. Taft of the Central Y. M. C. A. College, Chicago, and Lois Whitney of Vassar College; Mrs. Amy Carson Middleton, Mrs. Kathryn Nelson, Mrs. Florence Elizabeth Sanders, and Miss Dorothy E. Wilson; Messrs. W. H. Auden, Conrad Aiken, Walter de la Mare, T. S. Eliot, John Gould Fletcher, Wilfrid Gibson, Edgar Lee Masters, Siegfried Sassoon, James Stephens, and the late A. E. Housman, G. W. Russell, and W. B. Yeats.

Contents

ENGLISH AND IRISH POETS

AMERICAN POETS

The *English*
and
Irish Poets

Thomas Hardy

Thomas Hardy was born June 2, 1840, in the hamlet of Higher Bockhampton, three miles from Dorchester, in a house which he described as "low, but rambling and spacious, with a paddock and large stablings." His parents were Thomas and Jemima Hand Hardy, of whose four children—Thomas, Henry, Mary, and Katherine—he was the eldest. His father, a small landowner, and by trade a builder and master-mason, traced his descent from a bailiff of the island of Jersey, one Clement le Hardy, whose son John settled in Dorsetshire in the fifteenth century. His mother came of a long line of English yeomanry.

He was too frail to enter school until he was eight, but under the instruction of his mother he could read by the time he could walk. His precocity is shown by his ability in very early childhood to read such works as Johnson's *Rasselas* and Dryden's translation of the *Aeneid*. His formal training began at the village school at Bockhampton, but the next year he was transferred to a Dorchester day-school, which he attended until he was fifteen. After this, he studied French with a governess, and later, when living in London, he attended evening classes in French at King's College for one or two terms. His formal training ended here, but for some years, working alone or with a friend, he continued the study of Greek, Latin, and French.

Hardy's early predilection was for the Church, but when John Hicks, a Dorchester architect, offered to take him as a pupil, he accepted the offer without any expression of regret at the change of plans, and began the study of architecture. The term of his apprenticeship to Hicks was six years, from 1856 to 1862, and on its completion he left Dorchester for London to begin the practice of his profession. He soon found employment with Arthur Blomfield, a designer and restorer of churches, in whose offices he worked for five years until poor health forced him to leave London. Returning to Dorchester, he worked for Hicks and for Hicks's successor, until 1873, when he abandoned the profession of architecture.

During the years of his apprenticeship, Hardy began to write verse, and one of his poems and some prose sketches relating to architecture were published in a Dorchester paper; but as his work absorbed him, he gave up writing until 1865, when he again began to write verse. The poems, which he now submitted to magazines, were all returned, however, and reluctantly he concluded that if he wished a literary career, he would have to write prose. His first attempt at fiction was a social novel, *The Poor Man and the Lady*, but after it was rejected by two or three publishers he was discouraged from further attempts to dispose of it. One who read the manuscript, however, was George Meredith, who advised Hardy to write another novel with more plot. Following this suggestion, he wrote *Desperate Remedies*, but it was also rejected by several publishers before the firm of Tinsley Brothers accepted it on condition that Hardy advance £75 to insure the Company against loss. While waiting for this novel to be published, he wrote *Under the Greenwood Tree*, but adverse reviews of *Desperate Remedies* and one or two rejections of the new work had almost decided him against further attempts at writing when Tinsley Brothers requested another story. He submitted *Under the Greenwood Tree*, which upon publication won the praise of several critics. Subsequently he wrote *A Pair of Blue Eyes* for serial publication in *Tinsley's Magazine*, and *Far from the Madding Crowd* for the *Cornhill Magazine*, at the request of its editor, Leslie Stephen. From this time he applied himself diligently to the writing of fiction, and during the next twenty years he published eleven novels and three volumes of short stories. The appearance of *Jude the Obscure* (1895) evoked such a storm of criticism, however, that he determined to write no more fiction, but to devote the rest of his life to poetry, which had always been his first interest. Actually, he had never stopped writing poetry, but except for an occasional ballad he published no verse until the appearance of *Wessex Poems* in 1898. After this date, however, except for an occasional article and a volume of short stories, he published only poetry, his total output amounting to ten volumes, of which eight were lyric and two dramatic poetry. Of the latter, *The Queen of Cornwall* is a one-act play for mummers; the other, *The Dynasts*, a monumental work dealing with the Napoleonic wars, is usually considered his greatest single creation.

Hardy was twice married. In 1870, while working on plans for the restoration of St. Juliot Church, Cornwall, he met Emma Lavinia Gifford, daughter of a Plymouth solicitor, and sister-in-law of the rector of St. Juliot; and they were married on September 17, 1874. After a honeymoon on the Continent, they lived for a few months each in turn at Surbiton, London, Swanage, and Yeovil, then for longer periods each at Sturminster Newton, London, Wimborne, and Dorchester. Finally, Hardy bought a small plot of ground a mile from Dorchester, on which he built Max Gate, a house he designed himself. He moved to his new home in 1885, and there he spent the rest of his life, leaving only for a few months each year in London or for an occasional holiday on the Continent or at some seaside place. On November 27, 1912, his wife died; and on February 11, 1914, he married his secretary, Florence Emily Dugdale, an author of children's books.

In outward circumstance Hardy's life appears to have been a reasonably happy one, and the ironical occurrences and tragic happenings so prominent in his works seem to have been the product of an intellectual attitude towards life rather than a sublimation of personal experience. He was never wealthy, but at no time in his life was he in want; his parents and brother and sisters, to whom he was greatly attached, all lived to an advanced age; although he had frail health in childhood, severe headaches in his youth, and a critical illness in 1880, he was active and on the whole enjoyed good health throughout his long life; and although his novels, and sometimes his poetry, were condemned for their social and religious views, and he felt that his philosophy was often misinterpreted, he never lacked staunch friends and advocates. In his latter years he was the recipient of numerous honors: the Order of Merit (1910); the Gold Medal of the Royal Society of Literature (1912); an honorary fellowship in Magdalene College, Cambridge (1913), and in Queen's College, Oxford (1923); and honorary degrees from several universities—Aberdeen (LL.D., 1905), Cambridge (D.Litt., 1913), Oxford (D.Litt., 1920), St. Andrews (LL.D., 1922), and Bristol (D.Litt., 1925).

He died at Max Gate on January 11, 1928. His heart was removed and placed in the grave of his first wife at Stinsford

Church, and his body was cremated and the ashes buried in the Poets' Corner in Westminster Abbey.

Because Hardy dealt so often in his novels and poems with ironical turns of fortune, critics generally classed him as a pessimist. But perhaps the best statement of his position is his own explanation in the "Apology" with which he prefaced his volume, *Late Lyrics and Earlier:*

> While I am quite aware that a thinker is not expected . . . to state all that crosses his mind concerning existence in this universe, in his attempts to explain or excuse the presence of evil and the incongruity of penalizing the irresponsible, it must be obvious to open intelligences that . . . such disallowance of "obstinate questionings" and "blank misgivings" tends to a paralyzed intellectual stalemate. . . . And what is today, in allusions to the present author's pages, alleged to be "pessimism" is, in truth, only such "questionings" in the exploration of reality, and is the first step towards the soul's betterment, and the body's also.
>
> If I may be forgiven for quoting my own old words, let me repeat what I printed in this relation more than twenty years ago . . . :
>
> If way to the Better there be, it exacts a full look at the Worst:
>
> that is to say, by the exploration of reality, and its frank recognition stage by stage along the survey, with an eye to the best consummation possible: briefly, evolutionary meliorism. But it is called pessimism nevertheless; . . . and the subject is charitably left to decent silence, as if further comment were needless.
>
> Happily there are some who feel such Levitical passing-by to be, alas, by no means a permanent dismissal of the matter; that comment on where the world stands is very much the reverse of needless in these disordered years of our prematurely afflicted century: that amendment and not madness lies that way. And looking down the future these few hold fast to the same: that whether the human and kindred animal races survive till the exhaustion or destruction of the globe, or whether these races perish . . . pain to all upon it, tongued or dumb, shall be kept down to a minimum by loving-kindness, operating through scientific knowledge, and actuated by the modicum of free will conjecturally possessed by organic life when the mighty necessitating forces—unconscious or other—that have "the balancings of the clouds," happen to be in equilibrium, which may or may not be often.

HAP

If but some vengeful god would call to me
From up the sky, and laugh: "Thou suffering thing,
Know that thy sorrow is my ecstasy,
That thy love's loss is my hate's profiting!"
Then would I bear it, clench myself, and die,
Steeled by the sense of ire unmerited;
Half-eased in that a Powerfuller than I
Had willed and meted me the tears I shed.

But not so. How arrives it joy lies slain,
And why unblooms the best hope ever sown?
—Crass Casualty obstructs the sun and rain,
And dicing Time for gladness casts a moan. . . .
These purblind Doomsters had as readily strown
Blisses about my pilgrimage as pain.

1866, 1898

NEUTRAL TONES

We stood by a pond that winter day,
And the sun was white, as though chidden of God,
And a few leaves lay on the starving sod;
    —They had fallen from an ash, and were gray.

Your eyes on me were as eyes that rove
Over tedious riddles of years ago;
And some words played between us to and fro
    On which lost the more by our love.

The smile on your mouth was the deadest thing
Alive enough to have strength to die;
And a grin of bitterness swept thereby
    Like an ominous bird a-wing. . . .

Since then, keen lessons that love deceives,
And wrings with wrong, have shaped to me
Your face, and the God-curst sun, and a tree,
    And a pond edged with grayish leaves.

1867, 1898

THE IMPERCIPIENT

(AT A CATHEDRAL SERVICE)

That with this bright believing band
I have no claim to be,
That faiths by which my comrades stand
Seem fantasies to me,
And mirage-mists their Shining Land,
Is a strange destiny.

Why thus my soul should be consigned
To infelicity,
Why always I must feel as blind
To sights my brethren see,
Why joys they've found I cannot find,
Abides a mystery.

Since heart of mine knows not that ease
Which they know; since it be
That He who breathes All's Well to these
Breathes no All's-Well to me,
My lack might move their sympathies
And Christian charity!

I am like a gazer who should mark
An inland company
Standing upfingered, with, "Hark! hark!
The glorious distant sea!"
And feel, "Alas, 'tis but yon dark
And wind-swept pine to me!"

Yet I would bear my shortcomings
With meet tranquillity,
But for the charge that blessed things
I'd liefer not have be.
O doth a bird deprived of wings
Go earth-bound wilfully!

* * * * *

Enough. As yet disquiet clings
About us. Rest shall we.

1898

TO LIFE

O Life with the sad seared face,
I weary of seeing thee,
And thy draggled cloak, and thy hobbling pace,
And thy too-forced pleasantry!

I know what thou would'st tell
Of Death, Time, Destiny—
I have known it long, and know, too, well
What it all means for me.

But canst thou not array
Thyself in rare disguise,
And feign like truth, for one mad day,
That Earth is Paradise?

I'll tune me to the mood,
And mumm with thee till eve;
And maybe what as interlude
I feign, I shall believe!

1902

THE SUBALTERNS

"Poor wanderer," said the leaden sky,
"I fain would lighten thee,
But there are laws in force on high
Which say it must not be."

—"I would not freeze thee, shorn one," cried
The North, "knew I but how
To warm my breath, to slack my stride;
But I am ruled as thou."

—"Tomorrow I attack thee, wight,"
Said Sickness. "Yet I swear
I bear thy little ark no spite,
But am bid enter there."

—"Come hither, Son," I heard Death say;
"I did not will a grave
Should end thy pilgrimage today,
But I, too, am a slave!"

We smiled upon each other then,
And life to me had less
Of that fell look it wore ere when
They owned their passiveness.

1902

BY THE EARTH'S CORPSE

"O Lord, why grievest Thou?—
Since Life has ceased to be
Upon this globe, now cold
As lunar land and sea,
And humankind, and fowl, and fur
Are gone eternally,
All is the same to Thee as ere
They knew mortality."

"O Time," replied the Lord,
"Thou readest me ill, I ween;
Were all *the same*, I should not grieve
At that late earthly scene,
Now blestly past—though planned by me
With interest close and keen!—
Nay, nay: things now are *not* the same
As they have earlier been.

"Written indelibly
On my eternal mind
Are all the wrongs endured
By Earth's poor patient kind,
Which my too oft unconscious hand
Let enter undesigned.
No god can cancel deeds foredone,
Or thy old coils unwind!

"As when, in Noë's days,
I whelmed the plains with sea,
So at this last, when flesh
And herb but fossils be,
And, all extinct, their piteous dust
Revolves obliviously,
That I made Earth, and life, and man,
It still repenteth me!"

1902

MUTE OPINION

I traversed a dominion
Whose spokesmen spake out strong
Their purpose and opinion
Through pulpit, press, and song.
I scarce had means to note there
A large-eyed few, and dumb,
Who thought not as those thought there
That stirred the heat and hum.

When, grown a Shade, beholding
That land in lifetime trode,
To learn if its unfolding
Fulfilled its clamored code,
I saw, in web unbroken,
Its history outwrought
Not as the loud had spoken,
But as the mute had thought.

1902

"I NEED NOT GO"

I need not go
Through sleet and snow
To where I know
She waits for me;
She will tarry me there
Till I find it fair,
And have time to spare
From company.

When I've overgot
The world somewhat,
When things cost not
Such stress and strain,
Is soon enough
By cypress sough
To tell my Love
I am come again.

And if some day,
When none cries nay,
I still delay
To seek her side
(Though ample measure
Of fitting leisure
Await my pleasure),
She will not chide.

What—not upbraid me
That I delayed me,
Nor ask what stayed me
So long? Ah, no!—
New cares may claim me,
New loves inflame me,
She will not blame me,
But suffer it so.

1902

HIS IMMORTALITY

I saw a dead man's finer part
Shining within each faithful heart
Of those bereft. Then said I: "This must be
His immortality."

I looked there as the seasons wore,
And still his soul continuously bore
A life in theirs. But less its shine excelled
Than when I first beheld.

His fellow-yearsmen passed, and then
In later hearts I looked for him again;
And found him—shrunk, alas! into a thin
And spectral mannikin.

Lastly I ask—now old and chill—
If aught of him remain unperished still;
And find, in me alone, a feeble spark,
Dying amid the dark.

1899, 1902

THE LAST CHRYSANTHEMUM

Why should this flower delay so long
To show its tremulous plumes?
Now is the time of plaintive robin-song,
When flowers are in their tombs.

Through the slow summer, when the sun
Called to each frond and whorl
That all he could for flowers was being done,
Why did it not uncurl?

It must have felt that fervid call
Although it took no heed,
Waking but now, when leaves like corpses fall,
And saps all retrocede.

Too late its beauty, lonely thing,
The season's shine is spent,
Nothing remains for it but shivering
In tempests turbulent.

Had it a reason for delay,
Dreaming in witlessness
That for a bloom so delicately gay
Winter would stay its stress?

—I talk as if the thing were born
With sense to work its mind;
Yet it is but one mask of many worn
By the Great Face behind.

1902

THE DARKLING THRUSH

I leant upon a coppice gate
When Frost was spectre-gray,
And Winter's dregs made desolate
The weakening eye of day.

The tangled bine-stems scored the sky
    Like strings of broken lyres,
And all mankind that haunted nigh
    Had sought their household fires.

The land's sharp features seemed to be
    The Century's corpse outleant,
His crypt the cloudy canopy,
    The wind his death-lament.
The ancient pulse of germ and birth
    Was shrunken hard and dry,
And every spirit upon earth
    Seemed fervorless as I.

At once a voice arose among
    The bleak twigs overhead
In a full-hearted evensong
    Of joy illimited;
An aged thrush, frail, gaunt, and small,
    In blast-beruffled plume,
Had chosen thus to fling his soul
    Upon the growing gloom.

So little cause for carolings
    Of such ecstatic sound
Was written on terrestrial things
    Afar or nigh around,
That I could think there trembled through
    His happy good-night air
Some blessed Hope, whereof he knew
    And I was unaware.

Dec. 1900, 1902

THE DAME OF ATHELHALL

"Dear! Shall I see thy face," she said,
    "In one brief hour?
And away with thee from a loveless bed
To a far-off sun, to a vine-wrapt bower,
And be thine own unseparated,
    And challenge the world's white glower?"

She quickened her feet, and met him where
    They had predesigned:
And they clasped, and mounted, and cleft the air
Upon whirling wheels; till the will to bind
Her life with his made the moments there
    Efface the years behind.

Miles slid, and the port uprose to view
    As they sped on;
When slipping its bond the bracelet flew
From her fondled arm. Replaced anon,
Its cameo of the abjured one drew
    Her musings thereupon.

The gaud with his image once had been
    A gift from him:
And so it was that its carving keen
Refurbished memories wearing dim,
Which set in her soul a twinge of teen,
    And a tear on her lashes' brim.

"I may not go!" she at length outspake,
    "Thoughts call me back—
I would still lose all for your dear, true sake;
My heart is thine, friend! But my track
Home, home to Athelhall I must take
    To hinder household wrack!"

He was wroth. And they parted, weak and wan;
    And he left the shore;
His ship diminished, was low, was gone;
And she heard in the waves as the daytide wore,
And read in the leer of the sun that shone,
    That they parted for evermore.

She homed as she came, at the dip of eve
    On Athel Coomb
Regaining the Hall she had sworn to leave.
The house was soundless as a tomb,
And she stole to her chamber, there to grieve
    Lone, kneeling, in the gloom.

From the lawn without rose her husband's voice
To one his friend:
"Another her Love, another my choice,
Her going is good. Our conditions mend;
In a change of mates we shall both rejoice;
I hoped that it thus might end!

"A quick divorce; she will make him hers,
And I wed mine.
So Time rights all things in long, long years—
Or rather she, by her bold design!
I admire a woman no balk deters:
She has blessed my life, in fine.

"I shall build new rooms for my new true bride,
Let the bygone be:
By now, no doubt, she has crossed the tide
With the man to her mind. Far happier she
In some warm vineland by his side
Than ever she was with me."

1902

IN TENEBRIS

II

Considerabam ad dexteram, et videbam; et non erat qui cognosceret me. . . . Non est qui requirat animam meam.
Psalm cxlii.

When the clouds' swoln bosoms echo back the shouts of the many and strong
That things are all as they best may be, save a few to be right ere long,
And my eyes have not the vision in them to discern what to these is so clear,
The blot seems straightway in me alone; one better he were not here.

The stout upstanders say, All's well with us; ruers have nought to rue!
And what the potent say so oft, can it fail to be somewhat true?

Breezily go they, breezily come; their dust smokes around their
career,
Till I think I am one born out of due time, who has no calling
here.

Their dawns bring lusty joys, it seems; their evenings all that is
sweet;
Our times are blessed times, they cry: Life shapes it as is most
meet,
And nothing is much the matter; there are many smiles to a
tear;
Then what is the matter is I, I say. Why should such an one
be here? . . .

Let him in whose ears the low-voiced Best is killed by the
clash of the First,
Who holds that if way to the Better there be, it exacts a full
look at the Worst,
Who feels that delight is a delicate growth cramped by crook-
edness, custom, and fear,
Get him up and be gone as one shaped awry; he disturbs the
order here.

1895-96, 1902

SHUT OUT THAT MOON

Close up the casement, draw the blind,
Shut out that stealing moon,
She wears too much the guise she wore
Before our lutes were strewn
With years-deep dust, and names we read
On a white stone were hewn.

Step not out on the dew-dashed lawn
To view the Lady's Chair,
Immense Orion's glittering form,
The Less and Greater Bear:
Stay in; to such sights we were drawn
When faded ones were fair.

Brush not the bough for midnight scents
  That come forth lingeringly,
And wake the same sweet sentiments
  They breathed to you and me
When living seemed a laugh, and love
  All it was said to be.

Within the common lamp-lit room
  Prison my eyes and thought;
Let dingy details crudely loom,
  Mechanic speech be wrought:
Too fragrant was Life's early bloom,
  Too tart the fruit it brought!

1904, 1909

ON THE DEPARTURE PLATFORM

We kissed at the barrier; and passing through
She left me, and moment by moment got
Smaller and smaller, until to my view
    She was but a spot;

A wee white spot of muslin fluff
That down the diminishing platform bore
Through hustling crowds of gentle and rough
    To the carriage door.

Under the lamplight's fitful glowers,
Behind dark groups from far and near,
Whose interests were apart from ours,
    She would disappear,

Then show again, till I ceased to see
That flexible form, that nebulous white;
And she who was more than my life to me
    Had vanished quite. . . .

We have penned new plans since that fair fond day,
And in season she will appear again—
Perhaps in the same soft white array—
    But never as then!

—"And why, young man, must eternally fly
A joy you'll repeat, if you love her well?"
—O friend, nought happens twice thus; why,
I cannot tell!

1909

LET ME ENJOY

(MINOR KEY)

Let me enjoy the earth no less
Because the all-enacting Might
That fashioned forth its loveliness
Had other aims than my delight.

About my path there flits a Fair,
Who throws me not a word or sign;
I'll charm me with her ignoring air,
And laud the lips not meant for mine.

From manuscripts of moving song
Inspired by scenes and dreams unknown,
I'll pour out raptures that belong
To others, as they were my own.

And some day hence, towards Paradise
And all its blest—if such should be—
I will lift glad, afar-off eyes,
Though it contain no place for me.

1909

AT CASTERBRIDGE FAIR

THE BALLAD-SINGER

Sing, Ballad-singer, raise a hearty tune;
Make me forget that there was ever a one
I walked with in the meek light of the moon
When the day's work was done.

Rhyme, Ballad-rhymer, start a country song;
Make me forget that she whom I loved well
Swore she would love me dearly, love me long,
Then—what I cannot tell!

Sing, Ballad-singer, from your little book;
Make me forget those heart-breaks, achings, fears;
Make me forget her name, her sweet sweet look—
Make me forget her tears.

* * * * *

AFTER THE FAIR

The singers are gone from the Cornmarket-place
With their broadsheets of rhymes,
The street rings no longer in treble and bass
With their skits on the times,
And the Cross, lately thronged, is a dim naked space
That but echoes the stammering chimes.

From Clock-corner steps, as each quarter ding-dongs,
Away the folk roam
By the "Hart" and Grey's Bridge into byways and "drongs,"
Or across the ridged loam;
The younger ones shrilling the lately heard songs,
The old saying, "Would we were home."

The shy-seeming maiden so mute in the fair
Now rattles and talks,
And that one who looked the most swaggering there
Grows sad as she walks,
And she who seemed eaten by cankering care
In statuesque sturdiness stalks.

And midnight clears High Street of all but the ghosts
Of its buried burghees,
From the latest far back to those old Roman hosts
Whose remains one yet sees,
Who loved, laughed, and fought, hailed their friends, drank their toasts
At their meeting-times here, just as these!

1902, 1909

THE REMINDER

While I watch the Christmas blaze
Paint the room with ruddy rays,
Something makes my vision glide
To the frosty scene outside.

There, to reach a rotting berry,
Toils a thrush,—constrained to very
Dregs of food by sharp distress,
Taking such with thankfulness.

Why, O starving bird, when I
One day's joy would justify,
And put misery out of view,
Do you make me notice you!

1909

THE MAN HE KILLED

"Had he and I but met
By some old ancient inn,
We should have sat us down to wet
Right many a nipperkin!

"But ranged as infantry,
And staring face to face,
I shot at him as he at me,
And killed him in his place.

"I shot him dead because—
Because he was my foe,
Just so: my foe of course he was;
That's clear enough; although

"He thought he'd 'list, perhaps,
Offhand like—just as I—
Was out of work—had sold his traps—
No other reason why.

"Yes; quaint and curious war is!
You shoot a fellow down
You'd treat if met where any bar is,
Or help to half-a-crown."

1902, 1909

A PLAINT TO MAN

When you slowly emerged from the den of Time,
And gained percipience as you grew,
And fleshed you fair out of shapeless slime,

Wherefore, O Man, did there come to you
The unhappy need of creating me—
A form like your own—for praying to?

My virtue, power, utility,
Within my maker must all abide,
Since none in myself can ever be,

One thin as a phasm on a lantern-slide
Shown forth in the dark upon some dim sheet,
And by none but its showman vivified.

"Such a forced device," you may say, "is meet
For easing a loaded heart at whiles:
Man needs to conceive of a mercy-seat

Somewhere above the gloomy aisles
Of this wailful world, or he could not bear
The irk no local hope beguiles."

—But since I was framed in your first despair
The doing without me has had no play
In the minds of men when shadows scare;

And now that I dwindle day by day
Beneath the deicide eyes of seers
In a light that will not let me stay,

And to-morrow the whole of me disappears,
The truth should be told, and the fact be faced
That had best been faced in earlier years:

The fact of life with dependence placed
On the human heart's resource alone,
In brotherhood bonded close and graced

With loving-kindness fully blown,
And visioned help unsought, unknown.

1909-10, 1914

THE YEAR'S AWAKENING

How do you know that the pilgrim track
Along the belting zodiac
Swept by the sun in his seeming rounds
Is traced by now to the Fishes' bounds
And into the Ram, when weeks of cloud
Have wrapt the sky in a clammy shroud,
And never as yet a tinct of spring
Has shown in the Earth's apparelling;
  O vespering bird, how do you know,
    How do you know?

How do you know, deep underground,
Hid in your bed from sight and sound,
Without a turn in temperature,
With weather life can scarce endure,
That light has won a fraction's strength,
And day put on some moments' length,
Whereof in merest rote will come,
Weeks hence, mild airs that do not numb,
  O crocus root, how do you know,
    How do you know?

1910, 1914

THE BLINDED BIRD

So zestfully canst thou sing?
And all this indignity,
With God's consent, on thee!
Blinded ere yet a-wing
By the red-hot needle thou,[1]
I stand and wonder how
So zestfully thou canst sing!

Resenting not such wrong,
Thy grievous pain forgot,

[1] Cf. the statement by Dr. Axel Munthe in *The Story of San Michele* (p. 462): "Long before science knew anything about the localization of the various nerve-centers in the human brain, the devil had revealed to his disciple man his ghastly discovery that by stinging out the eyes of a bird with a red-hot needle the bird would sing automatically."

Eternal dark thy lot,
Groping thy whole life long,
After that stab of fire,
Enjailed in pitiless wire;
Resenting not such wrong!

Who hath charity? This bird.
Who suffereth long and is kind,
Is not provoked, though blind
And alive ensepulchred?
Who hopeth, endureth all things?
Who thinketh no evil, but sings?
Who is divine? This bird.

1917

THE OXEN

Christmas Eve, and twelve of the clock.
"Now they are all on their knees,"
An elder said as we sat in a flock
By the embers in hearthside ease.

We pictured the meek mild creatures where
They dwelt in their strawy pen,
Nor did it occur to one of us there
To doubt they were kneeling then.

So fair a fancy few would weave
In these years! Yet, I feel,
If someone said on Christmas Eve,
"Come; see the oxen kneel,

"In the lonely barton by yonder coomb
Our childhood used to know,"
I should go with him in the gloom,
Hoping it might be so.

1915, 1917

TRANSFORMATIONS

Portion of this yew
Is a man my grandsire knew,
Bosomed here at its foot:
This branch may be his wife,
A ruddy human life
Now turned to a green shoot.

These grasses must be made
Of her who often prayed,
Last century, for repose;
And the fair girl long ago
Whom I often tried to know
May be entering this rose.

So, they are not underground,
But as nerves and veins abound
In the growths of upper air,
And they feel the sun and rain,
And the energy again
That made them what they were!

1917

"FOR LIFE I HAD NEVER CARED GREATLY"

For Life I had never cared greatly,
As worth a man's while;
Peradventures unsought,
Peradventures that finished in nought,
Had kept me from youth and through manhood till lately
Unwon by its style.

In earliest years—why I know not—
I viewed it askance;
Conditions of doubt,
Conditions that leaked slowly out,
May haply have bent me to stand and to show not
Much zest for its dance.

With symphonies soft and sweet color
It courted me then,
Till evasions seemed wrong,
Till evasions gave in to its song,
And I warmed, until living aloofly loomed duller
Than life among men.

Anew I found nought to set eyes on,
When, lifting its hand,
It uncloaked a star,
Uncloaked it from fog-damps afar,
And showed its beams burning from pole to horizon
As bright as a brand.

And so, the rough highway forgetting,
I pace hill and dale
Regarding the sky,
Regarding the vision on high,
And thus re-illumed have no humor for letting
My pilgrimage fail.

1917

THE PITY OF IT

I walked in loamy Wessex lanes, afar
From rail-track and from highway, and I heard
In field and farmstead many an ancient word
Of local lineage like "Thu bist," "Er war,"
"Ich woll," "Er sholl," and by-talk similar,
Nigh as they speak who in this month's moon gird
At England's very loins, thereunto spurred
By gangs whose glory threats and slaughters are.

Then seemed a Heart crying: "Whosoever they be
At root and bottom of this, who flung this flame
Between kin folk kin tongued even as are we,
Sinister, ugly, lurid, be their fame;
May their familiars grow to shun their name,
And their brood perish everlastingly."

1915, 1917

IN TIME OF "THE BREAKING OF NATIONS"

(JEREMIAH li, 20)

Only a man harrowing clods
  In a slow silent walk
With an old horse that stumbles and nods
  Half asleep as they stalk.

Only thin smoke without flame
  From the heaps of couch-grass;
Yet this will go onward the same
  Though Dynasties pass.

Yonder a maid and her wight
  Come whispering by:
War's annals will fade into night
  Ere their story die.

1915, 1917

THE COMING OF THE END

    How it came to an end!
The meeting afar from the crowd,
And the love-looks and laughters unpenned,
The parting when much was avowed,
    How it came to an end!

    It came to an end;
Yes, the outgazing over the stream,
With the sun on each serpentine bend,
Or, later, the luring moon-gleam;
    It came to an end.

    It came to an end,
The housebuilding, furnishing, planting,
As if there were ages to spend
In welcoming, feasting, and jaunting;
    It came to an end.

    It came to an end,
That journey of one day a week:

("It always goes on," said a friend,
"Just the same in bright weathers or bleak;")
But it came to an end.

"*How* will come to an end
This orbit so smoothly begun,
Unless some convulsion attend?"
I often said. "What will be done
When it comes to an end?"

Well, it came to an end
Quite silently—stopped without jerk;
Better close no prevision could lend;
Working out as One planned it should work
Ere it came to an end.

1917

"THE CURTAINS NOW ARE DRAWN"

(SONG)

The curtains now are drawn,
And the spindrift strikes the glass,
Blown up the jaggèd pass
By the surly salt sou'-west,
And the sneering glare is gone
Behind the yonder crest,
While she sings to me:
"O the dream that thou art my Love, be it thine,
And the dream that I am thy Love, be it mine,
And death may come, but loving is divine."

I stand here in the rain,
With its smite upon her stone,
And the grasses that have grown
Over women, children, men,
And their texts that "Life is vain";
But I hear the notes as when
Once she sang to me:
"O the dream that thou art my Love, be it thine,
And the dream that I am thy Love, be it mine,
And death may come, but loving is divine."

1913, 1922

"ACCORDING TO THE MIGHTY WORKING"

When moiling seems at cease
    In the vague void of night-time,
    And heaven's wide roomage stormless
    Between the dusk and light-time,
    And fear at last is formless,
We call the allurement Peace.

Peace, this hid riot, Change,
    This revel of quick-cued mumming,
    This never truly being,
    This evermore becoming,
    This spinner's wheel onfleeing
Outside perception's range.

1917, 1922

GOING AND STAYING

The moving sun-shapes on the spray,
The sparkles where the brook was flowing,
Pink faces, plightings, moonlit May,
These were the things we wished would stay;
    But they were going.

Seasons of blankness as of snow,
The silent bleed of a world decaying,
The moan of multitudes in woe,
These were the things we wished would go;
    But they were staying.

Then we looked closelier at Time,
And saw his ghostly arms revolving
To sweep off woeful things with prime,
Things sinister with things sublime
    Alike dissolving.

1922

THE CONTRETEMPS

A forward rush by the lamp in the gloom,
And we clasped, and almost kissed;
But she was not the woman whom
I had promised to meet in the thawing brume
On that harbor-bridge; nor was I he of her tryst.

So loosening from me swift she said:
"O why, why feign to be
The one I had meant!—to whom I have sped
To fly with, being so sorrily wed!"
—'Twas thus and thus that she upbraided me.

My assignation had struck upon
Some others' like it, I found.
And her lover rose on the night anon;
And then her husband entered on
The lamplit, snowflaked, sloppiness around.

"Take her and welcome, man!" he cried:
"I wash my hands of her.
I'll find me twice as good a bride!"
—All this to me, whom he had eyed,
Plainly, as his wife's planned deliverer.

And next the lover: "Little I knew,
Madam, you had a third!
Kissing here in my very view!"
—Husband and lover then withdrew.
I let them; and I told them not they erred.

Why not? Well, there faced she and I—
Two strangers who'd kissed, or near,
Chancewise. To see stand weeping by
A woman once embraced, will try
The tension of a man the most austere.

So it began; and I was young,
She pretty, by the lamp,
As flakes came waltzing down among
The waves of her clinging hair, that hung
Heavily on her temples, dark and damp.

And there alone still stood we two;
  She one cast off for me,
Or so it seemed: while night ondrew,
Forcing a parley what should do
We twain hearts caught in one catastrophe.

In stranded souls a common strait
  Wakes latencies unknown,
Whose impulse may precipitate
A life-long leap. The hour was late,
And there was the Jersey boat with its funnel agroan.

"Is wary walking worth much pother?"
  It grunted, as still it stayed.
"One pairing is as good as another
Where all is venture! Take each other,
And scrap the oaths that you have aforetime made." . . .

—Of the four involved there walks but one
  On earth at this late day.
And what of the chapter so begun?
In that odd complex what was done?
Well; happiness comes in full to none:
Let peace lie on lulled lips: I will not say.

1922

THE FALLOW DEER AT THE LONELY HOUSE

One without looks in to-night
  Through the curtain-chink
From the sheet of glistening white;
One without looks in to-night
  As we sit and think
  By the fender-brink.

We do not discern those eyes
  Watching in the snow;
Lit by lamps of rosy dyes
We do not discern those eyes
  Wondering, aglow,
  Fourfooted, tiptoe.

1922

THE SELFSAME SONG

A bird sings the selfsame song,
With never a fault in its flow,
That we listened to here those long
    Long years ago.

A pleasing marvel is how
A strain of such rapturous rote
Should have gone on thus till now
    Unchanged in a note!

—But it's not the selfsame bird.—
No: perished to dust is he. . . .
As also are those who heard
    That song with me.

1922

FIRST OR LAST

(SONG)

If grief come early
Joy comes late,
If joy come early
Grief will wait;
  Aye, my dear and tender!

Wise ones joy them early
While the cheeks are red,
Banish grief till surly
Time has dulled their dread.

  And joy being ours
  Ere youth has flown,
  The later hours
  May find us gone;
    Aye, my dear and tender!

1922

AN ANCIENT TO ANCIENTS

Where once we danced, where once we sang,
Gentlemen,
The floors are sunken, cobwebs hang,
And cracks creep; worms have fed upon
The doors. Yea, sprightlier times were then
Than now, with harps and tabrets gone,
Gentlemen!

Where once we rowed, where once we sailed,
Gentlemen,
And damsels took the tiller, veiled
Against too strong a stare (God wot
Their fancy, then or anywhen!)
Upon that shore we are clean forgot,
Gentlemen!

We have lost somewhat, afar and near,
Gentlemen,
The thinning of our ranks each year
Affords a hint we are nigh undone,
That we shall not be ever again
The marked of many, loved of one,
Gentlemen.

In dance the polka hit our wish,
Gentlemen,
The paced quadrille, the spry schottische,
"Sir Roger."—And in opera spheres
The "Girl" (the famed "Bohemian"),
And "Trovatore," held the ears,
Gentlemen.

This season's paintings do not please,
Gentlemen,
Like Etty, Mulready, Maclise;
Throbbing romance has waned and wanned;
No wizard wields the witching pen
Of Bulwer, Scott, Dumas, and Sand,
Gentlemen.

The bower we shrined to Tennyson,
Gentlemen,
Is roof-wrecked; damps there drip upon
Sagged seats, the creeper-nails are rust,
The spider is sole denizen;
Even she who voiced those rhymes is dust,
Gentlemen!

We who met sunrise sanguine-souled,
Gentlemen,
Are wearing weary. We are old;
These younger press; we feel our rout
Is imminent to Aïdes' den,—
That evening shades are stretching out,
Gentlemen!

And vet, though ours be failing frames,
Gentlemen,
So were some others' history names,
Who trode their track light-limbed and fast
As these youth, and not alien
From enterprise, to their long last.
Gentlemen.

Sophocles, Plato, Socrates,
Gentlemen,
Pythagoras, Thucydides,
Herodotus, and Homer,—yea,
Clement, Augustin, Origen,
Burnt brightlier towards their setting-day,
Gentlemen.

And ve, red-lipped and smooth-browed: list,
Gentlemen;
Much is there waits you we have missed;
Much lore we leave you worth the knowing,
Much, much has lain outside our ken:
Nay, rush not: times serves: we are going,
Gentlemen.

1922

WAITING BOTH

A star looks down at me,
And says: "Here I and you
Stand, each in our degree:
What do you mean to do,—
   Mean to do?"

I say: "For all I know,
Wait, and let Time go by,
Till my change come,"—"Just so."
The star says: "So mean I:—
   So mean I."

1925

"THERE SEEMED A STRANGENESS"

(A PHANTASY)

There seemed a strangeness in the air,
Vermilion light on the land's lean face;
I heard a Voice from I knew not where:—
"The Great Adjustment is taking place!

"I set thick darkness over you
And fogged you all your years therein;
   At last I uncloud your view,
Which I am weary of holding in.

"Men have not heard, men have not seen
Since the beginning of the world
   What earth and heaven mean;
But now their curtains shall be furled,

"And they shall see what is, ere long,
Not through a glass, but face to face;
And Right shall disestablish Wrong:
The Great Adjustment is taking place."

1925

SNOW IN THE SUBURBS

Every branch big with it,
Bent every twig with it;
Every fork like a white web-foot;
Every street and pavement mute:
Some flakes have lost their way, and grope back upward, when
Meeting those meandering down they turn and descend again.
The palings are glued together like a wall,
And there is no waft of wind with the fleecy fall.

A sparrow enters the tree,
Whereon immediately
A snow-lump thrice his own slight size
Descends on him and showers his head and eyes,
And overturns him,
And near inurns him,
And lights on a nether twig, when its brush
Starts off a volley of other lodging lumps with a rush.

The steps are a blanched slope,
Up which, with feeble hope,
A black cat comes, wide-eyed and thin;
And we take him in.

1925

ON THE PORTRAIT OF A WOMAN ABOUT TO BE HANGED

Comely and capable one of our race,
Posing there in your gown of grace,
Plain, yet becoming;
Could subtlest breast
Ever have guessed
What was behind that innocent face,
Drumming, drumming!

Would that your Causer, ere knoll your knell
For this riot of passion, might deign to tell
Why, since It made you

Sound in the germ,
It sent a worm
To madden Its handiwork, when It might well
Not have assayed you,

Not have implanted, to your deep rue,
The Clytæmnestra spirit in you,
And with purblind vision
Sowed a tare
In a field so fair,
And a thing of symmetry, seemly to view,
Brought to derision!

Jan. 6, 1923, 1925

HE INADVERTENTLY CURES HIS LOVE-PAINS

(SONG)

I said: "O let me sing the praise
Of her who sweetly racks my days,—
Her I adore;
Her lips, her eyes, her moods, her ways!"

In miseries of pulse and pang
I strung my harp, and straightway sang
As none before:—
To wondrous words my quavers rang!

Thus I let heartaches lilt my verse,
Which suaged and soothed, and made disperse
The smarts I bore
To quiet like a sepulchre's.

But, eased, the days that thrilled ere then
Lost value; and I ask, O when,
And how, restore
Those old sweet agonies again!

1925

"WHY DO I?"

Why do I go on doing these things?
Why not cease?
Is it that you are yet in this world of welterings
And unease,
And that, while so, mechanic repetitions please?

When shall I leave off doing these things?—
When I hear
You have dropped your dusty cloak and taken you wondrous wings
To another sphere,
Where no pain is: Then shall I hush this dinning gear.

1925

Gerard Manley Hopkins

Gerard Manley Hopkins, eldest of the eight children of Manley and Catherine Smith Hopkins, was born at Stratford, Essex, June 11, 1844. His father, who was Consul General of the Hawaiian Islands to Great Britain, was cultured and literary; he wrote a history of Hawaii, a manual of marine insurance, and considerable verse, a volume of which he published privately late in his life. Gerard's mother, who was well educated, came of a talented family: her father, Samuel Smith, was a well-known physician, a brother was a landscape painter, and her sisters were musicians and artists.

As a child Gerard was tutored in music and drawing by his father's sister. His first formal training was received at a day-school in Hampstead, which he entered in the autumn of 1852. After two years he was transferred to the Highgate Grammar School, where earlier Lamb, Keats, Coleridge, and De Quincey were pupils. Here his record was brilliant: he won a scholarship and various prizes, two for English poetry, and finally an exhibition for Balliol College, Oxford, which he entered at the Christmas term of 1863.

At Balliol, Hopkins came under the instruction of Benjamin Jowett and Walter Pater, and he became a close friend of Robert Bridges, the future Poet Laureate. At first he tended towards liberalism in religion, but coming under the influence of H. P. Liddon, an associate of Dr. Pusey's in the Tractarian Movement, and later of Dr. Pusey himself, he became a Tractarian. Even the High Church principles of the Tractarians, however, did not long satisfy his ardent spirit, and by the summer of 1866 he had determined to become a Catholic. He wrote the Reverend John Henry Newman of this determination, and requested an audience with him. After several meetings with Newman, he was received into the Catholic Church on October 21, 1866, at Newman's Oratory at Birmingham. In the spring of 1867 he took his degree from Oxford, with a Double-first in "Greats." After spending his summer vacation on the Continent, Hopkins accepted an invitation of Newman to teach at the Oratory; but during the year he decided to become a priest, and the following September he entered the Jesuit Novitiate at Roehampton. He was ordained a priest in 1877, and began his duties first as preacher at Farm Street Church, London, then as sub-minister at Mount St. Mary's College, Chesterfield. In 1878 he was preacher at St. Aloysius Church, Oxford, and the following year at St. Francis Xavier's Church, Liverpool. In 1882 he was assigned to teach classics at Stonyhurst College, a Jesuit institution, and in 1884 was appointed to the Chair of Greek at the Royal University, Dublin, where he remained until his death of typhoid fever on June 8, 1889. He was buried in the Jesuit cemetery at Glasnevin.

Hopkins was frail from childhood, but he possessed an indomitable will, and often underwent self-imposed disciplines that must have required great fortitude to perform: when a pupil at Highgate, for instance, he went a week without drinking any liquid in order to prove a theory he then held that most people consume too many liquids; and after becoming a priest, he underwent many long periods of self-denial of one sort or another. He was precocious, and early gave evidence of exceptional originality in both thought and the use of words: an example of the latter survives in a description of a schoolmate as a "kaleidoscopic, parti-colored, harlequinesque, thaumatropic being," which he wrote at the age of twelve. Early diaries show that while at Highgate he was evaluating obscure passages of Servius, Oppian, and Aristotle's *Poetics*, and was reading Italian novels. At Oxford, in addition to the required work, he read extensively in English, French, and German literature, studied painting and architecture, and wrote poetry. He was a talented student of music, and towards the close of his life was giving much time to composing.

When Hopkins became a Jesuit, in 1868, he destroyed the manuscripts of all his poetry then in his possession. A few of his early poems were preserved by Robert Bridges, and some few poems and fragments survived from other sources; but the bulk of his slender output dates from 1876, when he again began to write verse. At his death his papers came into the hands of Robert Bridges, who already had copies of many of his poems. Bridges gradually created an interest in Hopkins's poetry, and in 1918 published that in his possession. Later a few more of his poems were discovered, and in 1930, under the editorship of Charles Williams, the second, and definitive, edition of his poetry was published. In addition, two volumes of his correspondence—with Robert Bridges and R. W. Dixon—containing much of his theory on prosody, were published.

Although Hopkins was a Victorian, his poetry belongs to the present age, both because of the accident of its late publication and because his theories and practice have exerted much influence on recent poets. In a preface to his poems which he left in manuscript to Bridges, he explained his theory of scansion (see *Poems*, 2nd ed., pp. 1-6), and this, together with Bridges' notes, should be read by those who wish a full understanding of his poetry. In brief, it may be said that he conceived of two types of rhythm, Running Rhythm (the common English rhythm in which each foot consists of two or three syllables and preferably should be falling—i.e., trochaic or dactylic) and Sprung Rhythm (in which the foot may have as many as four, or even more, syllables, and the stress always comes first, with pauses or heavy stresses taking the place of extra syllables in the shorter feet). Counterpoint Rhythm was the result of imposing a variant rhythm on the original pattern. Then in style, in an effort to secure condensation, he resorted to frequent ellipsis, especially the omission of relative pronouns, and to the placing of words in such positions that if considered grammatically and not logically the meaning is ambiguous. His rimes are sometimes strained: it is rare if not unique in serious poetry, for instance, to find such rimes as *rounded—town did*, *stupendous—overbend us—an end*, *as* (the *as* being part of *astray*, which he divides thus to gain the rime), and *handsome—and some*. But according to Bridges, in his latest poems he was "beginning to concentrate the force of all his luxuriant experiments in rhythm and diction, and castigate his art into a more reserved style";[1] and in spite of what Bridges considered flaws in Hopkins's poetry, he launched it with this exhortation:

> Go forth: amidst our chaffinch flock display
> Thy plumage of far wonder and heavenward flight! [2]

[1] *Poems*, 2nd ed., p. 99. [2] *Ibid.*, p. [xx].

HEAVEN-HAVEN

A NUN TAKES THE VEIL

I have desired to go
Where springs not fail,
To fields where flies no sharp and sided hail
And a few lilies blow.

And I have asked to be
Where no storms come,
Where the green swell is in the havens dumb,
And out of the swing of the sea.

1866, 1918

THE HABIT OF PERFECTION

Elected Silence, sing to me
And beat upon my whorlèd ear,
Pipe me to pastures still and be
The music that I care to hear.

Shape nothing, lips; be lovely-dumb:
It is the shut, the curfew sent
From there where all surrenders come
Which only makes you eloquent.

Be shellèd, eyes, with double dark
And find the uncreated light:
This ruck and reel which you remark
Coils, keeps, and teases simple sight.

Palate, the hutch of tasty lust,
Desire not to be rinsed with wine:
The can must be so sweet, the crust
So fresh that come in fasts divine!

Nostrils, your careless breath that spend
Upon the stir and keep of pride,
What relish shall the censers send
Along the sanctuary side!

O feel-of-primrose hands, O feet
That want the yield of plushy sward,
But you shall walk the golden street
And you unhouse and house the lord.

And, Poverty, be thou the bride
And now the marriage feast begun,
And lily-colored clothes provide
Your spouse not labored-at nor spun.
1866, 1918

GOD'S GRANDEUR

The world is charged with the grandeur of God.
  It will flame out, like shining from shook foil;
  It gathers to a greatness, like the ooze of oil
Crushed. Why do men then now not reck his rod?
Generations have trod, have trod, have trod;
  And all is seared with trade; bleared, smeared with toil;
  And wears man's smudge and shares man's smell: the soil
Is bare now, nor can foot feel, being shod.

And for all this, nature is never spent;
  There lives the dearest freshness deep down things;
And though the last lights off the black West went
  Oh, morning, at the brown brink eastward, springs—
Because the Holy Ghost over the bent
  World broods with warm breast and with ah! bright wings.
1877, 1918

THE LANTERN OUT OF DOORS

Sometimes a lantern moves along the night,
  That interests our eyes. And who goes there?
  I think; where from and bound, I wonder, where,
With, all down darkness wide, his wading light?

Men go by me whom either beauty bright
  In mould or mind or what not else makes rare:
  They rain against our much-thick and marsh air
Rich beams, till death or distance buys them quite.

Death or distance soon consumes them: wind
  What most I may eye after, be in at the end
I cannot, and out of sight is out of mind.

Christ minds; Christ's interest, what to avow or amend
  There, eyes them, heart wants, care haunts, foot follows kind,
Their ransom, their rescue, and first, fast, last friend.

1877, 1918

THE WINDHOVER:

TO CHRIST OUR LORD

I caught this morning morning's minion, king-
  dom of daylight's dauphin, dapple-dawn-drawn Falcon, in his riding
  Of the rolling level underneath him steady air, and striding
High there, how he rung upon the rein of a wimpling wing
In his ecstasy! then off, off forth on swing,
  As a skate's heel sweeps smooth on a bow-bend: the hurl and gliding
  Rebuffed the big wind. My heart in hiding
Stirred for a bird,—the achieve of, the mastery of the thing!

Brute beauty and valor and act, oh, air, pride, plume, here
  Buckle! And the fire that breaks from thee then, a billion
Times told lovelier, more dangerous, O my chevalier!

  No wonder of it: sheer plod makes plough down sillion
Shine, and blue-bleak embers, ah my dear,
  Fall, gall themselves, and gash gold-vermilion.

1877, 1918

PIED BEAUTY

Glory be to God for dappled things—
  For skies of couple-color as a brinded cow;
    For rose-moles all in stipple upon trout that swim;
Fresh-firecoal chestnut-falls; finches' wings;
  Landscape plotted and pieced—fold, fallow, and plough;
    And all trades, their gear and tackle and trim.

All things counter, original, spare, strange;
  Whatever is fickle, freckled (who knows how?)
    With swift, slow; sweet, sour; adazzle, dim;
He fathers-forth whose beauty is past change:
                                    Praise him.

1877, 1918

THE CAGED SKYLARK

As a dare-gale skylark scanted in a dull cage
  Man's mounting spirit in his bone-house, mean house, dwells—
  That bird beyond the remembering his free fells;
This in drudgery, day-laboring-out life's age.

Though aloft on turf or perch or poor low stage,
  Both sing sometimes the sweetest, sweetest spells,
  Yet both droop deadly sometimes in their cells
Or wring their barriers in bursts of fear or rage.

Not that the sweet-fowl, song-fowl, needs no rest—
Why, hear him, hear him babble and drop down to his nest,
  But his own nest, wild nest, no prison.

Man's spirit will be flesh-bound when found at best,
But uncumbered: meadow-down is not distressed
  For a rainbow footing it nor he for his bones risen.

1877, 1918

SPELT FROM SIBYL'S LEAVES

Earnest, earthless, equal, attunable, vaulty, voluminous, stupen-
    dous
Evening strains to be time's vast, womb-of-all, home-of-all,
    hearse-of-all night.
Her fond yellow hornlight wound to the west, her wild hollow
    hoarlight hung to the height
Waste; her earliest stars, earl-stars, stars principal, overbend us,
Fire-featuring heaven. For earth her being has unbound, her
    dapple is at an end, as-[1]

[1] Divided thus to show the rime. *Throughther* in the next line, Bridges said, is now confined to dialect and is the speech form of *through-other;* he cites another use in Burns's "Halloween," st. 5.

tray or aswarm, all throughther, in throngs; self in self steeped and pashed—quite
Disremembering, dismembering all now. Heart, you round me right
With: Our evening is over us; our night whelms, whelms, and will end us.
Only the beak-leaved boughs dragonish damask the tool-smooth bleak light; black,
Ever so black on it. Our tale, O our oracle! Let life, waned, ah let life wind
Off her once skeined stained veined variety upon, all on two spools; part, pen, pack
Now her all in two flocks, two folds—black, white; right, wrong; reckon but, reck but, mind
But these two; ware of a world where but these two tell, each off the other; of a rack
Where, selfwrung, selfstrung, sheathe- and shelterless, thoughts against thoughts in groans grind.

1918

INVERSNAID

This darksome burn, horseback brown,
His rollrock highroad roaring down,
In coop and in comb the fleece of his foam
Flutes and low to the lake falls home.

A windpuff-bonnet of fawn-froth
Turns and twindles over the broth
Of a pool so pitchblack, fell-frowning,
It rounds and rounds Despair to drowning.

Degged with dew, dappled with dew
Are the groins of the braes that the brook treads through,
Wiry heathpacks, flitches of fern,
And the beadbonny ash that sits over the burn.

What would the world be, once bereft
Of wet and of wildness? Let them be left,
O let them be left, wildness and wet;
Long live the weeds and the wilderness yet.

1881, 1918

THE LEADEN ECHO AND THE GOLDEN ECHO

MAIDENS' SONG FROM "ST. WINEFRED'S WELL"

THE LEADEN ECHO

How to keep—is there any any, is there none such, nowhere known
some, bow or brooch or braid or brace, lace, latch or catch
or key to keep
Back beauty, keep it, beauty, beauty, beauty, . . . from vanishing
away?
O is there no frowning of these wrinkles, rankèd wrinkles deep,
Down? no waving off of these most mournful messengers, still
messengers, sad and stealing messengers of grey?
No there's none, there's none, O no there's none,
Nor can you long be, what you now are, called fair,
Do what you may do, what, do what you may,
And wisdom is early to despair:
Be beginning; since, no, nothing can be done
To keep at bay
Age and age's evils, hoar hair,
Ruck and wrinkle, drooping, dying, death's worst, winding sheets,
tombs and worms and tumbling to decay;
So be beginning, be beginning to despair.
O there's none; no no no there's none:
Be beginning to despair, to despair,
Despair, despair, despair, despair.

THE GOLDEN ECHO

Spare!
There is one, yes I have one (Hush there!);
Only not within seeing of the sun,
Not within the singeing of the strong sun,
Tall sun's tingeing, or treacherous the tainting of the earth's air,
Somewhere elsewhere there is ah well where! one,
One. Yes I can tell such a key, I do know such a place,
Where whatever's prized and passes of us, everything that's fresh
and fast flying of us, seems to us sweet of us and swiftly
away with, done away with, undone,
Undone, done with, soon done with, and yet dearly and danger-
ously sweet
Of us, the wimpled-water-dimpled, not-by-morning-matched face,
The flower of beauty, fleece of beauty, too too apt to, ah! to fleet,

Never fleets more, fastened with the tenderest truth
To its own best being and its loveliness of youth: it is an ever-
    lastingness of, O it is an all youth!
Come then, your ways and airs and looks, locks, maiden gear,
    gallantry and gaiety and grace,
Winning ways, airs innocent, maiden manners, sweet looks, loose
    locks, long locks, lovelocks, gaygear, going gallant, girlgrace—
Resign them, sign them, seal them, send them, motion them with
    breath,
And with sighs soaring, soaring sighs deliver
Them; beauty-in-the-ghost, deliver it, early now, long before death
Give beauty back, beauty, beauty, beauty, back to God, beauty's
    self and beauty's giver.
See; not a hair is, not an eyelash, not the least lash lost; every hair
Is, hair of the head, numbered.
Nay, what we had lighthanded left in surly the mere mould
Will have waked and have waxed and have walked with the wind
    what while we slept,
This side, that side hurling a heavyheaded hundredfold
What while we, while we slumbered.
O then, weary then why should we tread? O why are we so hag-
    gard at the heart, so care-coiled, care-killed, so fagged, so
    fashed, so cogged, so cumbered,
When the thing we freely forfeit is kept with fonder a care,
Fonder a care kept than we could have kept it, kept
Far with fonder a care (and we, we should have lost it) finer,
    fonder
A care kept.—Where kept? Do but tell us where kept, where.—
Yonder.—What high as that! We follow, now we follow.
    —Yonder, yes yonder, yonder,
Yonder.

1882, 1918

[NO WORST, THERE IS NONE]

No worst, there is none. Pitched past pitch of grief,
More pangs will, schooled at forepangs, wilder wring.
Comforter, where, where is your comforting?
Mary, mother of us, where is your relief?
My cries heave, herds-long; huddle in a main, a chief
Woe, world-sorrow; on an age-old anvil wince and sing—
Then lull, then leave off. Fury had shrieked "No ling-
ering! Let me be fell: force I must be brief."

O the mind, mind has mountains; cliffs of fall
Frightful, sheer, no-man-fathomed. Hold them cheap
May who ne'er hung there. Nor does long our small
Durance deal with that steep or deep. Here! creep,
Wretch, under a comfort serves in a whirlwind: all
Life death does end and each day dies with sleep.
1918

[I WAKE AND FEEL THE FELL OF DARK]

I wake and feel the fell of dark, not day.
What hours, O what black hours we have spent
This night! what sights you, heart, saw; ways you went!
And more must, in yet longer light's delay.
With witness I speak this. But where I say
Hours I mean years, mean life. And my lament
Is cries countless, cries like dead letters sent
To dearest him that lives alas! away.

I am gall, I am heartburn. God's most deep decree
Bitter would have me taste: my taste was me;
Bones built in me, flesh filled, blood brimmed the curse.
Selfyeast of spirit a dull dough sours. I see
The lost are like this, and their scourge to be
As I am mine, their sweating selves; but worse.
c. 1885, 1918

[THOU ART INDEED JUST, LORD]

Justus quidem tu es, Domine, si disputem tecum: verumtamen justa loquar ad te: Quare via impiorum prosperatur? &c.[1]

Thou are indeed just, Lord, if I contend
With thee; but, sir, so what I plead is just.
Why do sinners' ways prosper? and why must
Disappointment all I endeavor end?
Wert thou my enemy, O thou my friend,
How wouldst thou worse, I wonder, than thou dost
Defeat, thwart me? Oh, the sots and thralls of lust
Do in spare hours more thrive than I that spend,

[1] The translation is in the first three lines of the sonnet. See *Jeremiah* 12:1.

Sir, life upon thy cause. See, banks and brakes
Now, leavèd how thick! lacèd they are again
With fretty chervil, look, and fresh wind shakes
Them; birds build—but not I build; no, but strain,
Time's eunuch, and not breed one work that wakes.
Mine, O thou lord of life, send my roots rain.

1889, 1918

Robert Bridges

Robert Seymour Bridges was born October 23, 1844, at Walmer, Kent. He was eighth of the nine children of John Thomas Bridges, of St. Nicholas Court, Isle of Thanet, and of Harriet Elizabeth, a daughter of the Reverend Sir Robert Affleck. His father's people had been substantial yeomen in the Isle of Thanet from the sixteenth century. In his childhood the family lived at Roselands, Walmer, but a year after his father's death—May 10, 1853—his mother married the Reverend John E. N. Molesworth, Vicar of Rochdale, a Lancashire manufacturing town, which for some years became Bridges's home.

He entered Eton in September, 1854, and remained there for nine years. In October, 1863, he went as a commoner to Corpus Christi College, Oxford, and four years later took his B.A. with honors. He was strong physically and was good at games; at Eton he played on the School Eleven, and at Oxford he rowed stroke on his College Eight. When at Eton he was interested in religion and held Puseyite views, but at Oxford this interest was soon displaced in favor of philosophy and natural science.

In November, 1869, he entered St. Bartholomew's Hospital, London, as a medical student, intending his studies "for knowledge and experience rather than to make a living"; but for some years he spent most of his time in travel: a lengthy, leisurely tour of Egypt, Greece, and Syria; a stay of some months in Germany to study the language; a tour of the Netherlands; two long periods in France, one a winter in Paris; and six months in Italy with his friend Ellis Wooldridge, afterwards Professor of Fine Arts at Oxford. But in 1871 he settled down at his studies and was graduated M.B. in 1874. He was House Physician at St. Bartholomew's in 1875-1876, Casualty Physician 1877-1879, Assistant Physician to the Hospital for Sick Children, Great Ormond Street,

1878, and later to the Great Northern Hospital, Holloway. In London he lived with Wooldridge at 50 Maddox Street until 1877; then, after the death of his stepfather, with his mother at 52 Bedford Square. He planned from the start to retire from the practice of medicine at 40, but in 1881 a severe attack of pneumonia and empyema took him to Italy and Sicily for some months to seek recovery, and upon his return to England he did not resume practice. Instead, he settled with his mother in the Manor House, Yattendon, where he lived a life of "joy in idleness," training the village choir, studying, and writing poetry. Here a neighbor was the architect and painter Alfred Waterhouse, whose eldest daughter, Mary Monica, Bridges married on September 3, 1884. He lived at Yattendon till 1905, when his wife's health required a stay of some months in Switzerland. On their return, they lived for two years in temporary abodes; then Bridges bought some land on Boar's Hill, Oxford, and there built Chilswell House, which was his home until his death. He had a son and two daughters, of whom one, Elizabeth Daryush, the wife of a Persian, is also a poet.

Bridges began writing verse at Eton, and in 1873 he published his first volume, *Poems*, which he had written during a two-weeks' holiday at the seaside, Seaford. Three years later he published a sonnet-sequence, *The Growth of Love* (consisting of twenty-four sonnets, but in later editions increased to seventy-nine); then followed two or three volumes of lyrics. At Yattendon he began a series of poetic dramas which occupied him for many years. His early work was issued for the most part in limited editions from private presses, and he was little known until the publication of his *Poetical Works* in six volumes, 1898-1905. Although never a "popular" poet, his appointment in 1913 to succeed Alfred Austin as Poet Laureate met with the general approval of other poets and of critics. During his remaining years he produced but little poetry until his eighty-fifth birthday, when he published *The Testament of Beauty*, for one of his years an amazing work in both quantity and quality, in which he summarized the wisdom of a lifetime of study, observation, and experience.

Bridges was greatly interested in language and prosody. He took the lead in organizing the Society for Pure English in 1913, and was its president until his death. He wrote numerous papers for it, and gave much time to the promotion of its interests. He wrote several critical studies, of which the best are *Milton's Prosody*

(1887, with subsequent revisions) and *John Keats, a Critical Essay* (1895); and he edited two anthologies—*The Spirit of Man* (1916) and *The Chilswell Book of English Poetry* (1924)—and, with Ellis Wooldridge, *The Yattendon Hymnal* (1899). In addition to these interests, he published many experiments in metrics. He was one of the most learned of English poets: he could write with facility on art, music, literature, medicine, science, history, and philosophy; he was an accomplished student of Greek and Latin, and was familiar with most modern European languages.

He received many honors: an Honorary Fellowship in Corpus Christi College, Oxford (1895); the honorary degrees of LL.D. from St. Andrews (1911), of D.Litt. from Oxford (1912) and from Harvard (1924), and of LL.D. from the University of Michigan (1924); and the Order of Merit (1929). He accepted a Fellowship in Creative Arts, offered him by the University of Michigan, and spent several months in 1924 at Ann Arbor.

After a brief illness, he died at his home on April 21, 1930.

ELEGY

The wood is bare: a river-mist is steeping
  The trees that winter's chill of life bereaves:
Only their stiffened boughs break silence, weeping
    Over their fallen leaves;

That lie upon the dank earth brown and rotten,
  Miry and matted in the soaking wet:
Forgotten with the spring, that is forgotten
    By them that can forget.

Yet it was here we walked when ferns were springing,
  And through the mossy bank shot bud and blade:—
Here found in summer, when the birds were singing,
    A green and pleasant shade.

'Twas here we loved in sunnier days and greener;
  And now, in this disconsolate decay,
I come to see her where I most have seen her,
    And touch the happier day.

For on this path, at every turn and corner,
  The fancy of her figure on me falls:
Yet walks she with the slow step of a mourner,
    Nor hears my voice that calls.

So through my heart there winds a track of feeling,
  A path of memory, that is all her own:
Whereto her phantom beauty ever stealing
    Haunts the sad spot alone.

About her steps the trunks are bare, the branches
  Drip heavy tears upon her downcast head;
And bleed from unseen wounds that no sun stanches,
    For the year's sun is dead.

And dead leaves wrap the fruits that summer planted:
  And birds that love the South have taken wing.
The wanderer, loitering o'er the scene enchanted,
    Weeps, and despairs of spring.

1873

[DEAR LADY, WHEN THOU FROWNEST]

Dear lady, when thou frownest,
  And my true love despisest,
And all thy vows disownest
  That sealed my venture wisest;
I think thy pride's displeasure
Neglects a matchless treasure
Exceeding price and measure.

But when again thou smilest,
  And love for love returnest,
And fear with joy beguilest,
  And takest truth in earnest;
Then, though I sheer adore thee,
The sum of my love for thee
Seems poor, scant, and unworthy.

1873

[I WILL NOT LET THEE GO]

I will not let thee go.
Ends all our month-long love in this?
Can it be summed up so,
Quit in a single kiss?
I will not let thee go.

I will not let thee go.
If thy words' breath could scare thy deeds,
As the soft south can blow
And toss the feathered seeds,
Then might I let thee go.

I will not let thee go.
Had not the great sun seen, I might;
Or were he reckoned slow
To bring the false to light,
Then might I let thee go.

I will not let thee go.
The stars that crowd the summer skies
Have watched us so below
With all their million eyes,
I dare not let thee go.

I will not let thee go.
Have we not chid the changeful moon,
Now rising late, and now
Because she set too soon,
And shall I let thee go?

I will not let thee go.
Have not the young flowers been content,
Plucked ere their buds could blow,
To seal our sacrament?
I cannot let thee go.

I will not let thee go.
I hold thee by too many bands:
Thou sayest farewell, and lo!
I have thee by the hands,
And will not let thee go.

1873

TRIOLET

When first we met we did not guess
That Love would prove so hard a master;
Of more than common friendliness
When first we met we did not guess.
Who could foretell this sore distress,
This irretrievable disaster
When first we met?—We did not guess
That Love would prove so hard a master.
1873

TRIOLET

All women born are so perverse
No man need boast their love possessing.
If nought seem better, nothing's worse:
All women born are so perverse.
From Adam's wife, that proved a curse
Though God had made her for a blessing,
All women born are so perverse
No man need boast their love possessing.
1873

[O WEARY PILGRIMS, CHANTING OF YOUR WOE]

O weary pilgrims, chanting of your woe,
That turn your eyes to all the peaks that shine,
Hailing in each the citadel divine
The which ye thought to have entered long ago;
Until at length your feeble steps and slow
Falter upon the threshold of the shrine,
And your hearts overburdened doubt in fine
Whether it be Jerusalem or no:

Disheartened pilgrims, I am one of you;
For, having worshipped many a barren face,
I scarce now greet the goal I journeyed to:
I stand a pagan in the holy place;
Beneath the lamp of truth I am found untrue,
And question with the God that I embrace.
1876

A PASSER-BY

Whither, O splendid ship, thy white sails crowding,
  Leaning across the bosom of the urgent West,
That fearest nor sea rising, nor sky clouding,
  Whither away, fair rover, and what thy quest?
  Ah! soon, when Winter has all our vales opprest,
When skies are cold and misty, and hail is hurling,
  Wilt thou glide on the blue Pacific, or rest
In a summer haven asleep, thy white sails furling.

I there before thee, in the country that well thou knowest,
  Already arrived am inhaling the odorous air:
I watch thee enter unerringly where thou goest,
  And anchor queen of the strange shipping there,
  Thy sails for awnings spread, thy masts bare:
Nor is aught from the foaming reef to the snow-capped, grandest
  Peak, that is over the feathery palms more fair
Than thou, so upright, so stately, and still thou standest.

And yet, O splendid ship, unhailed and nameless,
  I know not if, aiming a fancy, I rightly divine
That thou hast a purpose joyful, a courage blameless,
  Thy port assured in a happier land than mine.
  But for all I have given thee, beauty enough is thine,
As thou, aslant with trim tackle and shrouding,
  From the proud nostril curve of a prow's line
In the offing scatterest foam, thy white sails crowding.

1879

LONDON SNOW

When men were all asleep the snow came flying,
In large white flakes falling on the city brown,
Stealthily and perpetually settling and loosely lying,
    Hushing the latest traffic of the drowsy town;
Deadening, muffling, stifling its murmurs failing;
Lazily and incessantly floating down and down:
    Silently sifting and veiling road, roof and railing;
Hiding difference, making unevenness even,
Into angles and crevices softly drifting and sailing.

All night it fell, and when full inches seven
It lay in the depth of its uncompacted lightness,
The clouds blew off from a high and frosty heaven;
And all woke earlier for the unaccustomed brightness
Of the winter dawning, the strange unheavenly glare:
The eye marvelled—marvelled at the dazzling whiteness;
The ear hearkened to the stillness of the solemn air;
No sound of wheel rumbling nor of foot falling,
And the busy morning cries came thin and spare.
Then boys I heard, as they went to school, calling,
They gathered up the crystal manna to freeze
Their tongues with tasting, their hands with snowballing;
Or rioted in a drift, plunging up to the knees;
Or peering up from under the white-mossed wonder,
"O look at the trees!" they cried, "O look at the trees!"
With lessened load a few carts creak and blunder,
Following along the white deserted way,
A country company long dispersed asunder:
When now already the sun, in pale display
Standing by Paul's high dome, spread forth below
His sparkling beams, and awoke the stir of the day.
For now doors open, and war is waged with the snow;
And trains of somber men, past tale of number,
Tread long brown paths, as toward their toil they go:
But even for them awhile no cares encumber
Their minds diverted; the daily word is unspoken,
The daily thoughts of labor and sorrow slumber
At the sight of the beauty that greets them, for the charm they have broken.

1880

THE VOICE OF NATURE

I stand on the cliff and watch the veiled sun paling
A silver field afar in the mournful sea,
The scourge of the surf, and plaintive gulls sailing
At ease on the gale that smites the shuddering lea:
Whose smile severe and chaste
June never hath stirred to vanity, nor age defaced.
In lofty thought strive, O spirit, for ever:
In courage and strength pursue thine own endeavor.

Ah! if it were only for thee, thou restless ocean
  Of waves that follow and roar, the sweep of the tides;
Wer't only for thee, impetuous wind, whose motion
  Precipitate all o'errides, and turns, nor abides:
    For you, sad birds and fair,
  Or only for thee, bleak cliff, erect in the air;
Then well could I read wisdom in every feature,
O well should I understand the voice of Nature.

But far away, I think, in the Thames valley,
  The silent river glides by flowery banks:
And birds sing sweetly in branches that arch an alley
  Of cloistered trees, moss-grown in their ancient ranks:
    Where if a light air stray,
  'Tis laden with hum of bees and scent of may.
Love and peace be thine, O spirit, for ever:
Serve thy sweet desire: despise endeavor.

And if it were only for thee, entrancèd river,
  That scarce dost rock the lily on her airy stem,
Or stir a wave to murmur, or a rush to quiver;
  Wer't but for the woods, and summer asleep in them:
    For you my bowers green,
  My hedges of rose and woodbine, with walks between,
Then well could I read wisdom in every feature,
O well should I understand the voice of Nature.

1880

ON A DEAD CHILD

Perfect little body, without fault or stain on thee,
  With promise of strength and manhood full and fair!
    Though cold and stark and bare,
The bloom and the charm of life doth awhile remain on thee.

Thy mother's treasure wert thou;—alas! no longer
  To visit her heart with wondrous joy; to be
    Thy father's pride;—ah, he
Must gather his faith together, and his strength make stronger.

To me, as I move thee now in the last duty,
  Dost thou with a turn or gesture anon respond;
    Startling my fancy fond
With a chance attitude of the head, a freak of beauty.

Thy hand clasps, as 'twas wont, my finger, and holds it:
But the grasp is the clasp of Death, heartbreaking and stiff;
Yet feels to my hand as if
'Twas still thy will, thy pleasure and trust that enfolds it.

So I lay thee there, thy sunken eyelids closing,—
Go lie thou there in thy coffin, thy last little bed!—
Propping thy wise, sad head,
Thy firm, pale hands across thy chest disposing.

So quiet! doth the change content thee?—Death, whither hath he taken thee?
To a world, do I think, that rights the disaster of this?
The vision of which I miss,
Who weep for the body, and wish but to warm thee and awaken thee?

Ah! little at best can all our hopes avail us
To lift this sorrow, or cheer us, when in the dark,
Unwilling, alone we embark,
And the things we have seen and have known and have heard of, fail us.

1880

[THE VERY NAMES OF THINGS BELOVED]

The very names of things beloved are dear,
And sounds will gather beauty from their sense,
As many a face through love's long residence
Groweth to fair instead of plain and sere:
But when I say thy name it hath no peer,
And I suppose fortune determined thence
Her dower, that such beauty's excellence
Should have a perfect title for the ear.

Thus may I think the adopting Muses chose
Their sons by name, knowing none would be heard
Or writ so oft in all the world as those,—
Dan Chaucer, mighty Shakespeare, then for third
The classic Milton, and to us arose
Shelley with liquid music in the word.

1889

[ALL EARTHLY BEAUTY HATH ONE CAUSE]

All earthly beauty hath one cause and proof,
To lead the pilgrim soul to beauty above:
Yet lieth the greater bliss so far aloof,
That few there be are weaned from earthly love.

Joy's ladder it is, reaching from home to home,
The best of all the work that all was good;
Whereof 'twas writ the angels aye upclomb,
Down sped, and at the top the Lord God stood.

But I my time abuse, my eyes by day
Centered on thee, by night my heart on fire—
Letting my numbered moments run away—
Nor e'en 'twixt night and day to heaven aspire:

So true it is that what the eye seeth not
But slow is loved, and loved is soon forgot.

1889

[THE WORLD COMES NOT TO AN END]

The world comes not to an end: her city-hives
Swarm with the tokens of a changeless trade,
With rolling wheel, driver and flagging jade,
Rich men and beggars, children, priests, and wives.
New homes on old are set, as lives on lives;
Invention with invention overlaid:
But still or tool or toy or book or blade
Shaped for the hand, that holds and toils and strives.

The men to-day toil as their fathers taught,
With little bettered means; for works depend
On works and overlap, and thought on thought:
And through all change the smiles of hope amend
The weariest face, the same love changed in nought:
In this thing too the world comes not to an end.

1889

THE PHILOSOPHER TO HIS MISTRESS

Because thou canst not see,
Because thou canst not know
The black and hopeless woe
That hath encompassed me:
Because, should I confess
The thought of my despair,
My words would wound thee less
Than swords can hurt the air:

Because with thee I seem
As one invited near
To taste the faery cheer
Of spirits in a dream;
Of whom he knoweth nought
Save that they vie to make
All motion, voice and thought
A pleasure for his sake:

Therefore more sweet and strange
Has been the mystery
Of thy long love to me,
That doth not quit, nor change,
Nor tax my solemn heart,
That kisseth in a gloom,
Knowing not who thou art
That givest, nor to whom.

Therefore the tender touch
Is more; more dear the smile:
And thy light words beguile
My wisdom overmuch:
And O with swiftness fly
The fancies of my song
To happy worlds, where I
Still in thy love belong.

1890

[THE EVENING DARKENS OVER]

The evening darkens over.
After a day so bright
The windcapt waves discover
That wild will be the night.
There's sound of distant thunder.

The latest sea-birds hover
Along the cliff's sheer height;
As in the memory wander
Last flutterings of delight,
White wings lost on the white.

There's not a ship in sight;
And as the sun goes under
Thick clouds conspire to cover
The moon that should rise yonder.
Thou art alone, fond lover.

1890

[I LOVE ALL BEAUTEOUS THINGS]

I love all beauteous things,
    I seek and adore them;
God hath no better praise,
And man in his hasty days
    Is honored for them.

I too will something make
    And joy in the making;
Although to-morrow it seem
Like the empty words of a dream
    Remembered on waking.

1890

APRIL, 1885

Wanton with long delay the gay spring leaping cometh;
The blackthorn starreth now his bough on the eve of May:
All day in the sweet box-tree the bee for pleasure hummeth:
The cuckoo sends afloat his note on the air all day.

Now dewy nights again and rain in gentle shower
At root of tree and flower have quenched the winter's drouth:
On high the hot sun smiles, and banks of cloud uptower
In bulging heads that crowd for miles the dazzling south.

1890

[O LOVE, MY MUSE]

O love, my muse, how was't for me
    Among the best to dare,
In thy high courts that bowed the knee
    With sacrifice and prayer?

Their mighty offerings at thy shrine
    Shamed me, who nothing bore;
Their suits were mockeries of mine,
    I sued for so much more.

Full many I met that crowned with bay
    In triumph home returned,
And many a master on the way
    Proud of the prize I scorned.

I wished no garland on my head
    Nor treasure in my hand;
My gift the longing that me led,
    My prayer thy high command.

My love, my muse; and when I spake
    Thou mad'st me thine that day,
And more than hundred hearts could take
    Gav'st me to bear away.

1890

THE WINDMILL

The green corn waving in the dale,
The ripe grass waving on the hill:
I lean across the paddock pale
And gaze upon the giddy mill.

Its hurtling sails a mighty sweep
Cut through the air: with rushing sound
Each strikes in fury down the steep,
Rattles, and whirls in chase around.

Beside his sacks the miller stands
On high within the open door:
A book and pencil in his hands,
His grist and meal he reckoneth o'er.

His tireless merry slave the wind
Is busy with his work to-day:
From whencesoe'er, he comes to grind;
He hath a will and knows the way.

He gives the creaking sails a spin,
The circling millstones faster flee,
The shuddering timbers groan within,
And down the shoot the meal runs free.

The miller giveth him no thanks,
And doth not much his work o'erlook:
He stands beside the sacks, and ranks
The figures in his dusty book.

1890

[I NEVER SHALL LOVE THE SNOW AGAIN]

I never shall love the snow again
    Since Maurice died:
With corniced drift it blocked the lane
And sheeted in a desolate plain
    The country side.

The trees with silvery rime bedight
    Their branches bare.
By day no sun appeared; by night
The hidden moon shed thievish light
    In the misty air.

We fed the birds that flew around
    In flocks to be fed:

No shelter in holly or brake they found.
The speckled thrush on the frozen ground
    Lay frozen and dead.

We skated on stream and pond; we cut
    The crinching snow
To Doric temple or Arctic hut;
We laughed and sang at nightfall, shut
    By the fireside glow.

Yet grudged we our keen delights before
    Maurice should come.
We said, In-door or out-of-door
We shall love life for a month or more,
    When he is home.

They brought him home; 'twas two days late
    For Christmas day:
Wrapped in white, in solemn state,
A flower in his hand, all still and straight
    Our Maurice lay.

And two days ere the year outgave
    We laid him low.
The best of us truly were not brave,
When we laid Maurice down in his grave
    Under the snow.

1893

NIGHTINGALES

Beautiful must be the mountains whence ye come,
And bright in the fruitful valleys the streams, wherefrom
    Ye learn your song:
Where are those starry woods? O might I wander there,
Among the flowers, which in that heavenly air
    Bloom the year long!

Nay, barren are those mountains and spent the streams:
Our song is the voice of desire, that haunts our dreams,
    A throe of the heart,

Whose pining visions dim, forbidden hopes profound,
No dying cadence nor long sigh can sound,
For all our art.

Alone, aloud in the raptured ear of men
We pour our dark nocturnal secret; and then,
As night is withdrawn
From these sweet-springing meads and bursting boughs of May,
Dream, while the innumerable choir of day
Welcome the dawn.

1893

[MY DELIGHT AND THY DELIGHT]

My delight and thy delight
Walking, like two angels white,
In the gardens of the night:

My desire and thy desire
Twining to a tongue of fire,
Leaping live, and laughing higher;
Through the everlasting strife
In the mystery of life.

Love, from whom the world begun,
Hath the secret of the sun.

Love can tell, and love alone,
Whence the million stars were strewn,
Why each atom knows its own,
How, in spite of woe and death,
Gay is life, and sweet is breath:

This he taught us, this we knew,
Happy in his science true,
Hand in hand as we stood
Neath the shadows of the wood,
Heart to heart as we lay
In the dawning of the day.

1899

PATER FILIO [1]

Sense with keenest edge unusëd,
  Yet unsteeled by scathing fire;
Lovely feet as yet unbruisëd
  On the ways of dark desire;
Sweetest hope that lookest smiling
O'er the wilderness defiling!

Why such beauty, to be blighted
  By the swarm of foul destruction?
Why such innocence delighted,
  When sin stalks to thy seduction?
All the litanies e'er chaunted
Shall not keep thy faith undaunted.

I have prayed the sainted Morning
  To unclasp her hands to hold thee;
From resignful Eve's adorning
  Stol'n a robe of peace to enfold thee;
With all charms of man's contriving
Armed thee for thy lonely striving.

Me too once unthinking Nature,
  —Whence Love's timeless mockery took me,—
Fashioned so divine a creature,
  Yea, and like a beast forsook me.
I forgave, but tell the measure
Of her crime in thee, my treasure.

1899

MELANCHOLIA

The sickness of desire, that in dark days
Looks on the imagination of despair,
Forgetteth man, and stinteth God his praise;
Nor but in sleep findeth a cure for care.
Incertainty that once gave scope to dream
Of laughing enterprise and glory untold,

[1] Father to son.

Is now a blackness that no stars redeem,
A wall of terror in a night of cold.
Fool! thou that hast impossibly desired
And now impatiently despairest, see
How nought is changed: Joy's wisdom is attired
Splendid for others' eyes if not for thee:
Not love or beauty or youth from earth is fled:
If they delight thee not, 'tis thou art dead.

1905

FORTUNATUS NIMIUM [1]

I have lain in the sun;
I have toiled as I might;
I have thought as I would,
And now it is night.

My bed full of sleep,
My heart of content,
For friends that I met
The way that I went.

I welcome fatigue
While frenzy and care
Like thin summer clouds
Go melting in air.

To dream as I may
And awake when I will
With the song of the birds
And the sun on the hill.

Or death—were it death—
To what should I wake,
Who loved in my home
All life for its sake?

What good have I wrought?
I laugh to have learned
That joy cannot come
Unless it be earned;

[1] Very happy.

For a happier lot
Than God giveth me,
It never hath been,
Nor ever shall be.

1920

VISION

How should I be to Love unjust
    Since Love hath been so kind to me?
O how forget thy tender trust
    Or slight the bond that set me free?
How should thy spirit's blithe embrace,
    Thy loyalty, have been given in vain,
From the first beckoning of thy grace
    That made a child of me again,
And since hath still my manhood led
    Through scathe and trouble hour by hour,
And in probation perfected
    The explicit fruit of such a flower?

Not ev'n the Apostles, in the days
    They walked with Christ, loved Him so well
As we may now, who ken His praise
    Reading the story that they tell,
Writ by them when their vision grew
    And he, who fled and thrice denied
Christ to His face, was proven true
    And gladly for His memory died:
So strong the Vision, there was none
    O'er whom the Fisher's net was cast,
Ev'n of the fearfullest not one
    Who would have left Him at the last.

So 'tis with me; the time hath cleared
    Not dulled my loving: I can see
Love's passing ecstasies endeared
    In aspects of eternity:
I am like a miser—I can say
    That having hoarded all my gold
I must grow richer every day
    And die possessed of wealth untold.

1925

A. E. Housman

Alfred Edward Housman was born March 26, 1859, at the Valley House, Fockbury, two miles from Bromsgrove, Worcestershire. He was eldest of the seven children—five boys and two girls—of Edward and Sarah Jane Housman. His mother was a daughter of the Reverend John Williams, rector of Woodchester, whose people came from Devonshire. His paternal grandfather was the Reverend Thomas Housman, who went to Bromsgrove in 1836 as assistant curate of the parish church, and whose family was of Lancashire origin. His father, a solicitor, was an unpractical business man, who wrote poetry and devoted so much money to mechanical inventions on which he received no return that in Alfred's childhood the family was reduced to greatly straitened circumstances. Housman's mother died on his twelfth birthday, and in 1873 his father married a cousin, a woman of much charm, to whom Alfred was devoted, and to whom he gave much aid in caring for the younger children.

His education began under a governess, and was continued for about a year at a small dame-school. At the age of eleven he was elected to a Foundation Scholarship at Bromsgrove School, which he attended as a day pupil from 1870 to 1877. Here he took no part in games, but he was an apt pupil and won many prizes, among them three for English verse; and upon the completion of his training at Bromsgrove, he gained a scholarship, paying £100 a year, at St. John's College, Oxford, which he entered in the autumn of 1877. His career at Oxford began brilliantly with his winning a First in Moderations (the second-year examinations); but in his last two years he neglected the required curriculum, especially that part pertaining to classical prose, for the study of obscure Latin poets, with the result that he failed Greats (the fourth-year examinations). He returned to Oxford for one term to study for a pass degree, and then spent several months at home, preparing for an examination for entry to the Civil Service and teaching Greek and Latin at Bromsgrove School. In 1882 he entered the Government Patent Office as a Higher Division Clerk, a position he held for ten years. His work required but six hours a day of his time, however, and he was thus able to continue his classical studies at the British Museum. He began contributing to learned journals, and gradually became known as a brilliant classical scholar. In 1892 the chair of Latin in University College, London, became vacant, and he was appointed to fill it. He occupied this chair until 1911, when he was appointed Kennedy Professor of Latin in Trinity College, Cambridge, a position he held until his death. He was considered one of the best classical scholars of his age, being noted for the saneness of his critical writings and for the incisiveness of his comments on disputed points. He edited the works of Juvenal (1905), of Lucan (1926), and the *Astronomica* of Manilius (1903-1930), and contributed frequently to several classical journals.

He began writing verse at the age of eight. He wrote much in his 'teens, but little in his twenties (only three poems while at Oxford), and his most prolific period began at the age of thirty-five. It was his custom to go on a long walk each day, and during such walks when in London, he began composing lyrics that comprised his first volume, *A Shropshire Lad* (1896), each walk yielding a poem, though usually in an unfinished state which required considerable polishing before it satisfied his exacting standards. His next volume, *Last Poems*, was issued in 1922; and after his death, his brother and literary executor, Laurence Housman, published a final volume, *More Poems* (1936), and also included in a biography—*A. E. H.* (1937)—a few unpublished lyrics, some fragments, and some light verse which Housman wrote chiefly for the entertainment of members of his family.

As a boy Housman was full of fun and gaiety, but after his Oxford days he underwent a change and "became a silent and impenetrable recluse [even] in the midst of his own family." [1] In his later years he appeared austere and unbending to acquaintances, and was apt to be aloof and difficult even with close friends.[2] He liked good food and good wine, and was fond of

[1] *A. E. H.*, p. 56.

[2] See *A Buried Life: Personal Recollections of A. E. Housman*, 1940, by Percy Withers.

travel: it was his custom for many years before his death to make a trip each summer to the Continent, usually to France, where, selecting a different section each year, he would give particular attention to the food and to the ecclesiastical architecture, of which he was an enthusiastic student.

Of himself, Housman wrote, "I was brought up in the Church of England and in the High Church party, which is much the best religion I have ever come across. But Lemprière's Classical Dictionary, which fell into my hands when I was eight, attached my affections to paganism. I became a deist at 13 and an atheist at 21.[1] . . . I am not a pessimist but a pejorist . . . and that is owing to my observation of the world, not to personal circumstances . . . My poetry, so far as I can make out, sprang chiefly from physical conditions, such as a relaxed sore throat during my most prolific period, the first five months of 1895." [2]

In 1933 Housman was induced to deliver the Leslie Stephen Lecture at Cambridge, and chose for his subject "The Name and Nature of Poetry"; this lecture was later published under the same title. He was an Honorary Fellow of St. John's College, Oxford, and Fellow of Trinity College, Cambridge. He was offered many honors, among them the Order of Merit, all of which he refused. He was never married. His death, April 30, 1936, resulted from heart trouble. His body was cremated and the ashes buried in the parish church of Ludlow, Shropshire.

[INTO MY HEART AN AIR THAT KILLS]

Into my heart an air that kills
  From yon far country blows:
What are those blue remembered hills,
  What spires, what farms are those?

That is the land of lost content,
  I see it shining plain,
The happy highways where I went
  And cannot come again.

c. 1890, 1896

[1] *A. E. H.*, p. 21. [2] *Ibid.*, p. 72.

BREDON HILL

In summertime on Bredon
  The bells they sound so clear;
Round both the shires they ring them
  In steeples far and near,
  A happy noise to hear.

Here of a Sunday morning
  My love and I would lie,
And see the colored counties,
  And hear the larks so high
  About us in the sky.

The bells would ring to call her
  In valleys miles away:
"Come all to church, good people;
  Good people, come and pray."
  But here my love would stay.

And I would turn and answer
  Among the springing thyme,
"Oh, peal upon our wedding,
  And we will hear the chime,
  And come to church in time."

But when the snows at Christmas
  On Bredon top were strown,
My love rose up so early
  And stole out unbeknown
  And went to church alone.

They tolled the one bell only;
  Groom there was none to see;
The mourners followed after,
  And so to church went she,
  And would not wait for me.

The bells they sound on Bredon,
  And still the steeples hum,
"Come all to church, good people,"—
  Oh, noisy bells, be dumb;
  I hear you, I will come.

July 1891, 1896

[BE STILL, MY SOUL]

Be still, my soul, be still; the arms you bear are brittle,
  Earth and high heaven are fixt of old and founded strong.
Think rather,—call to thought, if now you grieve a little,
  The days when we had rest, O soul, for they were long.

Men loved unkindness then, but lightless in the quarry
  I slept and saw not; tears fell down, I did not mourn;
Sweat ran and blood sprang out and I was never sorry:
  Then it was well with me, in days ere I was born.

Now, and I muse for why and never find the reason,
  I pace the earth, and drink the air, and feel the sun.
Be still, be still, my soul; it is but for a season:
  Let us endure an hour and see injustice done.

Ay, look: high heaven and earth ail from the prime foundation;
  All thoughts to rive the heart are here, and all are vain:
Horror and scorn and hate and fear and indignation—
  Oh why did I awake? when shall I sleep again?

1892-93, 1896

[WITH RUE MY HEART IS LADEN]

With rue my heart is laden
  For golden friends I had,
For many a rose-lipt maiden
  And many a lightfoot lad.

By brooks too broad for leaping
  The lightfoot boys are laid;
The rose-lipt girls are sleeping
  In fields where roses fade.

Aug. 1893, 1896

[WHITE IN THE MOON THE LONG ROAD LIES]

White in the moon the long road lies,
  The moon stands blank above;
White in the moon the long road lies
  That leads me from my love.

Still hangs the hedge without a gust,
  Still, still the shadows stay:
My feet upon the moonlit dust
  Pursue the ceaseless way.

The world is round, so travellers tell,
  And straight though reach the track,
Trudge on, trudge on, 'twill all be well,
  The way will guide one back.

But ere the circle homeward hies
  Far, far must it remove:
White in the moon the long road lies
  That leads me from my love.

1894, 1896

[FAREWELL TO BARN AND STACK AND TREE]

"Farewell to barn and stack and tree,
  Farewell to Severn shore.
Terence, look your last at me,
  For I come home no more.

"The sun burns on the half-mown hill,
  By now the blood is dried;
And Maurice amongst the hay lies still
  And my knife is in his side.

"My mother thinks us long away;
  'Tis time the field were mown.
She had two sons at rising day,
  To-night she'll be alone.

"And here's a bloody hand to shake,
  And oh, man, here's good-bye;
We'll sweat no more on scythe and rake,
  My bloody hands and I.

"I wish you strength to bring you pride,
  And a love to keep you clean,
And I wish you luck, come Lammastide,
  At racing on the green.

"Long for me the rick will wait,
  And long will wait the fold,
And long will stand the empty plate,
  And dinner will be cold."
Aug. 1894, 1896

[NOW HOLLOW FIRES BURN OUT TO BLACK]

Now hollow fires burn out to black,
  And lights are guttering low:
Square your shoulders, lift your pack,
  And leave your friends and go.

Oh, never fear, man; nought's to dread;
  Look not left nor right:
In all the endless road you tread
  There's nothing but the night.
Autumn 1894, 1896

[WHEN I WAS ONE-AND-TWENTY]

When I was one-and-twenty
  I heard a wise man say,
"Give crowns and pounds and guineas
  But not your heart away;
Give pearls away and rubies
  But keep your fancy free."
But I was one-and-twenty,
  No use to talk to me.

When I was one-and-twenty
  I heard him say again,
"The heart out of the bosom
  Was never given in vain;
'Tis paid with sighs a plenty
  And sold for endless rue."
And I am two-and-twenty,
  And oh, 'tis true, 'tis true.
Jan. 1895, 1896

REVEILLE

Wake: the silver dusk returning
Up the beach of darkness brims,
And the ship of sunrise burning
Strands upon the eastern rims.

Wake: the vaulted shadow shatters,
Trampled to the floor it spanned,
And the tent of night in tatters
Straws the sky-pavilioned land.

Up, lad, up, 'tis late for lying:
Hear the drums of morning play;
Hark, the empty highways crying
"Who'll beyond the hills away?"

Towns and countries woo together,
Forelands beacon, belfries call;
Never lad that trod on leather
Lived to feast his heart with all.

Up, lad: thews that lie and cumber
Sunlit pallets never thrive;
Morns abed and daylight slumber
Were not meant for man alive.

Clay lies still, but blood's a rover;
Breath's a ware that will not keep.
Up, lad: when the journey's over
There'll be time enough to sleep.

Jan. 1895, 1896

[ON MOONLIT HEATH AND LONESOME BANK]

On moonlit heath and lonesome bank
The sheep beside me graze;
And yon the gallows used to clank
Fast by the four cross ways.

A careless shepherd once would keep
  The flocks by moonlight there,
And high amongst the glimmering sheep
  The dead man stood on air.

They hang us now in Shrewsbury jail:
  The whistles blow forlorn,
And trains all night groan on the rail
  To men that die at morn.

There sleeps in Shrewsbury jail to-night,
  Or wakes, as may betide,
A better lad, if things went right,
  Than most that sleep outside.

And naked to the hangman's noose
  The morning clocks will ring
A neck God made for other use
  Than strangling in a string.

And sharp the link of life will snap,
  And dead on air will stand
Heels that held up as straight a chap
  As treads upon the land.

So here I'll watch the night and wait
  To see the morning shine,
When he will hear the stroke of eight
  And not the stroke of nine;

And wish my friend as sound a sleep
  As lads' I did not know,
That shepherded the moonlit sheep
  A hundred years ago.

Feb. 1895, 1896

[WHEN I WATCH THE LIVING MEET]

When I watch the living meet,
  And the moving pageant file
Warm and breathing through the street
  Where I lodge a little while,

If the heats of hate and lust
  In the house of flesh are strong,
Let me mind the house of dust
  Where my sojourn shall be long.

In the nation that is not
  Nothing stands that stood before;
There revenges are forgot,
  And the hater hates no more;

Lovers lying two and two
  Ask not whom they sleep beside,
And the bridegroom all night through
  Never turns him to the bride.

c. *Feb.* 1895, 1896

THE DAY OF BATTLE

"Far I hear the bugle blow
To call me where I would not go,
And the guns begin the song,
'Soldier, fly or stay for long.'

"Comrade, if to turn and fly
Made a soldier never die,
Fly I would, for who would not?
'Tis sure no pleasure to be shot.

"But since the man that runs away
Lives to die another day,
And cowards' funerals, when they come,
Are not wept so well at home,

"Therefore, though the best is bad,
Stand and do the best, my lad;
Stand and fight and see your slain,
And take the bullet in your brain."

March 1895, 1896

TO AN ATHLETE DYING YOUNG

The time you won your town the race
We chaired you through the market-place;
Man and boy stood cheering by,
And home we brought you shoulder-high.

To-day, the road all runners come,
Shoulder-high we bring you home,
And set you at your threshold down,
Townsman of a stiller town.

Smart lad, to slip betimes away
From fields where glory does not stay,
And early though the laurel grows
It withers quicker than the rose.

Eyes the shady night has shut
Cannot see the record cut,
And silence sounds no worse than cheers
After earth has stopped the ears.

Now you will not swell the rout
Of lads that wore their honors out,
Runners whom renown outran
And the name died before the man.

So set, before its echoes fade,
The fleet foot on the sill of shade,
And hold to the low lintel up
The still-defended challenge-cup.

And round that early-laurelled head
Will flock to gaze the strengthless dead,
And find unwithered on its curls
The garland briefer than a girl's.

c. *March 1895*, 1896

[LOVELIEST OF TREES]

Loveliest of trees, the cherry now
Is hung with bloom along the bough,
And stands about the woodland ride,
Wearing white for Eastertide.

Now, of my threescore years and ten,
Twenty will not come again,
And take from seventy springs a score,
It only leaves me fifty more.

And since to look at things in bloom
Fifty springs are little room,
About the woodlands I will go
To see the cherry hung with snow.
c. *May 1895, 1896*

[IS MY TEAM PLOUGHING]

"Is my team ploughing,
  That I was used to drive
And hear the harness jingle
  When I was man alive?"

Ay, the horses trample,
  The harness jingles now;
No change though you lie under
  The land you used to plough.

"Is football playing
  Along the river shore,
With lads to chase the leather,
  Now I stand up no more?"

Ay, the ball is flying,
  The lads play heart and soul;
The goal stands up, the keeper
  Stands up to keep the goal.

"Is my girl happy,
 That I thought hard to leave,
And has she tired of weeping
 As she lies down at eve?"

Ay, she lies down lightly,
 She lies not down to weep:
Your girl is well contented.
 Be still, my lad, and sleep.

"Is my friend hearty,
 Now I am thin and pine,
And has he found to sleep in
 A better bed than mine?"

Yes, lad, I lie easy,
 I lie as lads would choose;
I cheer a dead man's sweetheart—
 Never ask me whose.
 May—autumn 1895, 1896

[WHEN SMOKE STOOD UP FROM LUDLOW]

When smoke stood up from Ludlow,
 And mist blew off from Teme,
And blithe afield to ploughing
 Against the morning beam
 I strode beside my team,

The blackbird in the coppice
 Looked out to see me stride,
And hearkened as I whistled
 The trampling team beside,
 And fluted and replied:

"Lie down, lie down, young yeoman;
 What use to rise and rise?
Rise man a thousand mornings
 Yet down at last he lies,
 And then the man is wise."

I heard the tune he sang me,
And spied his yellow bill;
I picked a stone and aimed it
And threw it with a will:
Then the bird was still.

Then my soul within me
Took up the blackbird's strain,
And still beside the horses
Along the dewy lane
It sang the song again:

"Lie down, lie down, young yeoman;
The sun moves always west;
The road one treads to labor
Will lead one home to rest,
And that will be the best."

c. *Aug.* 1895, 1896

[THINK NO MORE, LAD]

Think no more, lad; laugh, be jolly:
Why should men make haste to die?
Empty heads and tongues a-talking
Make the rough road easy walking,
And the feather pate of folly
Bears the falling sky.

Oh, 'tis jesting, dancing, drinking
Spins the heavy world around.
If young hearts were not so clever,
Oh, they would be young for ever:
Think no more; 'tis only thinking
Lays lads underground.

c. *Sept.* 1895, 1896

[TERENCE, THIS IS STUPID STUFF]

"Terence, this is stupid stuff:
You eat your victuals fast enough;
There can't be much amiss, 'tis clear,

To see the rate you drink your beer.
But oh, good Lord, the verse you make,
It gives a chap the belly-ache.
The cow, the old cow, she is dead;
It sleeps well, the hornèd head:
We poor lads, 'tis our turn now
To hear such tunes as killed the cow.
Pretty friendship 'tis to rhyme
Your friends to death before their time
Moping melancholy mad:
Come, pipe a tune to dance to, lad."

Why, if 'tis dancing you would be,
There's brisker pipes than poetry.
Say, for what were hop-yards meant,
Or why was Burton built on Trent?
Oh, many a peer of England brews
Livelier liquor than the Muse,
And malt does more than Milton can
To justify God's ways to man.
Ale, man, ale's the stuff to drink
For fellows whom it hurts to think:
Look into the pewter pot
To see the world as the world's not.
And faith, 'tis pleasant till 'tis past:
The mischief is that 'twill not last.
Oh, I have been to Ludlow fair
And left my necktie God knows where,
And carried half-way home, or near,
Pints and quarts of Ludlow beer:
Then the world seemed none so bad,
And I myself a sterling lad;
And down in lovely muck I've lain,
Happy till I woke again.
Then I saw the morning sky:
Heigho, the tale was all a lie;
The world, it was the old world yet,
I was I, my things were wet,
And nothing now remained to do
But begin the game anew.

Therefore, since the world has still
Much good, but much less good than ill,

And while the sun and moon endure
Luck's a chance, but trouble's sure,
I'd face it as a wise man would,
And train for ill and not for good.
'Tis true, the stuff I bring for sale
Is not so brisk a brew as ale:
Out of a stem that scored the hand
I wrung it in a weary land.
But take it: if the smack is sour,
The better for the embittered hour;
It should do good to heart and head
When your soul is in my soul's stead;
And I will friend you, if I may,
In the dark and cloudy day.

There was a king reigned in the East:
There, when kings will sit to feast,
They get their fill before they think
With poisoned meat and poisoned drink.
He gathered all that springs to birth
From the many-venomed earth;
First a little, thence to more,
He sampled all her killing store;
And easy, smiling, seasoned sound,
Sate the king when healths went round.
They put arsenic in his meat
And stared aghast to watch him eat;
They poured strychnine in his cup
And shook to see him drink it up:
They shook, they stared as white's their shirt:
Them it was their poison hurt.
—I tell the tale that I heard told.
Mithridates, he died old.

c. Sept. 1895, 1896

[YONDER SEE THE MORNING BLINK]

Yonder see the morning blink:
  The sun is up, and up must I,
To wash and dress and eat and drink
And look at things and talk and think
  And work, and God knows why.

Oh, often have I washed and dressed
  And what's to show for all my pain?
Let me lie abed and rest:
Ten thousand times I've done my best
  And all's to do again.

Dec. 1895, 1922

[THE CHESTNUT CASTS HIS FLAMBEAUX]

The chestnut casts his flambeaux, and the flowers
  Stream from the hawthorn on the wind away,
The doors clap to, the pane is blind with showers.
  Pass me the can, lad; there's an end of May.

There's one spoilt spring to scant our mortal lot,
  One season ruined of our little store.
May will be fine next year as like as not:
  Oh ay, but then we shall be twenty-four.

We for a certainty are not the first
  Have sat in taverns while the tempest hurled
Their hopeful plans to emptiness, and cursed
  Whatever brute and blackguard made the world.

It is in truth iniquity on high
  To cheat our sentenced souls of aught they crave,
And mar the merriment as you and I
  Fare on our long fool's-errand to the grave.

Iniquity it is; but pass the can.
  My lad, no pair of kings our mothers bore;
Our only portion is the estate of man:
  We want the moon, but we shall get no more.

If here to-day the cloud of thunder lours
  To-morrow it will hie on far behests;
The flesh will grieve on other bones than ours
  Soon, and the soul will mourn in other breasts.

The troubles of our proud and angry dust
  Are from eternity, and shall not fail.
Bear them we can, and if we can we must.
  Shoulder the sky, my lad, and drink your ale.

1896-1922, 1922

[NOW DREARY DAWNS THE EASTERN LIGHT]

Now dreary dawns the eastern light,
  And fall of eve is drear,
And cold the poor man lies at night,
  And so goes out the year.

Little is the luck I've had,
  And oh, 'tis comfort small
To think that many another lad
  Has had no luck at all.

1896-1922, 1922

[AS I GIRD ON FOR FIGHTING]

As I gird on for fighting
  My sword upon my thigh,
I think on old ill fortunes
  Of better men than I.

Think I, the round world over,
  What golden lads are low
With hurts not mine to mourn for
  And shames I shall not know.

What evil luck soever
  For me remains in store,
'Tis sure much finer fellows
  Have fared much worse before.

So here are things to think on
  That ought to make me brave,
As I strap on for fighting
  My sword that will not save.

c. *1900*, 1922

[THE RAIN, IT STREAMS ON STONE]

The rain, it streams on stone and hillock,
  The boot clings to the clay.
Since all is done that's due and right
Let's home; and now, my lad, good-night,
  For I must turn away.

Good-night, my lad, for nought's eternal;
  No league of ours, for sure.
To-morrow I shall miss you less,
And ache of heart and heaviness
  Are things that time should cure.

Over the hill the highway marches
  And what's beyond is wide:
Oh, soon enough will pine to nought
Remembrance and the faithful thought
  That sits the grave beside.

The skies, they are not always raining
  Nor grey the twelvemonth through;
And I shall meet good days and mirth,
And range the lovely lands of earth
  With friends no worse than you.

But oh, my man, the house is fallen
  That none can build again;
My man, how full of joy and woe
Your mother bore you years ago
  To-night to lie in the rain.

1902-22, 1922

[WAKE NOT FOR THE WORLD-HEARD THUNDER]

Wake not for the world-heard thunder
  Nor the chime that earthquakes toll.
Star may plot in heaven with planet,
Lightning rive the rock of granite,
Tempest tread the oakwood under:
  Fear not you for flesh nor soul.
Marching, fighting, victory past,
Stretch your limbs in peace at last.

Stir not for the soldiers drilling
  Nor the fever nothing cures:
Throb of drum and timbal's rattle
Call but man alive to battle,
And the fife with death-notes filling
  Screams for blood but not for yours.
Times enough you bled your best;
Sleep on now, and take your rest.

Sleep, my lad; the French are landed,
  London's burning, Windsor's down;
Clasp your cloak of earth about you,
We must man the ditch without you,
March unled and fight short-handed,
  Charge to fall and swim to drown.
Duty, friendship, bravery o'er,
Sleep away, lad; wake no more.

March 1922, 1922

[HO, EVERYONE THAT THIRSTETH]

Ho, everyone that thirsteth
  And hath the price to give,
Come to the stolen waters,
  Drink and your soul shall live.

Come to the stolen waters
  And leap the guarded pale,
And pull the flower in season
  Before desire shall fail.

It shall not last for ever,
  No more than earth and skies;
But he that drinks in season
  Shall live before he dies.

June suns, you cannot store them
  To warm the winter's cold,
The lad that hopes for heaven
  Shall fill his mouth with mould.

c. 1922, 1936

FOR MY FUNERAL

O thou that from thy mansion
  Through time and place to roam,
Dost send abroad thy children,
  And then dost call them home,

That men and tribes and nations
  And all thy hand hath made
May shelter them from sunshine
  In thine eternal shade:

We now to peace and darkness
  And earth and thee restore
Thy creature that thou madest
  And wilt cast forth no more.

1925, 1936

W. B. Yeats

William Butler Yeats, eldest son of the artist John Butler Yeats, was born at Sandymount, Dublin, June 13, 1865. His mother was a daughter of William Pollexfen, a shipowner of Sligo, in northwestern Ireland. He had two brothers, of whom one died in infancy, and two sisters; the surviving brother, Jack Butler Yeats, became a well-known artist, and one of his sisters founded the Cuala Press, Dublin, from which many of his books were first issued.

He spent much of his childhood with his grandparents in Sligo, where from servants and members of the family he heard stories of Celtic folklore which colored his thinking and animated his writings. Of those years he later wrote, "I remember little of childhood but its pain. I have grown happier with every year of life as though gradually conquering something in myself, for certainly my miseries were not made by others but were a part of my own mind." [1]

Because his thoughts were constantly straying, he found learning difficult; and only fear of his father, who on a visit to Sligo volunteered to teach him, made him master reading. For a short while he attended a dame-school, where he learned spelling and grammar. At the age of nine he went to live with his parents in London, and for the next six years he attended the Godolphin School, Hammersmith, but returned to Sligo each year for his vacations. He still learned with such difficulty that he had to spend a whole evening on one lesson if he was to know it. He said of himself at this time, "My thoughts were a great excitement, but when I tried to do anything with them, it was like trying to pack a balloon into a shed in a high wind. I was always near the bottom of my class, and always making excuses that but added to my timidity;

[1] *Autobiographies*, p. 13.

but no master was rough with me. I was known to collect moths and butterflies and to get into no worse mischief than hiding now and again an old tailless white rat in my coat-pocket or my desk."[1] In 1880 his family moved to Dublin, where for three years Yeats attended the Erasmus Smith School. From his eighteenth to twenty-first year he studied at the Metropolitan School of Art, but spent as much time writing and chanting poetry, and studying psychical phenomena and mystical philosophy, as in studying art.

His first liking for rime came when as a child he heard a stable-boy read some "Orange verse," and for poetry when at the age of eight or nine he heard his father read Macaulay's *Lays of Ancient Rome* and Scott's *Lay of the Last Minstrel*. He began when about seventeen to write plays in verse, using Shelley and Spenser as models; and two years later he published his first poem, a lyric, and shortly afterwards an arcadian play, *The Island of Statues*, in the *Dublin University Review*. From this time he contributed frequently to this magazine and to the *Irish Monthly*, but wrote his "first good lyrics and tolerable essays" some years later for the *National Observer*, of which W. E. Henley was editor. His first book was a volume of poems, *Mosada*, published by subscription in 1886, and his next a book of stories.

In 1887 he returned to London with his parents, and for the next few years was extremely busy writing poetry and earning a small income by writing literary gossip for provincial newspapers, compiling anthologies of Irish fairy stories, editing selections from Irish authors, and contributing to several journals. Despite all this, he found time to attend meetings of the Socialist League at the home of William Morris, to help found the Rhymers' Club, to study magic and spiritism, and to found the Irish Literary Society. Among his friends of those years were Henley, Lionel Johnson, Ernest Dowson, Arthur Symons, Oscar Wilde, the French poet Verlaine, and, most important of all, John O'Leary, the old Fenian leader, through association with whom, he said, came all he set his hand to later. The chief early influence on his work was that of the Pre-Raphaelites; the next influence was that of Blake, whose works he helped edit; and after the middle nineties he was influenced by Pater and the French poets Mallarmé and Villiers de L'Isle Adam. But from the beginning he went for material to Celtic sources; and, influenced partly by O'Leary and other polit-

[1] *Ibid.*, p. 50.

ical leaders and partly by his own convictions, gained by years of study and thought, he applied himself to creating a new national literature that should be peculiarly Irish. He gradually freed himself from his early influences, and in his own work developed a body of fresh subject matter and a style personal and distinctive.

Aside from his poetry, his most conspicuous contribution to Irish literature was in the drama. As early as 1887 he planned to create an Irish theatre, and about 1900, with the help of Lady Gregory and others, he succeeded in founding the Abbey Theatre in Dublin. He wrote many dramas for the Abbey Players, and he maintained an interest in the work of this group throughout his remaining years. He also wrote much prose, of which the more important volumes are *The Celtic Twilight* (1893), *Ideas of Good and Evil* (1903), *Discoveries* (1907), *The Cutting of an Agate* (1912), and several autobiographical works: *Reveries over Childhood and Youth* (1915), *Four Years* (1921), and *The Trembling of the Veil* (1922)—published together as *Autobiographies* (1927)—and *A Packet for Ezra Pound* (1929) and *Stories of Michael Robartes and His Friends* (1931).

During his later years his literary reputation mounted steadily. In 1923 he was awarded the Nobel prize for literature. The University of Dublin, Oxford, and other universities conferred honorary degrees on him. On his seventieth birthday Ireland gave him national recognition by honoring him at a dinner which was attended by over two hundred leading men of the country, as well as by representatives from England and other countries. And from 1922 to 1928 he was a senator of the Irish Free State.

On October 20, 1917, he married Miss Georgie Lees, a daughter of W. G. H. Lees of Wrexham, England; and they had two children, a daughter and a son. After his marriage, Yeats lived part of the time in western Ireland, where he used as a study one of the medieval square towers, of which a few still exist. For some years before his death, however, he lived in a suburb of Dublin. He visited the United States several times, and on these visits gave frequent lectures. In his last years he spent much time in Italy, Sicily, and southern France in search of health. In the last three years of his life he was afflicted with heart trouble, which finally caused his death. He died on January 28, 1939, at a country hotel on Cap Martin, on the French Riviera, and was buried in the cemetery above the little town of Roquebrune.

THE INDIAN UPON GOD

I passed along the water's edge below the humid trees,
My spirit rocked in evening light, the rushes round my knees,
My spirit rocked in sleep and sighs; and saw the moorfowl pace
All dripping on a grassy slope, and saw them cease to chase
Each other round in circles, and heard the eldest speak:
Who holds the world between His bill and made us strong or weak
Is an undying moorfowl, and He lives beyond the sky.
The rains are from His dripping wing, the moonbeams from His eye.
I passed a little further on and heard a lotus talk:
Who made the world and ruleth it, He hangeth on a stalk,
For I am in His image made, and all this tinkling tide
Is but a sliding drop of rain between His petals wide.
A little way within the gloom a roebuck raised his eyes
Brimful of starlight, and he said: *The Stamper of the Skies,*
He is a gentle roebuck; for how else, I pray, could He
Conceive a thing so sad and soft, a gentle thing like me?
I passed a little further on and heard a peacock say:
Who made the grass and made the worms and made my feathers gay,
He is a monstrous peacock, and He waveth all the night
His languid tail above us, lit with myriad spots of light.

1884, 1889

THE MADNESS OF KING GOLL[1]

I sat on cushioned otter skin:
My word was law from Ith to Emen,
And shook at Invar Amargin
The hearts of the world-troubling seamen,
And drove tumult and war away
From girl and boy and man and beast;
The fields grew fatter day by day,

[1] According to tradition, Goll was a prince of Ulster, and at the battle of Ventry Harbor between Finn McCumhail's bands and the King of the World he was roused to such a frenzy that he lost his reason. He found his way to the Gleann-na-n-gealt, where all lunatics must go if they can. Except for this suggestion, Yeats's poem owes little to the legend.

The wild fowl of the air increased;
And every ancient Ollave said,
While he bent down his fading head,
"He drives away the Northern cold."
They will not hush, the leaves a-flutter round me, the beech leaves old.

I sat and mused and drank sweet wine;
A herdsman came from inland valleys,
Crying, the pirates drove his swine
To fill their dark-beaked hollow galleys.
I called my battle-breaking men,
And my loud brazen battle-cars
From rolling vale and rivery glen;
And under the blinking of the stars
Fell on the pirates by the deep,
And hurled them in the gulf of sleep:
These hands won many a torque of gold.
They will not hush, the leaves a-flutter round me, the beech leaves old.

But slowly, as I shouting slew
And trampled in the bubbling mire,
In my most secret spirit grew
A whirling and a wandering fire:
I stood: keen stars above me shone,
Around me shone keen eyes of men:
I laughed aloud and hurried on
By rocky shore and rushy fen;
I laughed because birds fluttered by,
And starlight gleamed, and clouds flew high,
And rushes waved and waters rolled.
They will not hush, the leaves a-flutter round me, the beech leaves old.

And now I wander in the woods
When summer gluts the golden bees,
Or in autumnal solitudes
Arise the leopard-colored trees;
Or when along the wintry strands
The cormorants shiver on their rocks;
I wander on, and wave my hands,
And sing, and shake my heavy locks.

The grey wolf knows me; by one ear
I lead along the woodland deer;
The hares run by me growing bold.
They will not hush, the leaves a-flutter round me, the beech leaves old.

I came upon a little town,
That slumbered in the harvest moon,
And passed a-tiptoe up and down,
Murmuring, to a fitful tune,
How I have followed, night and day,
A tramping of tremendous feet,
And saw where this old tympan lay,
Deserted on a doorway seat,
And bore it to the woods with me;
Of some unhuman misery
Our married voices wildly trolled.
They will not hush, the leaves a-flutter round me, the beech leaves old.

I sang how, when day's toil is done,
Orchil shakes out her long dark hair
That hides away the dying sun
And sheds faint odors through the air:
When my hand passed from wire to wire
It quenched, with sound like falling dew,
The whirling and the wandering fire;
But lift a mournful ulalu,
For the kind wires are torn and still,
And I must wander wood and hill
Through summer's heat and winter's cold.
They will not hush, the leaves a-flutter round me, the beech leaves old.

1889

DOWN BY THE SALLEY GARDENS

Down by the salley gardens my love and I did meet;
She passed the salley gardens with little snow-white feet.
She bid me take love easy, as the leaves grow on the tree;
But I, being young and foolish, with her would not agree.

In a field by the river my love and I did stand,
And on my leaning shoulder she laid her snow-white hand.
She bid me take life easy, as the grass grows on the weirs;
But I was young and foolish, and now am full of tears.

1889.

CUCHULAIN'S FIGHT WITH THE SEA [1]

A man came slowly from the setting sun,
To Emer, raddling raiment in her dun,
And said, "I am that swineherd, whom you bid
Go dwell upon the cliffs and watch the tide;
But now I have no need to watch it more."

Then Emer cast the web upon the floor,
And raising arms all raddled with the dye,
Parted her lips with a loud sudden cry.

That swineherd stared upon her face and said:
"Not any god alive, nor mortal dead,
Has slain so mighty armies, so great kings,
Nor won the gold that now Cuchulain brings."

"Why do you tremble thus from feet to crown?"

He caught his breath and cast him weeping down
Upon the web-heaped floor, and thus his word:
"With him is one sweet-throated like a bird."

"You dare me to my face," and thereupon
She smote with raddled fist, and where her son
Herded the cattle came with stumbling feet,
And cried with angry voice, "It is not meet
To idle life away with flocks and herds."

"I have long waited, mother, for those words:
But wherefore now?"

"There is a man to die;
You have the heaviest arm under the sky."

[1] Cuchulain (pronounced ko͝o-ho͞o'lĭn) was the hero of a group of tales which date from the beginning of the Christian Era. The story of how he won Emer and of his other exploits may be read in Lady Gregory's *Cuchulain of Muirthemne.*

"No, somewhere under daylight or the stars
My father stands amid his battle cars."

"But you have grown to be the taller man."

"Yet somewhere under starlight or the sun
My father stands amid his battle cars."

"But he is old and sad with many wars."

"I only ask what way my journey lies.
For He who made you bitter, made you wise."

"The Red Branch gather a great company
Between the game and the horses of the sea.
Go there, and camp upon the forest's rim;
But tell your name and lineage to him
Whose blade compels, and bid them send you one
Who has a like vow from their triple dun."

Among those feasting kings Cuchulain dwelt,
And his young dear one close beside him knelt;
Stared like the Spring upon the ancient skies,
Upon the mournful wonder of his eyes,
And pondered on the glory of his days;
And all around the harp-string told his praise,
And Concobar, the Red Branch king of kings,
With his own fingers touched the brazen strings.

At last Cuchulain spake, "Some man has made
His evening fire amid the leafy shade.
I have often heard him singing to and fro,
I have often heard the sweet sound of his bow,
Seek out what man he is."

One went and came.
"He bade me let all know he gives his name
At the sword point, and bade me bring him one
Who had a like vow from our triple dun."

"I only of the Red Branch hosted now,"
Cuchulain cried, "have made and keep that vow."

After short fighting in the leafy shade,
He spake to the young man, "Is there no maid
Who loves you, no white arms to wrap you round,
Or do you long for the dim sleepy ground,
That you have come and dared me to my face?"

"The dooms of men are in God's hidden place."

"Your head a while seemed like a woman's head
That I loved once."

Again the fighting sped,
But now the war rage in Cuchulain woke,
And through that new blade's guard the old blade broke,
And pierced him.

"Speak before your breath is done."

"Cuchulain I, mighty Cuchulain's son."

"I put you from your pain. I can no more."

While day its burden on to evening bore,
With head bowed on his knees Cuchulain stayed;
Then Concobar sent that sweet-throated maid,
And she, to win him, his grey hair caressed;
In vain her arms, in vain her soft white breast.
Then Concobar, the subtlest of all men,
Ranking his Druids round him ten by ten,
Spake thus, "Cuchulain will dwell there and brood,
For three days more in dreadful quietude,
And then arise, and raving slay us all.
Chaunt in his ear delusions magical,
That he may fight the horses of the sea."
The Druids took them to their mystery,
And chanted for three days.

Cuchulain stirred,
Stared on the horses of the sea, and heard
The cars of battle and his own name cried;
And fought with the invulnerable tide.

1893

THE ROSE OF THE WORLD

Who dreamed that beauty passes like a dream?
For these red lips, with all their mournful pride,
Mournful that no new wonder may betide,
Troy passed away in one high funeral gleam,
And Usna's children died.[1]

We and the laboring world are passing by:
Amid men's souls, that waver and give place,
Like the pale waters in their wintry race,
Under the passing stars, foam of the sky,
Lives on this lonely face.

Bow down, archangels, in your dim abode:
Before you were, or any hearts to beat,
Weary and kind, one lingered by His seat;
He made the world to be a grassy road
Before her wandering feet.

1893

THE LAKE ISLE OF INNISFREE

I will arise and go now, and go to Innisfree,
And a small cabin build there, of clay and wattles made:
Nine bean rows will I have there, a hive for the honey bee,
And live alone in the bee-loud glade.

And I shall have some peace there, for peace comes dropping slow,
Dropping from the veils of the morning to where the cricket sings;
There midnight's all a glimmer, and noon a purple glow,
And evening full of the linnet's wings.

I will arise and go now, for always night and day
I hear lake water lapping with low sounds by the shore;
While I stand on the roadway, or on the pavements grey,
I hear it in the deep heart's core.

1893

[1] The sons of Usna—Naesi, Anli, and Ardan—lost their lives while fighting against the troops of Conor Mac Nessa, King of Ulster, who was seeking to regain his adopted daughter, Deirdre, whom Naesi had married. In Irish legend Deirdre's beauty is celebrated in much the way that Helen's is in Greek mythology.

THE PITY OF LOVE

A pity beyond all telling
Is hid in the heart of love:
The folk who are buying and selling,
The clouds on their journey above,
The cold wet winds ever blowing,
And the shadowy hazel grove
Where mouse-grey waters are flowing,
Threaten the head that I love.

1893

WHEN YOU ARE OLD

When you are old and grey and full of sleep,
And nodding by the fire, take down this book,
And slowly read, and dream of the soft look
Your eyes had once, and of their shadows deep;

How many loved your moments of glad grace,
And loved your beauty with love false or true;
But one man loved the pilgrim soul in you,
And loved the sorrows of your changing face.

And bending down beside the glowing bars
Murmur, a little sadly, how love fled
And paced upon the mountains overhead
And hid his face amid a crowd of stars.

1893

[THE SONG OF THE FAERIES]

[From *The Land of Heart's Desire*]

The wind blows out of the gates of the day,
The wind blows over the lonely of heart,
And the lonely of heart is withered away,
While the faeries dance in a place apart,
Shaking their milk-white feet in a ring,
Tossing their milk-white arms in the air:
For they hear the wind laugh and murmur and sing

Of a land where even the old are fair,
And even the wise are merry of tongue;
But I heard a reed of Coolaney say,
"When the wind has laughed and murmured and sung,
The lonely of heart is withered away!"

1894

RED HANRAHAN'S SONG ABOUT IRELAND [1]

The old brown thorn trees break in two high over Cummen
Strand,
Under a bitter black wind that blows from the left hand;
Our courage breaks like an old tree in a black wind and dies,
But we have hidden in our hearts the flame out of the eyes
Of Cathleen, the daughter of Houlihan.

The wind has bundled up the clouds high over Knocknarea,
And thrown the thunder on the stones for all that Maeve can say.
Angers that are like noisy clouds have set our hearts abeat;
But we have all bent low and low and kissed the quiet feet
Of Cathleen, the daughter of Houlihan.

The yellow pool has overflowed high up on Clooth-na-Bare,
For the wet winds are blowing out of the clinging air;
Like heavy flooded waters our bodies and our blood:
But purer than a tall candle before the Holy Rood
Is Cathleen, the daughter of Houlihan.

1897

THE LOVER TELLS OF THE ROSE IN HIS HEART

All things uncomely and broken, all things worn out and old,
The cry of a child by the roadway, the creak of a lumbering cart,
The heavy steps of the ploughman, splashing the wintry mould,
Are wronging your image that blossoms a rose in the deeps of
my heart.

[1] Red Hanrahan is the main character in Yeats's *Story of Red Hanrahan.* His making of the song about Ireland is told in the story "Hanrahan and Cathleen the Daughter of Hoolihan." Cathleen, obviously, is Ireland.

The wrong of unshapely things is a wrong too great to be told;
I hunger to build them anew and sit on a green knoll apart,
With the earth and the sky and the water, remade, like a casket
  of gold
For my dreams of your image that blossoms a rose in the deeps
  of my heart.

1899

INTO THE TWILIGHT

Out-worn heart, in a time out-worn,
Come clear of the nets of wrong and right;
Laugh, heart, again in the grey twilight,
Sigh, heart, again in the dew of the morn.

Your mother Eire is always young,
Dew ever shining and twilight grey;
Though hope fall from you and love decay,
Burning in fires of a slanderous tongue.

Come, heart, where hill is heaped upon hill:
For there the mystical brotherhood
Of sun and moon and hollow and wood
And river and stream work out their will;

And God stands winding His lonely horn,
And time and the world are ever in flight;
And love is less kind than the grey twilight,
And hope is less dear than the dew of the morn.

1899

THE SONG OF WANDERING AENGUS

I went out to the hazel wood,
Because a fire was in my head,
And cut and peeled a hazel wand,
And hooked a berry to a thread;
And when white moths were on the wing,
And moth-like stars were flickering out,
I dropped the berry in a stream
And caught a little silver trout.

When I had laid it on the floor
I went to blow the fire aflame,
But something rustled on the floor,
And some one called me by my name:
It had become a glimmering girl
With apple blossom in her hair
Who called me by my name and ran
And faded through the brightening air.

Though I am old with wandering
Through hollow lands and hilly lands,
I will find out where she has gone,
And kiss her lips and take her hands;
And walk among long dappled grass,
And pluck till time and times are done
The silver apples of the moon,
The golden apples of the sun.

1899

HE WISHES FOR THE CLOTHS OF HEAVEN

Had I the heavens' embroidered cloths,
Enwrought with golden and silver light,
The blue and the dim and the dark cloths
Of night and light and the half-light,
I would spread the cloths under your feet:
But I, being poor, have only my dreams;
I have spread my dreams under your feet;
Tread softly because you tread on my dreams.

1899

IN THE SEVEN WOODS

I have heard the pigeons of the Seven Woods
Make their faint thunder, and the garden bees
Hum in the lime-tree flowers; and put away
The unavailing outcries and the old bitterness
That empty the heart. I have forgot awhile
Tara uprooted, and new commonness
Upon the throne and crying about the streets
And hanging its paper flowers from post to post,

Because it is alone of all things happy.
I am contented, for I know that Quiet
Wanders laughing and eating her wild heart
Among pigeons and bees, while that Great Archer,
Who but awaits His hour to shoot, still hangs
A cloudy quiver over Parc-na-lee.

1904

NEVER GIVE ALL THE HEART

Never give all the heart, for love
Will hardly seem worth thinking of
To passionate women if it seem
Certain, and they never dream
That it fades out from kiss to kiss;
For everything that's lovely is
But a brief, dreamy, kind delight.
O never give the heart outright,
For they, for all smooth lips can say,
Have given their hearts up to the play.
And who could play it well enough
If deaf and dumb and blind with love?
He that made this knows all the cost,
For he gave all his heart and lost.

1904

NO SECOND TROY

Why should I blame her that she filled my days
With misery, or that she would of late
Have taught to ignorant men most violent ways,
Or hurled the little streets upon the great,
Had they but courage equal to desire?
What could have made her peaceful with a mind
That nobleness made simple as a fire,
With beauty like a tightened bow, a kind
That is not natural in an age like this,
Being high and solitary and most stern?
Why, what could she have done, being what she is?
Was there another Troy for her to burn?

1910

SEPTEMBER 1913

What need you, being come to sense,
But fumble in a greasy till
And add the halfpence to the pence
And prayer to shivering prayer, until
You have dried the marrow from the bone;
For men were born to pray and save:
Romantic Ireland's dead and gone,
It's with O'Leary [1] in the grave.

Yet they were of a different kind,
The names that stilled your childish play,
They have gone about the world like wind,
But little time had they to pray
For whom the hangman's rope was spun,
And what, God help us, could they save?
Romantic Ireland's dead and gone,
It's with O'Leary in the grave.

Was it for this the wild geese spread
The grey wing upon every tide;
For this that all that blood was shed,
For this Edward Fitzgerald died,
And Robert Emmet and Wolfe Tone,
All that delirium of the brave?
Romantic Ireland's dead and gone,
It's with O'Leary in the grave.

Yet could we turn the years again,
And call those exiles as they were
In all their loneliness and pain,
You'd cry, "Some woman's yellow hair
Has maddened every mother's son":
They weighed so lightly what they gave.
But let them be, they're dead and gone,
They're with O'Leary in the grave.

1914

[1] John O'Leary, the Fenian leader, for many years a friend of Yeats.

THE WILD SWANS AT COOLE

The trees are in their autumn beauty,
The woodland paths are dry,
Under the October twilight the water
Mirrors a still sky;
Upon the brimming water among the stones
Are nine-and-fifty swans.

The nineteenth autumn has come upon me
Since I first made my count;
I saw, before I had well finished,
All suddenly mount
And scatter wheeling in great broken rings
Upon their clamorous wings.

I have looked upon those brilliant creatures,
And now my heart is sore.
All's changed since I, hearing at twilight,
The first time on this shore,
The bell-beat of their wings above my head,
Trod with a lighter tread.

Unwearied still, lover by lover,
They paddle in the cold,
Companionable streams or climb the air;
Their hearts have not grown old;
Passion or conquest, wander where they will,
Attend upon them still.

But now they drift on the still water
Mysterious, beautiful;
Among what rushes will they build,
By what lake's edge or pool
Delight men's eyes when I awake some day
To find they have flown away?

1919

TO A YOUNG BEAUTY

Dear fellow-artist, why so free
With every sort of company,
With every Jack and Jill?
Choose your companions from the best;
Who draws a bucket with the rest
Soon topples down the hill.

You may, that mirror for a school,
Be passionate, not bountiful
As common beauties may,
Who were not born to keep in trim
With old Ezekiel's cherubim
But those of Beauvarlet.

I know what wages beauty gives,
How hard a life her servant lives,
Yet praise the winters gone:
There is not a fool can call me friend,
And I may dine at journey's end
With Landor and with Donne.

1919

TOM O'ROUGHLEY

"Though logic choppers rule the town,
And every man and maid and boy
Has marked a distant object down,
An aimless joy is a pure joy,"
Or so did Tom O'Roughley say
That saw the surges running by,
"And wisdom is a butterfly
And not a gloomy bird of prey.

"If little planned is little sinned
But little need the grave distress.
What's dying but a second wind?
How but in zig-zag wantonness

Could trumpeter Michael be so brave?"
Or something of that sort he said,
"And if my dearest friend were dead
I'd dance a measure on his grave."

1919

THE PEOPLE

"What have I earned for all that work," I said,
"For all that I have done at my own charge?
The daily spite of this unmannerly town,
Where who has served the most is most defamed,
The reputation of his lifetime lost
Between the night and morning. I might have lived,
And you know well how great the longing has been,
Where every day my footfall should have lit
In the green shadow of Ferrara wall;
Or climbed among the images of the past—
The unperturbed and courtly images—
Evening and morning, the steep street of Urbino
To where the duchess and her people talked
The stately midnight through until they stood
In their great window looking at the dawn;
I might have had no friend that could not mix
Courtesy and passion into one like those
That saw the wicks grow yellow in the dawn;
I might have used the one substantial right
My trade allows: chosen my company,
And chosen what scenery had pleased me best."
Thereon my phoenix answered in reproof,
"The drunkards, pilferers of public funds,
All the dishonest crowd I had driven away,
When my luck changed and they dared meet my face,
Crawled from obscurity, and set upon me
Those I had served and some that I had fed;
Yet never have I, now nor any time,
Complained of the people."
All I could reply
Was: "You, that have not lived in thought but deed,
Can have the purity of a natural force,
But I, whose virtues are the definitions
Of the analytic mind, can neither close

The eye of the mind nor keep my tongue from speech."
And yet, because my heart leaped at her words,
I was abashed, and now they come to mind
After nine years, I sink my head abashed.

1919

EGO DOMINUS TUUS

Hic. On the grey sand beside the shallow stream
Under your old wind-beaten tower, where still
A lamp burns on beside the open book
That Michael Robartes left, you walk in the moon,
And, though you have passed the best of life, still trace,
Enthralled by the unconquerable delusion,
Magical shapes.
Ille. By the help of an image
I call to my own opposite, summon all
That I have handled least, least looked upon.
Hic. And I would find myself and not an image.
Ille. That is our modern hope and by its light
We have lit upon the gentle, sensitive mind,
And lost the old nonchalance of the hand;
Whether we have chosen chisel, pen or brush,
We are but critics, or but half create,
Timid, entangled, empty and abashed,
Lacking the countenance of our friends.
Hic. And yet
The chief imagination of Christendom,
Dante Alighieri, so utterly found himself
That he has made that hollow face of his
More plain to the mind's eye than any face
But that of Christ.
Ille. And did he find himself,
Or was the hunger that had made it hollow
A hunger for the apple on the bough
Most out of reach? and is that spectral image
The man that Lapo and that Guido knew?
I think he fashioned from his opposite
An image that might have been a stony face,
Staring upon a bedouin's horse-hair roof
From doored and windowed cliff, or half upturned
Among the coarse grass and the camel dung.

He set his chisel to the hardest stone.
Being mocked by Guido for his lecherous life,
Derided and deriding, driven out
To climb that stair and eat that bitter bread,
He found the unpersuadable justice, he found
The most exalted lady loved by a man.
Hic. Yet surely there are men who have made their art
Out of no tragic war, lovers of life,
Impulsive men that look for happiness
And sing when they have found it.
Ille. No, not sing,
For those that love the world serve it in action,
Grow rich, popular and full of influence,
And should they paint or write still it is action:
The struggle of the fly in marmalade.
The rhetorician would deceive his neighbors,
The sentimentalist himself; while art
Is but a vision of reality.
What portion in the world can the artist have
Who has awakened from the common dream
But dissipation and despair?
Hic. And yet
No one denies to Keats love of the world;
Remember his deliberate happiness.
Ille. His art is happy but who knows his mind?
I see a schoolboy when I think of him
With face and nose pressed to a sweet-shop window,
For certainly he sank into his grave
His senses and his heart unsatisfied,
And made—being poor, ailing and ignorant,
Shut out from all the luxury of the world,
The coarse-bred son of a livery-stable keeper—
Luxuriant song.
Hic. Why should you leave the lamp
Burning alone beside an open book,
And trace these characters upon the sands?
A style is found by sedentary toil
And by the imitation of great masters.
Ille. Because I seek an image, not a book.
Those men that in their writings are most wise
Own nothing but their blind, stupefied hearts.
I call to the mysterious one who yet
Shall walk the wet sands by the edge of the stream

And look most like me, being indeed my double,
And prove of all imaginable things
The most unlike, being my anti-self,
And standing by these characters disclose
All that I seek; and whisper it as though
He were afraid the birds, who cry aloud
Their momentary cries before it is dawn,
Would carry it away to blasphemous men.

1919

A PRAYER FOR MY DAUGHTER

Once more the storm is howling, and half hid
Under this cradle-hood and coverlid
My child sleeps on. There is no obstacle
But Gregory's wood and one bare hill
Whereby the haystack-and-roof-levelling wind,
Bred on the Atlantic, can be stayed;
And for an hour I have walked and prayed
Because of the great gloom that is in my mind.

I have walked and prayed for this young child an hour
And heard the sea-wind scream upon the tower,
And under the arches of the bridge, and scream
In the elms above the flooded stream;
Imagining in excited reverie
That the future years had come,
Dancing to a frenzied drum,
Out of the murderous innocence of the sea.

May she be granted beauty and yet not
Beauty to make a stranger's eye distraught,
Or hers before a looking-glass, for such,
Being made beautiful overmuch,
Consider beauty a sufficient end,
Lose natural kindness and may be
The heart-revealing intimacy
That chooses right, and never find a friend.

Helen being chosen found life flat and dull
And later had much trouble from a fool,
While that great Queen, that rose out of the spray,
Being fatherless could have her way,

Yet chose a bandy-legged smith for man.
It's certain that fine women eat
A crazy salad with their meat,
Whereby the Horn of Plenty is undone.

In courtesy I'd have her chiefly learned;
Hearts are not had as a gift, but hearts are earned
By those that are not entirely beautiful;
Yet many, that have played the fool
For beauty's very self, has charm made wise,
And many a poor man that has roved,
Loved and thought himself beloved,
From a glad kindness cannot take his eyes.

May she become a flourishing hidden tree
That all her thoughts may like the linnet be,
And have no business but dispensing round
Their magnanimities of sound,
Nor but in merriment begin a chase,
Nor but in merriment a quarrel.
Oh, may she live like some green laurel
Rooted in one dear perpetual place.

My mind, because the minds that I have loved,
The sort of beauty that I have approved,
Prosper but little, has dried up of late,
Yet knows that to be choked with hate
May well be of all evil chances chief.
If there's no hatred in a mind
Assault and battery of the wind
Can never tear the linnet from the leaf.

An intellectual hatred is the worst,
So let her think opinions are accursed.
Have I not seen the loveliest woman born
Out of the mouth of Plenty's horn,
Because of her opinionated mind
Barter that horn and every good
By quiet natures understood
For an old bellows full of angry wind?

Considering that, all hatred driven hence,
The soul recovers radical innocence

And learns at last that it is self-delighting,
Self-appeasing, self-affrighting,
And that its own sweet will is heaven's will;
She can, though every face should scowl
And every windy quarter howl
Or every bellows burst, be happy still.

And may her bridegroom bring her to a house
Where all's accustomed, ceremonious;
For arrogance and hatred are the wares
Peddled in the thoroughfares.
How but in custom and in ceremony
Are innocence and beauty born?
Ceremony's a name for the rich horn,
And custom for the spreading laurel tree.

June 1919, 1921

SAILING TO BYZANTIUM

That is no country for old men. The young
In one another's arms, birds in the trees
(Those dying generations) at their song,
The salmon-falls, the mackerel-crowded seas,
Fish, flesh, or fowl, commend all summer long
Whatever is begotten, born, and dies.
Caught in that sensual music, all neglect
Monuments of unaging intellect.

An aged man is but a paltry thing,
A tattered coat upon a stick, unless
Soul clap its hands and sing, and louder sing
For every tatter in its mortal dress;
Nor is there singing school but studying
Monuments of its own magnificence;
And therefore I have sailed the seas and come
To the holy city of Byzantium.

O sages, standing in God's holy fire
As in the gold mosaic of a wall,
Come from the holy fire, perne in a gyre,
And be the singing-masters of my soul.
Consume my heart away—sick with desire

And fastened to a dying animal
It knows not what it is—and gather me
Into the artifice of eternity.

Once out of nature I shall never take
My bodily form from any natural thing,
But such a form as Grecian goldsmiths make
Of hammered gold and gold enamelling
To keep a drowsy emperor awake;
Or set upon a golden bough to sing
To lords and ladies of Byzantium
Of what is past, or passing, or to come.

1928

THE TOWER [1]

I

What shall I do with this absurdity—
O heart, O troubled heart—this caricature,
Decrepit age that has been tied to me
As to a dog's tail?
                    Never had I more
Excited, passionate, fantastical
Imagination, nor an ear and eye
That more expected the impossible—
No, not in boyhood when with rod and fly,
Or the humbler worm, I climbed Ben Bulben's back
And had the livelong summer day to spend.
It seems that I must bid the Muse go pack,
Choose Plato and Plotinus for a friend
Until imagination, ear and eye,
Can be content with argument and deal

[1] "The persons mentioned are associated by legend, story, and tradition with the neighborhood of . . . Ballylee Castle, where the poem was written. Mrs. French lived at Peterswell in the eighteenth century and was related to Sir Jonah Barrington, who described the incident of the ear . . . The peasant beauty and the blind poet are Mary Hynes and Raftery, and the incident of the man drowned in Cloone Bog is recorded in my *Celtic Twilight*. Hanrahan's pursuit of the phantom hare and hounds is from my *Stories of Red Hanrahan*. The ghosts have been seen at their game of dice in what is now my bedroom, and the old bankrupt man lived about a hundred years ago. . . ." —*Author's note*. The Tower is one in which the poet had a workshop for some years. It is here also symbolical of age; hence in the third part the transition to the making of the will is a natural one.

In abstract things; or be derided by
A sort of battered kettle at the heel.

II

I pace upon the battlements and stare
On the foundations of a house, or where
Tree, like a sooty finger, starts from the earth;
And send imagination forth
Under the day's declining beam, and call
Images and memories
From ruin or from ancient trees,
For I would ask a question of them all.

Beyond that ridge lived Mrs. French, and once
When every silver candlestick or sconce
Lit up the dark mahogany and the wine,
A serving man that could divine
That most respected lady's every wish,
Ran and with the garden shears
Clipped an insolent farmer's ears
And brought them in a little covered dish.

Some few remembered still when I was young,
A peasant girl commended by a song,
Who'd lived somewhere upon that rocky place,
And praised the color of her face,
And had the greater joy in praising her,
Remembering that, if walked she there,
Farmers jostled at the fair
So great a glory did the song confer.

And certain men, being maddened by those rhymes,
Or else by toasting her a score of times,
Rose from the table and declared it right
To test their fancy by their sight;
But they mistook the brightness of the moon
For the prosaic light of day—
Music had driven their wits astray—
And one was drowned in the great bog of Cloone.

Strange, but the man who made the song was blind,
Yet, now I have considered it, I find
That nothing strange; the tragedy began

With Homer that was a blind man,
And Helen has all living hearts betrayed.
O may the moon and sunlight seem
One inextricable beam,
For if I triumph I must make men mad.

And I myself created Hanrahan
And drove him drunk or sober through the dawn
From somewhere in the neighboring cottages.
Caught by an old man's juggleries
He stumbled, tumbled, fumbled to and fro
And had but broken knees for hire
And horrible splendor of desire;
I thought it all out twenty years ago:

Good fellows shuffled cards in an old bawn;
And when that ancient ruffian's turn was on
He so bewitched the cards under his thumb
That all, but the one card, became
A pack of hounds and not a pack of cards,
And that he changed into a hare.
Hanrahan rose in frenzy there
And followed up those baying creatures towards—

O towards I have forgotten what—enough!
I must recall a man that neither love
Nor music nor an enemy's clipped ear
Could, he was so harried, cheer;
A figure that has grown so fabulous
There's not a neighbor left to say
When he finished his dog's day:
An ancient bankrupt master of this house.

Before that ruin came, for centuries,
Rough men-at-arms, cross-gartered to the knees
Or shod in iron, climbed the narrow stairs,
And certain men-at-arms there were
Whose images, in the Great Memory stored,
Come with loud cry and panting breast
To break upon a sleeper's rest
While their great wooden dice beat on the board.

As I would question all, come all who can;
Come old, necessitous, half-mounted man;

And bring beauty's blind rambling celebrant;
The red man the juggler sent
Through God-forsaken meadows; Mrs. French,
Gifted with so fine an ear;
The man drowned in a bog's mire,
When mocking muses chose the country wench.

Did all old men and women, rich and poor,
Who trod upon these rocks or passed this door,
Whether in public or in secret rage
As I do now against old age?
But I have found an answer in those eyes
That are impatient to be gone;
Go therefore; but leave Hanrahan,
For I need all his mighty memories.

Old lecher with a love on every wind
Bring up out of that deep considering mind
All that you have discovered in the grave,
For it is certain that you have
Reckoned up every unforeknown, unseeing
Plunge, lured by a softening eye,
Or by a touch or a sigh,
Into the labyrinth of another's being;

Does the imagination dwell the most
Upon a woman won or woman lost?
If on the lost, admit you turned aside
From a great labyrinth out of pride,
Cowardice, some silly over-subtle thought
Or anything called conscience once;
And that if memory recur, the sun's
Under eclipse and the day blotted out.

III

It is time that I wrote my will;
I choose upstanding men,
That climb the streams until
The fountain leap, and at dawn
Drop their cast at the side
Of dripping stone; I declare
They shall inherit my pride,
The pride of people that were

Bound neither to Cause nor to State,
Neither to slaves that were spat on,
Nor to the tyrants that spat,
The people of Burke and of Grattan
That gave, though free to refuse—
Pride, like that of the morn,
When the headlong light is loose,
Or that of the fabulous horn,
Or that of the sudden shower
When all streams are dry,
Or that of the hour
When the swan must fix his eye
Upon a fading gleam,
Float out upon a long
Last reach of glittering stream
And there sing his last song.
And I declare my faith;
I mock Plotinus' thought
And cry in Plato's teeth,
Death and life were not
Till man made up the whole,
Made lock, stock and barrel
Out of his bitter soul,
Aye, sun and moon and star, all,
And further add to that
That, being dead, we rise,
Dream and so create
Translunar Paradise.
I have prepared my peace
With learned Italian things
And the proud stones of Greece,
Poet's imaginings
And memories of love,
Memories of the words of women,
All those things whereof
Man makes a superhuman,
Mirror-resembling dream.

As at the loophole there,
The daws chatter and scream,
And drop twigs layer upon layer.
When they have mounted up,
The mother bird will rest

On their hollow top,
And so warm her wild nest.

I leave both faith and pride
To young upstanding men
Climbing the mountain side,
That under bursting dawn
They may drop a fly;
Being of that metal made
Till it was broken by
This sedentary trade.

Now shall I make my soul,
Compelling it to study
In a learned school
Till the wreck of body,
Slow decay of blood,
Testy delirium
Or dull decrepitude,
Or what worse evil come—
The death of friends, or death
Of every brilliant eye
That made a catch in the breath—
Seem but the clouds of the sky
When the horizon fades;
Or a bird's sleepy cry
Among the deepening shades.

1928

AMONG SCHOOL CHILDREN

I walk through the long schoolroom questioning,
A kind old nun in a white hood replies;
The children learn to cipher and to sing,
To study reading-books and history,
To cut and sew, be neat in everything
In the best modern way—the children's eyes
In momentary wonder stare upon
A sixty year old smiling public man.

I dream of a Ledæan body, bent
Above a sinking fire, a tale that she

Told of a harsh reproof, or trivial event
That changed some childish day to tragedy—
Told, and it seemed that our two natures blent
Into a sphere from youthful sympathy,
Or else, to alter Plato's parable,
Into the yolk and white of the one shell.

And thinking of that fit of grief or rage
I look upon one child or t'other there
And wonder if she stood so at that age—
For even daughters of the swan can share
Something of every paddler's heritage—
And had that color upon cheek or hair;
And thereupon my heart is driven wild:
She stands before me as a living child.

Her present image floats into the mind—
Did quattrocento finger fashion it
Hollow of cheek as though it drank the wind
And took a mess of shadows for its meat?
And I though never of Ledæan kind
Had pretty plumage once—enough of that,
Better to smile on all that smile, and show
There is a comfortable kind of old scarecrow.

What youthful mother, a shape upon her lap
Honey of generation had betrayed,
And that must sleep, shriek, struggle to escape
As recollection or the drug decide,
Would think her son, did she but see that shape
With sixty or more winters on its head,
A compensation for the pang of his birth,
Or the uncertainty of his setting forth?

Plato thought nature but a spume that plays
Upon a ghostly paradigm of things;
Solider Aristotle played the taws
Upon the bottom of a king of kings;
World-famous golden-thighed Pythagoras
Fingered upon a fiddle stick or strings
What a star sang and careless Muses heard:
Old clothes upon old sticks to scare a bird.

Both nuns and mothers worship images,
But those the candles light are not as those
That animate a mother's reveries,
But keep a marble or a bronze repose.
And yet they too break hearts—O Presences
That passion, piety or affection knows,
And that all heavenly glory symbolize—
O self-born mockers of man's enterprise;

Labor is blossoming or dancing where
The body is not bruised to pleasure soul,
Nor beauty born out of its own despair,
Nor blear-eyed wisdom out of midnight oil.
O chestnut tree, great rooted blossomer,
Are you the leaf, the blossom or the bole?
O body swayed to music, O brightening glance,
How can we know the dancer from the dance?

1928

COOLE AND BALLYLEE, 1931

Under my window-ledge the waters race,
Otters below and moor-hens on the top,
Run for a mile undimmed in Heaven's face
Then darkening through "dark" Raftery's "cellar" drop,
Run underground, rise in a rocky place
In Coole demesne, and there to finish up
Spread to a lake and drop into a hole.
What's water but the generated soul?

Upon the border of that lake's a wood
Now all dry sticks under a wintry sun,
And in a copse of beeches there I stood,
For Nature's pulled her tragic buskin on
And all the rant's a mirror of my mood:
At sudden thunder of the mounting swan
I turned about and looked where branches break
The glittering reaches of the flooded lake.

Another emblem there! That stormy white
But seems a concentration of the sky;
And, like the soul, it sails into the sight

And in the morning's gone, no man knows why;
And is so lovely that it sets to right
What knowledge or its lack had set awry,
So arrogantly pure, a child might think
It can be murdered with a spot of ink.

Sound of a stick upon the floor, a sound
From somebody that toils from chair to chair;
Beloved books that famous hands have bound,
Old marble heads, old pictures everywhere;
Great rooms where travelled men and children found
Content or joy; a last inheritor
Where none has reigned that lacked a name and fame
Or out of folly into folly came.

A spot whereon the founders lived and died
Seemed once more dear than life; ancestral trees,
Or gardens rich in memory glorified
Marriages, alliances, and families,
And every bride's ambition satisfied.
Where fashion or mere fantasy decrees
Man shifts about—all that great glory spent—
Like some poor Arab tribesman and his tent.

We were the last romantics—chose for theme
Traditional sanctity and loveliness;
Whatever's written in what poets name
The book of the people; whatever most can bless
The mind of man or elevate a rhyme;
But all is changed, that high horse riderless,
Though mounted in that saddle Homer rode
Where the swan drifts upon a darkening flood.

1933

WHAT THEN?

His chosen comrades thought at school
He must grow a famous man;
He thought the same and lived by rule,
All his twenties crammed with toil;
"What then?" sang Plato's ghost. "What then?"

Everything he wrote was read,
After certain years he won
Sufficient money for his need,
Friends that have been friends indeed;
"What then?" sang Plato's ghost. "What then?"

All his happier dreams came true—
A small old house, wife, daughter, son,
Grounds where plum and cabbage grew,
Poets and Wits about him drew;
"What then?" sang Plato's ghost. "What then?"

"The work is done," grown old he thought,
"According to my boyish plan;
Let the fools rage, I swerved in naught,
Something to perfection brought;"
But louder sang that ghost, "What then?"

1938

THE CIRCUS ANIMALS' DESERTION

I

I sought a theme and sought for it in vain,
I sought it daily for six weeks or so.
Maybe at last, being but a broken man,
I must be satisfied with my heart, although
Winter and summer till old age began
My circus animals were all on show,
Those stilted boys, that burnished chariot,
Lion and woman and the Lord knows what.

II

What can I but enumerate old themes?
First that sea-rider Oisin led by the nose
Through three enchanted islands, allegorical dreams,
Vain gaiety, vain battle, vain repose,
Themes of the embittered heart, or so it seems,
That might adorn old songs or courtly shows;
But what cared I that set him on to ride,
I, starved for the bosom of his faery bride?

And then a counter-truth filled out its play,
The Countess Cathleen was the name I gave it;
She, pity-crazed, had given her soul away,
But masterful Heaven had intervened to save it.
I thought my dear must her own soul destroy,
So did fanaticism and hate enslave it,
And this brought forth a dream and soon enough
This dream itself had all my thought and love.

And when the Fool and Blind Man stole the bread
Cuchulain fought the ungovernable sea;
Heart-mysteries there, and yet when all is said
It was the dream itself enchanted me:
Character isolated by a deed
To engross the present and dominate memory.
Players and painted stage took all my love,
And not those things that they were emblems of.

III

Those masterful images because complete
Grew in pure mind, but out of what began?
A mound of refuse or the sweepings of a street,
Old kettles, old bottles, and a broken can,
Old iron, old bones, old rags, that raving slut
Who keeps the till. Now that my ladder's gone,
I must lie down where all the ladders start,
In the foul rag-and-bone shop of the heart.

1940

POLITICS

"In our time the destiny of man presents its meaning in political terms."—Thomas Mann

How can I, that girl standing there,
My attention fix
On Roman or on Russian
Or on Spanish politics?
Yet here's a travelled man that knows
What he talks about,
And there's a politician
That has read and thought,
And maybe what they say is true

Of war and war's alarms,
But O that I were young again
And held her in my arms!

1940

THE BLACK TOWER

Say that the men of the old black tower,
Though they but feed as the goatherd feeds,
Their money spent, their wine gone sour,
Lack nothing that a soldier needs,
That all are oath-bound men:
Those banners come not in.

There in the tomb stand the dead upright,
But winds come up from the shore:
They shake when the winds roar,
Old bones upon the mountain shake.

Those banners come to bribe or threaten,
Or whisper that a man's a fool
Who, when his own right king's forgotten,
Cares what king sets up his rule.
If he died long ago
Why do you dread us so?

There in the tomb drops the faint moonlight,
But wind comes up from the shore:
They shake when the winds roar,
Old bones upon the mountain shake.

The tower's old cook that must climb and clamber
Catching small birds in the dew of the morn
When we hale men lie stretched in slumber
Swears that he hears the king's great horn.
But he's a lying hound:
Stand we on guard oath-bound!

There in the tomb the dark grows blacker,
But wind comes up from the shore:
They shake when the winds roar,
Old bones upon the mountain shake.

Jan. 21, 1939, 1940

Rudyard Kipling

Joseph Rudyard Kipling was born in Bombay, India, December 30, 1865. His father, John Lockwood Kipling, had been a designer of terra cotta in the Burslem Potteries, but after his marriage he accepted an appointment as professor of Architectural Sculpture in the British School of Art, Bombay, and later became director of the museum at Lahore. His mother, a daughter of the Reverend G. B. Macdonald, a Methodist minister, was one of four sisters, each of whom married or became the mother of a famous man: the eldest married the Pre-Raphaelite artist Edward Burne-Jones; the second married Edward Poynter, afterwards president of the Royal Academy; the third, Alice, was Kipling's mother; and the fourth was the mother of Stanley Baldwin, who became Prime Minister of England.

From native servants, Kipling in his early childhood heard much of Indian folklore and learned to speak Hindustani. When he was about seven, he was taken to England to be educated, and was placed in charge of the wife of a retired navy captain at Southsea, near Portsmouth. Here, except for brief holiday visits with the Burne-Joneses, he spent the next six years, attending a day school, and when at home being subjected to an almost insane brutality by his landlady and her son. The harsh treatment he underwent finally brought on a nervous breakdown, which led to an investigation by his family and his removal. In the spring of 1878 he was sent to a preparatory school, the United Services College, Westward Ho, on the north coast of Devonshire, where he remained four years. Here because of poor eyesight he took no part in games, but in his second year he began to write verse, and in his last two years he edited the school paper, the *U. S. C. Chronicle*. This helped him determine on writing as a profession, and at the end of his school days he left for India, at the age of sixteen years and nine months, to become a journalist.

From 1882 to 1887 he was reporter and sub-editor on the Lahore *Civil and Military Gazette*, and from 1887 to 1889 on the larger Allahabad *Pioneer*. His assignments took him to all parts of India and made him acquainted with most of the civil and military leaders of the time. In his work, moreover, he had much latitude, and when fillers were needed to supplement the news, he began to use his own verse and prose. Thus in 1885 he began the series of stories called *Plain Tales from the Hills*, and by 1886 he had enough verse for a volume, *Departmental Ditties*. After six and a half years of newspaper work, he quit to give all his time to creative work. Some of his stories had been published in paper-backed volumes for sale at railway bookstalls in India, and he sold the rights to these, for £250 and a small royalty, to the man who controlled the bookstalls, and with the proceeds set out for the United States and England. He received no encouragement in America, but in London his success was better: a publisher brought out several volumes of his tales, *Macmillan's Magazine* and the *St. James's Gazette* took contributions, and W. E. Henley, editor of the *National Observer*, began publishing his *Barrack-room Ballads*.

In 1891 he went to Italy to recover from a serious illness, and from there traveled to Cape Town, Australia, and New Zealand; but in January, 1892, he returned to London to marry Caroline Balestier, a native of Vermont, who at the time was living in London. They started, by way of Canada, on a trip around the world, but when they were in Yokohama, a bank failed in which they had their funds, and they were forced to cancel the rest of the trip. They returned to Mrs. Kipling's old home, near Brattleboro, Vermont, where they lived for the next four years. They bought land and built a house, and their two eldest children were born there, and there Kipling did some of his best work: *Many Inventions, Captains Courageous*, the two *Jungle Books*, and most of the poems of *The Seven Seas*. A quarrel between Kipling and one of his wife's brothers led to a good deal of unpleasant notoriety, however, and this, coupled with a feeling by Kipling that the environment in general was inhospitable, led them, in the spring of 1896, to return to England. They lived for a while at Rottingdean, on the Sussex coast, but spent considerable time in travel: in the winter of 1897 they went to South Africa, where for some months Kipling did war work; and in 1899 they made a trip to New York, where Kipling and both his daughters became desperately ill with pneumonia, of which his eldest child died. To escape the English winters, they went to South Africa for several months each year from 1900 to 1907. In 1902 they bought Bateman's, an estate near Burwash, East Sussex, which was their home for the rest of their lives.

Kipling was awarded the Nobel prize for literature in 1907, and the Gold Medal of the Royal Society of Literature in 1926; and in 1933 he was made an associate member of the French Academy. He received many honorary degrees: the LL. D. from McGill (1899), the Litt. D. from Durham and Oxford (1907), Cambridge (1908), Edinburgh (1920), and Paris and Strasbourg (1921), and the Ph. D. from Athens (1924). He was Rector of the University of St. Andrews from 1922 to 1925, and in 1932 was made an Honorary Fellow of Magdalene College, Cambridge.

Of his three children only one survived him; his only son was killed in the World War. He died, following an operation for a perforated stomach ulcer, on January 18, 1936, and was buried in Westminster Abbey. By Mrs. Kipling's will, Bateman's with its three hundred acres was left at her death, in 1939, to the country as a national shrine.

THE BALLAD OF EAST AND WEST

Oh, East is East, and West is West, and never the twain shall meet,
Till Earth and Sky stand presently at God's great Judgment Seat;
But there is neither East nor West, Border, nor Breed, nor Birth,
When two strong men stand face to face, though they come from the ends of the earth!

Kamal is out with twenty men to raise the Border-side,
And he has lifted the Colonel's mare that is the Colonel's pride.
He has lifted her out of the stable-door between the dawn and the day,
And turned the calkins upon her feet, and ridden her far away.
Then up and spoke the Colonel's son that led a troop of the Guides:
"Is there never a man of all my men can say where Kamal hides?"
Then up and spoke Mohammed Khan, the son of the Ressaldar:

"If ye know the track of the morning-mist, ye know where his pickets are.
"At dusk he harries the Abazai—at dawn he is into Bonair,
"But he must go by Fort Bukloh to his own place to fare.
"So if ye gallop to Fort Bukloh as fast as a bird can fly,
"By the favor of God ye may cut him off ere he win to the Tongue of Jagai.
"But if he be past the Tongue of Jagai, right swiftly turn ye then,
"For the length and the breadth of that grisly plain is sown with Kamal's men.
"There is rock to the left, and rock to the right, and low lean thorn between,
"And ye may hear a breech-bolt snick where never a man is seen."
The Colonel's son has taken horse, and a raw rough dun was he,
With the mouth of a bell and the heart of Hell and the head of a gallows-tree.
The Colonel's son to the Fort has won, they bid him stay to eat—
Who rides at the tail of a Border thief, he sits not long at his meat.
He's up and away from Fort Bukloh as fast as he can fly,
Till he was aware of his father's mare in the gut of the Tongue of Jagai,
Till he was aware of his father's mare with Kamal upon her back,
And when he could spy the white of her eye, he made the pistol crack.
He has fired once, he has fired twice, but the whistling ball went wide.
"Ye shoot like a soldier," Kamal said. "Show now if ye can ride."
It's up and over the Tongue of Jagai, as blown dust-devils go,
The dun he fled like a stag of ten, but the mare like a barren doe.
The dun he leaned against the bit and slugged his head above,
But the red mare played with the snaffle-bars, as a maiden plays with a glove.
There was rock to the left and rock to the right, and low lean thorn between,
And thrice he heard a breech-bolt snick tho' never a man was seen.
They have ridden the low moon out of the sky, their hoofs drum up the dawn,
The dun he went like a wounded bull, but the mare like a new-roused fawn.
The dun he fell at a water-course—in a woeful heap fell he,

And Kamal has turned the red mare back, and pulled the rider
free.
He has knocked the pistol out of his hand—small room was
there to strive,
" 'T was only by favor of mine," quoth he, "ye rode so long alive:
"There was not a rock for twenty mile, there was not a clump
of tree,
"But covered a man of my own men with his rifle cocked on his
knee.
"If I had raised my bridle-hand, as I have held it low,
"The little jackals that flee so fast were feasting all in a row.
"If I had bowed my head on my breast, as I have held it high,
"The kite that whistles above us now were gorged till she could
not fly."
Lightly answered the Colonel's son: "Do good to bird and beast,
"But count who come for the broken meats before thou makest a
feast.
"If there should follow a thousand swords to carry my bones away,
"Belike the price of a jackal's meal were more than a thief
could pay.
"They will feed their horse on the standing crop, their men on
the garnered grain.
"The thatch of the byres will serve their fires when all the
cattle are slain.
"But if thou thinkest the price be fair,—thy brethren wait to sup,
"The hound is kin to the jackal-spawn,—howl, dog, and call
them up!
"And if thou thinkest the price be high, in steer and gear and
stack,
"Give me my father's mare again, and I'll fight my own way
back!"
Kamal has gripped him by the hand and set him upon his feet.
"No talk shall be of dogs," said he, "when wolf and grey wolf
meet.
"May I eat dirt if thou hast hurt of me in deed or breath;
"What dam of lances brought thee forth to jest at the dawn
with Death?"
Lightly answered the Colonel's son: "I hold by the blood of
my clan:
"Take up the mare for my father's gift—by God, she has carried a
man!"
The red mare ran to the Colonel's son, and nuzzled against his
breast;

"We be two strong men," said Kamal then, "but she loveth the younger best.
"So she shall go with a lifter's dower, my turquoise-studded rein,
"My 'broidered saddle and saddle-cloth, and silver stirrups twain."
The Colonel's son a pistol drew, and held it muzzle-end,
"Ye have taken the one from a foe," said he. "Will ye take the mate from a friend?"
"A gift for a gift," said Kamal straight; "a limb for the risk of a limb.
"Thy father has sent his son to me, I'll send my son to him!"
With that he whistled his only son, that dropped from a mountain-crest—
He trod the ling like a buck in spring, and he looked like a lance in rest.
"Now here is thy master," Kamal said, "who leads a troop of the Guides,
"And thou must ride at his left side as shield on shoulder rides.
"Till Death or I cut lose the tie, at camp and board and bed,
"Thy life is his—thy fate it is to guard him with thy head.
"So, thou must eat the White Queen's meat, and all her foes are thine,
"And thou must harry thy father's hold for the peace of the Border-line,
"And thou must make a trooper tough and hack thy way to power—
"Belike they will raise thee to Ressaldar when I am hanged in Peshawur."
They have looked each other between the eyes, and there they found no fault,
They have taken the Oath of the Brother-in-Blood on leavened bread and salt:
They have taken the Oath of the Brother-in-Blood on fire and fresh-cut sod,
On the hilt and the haft of the Khyber knife, and the Wondrous Names of God.
The Colonel's son he rides the mare and Kamal's boy the dun,
And two have come back to Fort Bukloh where there went forth but one.
And when they drew to the Quarter-Guard, full twenty swords flew clear—
There was not a man but carried his feud with the blood of the mountaineer.

"Ha' done! ha' done!" said the Colonel's son. "Put up the steel at your sides!
"Last night ye had struck at a Border thief—to-night 't is a man of the Guides!"

Oh, East is East, and West is West, and never the twain shall meet,
Till Earth and Sky stand presently at God's great Judgment Seat;
But there is neither East nor West, Border, nor Breed, nor Birth,
When two strong men stand face to face, though they come from the ends of the earth!

1889, 1892

TOMLINSON

Now Tomlinson gave up the ghost in his house in Berkeley Square,
And a Spirit came to his bedside and gripped him by the hair—
A Spirit gripped him by the hair and carried him far away,
Till he heard as the roar of a rain-fed ford the roar of the Milky Way:
Till he heard the roar of the Milky Way die down and drone and cease,
And they came to the Gate within the Wall where Peter holds the keys.
"Stand up, stand up now, Tomlinson, and answer loud and high
"The good that ye did for the sake of men or ever ye came to die—
"The good that ye did for the sake of men on little earth so lone!"
And the naked soul of Tomlinson grew white as a rain-washed bone.
"O I have a friend on earth," he said, "that was my priest and guide,
"And well would he answer all for me if he were at my side."
—"For that ye strove in neighbor-love it shall be written fair,
"But now ye wait at Heaven's Gate and not in Berkeley Square:
"Though we called your friend from his bed this night, he could not speak for you,
"For the race is run by one and one and never by two and two."
Then Tomlinson looked up and down, and little gain was there,
For the naked stars grinned overhead, and he saw that his soul was bare.

The Wind that blows between the Worlds, it cut him like a knife,
And Tomlinson took up the tale and spoke of his good in life.
"O this I have read in a book," he said, "and that was told to me,
"And this I have thought that another man thought of a Prince
in Muscovy."
The good souls flocked like homing doves and bade him clear
the path,
And Peter twirled the jangling keys in weariness and wrath.
"Ye have read, ye have heard, ye have thought," he said, "and
the tale is yet to run:
"By the worth of the body that once ye had, give answer—what
ha' ye done?"
Then Tomlinson looked back and forth, and little good it bore,
For the darkness stayed at his shoulder-blade and Heaven's
Gate before:—
"O this I have felt, and this I have guessed, and this I have
heard men say,
"And this they wrote that another man wrote of a carl in
Norroway."
"Ye have read, ye have felt, ye have guessed, good lack! Ye
have hampered Heaven's Gate;
"There's little room between the stars in idleness to prate!
"For none may reach by hired speech of neighbor, priest, and kin
"Through borrowed deed to God's good meed that lies so fair
within;
"Get hence, get hence to the Lord of Wrong, for the doom has
yet to run,
"And . . . the faith that ye share with Berkeley Square
uphold you, Tomlinson!"

* * * * *

The Spirit gripped him by the hair, and sun by sun they fell
Till they came to the belt of Naughty Stars that rim the mouth
of Hell.
The first are red with pride and wrath, the next are white with
pain,
But the third are black with clinkered sin that cannot burn again.
They may hold their path, they may leave their path, with never
a soul to mark:
They may burn or freeze, but they must not cease in the Scorn
of the Outer Dark.
The Wind that blows between the Worlds, it nipped him to
the bone,

And he yearned to the flare of Hell-gate there as the light of his
own hearth-stone.
The Devil he sat behind the bars, where the desperate legions
drew,
But he caught the hasting Tomlinson and would not let him
through.
"Wot ye the price of good pit-coal that I must pay?" said he,
"That ye rank yoursel' so fit for Hell and ask no leave of me?
"I am all o'er-sib to Adam's breed that ye should give me scorn,
"For I strove with God for your First Father the day that he
was born.
"Sit down, sit down upon the slag, and answer loud and high
"The harm that ye did to the Sons of Men or ever you came to
die."
And Tomlinson looked up and up, and saw against the night
The belly of a tortured star blood-red in Hell-Mouth light;
And Tomlinson looked down and down, and saw beneath his feet
The frontlet of a tortured star milk-white in Hell-Mouth heat.
"O I had a love on earth," said he, "that kissed me to my fall;
"And if ye would call my love to me I know she would answer
all."
—"All that ye did in love forbid it shall be written fair,
"But now ye wait at Hell-Mouth Gate and not in Berkeley
Square:
"Though we whistled your love from her bed to-night, I trow she
would not run,
"For the sin ye do by two and two ye must pay for one by one!"
The Wind that blows between the Worlds, it cut him like a knife,
And Tomlinson took up the tale and spoke of his sins in life:—
"Once I ha' laughed at the power of love and twice at the grip
of the Grave,
"And thrice I ha' patted my God on the head that men might
call me brave."
The Devil he blew on a brandered soul and set it aside to cool:—
"Do ye think I would waste my good pit-coal on the hide of a
brain-sick fool?
"I see no worth in the hobnailed mirth or the jolthead jest ye did
"That I should waken my gentlemen that are sleeping three on a
grid."
Then Tomlinson looked back and forth, and there was little
grace,
For Hell-Gate filled the houseless Soul with the Fear of Naked
Space.

"Nay, this I ha' heard," quo' Tomlinson, "and this was noised abroad,
"And this I ha' got from a Belgian book on the word of a dead French lord."
—"Ye ha' heard, ye ha' read, ye ha' got, good lack! and the tale begins afresh—
"Have ye sinned one sin for the pride o' the eye or the sinful lust of the flesh?"
Then Tomlinson he gripped the bars and yammered, "Let me in—
"For I mind that I borrowed my neighbor's wife to sin the deadly sin."
The Devil he grinned behind the bars, and banked the fires high:
"Did ye read of that sin in a book?" said he; and Tomlinson said, "Ay!"
The Devil he blew upon his nails, and the little devils ran,
And he said: "Go husk this whimpering thief that comes in the guise of a man:
"Winnow him out 'twixt star and star, and sieve his proper worth:
"There's sore decline in Adam's line if this be spawn of Earth."
Empusa's crew, so naked-new they may not face the fire,
But weep that they bin too small to sin to the height of their desire,
Over the coal they chased the Soul, and racked it all abroad,
As children rifle a caddis-case or the raven's foolish hoard.
And back they came with the tattered Thing, as children after play,
And they said: "The soul that he got from God he has bartered clean away.
"We have threshed a stook of print and book, and winnowed a chattering wind
"And many a soul wherefrom he stole, but his we cannot find.
"We have handled him, we have dandled him, we have seared him to the bone,
"And, Sire, if tooth and nail show truth he has no soul of his own."
The Devil he bowed his head on his breast and rumbled deep and low:—
"I'm all o'er-sib to Adam's breed that I should bid him go.
"Yet close we lie, and deep we lie, and if I gave him place,
"My gentlemen that are so proud would flout me to my face;
"They'd call my house a common stews and me a careless host,

"And—I would not anger my gentlemen for the sake of a shiftless ghost."
The Devil he looked at the mangled Soul that prayed to feel the flame,
And he thought of Holy Charity, but he thought of his own good name:—
"Now ye could haste my coal to waste, and sit ye down to fry:
"Did ye think of that theft for yourself?" said he; and Tomlinson said, "Ay!"
The Devil he blew an outward breath, for his heart was free from care:—
"Ye have scarce the soul of a louse," he said, "but the roots of sin are there,
"And for that sin should ye come in were I the lord alone.
"But sinful pride has rule inside—ay, mightier than my own.
"Honor and Wit, fore-damned they sit, to each his Priest and Whore:
"Nay, scarce I dare myself go there, and you they'd torture sore.
"Ye are neither spirit nor spirk," he said; "ye are neither book nor brute—
"Go, get ye back to the flesh again for the sake of Man's repute.
"I'm all o'er-sib to Adam's breed that I should mock your pain,
"But look that ye win to worthier sin ere ye come back again.
"Get hence, the hearse is at your door—the grim black stallions wait—
"They bear your clay to place to-day. Speed, lest ye come too late!
"Go back to Earth with a lip unsealed—go back with an open eye,
"And carry my word to the Sons of Men or ever ye come to die:
"That the sin they do by two and two they must pay for one by one,
"And . . . the God that you took from a printed book be with you, Tomlinson!"

1891, 1892

DANNY DEEVER

"What are the bugles blowin' for?" said Files-on-Parade.
"To turn you out, to turn you out," the Color-Sergeant said.
"What makes you look so white, so white?" said Files-on-Parade.
"I'm dreadin' what I've got to watch," the Color-Sergeant said.
For they're hangin' Danny Deever, you can hear the Dead March play,

The regiment's in 'ollow square—they're hangin' him to-day;
They've taken of his buttons off an' cut his stripes away,
An' they're hangin' Danny Deever in the mornin'.

"What makes the rear-rank breathe so 'ard?" said Files-on-Parade.
"It's bitter cold, it's bitter cold," the Color-Sergeant said.
"What makes that front-rank man fall down?" says
Files-on-Parade.
"A touch o' sun, a touch o' sun," the Color-Sergeant said.
They are hangin' Danny Deever, they are marchin' of 'im
round,
They 'ave 'alted Danny Deever by 'is coffin on the ground;
An' 'e'll swing in 'arf a minute for a sneakin' shootin'
hound—
O they're hangin' Danny Deever in the mornin'!

" 'Is cot was right-'and cot to mine," said Files-on-Parade.
" 'E's sleepin' out an' far to-night," the Color-Sergeant said.
"I've drunk 'is beer a score o' times," said Files-on-Parade.
" 'E's drinkin' bitter beer alone," the Color-Sergeant said.
They are hangin' Danny Deever, you must mark 'im to 'is
place,
For 'e shot a comrade sleepin'—you must look 'im in the face;
Nine 'undred of 'is county an' the regiment's disgrace,
While they're hangin' Danny Deever in the mornin'.

"What's that so black agin the sun?" said Files-on-Parade.
"It's Danny fightin' 'ard for life," the Color-Sergeant said.
"What's that that whimpers over'ead?" said Files-on-Parade.
"It's Danny's soul that's passin' now," the Color-Sergeant said.
For they're done with Danny Deever, you can 'ear the
quickstep play,
The Regiment's in column, an' they're marchin' us away;
Ho! the young recruits are shakin', an' they'll want their
beer to-day,
After hangin' Danny Deever in the mornin'.

1892

GUNGA DIN

You may talk o' gin and beer
When you're quartered safe out 'ere,
An' you're sent to penny-fights an' Aldershot it;

But when it comes to slaughter
You will do your work on water,
An' you'll lick the bloomin' boots of 'im that's got it.
Now in Injia's sunny clime,
Where I used to spend my time
A-servin' of 'Er Majesty the Queen,
Of all them blackfaced crew
The finest man I knew
Was our regimental bhisti, Gunga Din.
He was "Din! Din! Din!
"You limpin' lump o' brick-dust, Gunga Din!
"Hi! Slippy *hitherao!*
"Water, get it! *Panee lao!* [1]
"You squidgy-nosed old idol, Gunga Din."

The uniform 'e wore
Was nothin' much before,
An' rather less than 'arf o' that be'ind,
For a piece o' twisty rag
An 'a goatskin water-bag
Was all the field-equipment 'e could find.
When the sweatin' troop-train lay
In a sidin' through the day,
Where the 'eat would make your bloomin' eyebrows crawl,
We shouted "Harry By!" [2]
Till our throats were bricky-dry,
Then we wopped 'im 'cause 'e couldn't serve us all.
It was "Din! Din! Din!
"You 'eathen, where the mischief 'ave you been?
"You put some *juldee* [3] in it
"Or I'll *marrow* [4] you this minute
"If you don't fill up my helmet, Gunga Din!"

'E would dot an' carry one
Till the longest day was done;
An' 'e didn't seem to know the use o' fear.
If we charged or broke or cut,
You could bet your bloomin' nut,
'E 'd be waitin' fifty paces right flank rear.
With 'is mussick [5] on 'is back,

[1] Bring water swiftly (the notes throughout the poem are the author's).
[2] O Brother.
[3] Be quick.
[4] Hit you.
[5] Water-skin.

'E would skip with our attack,
An' watch us till the bugles made "Retire."
An' for all 'is dirty 'ide
'E was white, clear white, inside
When 'e went to tend the wounded under fire!
        It was "Din! Din! Din!"
    With the bullets kickin' dust-spots on the green.
        When the cartridges ran out,
        You could hear the front-ranks shout,
    "Hi! ammunition-mules an' Gunga Din!"

I shan't forgit the night
When I dropped be'ind the fight
With a bullet where my belt-plate should 'a' been.
I was chokin' mad with thirst,
An' the man that spied me first
Was our good old grinnin', gruntin' Gunga Din.
'E lifted up my 'ead,
An' he plugged me where I bled,
An' 'e guv me 'arf-a-pint o' water green:
It was crawlin' and it stunk,
But of all the drinks I've drunk,
I'm gratefullest to one from Gunga Din.
        It was "Din! Din! Din!
    " 'Ere's a beggar with a bullet through 'is spleen;
        " 'E's chawin' up the ground,
        "An' 'e's kickin' all around:
    "For Gawd's sake git the water, Gunga Din!"

'E carried me away
To where a dooli lay,
An' a bullet come an' drilled the beggar clean.
'E put me safe inside,
An' just before 'e died,
"I 'ope you liked your drink," sez Gunga Din.
So I'll meet 'im later on
At the place where 'e is gone—
Where it's always double drill and no canteen;
'E'll be squattin' on the coals
Givin' drink to poor damned souls,
An' I'll get a swig in hell from Gunga Din!
        Yes, Din! Din! Din!

You Lazarushian-leather Gunga Din!
Though I've belted you and flayed you,
By the livin' Gawd that made you,
You're a better man than I am, Gunga Din!
1892

MANDALAY

By the old Moulmein Pagoda, lookin' lazy at the sea,
There's a Burma girl a-settin', and I know she thinks o' me;
For the wind is in the palm-trees, and the temple-bells they say:
"Come you back, you British soldier; come you back to Mandalay!"
Come you back to Mandalay,
Where the old Flotilla lay:
Can't you 'ear their paddles chunkin' from Rangoon to Mandalay?
On the road to Mandalay,
Where the flyin'-fishes play,
An' the dawn comes up like thunder outer China 'crost the Bay!

'Er petticoat was yaller an' 'er little cap was green,
An' 'er name was Supi-yaw-lat—jes' the same as Theebaw's Queen,
An' I seed her first a-smokin' of a whackin' white cheroot,
An' a-wastin' Christian kisses on an 'eathen idol's foot:
Bloomin' idol made o' mud—
Wot they called the Great Gawd Budd—
Plucky lot she cared for idols when I kissed 'er where she stud!
On the road to Mandalay . . .

When the mist was on the rice-fields an' the sun was droppin' slow,
She'd git 'er little banjo an' she'd sing "*Kulla-lo-lo!*"
With 'er arm upon my shoulder an' 'er cheek agin my cheek
We useter watch the steamers an' the *hathis* pilin' teak.
Elephints a'pilin' teak
In the sludgy, squdgy creek,
Where the silence 'ung that 'eavy you was 'arf afraid to speak!
On the road to Mandalay . . .

But that's all shove be'ind me—long ago an' fur away,
An' there ain't no 'busses runnin' from the Bank to Mandalay;
An' I'm learnin' 'ere in London what the ten-year soldier tells:
"If you've 'eard the East a-callin', you won't never 'eed
naught else."
No! you won't 'eed nothin' else
But them spicy garlic smells,
An' the sunshine an' the palm-trees an' the tinkly
temple-bells;
On the road to Mandalay . . .

I am sick o' wastin' leather on these gritty pavin'-stones,
An' the blasted English drizzle wakes the fever in my bones;
Tho' I walks with fifty 'ousemaids outer Chelsea to the Strand,
An' they talks a lot o' lovin,' but wot do they understand?
Beefy face an' grubby 'and—
Law! wot do they understand?
I've a neater, sweeter maiden in a cleaner, greener land!
On the road to Mandalay . . .

Ship me somewheres east of Suez, where the best is like the worst
Where there aren't no Ten Commandments an' a man can
raise a thirst;
For the temple-bells are callin', an' it's there that I would be—
By the old Moulmein Pagoda, looking lazy at the sea;
On the road to Mandalay,
Where the old Flotilla lay,
With our sick beneath the awnings when we went to
Mandalay!
O the road to Mandalay,
Where the flyin'-fishes play,
An' the dawn comes up like thunder outer China 'crost
the Bay!

1892

THE LAST CHANTEY

"And there was no more sea"

Thus said the Lord in the Vault above the Cherubim,
Calling to the Angels and the Souls in their degree:
"Lo! Earth has passed away
On the smoke of Judgment Day.
That Our word may be established shall We gather up the sea?"

Loud sang the souls of the jolly, jolly mariners:
  "Plague upon the hurricane that made us furl and flee!
    But the war is done between us,
    In the deep the Lord hath seen us—
  Our bones we'll leave the barracout', and God may sink the
      sea!"

Then said the soul of Judas that betrayèd Him:
  "Lord, hast Thou forgotten Thy covenant with me?
    How once a year I go
    To cool me on the floe?
  And Ye take my day of mercy if Ye take away the sea!"

Then said the soul of the Angel of the Off-Shore Wind:
  (He that bits the thunder when the bull-mouthed breakers
      flee):
    "I have watch and ward to keep
    O'er Thy wonders on the deep,
  And Ye take mine honor from me if Ye take away the sea!"

Loud sang the souls of the jolly, jolly mariners:
  "Nay, but we were angry, and a hasty folk are we!
    If we worked the ship together
    Till she foundered in foul weather,
  Are we babes that we should clamor for a vengeance on the
      sea?"

Then said the souls of the slaves that men threw overboard:
  "Kennelled in the picaroon a weary band were we;
    But Thy arm was strong to save,
    And it touched us on the wave,
  And we drowsed the long tides idle till Thy Trumpets tore
      the sea."

Then cried the soul of the stout Apostle Paul to God:
  "Once we frapped a ship, and she labored woundily.
    There were fourteen score of these,
    And they blessed Thee on their knees,
  When they learned Thy Grace and Glory under Malta by the
      sea!"

Loud sang the souls of the jolly, jolly mariners,
  Plucking at their harps, and they plucked unhandily:

"Our thumbs are rough and tarred,
And the tune is something hard—
May we lift a Deepsea Chantey such as seamen use at sea?"

Then said the souls of the gentlemen-adventurers—
Fettered wrist to bar all for red iniquity:
"Ho, we revel in our chains
O'er the sorrow that was Spain's;
Heave or sink it, leave or drink it, we were masters of the sea!"

Up spake the soul of a grey Gothavn 'speckshioner—
(He that led the flinching in the fleets of fair Dundee):
"Oh, the ice-blink white and near,
And the bowhead breaching clear!
Will Ye whelm them all for wantonness that wallow in the sea?"

Loud sang the souls of the jolly, jolly mariners,
Crying: "Under Heaven, here is neither lead nor lee!
Must we sing for evermore
On the windless, glassy floor?
Take back your golden fiddles and we'll beat to open sea!"

Then stooped the Lord, and He called the good sea up to Him,
And 'stablishèd its borders unto all eternity,
That such as have no pleasure
For to praise the Lord by measure,
They may enter into galleons and serve Him on the sea.

Sun, wind, and cloud shall fail not from the face of it,
Stinging, ringing spindrift, nor the fulmar flying free;
And the ships shall go abroad
To the Glory of the Lord
Who heard the silly sailor-folk and gave them back their sea!

1892, 1896

WHEN EARTH'S LAST PICTURE IS PAINTED

When Earth's last picture is painted and the tubes are twisted and dried,
When the oldest colors have faded, and the youngest critic has died,

We shall rest, and, faith, we shall need it—lie down for an æon
  or two,
Till the Master of All Good Workmen shall put us to work anew.

And those that were good shall be happy: they shall sit in a
  golden chair;
They shall splash at a ten-league canvas with brushes of comets'
  hair.
They shall find real saints to draw from—Magdalene, Peter, and
  Paul;
They shall work for an age at a sitting and never be tired at all!

And only the Master shall praise us, and only the Master shall
  blame;
And no one shall work for money, and no one shall work for fame,
But each for the joy of the working, and each, in his separate star,
Shall draw the Thing as he sees It for the God of Things as
  They are!

1892, 1896

RECESSIONAL

God of our fathers, known of old,
  Lord of our far-flung battle-line,
Beneath whose awful Hand we hold
  Dominion over palm and pine—
Lord God of Hosts, be with us yet,
Lest we forget—lest we forget!

The tumult and the shouting dies;
  The Captains and the Kings depart:
Still stands Thine ancient sacrifice,
  An humble and a contrite heart.
Lord God of Hosts, be with us yet,
Lest we forget—lest we forget!

Far-called, our navies melt away;
  On dune and headland sinks the fire:
Lo, all our pomp of yesterday
  Is one with Nineveh and Tyre!
Judge of the Nations, spare us yet,
Lest we forget—lest we forget!

If, drunk with sight of power, we loose
  Wild tongues that have not Thee in awe,
Such boastings as the Gentiles use,
  Or lesser breeds without the Law—
Lord God of Hosts, be with us yet,
Lest we forget—lest we forget!

For heathen heart that puts her trust
  In reeking tube and iron shard,
All valiant dust that builds on dust,
  And guarding, calls not Thee to guard,
For frantic boast and foolish word—
Thy Mercy on Thy People, Lord!

1897, 1903

THE DYKES

We have no heart for the fishing, we have no hand for the oar—
All that our fathers taught us of old pleases us now no more;
All that our own hearts bid us believe we doubt where we do
  not deny—
There is no proof in the bread we eat or rest in the toil we ply.

Look you, our foreshore stretches far through sea-gate, dyke, and
  groin—
Made land all, that our fathers made, where the flats and the
  fairway join.
They forced the sea a sea-league back. They died, and their work
  stood fast.
We were born to peace in the lee of the dykes, but the time of
  our peace is past.

Far off, the full tide clambers and slips, mouthing and testing all,
Nipping the flanks of the water-gates, baying along the wall;
Turning the shingle, returning the shingle, changing the set of
  the sand . . .
We are too far from the beach, men say, to know how the
  outworks stand.

So we come down, uneasy, to look, uneasily pacing the beach.
These are the dykes our fathers made: we have never known a
  breach.

Time and again has the gale blown by and we were not afraid;
Now we come only to look at the dykes—at the dykes our
fathers made.

O'er the marsh where the homesteads cower apart the harried
sunlight flies,
Shifts and considers, wanes and recovers, scatters and sickens
and dies—
An evil ember bedded in ash—a spark blown west by the
wind . . .
We are surrendered to night and the sea—the gale and the
tide behind!

At the bridge of the lower saltings the cattle gather and blare,
Roused by the feet of running men, dazed by the lantern glare.
Unbar and let them away for their lives—the levels drown as they
stand,
Where the flood-wash forces the sluices aback and the ditches
deliver inland.

Ninefold deep to the top of the dykes the galloping breakers
stride,
And their overcarried spray is a sea—a sea on the landward side.
Coming, like stallions they paw with their hooves, going they
snatch with their teeth,
Till the bents and the furze and the sand are dragged out, and
the old-time hurdles beneath!

Bid men gather fuel for fire, the tar, the oil, and the tow—
Flame we shall need, not smoke, in the dark if the riddled
sea-banks go.
Bid the ringers watch in the tower (who knows how the dawn
shall prove?)
Each with his rope between his feet and the trembling bells above.

Now we can only wait till the day, wait and apportion our shame.
These are the dykes our fathers left, but we would not look to
the same.
Time and again were we warned of the dykes, time and again
we delayed:
Now, it may fall, we have slain our sons, as our fathers we have
betrayed.

* * * * *

Walking along the wreck of the dykes, watching the work of
the seas!
These were the dykes our fathers made to our great profit and
ease.
But the peace is gone and the profit is gone, and the old sure
day withdrawn . . .
That our own houses show as strange when we come back in
the dawn!

1902, 1903

IF—

If you can keep your head when all about you
Are losing theirs and blaming it on you,
If you can trust yourself when all men doubt you,
But make allowance for their doubting too;
If you can wait and not be tired by waiting,
Or being lied about, don't deal in lies,
Or being hated, don't give way to hating,
And yet don't look too good, nor talk too wise:

If you can dream—and not make dreams your master;
If you can think—and not make thoughts your aim;
If you can meet with Triumph and Disaster
And treat those two impostors just the same;
If you can bear to hear the truth you've spoken
Twisted by knaves to make a trap for fools,
Or watch the things you gave your life to, broken,
And stoop and build 'em up with worn-out tools:

If you can make one heap of all your winnings
And risk it on one turn of pitch-and-toss,
And lose, and start again at your beginnings
And never breathe a word about your loss;
If you can force your heart and nerve and sinew
To serve your turn long after they are gone,
And so hold on when there is nothing in you
Except the Will which says to them: "Hold on!"

If you can talk with crowds and keep your virtue,
Or walk with Kings—nor lose the common touch,
If neither foes nor loving friends can hurt you,

If all men count with you, but none too much;
If you can fill the unforgiving minute
With sixty seconds' worth of distance run,
Yours is the Earth and everything that's in it,
And—which is more—you'll be a Man, my son!

1910

G. W. Russell (A. E.)

George William Russell, second son of Thomas Ebas and Mary Ann Armstrong Russell, was born April 10, 1867, in Lurgan, County Armagh, Ireland. His father, a cultured man of deep religious convictions, was bookkeeper in a firm of cambric manufacturers. His mother came from the country near Lurgan and was working in a general store when she met Thomas Russell, then a bookkeeper there. When George was three years and ten months old, he was sent to the Lurgan Model School, which he attended for seven years, until the family moved to Dublin, where his father had accepted a better position. After two or three more years of elementary training, he enrolled, in 1880, at the Metropolitan School of Art, where he studied for a few months each year till 1900; and for two years, 1882-1884, he attended the Rathmines School. Although he now showed high literary and artistic ability, he could not rely on the limited means of his father for support, and therefore had to go to work. His father obtained an excellent situation for him at Guinness's Brewery, but because after he became a Theosophist his "ethical sense was outraged" at working in a brewery, he gave it up, and in 1890 took a clerkship in the warehouse of a Dublin drapery firm, where he worked for the next six years at a salary of £30 to £60 a year.

When at school he was accustomed to spend his holidays with an aunt in Armagh, and while walking about the Armagh countryside, he found awakening in himself a visionary faculty. While lying on a hill one day, he suddenly saw the earth as a living organism, the rocks and clay appearing "lovelier and lordlier beings" than any person he had known. He "began to run in and out of the house of dream" [1] and to live much of the time in a world

[1] *Song and Its Fountains*, p. 15. The quotation in the preceding sentence is from the same work, p. 7.

apart from that of ordinary practical persons. Through W. B. Yeats, a fellow-pupil at the Art School, he was brought into the Theosophical Society, a branch of which Yeats and his friends had been instrumental in founding in Dublin. Russell became an eager student of eastern philosophy, and was soon one of the leaders of the group, which lived a sort of communal life at a house in Ely Place. The Society published a little magazine, the *Irish Theosophist,* to which Russell became a frequent contributor of both verse and prose, and in which his first published work appeared.[1]

In 1897 Sir Horace Plunkett was seeking a man to help with the work of the Irish Agricultural Organization Society, and Yeats strongly recommended Russell as just the person needed. Russell was approached, and after some hesitation and strong persuasion by Yeats, he joined the Society as organizer. For the next few years, traveling most of the time on bicycle, he went all over the country, helping to found co-operative poultry and creamery societies and co-operative credit societies, and studying the economic needs of Ireland. After working as organizer for several years, he became Assistant Secretary of the Society, and in 1904 became editor of its official organ, the *Irish Homestead*—after 1923 the *Irish Statesman*—a position he retained till 1930, when financial difficulties forced its suspension.

Russell wrote verse from boyhood. He said a volume of Tennyson's poems, which his father gave him when a child, was his first revelation of the art of poetry. His first volume of poetry, *Homeward, Songs by the Way,* was published in 1894; and between this time and the publication forty years later of *The House of the Titans and Other Poems,* despite his labors as organizer and editor for the Agricultural Society, he published nearly a dozen volumes of poetry and a number of prose works, and became widely and favorably known as an artist. Of his prose works, four are espe-

[1] His use of the pseudonym "A. E." dates from these days. He contributed so many items to the magazine that modesty led him to sign pseudonyms to some of them. One such was AEon, a term for which he felt a peculiar fascination. His handwriting was such, however, that the printer could not decipher the word, but set up the first two letters with a question mark. Russell struck out the question mark and let the letters stand, and thereafter he published his poetry under these initials. Although there was never any mystery, everyone knowing who "A. E." was, to the end Russell thought of himself as having a sort of double identity, "A. E." representing the poetic and mystic side of his nature, and his own name the practical side as evidenced in his journalistic and organizational work.

cially valuable as throwing light on his philosophy, his thought, and his poetry: *Imaginations and Reveries* (1915), *The Interpreters* (1922), *Song and Its Fountains*[1] (1932), and *The Avatars* (1933). He also helped Yeats and Lady Gregory in establishing the Abbey Theatre in Dublin, and wrote a play, *Deirdre,* which was produced there. His poetry is largely the product of his mysticism and his love of nature: all his poems in *Collected Poems,* save one, were conceived and written in the open air.

Russell's work occupied his time so fully that until 1928 he had been away from Ireland but three times, twice on trips to London and once, in 1926, to Paris. In January, 1928, he made a trip to the United States to raise funds for the *Irish Statesman.* Thereafter he visited the United States on three other occasions: in June, 1928, to receive an honorary degree from Yale; from September, 1930, to May, 1931, for a lecture tour which took him as far as California; and from December, 1934, to March, 1935, upon the request of Henry Wallace, Secretary of Agriculture, to lecture and "advise about rural policies." After August, 1933, London became his headquarters, but he returned for occasional short visits to Dublin, and spent the summer of 1934 in Donegal. In 1929 Dublin University made him a Doctor of Letters in recognition of his service to Irish literature. Earlier he was offered a seat in the Senate of the Irish Free State, but he refused this on the ground that he could not earn the money he would receive.

In June, 1898, he married Violet North, then an assistant on the *Irish Theosophist;* and for many years their home was the center of artistic and cultural interests in Dublin: on Sunday evenings "almost every one worth knowing in Dublin" gathered there. They had three children, one who died in infancy, and two sons who survived their parents. His wife died on February 13, 1932. Russell's own health began to fail in the spring of 1935, and his trouble proved to be cancer. An operation failed to save him, and he died at Bournemouth, England, on July 17, 1935, and on July 20 was buried in Mount Jerome Cemetery, Dublin.

[1] This volume especially traces his poetic development and explains the source and idea of many of his poems, among them the following which are included in this volume: "Sacrifice" (pp. 64-67); "Resurrection" (pp. 45-48), and "Promise" (p. 84).

THE UNKNOWN GOD

Far up the dim twilight fluttered
Moth-wings of vapor and flame:
The lights danced over the mountains,
Star after star they came.

The lights grew thicker unheeded,
For silent and still were we;
Our hearts were drunk with a beauty
Our eyes could never see.

1894

OVERSOUL

I am Beauty itself among beautiful things.
Bhagavad-Gita

The East was crowned with snow-cold bloom
And hung with veils of pearly fleece:
They died away into the gloom,
Vistas of peace—and deeper peace.

And earth and air and wave and fire
In awe and breathless silence stood;
For One who passed into their choir
Linked them in mystic brotherhood.

Twilight of amethyst, amid
Thy few strange stars that lit the heights,
Where was the secret spirit hid?
Where was Thy place, O Light of Lights?

The flame of Beauty far in space—
Where rose the fire: in Thee? in Me?
Which bowed the elemental race
To adoration silently?

1894

SACRIFICE

Those delicate wanderers,
The wind, the star, the cloud,
Ever before mine eyes,
As to an altar bowed,
Light and dew-laden airs
Offer in sacrifice.

The offerings arise:
Hazes of rainbow light,
Pure crystal, blue, and gold,
Through dreamland take their flight;
And 'mid the sacrifice
God moveth as of old.

In miracles of fire
He symbols forth his days;
In gleams of crystal light
Reveals what pure pathways
Lead to the soul's desire,
The silence of the height.

1894

INHERITANCE

As flow the rivers to the sea
Adown from rocky hill or plain,
A thousand ages toiled for thee
And gave thee harvest of their gain;
And weary myriads of yore
Dug out for thee earth's buried ore.

The shadowy toilers for thee fought
In chaos of primeval day
Blind battles with they knew not what;
And each before he passed away
Gave clear articulate cries of woe:
Your pain is theirs of long ago.

And all the old heart sweetness sung,
The joyous life of man and maid

In forests when the earth was young,
In rumors round your childhood strayed:
The careless sweetness of your mind
Comes from the buried years behind.

And not alone unto your birth
Their gifts the weeping ages bore,
The old descents of God on earth
Have dowered thee with celestial lore:
So, wise, and filled with sad and gay
You pass unto the further day.

1894

THE GIFT

I thought, belovèd, to have brought to you
A gift of quietness and ease and peace,
Cooling your brow as with the mystic dew
    Dropping from twilight trees.

Homeward I go not yet; the darkness grows;
Not mine the voice to still with peace divine:
From the first fount the stream of quiet flows
    Through other hearts than mine.

Yet of my night I give to you the stars,
And of my sorrow here the sweetest gains,
And out of hell, beyond its iron bars,
    My scorn of all its pains.

1897

REFUGE

Twilight, a timid fawn, went glimmering by,
    And Night, the dark-blue hunter, followed fast,
Ceaseless pursuit and flight were in the sky,
    But the long chase had ceased for us at last.

We watched together while the driven fawn
    Hid in the golden thicket of the day.
We, from whose hearts pursuit and flight were gone,
    Knew on the hunter's breast her refuge lay.

1904

CARROWMORE

It's a lonely road through bogland to the lake at Carrowmore,
And a sleeper there lies dreaming where the water laps the shore;
Though the moth-wings of the twilight in their purples are unfurled,
Yet his sleep is filled with music by the masters of the world.

There's a hand is white as silver that is fondling with his hair:
There are glimmering feet of sunshine that are dancing by him there:
And half-open lips of faery that were dyed a faery red
In their revels where the Hazel Tree its holy clusters shed.

"Come away," the red lips whisper, "all the world is weary now;
'Tis the twilight of the ages and it's time to quit the plough.
Oh, the very sunlight's weary ere it lightens up the dew,
And its gold is changed and faded before it falls to you.

"Though your colleen's heart be tender, a tenderer heart is near.
What's the starlight in her glances when the stars are shining clear?
Who would kiss the fading shadow when the flower-face glows above?
'Tis the beauty of all Beauty that is calling for your love."

Oh, the great gates of the mountain have opened once again,
And the sound of song and dancing falls upon the ears of men,
And the Land of Youth lies gleaming, flushed with rainbow light and mirth,
And the old enchantment lingers in the honey-heart of earth.

1904

THE SILENCE OF LOVE

I could praise you once with beautiful words ere you came
And entered my life with love in a wind of flame.
I could lure with a song from afar my bird to its nest,
But with pinions drooping together silence is best.

In the land of beautiful silence the winds are laid,
And life grows quietly one in the cloudy shade.
I will not waken the passion that sleeps in the heart,
For the winds that blew us together may blow us apart.

Fear not the stillness; for doubt and despair shall cease
With the gentle voices guiding us into peace.
Our dreams will change as they pass through the gates of gold,
And Quiet, the tender shepherd, shall keep the fold.

1904

THE TWILIGHT OF EARTH

The wonder of the world is o'er:
    The magic from the sea is gone:
There is no unimagined shore,
    No islet yet to venture on.
The Sacred Hazels' blooms are shed,
The Nuts of Knowledge harvested.[1]

Oh, what is worth this lore of age
    If time shall never bring us back
Our battle with the gods to wage
    Reeling along the starry track.
The battle rapture here goes by
In warring upon things that die.

Let be the tale of him whose love
    Was sighed between white Deirdre's breasts,
It will not lift the heart above
    The sodden clay on which it rests.
Love once had power the gods to bring
All rapt on its wild wandering.

We shiver in the falling dew,
    And seek a shelter from the storm:
When man these elder brothers knew
    He found the mother nature warm,

[1] The Sacred Hazel is the Celtic tree of life. It grew over Connla's Well, and the fruit which fell from it were the Nuts of Knowledge which give wisdom and inspiration. Connla's Well is a Celtic equivalent of the First Fountain of mysticism.—*Author's note.*

A hearth fire blazing through it all,
A home without a circling wall.

We dwindle down beneath the skies,
    And from ourselves we pass away:
The paradise of memories
    Grows ever fainter day by day.
The shepherd stars have shrunk within,
The world's great night will soon begin.

Will no one, ere it is too late,
    Ere fades the last memorial gleam,
Recall for us our earlier state?
    For nothing but so vast a dream
That it would scale the steeps of air
Could rouse us from so vast despair.

The power is ours to make or mar
    Our fate as on the earliest morn,
The Darkness and the Radiance are
    Creatures within the spirit born.
Yet, bathed in gloom too long, we might
Forget how we imagined light.

Not yet are fixed the prison bars;
    The hidden light the spirit owns
If blown to flame would dim the stars
    And they who rule them from their thrones:
And the proud sceptred spirits thence
Would bow to pay us reverence.

Oh, while the glory sinks within
    Let us not wait on earth behind,
But follow where it flies, and win
    The glow again, and we may find
Beyond the Gateways of the Day
Dominion and ancestral sway.

1904

AN IRISH FACE

Not her own sorrow only that hath place
Upon yon gentle face.
Too slight have been her childhood's years to gain
The imprint of such pain.
It hid behind her laughing hours, and wrought
Each curve in saddest thought
On brow and lips and eyes. With subtle art
It made that little heart
Through its young joyous beatings to prepare
A quiet shelter there,
Where the immortal sorrows might find a home.
And many there have come;
Bowed in a mournful mist of golden hair
Deirdre hath entered there.
And shrouded in a fall of pitying dew,
Weeping the friend he slew,
The Hound of Ulla [1] lies, with those who shed
Tears for the Wild Geese fled.
And all the lovers on whom fate had warred
Cutting the silver cord
Enter, and softly breath by breath they mould
The young heart to the old,
The old protest, the old pity, whose power
Are gathering to the hour
When their knit silence shall be mightier far
Than leagued empires are.
And dreaming of the sorrow on this face
We grow of lordlier race,
Could shake the rooted rampart of the hills
To shield her from all ills,
And through a deep adoring pity won
Grow what we dream upon.

1904

[1] Cuchulain, the great champion of the Red Branch cycle of tales.—*Author's note.*

RECONCILIATION

I begin through the grass once again to be bound to the Lord;
    I can see, through a face that has faded, the face full of rest
Of the earth, of the mother, my heart with her heart in accord,
    As I lie 'mid the cool green tresses that mantle her breast.
I begin with the grass once again to be bound to the Lord.

By the hand of a child I am led to the throne of the King
    For a touch that now fevers me not is forgotten and far,
And His infinite sceptred hands that sway us can bring
    Me in dreams from the laugh of a child to the song of a star.
On the laugh of a child I am borne to the joy of the King.

1904

THE EARTH

They tell me that the earth is still the same
Although the Red Branch now is but a name,
That yonder peasant lifting up his eyes
Can see the marvel of the morning rise,
The wonder Deirdre gazed on when she came.

I cannot think the hearts that beat so high
Had not a lordlier palace roof of sky,
And that the earth on which the heroes trod
Seemed not to live beneath them like a god
Who loved them and could answer to their cry.

Who said the sun will shine with equal face
Alike upon the noble and the base?
The mighty only to the mighty seems;
The world that loomed through proud and golden dreams
Has dropped behind this world and left no trace.

When that the proud and golden race passed by,
This cold paternal majesty on high,
This unresponsive earth beneath the feet,
Replaced the dear brown breasts that were so sweet,
The face of brooding love within the sky.

How could a beggar wear the kingly crown,
Or those who weakly laid the sceptre down,
Walk 'mid the awful beauty God had made
For those whose hearts were proud and unafraid,
Careless if on His face were smile or frown?

1913

THE WINDS OF ANGUS [1]

The grey road whereupon we trod became as holy ground:
The eve was all one voice that breathed its message with no
sound:
And burning multitudes pour through my heart, too bright,
too blind,
Too swift and hurried in their flight to leave their tale behind.
Twin gates unto that living world, dark honey-colored eyes,
The lifting of whose lashes flushed the face with Paradise,
Beloved, there I saw within their ardent rays unfold
The likeness of enraptured birds that flew from deeps of gold
To deeps of gold within my breast to rest, or there to be
Transfigured in the light, or find a death to life in me.
So love, a burning multitude, a seraph wind that blows
From out the deep of being to the deep of being goes.
And sun and moon and starry fires and earth and air and sea
Are creatures from the deep let loose, who pause in ecstasy,
Or wing their wild and heavenly way until again they find
The ancient deep, and fade therein, enraptured, bright, and blind.

1913

THE VIRGIN MOTHER

Who is that goddess to whom men should pray,
But her from whom their hearts have turned away,
Out of whose virgin being they were born,
Whose mother nature they have named with scorn
Calling its holy substance common clay.

Yet from this so despisèd earth was made
The milky whiteness of those queens who swayed

[1] Angus is the Celtic Eros. In the bardic stories he is described as a tall, golden-haired youth playing on a harp and surrounded by singing birds. The kisses of these birds brought love and after that death.—*Author's note.*

Their generations with a light caress,
And from some image of whose loveliness
The heart built up high heaven when it prayed.

Lover, your heart, the heart on which it lies,
Your eyes that gaze and those alluring eyes,
Your lips, the lips they kiss, alike had birth
Within that dark divinity of earth,
Within that mother being you despise.

Ah, when I think this earth on which I tread
Hath borne these blossoms of the lovely dead,
And makes the living heart I love to beat,
I look with sudden awe beneath my feet
As you with erring reverence overhead.

1913

IN AS MUCH . . .

When for love it was fain of
The wild heart was chidden,
When the white limbs were clothed
And the beauty was hidden;

For the scorn that was done to
The least of her graces,
The Mother veiled over
And hid from our faces

The high soul of nature,
The deep and the wonder,
Her towers up in heaven,
And the fairyland under.

The Mother then whispered,
"The wrong done by thee
To the least limb of beauty
Was done unto me."

1913

WHEN

When mine hour is come
Let no teardrop fall
And no darkness hover
Round me where I lie.
Let the vastness call
One who was its lover,
Let me breathe the sky.

Where the lordly light
Walks along the world,
And its silent tread
Leaves the grasses bright,
Leaves the flowers uncurled,
Let me to the dead
Breathe a gay goodnight.

1913

CONTINUITY

No sign is made while empires pass.[1]
The flowers and stars are still His care,
The constellations hid in grass,
The golden miracles in air.

Life in an instant will be rent
Where death is glittering blind and wild—
The Heavenly Brooding is intent
To that last instant on Its child.

It breathes the glow in brain and heart,
Life is made magical. Until
Body and spirit are apart
The Everlasting works Its will.

In that wild orchid that your feet
In their next falling shall destroy,
Minute and passionate and sweet
The Mighty Master holds His joy.

[1] This was written during the first World War.

Though the crushed jewels droop and fade
The Artist's labors will not cease,
And of the ruins shall be made
Some yet more lovely masterpiece.

1918

MUTINY

That blazing galleon the sun,
This dusky coracle I ride,
Both under secret orders sail,
And swim upon the selfsame tide.

The fleet of stars, my boat of soul,
By perilous magic mountains pass,
Or lie where no horizons gleam
Fainting upon a sea of glass.

Come, break the seals and tell us now
Upon what enterprise we roam:
To storm what city of the gods,
Or—sail for the green fields of home!

1925

TIME

At every heart-beat
Through the magic day
A lovely laughing creature
Ran away.
Where have they wandered,
The flock so gay?

I had but looked on them
And away they ran,
The exquisite lips untouched.
As they began
To part, Time swept them
On his caravan.

These new-born beauties
The tyrant took.

Their gaze was on mine
And mine forsook.
I could not stay even
One lovely look.

In what fold are they?
Could I pursue
Through the Everliving
And know anew
All those golden motions
That were you?

Were beauty only
A day the same,
We could know the Maker
And name His name.
We would know the substance
Was holy flame.

Is there an oasis
Where Time stands still,
Where the fugitive beauty
Stays as we will?
Is there an oasis
Where Time stands still?

1925

RESURRECTION

Not by me these feet were led
  To the path beside the wave,
Where the naiad lilies shed
  Moonfire o'er a lonely grave.

Let the dragons of the past
  In their caverns sleeping lie.
I am dream-betrayed, and cast
  Into that old agony.

And an anguish of desire
  Burns as in the sunken years,
And the soul sheds drops of fire
  All unquenchable by tears.

I, who sought on high for calm,
  In the Everliving find
All I was in what I am,
  Fierce with gentle intertwined;

Hearts which I had crucified
  With my heart that tortured them:
Penitence, unfallen pride—
  These my thorny diadem!

Thou would'st ease in heaven thy pain,
  Oh, thou fiery, bleeding thing!
All thy wounds will wake again
  At the heaving of a wing.

All thy dead with thee shall rise,
  Dies Irae. If the soul
To the Everliving flies,
  There shall meet it at the goal

Love that Time had overlaid,
  Deaths that we again must die—
Let the dragons we have made
  In their caverns sleeping lie.

1925

PROMISE

Be not so desolate
Because thy dreams have flown
And the hall of the heart is empty
And silent as stone,
As age left by children
Sad and alone.

Those delicate children,
Thy dreams, still endure:
All pure and lovely things
Wend to the Pure.
Sigh not: unto the fold
Their way was sure.

Thy gentlest dreams, thy frailest,
Even those that were
Born and lost in a heart-beat,
Shall meet thee there.
They are become immortal
In shining air.

The unattainable beauty
The thought of which was pain,
That flickered in eyes and on lips
And vanished again:
That fugitive beauty
Thou shalt attain.

The lights innumerable
That led thee on and on,
The Masque of Time ended,
Shall glow into one.
It shall be with thee for ever
Thy travel done.

1925

A MURMUR IN THE GRASS

O pale-lipped blossom
Why do you sigh?
"For the many million
Times I must die
Ere I be as that glory
Up in the sky."

Your sisters with beauty
Are satisfied.
Is it not envy
Dreams of such pride?
"No, there is nothing
To life denied.

"It would be unjust,
Unjust, if we
Could dream of a beauty
We might not be.

Life is becoming
All we see.

"I shall rise from the grass,
I shall fill all the blue,
And I shall be blossom
And fire and dew
In the boundlessness
We travel through."

1925

VALE [1]

This was the heavenly hiding place
Wherein the spirit laughed a day,
All its proud ivories and fires
Shrunk to a shovelful of clay.

It must have love, this silent earth,
To leap up at the King's desire,
Moving in such a noble dance
Of wreathèd ivory and fire.

It will not stir for me at all,
Nor answer me with voice or gleam.
Adieu, sweet-memoried dust, I go
After the Master for His dream.

1931

FORGOTTEN

The hills have vanished in dark air;
And night, without an eye, is blind.
I too am starless. Time has blurred
The aeons of my life behind.

Oh, what in those dark aeons lay?
What tumult, beauty and desire?
I know not, all are lost beyond
Sunsets of anguish and of fire.

1931

[1] The Latin word *farewell.*

COMFORT

The skies were dim and vast and deep
Above the vale of rest.
They seemed to rock the stars to sleep
Beyond the mountain's crest.

I sought for graves I had mourned, but found
The roads were blind. The grave,
Even of love, heart-lost, was drowned
Under time's brimming wave.

Huddled beneath the wheeling sky,
Strange was my comfort there:
That stars and stones and love and I
Drew to one sepulchre.

1934

INNOCENCE

How could she know, that child who thought
So lovely pure the tale I told,
Within what obscene pits were wrought
The ores to make her fairy gold?

How could she know through what dire strife,
From what dark martyrdoms, there spring
The resurrection and the life,
The glow within the psyche's wing?

1934

TO ONE WHO WANTED A PHILOSOPHY FROM ME

You tell me of my songs you cannot fit
Their thought together, so contrary the lights.
I cannot help you to the sense of it.
We rise and fall, have many days and nights,
Make songs in both; and when we are in our pit
Gaze back in wonder at our own endless heights.

1934

W. H. Davies

William Henry Davies, a son of poor Welsh parents, was born April 20, 1871, in Newport, Wales, in the Church House, a "pub" kept by his grandfather Francis Davies, a retired sea-captain. His father died when William was a child, and when, shortly afterwards, his mother re-married, he and a sister and half-witted older brother were adopted by Francis Davies and his wife. He attended school for some years until he organized a gang of his schoolmates to steal from merchants of the neighborhood, was caught, and dismissed from school. He then took a job with an ironmonger at five shillings a week, but later was apprenticed to a picture-frame maker. At this time, through the encouragement of a young woman, he began reading Marlowe, Shakespeare, Byron, Shelley, and other poets, and writing verse himself; but her death brought an end to his interest in literature, and he determined to go to America as soon as he had completed his apprenticeship. Upon his grandmother's refusal to supply him with funds for a trip to America, he left home for Bristol, where he worked for six months till his grandmother's death brought him a small legacy. Securing £15 of his inheritance, he sailed, at the age of twenty-three, for the United States.

He arrived in New York with ten dollars, and after a few days in a small Connecticut town, he determined to go to Chicago to look for work. Knowing nothing of American geography, he asked directions of a man he met in a park. This man turned out to be a noted tramp, who suggested that Davies join him in his wanderings. Davies accepted the proposal, was introduced to the ways of hoboes and beggars, and for the next six years was a professional tramp, riding the rails from coast to coast, and occasionally working in the berry fields of Michigan or as cattleman on freighters between Baltimore and England. In his thirtieth year, after a short stay in England, he set out for the Klondike, where he supposed gold lay around on top of the ground and might be had for the picking up. When on his way in Canada, he was persuaded by a fellow-tramp to steal a ride on a passenger train instead of a freight, as he had always done before. In boarding the train, he fell under a wheel and had his right foot cut off. As he lay recovering from this accident and reflecting on his condition, he realized that his life as a tramp was ended and that he must find an occupation; and remembering his early attempts at writing, he determined to go back to England and become a poet.

Eventually he drifted to a cheap London lodging house, where he could live for six pence a day, and started writing. Soon he had produced a blank verse drama, a long poem about birds and beasts, a hundred sonnets, and several other works; but for none of these could he find a publisher. To raise money to publish them himself, he took to the road again, this time as a peddler of shoe laces, pins, and needles; but he had no success, and was forced to secure an advance on his small income from his grandmother's estate. With the sum thus obtained, he hired a printer, for £19, to print 250 copies of *The Soul's Destroyer and Other Poems* (1905), which he began sending to various important people with the request to purchase the book or return it. One of those to whom he sent a copy was Bernard Shaw, who recognized its merit, and with the help of one or two friendly critics introduced Davies to the public, and aroused interest in him and his work.

Davies now began issuing books in rapid succession, and during his remaining years he published more than twenty volumes of poetry, besides collected and selected editions, and a number of prose works. Among the latter were three novels, two books on nature, and three autobiographical works; but these were inferior to his poetry, and except for *The Autobiography of a Super-Tramp* (1908), his prose displayed little merit. In 1921 he was editor of the magazine *Form*, and he compiled two anthologies: *Shorter Lyrics of the Twentieth Century* (1922) and *Jewels of Song* (1930).

Soon after the publication of his first poetry he was given a Civil List Pension of £50 a year, and the amount was twice increased later. In 1926 the University of Wales gave him an honorary D.Litt. degree. In 1924 he married Helen Payne, and for some years they lived at Oxted, Surrey, and then moved to Nailsworth,

Gloucester, where Davies made his home henceforth. He was in poor health for sometime before his death on September 26, 1940.

THE WAYS OF TIME

As butterflies are but winged flowers,
    Half sorry for their change, who fain,
So still and long they lie on leaves,
    Would be thought flowers again—

E'en so my thoughts, that should expand,
    And grow to higher themes above,
Return like butterflies to lie
    On the old things I love.

1907

THE RAIN

I hear leaves drinking Rain;
    I hear rich leaves on top
Giving the poor beneath
    Drop after drop;
'Tis a sweet noise to hear
These green leaves drinking near.

And when the Sun comes out,
    After this Rain shall stop,
A wondrous Light will fill
    Each dark, round drop;
I hope the Sun shines bright:
'Twill be a lovely sight.

1908

TRULY GREAT

My walls outside must have some flowers,
    My walls within must have some books;
A house that's small; a garden large,
    And in it leafy nooks.

A little gold that's sure each week;
 That comes not from my living kind,
But from a dead man in his grave,
 Who cannot change his mind.

A lovely wife, and gentle too;
 Contented that no eyes but mine
Can see her many charms, nor voice
 To call her beauty fine.

Where she would in that stone cage live,
 A self-made prisoner, with me;
While many a wild bird sang around,
 On gate, on bush, on tree.

And she sometimes to answer them,
 In her far sweeter voice than all;
Till birds, that loved to look on leaves,
 Will doat on a stone wall.

With this small house, this garden large,
 This little gold, this lovely mate,
With health in body, peace at heart—
 Show me a man more great.

1908

IN THE COUNTRY

This life is sweetest; in this wood
I hear no children cry for food;
I see no woman white with care,
No man with muscles wasting here.

No doubt it is a selfish thing
To fly from human suffering;
No doubt he is a selfish man,
Who shuns poor creatures sad and wan.

But 'tis a wretched life to face
Hunger in almost every place;
Cursed with a hand that's empty, when
The heart is full to help all men.

Can I admire the statue great,
When living men starve at its feet!
Can I admire the park's green tree,
A roof for homeless misery!

When I can see few men in need,
I then have power to help by deed,
Nor lose my cheerfulness in pity—
Which I must do in every city.

For when I am in those great places,
I see ten thousand suffering faces;
Before me stares a wolfish eye,
Behind me creeps a groan or sigh.

1910

THE EXAMPLE

Here's an example from
    A Butterfly;
That on a rough, hard rock
    Happy can lie;
Friendless and all alone
On this unsweetened stone.

Now let my bed be hard,
    No care take I;
I'll make my joy like this
    Small Butterfly;
Whose happy heart has power
To make a stone a flower.

1911

LEISURE

What is this life if, full of care,
We have no time to stand and stare.

No time to stand beneath the boughs
And stare as long as sheep or cows.

No time to see, when woods we pass,
Where squirrels hide their nuts in grass.

No time to see, in broad daylight,
Streams full of stars, like stars at night.

No time to turn at Beauty's glance,
And watch her feet, how they can dance.

No time to wait till her mouth can
Enrich that smile her eyes began.

A poor life this if, full of care,
We have no time to stand and stare.

1911

FANCY'S HOME

Tell me, Fancy, sweetest child,
Of thy parents and thy birth;
Had they silk, and had they gold,
And a park to wander forth,
With a castle green and old?

In a cottage I was born,
My kind father was Content,
My dear mother Innocence;
On wild fruits of wonderment
I have nourished ever since.

1911

SHEEP

When I was once in Baltimore,
A man came up to me and cried,
"Come, I have eighteen hundred sheep,
And we will sail on Tuesday's tide.

"If you will sail with me, young man,
I'll pay you fifty shillings down;
These eighteen hundred sheep I take
From Baltimore to Glasgow town."

He paid me fifty shillings down,
    I sailed with eighteen hundred sheep;
We soon had cleared the harbor's mouth,
    We soon were in the salt sea deep.

The first night we were out at sea
    Those sheep were quiet in their mind;
The second night they cried with fear—
    They smelt no pastures in the wind.

They sniffed, poor things, for their green fields,
    They cried so loud I could not sleep:
For fifty thousand shillings down
    I would not sail again with sheep.

1911

CHRIST THE MAN

Lord, I say nothing; I profess
    No faith in Thee nor Christ Thy Son:
Yet no man ever heard me mock
    A true believing one.

If knowledge is not great enough
    To give a man believing power,
Lord, he must wait in Thy great hand
    Till revelation's hour.

Meanwhile he'll follow Christ the man,
    In that humanity He taught,
Which to the poor and the oppressed,
    Gives its best time and thought.

1911

THE SLEEPERS

As I walked down the waterside
    This silent morning, wet and dark;
Before the cocks in farmyards crowed,
    Before the dogs began to bark;
Before the hour of five was struck
By old Westminster's mighty clock:

As I walked down the waterside
    This morning, in the cold damp air,
I saw a hundred women and men
    Huddled in rags and sleeping there:
These people have no work, thought I,
And long before their time they die.

That moment, on the waterside,
    A lighted car came at a bound;
I looked inside, and saw a score
    Of pale and weary men that frowned;
Each man sat in a huddled heap,
Carried to work while fast asleep.

Ten cars rushed down the waterside,
    Like lighted coffins in the dark;
With twenty dead men in each car,
    That must be brought alive by work:
These people work too hard, thought I,
And long before their time they die.

1911

WINTER'S BEAUTY

Is it not fine to walk in spring,
When leaves are born, and hear birds sing?
And when they lose their singing powers,
In summer, watch the bees at flowers?
Is it not fine, when summer's past,
To have the leaves, no longer fast,
Biting my heel where'er I go,
Or dancing lightly on my toe?
Now winter's here and rivers freeze;
As I walk out I see the trees,
Wherein the pretty squirrels sleep,
All standing in the snow so deep:
And every twig, however small,
Is blossomed white and beautiful.
Then welcome, winter, with thy power
To make this tree a big white flower;
To make this tree a lovely sight,
With fifty brown arms draped in white,

While thousands of small fingers show
In soft white gloves of purest snow.
1913

MY LOVE COULD WALK

My love could walk in richer hues
Than any bird of paradise,
And no one envy her her dress:
Since in her looks the world would see
A robin's love and friendliness.

And she could be the lily fair,
More richly dressed than all her kind,
And no one envy her her gain:
Since in her looks the world would see
A daisy that was sweet and plain.

Oh, she could sit like any queen
That's nailed by diamonds to a throne,
Her splendor envied by not one:
Since in her looks the world would see
A queen that's more than half a nun.
1918

BIRDS

When our two souls have left this mortal clay,
And, seeking mine, you think that mine is lost—
Look for me first in that Elysian glade
Where Lesbia is, for whom the birds sing most.

What happy hearts those feathered mortals have,
That sing so sweet when they're wet through in spring!
For in that month of May when leaves are young,
Birds dream of song, and in their sleep they sing.

And when the spring has gone and they are dumb,
Is it not fine to watch them at their play:
Is it not fine to see a bird that tries
To stand upon the end of every spray?

See how they tilt their pretty heads aside:
    When women make that move they always please.
What cosy homes birds make in leafy walls
    That Nature's love has ruined—and the trees.

Oft have I seen in fields the little birds
    Go in between a bullock's legs to eat;
But what gives me most joy is when I see
    Snow on my doorstep, printed by their feet.

1918

FORGIVENESS

Stung by a spiteful wasp,
    I let him go life free:
That proved the difference
    In him and me.

For, had I killed my foe,
    It had proved me at once
The stronger wasp, and no
    More difference.

1918

THE BELL

It is the bell of death I hear,
Which tells me my own time is near,
When I must join those quiet souls
Where nothing lives but worms and moles;
And not come through the grass again,
Like worms and moles, for breath or rain;
Yet let none weep when my life's through,
For I myself have wept for few.

The only things that knew me well
Were children, dogs, and girls that fell;
I bought poor children cakes and sweets,
Dogs heard my voice and danced the streets;
And, gentle to a fallen lass,
I made her weep for what she was.

Good men and women know not me,
Nor love nor hate the mystery.

1918

RAGS AND BONES

This morning, as I wandered forth,
I heard a man cry, "Rags and Bones!"
And little children in the streets
Went home for bottles, bones, and rags,
To barter for his toys and sweets.

And then I thought of grown-up man,
That in our dreams we trust a God
Will think our rags and bones a boon,
And give us His immortal sweets
For these poor lives cast off so soon.

The mind, they say, will gather strength
That broods on what is hard to know:
The fear of unfamiliar things
Is better than their parents' love,
To teach young birds to use their wings.

But riddles are not made for me,
My joy's in beauty, not its cause:
Then give me but the open skies,
And birds that sing in a green wood
That's snow-bound by anemones.

1918

THE CAPTIVE LION

Thou that in fury with thy knotted tail
Hast made this iron floor thy beaten drum;
That now in silence walks thy little space—
Like a sea-captain—careless what may come:

What power has brought your majesty to this,
Who gave those eyes their dull and sleepy look;
Who took their lightning out, and from thy throat
The thunder when the whole wide forest shook?

It was that man who went again, alone,
Into thy forest dark—Lord, he was brave!
That man a fly has killed, whose bones are left
Unburied till an earthquake digs his grave.

1920

TELLING FORTUNES

"You'll have a son," the old man said—
 "And then a daughter fair to meet
As any summer nights that dance
 Upon a thousand silver feet."
"You dear old man, now can you tell
If my fair daughter'll marry well?"
The old man winked his eye and said,
 "Well, knowing men for what they are,
She'll break their hearts, because she'll not
 Be half as good as she is fair."
The new-made wife was full of pain,
And raised her head and hoped again.
"And will my son be fine and smart
And win a noble lady's heart?"
The old man winked his other eye—
"Well, knowing women as we do,
 The kind of man they most prefer,
He'll break their hearts, because he'll be
 A fool, a coxcomb, and a cur."

1922

LOVE, LIKE A DROP OF DEW

When I pass down the street and see
 The people smiling so,
It's clear enough that my true love
 Was there awhile ago.

Her lips that, following her two eyes,
 Go smiling here and there,
Seem newly kissed—but 'tis my faith
 That none but I would dare.

Love, like a drop of dew that joins
    Two blades of grass together,
Has made her mine, as I am hers,
    For ever and for ever.

1924

ONE TOKEN

The power was given at birth to me
To stare at a rainbow, bird or tree,
    Longer than any man alive;
And from these trances, when they're gone,
My songs of joy come, one by one.

But what I want I cannot have:
One token from beyond the grave,
    That hour I neither dream nor sleep,
To prove death but a veil to hide
Another life on the other side.

1924

THE RIVALS

Pleasure is not the one I love:
    Her laughter in the market-place
Makes every fool her echo there;
    And from her finger-tips she throws
Wild kisses in the open air.

Give me that little miser, Joy,
    Who hoards at home her quiet charms;
And offers with her two soft lips
    A warmer kiss than any thrown
By Pleasure, from her finger-tips.

1924

THE TWO STARS

Day has her star, as well as Night,
One star is black, the other white.
I saw a white star burn and pant
    And swirl with such a wildness, once—

That I stood still, and almost stared
    Myself into a trance!
The star of Day, both seen and heard,
Is but a little English bird;
The Lark, whose wings beat time to his
    Wild rapture, sings, high overhead;
When silence comes, we almost fear
    That Earth receives its dead.

1924

THE SNOWFLAKE

When we are young and wake from sleep,
    What pillow-fights we share with Life!
We laugh and punch, and never dream
    How Death can end that joyful strife.

We'll not let Time destroy that dream,
    But in old age our spirit brave
Shall, like a snowflake in its fall,
    Dance while it hovers o'er the grave.

Contented men are still my theme,
    Who—though too poor for ivory keys—
Still whistle with their naked lips
    Their happy tunes of careless ease.

1924

THE JOY OF LIFE

How sweet is Life, how beautiful,
    When lying curled in innocent sleep!
Without one thought that, soon or late,
    Death will unbend that graceful curve
And stretch him out, all stiff and straight.

Go, happy Life, and say to Death—
    "I gave this man sufficient joy
To last him for a thousand years."
    Then ask him why my time's as short
As one whose breath is full of tears.

1924

THE WORMS' CONTEMPT

What do we earn for all our gentle grace?
A body stiff and cold from foot to face.

If you have beauty, what is beauty worth?
A mask to hide it, made of common earth.

What do we get for all our song and prattle?
A gasp for longer breath, and then a rattle.

What do we earn for dreams, and our high teaching?
The worms' contempt, that have no time for preaching.

1939

LIFE

The quality of life on earth
    Is all that dreams could make it be;
And all I ask for in this world
    Is but increase in quantity.
My corn and wine—how sweet are these!
    How precious is this living breath!
Is it not Man's ingratitude
    That looks for better after death?

1939

Ralph Hodgson

Ralph Hodgson was born at Bradford, Yorkshire, March 12, 1872. In his early years he worked as a pressman in Fleet Street, the newspaper center in London, then as a draughtsman on the pictorial staff of an evening paper, and for a while he edited *Fry's Magazine*. In 1913 he formed a partnership with the artist, Lovat Fraser, and Holbrook Jackson to publish broadsides and chapbooks; and from their press, "The Sign of Flying Fame," were issued a number of Hodgson's poems. In 1924 he was given a three-year appointment as lecturer on English literature at the Imperial University, Sendai, Japan, and the appointment was twice renewed, Hodgson being the first to receive the appointment more than once.

Although he has been a lifelong devotee of poetry, he has regarded the writing of it as an avocation. In 1907 he published his first book of verse, *The Blackbird and Other Lines;* then in 1913 he issued several pamphlets of his verse at "The Sign of Flying Fame" press, and for these received the Edmond de Polignac Prize in 1914; and finally he published a small collection, *Poems,* in 1922. Besides poetry, his hobbies have been the breeding and showing of bull terriers (on which he is a recognized authority), prize fighting, and the protection and care of animals and birds.

Hodgson has been married three times, his third wife being an American. He now lives near Minerva, Ohio, and occupies himself in raising dogs and in giving occasional lectures. He has of late years been printing his poetry in chapbooks, which are issued from a private press in Minerva.

THE LINNET

They say the world's a sham, and life a lease
Of nightmare nothing nicknamed Time, and we
Ghost voyagers in undiscovered seas
Where fact is feign; mirage, reality:

Where all is vain and vanity is all,
And eyes look out and only know they stare
At conjured coasts whose beacons rise and fall
And vanish with the hopes that feigned them there:

Where sea-shell measures urge a phantom dance
Till fancied pleasure drowns imagined pain—
Till Death stares madness out of countenance,
And vanity is all and all is vain.

It may be even as my friends allege.
I'm pressed to prove that life is something more—
And yet a linnet on a hawthorn hedge
Still wants explaining and accounting for.

1907

THE NIGHT

Fond muse surrender, weary as thou art,
To sleep at last; a meadow's breadth from thee,
In yon dim copse and still, a sister heart
Hath respite from its old sweet agony.

The wall of night is up; around, across,
Above nor sound nor sense of day remains;
Comes only now the fitful drive and toss
Of moths upon the yellow window-panes.

1907

THE BULL

See an old unhappy bull,
Sick in soul and body both,
Slouching in the undergrowth

Of the forest beautiful,
Banished from the herd he led,
Bulls and cows a thousand head.

Cranes and gaudy parrots go
Up and down the burning sky;
Tree-top cats purr drowsily
In the dim-day green below;
And troops of monkeys, nutting, some,
All disputing, go and come;

And things abominable sit
Picking offal buck or swine,
On the mess and over it
Burnished flies and beetles shine,
And spiders big as bladders lie
Under hemlocks ten foot high;

And a dotted serpent curled
Round and round and round a tree,
Yellowing its greenery
Keeps a watch on all the world,
All the world and this old bull
In the forest beautiful.

Bravely by his fall he came:
One he led, a bull of blood
Newly come to lustihood
Fought and put his prince to shame,
Snuffed and pawed the prostrate head
Tameless even while it bled.

There they left him, every one,
Left him there without a lick,
Left him for the birds to pick,
Left him there for carrion,
Vilely from their bosom cast
Wisdom, worth and love at last.

When the lion left his lair
And roared his beauty through the hills,
And the vultures pecked their quills
And flew into the middle air,

Then this prince no more to reign
Came to life and lived again.

He snuffed the herd in far retreat,
He saw the blood upon the ground,
And snuffed the burning airs around
Still with beevish odors sweet,
While the blood ran down his head
And his mouth ran slaver red.

Pity him, this fallen chief,
All his splendor, all his strength,
All his body's breadth and length
Dwindled down with shame and grief,
Half the bull he was before,
Bones and leather, nothing more.

See him standing dewlap-deep
In the rushes at the lake,
Surly, stupid, half asleep,
Waiting for his heart to break
And the birds to join the flies
Feasting at his bloodshot eyes;

Standing with his head hung down
In a stupor, dreaming things:
Green savannas, jungles brown,
Battlefields and bellowings,
Bulls undone and lions dead
And vultures flapping overhead.

Dreaming things: of days he spent
With his mother gaunt and lean
In the valley warm and green,
Full of baby wonderment,
Blinking out of silly eyes
At a hundred mysteries;

Dreaming over once again
How he wandered with a throng
Of bulls and cows a thousand strong,
Wandered on from plain to plain,
Up the hill and down the dale,
Always at his mother's tail;

How he lagged behind the herd,
Lagged and tottered, weak of limb,
And she turned and ran to him
Blaring at the loathly bird
Stationed always in the skies,
Waiting for the flesh that dies.

Dreaming maybe of a day
When her drained and drying paps
Turned him to the sweets and saps,
Richer fountains by the way,
And she left the bull she bore
And he looked to her no more;

And his little frame grew stout,
And his little legs grew strong,
And the way was not so long;
And his little horns came out,
And he played at butting trees
And boulder-stones and tortoises,

Joined a game of knobby skulls
With the youngsters of his year,
All the other little bulls,
Learning both to bruise and bear,
Learning how to stand a shock
Like a little bull of rock.

Dreaming of a day less dim,
Dreaming of a time less far,
When the faint but certain star
Of destiny burned clear for him,
And a fierce and wild unrest
Broke the quiet of his breast,

And the gristles of his youth
Hardened in his comely pow,
And he came to fighting growth,
Beat his bull and won his cow,
And flew his tail and trampled off
Past the tallest, vain enough,

And curved about in splendor full
And curved again and snuffed the airs

As who should say, Come out who dares!
And all beheld a bull, a Bull,
And knew that here was surely one
That backed for no bull, fearing none.

And the leader of the herd
Looked and saw, and beat the ground,
And shook the forest with his sound,
Bellowed at the loathly bird
Stationed always in the skies,
Waiting for the flesh that dies.

Dreaming, this old bull forlorn,
Surely dreaming of the hour
When he came to sultan power,
And they owned him master-horn,
Chiefest bull of all among
Bulls and cows a thousand strong;

And in all the tramping herd
Not a bull that barred his way,
Not a cow that said him nay,
Not a bull or cow that erred
In the furnace of his look
Dared a second, worse rebuke;

Not in all the forest wide,
Jungle, thicket, pasture, fen,
Not another dared him then,
Dared him and again defied;
Not a sovereign buck or boar
Came a second time for more;

Not a serpent that survived
Once the terrors of his hoof
Risked a second time reproof,
Came a second time and lived,
Not a serpent in its skin
Came again for discipline;

Not a leopard bright as flame,
Flashing fingerhooks of steel,
That a wooden tree might feel,

Met his fury once and came
For a second reprimand,
Not a leopard in the land;

Not a lion of them all,
Not a lion of the hills,
Hero of a thousand kills,
Dared a second fight and fall,
Dared that ram terrific twice,
Paid a second time the price.

Pity him, this dupe of dream,
Leader of the herd again
Only in his daft old brain,
Once again the bull supreme
And bull enough to bear the part
Only in his tameless heart.

Pity him that he must wake;
Even now the swarm of flies
Blackening his bloodshot eyes
Bursts and blusters round the lake,
Scattered from the feast half-fed,
By great shadows overhead;

And the dreamer turns away
From his visionary herds
And his splendid yesterday,
Turns to meet the loathly birds
Flocking round him from the skies,
Waiting for the flesh that dies.

1913

TIME, YOU OLD GIPSY MAN

Time, you old gipsy man,
Will you not stay,
Put up your caravan
Just for one day?

All things I'll give you
Will you be my guest,
Bells for your jennet
Of silver the best,
Goldsmiths shall beat you
A great golden ring,
Peacocks shall bow to you,
Little boys sing.
Oh, and sweet girls will
Festoon you with may,
Time, you old gipsy,
Why hasten away?

Last week in Babylon,
Last night in Rome,
Morning, and in the crush
Under Paul's dome;
Under Paul's dial
You tighten your rein—
Only a moment,
And off once again;
Off to some city
Now blind in the womb,
Off to another
Ere that's in the tomb.

Time, you old gipsy man,
  Will you not stay,
Put up your caravan
  Just for one day?

1913

EVE

Eve, with her basket, was
Deep in the bells and grass,
Wading in bells and grass
Up to her knees,
Picking a dish of sweet
Berries and plums to eat,
Down in the bells and grass
Under the trees.

Mute as a mouse in a
Corner the cobra lay,
Curled round a bough of the
Cinnamon tall. . . .
Now to get even and
Humble proud heaven and
Now was the moment or
Never at all.

"Eva!" Each syllable
Light as a flower fell;
"Eva!" he whispered the
Wondering maid;
Soft as a bubble sung
Out of a linnet's lung,
Soft and most silverly
"Eva!" he said.

Picture that orchard sprite,
Eve, with her body white,
Supple and smooth to her
Slim finger tips,
Wondering, listening,
Listening, wondering,
Eve with a berry
Half-way to her lips.

Oh, had our simple Eve
Seen through the make-believe!
Had she but known the
Pretender he was!
Out of the boughs he came,
Whispering still her name,
Tumbling in twenty rings
Into the grass.

Here was the strangest pair
In the world anywhere,
Eve in the bells and grass
Kneeling, and he
Telling his story low. . . .
Singing birds saw them go
Down the dark path to
The Blasphemous Tree.

Oh, what a clatter when
Titmouse and Jenny Wren
Saw him successful and
Taking his leave!
How the birds rated him,
How they all hated him!
How they all pitied
Poor motherless Eve!

Picture her crying
Outside in the lane,
Eve, with no dish of sweet
Berries and plums to eat,
Haunting the gate of the
Orchard in vain. . . .
Picture the lewd delight
Under the hill to-night—
"Eva!" the toast goes round,
"Eva!" again.

1913

THE SONG OF HONOR

I climbed a hill as light fell short,
And rooks came home in scramble sort,
And filled the trees and flapped and fought
And sang themselves to sleep;
An owl from nowhere with no sound
Swung by and soon was nowhere found,
I heard him calling half-way round,
Holloing loud and deep;
A pair of stars, faint pins of light,
Then many a star, sailed into sight,
And all the stars, the flower of night,
Were round me at a leap;
To tell how still the valleys lay
I heard a watchdog miles away,
And bells of distant sheep.
I heard no more of bird or bell,
The mastiff in a slumber fell,
I stared into the sky,
As wondering men have always done

Since beauty and the stars were one,
Though none so hard as I.

It seemed, so still the valleys were,
As if the whole world knelt at prayer,
Save me and me alone;
So pure and wide that silence was
I feared to bend a blade of grass,
And there I stood like stone.

There, sharp and sudden, there I heard—
Ah! some wild lovesick singing bird
Woke singing in the trees?
The nightingale and babble-wren
Were in the English greenwood then,
And you heard one of these?
The babble-wren and nightingale
Sang in the Abyssinian vale
That season of the year!
Yet, true enough, I heard them plain,
I heard them both again, again,
As sharp and sweet and clear
As if the Abyssinian tree
Had thrust a bough across the sea,
Had thrust a bought across to me
With music for my ear!

I heard them both, and oh! I heard
The song of every singing bird
That sings beneath the sky,
And with the song of lark and wren
The song of mountains, moths and men
And seas and rainbows vie!

I heard the universal choir,
The Sons of Light exalt their Sire
With universal song,
Earth's lowliest and loudest notes,
Her million times ten million throats
Exalt Him loud and long,
And lips and lungs and tongues of Grace
From every part and every place
Within the shining of His face,
The universal throng.

I heard the hymn of being sound
From every well of honor found
In human sense and soul:
The song of poets when they write
The testament of Beauty sprite
Upon a flying scroll,
The song of painters when they take
A burning brush for Beauty's sake
And limn her features whole—

The song of men divinely wise
Who look and see in starry skies
Not stars so much as robins' eyes,
And when these pale away
Hear flocks of shiny pleiades
Among the plums and apple trees
Sing in the summer day—

The song of all both high and low
To some blest vision true,
The song of beggars when they throw
The crust of pity all men owe
To hungry sparrows in the snow,
Old beggars hungry too—
The song of kings of kingdoms when
They rise above their fortune Men,
And crown themselves anew—

The song of courage, heart and will
And gladness in a fight,
Of men who face a hopeless hill
With sparkling and delight,
The bells and bells of song that ring
Round banners of a cause or king
From armies bleeding white—

The song of sailors every one
When monstrous tide and tempest run
At ships like bulls at red,
When stately ships are twirled and spun
Like whipping tops and help there's none
And mighty ships ten thousand ton
Go down like lumps of lead—

And song of fighters stern as they
At odds with fortune night and day,
Crammed up in cities grim and grey
As thick as bees in hives,
Hosannas of a lowly throng
Who sing unconscious of their song,
Whose lips are in their lives—

And song of some at holy war
With spells and ghouls more dread by far
Than deadly seas and cities are
Or hordes of quarrelling kings—
The song of fighters great and small,
The song of pretty fighters all
And high heroic things—

The song of lovers—who knows how
Twitched up from place and time
Upon a sigh, a blush, a vow,
A curve or hue of cheek or brow,
Borne up and off from here and now
Into the void sublime!
And crying loves and passions still
In every key from soft to shrill
And numbers never done,
Dog-loyalties to faith and friend,
And loves like Ruth's of old no end,
And intermission none—

And burst on burst for beauty and
For numbers not behind,
From men whose love of motherland
Is like a dog's for one dear hand,
Sole, selfless, boundless, blind—
And song of some with hearts beside
For men and sorrows far and wide,
Who watch the world with pity and pride
And warm to all mankind—

And endless joyous music rise
From children at their play,
And endless soaring lullabies
From happy, happy mothers' eyes,

And answering crows and baby-cries,
How many who shall say!
And many a song as wondrous well
With pangs and sweets intolerable
From lonely hearths too grey to tell,
God knows how utter grey!
And song from many a house of care
When pain has forced a footing there,
And there's a Darkness on the stair
Will not be turned away—

And song—that song whose singers come
With old kind tales of pity from
The Great Compassion's lips,
That make the bells of Heaven to peal
Round pillows frosty with the feel
Of Death's cold finger tips—

The song of men all sorts and kinds,
As many tempers, moods and minds
As leaves are on a tree,
As many faiths and castes and creeds,
As many human bloods and breeds
As in the world may be;

The song of each and all who gaze
On Beauty in her naked blaze,
Or see her dimly in a haze,
Or get her light in fitful rays
And tiniest needles even,
The song of all not wholly dark,
Not wholly sunk in stupor stark
Too deep for groping Heaven—

And alleluias sweet and clear
And wild with beauty men mishear,
From choirs of song as near and dear
To Paradise as they,
The everlasting pipe and flute
Of wind and sea and bird and brute,
And lips deaf men imagine mute
In wood and stone and clay,

The music of a lion strong
That shakes a hill a whole night long,
A hill as loud as he,
The twitter of a mouse among
Melodious greenery,
The ruby's and the rainbow's song,
The nightingale's—all three,
The song of life that wells and flows
From every leopard, lark and rose
And everything that gleams or goes
Lack-lustre in the sea.

I heard it all, each, every note
Of every lung and tongue and throat,
Ay, every rhythm and rhyme
Of everything that lives and loves
And upward, ever upward moves
From lowly to sublime!
Earth's multitudinous Sons of Light,
I heard them lift their lyric might
With each and every chanting sprite
That lit the sky that wondrous night
As far as eye could climb!
I heard it all, I heard the whole
Harmonious hymn of being roll
Up through the chapel of my soul
And at the altar die,
And in the awful quiet then
Myself I heard, Amen, Amen,
Amen I heard me cry!
I heard it all and then although
I caught my flying senses, Oh,
A dizzy man was I!
I stood and stared; the sky was lit,
The sky was stars all over it,
I stood, I knew not why,
Without a wish, without a will,
I stood upon that silent hill
And stared into the sky until
My eyes were blind with stars, and still
I stared into the sky.

1913

THE MYSTERY

He came and took me by the hand
  Up to a red rose tree,
He kept His meaning to Himself
  But gave a rose to me.

I did not pray Him to lay bare
  The mystery to me.
Enough the rose was Heaven to smell,
  And His own face to see.

1913

STUPIDITY STREET

I saw with open eyes
Singing birds sweet
Sold in the shops
For the people to eat,
Sold in the shops of
Stupidity Street.

I saw in vision
The worm in the wheat,
And in the shops nothing
For people to eat;
Nothing for sale in
Stupidity Street.

1913

AFTER

"How fared you when you mortal were?
  What did you see on my peopled star?"
"Oh, well enough," I answered her,
  "It went for me where mortals are!

"I saw blue flowers and the merlin's flight
  And the rime on the wintry tree,
Blue doves I saw and summer light
  On the wings of the cinnamon bee."

1913

THE BELLS OF HEAVEN

'Twould ring the bells of Heaven
The wildest peal for years,
If Parson lost his senses
And people came to theirs,
And he and they together
Knelt down with angry prayers
For tamed and shabby tigers
And dancing dogs and bears,
And wretched, blind pit ponies,
And little hunted hares.

1922

Walter de la Mare

Walter John de la Mare was born April 25, 1873, in Charlton, Kent. His father, James Edward Delamare (as he wrote the name), descended from a Huguenot family that settled in England in 1730. His mother, Lucy Sophia Browning, was the daughter of a physician and a distant relative of Robert Browning.

At an early age he entered the St. Paul's Cathedral Choir School, where he remained till 1890. He was an excellent pupil, ranking among the first three or four of his class, and during his last three terms standing at the top. In his last year there he was one of those responsible for founding a school magazine, the *Choristers' Journal.*

On leaving school he entered the offices of the Anglo-American Oil Company, where he worked as a clerk for eighteen years, chiefly in the statistics department. His aim, however, was to become an author, and in his spare time he worked steadily at literary composition. In 1895 one of his short stories, "Kismet," was published in the *Sketch.* The next year he began contributing stories to the *Cornhill Magazine,* contact with which he owed to his brother-in-law, Roger Ingpen, then on the staff of the publishers. Meanwhile he was also writing poetry; and in 1902 appeared *Songs of Childhood,* his first book. Next came a novel, *Henry Brocken* (1904), and this was followed by another book of verse, *Poems* (1906). Until 1904 he published his work under the pseudonym Walter Ramal, an anagram of de la Mare.

Through the efforts of Sir Henry Newbolt, he received from the government in 1908 a grant from the Privy Purse of £200, and later was given a Civil List Pension of £100 a year. This and some journalistic work—mostly reviewing books for the *Saturday Westminster,* the *Bookman,* and the *London Times Literary Supplement*—enabled him in 1908 to give up his post with the oil company. Presently he was able to escape even the task of reviewing books and to devote all his time to creative writing. He has published more than a dozen volumes of poetry, and several novels and volumes of short stories and essays. Among his prose works are *The Three Mulla-Mulgars* (1910), *Memoirs of a Midget* (1921), *The Riddle and Other Stories* (1923), *Broomsticks and Other Tales* (1925), *The Connoisseur and Other Stories* (1926), *On the Edge* (1930), *Desert Islands* (1930), *The Lord Fish and Other Stories* (1933), and *Early One Morning in the Spring* (1935). He has also edited several books and compiled an anthology of children's verse, *Come Hither!* (1923).

He has received honorary degrees from Cambridge (Litt.D.), Bristol (Litt.D.), and St. Andrews (LL.D.); and he was the first recipient of the Edmond de Polignac Prize for Literature, awarded in 1911 for his novel *The Return.*

He spent the winter of 1916-1917 lecturing in the United States, and he has visited this country two or three times since. In the early nineties he married Constance Elfrida Ingpen, and they had four children. For many years he has lived at Hill House, Taplow, Buckinghamshire, a few miles from London.

SHADOW

Even the beauty of the rose doth cast,
When its bright, fervid noon is past,
A still and lengthening shadow in the dust,
    Till darkness come
    And take its strange dream home.

The transient bubbles of the water paint
'Neath their frail arch a shadow faint;
The golden nimbus of the windowed saint,
    Till shine the stars,
    Casts pale and trembling bars.

The loveliest thing earth hath, a shadow hath,
A dark and livelong hint of death,
Haunting it ever till its last faint breath.
    Who, then, may tell
The beauty of heaven's shadowless asphodel?

1906

UNREGARDING

Put by thy days like withered flowers
  In twilight hidden away:
Memory shall upbuild thee bowers
  Sweeter than they.

Hoard not from swiftness of thy stream
  The shallowest cruse of tears:
Pools still as heaven shall lovelier dream
  In future years.

Squander thy love as she that flings
  Her soul away on night;
Lovely are love's far echoings,
  Height unto height.

O, make no compact with the sun,
  No compact with the moon!
Night falls full-cloaked, and light is gone
  Sudden and soon.

1906

REMEMBRANCE

The sky was like a waterdrop
  In shadow of a thorn,
Clear, tranquil, beautiful,
  Forlorn.

Lightning along its margin ran;
  A rumor of the sea
Rose in profundity and sank
  Into infinity.

Lofty and few the elms, the stars
  In the vast boughs most bright;
I stood a dreamer in a dream
  In the unstirring night.

Not wonder, worship, not even peace
  Seemed in my heart to be:
Only the memory of one,
  Of all most dead to me.

1906

THE THREE CHERRY TREES

  There were three cherry trees once,
  Grew in a garden all shady;
And there for delight of so gladsome a sight,
  Walked a most beautiful lady,
  Dreamed a most beautiful lady.

  Birds in those branches did sing,
  Blackbird and throstle and linnet,
But she walking there was by far the most fair—
  Lovelier than all else within it,
  Blackbird and throstle and linnet.

  But blossoms to berries do come,
  All hanging on stalks light and slender,
And one long summer's day charmed that lady away,
  With vows sweet and merry and tender;
  A lover with voice low and tender.

  Moss and lichen the green branches deck;
  Weeds nod in its paths green and shady;
Yet a light footstep seems there to wander in dreams,
  The ghost of that beautiful lady,
  That happy and beautiful lady.

1912

OLD SUSAN

When Susan's work was done, she would sit,
With one fat guttering candle lit,
And window opened wide to win
The sweet night air to enter in.
There, with a thumb to keep her place,
She would read, with stern and wrinkled face,

Her mild eyes gliding very slow
Across the letters to and fro,
While wagged the guttering candle flame
In the wind that through the window came.
And sometimes in the silence she
Would mumble a sentence audibly,
Or shake her head as if to say,
"You silly souls, to act this way!"
And never a sound from night I would hear,
Unless some far-off cock crowed clear;
Or her old shuffling thumb should turn
Another page; and rapt and stern,
Through her great glasses bent on me,
She would glance into reality;
And shake her round old silvery head,
With—"You!—I thought you was in bed!"—
Only to tilt her book again,
And rooted in Romance remain.

1912

MISS LOO

When thin-strewn memory I look through,
I see most clearly poor Miss Loo,
Her tabby cat, her cage of birds,
Her nose, her hair, her muffled words,
And how she would open her green eyes,
As if in some immense surprise,
Whenever as we sat at tea
She made some small remark to me.

'Tis always drowsy summer when
From out the past she comes again;
The westering sunshine in a pool
Floats in her parlor still and cool;
While the slim bird its lean wires shakes,
As into piercing song it breaks;
Till Peter's pale-green eyes ajar
Dream, wake; wake, dream, in one brief bar.
And I am sitting, dull and shy,
And she with gaze of vacancy,

And large hands folded on the tray,
Musing the afternoon away;
Her satin bosom heaving slow
With sighs that softly ebb and flow;
And her plain face in such dismay,
It seems unkind to look her way:
Until all cheerful back will come
Her gentle gleaming spirit home:
And one would think that poor Miss Loo
Asked nothing else, if she had you.

1912

THE LISTENERS

"Is there anybody there?" said the Traveller,
  Knocking on the moonlit door;
And his horse in the silence champed the grasses
  Of the forest's ferny floor:
And a bird flew up out of the turret,
  Above the Traveller's head:
And he smote upon the door again a second time;
  "Is there anybody there?" he said.
But no one descended to the Traveller;
  No head from the leaf-fringed sill
Leaned over and looked into his grey eyes,
  Where he stood perplexed and still.
But only a host of phantom listeners
  That dwelt in the lone house then
Stood listening in the quiet of the moonlight
  To that voice from the world of men:
Stood thronging the faint moonbeams on the dark stair,
  That goes down to the empty hall,
Hearkening in an air stirred and shaken
  By the lonely Traveller's call.
And he felt in his heart their strangeness,
  Their stillness answering his cry,
While his horse moved, cropping the dark turf,
  'Neath the starred and leafy sky;
For he suddenly smote on the door, even
  Louder, and lifted his head:—
"Tell them I came, and no one answered,
  That I kept my word," he said.

Never the least stir made the listeners,
  Though every word he spake
Fell echoing through the shadowiness of the still house
  From the one man left awake:
Ay, they heard his foot upon the stirrup,
  And the sound of iron on stone,
And how the silence surged softly backward,
  When the plunging hoofs were gone.

1912

THE TRUANTS

Ere my heart beats too coldly and faintly
  To remember sad things, yet be gay,
I would sing a brief song of the world's little children
    Magic hath stolen away.

The primroses scattered by April,
  The stars of the wide Milky Way,
Cannot outnumber the hosts of the children
    Magic hath stolen away.

The buttercup green of the meadows,
  The snow of the blossoming may,
Lovelier are not than the legions of children
    Magic hath stolen away.

The waves tossing surf in the moonbeam,
  The albatross lone on the spray,
Alone know the tears wept in vain for the children
    Magic hath stolen away.

In vain: for at hush of the evening
  When the stars twinkle into the grey,
Seems to echo the far-away calling of children
    Magic hath stolen away.

1913

SAM'S THREE WISHES: *or* LIFE'S LITTLE WHIRLIGIG

"I'm thinking and thinking," said old Sam Shore,
" 'Twere somebody *knocking* I heard at the door."

From the clock popped the cuckoo and cuckooed out eight,
As there in his chair he wondering sate . . .
"There's no one I knows on would come so late,
A-clicking the latch of an empty house
With nobbut inside 'un but me and a mouse. . . .
Maybe a-waking in sleep I be,
And 'twere out of a dream came that tapping to me."
At length he cautiously rose, and went,
And with thumb upon latch awhile listening bent,
Then slowly drew open the door. And behold!
There stood a Fairy!—all green and gold,
Mantled up warm against dark and cold,
And smiling up into his candle shine,
Lips like wax, and cheeks like wine,
As saucy and winsome a thing to see
As are linden buds on a linden tree.

Stock-still in the doorway stood simple Sam,
A-ducking his head, with "Good-e'en to 'ee, Ma'am."

Dame Fairy she nods, and cries clear and sweet,
" 'Tis a *very* good-e'en, sir, when such folks meet.
I know thee, Sam, though thou wist not of me,
And I'm come in late gloaming to speak with thee;
Though my eyes do dazzle at glint of your rush,
All under this pretty green fuchsia bush."

Sam ducked once more, smiling simple and slow.
Like the warbling of birds her words did flow,
And she laughed, very merry, to see how true
Shone the old man's kindness his courtesy through.
And she nodded her head, and the stars on high
Sparkled down on her smallness from out of the sky.

"A friend is a friend, Sam, and wonderful pleasant,
And I'm come for old sake's sake to bring thee a present.

Three wishes, three wishes are thine, Sam Shore,
Just three wishes—and wish no more,
All for because, ruby-ripe to see,
The pixy-pears burn in yon hawthorn tree,
And your old milch cow, wheresoever she goes
Never crops over the fairy-knowes.
Ay, Sam, thou art old and thy house is lone,
But there's Potencies round thee, and here is one!"

Poor Sam, he stared: and the stars o'erhead
A shimmering light on the elm-tops shed.
Like rilling of water her voice rang sweet,
And the night-wind sighed at the sound of it.
He frowned—glanced back at the empty grate,
And shook very slowly his grey old pate:
"Three wishes, my dear! Why, I scarcely knows
Which be my crany and which my toes!
But I thank 'ee, Ma'am, kindly, and this I'd say,
That the night of your passing is Michaelmas Day;
And if it were company come on a sudden,
Why, I'd ax for a fat goose to fry in the oven!"

And lo, and forsooth! as the words he was uttering,
A rich puff of air set his candle a-guttering,
And there rose in the kitchen a sizzling and sputtering,
With a crackling of sparks and of flames a great fluttering,
And—of which here could not be two opinions—
A smoking-hot savor of sage and onions.
Beam, wall and flagstones the kitchen was lit,
Every dark corner and cranny of it
With the blaze from the hearthstone. Copper and brass
Winked back the winking of platter and glass.
And a wonderful squeaking of mice went up
At the smell of a Michaelmas supper to sup—
Unctuous odors that wreathed and swirled
Where'er frisked a whisker or mouse-tail twirled,
While out of the chimney up into the night
That ne'er-to-be-snuffed-too-much smoke took flight.

"That's one," says the Fairy, finger on thumb,
"So now, Mister Sam, there's but two to come!"
She leaned her head sidelong; she lifted her chin,
With a twinkling of eye from the radiance within.

Poor Sam stood stounded; he says, says he,
"I *wish* my old Mother was back with me,
For if there was one thing she couldn't refuse
'Twas a sweet thick slice from the breast of a goose."
But his cheek grew stiff and his eyes stared bright,
For there, on her stick, pushing out of the night,
Tap-tapping along, herself and no other,
Came who but the shape of his dear old Mother!
Straight into the kitchen she hastened and went,
Her breath coming quick as if all but spent.
"Why, Sam," says she, "the bird be turning,
For my nose tells I that the skin's a-burning!"
And down at the oven the ghost of her sat
And basted the goose with the boiling fat.

"Oho," cries the Fairy, sweet and small,
"Another wish gone will leave nothing at all."
And Sam sighs, "Bless 'ee, Ma'am, keep the other,
There's nowt that I want now I have my Mother."
But the Fairy laughs softly, and says, says she,
"There's one wish left, Sam, I promised 'ee three.
Hasten your wits, the hour creeps on,
There's calling afield and I'm soon to be gone.
Soon as haps midnight the cocks will crow
And me to the gathering and feasting must go."

Sam gazed at his Mother—withered and wan,
The rose in her cheek, her bright hair, gone,
And her poor old back bent double with years—
And he scarce could speak for the salt, salt tears.
"Well, well," he says, "I'm unspeakable glad:
But—it bain't quite the same as when I was a lad.
There's joy and there's joy, Ma'am, but to tell 'ee the truth
There's none can compare with the joy of one's youth.
And if it was possible, how could I choose
But be back in boy's breeches to eat the goose;
And all the old things—and my Mother the most,
To shine again real as my own gatepost.
What wouldn't I give, too, to see again wag
The dumpity tail of my old dog, Shag!
Your kindness, Ma'am, but all wishing was vain
Unless us can both be young again."
A shrill, faint laughter from nowhere came . . .

Empty the dark in the candle-flame. . . .
And there stood our Sam, about four foot high,
Snub nose, shock hair, and round blue eye.
Breeches and braces and coat of him too,
Shirt on his back, and each clodhopping shoe
Had shrunk to a nicety—button and hem
To fit the small Sammie tucked up into them.

There was his Mother, too; smooth, clear cheek,
Lips as sooth as a blackbird's beak,
Pretty arched eyebrows, the daintiest nose—
While the smoke of the baking deliciously rose.

"Come, Sammie," she cries, "your old Mammikin's joy,
Climb up on your stool, supper's ready, my boy.
Bring in the candle, and shut out the night;
There's goose, baked taties and cabbage to bite.
Why, bless the wee lamb, he's all shiver and shake,
And you'd think from the look of him scarcely awake!
If 'ee glour wi' those eyes, Sam, so dark and round,
The elves will away with 'ee, I'll be bound!"
So Sam and his Mother by wishes three
Were made just as happy as happy can be.
And there—with a bumpity tail to wag—
Sat laughing, with tongue out, their old dog, Shag.
To clatter of platter, bones, giblets and juice,
Between them they ate up the whole of the goose.

But time is a river for ever in flow,
The weeks went by as the weeks must go.
Soon fifty-two to a year did grow.
The long years passed, one after another,
Making older and older our Sam and his Mother;
And, alas and alack, with nine of them gone,
Poor Shag lay asleep again under a stone.
And a sorrowful dread would sometimes creep
Into Sam's dreams, as he lay asleep,
That his Mother was lost, and away he'd fare,
Calling her, calling her, everywhere,
In dark, in rain, by roads unknown,
Under echoing hills, and alone, alone.
What bliss in the morning to wake and see
The sun shining green in the linden tree,

And out of that dream's dark shadowiness
To slip in on his Mother and give her a kiss,
Then go whistling off in the dew to hear
The thrushes all mocking him, sweet and clear.

Still, moon after moon from heaven above
Shone on Mother and son, and made light of love.
Her roses faded, her pretty brown hair
Had sorrowful grey in it everywhere.
And at last she died, and was laid to rest,
Her tired hands crossed on her shrunken breast.
And Sam, now lonely, lived on and on
Till most of his workaday life seemed gone.

Yet spring came again with its green and blue,
And presently summer's wild roses too,
Pinks, Sweet William, and sops-in-wine,
Blackberry, lavender, eglantine.
And when these had blossomed and gone their way,
'Twas apples, and daisies and Michaelmas Day—
Yes, spider-webs, dew, and haws in the may,
And seraphs singing in Michaelmas Day.

Sam worked all morning and *couldn't* get rest
For a kind of a feeling of grief in his breast.
And yet, not grief, but something more
Like the thought that what happens has happened before.
He fed the chickens, he fed the sow,
On a three-legged stool sate down to the cow,
With a pail 'twixt his legs in the green in the meadow,
Under the elm trees' lengthening shadow;
And woke at last with a smile and a sigh
To find he had milked his poor Jingo dry.

As dusk set in, even the birds did seem
To be calling and calling from out of a dream.
He chopped up kindling, shut up his shed,
In a bucket of well-water soused his head
To freshen his eyes up a little and make
The drowsy old wits of him wider awake.
As neat as a womanless creature is able
He swept up his hearthstone and laid the table.
And then o'er his platter and mug, if you please,

Sate gloomily gooming at loaf and cheese—
Gooming and gooming as if the mere sight
Of his victuals could satisfy appetite!
And the longer and longer he looked at them
The slimmer slimmed upward his candle flame,
Blue in the air. And when squeaked a mouse
'Twas loud as a trump in the hush of the house.
Then, sudden, a soft little wind puffed by,
'Twixt the thick-thatched roof and the star-sown sky;
And died. And then
That deep, dead, wonderful silence again.

Then—soft as a rattle a-counting her seeds
In the midst of a tangle of withered-up weeds—
Came a faint, faint knocking, a rustle like silk,
And a breath at the keyhole as soft as milk—
Still as the flit of a moth. And then . . .
That infinitesimal knocking again.

Sam lifted his chin from his fists. He listened.
His wandering eyes in the candle glistened,
Then slowly, slowly, rolled round by degrees—
And there sat a mouse on the top of his cheese.
He stared at this Midget, and it at him,
Over the edge of his mug's round rim,
And—as if it were Christian—he says, "Did 'ee hear
A faint little tap-tap-tap-tapping, my dear?
You was at supper and me in a maze;
'Tis dark for a caller in these lone days;
There's nowt in the larder. We're both of us old.
And all of my loved ones sleep under the mould,
And yet—and yet—as I've told 'ee before . . ."

But if Sam's story you'd read to the end,
Turn back to page 1, and press onward, dear friend;
Yes, if you would stave the last note of this song,
Turn back to page primus, and warble along!
For all sober records of life (come to write 'em),
Are bound to continue—well—ad infinitum!

1913

SILVER

Slowly, silently, now the moon
Walks the night in her silver shoon;
This way, and that, she peers, and sees
Silver fruit upon silver trees;
One by one the casements catch
Her beams beneath the silvery thatch;
Couched in his kennel, like a log,
With paws of silver sleeps the dog;
From their shadowy cote the white breasts peep
Of doves in a silver-feathered sleep;
A harvest mouse goes scampering by,
With silver claws, and silver eye;
And moveless fish in the water gleam,
By silver reeds in a silver stream.

1913

THE SONG OF SHADOWS

Sweep thy faint strings, Musician,
  With thy long lean hand;
Downward the starry tapers burn,
  Sinks soft the waning sand;
The old hound whimpers couched in sleep,
  The embers smolder low;
Across the walls the shadows
    Come, and go.

Sweep softly thy strings, Musician,
  The minutes mount to hours;
Frost on the windless casement weaves
  A labyrinth of flowers;
Ghosts linger in the darkening air,
  Hearken at the open door;
Music hath called them, dreaming,
    Home once more.

1913

THE GHOST

"Who knocks?" "I, who was beautiful,
Beyond all dreams to restore,
I, from the roots of the dark thorn am hither,
And knock on the door."

"Who speaks?" "I—once was my speech
Sweet as the bird's on the air,
When echo lurks by the waters to heed;
'Tis I speak thee fair."

"Dark is the hour!" "Ay, and cold."
"Lone is my house." "Ah, but mine?"
"Sight, touch, lips, eyes yearned in vain."
"Long dead these to thine . . ."

Silence. Still faint on the porch
Brake the flames of the stars.
In gloom groped a hope-wearied hand
Over keys, bolts, and bars.

A face peered. All the grey night
In chaos of vacancy shone;
Nought but vast sorrow was there—
The sweet cheat gone.

1918

THE DREAMER

O thou who giving helm and sword,
Gavest the rusting rain,
And starry dark's all tender dews
To blunt and stain:

Out of the battle I am sped,
Unharmed yet stricken sore;
A living shape amid whispering shades
On Lethe's shore.

No trophy in my hands I bring,
  To this sad, sighing stream,
The neighings and the trumps and cries
  Were but a dream.

Traitor to life, of life betrayed:
  O, of thy mercy deep,
A dream my all, the all I ask
  Is sleep.

1918

THE SCRIBE

What lovely things
  Thy hand hath made:
The smooth-plumed bird
  In its emerald shade,
The seed of the grass,
  The speck of stone
Which the wayfaring ant
  Stirs—and hastes on!

Though I should sit
  By some tarn in thy hills,
Using its ink
  As the spirit wills
To write of Earth's wonders,
  Its live, willed things,
Flit would the ages
  On soundless wings
Ere unto Z
  My pen drew nigh;
Leviathan told,
  And the honey-fly:
And still would remain
  My wit to try—
My worn reeds broken,
  The dark tarn dry,
All words forgotten—
  Thou, Lord, and I.

1918

THE VEIL

I think and think; yet still I fail—
Why does this lady wear a veil?
Why thus elect to mask her face
Beneath that dainty web of lace?
The tip of a small nose I see,
And two red lips, set curiously
Like twin-born cherries on one stem,
And yet she has netted even them.
Her eyes, it's plain, survey with ease
Whatever to glance upon they please.
Yet, whether hazel, grey, or blue,
Or that even lovelier lilac hue,
I cannot guess: why—why deny
Such beauty to the passer-by?
Out of a bush a nightingale
May expound his song; beneath that veil
A happy mouth no doubt can make
English sound sweeter for its sake.
But then, why muffle in, like this,
What every blossomy wind would kiss?
Why in that little night disguise
A daybreak face, those starry eyes?

1921

THE QUIET ENEMY

Hearken!—now the hermit bee
Drones a quiet threnody;
Greening on the stagnant pool
The criss-cross light slants silken-cool;
In the venomed yew tree wings
Preen and flit. The linnet sings.

Gradually the brave sun
Drops to a day's journey done;
In the marshy flats abide
Mists to muffle midnight-tide.
Puffed within the belfry tower
Hungry owls drowse out their hour. . .

Walk in beauty. Vaunt thy rose.
Flaunt thy transient loveliness.
Pace for pace with thee there goes
A shape that hath not come to bless.
I thine enemy? . . . Nay, nay.
I can only watch and wait
Patient treacherous time away,
Hold ajar the wicket gate.

1921

THE CATECHISM

"Hast thou then nought wiser to bring
Than worn-out songs of moon and of rose?"
"Cracked my voice, and broken my wing,
God knows."

"Tell'st thou no truth of the life that *is*;
Seek'st thou from heaven no pitying sign?"
"Ask thine own heart these mysteries,
Not mine."

"Where then the faith thou hast brought to seed?
Where the sure hope thy soul would feign?"
"Never ebbed sweetness—even out of a weed—
In vain."

"Fool. The night comes. . . . 'Tis late. Arise.
Cold lap the waters of Jordan stream."
"Deep be their flood, and tranquil thine eyes
With a dream."

1921

THE HOLLY

The sturdiest of forest trees
With acorns is inset;
Wan white blossoms the elder brings
To fruit as black as jet;
But O, in all green English woods
Is aught so fair to view

As the sleek, sharp, dark-leaved holly tree
And its berries burning through?

Towers the ash; and dazzling green
The larch her tassels wears;
Wondrous sweet are the clots of may
The tangled hawthorn bears;
But O, in heath or meadow or wold
Springs aught beneath the blue
As brisk and trim as the holly-tree bole
With its berries burning through?

When hither, thither, falls the snow,
And blazes small the frost,
Naked amid the winter stars
The elm's vast boughs are tossed;
But O, of all that summer showed
What now to winter's true
As the prickle-beribbed dark holly tree,
With berries burning through!

1930

LUCY

Strange—as I sat brooding here,
While memory plied her quiet thread,
Your once-loved face came back, my dear,
  Amid the distant dead.

That pleasant cheek, hair smooth and brown,
Clear brows, and wistful eyes—yet gay:
You stand, in your alpaca gown,
  And ghost my heart away.

I was a child then; nine years old—
And you a woman. Well, stoop close,
To heed a passion never told
  Under how faded a rose!

Do you remember? Few my pence:
I hoarded them with a miser's care,
And bought you, in passionate innocence,
  A birthday maidenhair.

I see its fronds. Again I sit,
Hunched up in bed, in the dark, alone,
Crazed with those eyes that, memory-lit,
    Now ponder on my own.

You gave me not a thought, 'tis true—
Precocious, silly child; and yet,
Perhaps of all you have loved—loved you,
    I may the last forget.

And though no single word of this
You heed—a lifetime gone—at rest;
I would that all remembrances
    As gently pierced my breast!

1931

FORESTS

Turn, now, tired mind unto your rest,
Within your secret chamber lie,
Doors shut, and windows curtained, lest
Footfall or moonbeam, stealing by,
Wake you, or night-wind sigh.

Now, Self, we are at peace—we twain;
The house is silent, except that—hark!—
Against its walls wells out again
That rapture in the empty dark;
Where, softly beaming, spark by spark,

The glow-worms stud the leaves with light;
And unseen flowers, refreshed with dew—
Jasmine, convolvulus, glimmering white,
The air with their still life endue,
And sweeten night for me and you.

Be mute all speech; and not of love
Talk we, nor call on hope, but be—
Calm as the constant stars above—
The friends of fragile memory,
Shared only now by you and me.

Thus hidden, thus silent, while the hours
From gloom to gloom their wings beat on,
Shall not a moment's peace be ours,
Till, faint with day, the east is wan,
And terrors of the dark are gone?

Nay—in the forests of the mind
Lurk beasts as fierce as those that tread
Earth's rock-strown wilds, to night resigned,
There stars of heaven no radiance shed—
Bleak-eyed Remorse, Despair becowled in lead.

With dawn these ravening shapes will go
Though One at watch will still remain:
Till knell the sunset hour, and lo!
The listening soul once more will know
Death and his pack are hot afield again.

1933

A ROBIN

Ghost-grey the fall of night,
  Ice-bound the lane,
Lone in the dying light
  Flits he again,
Lurking where shadows steal,
Perched in his coat of blood,
Man's homestead at his heel,
  Death-still in the wood.

Where shall such creature rest?
  Where shall he hide
So wild, so strange a breast,
  What mate beside?
What bond can that bead eye—
Searching for worm or crumb—
Find with humanity
  Monstrous and mum?

Haunting the clod-bound plough,
  The rust-worn spade,
Delving beneath the bough,
  Infinite shade,

Black as the pit to see,
Winter and waste and woe—
Mate for the sexton, he
  Hops o'er the snow.

Odd restless child; it's dark;
  All wings are flown
But this one wizard's—hark!—
  Stone clapped on stone.
Changeling and solitary,
Secret and sharp and small,
Flits he from tree to tree,
  Calling on all.

1933

SOLITUDE

Ghosts there must be with me in this old house,
Deepening its midnight as the clock beats on.
Whence else upwelled—strange, sweet, yet ominous—
That moment of happiness, and then was gone?

Nimbler than air-borne music, heart may call
A speechless message to the inward ear,
As secret even as that which then befell,
Yet nought that listening could make more clear.

Delicate, subtle senses, instant, fleet!—
But oh, how near the verge at which they fail!
In vain, self hearkens for the fall of feet
Soft as its own may be, beyond the pale.

1938

THE LAST CHAPTER

I am living more alone now than I did;
This life tends inward, as the body ages;
And what is left of its strange book to read
Quickens in interest with the last few pages.

Problems abound. Its authorship? A sequel?
Its hero-villain, whose ways so little mend?
The plot? still dark. The style? a shade unequal.
And what of the denouement? And, the end?

No, no, have done! Lay the thumbed thing aside;
Forget its horrors, folly, incitements, lies;
In silence and in solitude abide,
And con what yet may bless your inward eyes.

Pace, still, for pace with you, companion goes,
Though now, through dulled and inattentive ear,
No more—as when a child's—your sick heart knows
His infinite energy and beauty near.

His, too, a World, though viewless save in glimpse;
He, too, a book of imagery bears;
And as your halting foot beside him limps,
Mark you whose badge and livery he wears.

1938

THE OLD SUMMERHOUSE

This blue-washed, old, thatched summerhouse—
Paint scaling, and fading from its walls—
How often from its hingeless door
I have watched—dead leaf, like the ghost of a mouse,
Rasping the worn brick floor—
The snows of the weir descending below,
And their thunderous waterfall.

Fall—fall: dark, garrulous rumor,
Until I could listen no more.
Could listen no more—for beauty with sorrow
Is a burden hard to be borne:
The evening light on the foam, and the swans, there;
That music, remote, forlorn.

1938

AWAY

There is no sorrow
Time heals never;
No loss, betrayal,
Beyond repair.
Balm for the soul, then,
Though grave shall sever
Lover from loved
And all they share;
See, the sweet sun shines,
The shower is over,
Flowers preen their beauty,
The day how fair!

Brood not too closely
On love, or duty;
Friends long forgotten
May wait you where
Life with death
Brings all to an issue;
None will long mourn for you,
Pray for you, miss you,
Your place left vacant,
You not there.

1938

John Masefield

John Edward Masefield was born June 1, 1878, in a house called The Knapp, at Ledbury, Herefordshire. His father, George Edward Masefield, was a solicitor, who married Caroline Louisa Parker. Both parents died when he was a child, and the Masefield children were reared by an aunt who lived at "the Priory," Ledbury. He attended a local school till he was thirteen, when he entered service on the training ship *Conway* at Liverpool to prepare for an officer's berth in the mercantile marine. But after two and a half years of training and one sea voyage, he left the service in the hope of better advancement in some other profession.

In April, 1895, he went ashore at New York with five dollars in his pocket, and rented a tiny room in Greenwich Village. For four months he worked at odd jobs—as baker's assistant, as livery stable boy, as dishwasher in a saloon; then for two years he found steady employment at a carpet factory in Yonkers, during which time he lived at 8 Maple Street. In spare hours he read, at first desultorily, but in 1896, after picking up a copy of Chaucer at a second-hand book shop, he began to read "with passion and system," and in rapid sequence went through Chaucer, Shakespeare, Milton, Shelley, and Keats. Up to this time he planned to study medicine, for though he had written verse from his ninth year, he had never thought of becoming an author; but his reading changed his plan, and in 1897 he returned to England with the idea of becoming a poet. He was able to sell some of his verse and stories, and to find work with newspapers. Later he became literary editor of the *Speaker*, and in 1904 he worked on the *Manchester Guardian*.

In 1902 he published his first volume, *Salt Water Ballads*, which brought him to the notice of literary men. Among those who encouraged him were John Synge, the Irish playwright, and W. B.

Yeats, with whom he spent a summer in Devonshire. In addition to poetry, he has written much prose, beginning with a book of sea tales, *A Mainsail Haul* (1905), and a novel, *Captain Margaret* (1908); and he has written a succession of poetic dramas. His first conspicuously successful work, however, was a long narrative poem, *The Everlasting Mercy*, which appeared in the *English Review* in 1911. After this he wrote in rapid succession several other long poems: *The Widow in the Bye Street* (1912), *Dauber* (1913), and *The Daffodil Fields* (1913), and later *Reynard the Fox* (1919), *Right Royal* (1920), *King Cole* (1921), and others less successful. Besides novels, stories, plays, and lyric and narrative poetry, he has written several books dealing with the World War, and has edited many works. Altogether, he is one of the most prolific of contemporary authors.

During World War I he served with the Red Cross in France and at Gallipoli and was appointed official historian of the Somme. He also lectured in the United States in 1916 and 1918.

Among other honors he has received the Edmond de Polignac prize for poetry (1912), the honorary degrees of D. Litt. from Oxford (1922) and LL. D. from St. Andrews (1922), and the Order of Merit (1935). Upon the death of Robert Bridges in 1930, he was appointed Poet Laureate.

In 1903 he married Constance de la Cherois-Crommelin, of Cushendun, County Antrim, Ireland. They have two children, a daughter, Judith, who is an artist, and a son. Masefield lives at Boar's Hill, near Oxford, within half a mile of the home of the late Laureate, Bridges.

A CONSECRATION

Not of the princes and prelates with periwigged charioteers
Riding triumphantly laurelled to lap the fat of the years,—
Rather the scorned—the rejected—the men hemmed in with
the spears;

The men of the tattered battalion which fights till it dies,
Dazed with the dust of the battle, the din and the cries,
The men with the broken heads and the blood running into
their eyes.

Not the be-medalled Commander, beloved of the throne,
Riding cock-horse to parade when the bugles are blown,
But the lads who carried the koppie and cannot be known.

Not the ruler for me, but the ranker, the tramp of the road,
The slave with the sack on his shoulders pricked on with the goad,
The man with too weighty a burden, too weary a load.

The sailor, the stoker of steamers, the man with the clout,
The chantyman bent at the halliards putting a tune to the shout,
The drowsy man at the wheel and the tired lookout.

Others may sing of the wine and the wealth and the mirth,
The portly presence of potentates goodly in girth;—
Mine be the dirt and the dross, the dust and scum of the earth!

THEIRS be the music, the color, the glory, the gold;
Mine be a handful of ashes, a mouthful of mold.
Of the maimed, of the halt and the blind in the rain
and the cold—
Of these shall my songs be fashioned, my tales be told.

1902

SEA-FEVER

I must go down to the seas again, to the lonely sea and the sky,
And all I ask is a tall ship and a star to steer her by,
And the wheel's kick and the wind's song and the white
sail's shaking,
And a grey mist on the sea's face and a grey dawn breaking.

I must go down to the seas again, for the call of the running tide
Is a wild call and a clear call that may not be denied;
And all I ask is a windy day with the white clouds flying,
And the flung spray and the blown spume, and the sea-gulls
crying.

I must go down to the seas again to the vagrant gypsy life,
To the gull's way and the whale's way where the wind's like a
whetted knife;
And all I ask is a merry yarn from a laughing fellow-rover,
And quiet sleep and a sweet dream when the long trick's over.

1902

THE WEST WIND

It's a warm wind, the west wind, full of birds' cries;
I never hear the west wind but tears are in my eyes.
For it comes from the west lands, the old brown hills,
And April's in the west wind, and daffodils.

It's a fine land, the west land, for hearts as tired as mine;
Apple orchards blossom there, and the air's like wine.
There is cool green grass there, where men may lie at rest,
And the thrushes are in song there, fluting from the nest.

"Will you not come home, brother? You have been long away,
It's April, and blossom time, and white is the spray;
And bright is the sun, brother, and warm is the rain,—
Will you not come home, brother, home to us again?

"The young corn is green, brother, where the rabbits run,
It's blue sky, and white clouds, and warm rain and sun.
It's song to a man's soul, brother, fire to a man's brain,
To hear the wild bees and see the merry spring again.

"Larks are singing in the west, brother, above the green wheat,
So will you not come home, brother, and rest your tired feet?
I've a balm for bruised hearts, brother, sleep for aching eyes,"
Says the warm wind, the west wind, full of birds' cries.

It's the white road westwards is the road I must tread
To the green grass, the cool grass, and rest for heart and head,
To the violets and the brown brooks and the thrushes' song,
In the fine land, the west land, the land where I belong.

1902

"ALL YE THAT PASS BY"

On the long dusty ribbon of the long city street,
The pageant of life is passing me on multitudinous feet,
With a word here of the hills, and a song there of the sea,
And—the great movement changes—the pageant passes me.

Faces—passionate faces—of men I may not know,
They haunt me, burn me to the heart, as I turn aside to go:
The king's face and the cur's face, and the face of the
stuffed swine,
They are passing, they are passing, their eyes look into mine.

I never can tire of the music of the noise of many feet,
The thrill of the blood pulsing, the tick of the heart's beat,
Of the men many as sands, of the squadrons ranked and massed
Who are passing, changing always, and never have changed
or passed.

1902

BIOGRAPHY

When I am buried, all my thoughts and acts
Will be reduced to lists of dates and facts,
And long before this wandering flesh is rotten
The dates which made me will be all forgotten;
And none will know the gleam there used to be
About the feast days freshly kept by me,
But men will call the golden hour of bliss
"About this time," or "shortly after this."

Men do not heed the rungs by which men climb
Those glittering steps, those milestones upon Time,
Those tombstones of dead selves, those hours of birth,
Those moments of the soul in years of earth;
They mark the height achieved, the main result,
The power of freedom in the perished cult,
The power of boredom in the dead man's deeds,
Not the bright moments of the sprinkled seeds.

By many waters and on many ways
I have known golden instants and bright days;
The day on which, beneath an arching sail,
I saw the Cordilleras and gave hail;
The summer day on which in heart's delight
I saw the Swansea Mumbles bursting white,
The glittering day when all the waves wore flags
And the ship *Wanderer* came with sails in rags;
That curlew-calling time in Irish dusk
When life became more splendid than its husk,

When the rent chapel on the brae at Slains
Shone with a doorway opening beyond brains;
The dawn when, with a brace-block's creaking cry,
Out of the mist a little barque slipped by,
Spilling the mist with changing gleams of red,
Then gone, with one raised hand and one turned head;
The howling evening when the spindrift's mists
Broke to display the four Evangelists,
Snow-capped, divinely granite, lashed by breakers,
Wind-beaten bones of long since buried acres;
The night alone near water when I heard
All the sea's spirit spoken by a bird;
The English dusk when I beheld once more
(With eyes so changed) the ship, the citied shore,
The lines of masts, the streets so cheerly trod
(In happier seasons) and gave thanks to God.
All had their beauty, their bright moments' gift,
Their something caught from Time, the ever-swift.

All of those gleams were golden; but life's hands
Have given more constant gifts in changing lands,
And when I count those gifts, I think them such
As no man's bounty could have bettered much:
The gift of country life, near hills and woods
Where happy waters sing in solitudes,
The gift of being near ships, of seeing each day
A city of ships with great ships under weigh,
The great street paved with water, filled with shipping,
And all the world's flags flying and seagulls dipping.

Yet when I am dust my penman may not know
Those water-trampling ships which made me glow,
But think my wonder mad and fail to find
Their glory, even dimly, from my mind,
And yet they made me:
                                        not alone the ships
But men hard-palmed from tallying-on to whips,
The two close friends of nearly twenty years,
Sea-followers both, sea-wrestlers and sea-peers,
Whose feet with mine wore many a bolt-head bright
Treading the decks beneath the riding light.
Yet death will make that warmth of friendship cold
And who'll know what one said and what one told

Our hearts' communion and the broken spells
When the loud call blew at the strike of bells?
No one, I know, yet let me be believed:
A soul entirely known is life achieved.

Years blank with hardship never speak a word
Live in the soul to make the being stirred,
Towns can be prisons where the spirit dulls
Away from mates and ocean-wandering hulls,
Away from all bright water and great hills
And sheep-walks where the curlews cry their fills,
Away in towns, where eyes have nought to see
But dead museums and miles of misery
And floating life unrooted from man's need
And miles of fish-hooks baited to catch greed
And life made wretched out of human ken
And miles of shopping women served by men.
So, if the penman sums my London days,
Let him but say that there were holy ways,
Dull Bloomsbury streets of dull brick mansions old,
With stinking doors where women stood to scold,
And drunken waits at Christmas with their horn
Droning the news, in snow, that Christ was born;
And windy gas lamps and the wet roads shining
And that old carol of the midnight whining,
And that old room (above the noisy slum)
Where there was wine and fire and talk with some
Under strange pictures of the wakened soul
To whom this earth was but a burnt-out coal.

O Time, bring back those midnights and those friends,
Those glittering moments that a spirit lends
That all may be imagined from the flash,
The cloud-hid god-game through the lightning gash,
Those hours of stricken sparks from which men took
Light to send out to men in song or book.
Those friends who heard St. Pancras' bells strike two
Yet stayed until the barber's cockerel crew,
Talking of noble styles, the Frenchman's best,
The thought beyond great poets not expressed,
The glory of mood where human frailty failed,
The forts of human light not yet assailed,
Till the dim room had mind and seemed to brood,

Binding our wills to mental brotherhood,
Till we become a college, and each night
Was discipline and manhood and delight,
Till our farewells and winding down the stairs
At each grey dawn had meaning that Time spares
That we, so linked, should roam the whole world round,
Teaching the ways our brooding minds had found,
Making that room our Chapter, our one mind
Where all that this world soiled should be refined.

Often at night I tread those streets again
And see the alley glimmering in the rain,
Yet now I miss that sight of earlier tramps,
A house with shadows of plane-boughs under lamps,
The secret house where once a beggar stood
Trembling and blind to show his woe for food.
And now I miss that friend who used to walk
Home to my lodgings with me, deep in talk,
Wearing the last of night out in still streets
Trodden by us and policemen on their beats
And cats, but else deserted; now I miss
That lively mind and guttural laugh of his
And that strange way he had of making gleam,
Like something real, the art we used to dream.
London has been my prison; but my books
Hills and great waters, laboring men and brooks,
Ships and deep friendships and remembered days
Which even now set all my mind ablaze
As that June day when, in the red bricks' chinks,
I saw the old Roman ruins white with pinks
And felt the hillside haunted even then
By not dead memory of the Roman men;
And felt the hillside thronged by souls unseen
Who knew the interest in me and were keen
That man alive should understand man dead
So many centuries since the blood was shed;
And quickened with strange hush because this comer
Sensed a strange soul alive behind the summer:
That other day on Ercall when the stones
Were sunbleached white, like long unburied bones,
While the bees droned and all the air was sweet
From honey buried underneath my feet,
Honey of purple heather and white clover

Sealed in its gummy bags till summer's over:
Then other days by water, by bright sea,
Clear as clean glass, and my bright friend with me,
The cove clean bottomed where we saw the brown
Red spotted plaice go skimming six feet down,
And saw the long fronds waving, white with shells,
Waving, unfolding, drooping, to the swells:
That sadder day when we beheld the great
And terrible beauty of a Lammas spate
Roaring white-mouthed in all the great cliff's gaps
Headlong, tree-tumbling fury of collapse,
While drenching clouds drove by, and every sense
Was water roaring or rushing or in offence,
And mountain sheep stood huddled, and blown gaps gleamed
Where torn white hair of torrents shook and streamed:
That sadder day when we beheld again
A spate going down in sunshine after rain,
When the blue reach of water leaping bright
Was one long ripple and clatter, flecked with white:
And that far day, that never blotted page,
When youth was bright like flowers about old age,
Fair generations bringing thanks for life
To that old kindly man and trembling wife
After their sixty years: Time never made
A better beauty since the Earth was laid
Than that thanksgiving given to grey hair
For the great gift of life which brought them there.

Days of endeavor have been good: the days
Racing in cutters for the comrades' praise;
The day they led my cutter at the turn,
Yet could not keep the lead and dropped astern;
The moment in the spurt when both boats' oars
Dipped in each other's wash and throats grew hoarse
And teeth ground into teeth and both strokes quickened,
Lashing the sea, and gasps came, and hearts sickened,
And coxswains damned us, dancing, banking stroke,
To put our weights on, though our hearts were broke,
And both boats seemed to stick and sea seemed glue,
The tide a mill race we were struggling through,
And every quick recover gave us squints
Of them still there, and oar tossed water-glints;
And cheering came, our friends, our foemen cheering,

A long, wild, rallying murmur on the hearing—
"Port Fore!" and "Starboard Fore!" "Port Fore." "Port Fore!"
"Up with her, Starboard," and at that each oar
Lightened, though arms were bursting, and eyes shut,
And the oak stretchers grunted in the strut,
And the curse quickened from the cox, our bows
Crashed, and drove talking water, we made vows,
Chastity vows and temperance; in our pain
We numbered things we'd never eat again
If we could only win; then came the yell,
"Starboard," "Port Fore," and then a beaten bell
Rung as for fire to cheer us. "Now." Oars bent;
Soul took the looms now body's bolt was spent,
"Damn it, come on now," "On now," "On now," "Starboard."
"Port Fore." "Up with her, Port"; each cutter harbored
Ten eye-shut painsick strugglers, "Heave, oh, heave,"
Catcalls waked echoes like a shrieking sheave.
"Heave," and I saw a back, then two. "Port Fore."
"Starboard." "Come on." I saw the midship oar
And knew we had done them. "Port Fore." "Starboard." "Now."
I saw bright water spurting at their bow,
Their cox' full face an instant. They were done.
The watcher's cheering almost drowned the gun.
We had hardly strength to toss our oars; our cry
Cheering the losing cutter was a sigh.
Other bright days of action have seemed great:
Wild days in a pampero off the Plate;
Good swimming days, at Hog Back or the Coves
Which the young gannet and the corbie loves;
Surf-swimming between rollers, catching breath
Between the advancing grave and breaking death,
Then shooting up into the sunbright smooth
To watch the advancing roller bare her tooth,
And days of labor also, loading, hauling;
Long days at winch or capstan, heaving, pawling;
The days with oxen, dragging stone from blasting,
And dusty days in mills, and hot days masting;
Trucking on dust-dry deckings smooth like ice,
And hunts in mighty wool-racks after mice;
Mornings with buckwheat when the fields did blanch
With White Leghorns come from the chicken ranch;
Days near the spring upon the sunburnt hill,
Plying the maul or gripping tight the drill;

Delights of work most real, delights that change
The headache life of towns to rapture strange
Not known by townsmen, nor imagined; health
That puts new glory upon mental wealth
And makes the poor man rich.
                                        But that ends, too,
Health with its thoughts of life; and that bright view,
That sunny landscape from life's peak, that glory,
And all a glad man's comments on life's story
And thoughts of marvellous towns and living men
And what pens tell and all beyond the pen
End, and are summed in words so truly dead
They raise no image of the heart and head,
The life, the man alive, the friend we knew,
The mind ours argued with or listened to,
None; but are dead, and all life's keenness, all,
Is dead as print before the funeral,
Even deader after, when the dates are sought,
And cold minds disagree with what we thought.
This many pictured world of many passions
Wears out the nations as a woman fashions,
And what life is is much to very few,
Men being so strange, so mad, and what men do
So good to watch or share; but when men count
Those hours of life that were a bursting fount,
Sparkling the dusty heart with living springs,
There seems a world, beyond our earthly things,
Gated by golden moments, each bright time
Opening to show the city white like lime,
High towered and many peopled. This made sure,
Work that obscures those moments seems impure,
Making our not-returning time of breath
Dull with the ritual and records of death,
That frost of fact by which our wisdom gives
Correctly stated death to all that lives.

Best trust the happy moments. What they gave
Makes man less fearful of the certain grave,
And gives his work compassion and new eyes.
The days that make us happy make us wise.

1903

SPANISH WATERS

Spanish waters, Spanish waters, you are ringing in my ears,
Like a slow sweet piece of music from the grey forgotten years;
Telling tales, and beating tunes, and bringing weary thoughts to
me
Of the sandy beach at Muertos, where I would that I could be.

There's a surf breaks on Los Muertos, and it never stops to roar,
And it's there we came to anchor, and it's there we went ashore,
Where the blue lagoon is silent amid snags of rotting trees,
Dropping like the clothes of corpses cast up by the seas.

We anchored at Los Muertos when the dipping sun was red,
We left her half-a-mile to sea, to west of Nigger Head;
And before the mist was on the Cay, before the day was done,
We were all ashore on Muertos with the gold that we had won.

We bore it through the marshes in a half-score battered chests,
Sinking, in the sucking quagmires, to the sunburn on our breasts,
Heaving over tree-trunks, gasping, damning at the flies and heat,
Longing for a long drink, out of silver, in the ship's cool lazareet.

The moon came white and ghostly as we laid the treasure down,
There was gear there'd make a beggarman as rich as Lima Town,
Copper charms and silver trinkets from the chests of Spanish
crews,
Gold doubloons and double moydores, louis d'ors and portagues.

Clumsy yellow-metal earrings from the Indians of Brazil,
Uncut emeralds out of Rio, bezoar stones from Guayaquil;
Silver, in the crude and fashioned, pots of old Arica bronze,
Jewels from the bones of Incas desecrated by the Dons.

We smoothed the place with mattocks, and we took and
blazed the tree,
Which marks yon where the gear is hid that none will ever see,
And we laid aboard the ship again, and south away we steers,
Through the loud surf of Los Muertos which is beating in my
ears.

I'm the last alive that knows it. All the rest have gone their ways,
Killed, or died, or come to anchor in the old Mulatas Cays,
And I go singing, fiddling, old and starved and in despair,
And I know where all that gold is hid, if I were only there.

It's not the way to end it all. I'm old, and nearly blind,
And an old man's past's a strange thing, for it never leaves his
mind.
And I see in dreams, awhiles, the beach, the sun's disc dipping
red,
And the tall ship, under topsails, swaying in past Nigger Head.

I'd be glad to step ashore there. Glad to take a pick and go
To the lone blazed coco-palm tree in the place no others know,
And lift the gold and silver that has moldered there for years
By the loud surf of Los Muertos which is beating in my ears.

1903

CARGOES

Quinquireme of Nineveh from distant Ophir,
Rowing home to haven in sunny Palestine,
With a cargo of ivory,
And apes and peacocks,
Sandalwood, cedarwood, and sweet white wine.

Stately Spanish galleon coming from the Isthmus,
Dipping through the Tropics by the palm-green shores,
With a cargo of diamonds,
Emeralds, amethysts,
Topazes, and cinnamon, and gold moidores.

Dirty British coaster with a salt-caked smoke stack,
Butting through the Channel in the mad March days,
With a cargo of Tyne coal,
Road-rails, pig-lead,
Firewood, iron-ware, and cheap tin trays.

1903

LONDON TOWN

Oh, London Town's a fine town, and London sights are rare,
And London ale is right ale, and brisk's the London air,
And busily goes the world there, but crafty grows the mind,
And London Town of all towns I'm glad to leave behind.

Then hey for croft and hop-yard, and hill, and field, and pond,
With Bredon Hill before me and Malvern Hill beyond.
The hawthorn white i' the hedgerow, and all the spring's attire
In the comely land of Teme and Lugg, and Clent, and Clee,
and Wyre.

Oh, London girls are brave girls, in silk and cloth o' gold,
And London shops are rare shops where gallant things are sold,
And bonnily clinks the gold there, but drowsily blinks the eye,
And London Town of all towns I'm glad to hurry by.

Then hey for covert and woodland, and ash and elm and oak,
Tewkesbury inns, and Malvern roofs, and Worcester chimney
smoke,
The apple trees in the orchard, the cattle in the byre,
And all the land from Ludlow town to Bredon church's spire.

Oh, London tunes are new tunes, and London books are wise,
And London plays are rare plays, and fine to country eyes,
But wretchedly fare the most there and merrily fare the few,
And London Town of all towns I'm glad to hurry through.

So hey for the road, the west road, by mill and forge and fold,
Scent of the fern and song of the lark by brook, and field, and
wold,
To the comely folk at the hearth-stone and the talk beside the
fire,
In the hearty land, where I was bred, my land of heart's desire.

1903

C. L. M.

In the dark womb where I began
My mother's life made me a man.
Through all the months of human birth
Her beauty fed my common earth.
I cannot see, nor breathe, nor stir,
But through the death of some of her.

Down in the darkness of the grave
She cannot see the life she gave.
For all her love, she cannot tell
Whether I use it ill or well,
Nor knock at dusty doors to find
Her beauty dusty in the mind.

If the grave's gates could be undone,
She would not know her little son,
I am so grown. If we should meet
She would pass by me in the street,
Unless my soul's face let her see
My sense of what she did for me.

What have I done to keep in mind
My debt to her and womankind?
What woman's happier life repays
Her for those months of wretched days?
For all my mouthless body leeched
Ere Birth's releasing hell was reached?

What have I done, or tried, or said
In thanks to that dear woman dead?
Men triumph over women still,
Men trample women's rights at will,
And man's lust roves the world untamed.

* * * * *

O grave, keep shut lest I be shamed.

1910

From DAUBER

(SECTION VI) [1]

All through the windless night the clipper rolled
In a great swell with oily gradual heaves
Which rolled her down until her time-bells tolled,
Clang, and the weltering water moaned like beeves.
The thundering rattle of slatting shook the sheaves,
Startles of water made the swing ports gush,
The sea was moaning and sighing and saying "Hush!"

It was all black and starless. Peering down
Into the water, trying to pierce the gloom,
One saw a dim, smooth, oily glitter of brown
Heaving and dying away and leaving room
For yet another. Like the march of doom
Came those great powers of marching silences;
Then fog came down, dead-cold, and hid the seas.

They set the Dauber to the foghorn. There
He stood upon the poop, making to sound
Out of the pump the sailor's nasal blare,
Listening lest ice should make the note resound.
She bayed there like a solitary hound
Lost in a covert; all the watch she bayed.
The fog, come closelier down, no answer made.

Denser it grew, until the ship was lost.
The elemental hid her; she was merged
In mufflings of dark death, like a man's ghost,
New to the change of death, yet thither urged.
Then from the hidden waters something surged—
Mournful, despairing, great, greater than speech,
A noise like one slow wave on a still beach.

Mournful, and then again mournful, and still
Out of the night that mighty voice arose;
The Dauber at his foghorn felt the thrill.
Who rode that desolate sea? What forms were those?

[1] *Dauber* is a tale of a poor boy who wanted to be an artist, and turned sailor to learn to paint the sea. The episode related in this section, though an integral part of the whole narrative, is complete in itself.

Mournful, from things defeated, in the throes
Of memory of some conquered hunting-ground,
Out of the night of death arose the sound.

"Whales!" said the Mate. They stayed there all night long
Answering the horn. Out of the night they spoke,
Defeated creatures who had suffered wrong,
But were still noble underneath the stroke.
They filled the darkness when the Dauber woke;
The men came peering to the rail to hear,
And the sea sighed, and the fog rose up sheer.

A wall of nothing at the world's last edge,
Where no life came except defeated life.
The Dauber felt shut in within a hedge,
Behind which form was hidden and thought was rife,
And that a blinding flash, a thrust, a knife
Would sweep the hedge away and make all plain,
Brilliant beyond all words, blinding the brain.

So the night passed, but then no morning broke—
Only a something showed that night was dead.
A sea-bird, cackling like a devil, spoke,
And the fog drew away and hung like lead.
Like mighty cliffs it shaped, sullen and red;
Like glowering gods at watch it did appear,
And sometimes drew away, and then drew near.

Like islands, and like chasms, and like hell,
But always mighty and red, gloomy and ruddy,
Shutting the visible sea in like a well;
Slow heaving in vast ripples, blank and muddy,
Where the sun should have risen it streaked bloody.
The day was still-born; all the sea-fowl scattering
Splashed the still water, mewing, hovering, clattering.

Then Polar snow came down little and light,
Till all the sky was hidden by the small,
Most multitudinous drift of dirty white
Tumbling and wavering down and covering all—
Covering the sky, the sea, the clipper tall,
Furring the ropes with white, casing the mast,
Coming on no known air, but blowing past.

And all the air seemed full of gradual moan,
As though in those cloud-chasms the horns were blowing
The mort for gods cast out and overthrown,
Or for the eyeless sun plucked out and going.
Slow the low gradual moan came in the snowing;
The Dauber felt the prelude had begun.
The snowstorm fluttered by; he saw the sun

Show and pass by, gleam from one towering prison
Into another, vaster and more grim,
Which in dull crags of darkness had arisen
To muffle-to a final door on him.
The gods upon the dull crags lowered dim,
The pigeons chattered, quarrelling in the track.
In the south-west the dimness dulled to black.

Then came the cry of "Call all hands on deck!"
The Dauber knew its meaning; it was come:
Cape Horn, that tramples beauty into wreck,
And crumples steel and smites the strong man dumb.
Down clattered flying kites and staysails: some
Sang out in quick, high calls: the fair-leads skirled,
And from the south-west came the end of the world.

"Caught in her ball-dress," said the Bosun, hauling;
"Lee-ay, lee-ay!" quick, high, come the men's call;
It was all wallop of sails and startled calling.
"Let fly!" "Let go!" "Clew up!" and "Let go all!"
"Now up and make them fast!" "Here, give us a haul!"
"Now up and stow them! Quick! By God! we're done!"
The blackness crunched all memory of the sun.

"Up!" said the Mate. "Mizen top-gallants. Hurry!"
The Dauber ran, the others ran, the sails
Slatted and shook; out of the black a flurry
Whirled in fine lines, tattering the edge to trails.
Painting and art and England were old tales
Told in some other life to that pale man,
Who struggled with white fear and gulped and ran.

He struck a ringbolt in his haste and fell—
Rose, sick with pain, half-lamed in his left knee;
He reached the shrouds where clambering men pell-mell

Hustled each other up and cursed him; he
Hurried aloft with them: then from the sea
Came a cold, sudden breath that made the hair
Stiff on the neck, as though Death whispered there.

A man below him punched him in the side.
"Get up, you Dauber, or let me get past."
He saw the belly of the skysail skied,
Gulped, and clutched tight, and tried to go more fast.
Sometimes he missed his ratline and was grassed,
Scraped his shin raw against the rigid line;
The clamberers reached the futtock-shrouds' incline.

Cursing they came; one, kicking out behind,
Kicked Dauber in the mouth, and one below
Punched at his calves; the futtock-shrouds inclined;
It was a perilous path for one to go.
"Up, Dauber, up!" A curse followed a blow.
He reached the top and gasped, then on, then on.
And one voice yelled "Let go!" and one "All gone!"

Fierce clamberers, some in oilskins, some in rags,
Hustling and hurrying up, up the steep stairs.
Before the windless sails were blown to flags,
And whirled like dirty birds athwart great airs,
Ten men in all, to get this mast of theirs
Snugged to the gale in time. "Up! Damn you, run!"
The mizzen topmast head was safely won.

"Lay out!" the Bosun yelled. The Dauber laid
Out on the yard, gripping the yard and feeling
Sick at the mighty space of air displayed
Below his feet, where mewing birds were wheeling.
A giddy fear was on him; he was reeling.
He bit his lip half through, clutching the jack.
A cold sweat glued the shirt upon his back.

The yard was shaking, for a brace was loose.
He felt that he would fall; he clutched, he bent,
Clammy with natural terror to the shoes
While idiotic promptings came and went.
Snow fluttered on a wind-flaw and was spent;
He saw the water darken. Someone yelled,
"Frap it; don't stay to furl! Hold on!" He held.

Darkness came down—half darkness—in a whirl;
The sky went out, the waters disappeared.
He felt a shocking pressure of blowing hurl
The ship upon her side. The darkness speared
At her with wind; she staggered, she careered,
Then down she lay. The Dauber felt her go;
He saw his yard tilt downwards. Then the snow

Whirled all about—dense, multitudinous, cold—
Mixed with the wind's one devilish thrust and shriek,
Which whiffled out men's tears, deafened, took hold,
Flattening the flying drift against the cheek
The yards buckled and bent, man could not speak.
The ship lay on her broadside; the wind's sound
Had devilish malice at having got her downed.

* * * * *

How long the gale had blown he could not tell,
Only the world had changed, his life had died.
A moment now was everlasting hell.
Nature, an onslaught from the weather side,
A withering rush of death, a frost that cried,
Shrieked, till he withered at the heart; a hail
Plastered his oilskins with an icy mail.

"Cut!" yelled his mate. He looked—the sail was gone,
Blown into rags in the first furious squall;
The tatters drummed the devil's tattoo. On
The buckling yard a block thumped like a mall.
The ship lay—the sea smote her, the wind's bawl
Came, "loo, loo, loo!" The devil cried his hounds
On to the poor spent stag strayed in his bounds.

"Cut! Ease her!" yelled his mate; the Dauber heard.
His mate wormed up the tilted yard and slashed,
A rag of canvas skimmed like a darting bird.
The snow whirled, the ship bowed to it, the gear lashed,
The sea-tops were cut off and flung down smashed;
Tatters of shouts were flung, the rags of yells—
And clang, clang, clang, below beat the two bells.

"O God!" the Dauber moaned. A roaring rang,
Blasting the royals like a cannonade;

The backstays parted with a crackling clang,
The upper spars were snapped like twigs decayed—
Snapped at their heels, their jagged splinters splayed,
Like white and ghastly hairs erect with fear.
The Mate yelled, "Gone, by God, and pitched them clear!"

"Up!" yelled the Bosun; "up and clear the wreck!"
The Dauber followed where he led: below
He caught one giddy glimpsing of the deck
Filled with white water, as though heaped with snow.
He saw the streamers of the rigging blow
Straight out like pennons from the splintered mast,
Then, all sense dimmed, all was an icy blast,

Roaring from nether hell and filled with ice,
Roaring and crashing on the jerking stage,
An utter bridle given to utter vice,
Limitless power mad with endless rage
Withering the soul; a minute seemed an age.
He clutched and hacked at ropes, at rags of sail,
Thinking that comfort was a fairy-tale

Told long ago—long, long ago—long since
Heard of in other lives—imagined, dreamed—
There where the basest beggar was a prince
To him in torment where the tempest screamed.
Comfort and warmth and ease no longer seemed
Things that a man could know: soul, body, brain,
Knew nothing but the wind, the cold, the pain.

"Leave that!" the Bosun shouted; "Crojick save!"
The splitting crojick, not yet gone to rags,
Thundered below, beating till something gave,
Bellying between its buntlines into bags.
Some birds were blown past, shrieking: dark, like shags,
Their backs seemed, looking down. "Leu, leu!" they cried.
The ship lay, the seas thumped her; she had died.

They reached the crojick yard, which buckled, buckled
Like a thin whalebone to the topsail's strain.
They laid upon the yard and heaved and knuckled,
Pounding the sail, which jangled and leapt again.
It was quite hard with ice, its rope like chain,

Its strength like seven devils; it shook the mast.
They cursed and toiled and froze: a long time passed.

Two hours passed, then a dim lightening came.
Those frozen ones upon the yard could see
The mainsail and the foresail still the same,
Still battling with the hands and blowing free,
Rags tattered where the staysails used to be.
The lower topsails stood; the ship's lee deck
Seethed with four feet of water filled with wreck.

An hour more went by; the Dauber lost
All sense of hands and feet, all sense of all
But of a wind that cut him to the ghost,
And of a frozen fold he had to haul,
Of heavens that fell and never ceased to fall,
And ran in smoky snatches along the sea,
Leaping from crest to wave-crest, yelling. He

Lost sense of time; no bells went, but he felt
Ages go over him. At last, at last
They frapped the cringled crojick's icy pelt;
In frozen bulge and bunt they made it fast.
Then, scarcely live, they laid in to the mast.
The Captain's speaking trumpet gave a blare,
"Make fast the topsail, Mister, while you're there."

Some seamen cursed, but up they had to go—
Up to the topsail yard to spend an hour
Stowing a topsail in a blinding snow,
Which made the strongest man among them cower.
More men came up, the fresh hands gave them power,
They stowed the sail; then with a rattle of chain
One half the crojick burst its bonds again.

* * * * *

They stowed the sail, frapping it round with rope,
Leaving no surface for the wind, no fold,
Then down the weather shrouds, half dead, they grope;
That struggle with the sail had made them old.
They wondered if the crojick furl would hold.
"Lucky," said one, "it didn't spring the spar."
"Lucky!" the Bosun said, "Lucky! We are!"

She came within two shakes of turning top
Or stripping all her shroud-screws, that first quiff.
"Now fish those wash-deck buckets out of the slop.
Here's Dauber says he doesn't like Cape Stiff.
This isn't wind, man, this is only a whiff.
Hold on, all hands, hold on!" a sea, half seen,
Paused, mounted, burst, and filled the main-deck green.

The Dauber felt a mountain of water fall.
It covered him deep, deep, he felt it fill,
Over his head, the deck, the fife-rails, all,
Quieting the ship; she trembled and lay still.
Then with a rush and shatter and clanging shrill
Over she went; he saw the water cream
Over the bitts; he saw the half-deck stream.

Then in the rush he swirled, over she went;
Her lee-rail dipped, he struck, and something gave;
His legs went through a port as the roll spent;
She paused, then rolled, and back the water drave.
He drifted with it as a part of the wave,
Drowning, half-stunned, exhausted, partly frozen,
He struck the booby hatchway; then the Bosun

Leaped, seeing his chance, before the next sea burst,
And caught him as he drifted, seized him, held,
Up-ended him against the bitts, and cursed.
"This ain't the George's Swimming Baths," he yelled;
"Keep on your feet!" Another grey-back felled
The two together, and the Bose, half-blind,
Spat: "One's a joke," he cursed, "but two's unkind."

"Now, damn it, Dauber!" said the Mate. "Look out,
Or you'll be over the side!" The water freed;
Each clanging freeing-port became a spout.
The men cleared up the decks as there was need.
The Dauber's head was cut, he felt it bleed
Into his oilskins as he clutched and coiled.
Water and sky were devil's brews which boiled,

Boiled, shrieked, and glowered; but the ship was saved.
Snugged safely down, though fourteen sails were split.
Out of the dark a fiercer fury raved.

The grey-backs died and mounted, each crest lit
With a white toppling gleam that hissed from it
And slid, or leaped, or ran with whirls of cloud,
Mad with inhuman life that shrieked aloud.

The watch was called; Dauber might go below.
"Splice the main brace!" the Mate called. All laid aft
To get a gulp of momentary glow
As some reward for having saved the craft.
The steward ladled mugs, from which each quaff'd
Whisky, with water, sugar, and lime-juice, hot,
A quarter of a pint each made the tot.

Beside the lamp-room door the steward stood
Ladling it out, and each man came in turn,
Tipped his sou'-wester, drank it, grunted "Good!"
And shambled forward, letting it slowly burn:
When all were gone the Dauber lagged astern,
Torn by his frozen body's lust for heat,
The liquor's pleasant smell, so warm, so sweet,

And by a promise long since made at home
Never to taste strong liquor. Now he knew
The worth of liquor; now he wanted some.
His frozen body urged him to the brew;
Yet it seemed wrong, an evil thing to do
To break that promise. "Dauber," said the Mate,
"Drink, and turn in, man; why the hell d'ye wait?"

"Please, sir, I'm temperance." "Temperance are you, hey?
That's all the more for me! So you're for slops?
I thought you'd had enough slops for to-day.
Go to your bunk and ease her when she drops.
And—damme, steward! you brew with too much hops!
Stir up the sugar, man!—and tell your girl
How kind the Mate was teaching you to furl."

Then the Mate drank the remnants, six men's share,
And ramped into his cabin, where he stripped
And danced unclad, and was uproarious there.
In waltzes with the cabin cat he tripped,
Singing in tenor clear that he was pipped—
That "he who strove the tempest to disarm,
Must never first embrail the lee yard-arm,"

And that his name was Ginger. Dauber crept
Back to the round-house, gripping by the rail.
The wind howled by; the passionate water leapt;
The night was all one roaring with the gale.
Then at the door he stopped, uttering a wail;
His hands were perished numb and blue as veins,
He could not turn the knob for both the Spains.

A hand came shuffling aft, dodging the seas,
Singing "her nut-brown hair" between his teeth;
Taking the ocean's tumult at his ease
Even when the wash about his thighs did seethe.
His soul was happy in its happy sheath;
"What, Dauber, won't it open? Fingers cold?
You'll talk of this time, Dauber, when you're old."

He flung the door half open, and a sea
Washed them both in, over the splashboard, down;
"You silly, salt miscarriage!" sputtered he.
"Dauber, pull out the plug before we drown!
That's spoiled my laces and my velvet gown.
Where is the plug?" Groping in pitch dark water,
He sang between his teeth "The Farmer's Daughter."

It was pitch dark within there; at each roll
The chests slid to the slant; the water rushed,
Making full many a clanging tin pan bowl
Into the black below-bunks as it gushed.
The dog-tired men slept through it; they were hushed.
The water drained, and then with matches damp
The man struck heads off till he lit the lamp.

"Thank you," the Dauber said; the seaman grinned.
"This is your first foul weather?" "Yes." "I thought
Up on the yard you hadn't seen much wind.
Them's rotten sea-boots, Dauber, that you brought.
Now I must cut on deck before I'm caught."
He went; the lamp-flame smoked; he slammed the door;
A film of water loitered across the floor.

The Dauber watched it come and watched it go;
He had had revelation of the lies
Cloaking the truth men never choose to know;

He could bear witness now and cleanse their eyes.
He had beheld in suffering; he was wise;
This was the sea, this searcher of the soul—
This never-dying shriek fresh from the Pole.

He shook with cold; his hands could not undo
His oilskin buttons, so he shook and sat,
Watching his dirty fingers, dirty blue,
Hearing without the hammering tackle slat;
Within, the drops from dripping clothes went pat,
Running in little patters, gentle, sweet,
And "Ai, ai!" went the wind, and the seas beat.

His bunk was sopping wet; he clambered in,
None of his clothes were dry: his fear recurred.
Cramps bunched the muscles underneath his skin.
The great ship rolled until the lamp was blurred.
He took his Bible and tried to read a word;
Trembled at going aloft again, and then
Resolved to fight it out and show it to men.

Faces recurred, fierce memories of the yard,
The frozen sail, the savage eyes, the jests,
The oaths of one great seaman, syphilis-scarred,
The tug of leeches jammed beneath their chests,
The buntlines bellying bunts out into breasts,
The deck so desolate-grey, the sky so wild.
He fell asleep, and slept like a young child.

But not for long; the cold awoke him soon,
The hot-ache and the skin-cracks and the cramp,
The seas thundering without, the gale's wild tune,
The sopping misery of the blankets damp.
A speaking-trumpet roared; a sea-boot's stamp
Clogged at the door. A man entered to shout:
"All hands on deck! Arouse here! Tumble out!"

The caller raised the lamp; his oilskins clicked
As the thin ice upon them cracked and fell.
"Rouse out!" he said. "This lamp is frozen wick'd.
Rouse out!" His accent deepened to a yell.
"We're among ice; it's blowing up like hell.
We're going to hand both topsails. Time, I guess,
We're sheeted up. Rouse out! Don't stay to dress!"

"Is it cold on deck?" said Dauber. "Is it cold?
We're sheeted up, I tell you, inches thick!
The fo'c'sle's like a wedding-cake, I'm told.
Now tumble out, my sons; on deck here, quick!
Rouse out, away, and come and climb the stick.
I'm going to call the half-deck. Bosun! Hey!
Both topsails coming in. Heave out! Away!"

He went; the Dauber tumbled from his bunk,
Clutching the side. He heard the wind go past,
Making the great ship wallow as if drunk.
There was a shocking tumult up the mast.
"This is the end," he muttered, "come at last!
I've got to go aloft, facing this cold.
I can't. I can't. I'll never keep my hold.

"I cannot face the topsail yard again.
I never guessed what misery it would be."
The cramps and hot-ache made him sick with pain.
The ship stopped suddenly from a devilish sea,
Then, with a triumph of wash, a rush of glee,
The door burst in, and in the water rolled,
Filling the lower bunks, black, creaming, cold.

The lamp sucked out. "Wash!" went the water back,
Then in again, flooding; the Bosun swore.
"You useless thing! You Dauber! You lee slack!
Get out, you heekapoota! Shut the door!
You coo-ilyaira, what are you waiting for?
Out of my way, you thing—you useless thing!"
He slammed the door indignant, clanging the ring.

And then he lit the lamp, drowned to the waist:
"Here's a fine house! Get at the scupper-holes"—
He bent against it as the water raced—
"And pull them out to leeward when she rolls.
They say some kinds of landsmen don't have souls.
I well believe. A Port Mahon baboon
Would make more soul then you got with a spoon."

Down in the icy water Dauber groped
To find the plug; the racing water sluiced
Over his head and shoulders as she sloped.

Without, judged by the sound, all hell was loosed.
He felt cold Death about him tightly noosed.
That Death was better than the misery there
Iced on the quaking foothold high in air.

And then the thought came: "I'm a failure. All
My life has been a failure. They were right.
It will not matter if I go and fall;
I should be free then from this hell's delight.
I'll never paint. Best let it end to-night.
I'll slip over the side. I've tried and failed."
So in the ice-cold in the night he quailed.

Death would be better, death, than this long hell
Of mockery and surrender and dismay—
This long defeat of doing nothing well,
Playing the part too high for him to play.
"O Death! who hides the sorry thing away,
Take me; I've failed. I cannot play these cards."
There came a thundering from the topsail yards.

And then he bit his lips, clenching his mind,
And staggered out to muster, beating back
The coward frozen self of him that whined.
Come what cards might he meant to play the pack.
"Ai!" screamed the wind; the topsail sheet went clack;
Ice filled the air with spikes; the grey-backs burst.
"Here's Dauber," said the Mate, "on deck the first.

"Why, holy sailor, Dauber, you're a man!
I took you for a soldier. Up now, come!"
Up on the yards already they began
That battle with the gale which strikes men dumb.
The leaping topsail thundered like a drum.
The frozen snow beat in the face like shots.
The wind spun whipping wave-crests into clots.

So up upon the topsail yard again,
In the great tempest's fiercest hour, began
Probation to the Dauber's soul, of pain
Which crowds a century's torment in a span.
For the next month the ocean taught this man,
And he, in that month's torment, while she wested,
Was never warm nor dry, nor full nor rested;

But still it blew, or, if it lulled, it rose
Within the hour and blew again; and still
The water as it burst aboard her froze.
The wind blew off an ice-field, raw and chill,
Daunting man's body, tampering with his will;
But after thirty days a ghostly sun
Gave sickly promise that the storms were done.

1912

REVELATION

If I could come again to that dear place
Where once I came, where Beauty lived and moved,
Where, by the sea, I saw her face to face,
That soul alive by which the world has loved;
If, as I stood at gaze among the leaves,
She would appear again, as once before,
While the red herdsman gathered up his sheaves
And brimming waters trembled up the shore;
If, as I gazed, her Beauty that was dumb,
In that old time, before I learned to speak,
Would lean to me and revelation come,
Words to the lips and color to the cheek,
    Joy with its searing-iron would burn me wise,
    I should know all; all powers, all mysteries.

1915

THE END

There, on the darkened deathbed, dies the brain
That flared three several times in seventy years;
It cannot lift the silly hand again,
Nor speak, nor sing; it neither sees nor hears.
And muffled mourners put it in the ground
And then go home, and in the earth it lies,
Too dark for vision and too deep for sound,
The million cells that made a good man wise.
Yet for a few short years an influence stirs

A sense or wraith or essence of him dead,
Which makes insensate things its ministers
To those beloved, his spirit's daily bread;
    Then that, too, fades; in book or deed a spark
    Lingers, then that, too, fades; then all is dark.

1915

[I NEVER SEE THE RED ROSE]

I never see the red rose crown the year,
Nor feel the young grass underneath my tread,
Without the thought, "This living beauty here
Is earth's remembrance of a beauty dead.
Surely where all this glory is displayed
Love has been quick, like fire, to high ends,
Here, in this grass, an altar has been made
For some white joy, some sacrifice of friends;
Here, where I stand, some leap of human brains
Has touched immortal things and left its trace,
The earth is happy here, the gleam remains;
Beauty is here, the spirit of the place,
    I touch the faith which nothing can destroy,
    The earth, the living church of ancient joy."

1916

[THERE IS NO GOD, AS I WAS TAUGHT]

There is no God, as I was taught in youth,
Though each, according to his stature, builds
Some covered shrine for what he thinks the truth,
Which day by day his reddest heart-blood gilds.
There is no God; but death, the clasping sea,
In which we move like fish, deep over deep
Made of men's souls that bodies have set free,
Floods to a Justice though it seems asleep.
There is no God, but still, behind the veil,
The hurt thing works, out of its agony.
Still, like a touching of a brimming Grail,
Return the pennies given to passers-by.
    There is no God, but we, who breathe the air,
    Are God ourselves and touch God everywhere.

1916

[THE COUNTRYMEN]

[From *Reynard the Fox*]

Ock Gurney and old Pete were there,
Riding their bonny cobs and swearing.
Ock's wife had giv'n them both a fairing,
A horse-rosette, red, white, and blue.
Their cheeks were brown as any brew,
And every comer to the meet
Said "Hello, Ock" or "Morning, Pete;
Be you a going to a wedding?"
"Why, noa," they said, "we'm going a bedding;
Now ben't us, uncle, ben't us, Ock?"
Pete Gurney was a lusty cock
Turned sixty-three, but bright and hale,
A dairy-farmer in the vale,
Much like a robin in the face,
Much character in little space,
With little eyes like burning coal.
His mouth was like a slit or hole
In leather that was seamed and lined.
He had the russet-apple mind
That betters as the weather worsen.
He was a manly English person,
Kind to the core, brave, merry, true;
One grief he had, a grief still new,
That former Parson joined with Squire
In putting down the Playing Quire,
In church, and putting organ in.
"Ah, boys, that was a pious din
That Quire was; a pious praise
The noise was that we used to raise;
I and my serpent, George with his'n,
On Easter Day in He is Risen,
Or blessed Christmas in Venite;
And how the trombone came in mighty,
In Alleluias from the heart—
Pious, for each man played his part,
Not like 'tis now." Thus he, still sore
For changes forty years before,
When all (that could) in time and tune,
Blew trumpets to the newë moon.

He was a bachelor, from choice.
He and his nephew farmed the Boyce,
Prime pasture land for thirty cows.
Ock's wife, Selina Jane, kept house,
And jolly were the three together.

Ock had a face like summer weather,
A broad red sun, split by a smile.
He mopped his forehead all the while,
And said "By damn," and "Ben't us, Unk?"
His eyes were close and deeply sunk.
He cursed his hunter like a lover,
"Now blast your soul, my dear, give over.
Woa, now, my pretty, damn your eyes."
Like Pete he was of middle size,
Dean-oak-like, stuggy, strong in shoulder,
He stood a wrestle like a boulder,
He had a back for pitching hay.
His singing voice was like a bay.
In talk he had a sideways spit,
Each minute, to refresh his wit.
He cracked Brazil nuts with his teeth.
He challenged Cobbett of the Heath
(Weight-lifting champion) once, but lost.
Hunting was what he loved the most,
Next to his wife and Uncle Pete.
With beer to drink and cheese to eat,
And rain in May to fill the grasses,
This life was not a dream that passes
To Ock, but like the summer flower.

1919

ON GROWING OLD

Be with me, Beauty, for the fire is dying;
My dog and I are old, too old for roving;
Man, whose young passion sets the spindrift flying,
Is soon too lame to march, too cold for loving.
I take the book and gather to the fire,
Turning old yellow leaves; minute by minute,
The clock ticks to my heart; a withered wire
Moves a thin ghost of music in the spinet.

I cannot sail your seas, I cannot wander
Your cornland, nor your hill-land nor your valleys,
Ever again, nor share the battle yonder
Where the young knight the broken squadron rallies.
    Only stay quiet while my mind remembers
    The beauty of fire from the beauty of embers.

Beauty, have pity, for the strong have power,
The rich their wealth, the beautiful their grace,
Summer of man its sunlight and its flower,
Spring time of man all April in a face.
Only, as in the jostling in the Strand,
Where the mob thrusts or loiters or is loud
The beggar with the saucer in his hand
Asks only a penny from the passing crowd,
So, from this glittering world with all its fashion,
Its fire and play of men, its stir, its march,
Let me have wisdom, Beauty, wisdom and passion,
Bread to the soul, rain where the summers parch.
    Give me but these, and though the darkness close
    Even the night will blossom as the rose.

1919

THE LEMMINGS

Once in a hundred years the Lemmings come
Westward, in search of food, over the snow,
Westward, until the salt sea drowns them dumb,
Westward, till all are drowned, those Lemmings go.
Once, it is thought, there was a westward land,
(Now drowned) where there was food for those starved things,
And memory of the place has burnt its brand
In the little brains of all the Lemming Kings.
Perhaps, long since, there was a land beyond
Westward from death, some city, some calm place,
Where one could taste God's quiet and be fond
With the little beauty of a human face;
    But now the land is drowned, yet still we press
    Westward, in search, to death, to nothingness.

1920

Wilfrid Gibson

Wilfrid Wilson Gibson was born October 2, 1878, at Battle Hill Terrace, Hexham, Northumberland. He was one of several children of John Pattison Gibson and his wife, Elizabeth Judith Frances Walton. His father was a pharmacist, whose hobby was archaeology.

His early training was at dame schools, but when the school he was attending at the age of fourteen failed, his formal training ended. He was studious, however, and thereafter taught himself. He began early to write verse, being encouraged in this by a sister who married an Oxford professor. A small inheritance which came to him when his father died enabled him to give all his time to writing; and life in a garret at Glasgow and near the common folk of whom he wrote furnished him with material for his poems. After the appearance of his poem "Blind" in the *Spectator,* September 4, 1897, he contributed frequently to various periodicals. He published his first volume, *Urlyn the Harper and Other Song,* in 1902, and since then he has published more than thirty volumes of lyric and dramatic poetry.

In 1912 he went to live in London, and there met Geraldine Townshend, whom he married the following year. Thereafter he lived for some time in Hertfordshire, where he had as neighbors Robert Frost and Lascelles Abercrombie. He visited the United States in January, 1917, and for the next six months he lectured in various cities and at several colleges. After being kept out of the army for some years because of an operation, he was finally accepted in October, 1917, and served until the end of the war as a private in the Army Service Corps.

He had a son and two daughters. For many years his home has been in a suburb of London.

[ALL LIFE MOVING TO ONE MEASURE]

All life moving to one measure—
Daily bread, daily bread—
Bread of life, and bread of labor,
Bread of bitterness and sorrow,
Hand-to-mouth and no to-morrow,
Dearth for housemate, death for neighbor . . .

"Yet, when all the babes are fed,
Love, are there not crumbs to treasure?"

1910

THE FLUTE

"Good-night!" he sang out cheerily:
"Good-night!" and yet again: "Good-night!"

And I was gay that night to be
Once more in my clean countryside,
Among the windy hills and wide.
Six days of city slush and mud,
Of hooting horn, and spattering wheel,
Made me rejoice again to feel
The tingling frost that fires the blood,
And sets life burning keen and bright;
And down the ringing road to stride
The eager swinging stride that braces
The straining thews from hip to heel:
To breathe again the wind that sweeps
Across the grassy, Northern steeps,
From crystal deeps and starry spaces.

And I was glad again to hear
The old man's greeting of good cheer:
For every night for many a year
At that same corner we had met,
Summer and Winter, dry and wet:
And though I never once had heard
The old man speak another word,
His cheery greeting at the bend
Seemed like the welcome of a friend.

But, as we neared to-night, somehow,
I felt that he would stop and speak—
Though he went by: and when I turned,
I saw him standing in the road,
And looking back, with hand to brow,
As if to shade old eyes, grown weak
Awaiting the long sleep they'd earned:
Though, as again towards him I strode,
A friendly light within them burned.
And then, as I drew nigh, he spoke
With shaking head, and voice that broke:
"I've missed you these last nights," he said:
"And I have not so many now
That I can miss friends easily . . .
Ay: friends grow scarce, as you grow old:
And roads are rough: and winds are cold:
And when you feel you're losing hold,
Life does not go too merrily."

And then he stood with nodding head,
And spoke no more. And so I told
How I had been, six days and nights,
Exiled from pleasant sounds and sights.
And now, as though my voice had stirred
His heart to speech, he told right out,
With quickening eye and quavering word,
The things I care to hear about,
The little things that make up life:
How he'd been lonesome, since his wife
Had died, some thirty year ago:
And how he trudged three mile or so
To reach the farmstead where he worked,
And three mile back to his own door . . .
For he dwelt outby on the moor:
And every day the distance irked
More sorely still his poor, old bones;
And all the road seemed strewn with stones
To trip you up, when you were old—
When you were old, and friends were few:
How, since the farmstead had been sold,
The master and the men were new,
All save himself; and they were young;
And Mistress had a raspy tongue:

So, often, he would hardly speak
A friendly word from week to week
With any soul. Old friends had died,
Or else had quit the countryside:
And since his wife was taken, he
Had lived alone, this thirty year:
And there were few who cared to hear
An old man's jabber . . . and too long
He'd kept me, standing in the cold,
With his long tongue, and such a song
About himself! And I would be . . .

I put my arm through his; and turned
To go upon his way with him:
And once again that warm light burned
In those old eyes, so weak and dim:
While, with thin, piping voice, he told
How much it meant to him each night
To change a kindly word with me:
To think that he'd at least one friend
Who'd maybe miss him, in the end.

Then, as we walked, he said no more:
And, silent, in the starry light,
Across the wide, sweet-smelling bent,
Between the grass and stars we went
In quiet, friendly company:
And, all the way, we only heard
A chirrup where some partridge stirred,
And ran before us through the grass,
To hide his head till we should pass.

At length we reached the cottage-door:
But when I stopped, and turned to go,
His words came falteringly and slow:
If I would step inside, and rest,
I'd be right welcome: not a guest
Had crossed his threshold, thirty year . . .
He'd naught but bread and cheese and beer
To offer me . . . but, I'd know best . . .
He spoke with hand upon the latch;
And when I answered, opened wide
The cottage-door, and stepped inside;

And, as I followed, struck a match,
And lit a tallow-dip: and stirred
The banked-up peats into a glow:
And then with shuffling step and slow
He moved about: and soon had set
Two mugs of beer, and bread and cheese:
And while we made a meal off these,
The old man never spoke a word;
But, brooding in the ingle-seat,
With eyes upon the kindling peat,
He seemed a while to quite forget
He was not sitting by himself
To-night, like any other night;
When, as in the dim candle-light
I glanced around me, with surprise
I saw upon the rafter-shelf
A flute, nigh hidden in the shade.

And when I asked him if he played,
The light came back into his eyes:
Ay, ay, he sometimes piped a bit,
But not so often since she died.
And then, as though old memories lit
His poor, old heart, and made it glad,
He told how he, when quite a lad,
Had taught himself: and they would play
On penny whistles all the day—
He and the miller's son, beside
The millpool, chirping all they knew,
Till they could whistle clean and true:
And how, when old enough to earn,
They both saved up to buy a flute:
And they had played it, turn for turn:
But Jake was dead, this long while back . . .
Ah! if I'd only heard him toot,
I'd know what music meant. Ay, ay . . .
He'd play me something, bye-and-bye;
Though he was nought to Jake . . . and now
His breath was scant, and fingering slack . . .
He used to play to her at night
The melodies that she liked best,
While she worked on: she'd never rest
By daylight, or by candle-light . . .

And then, with hand upon his brow,
He brooded, quiet in his chair,
With eyes upon the red peat-glare;
Until, at length, he roused himself,
And reached the flute down from the shelf;
And, carrying it outside the door,
I saw him take a can, and pour
Fresh water through the instrument,
To make it sweet of tone, he said.
Then in his seat, so old and bent,
With kindling eyes and swaying head,
He played the airs he used to play
To please his wife, before she died.

And as I watched his body sway
In time and tune, from side to side—
So happy, just to play, and please
With old familiar melodies—
His eyes grew brighter and more bright,
As though they saw some well-loved sight:
And, following his happy gaze,
I turned, and saw, without amaze,
A woman standing, young and fair,
With hazel eyes, and thick, brown hair
Brushed smoothly backward from the brow,
Beside the table that but now,
Save for the empty mugs, was bare.
Upon it she had spread a sheet,
And stood there, ironing a shirt,
Her husband's, as he played to her
Her favorite tunes, so old and sweet.
I watched her move with soundless stir;
Then stand with listening eyes, and hold
The iron near her glowing cheek,
Lest it, too hot, should do some hurt,
And she, so careful not to burn
The well-darned shirt, so worn and old.
Then, something seemed to make me turn
To look on the old man again:
And, as I looked, the playing stopped;
And now I saw that he had dropped
Into his brooding mood once more,
With eyes again grown dull and weak.

He seemed the oldest of old men
Who grope through life with sight worn dim:
And, even as I looked at him,
Too full of tender awe to speak,
I knew once more the board was bare,
With no young woman standing there
With hazel eyes and thick, brown hair.

And so, at last, I rose, and took
His hand: and as he clasped mine tight,
I saw again that friendly look
Fill his old weary eyes with light,
And wish me, without words, good-night.
And in my heart, that look glowed bright
Till I reached home across the moor.

And, at the corner of the lane,
Next night, I heard the old voice cry
In greeting, as I struggled by,
Head-down against the wind and rain.
And so each night, until one day,
His master chanced across my way:
But, when I spoke of him, he said:
Did I not know the man was dead,
And had been dead a week or so?
One morn he'd not turned up to work,
And never having known him shirk,
And hearing that he lived alone,
He thought it best himself to go
And see what ailed: and coming there,
He found the old man in his chair,
Stone-dead beside the cold hearthstone.
It must be full a week, or more . . .
Ay, just two weeks, come Saturday,
He'd found him; but he must have died
O'ernight—(the night I heard him play!)
And they had found, dropt by his side,
A broken flute upon the floor.

Yet, every night, his greeting still
At that same corner of the hill,
Summer and Winter, wet or dry,
'Neath cloud, or moon, or cold starlight,

Is waiting there to welcome me:
And ever as I hurry by,
The old voice sings out cheerily:
"Good-night!" and yet again, "Good-night!"

1912

SIGHT

By the lamplit stall I loitered, feasting my eyes
On colors ripe and rich for the heart's desire—
Tomatoes, redder than Krakatoa's fire,
Oranges like old sunsets over Tyre,
And apples golden-green as the glades of Paradise.

And as I lingered, lost in divine delight,
My heart thanked God for the goodly gift of sight
And all youth's lively senses keen and quick . . .
When suddenly, behind me in the night,
I heard the tapping of a blind man's stick.

1914

[SO LONG HAD I TRAVELLED]

So long had I travelled the lonely road,
Though, now and again, a wayfaring friend
Walked shoulder to shoulder, and lightened the load,
I often would think to myself as I strode,
No comrade will journey with you to the end.

And it seemed to me, as the days went past,
And I gossiped with cronies, or brooded alone,
By wayside fires, that my fortune was cast
To sojourn by other men's hearths to the last,
And never to come to my own hearthstone.

The lonely road no longer I roam.
We met, and were one in the heart's desire.
Together we came through the wintry gloam
To the little old house by the cross-ways, home;
And crossed the threshold, and kindled the fire.

1914

BEFORE ACTION

I sit beside the brazier's glow,
And, drowsing in the heat,
I dream of daffodils that blow
And lambs that frisk and bleat—

Black lambs that frolic in the snow
Among the daffodils,
In a far orchard that I know
Beneath the Malvern hills.

Next year the daffodils will blow,
And lambs will frisk and bleat;
But I'll not feel the brazier's glow,
Nor any cold or heat.

1915

THE RETURN

He went, and he was gay to go;
And I smiled on him as he went.
My son—'twas well he couldn't know
My darkest dread, nor what it meant—

Just what it meant to smile and smile
And let my son go cheerily—
My son . . . and wondering all the while
What stranger would come back to me.

1915

COMRADES

As I was marching in Flanders
A ghost kept step with me—
Kept step with me and chuckled
And muttered ceaselessly:

"Once I too marched in Flanders,
The very spit of you,
And just a hundred years since,
To fall at Waterloo.

"They buried me in Flanders
Upon the field of blood,
And long I've lain forgotten
Deep in the Flemish mud.

"But now you march in Flanders,
The very spit of me;
To the ending of the day's march
I'll bear you company."

1915

THE LARK

A lull in the racket and brattle,
And a lark soars into the light—
And its song seems the voice of the light
Quelling the voices of night
And the shattering fury of battle.

But again the fury of battle
Breaks out, and he drops from the height—
Dead as a stone from the height—
Drops dead, and the voice of the light
Is drowned in the shattering brattle.

1915

BACK

They ask me where I've been,
And what I've done and seen.
But what can I reply
Who know it wasn't I,
But someone just like me,
Who went across the sea
And with my head and hands
Killed men in foreign lands . . .
Though I must bear the blame
Because he bore my name.

1915

THE MESSAGES

"I cannot quite remember. . . . There were five
Dropt dead beside me in the trench—and three
Whispered their dying messages to me. . . ."

Back from the trenches, more dead than alive,
Stone-deaf and dazed, and with a broken knee,
He hobbled slowly, muttering vacantly:

"I cannot quite remember. . . . There were five
Dropt dead beside me in the trench, and three
Whispered their dying messages to me. . . .

"Their friends are waiting, wondering how they thrive—
Waiting a word in silence patiently. . . .
But what they said, or who their friends may be

"I cannot quite remember. . . . There were five
Dropt dead beside me in the trench,—and three
Whispered their dying messages to me. . . ."

1915

RUPERT BROOKE

Once in my garret—you being far away
Tramping the hills and breathing upland air,
Or so I fancied—brooding in my chair,
I watched the London sunshine feeble and grey
Dapple my desk, too tired to labor more,
When, looking up, I saw you standing there—
Although I'd caught no footstep on the stair,—
Like sudden April at my open door.

Though now beyond earth's farthest hills you fare,
Song-crowned, immortal, sometimes it seems to me
That, if I listen very quietly,
Perhaps I'll hear a light foot on the stair
And see you, standing with your angel air,
Fresh from the uplands of eternity.

1916

TENANTS

Suddenly, out of dark and leafy ways,
We came upon the little house asleep
In cold blind stillness, shadowless and deep,
In the white magic of the full moon-blaze:
Strangers without the gate, we stood agaze,
Fearful to break that quiet, and to creep
Into the house that had been ours to keep
Through a long year of happy nights and days.

So unfamiliar in the white moon-gleam,
So old and ghostly like a house of dream
It seemed, that over us there stole the dread
That even as we watched it, side by side,
The ghosts of lovers, who had lived and died
Within its walls, were sleeping in our bed.

1916

SEA-CHANGE

Wind-flicked and ruddy her young body glowed
In sunny shallows, splashing them to spray:
But when on rippled silver sand she lay,
And over her the little green waves flowed,
Coldly translucent and moon-colored showed
Her frail young beauty, as if rapt away
From all the light and laughter of the day
To some twilit, forlorn sea-god's abode.

Again into the sun with happy cry
She leapt alive and sparkling from the sea,
Sprinkling white spray against the hot blue sky,
A laughing girl . . . and yet, I see her lie
Under a deeper tide eternally
In cold moon-colored immortality.

1916

GIRL'S SONG

I saw three black pigs riding
In a blue and yellow cart—
Three black pigs riding to the fair
Behind the old grey dappled mare—
But it wasn't black pigs riding
In a gay and gaudy cart
That sent me into hiding
With a flutter in my heart.

I heard the cart returning,
The jolting, jingling cart—
Returning empty from the fair
Behind the old jog-trotting mare—
But it wasn't the returning
Of a clattering, empty cart
That sent the hot blood burning
And throbbing through my heart.
1916

THE MUGGER'S SONG

Driving up the Mallerstang,
The mugger cracked his whip and sang—
And all his crocks went rattle, rattle—

"The road runs fair and smooth and even
From Appleby to Kirkby Stephen—
And womenfolk are kittle cattle.

"And Kirkby Stephen's fair to see,
And inns are good in Appleby"—
And all his crocks went rattle, rattle.

"But what care I for Kirkby Stephen,
Or whether roads are rough or even—
And womenfolk are kittle cattle?

"And what care I for Appleby,
Since Bess of the Blue Bell jilted me?"—
And all his crocks went rattle, rattle.

"And wed to-day in Kirkby Stephen,
A sweep whose legs are odd and even?—
And womenfolk are kittle cattle."

1918

CURLEW CALLING

Curlew calling down the slack,
When grey rains are falling,
From the bitter town and black,
Curlew, I am coming back,
Curlew calling!

Hawk a-hover on the wind,
Look for me, your lover,
Come from barren ways and blind,
Where men seek but never find,—
Hawk a-hover!

Grey snipe drumming in the gloam,
I am coming, coming,
Never from my kind to roam.
Grey snipe, I am coming home,
Grey snipe drumming.

1918

THE EMPTY PURSE

One song leads on to another,
One friend to another friend,
So I'll travel along
With a friend and a song—
I'll travel along
Ten thousand strong—
To the end.

But if all songs should fail me,
And friend fail after friend,
I'll still have you,
O tried and true—

I'll still have you,
And a stone in my shoe,
To the end.

1918

LAMENT

We who are left, how shall we look again
Happily on the sun, or feel the rain,
Without remembering how they who went
Ungrudgingly, and spent
Their all for us, loved, too, the sun and rain?

A bird among the rain-wet lilac sings—
But we, how shall we turn to little things
And listen to the birds and winds and streams
Made holy by their dreams,
Nor feel the heart-break in the heart of things?

1918

THE PAISLEY SHAWL

What were his dreams who wove this colored shawl—
The grey, hard-bitten weaver, gaunt and dour,
Out of whose grizzled memory, even as a flower
Out of bleak Winter at young April's call
In the old tradition of flowers breaks into bloom,
Blossomed the ancient intricate design
Of softly-glowing hues and exquisite line—
What were his dreams, crouched at his cottage loom?

What were her dreams, the laughing April lass
Who first, in the flowering of young delight,
With parted lips and eager tilted head
And shining eyes, about her shoulders white
Drew the soft fabric of kindling green and red,
Standing before the candle-lighted glass?

1920

THE PUFFIN

He stooped down suddenly and thrust his hand
Into a tunnel in the shallow sand
Beneath a campion-clump, and brought to light
A brooding puffin with black wings clasped tight
To her white breast: but twisting round her sleek,
Pied, darting head, her scarlet razor-beak
She snapped in anger, cutting his finger clean
To the very bone; and on the clump of green
Among the campion blossoms white as foam
He dropped the bird and watched her scurry home;
And laughed, while from the wounded finger dripped
Blood redder even than the beak that ripped
The flesh so cruelly, and, chuckling, said:
"Well, anyway, the blood still runs as red
In my old veins as when I saw it spill
The first time that I felt a puffin's bill
Long years since: and it seems as though I had
As little sense as when I was a lad
To let myself be caught so easily
And that brave bird make such a fool of me
Who thought myself as wise as Solomon.
Yet it is better to feel a fool's blood run
Still quick and lively in the veins and be
A living fool beside the April sea
Than lie like Solomon in his unknown grave,
A pinch of dry dust that no wit could save."

1920

THE CONSCRIPT

Indifferent, flippant, earnest, but all bored,
The doctors sit in the glare of electric light
Watching the endless stream of naked white
Bodies of men for whom their hasty award
Means life or death maybe or the living death
Of mangled limbs, blind eyes or a darkened brain:
And the chairman as his monocle falls again
Pronounces each doom with easy indifferent breath.

Then suddenly I shudder as I see
A young man move before them wearily,
Cadaverous as one already dead:
But still they stare untroubled as he stands
With arms outstretched and drooping thorn-crowned head,
The nail-marks glowing in his feet and hands.

1920

REVEILLE

Still bathed in its moonlight slumber, the little white house by the cedar
Stands silent against the red dawn;
And nothing I know of who sleeps there, to the travail of day yet unwakened,
Behind the blue curtains undrawn:

But I dream as we march down the roadway, ringing loud and rime-white in the moonlight,
Of a little dark house on a hill
Wherein when the battle is over, to the rapture of day yet unwakened,
We shall slumber as soundless and still.

1920

ON BROADWAY

Daffodils dancing by moonlight in English meadows,
Moon-pale daffodils under the April moon—
Here in the throng and clangor and hustle of Broadway,
Broadway brawling and loud in the glare of the noon,
Comes to me now as a half-remembered tune
The silence and wonder of daffodils dancing by moonlight,
Dreamily dancing in dew-sprinkled moonshiny meadows,
Ghostly daffodils under a ghostly moon.

1920

IN COURSE OF TIME

The sarsen-stone
Door-post of temple, altar-throne
Of some old god, or monument
Erected by a warrior-host
To mark the fallen chieftain's tomb,
In course of time has come
To serve the old black sow for scratching-post.

A lad's light word,
Breathed low and scarcely heard
Or heeded in the babblement
And blare of other tongues, has time
Remembered, and the souls of men
Again and yet again
Take fire at that dead lad's undying rhyme.

1925

THE VOYAGE

In sailing it were good to have a chart
To steer a course by, and keep us in good heart
Throughout the voyage, even if in the end
We founder on unnoted shoals: but we,
Pressed for life's voyage, must venture recklessly,
Without a chart or compass, on and on,
Keeping precarious foothold on the slant
And slippery deck, o'er swallowing deeps, and run
Before the wind of hazard, ignorant
Even of the airt from which the wind is blowing
That drives us onward, and not even knowing
If there be any harbor to be won.

1930

IMMORTALITY

They tell us there is no stability,
That naught abides for ever anywhere;
The everlasting hills dissolve in air,
Frittered by wind and rain incessantly;

The solid rock is but a whirling motion
Of perishing dust; the sun, a failing fire;
A fleet evaporation, the old ocean;
And love, a self-consuming brief desire.

And yet, if evanescence be eternal—
Change, the one constant, this body of our death
Exists not: death were immobility;
And change is life, the spirit's very breath
Of being; and we are one with the supernal
Swirl of ever-living ecstasy.

1930

THE SWOOPING WINGS

Suddenly, as I crouched low on a ledge
For shelter as a hailstorm raked the crag,
An eagle swooped, the gust of his descent
Fanning me as he passed, and smote a stag
That unaware belled on the precipice edge
A blinding blow with his death-dealing wing,
And toppled him from his precarious perch
Where he had stood exultant, challenging
The stags of all the earth in royal pride,
And sent him hurtling down the mountain-side,
Helplessly crashing through the silver birch;
Then, swerving to recover poise, once more
Swooped on his mangled victim, lying spent
Among the boulders of the Atlantic shore,
Soused in the spindrift of the flowing tide.
The squall ceased; and the wet walls of the pass
In instant sunshine gleamed like burnished glass:
But still I huddled there with sobbing breath,
My soul still shaken by the winnowing
Of the down-rushing of the wings of death.

1932

HER DEATH

Now death at last had taken her; and they
Were free to live and let love have its way,
They who had held themselves in check so long
Lest they should hurt that tender heart, and wrong
Their love itself by letting it destroy
The affection that had been the only joy
Of her poor crippled life. . . . Now they were free—
And yet they stood there, hesitatingly,
And realized their love held in restraint
By tenderness had with the years grown faint,
That now between them there could only be
The affection of familiarity
And old habitual kindness. . . . Side by side
Speechless they stood, regretting she had died.

1932

THE DARK FOREST

You knew him?
Knew him? Who can thread with ease
The implications and intricacies
Of the dark forest of another's mind?
Why, even in my own, I stumble blind
And baffled through crass midnight and the dense
Thicket of cobwebbed branches, with no sense
Of sure direction, tangled in the brake,
Ever uncertain of the road to take
Through thorn and brambled sprays that trip and rasp:
And only rarely is it mine to grasp
The trenchant thought that cuts a pathway clear
Through matted undergrowths of doubt and fear.

1932

TIME, GENTLEMEN, PLEASE! [1]

"Time, gentlemen, please!" The inexorable host
Calls out above the chattering and the laughter,
Flinging the door wide open to the night;

[1] The tavern keeper's warning to clients that it is closing time.

And out we stumble from the warmth and light
Into Hereafter—

One after one we go into the cold
Lampless oblivion that so long has haunted
Our hearts in pauses of the revelry,
Our bosoms emptied of the pride that we
So bravely flaunted.

"Time, gentlemen, time!" And we who long hobnobbed
With boon companions in the light and laughter,
Each, willy-nilly, must set out alone,
Stript to the naked soul, through the unknown
Homeless Hereafter.

1932

Harold Monro

Harold Edward Monro was born March 14, 1879, in Brussels, Belgium. He was of Scotch descent, and his family belonged to the professional class: many of its members were physicians, and his father and his mother's father were engineers. At the age of seven he was taken to Wells, Somerset, and sent to a dame school. Later he attended Radley, a school in Berkshire, till 1897; then after a year in France he entered Caius College, Cambridge, where he specialized in the modern languages, lost a good deal at horse-racing, wrote some comic operas, and became a devotee of Shelley. After taking second class honors in 1901, he began the study of law; but while on a walking tour in the Hartz Mountains in 1902, he met a woman whom he married the following year, a move that necessitated his going to work.

His first job was as a real estate agent and poultry farmer in Ireland, but after some three years of this, he moved to the neighborhood of Haslemere and founded the Samurai Press. This venture only plunged him in debt, however, and after a year or two he gave it up and moved to the Continent, where he made a walking tour from Paris to Milan, settled for a while in Florence, and then bought a mill in Switzerland, from which he was presently driven out by a flood. Late in 1911 he returned to England with a new idea: he would found a magazine in which "poetry should be . . . discussed in its relation to life, and the same tests and criteria applied to it as to the other arts." In January, 1912, appeared the first number of this periodical, the *Poetry Review*, but after a few months, difficulties over its management arose among members of the Poetry Society, in collaboration with whom he was working, and Monro withdrew from the venture.

His next move proved to be the turning point of his life. In

January, 1913, he opened the Poetry Bookshop, to provide a center of interest for poetry. Here poets could gather and read their work, and any book of poetry could be purchased from a man who knew its contents and could discuss poetry intelligently. Except for the war years, when he served in the army first as officer in an anti-aircraft battery and later as an attaché of the War Office, he ran the Bookshop till his death. He also founded a quarterly, *Poetry and Drama*, which ran for eight numbers, till its publication was interrupted by World War I; and after the war he published for some time another magazine, the *Chapbook*.

He wrote verse from his early school days, but not until his study of Shelley, at Cambridge, did he have any serious intention of becoming a poet. His first volume, *Poems*, was published in 1906, and this was followed a year later by a long poem, *Judas*. His next works were prose: *Proposals for a Voluntary Nobility* (1907), *The Evolution of a Soul* (1907), and *The Chronicle of a Pilgrimage* (1909). None of this early work was important, however, and it was not till the appearance of *Children of Love* (1914) that the distinctive qualities of his style became evident. His remaining work consisted of a book of criticism, *Some Contemporary Poets* (1920); a morality play, *One Day Awake* (1922); an anthology, *Twentieth Century Poetry* (1929); and four or five slender volumes of poetry.

Monro had one son, Nigel, who was born in 1904. He was divorced in 1916, and in 1920 he married Alida Klemantaski, whom he had met in 1913, and who assisted him in running the Poetry Bookshop. Following a long and painful illness, he died of cancer at a nursing home at Broadstairs, on the Kentish coast, on March 15, 1932; and on March 19, his body was cremated at Golders Green, London.

Of Monro's poetry, T. S. Eliot said, in closing a critical article on his work, "I think that his poetry, as a whole, is more nearly the real right thing than any of the poetry of a somewhat older generation than mine except Mr. Yeats's. . . . In the end, it will remain because, like every other good poet, he has not simply done something better than anyone else, but done something that no one else has done at all." [1]

[1] *The Collected Poems of Harold Monro*, p. xvi.

LONDON INTERIOR

Autumn is in the air,
The children are playing everywhere.

One dare not open this old door too wide;
It is so dark inside.
The hall smells of dust;
A narrow squirt of sunlight enters high,
Cold, yellow.
The floor creaks, and I hear a sigh,
Rise in the gloom and die.

Through the hall, far away,
I just can see
The dingy garden with its wall and tree.
A yellow cat is sitting on the wall
Blinking toward the leaves that fall.
And now I hear a woman call
Some child from play.

Then all is still. Time must go
Ticking slow, glooming slow.

The evening will turn grey.
It is sad in London after two.
All, all the afternoon
What can old men, old women do?

It is sad in London when the gloom
Thickens, like wool,
In the corners of the room;
The sky is shot with steel,
Shot with blue.

The bells ring the slow time;
The chairs creak, the hours climb;
The sunlight lays a streak upon the floor.

1914

SUBURB

Dull and hard the low wind creaks
Among the rustling pampas plumes.
Drearily the year consumes
Its fifty-two insipid weeks.

Most of the grey-green meadow land
Was sold in parsimonious lots;
The dingy houses stand
Pressed by some stout contractor's hand
Tightly together in their plots.

Through builded banks the sullen river
Gropes, where its houses crouch and shiver.
Over the bridge the tyrant train
Shrieks, and emerges on the plain.

In all the better gardens you may pass,
(Product of many careful Saturdays),
Large red geraniums and tall pampas grass
Adorn the plots and mark the gravelled ways.

Sometimes in the background may be seen
A private summer-house in white or green.
Here on warm nights the daughter brings
Her vacillating clerk,
To talk of small exciting things
And touch his fingers through the dark.

He, in the uncomfortable breach
Between her trilling laughters,
Promises, in halting speech,
Hopeless immense Hereafters.
She trembles like the pampas plumes.
Her strained lips haggle. He assumes
The serious quest . . .

Now as the train is whistling past
He takes her in his arms at last.

It's done. She blushes at his side
Across the lawn—a bride, a bride.

* * * * *

The stout contractor will design,
The lazy laborers will prepare,
Another villa on the line;
In the little garden-square
Pampas grass will rustle there.

1914

EVERY THING

Since man has been articulate,
Mechanical, improvidently wise
(Servant of Fate),
He has not understood the little cries
And foreign conversations of the small
Delightful creatures that have followed him
Not far behind;
Has failed to hear the sympathetic call
Of Crockery and Cutlery, those kind
Reposeful Teraphim
Of his domestic happiness; the Stool
He sat on, or the Door he entered through:
He has not thanked them, overbearing fool!
What is he coming to?

But you should listen to the talk of these.
Honest they are, and patient they have kept,
Served him without his *Thank-you* or his *Please* . . .
I often heard
The gentle Bed, a sigh between each word,
Murmuring, before I slept.
The Candle, as I blew it, cried aloud,
Then bowed,
And in a smoky argument
Into the darkness went.
The Kettle puffed a tentacle of breath:—
"Pooh! I have boiled his water, I don't know
Why; and he always says I boil too slow.
He never calls me 'Sukie dear,' and oh,

I wonder why I squander my desire
Sitting submissive on his kitchen fire."

Now the old Copper Basin suddenly
Rattled and tumbled from the shelf,
Bumping and crying: "I can fall by myself;
Without a woman's hand
To patronize and coax and flatter me,
I understand
The lean and poise of gravitable land."
It gave a raucous and tumultuous shout,
Twisted itself convulsively about,
Rested upon the floor, and, while I stare,
It stares and grins at me.
The old impetuous Gas above my head
Begins irascibly to flare and fret,
Wheezing into its epileptic jet,
Reminding me I ought to go to bed.

The Rafters creak; an Empty-Cupboard door
Swings open; now a wild Plank of the floor
Breaks from its joist, and leaps behind my foot.
Down from the chimney half a pound of Soot
Tumbles, and lies, and shakes itself again.
The Putty cracks against the window-pane.
A piece of Paper in the basket shoves
Another piece, and toward the bottom moves.
My independent Pencil, while I write,
Breaks at the point: the ruminating Clock
Stirs all its body and begins to rock,
Warning the waiting presence of the Night,
Strikes the dead hour, and tumbles to the plain
Ticking of ordinary work again.

You do well to remind me, and I praise
Your strangely individual foreign ways.
You call me from myself to recognize
Companionship in your unselfish eyes.
I want your dear acquaintances, although
I pass you arrogantly over, throw
Your lovely sounds, and squander them along
My busy days. I'll do you no more wrong.
Purr for me, Sukie, like a faithful cat.

You, my well trampled Boots, and you, my Hat,
Remain my friends: I feel, though I don't speak,
Your touch grow kindlier from week to week.

It well becomes our mutual happiness
To go toward the same end more or less.
There is not much dissimilarity,
Not much to choose, I know it well, in fine,
Between the purposes of you and me,
And your eventual Rubbish Heap, and mine.

1917

THE SILENT POOL

I

I have discovered finally to-day
This house that I have called my own
Is built of straw and clay,
Not, as I thought, of stone.

I wonder who the architect could be,
What builder made it of that stuff;
When it was left to me
The house seemed good enough.

Yet, slowly, as its roof began to sink,
And as its walls began to split,
And I began to think,
Then I suspected it;

But did not clearly know until to-day
That it was only built of straw and clay.

II

Now I will go about on my affairs
As though I had no cares,
Nor ever think at all
How one day soon that house is bound to fall,
So when I'm told the wind has blown it down
I may have something else to call my own.

I have enquired who was the architect,
What builder did erect.
I'm told they did design
Million and million others all like mine,
And argument with all men ends the same:—
It is impossible to fix the blame.

I am so glad that underneath our talk
Our minds together walk.
We argue all the while,
But down below our argument we smile.
We have our houses, but we understand
That our real property is common land.

III

At night we often go
With happy comrades to that real estate,
Where dreams in beauty grow,
And every man enjoys a common fate.

At night in sleep one flows
Below the surface of all argument;
The brain, with all it knows,
Is covered by the waters of content.

But when the dawn appears
Brain rises to the surface with a start,
And, waking, quickly sneers
At the old natural brightness of the heart.

Oh, that a man might choose
To live unconsciously like beast or bird,
And our clear thought not lose
Its beauty when we turn it into word.

IV

Those quarrelings between my brain and heart
(In which I'd take no part)
Pursue their violent course
Corrupting my most vital force
So that my natural property is spent
In fees to keep alive their argument.

V

Look downward in the silent pool:
The weeds cling to the ground they love;
They live so quietly, are so cool;
They do not need to think, or move.

Look down in the unconscious mind:
There everything is quiet too
And deep and cool, and you will find
Calm growth and nothing hard to do,
And nothing that need trouble you.

1922

REAL PROPERTY

Tell me about that harvest field.
Oh! Fifty acres of living bread.
The color has painted itself in my heart.
The form is patterned in my head.

So now I take it everywhere;
See it whenever I look round;
Hear it growing through every sound,
Know exactly the sound it makes—
Remembering, as one must all day,
Under the pavement the live earth aches.

Trees are at the farther end,
Limes all full of the mumbling bee:
So there must be a harvest field
Whenever one thinks of a linden tree.

A hedge is about it, very tall,
Hazy and cool, and breathing sweet.
Round paradise is such a wall
And all the day, in such a way,
In paradise the wild birds call.

You only need to close your eyes
And go within your secret mind,
And you'll be into paradise:

I've learnt quite easily to find
Some linden trees and drowsy bees,
A tall sweet hedge with the corn behind.

I will not have that harvest mown:
I'll keep the corn and leave the bread.
I've bought that field; it's now my own:
I've fifty acres in my head.
I take it as a dream to bed.
I carry it about all day. . . .

Sometimes when I have found a friend
I give a blade of corn away.

1922

LIVING

Slow bleak awakening from the morning dream
Brings me in contact with the sudden day.
I am alive—this I.
I let my fingers move along my body.
Realization warns them, and my nerves
Prepare their rapid messages and signals.
While Memory begins recording, coding,
Repeating; all the time Imagination
Mutters: You'll only die.

Here's a new day. O Pendulum move slowly!
My usual clothes are waiting on their peg.
I am alive—this I.
And in a moment Habit, like a crane,
Will bow its neck and dip its pulleyed cable,
Gathering me, my body, and our garment,
And swing me forth, oblivious of my question,
Into the daylight—why?

I think of all the others who awaken,
And wonder if they go to meet the morning
More valiantly than I;
Nor asking of this Day they will be living:
What have I done that I should be alive?
O, can I not forget that I am living?

How shall I reconcile the two conditions:
Living, and yet—to die?

Between the curtains the autumnal sunlight
With lean and yellow finger points me out;
The clock moans: Why? Why? Why?
But suddenly, as if without a reason,
Heart, Brain, and Body, and Imagination
All gather in tumultuous joy together,
Running like children down the path of morning
To fields where they can play without a quarrel:
A country I'd forgotten, but remember,
And welcome with a cry.

O cool glad pasture; living tree, tall corn,
Great cliff, or languid sloping sand, cold sea,
Waves; rivers curving: you, eternal flowers,
Give me content, while I can think of you:
Give me your living breath!
Back to your rampart, Death.

1928

MIDNIGHT LAMENTATION

When you and I go down
Breathless and cold,
Our faces both worn back
To earthly mold,
How lonely we shall be!
What shall we do,
You without me,
I without you?

I cannot bear the thought
You, first, may die,
Nor of how you will weep,
Should I.
We are too much alone;
What can we do
To make our bodies one:
You, me; I, you?

We are most nearly born
Of one same kind;
We have the same delight,
The same true mind.
Must we then part, we part;
Is there no way
To keep a beating heart,
And light of day?

I could now rise and run
Through street on street
To where you are breathing—you,
That we might meet,
And that your living voice
Might sound above
Fear, and we two rejoice
Within our love.

How frail the body is,
And we are made
As only in decay
To lean and fade.
I think too much of death;
There is a gloom
When I can't hear your breath
Calm in some room.

Oh, but how suddenly
Either may droop;
Countenance be so white,
Body stoop.
Then there may be a place
Where fading flowers
Drop on a lifeless face
Through weeping hours.

Is then nothing safe?
Can we not find
Some everlasting life
In our one mind?
I feel it like disgrace
Only to understand
Your spirit through your word,
Or by your hand.

I cannot find a way
Through love and through;
I cannot reach beyond
Body, to you.
When you or I must go
Down evermore,
There'll be no more to say
—But a locked door.

1928

HOLY MATRIMONY

I

It was a fatal trick to play upon him.
With lusty life all pointing to one aim,
And his whole body watchful:
She at the moment came.

Could he resist? Could she? That one blue glance
Was not her own: oh, a far stronger power
Than hers shone at him through her
And fixed their mating hour.

II

Words, hardly needed, then were spoken,
All having only one intent.
They walked like children staring downward,
With body toward body bent.

Now all the others mumble darkly,
Wonder and enviously stare.
There is a glowing in the household:
Desire will dwell a moment here.

But older eyes gleam coldly on them;
Stiffer bodies step between.
Now while the preparations start
They must be cleanly kept apart:
So has the custom always been.

"You cannot kneel before the altar
Until we've trimmed the lamp for you.

Meanwhile you may a little woo;
We've much to do:
We'll bake and sew and watch you sidelong,
And make your wedding bed for you."

III

But he and she
They hear, they stare,
And they are asking:
Who are we?

They cling and cry:
What have we done?
Through us what ceremonial
Is begun?

The dark doors close
Upon the sky.
They shall be locked within
Till they do die.

IV

O prison church! O warder-priest!
Now they who used to walk the wind of freedom
Are living in your gloomy house of stone;
And they and it are growing older;
She is becoming every day less fair.
The more together, they are more alone:
They pile the fire and yet the hearth is colder.

1928

THE EARTH FOR SALE

I

How perilous life will become on earth
When the great breed of man has covered all.
The world, that was too large, will be too small.
Deserts and mountains will have been explored,
Valleys swarmed through; and our prolific breed,
Exceeding death ten million times by birth,
Will halt (bewildered, bored),
And then may droop and dwindle like an autumn weed.

How shall we meet that moment when we know
There is no room to grow;
We, conscious, and with lonely startled eyes
Glaring upon ourselves, and with no Lord
To pray to: judged, without appeal,
What shall we feel?
He, being withdrawn, no supplicating cries
Will call Him back. He'll speak no further word.

Can special vision be required to see
What few pale centuries will take us there,
Where, at the barrier of the future, we
Shall stand condemned, in serried ranks, and stare
At Nothing—fearing Something may appear?

The Earth is covered with large auction boards,
And all her lands are reckoned up for sale.
The spaces that are now called virgin soil
Will soon be bought, and covered with great breed
Of human seed;
And, when the driven hordes
Cry "Food!"—but find no more for any toil,
Fear, fear will strike all eyes and faces pale.
Then no one more will speak,
But, rising from a murmur to a wail,
One voice, for all, will, like a Siren, shriek.

II

Is there no pledge to make at once with Earth
While yet we have not murdered all her trees;
Before it is too late for oath or pledge;
While yet man may be happy in his birth—
Before we have to fall upon our knees,
Clinging for safety to her farthest edge?
It is not very noble that we kill
Her lions and tigers, all. Is that our reign?—
Then let us build ourselves on earth again.
What is the human will?
Is it so clearly better than the ant's?
And is our life more holy than the plants'?
They do fulfil their purpose every year,
And bring no pain, nor fear.

III

Woe to that miserable last mankind;
And, when I think of that, I have a dread
I may awake on earth, again, to find
Myself, among it, living, oh, not dead.

IV

I had been thinking of that final Earth.
Then I remembered she herself would lick
Her own lithe body clean, and from her girth
Wipe any vermin that might cling too thick.

Damned! Damned! Apparent conqueror to-day—
Oh, evanescent sway!
O drunken lust!
O swarming dust!

Man makes himself believe he has a claim
To plant bright flags on every hill he swarms;
But in the end, and in his own wild name,
And for the better prospect of his fame,
Whether it be a person or a race,
Earth, with a smiling face,
Will hold and smother him in her large arms.

1928

NEW DAY

And how will fancy lead his life to-day?
Eyes lift their shutters. Still the room is grey.
But slowly it reveals (with blankets back)
Omens all clothed in blue; or green; or black.
How will the small things of the day behave?
Will hope be calm, or petulantly rave?

There'll be no great decision. Time will knit,
And multiply the stitches while we look.
A few hours we shall stand, a few hours sit,
A few hours talk, or walk, or read a book.
The dishes will be washed, the table laid.
Smells of sweet food will spread delicious wings.

The daily commonplaces will be said,
And we shall handle all the daily things.

And so the time will pass.
Yet is there not a meaning in our looks
That makes us kindred as the blades of grass,
Or tree-leaves leaning over country brooks?
May we not be aware somehow
Among the cool small habits we have made
Of calm hands or a sympathetic brow,
Or of a guiding motive in the shade?

Yes! Yes! Oh what delusion have I had?—
Only to-day discovered you?
No wonder yesterday remained so sad.
Let us find out what Love intends to do.
Meanwhile for me
The moments will be only two or three.
Some little glance of yours will send me mad;
Some other look of yours will set me free;
Some word you drop make my whole body sad.
Some thing you do will send my spirit flying
Into the blue of wild delight;
And next the thought of you will leave my body lying
In passionate waking dreams all through to-night.

1933

BITTER SANCTUARY

I

She lives in the porter's room; the plush is nicotined.
Clients have left their photos there to perish.
She watches through green shutters those who press
To reach unconsciousness.
She licks her varnished thin magenta lips,
She picks her foretooth with a finger nail,
She pokes her head out to greet new clients, or
To leave them (to what torture) waiting at the door.

II

Heat has locked the heavy earth,
Given strength to every sound,

He, where his life still holds him to the ground,
In anæsthesia, groaning for re-birth,
Leans at the door.
From out the house there comes the dullest flutter;
A lackey; and thin giggling from behind that shutter.

III

His lost eyes lean to find and read the number.
Follows his knuckled rap, and hesitating curse.
He cannot wake himself; he may not slumber;
While on the long white wall across the road
Drives the thin outline of a dwindling hearse.

IV

Now the door opens wide.

He: "Is there room inside?"
She: "Are you past the bounds of pain?"
He: "May my body lie in vain
    Among the dreams I cannot keep!"
She: "Let him drink the cup of sleep."

V

Thin arms and ghostly hands; faint sky-blue eyes;
Long drooping lashes, lids like full-blown moons,
Clinging to any brink of floating skies:
What hope is there? What fear?—Unless to wake and see
Lingering flesh, or cold eternity.

O yet some face, half living, brings
Far gaze to him and croons:
She: "You're white. You are alone.
    Can you not approach my sphere?"
He: "I'm changing into stone."
She: "Would I were! Would *I* were!"
Then the white attendants fill the cup.

VI

In the morning through the world,
Watch the flunkeys bring the coffee;
Watch the shepherds on the downs,
Lords and ladies at their toilet,
Farmers, merchants, frothing towns.

But look how he, unfortunate, now fumbles
Through unknown chambers, unheedful stumbles.
Can he evade the overshadowing night?
Are there not somewhere chinks of braided light?

VII

How do they leave who once are in those rooms?
Some may be found, they say, deeply asleep
In ruined tombs.
Some in white beds, with faces round them. Some
Wander the world, and never find a home.

1933

Alfred Noyes

Alfred Noyes, the eldest son of Alfred and Amelia Adams Rowley Noyes, was born September 16, 1880, at Wolverhampton, Staffordshire. He attended Exeter College, Oxford, from October, 1898, to 1903, but did not take a degree. He wrote verse from childhood, and published his first volume, *The Loom of Years*, in 1902, and his second, *The Flower of Old Japan*, a year later. Thereafter for many years he published poetry and prose at the rate of about a volume a year.

In 1913 he visited the United States to lecture at the Lowell Institute, Boston, and for his subject chose "The Sea in English Poetry." He was cordially received in America: Yale gave him an honorary D. Litt. degree (1913); he had many requests to lecture; and in 1914 Princeton appointed him Professor of Modern English Literature, a position he held till 1923.

Poor eyesight kept him out of the army during the first World War, but for meritorious service with the British Foreign Office, to which he was attached for a time in 1916, he was made a Commander of the Order of the British Empire in 1918. In 1923 he gave up his appointment at Princeton to live in England and devote his time to writing. On several occasions, however, he has returned to America to lecture.

In addition to more than twenty books of poetry, he has written much prose: a life of William Morris (1908); some volumes of short stories, *Walking Shadows* (1917) and *The Hidden Player* (1924); several novels, among them *The Sun Cure* (1929) and *The Return of the Scarecrow* (1929); such critical works as *Some Aspects of Modern Poetry* (1924), *New Essays and American Impressions* (1927), and *The Opalescent Parrot* (1929); a work dealing with his religious experiences, *The Unknown God* (1934); and many magazine articles. He has also edited several anthologies.

In 1925 Noyes became a Roman Catholic. In 1907 he married Garnett Daniels, the daughter of a United States army colonel, and they had a son and two daughters. His wife died on October 8, 1926, and on September 27, 1927, he married Mrs. Mary Weld-Blundell, a widow who was the daughter of Captain J. G. Mayne. He lives much of the time now on the Isle of Wight.

THE BARREL-ORGAN

There's a barrel-organ carolling across a golden street
  In the City as the sun sinks low;
And the music's not immortal; but the world has made it sweet
  And fulfilled it with the sunset glow;
And it pulses through the pleasures of the City and the pain
  That surround the singing organ like a large eternal light;
And they've given it a glory and a part to play again
  In the Symphony that rules the day and night.

And now it's marching onward through the realms of old romance,
  And trolling out a fond familiar tune,
And now it's roaring cannon down to fight the King of France,
  And now it's prattling softly to the moon,
And all around the organ there's a sea without a shore
  Of human joys and wonders and regrets,
To remember and to recompense the music evermore
  For what the cold machinery forgets. . . .

Yes; as the music changes,
  Like a prismatic glass,
It takes the light and ranges
  Through all the moods that pass;
Dissects the common carnival
  Of passions and regrets,
And gives the world a glimpse of all
  The colors it forgets.

And there *La Traviata* sighs
  Another sadder song;
And there *Il Trovatore* cries
  A tale of deeper wrong;
And bolder knights to battle go
  With sword and shield and lance,

Than ever here on earth below
Have whirled into—a *dance!*—

Go down to Kew in lilac-time, in lilac-time, in lilac-time;
Go down to Kew in lilac-time (it isn't far from London!),
And you shall wander hand in hand with love in summer's wonderland;
Go down to Kew in lilac-time (it isn't far from London!).

The cherry-trees are seas of bloom and soft perfume and sweet perfume,
The cherry-trees are seas of bloom (and oh, so near to London!),
And there they say, when dawn is high and all the world's a blaze of sky
The cuckoo, though he's very shy, will sing a song for London.

The Dorian nightingale is rare, and yet they say you'll hear him there
At Kew, at Kew in lilac-time (and oh, so near to London!),
The linnet and the throstle, too, and after dark the long halloo
And golden-eyed *tu-whit, tu-whoo* of owls that ogle London.

For Noah hardly knew a bird of any kind that isn't heard
At Kew, at Kew in lilac-time (and oh, so near to London!),
And when the rose begins to pout and all the chestnut spires are out
You'll hear the rest without a doubt, all chorussing for London:—

Come down to Kew in lilac-time, in lilac-time, in lilac-time;
Come down to Kew in lilac-time (it isn't far from London!),
And you shall wander hand in hand with love in summer's wonderland;
Come down to Kew in lilac-time (it isn't far from London!).

And then the troubadour begins to thrill the golden street,
In the City as the sun sinks low;
And in all the gaudy busses there are scores of weary feet
Marking time, sweet time, with a dull mechanic beat,
And a thousand hearts are plunging to a love they'll never meet,
Through the meadows of the sunset, through the poppies and the wheat,
In the land where the dead dreams go.

Verdi, Verdi, when you wrote *Il Trovatore* did you dream
  Of the City when the sun sinks low,
Of the organ and the monkey and the many-colored stream
On the Piccadilly pavement, of the myriad eyes that seem
To be litten for a moment with a wild Italian gleam
As *A che la morte* parodies the world's eternal theme
  And pulses with the sunset-glow?

There's a thief, perhaps, that listens with a face of frozen stone
  In the City as the sun sinks low;
There's a portly man of business with a balance of his own,
There's a clerk and there's a butcher of a soft reposeful tone.
And they're all of them returning to the heavens they have
    known:
They are crammed and jammed in busses and—they're each of
    them alone
  In the land where the dead dreams go.

There's a very modish woman and her smile is very bland
  In the City as the sun sinks low;
And her hansom jingles onward, but her little jewelled hand
Is clenched a little tighter and she cannot understand
What she wants or why she wanders to that undiscovered land,
For the parties there are not at all the sort of thing she planned,
  In the land where the dead dreams go.

There's a rowing man that listens and his heart is crying out
  In the City as the sun sinks low;
For the barge, the eight, the Isis, and the coach's whoop and
    shout,
For the minute-gun, the counting, and the long dishevelled rout,
For the howl along the tow-path and a fate that's still in doubt,
For a roughened oar to handle and a race to think about
  In the land where the dead dreams go.

There's a laborer that listens to the voices of the dead
  In the City as the sun sinks low;
And his hand begins to tremble and his face to smolder red
As he sees a loafer watching him and—there he turns his head
And stares into the sunset where his April love is fled,
For he hears her softly singing and his lonely soul is led
  Through the land where the dead dreams go.

There's an old and haggard demi-rep, it's ringing in her ears,
  In the City as the sun sinks low;
With the wild and empty sorrow of the love that blights and sears,
Oh, and if she hurries onward, then be sure, be sure she hears,
Hears and bears the bitter burden of the unforgotten years,
And her laugh's a little harsher and her eyes are brimmed with tears
  For the land where the dead dreams go.

There's a barrel-organ carolling across a golden street
  In the City as the sun sinks low;
Though the music's only Verdi there's a world to make it sweet
Just as yonder yellow sunset where the earth and heaven meet
Mellows all the sooty City! Hark, a hundred thousand feet
Are marching on to glory through the poppies and the wheat
  In the land where the dead dreams go.

So it's Jeremiah, Jeremiah,
  What have you to say
When you meet the garland girls
  Tripping on their way?

All around my gala hat
  I wear a wreath of roses
(A long and lonely year it is
  I've waited for the May!).
If any one should ask you,
  The reason why I wear it is—
My own love, my true love,
  Is coming home to-day.

And it's buy a bunch of violets for the lady
  (*It's lilac-time in London; it's lilac-time in London!*),
Buy a bunch of violets for the lady
  While the sky burns blue above:

On the other side the street you'll find it shady
  (*It's lilac-time in London; it's lilac-time in London!*),
But buy a bunch of violets for the lady,
  And tell her she's your own true love.

There's a barrel-organ carolling across a golden street
  In the City as the sun sinks glittering and slow;

And the music's not immortal; but the world has made it sweet
And enriched it with the harmonies that make a song complete
In the deeper heavens of music where the night and morning
        meet,
   As it dies into the sunset-glow;
And it pulses through the pleasures of the City and the pain
   That surround the singing organ like a large eternal light,
And they've given it a glory and a part to play again
   In the Symphony that rules the day and night.

And there, as the music changes,
   The song runs round again.
Once more it turns and ranges
   Through all its joy and pain,
Dissects the common carnival
   Of passions and regrets;
And the wheeling world remembers all
   The wheeling song forgets.

Once more *La Traviata* sighs
   Another sadder song:
Once more *Il Trovatore* cries
   A tale of deeper wrong;
Once more the knights to battle go
   With sword and shield and lance
Till once, once more, the shattered foe
   Has whirled into—*a dance!*

Come down to Kew in lilac-time, in lilac-time, in lilac-time;
   Come down to Kew in lilac-time (it isn't far from London!),
And you shall wander hand in hand with love in summer's
        wonderland;
   Come down to Kew in lilac-time (it isn't far from London!).

1904

SONG

[From *Drake*]

Now the purple night is past,
   Now the moon more faintly glows,
Dawn has through thy casement cast
   Roses on thy breast, a rose;

Now the kisses are all done,
  Now the world awakes anew,
Now the charmèd hour is gone,
  Let not love go, too.

When old winter, creeping nigh,
  Sprinkles raven hair with white,
Dims the brightly glancing eye,
  Laughs away the dancing light,
Roses may forget their sun,
  Lilies may forget their dew,
Beauties perish, one by one,
  Let not love go, too.

Palaces and towers of pride
  Crumble year by year away;
Creeds like robes are laid aside,
  Even our very tombs decay!
When the all-conquering moth and rust
  Gnaw the goodly garment through,
When the dust returns to dust,
  Let not love go, too.

Kingdoms melt away like snow,
  Gods are spent like wasting flames,
Hardly the new peoples know
  Their divine thrice-worshipped names!
At the last great hour of all,
  When thou makest all things new,
Father, hear Thy children call,
  Let not love go, too.

1906

THE HIGHWAYMAN

PART ONE

The wind was a torrent of darkness among the gusty trees,
The moon was a ghostly galleon tossed upon cloudy seas,
The road was a ribbon of moonlight over the purple moor,
And the highwayman came riding—
        Riding—riding—
The highwayman came riding, up to the old inn door.

He'd a French cocked-hat on his forehead, a bunch of lace at his
chin,
A coat of the claret velvet, and breeches of brown doe-skin;
They fitted with never a wrinkle: his boots were up to the thigh!
And he rode with a jewelled twinkle,
His pistol butts a-twinkle,
His rapier hilt a-twinkle, under the jewelled sky.

Over the cobbles he clattered and clashed in the dark inn-yard,
And he tapped with his whip on the shutters, but all was
locked and barred;
He whistled a tune to the window, and who should be
waiting there
But the landlord's black-eyed daughter,
Bess, the landlord's daughter,
Plaiting a dark red love-knot into her long black hair.

And dark in the dark old inn-yard a stable-wicket creaked
Where Tim the ostler listened; his face was white and peaked;
His eyes were hollows of madness, his hair like moldy hay,
But he loved the landlord's daughter,
The landlord's red-lipped daughter;
Dumb as a dog he listened, and he heard the robber say—

"One kiss, my bonny sweetheart, I'm after a prize to-night,
But I shall be back with the yellow gold before the morning light;
Yet, if they press me sharply, and harry me through the day,
Then look for me by moonlight,
Watch for me by moonlight,
I'll come to thee by moonlight, though hell should bar the way."

He rose upright in the stirrups; he scarce could reach her hand,
But she loosened her hair i' the casement! His face burnt like a
brand
As the black cascade of perfume came tumbling over his breast;
And he kissed its waves in the moonlight,
(Oh, sweet black waves in the moonlight!)
Then he tugged at his rein in the moonlight, and galloped away
to the West.

PART TWO

He did not come in the dawning; he did not come at noon;
And out o' the tawny sunset, before the rise o' the moon,

When the road was a gipsy's ribbon, looping the purple moor,
A red-coat troop came marching—
Marching—marching—
King George's men came marching, up to the old inn-door.

They said no word to the landlord, they drank his ale instead,
But they gagged his daughter and bound her to the foot of her narrow bed;
Two of them knelt at her casement, with muskets at their side!
There was death at every window;
And hell at one dark window;
For Bess could see, through her casement, the road that *he* would ride.

They had tied her up to attention, with many a sniggering jest;
They had bound a musket beside her, with the barrel beneath her breast!
"Now keep good watch!" and they kissed her.
She heard the dead man say—
Look for me by moonlight;
Watch for me by moonlight;
I'll come to thee by moonlight, though hell should bar the way!

She twisted her hands behind her; but all the knots held good!
She writhed her hands till her fingers were wet with sweat or blood!
They stretched and strained in the darkness, and the hours crawled by like years,
Till, now, on the stroke of midnight,
Cold, on the stroke of midnight,
The tip of one finger touched it! The trigger at least was hers!

The tip of one finger touched it; she strove no more for the rest!
Up, she stood up to attention, with the barrel beneath her breast,
She would not risk their hearing; she would not strive again;
For the road lay bare in the moonlight;
Blank and bare in the moonlight;
And the blood of her veins in the moonlight throbbed to her love's refrain.

Tlot-tlot; tlot-tlot! Had they heard it? The horse-hoofs ringing clear;
Tlot-tlot, tlot-tlot, in the distance? Were they deaf that they did not hear?

Down the ribbon of moonlight, over the brow of the hill,
The highwayman came riding,
Riding, riding!
The red-coats looked to their priming! She stood up, straight and still!

Tlot-tlot, in the frosty silence! *Tlot-tlot,* in the echoing night!
Nearer he came and nearer! Her face was like a light!
Her eyes grew wide for a moment; she drew one last deep breath,
Then her finger moved in the moonlight,
Her musket shattered the moonlight,
Shattered her breast in the moonlight and warned him—with her death.

He turned; he spurred to the West; he did not know who stood
Bowed, with her head o'er the musket, drenched with her own red blood!
Not till the dawn he heard it, his face grew grey to hear
How Bess, the landlord's daughter,
The landlord's black-eyed daughter,
Had watched for her love in the moonlight, and died in the darkness there.

Back, he spurred like a madman, shrieking a curse to the sky,
With the white road smoking behind him and his rapier brandished high!
Blood-red were his spurs i' the golden noon; wine-red was his velvet coat,
When they shot him down on the highway,
Down like a dog on the highway,
And he lay in his blood on the highway, with the bunch of lace at his throat.

* * * * *

And still of a winter's night, they say, when the wind is in the trees,
When the moon is a ghostly galleon tossed upon cloudy seas,
When the road is a ribbon of moonlight over the purple moor,
A highwayman comes riding—
Riding—riding—
A highwayman comes riding, up to the old inn-door.

Over the cobbles he clatters and clangs in the dark inn-yard;
He taps with his whip on the shutters, but all is locked and barred;

He whistles a tune to the window, and who should be waiting
there
But the landlord's black-eyed daughter,
Bess, the landlord's daughter,
Plaiting a dark red love-knot into her long black hair.

1906

FORTY SINGING SEAMEN

"*In our lands be Beeres and Lyons of dyvers colours as ye redd, grene, black, and white. And in our land be also unicornes and these Unicornes slee many Lyons. . . . Also there dare no man make a lye in our lande, for if he dyde he sholde incontynent be sleyn.*"—Mediaeval Epistle, of Pope Prester John.

Across the seas of Wonderland to Mogadore we plodded,
Forty singing seamen in an old black barque,
And we landed in the twilight where a Polyphemus nodded
With his battered moon-eye winking red and yellow through
the dark!
For his eye was growing mellow,
Rich and ripe and red and yellow,
As was time, since old Ulysses made him bellow in the dark!
Cho.—Since Ulysses bunged his eye up with a pine-torch in
the dark!

Were they mountains in the gloaming or the giant's ugly
shoulders
Just beneath the rolling eyeball, with its bleared and vinous
glow,
Red and yellow o'er the purple of the pines among the boulders
And the shaggy horror brooding on the sullen slopes below,
Were they pines among the boulders
Or the hair upon his shoulders?
We were only simple seamen, so of course we didn't know.
Cho.—We were simple singing seamen, so of course we couldn't
know.

But we crossed a plain of poppies, and we came upon a fountain
Not of water, but of jewels, like a spray of leaping fire;
And behind it, in an emerald glade, beneath a golden mountain
There stood a crystal palace, for a sailor to admire;

For a troop of ghosts came round us,
Which with leaves of bay they crowned us,
Then with grog they well nigh drowned us, to the depth of our desire!
Cho.—And 'twas very friendly of them, as a sailor can admire!

There was music all about us, we were growing quite forgetful
We were only singing seamen from the dirt of Londontown,
Though the nectar that we swallowed seemed to vanish half regretful
As if we wasn't good enough to take such vittles down,
When we saw a sudden figure,
Tall and black as any nigger,
Like the devil—only bigger—drawing near us with a frown!
Cho.—Like the devil—but much bigger—and he wore a golden crown!

And "What's all this?" he growls at us! With dignity we chaunted,
"Forty singing seamen, sir, as won't be put upon!"
"What? Englishmen?" he cries, "Well, if ye don't mind being haunted,
Faith you're welcome to my palace; I'm the famous Prester John!
Will ye walk into my palace?
I don't bear 'ee any malice!
One and all ye shall be welcome in the halls of Prester John!"
Cho.—So we walked into the palace and the halls of Prester John!

Now the door was one great diamond and the hall a hollow ruby—
Big as Beachy Head, my lads, nay bigger by a half!
And I sees the mate wi' mouth agape, a-staring like a booby,
And the skipper close behind him, with his tongue out like a calf!
Now the way to take it rightly
Was to walk along politely
Just as if you didn't notice—so I couldn't help but laugh!
Cho.—For they both forgot their manners and the crew was bound to laugh!

But he took us through his palace and, my lads, as I'm a sinner,
We walked into an opal like a sunset-colored cloud—
"My dining-room," he says, and, quick as light we saw a dinner

Spread before us by the fingers of a hidden fairy crowd;
And the skipper, swaying gently
After dinner, murmurs faintly,
"I looks to-wards you, Prester John, you've done us very proud!"
Cho.—And we drank his health with honors, for he *done* us very proud!

Then he walks us to his garden where we sees a feathered demon
Very splendid and important on a sort of spicy tree!
"That's the Phœnix," whispers Prester, "which all eddicated seamen
Knows the only one existent, and *he's* waiting for to flee!
When his hundred years expire
Then he'll set hisself a-fire
And another from his ashes rise most beautiful to see!"
Cho.—With wings of rose and emerald most beautiful to see!

Then he says, "In younder forest there's a little silver river,
And whosoever drinks of it, his youth shall never die!
The centuries go by, but Prester John endures for ever
With his music in the mountains and his magic on the sky!
While your hearts are growing colder,
While your world is growing older,
There's a magic in the distance, where the sea-line meets the sky."
Cho.—It shall call to singing seamen till the fount o' song is dry!

So we thought we'd up and seek it, but that forest fair defied us,—
First a crimson leopard laughs at us most horrible to see,
Then a sea-green lion came and sniffed and licked his chops and eyed us,
While a red and yellow unicorn was dancing round a tree!
We was trying to look thinner,
Which was hard, because our dinner
Must ha' made us very tempting to a cat o' high degree!
Cho.—Must ha' made us very tempting to the whole menarjeree!

So we scuttled from that forest and across the poppy meadows
Where the awful shaggy horror brooded o'er us in the dark!
And we pushes out from shore again a-jumping at our shadows,
And pulls away most joyful to the old black barque!
And home again we plodded
While the Polyphemus nodded

With his battered moon-eye winking red and yellow through
the dark.
Cho.—Oh, the moon above the mountains, red and yellow
through the dark!

Across the seas of Wonderland to London-town we blundered,
Forty singing seamen as was puzzled for to know
If the visions that we saw was caused by—here again we
pondered—
A tipple in a vision forty thousand years ago.
Could the grog we *dreamt* we swallowed
Make us *dream* of all that followed?
We were only simple seamen, so of course we didn't know!
Cho.—We were simple singing seamen, so of course we could not
know!

1907

[THOMAS DEKKER'S SONG]

[From *Tales of the Mermaid Tavern*]

Seven wise men on an old black settle,
Seven wise men of the Mermaid Inn,
Ringing blades of the one right metal,
What is the best that a blade can win?
Bread and cheese, and a few small kisses?
Ha! ha! ha! Would you take them—you?
—Ay, if Dame Venus would add to her blisses
A roaring fire and a friend or two!
Chorus: Up now, answer me, tell me true!—
—Ay, if the hussy would add to her blisses
A roaring fire and a friend or two!

What will you say when the world is dying?
What, when the last wild midnight falls
Dark, too dark for the bat to be flying
Round the ruins of old St. Paul's?
What will be last of the lights to perish?
What but the little red ring we knew,
Lighting the hands and the hearts that cherish
A fire, a fire, and a friend or two!
Chorus: Up now, answer me, tell me true!
What will be last of the stars to perish?
—The fire that lighteth a friend or two!

Up now, answer me, on your mettle,
  Wisest man of the Mermaid Inn,
Soberest man on the old black settle,
  Out with the truth! It was never a sin.—
Well, if God saved me alone of the seven,
  Telling me you must be damned, or you,
"This," I would say, "This is hell, not heaven!
  Give me the fire and a friend or two!"
Chorus: Steel was never so ringing true:
    "God," we would say, "this is hell, not heaven!
    Give us the fire, and a friend or two!"

1913

THE SILVER CROOK

I was mistuk, once, for the Poape of Roame . . .
The drawled fantastic words came floating down
Behind me, five long years ago, when last
I left the old shepherd, Bramble, by his fold.
  Bramble was fond, you'll judge, of his own tales,
And cast a gorgeous fly for the unwary:
But I was late, and could not listen then,
Despite his eager leer.
                Yet, many a night,
And many a league from home, out of a dream
Of white chalk coasts, and roofs of Horsham stone,
Colored like russet apples, there would come
Music of sheep-bells, baaing of black-nosed lambs,
Barking of two wise dogs, crushed scents of thyme,
A silver crook, bright as the morning star,
Above the naked downs.
                Then—Bramble's voice,
I was mistuk, once, for the Poape of Roame,
Would almost wake me, wondering what he meant.
  Now, five years later, while the larks went up
Over the dew-ponds in a wild-winged glory,
And all the Sussex downs, from weald to sea,
Were patched like one wide crazy quilt, in squares
Of yellow and crimson, clover and mustard-flower,
Edged with white chalk, I found him once again.
He leaned upon his crook, unbudged by war,
Unchanged, and leering eagerly as of old.

How should I paint old Bramble—the shrewd face,
Brown as the wrinkled loam, the bright brown eyes,
The patriarchal beard, the moleskin cap,
The boots that looked like tree-stumps, the loose cloak
Tanned by all weathers,—every inch of him
A growth of Sussex soil. His back was bent
Like wind-blown hawthorn, turning from the sea,
With roots that strike the deeper.
Well content
With all his world, and boastful as a child,
In splendid innocence of the worldling's way,
Whose murderous ego skulks behind a hedge
Of modest privet,—no, I cannot paint him.
Better to let him talk, and paint himself.
"Marnin'," he said; and swept away five years.
Then, with complete dominion over time,
Waiving all prelude, he picked up the thread
We dropped that day, and cast his bait again:—
I was mistuk, once, for the Poape of Roame.—
"Tell me," I said. "Explain. I've dreamed of it."—
"I rackon you doan't believe it. Drunken Dick,
'Ull tell you 'tis as true's I'm stannin' here.
It happened along of this old silver crook.
I call it silver 'cos it shines so far.
My wife can see it over at Ovingdean
When I'm on Telscombe Tye. They doan't mek crooks
Like this in Sussex now. They've lost the way
To shape 'em. That's what they French papists knowed
Over at Arundel. They tried to buy
My crook, to carry in church. But I woan't sell 'en.
I've heerd there's magic in a crook like this.—
White magic. Well, I rackon it did save Dick
More ways than one, that night, from the old Black Ram.
I've med a song about it. There was once
A Lunnon poet, down here for his health,
Asked me to sing it to 'un, an' I did.
It med him laff, too. 'Sing it again,' he says,
'But go slow, this time.' 'No, I woan't,' I says
(I knowed what *he* was trying). 'No,' I says,
'I woan't go slow. You'll ketch 'un if I do.'
You see, he meks a tedious mort of money
From these here ballad books, an' I wer'n't goin'
To let these Lunnon chuckle-heads suck my brains.

I med it to thet ancient tune you liked,
The Brown Girl. 'Member it?"
Bramble cleared his throat,
Spat at a bee, leaned forward on his crook,
Fixed his brown eyes upon a distant spire,
Solemnly swelled his lungs, once, twice, and thrice;
Then, like an old brown thrush, began to sing:—

"The Devil turns round when he hears the sound
Of bells in a Sussex foald.
One crack, I rackon, from this good crook
Would make old Scratch leave hoald.
They can't shape crooks to-day like mine,
For the liddle folk helped 'em then.
I've heerd some say as they've see'd 'en shine
From Ditchling to Fairlight Glen.

"I loaned 'em a loanst o' my crook one day
To carry in Arundel.
They'd buy 'en to show in their church, they say;
But goald woan't mek me sell.
I never should find a crook so slick,
So silver in the sun;
And, if you talk to Drunken Dick,
He'll tell you what it's done.

"You'll find him spannelling round the Plough;
And, Lord! when Dick was young,
He'd drink enough to draown a cow,
And roughen a tiger's tongue.
He'd drink Black Ram till his noäse turned blue,
And the liddle black mice turned white.
You ask 'en what my crook can do,
An' what he see'd that night.

"He says, as through the fern he ran
('Twas Pharisees' fern, say, I),
A wild potatur, as big as a man,
Arose and winked its eye.
He says it took his arm that night,
And waggled its big brown head,
Then sang: '*This world will never go right*
Till Drunken Dick be dead.'

"He shooked it off and, rambling round,
  Among the goalden gorse,
He heers a kin' of sneering sound
  Pro-ciddin' from a horse,
Which reared upright, then said out loud
  (While Dick said, 'I'll be danged!')
'*His parents will be tedious proud*
  When Drunken Dick is hanged!'

"I rackon 'twould take a barrel of ale,
  Betwix' my dinner and tea,
To mek me see the very nex' thing
  That Drunken Dick did see;
For first he thought 'twas elephants walked
  Behind him on the Tye,
And then he saw fowei ricks of straw
  That heaved against the sky.

"He saw 'em lift. He saw 'em shift.
  He saw gurt beards arise,
He saw 'em slowly lumbering down
  A hundred times his size;
And, as he ran, he heer'd 'em say,
  Whenever his head he turned,
'*This world will never be bright and gay*
  Till Drunken Dick be burned.'

"And then as Dick escaped again
  And squirmed the churchyard through,
The cock that crowns the weather-vane
  Cried '*How d'ye doodle doo?*'
'Why, how d'ye doodle doo?' says Dick,
  'I know why you go round.'
'*There'll be no luck*,' that rooster shruck,
  '*Till Drunken Dick be drowned!*'

"And then, as Dick dodged round they barns,
  And med for the white chalk coast,
He meets Himself, with the two black horns,
  And eyes 'twud mek you roast.
'Walcome! walcome!' old Blackamoor cried,
  ' 'Tis muttonless day in hell,
So I think I'll have your kidneys, fried,
  And a bit of your liver as well.'

"Then Dick he loosed a tarr'ble shout,
And the Devil stopped dead to look;
And the sheep-bells rang, and the moon came out,
And it shone on my silver crook.
'I rackon,' says Dick, 'if you're oald Nick,
You'd batter be scramblin' home;
For *those* be the ringers of Arundel,
And *that* is the Poape of Roame.' "

1920

James Stephens

James Stephens, the son of poor Irish parents, was born in Dublin in February, 1882. He received little formal education, being thrown at an early age on his own resources and compelled to make a living. He married, became the father of two children, and supported his family by working as a typist in the office of a solicitor. In his spare time, however, he began to write verse and prose, but at first he offered only the prose to editors. Some of his articles, "Jottings of a Philosopher," were published in a magazine to which G. W. Russell (A. E.) was contributing poetry; and wishing to have Russell's opinion of his verse before attempting to sell it, Stephens sent him half a dozen poems and asked to be told if they were any good. In reply he received an invitation to Russell's home on the following Sunday evening, and arrived to find half the celebrities of Dublin there to hear him read his poetry. This marked the beginning of his literary success. He made the acquaintance of publishers and became an accepted member of the literary circle in Dublin. Soon, at the instance of Russell and others, he was appointed Assistant to the Director of the National Gallery of Ireland, and was able to give up his clerical position with the solicitor.

In 1909 he published two volumes of poetry, *Insurrections* and *The Lonely God and Other Poems,* and in 1912 another volume of poetry, *The Hill of Vision,* and two prose works, *The Charwoman's Daughter,* a novel, and *The Crock of Gold,* an elaboration of his early "Jottings of a Philosopher." For the latter he was awarded the Edmond de Polignac prize in 1913. He now took his family to Paris, and while living there published a book of sketches and verse, *Here Are Ladies* (1913). Since 1912 he has published eight or nine volumes of poetry. He says jestingly that he is the only real poet living, because he writes poetry only when he feels an impelling urge to do so, while others write because they have a reputation to sustain or for some other considered reason. Among his later prose works are *The Demi-Gods* (1914), a highly imaginative novel; *Deirdre* (1923), for which he received the Tailltean Gold Medal; *In the Land of Youth* (1924), an adaptation of the old bardic tales of Ireland; and *Etched in Moonlight* (1928), a volume of short stories. He has also edited, or assisted in editing, several volumes of poetry.

Stephens is a cosmopolite. He has a home in London, but uses it "as a place to take off from" rather than to live in. He spends some of his time in Dublin, but is frequently in the United States, where he is much in demand as a lecturer.

WHAT TOMAS SAID IN A PUB

I saw God! Do you doubt it?
Do you dare to doubt it?
I saw the Almighty Man! His hand
Was resting on a mountain! And
He looked upon the World, and all about it:
I saw Him plainer than you see me now
—You mustn't doubt it!

He was not satisfied;
His look was all dissatisfied!
His beard swung on a wind, far out of sight
Behind the world's curve! And there was light
Most fearful from His forehead! And He sighed
—That star went always wrong, and from the start
I was dissatisfied!—

He lifted up His hand!
I say He heaved a dreadful hand
Over the spinning earth! Then I said,—Stay,
You must not strike it, God! I'm in the way!
And I will never move from where I stand!—
He said,—Dear child, I feared that you were dead,—
. . . And stayed His hand!

1909

CHILL OF THE EVE

A long green swell
Slopes soft to the sea;
And a far-off bell
Swings sweet to me;
As the grey
Chill day
Slips away
From the lea.

Spread cold and far,
Without one glow
From a mild pale star,
Is the sky's steel bow;
And the grey
Chill day
Slips away
Below.

Yon green tree grieves
To the air around;
And the whispering leaves
Have a lonely sound;
As the grey
Chill day
Slips away
From the ground.

And dark, more dark,
The shades settle down;
Far off is a spark
From the lamp-lit town;
And the grey
Chill day
Slips away
With a frown.

1909

HATE

My enemy came nigh;
And I
Stared fiercely in his face:
My lips went writhing back in a grimace,
And stern I watched him from a narrowed eye:
Then, as I turned away,
My enemy,
That bitter-heart, and savage, said to me:

—Some day, when this is past;
When all the arrows that we have are cast;
We may ask one another why we hate?
And fail to find a story to relate:
It may seem to us, then, a mystery
That we could hate each other—
Thus said he; and did not turn away;
Waiting to hear what I might have to say!

But I fled quickly: fearing, if I stayed,
I might have kissed him, as I would a maid.

1909

THE SHELL

I

And then I pressed the shell
Close to my ear,
And listened well.

And straightway, like a bell,
Came low and clear
The slow, sad murmur of far distant seas,

Whipped by an icy breeze
Upon a shore
Wind-swept and desolate.

It was a sunless strand that never bore
The footprint of a man,
Nor felt the weight

Since time began
Of any human quality or stir,
Save what the dreary winds and wave incur.

II

And in the hush of waters was the sound
Of pebbles, rolling round;
For ever rolling, with a hollow sound:

And bubbling sea-weeds, as the waters go,
Swish to and fro
Their long cold tentacles of slimy grey;

There was no day;
Nor ever came a night
Setting the stars alight

To wonder at the moon:
Was twilight only, and the frightened croon,
Smitten to whimpers, of the dreary wind

And waves that journeyed blind . . .
And then I loosed my ear.—Oh, it was sweet
To hear a cart go jolting down the street!

1909

OPTIMIST

I

All ye that labor! Every broken man
Bending beneath his load! Each tired heart
That cannot quit its burden! All the clan
Black-browed and fierce, who feel the smart

Of fortune's lances, wayward, uncontrolled!
All ye who writhe in silence 'neath the sin
That no man knows about! And ye that sold
The freedom of your souls if ye might win

A little ease from strife, and hate the thing
That bought it! Ye that droop, trembling with pain,

And hunger-haunted, lacking everything
That dignifies existence, and are fain

To lay ye down and die! Hear the behest
—All ye that labor, come to Me, and rest—

II

Let ye be still, ye tortured ones! Nor strive
Where striving's futile! Ye can ne'er attain
To lay your burdens down! All things alive
Must bear the woes of life, and if the pain

Be more than ye can bear, then ye can die!
That is the law! And bootless 'tis to seek
In the deeps of space; beyond the high
Pearl-tincted clouds; out where the moon doth peak

Her silver horns; for all that vastness bows
To Tyrant Toil, and weeps to find
Somewhere an aid. Be ye patient! Rouse
Your shoulders to the load to ye assigned,

And dree your weird! Be sure ye shall not moan
Stretched in the narrow bed, beneath the stone!

III

Lo, we are mocked with fancies! And we stretch
Our unavailing arms to anywhere
Where help is none. The north wind will not fetch
An answer to our cries! Nor on the air,

Fanned by the south wind's fan, is friend or aid!
What then is left, but this—that we be brave,
And steadfast in our places! Not afraid
However fell our lot! And we will lave

Us deep in human waters, till the mind
Grows wise and kindly, and we haply steal
A paradise from Nature. Naught can bind
Man closer unto man than that he feel

The trouble of his comrade! So we grope
Through courage, truth, and kindness, back to Hope.

1909

DANCE

(1)

Left and right and swing around!
Soar and dip and fall for glee!
Happy sky, and bird, and ground!
Happy wind, and happy tree!

Happy minions, dancing mad!
Joy is guide enough for you;
Cure the world of good and bad;
And teach us innocence anew!

(2)

Good and bad and right and wrong!
Wave the silly words away!
This is wisdom—to be strong!
This is virtue—to be gay!

Let us sing and dance, until
We shall know the final art;
How to banish good and ill
With the laughter of the heart!

1912

BESSIE BOBTAIL

As down the road she wambled slow,
She had not got a place to go:
She had not got a place to fall
And rest herself—no place at all!
She stumped along, and wagged her pate;
And said a thing was desperate.

Her face was screwed and wrinkled tight
Just like a nut—and, left and right,
On either side, she wagged her head
And said a thing; and what she said
Was desperate as any word
That ever yet a person heard.

I walked behind her for a while,
And watched the people nudge and smile:
But ever, as she went, she said,
As left and right she swung her head,
—O God He knows: And, God He knows!
And, surely God Almighty knows!

1912

WHY TOMAS CAM WAS GRUMPY

If I were rich what would I do?
I'd leave the horse just ready to shoe;
I'd leave the pail beside the cow;
I'd leave the furrow beneath the plough;
I'd leave the ducks, tho' they should quack,
"Our eggs will be stolen before you're back";
I'd buy a diamond brooch, a ring,
A chain of gold that I would fling
Around her neck. . . . Ah, what an itch,
If I were rich!

What would I do if I were wise?
I would not debate about the skies;
Nor would I try a book to write;
Or find the wrong in the tangled right;
I would not debate with learned men
Of how, and what, and why, and when;
—I'd train my tongue to a linnet's song,
I'd learn the words that couldn't go wrong—
And then I'd say . . . And win the prize,
If I were wise!

But I'm not that nor t'other, I bow
My back to the work that's waiting now:
I'll shoe the horse that's standing ready;
I'll milk the cow if she'll be steady;
I'll follow the plough that turns the loam;
I'll watch the ducks don't lay from home:
—And I'll curse, and curse, and curse again
Till the devil joins in with his big amen;
And none but he and I will wot
When the heart within me starts to rot;

To fester and churn its ugly brew
. . . Where's my spade! I've work to do!

1912

SHAME

I was ashamed! I dared not lift my eyes!
I could not bear to look upon the skies!
What I had done! sure, everybody knew!
From everywhere hands pointed where I stood,
And scornful eyes were piercing through and through
The moody armor of my hardihood!

I heard their voices too, each word an asp
That buzz'd and stung me sudden as a flame!
And all the world was jolting on my name!
And now and then there came a wicked rasp
Of laughter, jarring me to deeper shame!

And then I looked, and there was no one nigh!
No eyes that stabbed like swords or glinted sly!
No laughter creaking on the silent air!
—And then I saw that I was all alone
Facing my soul! And next I was aware
That this mad mockery was all my own!

1912

WHAT THE DEVIL SAID

It was night time! God, the Father Good,
Weary of praises, on a sudden stood
From His great Throne, and leaned upon the sky:
For He had heard a sound; a little cry,
Thin as a whisper, climbing up the Steep.

And so He looked to where the Earth, asleep,
Rocked with the moon: He saw the whirling sea
Swing round the world in surgent energy,
Tangling the moonlight in its netted foam;
And, nearer, saw the white and fretted dome
Of the ice-capped pole spin back again a ray
To whistling stars, bright as a wizard's day.

But these He passed, with eyes intently wide,
Till, closer still, the mountains He espied
Squatting tremendous on the broad-backed Earth,
Each nursing twenty rivers at a birth!
And then, minutely, sought He for the cry
That had climbed the slant of space so hugely high.

He found it in a ditch outside a town:
A tattered hungry woman, crouching down
By a dead babe—So there was nought to do,
For what is done is done! And sad He drew
Back to His Heaven of ivory and gold:
And, as He sat, all suddenly there rolled,
From where the woman wept upon the sod,
Satan's deep voice—*O thou unhappy God!*

1912

A WOMAN IS A BRANCHY TREE

A woman is a branchy tree
And man a singing wind;
And from her branches carelessly
He takes what he can find:

Then wind and man go far away,
While winter comes with loneliness;
With cold, and rain, and slow decay,
On woman and on tree till they

Droop to the earth again, and be
A withered woman, a withered tree;
While wind and man woo in the glade
Another tree, another maid.

1912

SWEET APPLE

At the end of the bough!
At the top of the tree!
—As fragrant, as high,
And as lovely, as thou—

One sweet apple reddens,
Which all men may see,
—At the end of the bough!

Swinging full to the view!
Though the harvesters now
Overlook it, repass it,
And pass busily:
Overlook it!
Nay, pluck it!
They do not know how!

For it swings out of reach
Like a cloud! And as free
As a star; or thy beauty,
That seems too, I vow,
Remote as the sweet apple swinging
—Ah me!
At the end of the bough!

1913

DEIRDRE

Do not let any woman read this verse!
It is for men, and after them their sons,
And their sons' sons!

The time comes when our hearts sink utterly;
When we remember Deirdre, and her tale,
And that her lips are dust.

Once she did tread the earth: men took her hand;
They looked into her eyes and said their say,
And she replied to them.

More than two thousand years it is since she
Was beautiful: she trod the waving grass;
She saw the clouds.

Two thousand years! The grass is still the same;
The clouds as lovely as they were that time
When Deirdre was alive.

But there has been again no woman born
Who was so beautiful; not one so beautiful
Of all the women born.

Let all men go apart and mourn together!
No man can ever love her! Not a man
Can dream to be her lover!

No man can bend before her! No man say—
What could one say to her? There are no words
That one could say to her!

Now she is but a story that is told
Beside the fire! No man can ever be
The friend of that poor queen!

1915

THE GOAT PATHS

The crooked paths go every way
  Upon the hill—they wind about
  Through the heather, in and out
Of a quiet sunniness.
And the goats, day after day,
  Stray in sunny quietness,
Cropping here and cropping there,
  As they pause and turn and pass,
Now a bit of heather spray,
  Now a mouthful of the grass.

In the deeper sunniness,
  In the place where nothing stirs,
Quietly in quietness,
  In the quiet of the furze,
They stand a while; they dream; they lie;
They stare upon the roving sky.

If you approach they run away,
  They will stare and stamp and bound,
  With a sudden angry sound,
To the sunny quietude:

To crouch again where nothing stirs
In the quiet of the furze,
To crouch them down again and brood
In the sunny solitude.

Were I but as free as they
I would stray away and brood,
I would beat a hidden way
Through the quiet heather spray
To a sunny solitude;
And should you come I'd run away,
I would make an angry sound,
I would stare and stamp and bound
To the deeper quietude,
To the place where nothing stirs
In the quiet of the furze.

In that airy quietness
I would dream as long as they;
Through the quiet sunniness
I would stray away and brood
All among the heather spray
In a sunny solitude.

I would think until I found
Something I can never find,
Something lying on the ground,
In the bottom of my mind.

1915

THE WASTE PLACES

As a naked man I go
Through the desert sore afraid,
Holding up my head, although
I am as frightened as a maid.

The couching lion there I saw
From barren rocks lift up his eye,
He parts the cactus with his paw,
He stares at me as I go by.

He would follow on my trace
 If he knew I was afraid,
If he knew my hardy face
 Hides the terrors of a maid.

In the night he rises, and
 He stretches forth, he snuffs the air,
He roars and leaps along the sand,
 He creeps and watches everywhere.

His burning eyes, his eyes of bale,
 Through the darkness I can see;
He lashes fiercely with his tail,
 He would love to spring at me.

I am the lion in his lair,
 I am the fear that frightens me,
I am the desert of despair,
 And the nights of agony.

Night or day, whate'er befall,
 I must walk that desert land,
Until I can dare to call
 The lion out to lick my hand.

1915

THE SNARE

I hear a sudden cry of pain!
There is a rabbit in a snare:
Now I hear the cry again,
But I cannot tell from where.

But I cannot tell from where
He is calling out for aid!
Crying on the frightened air,
Making everything afraid!

Making everything afraid!
Wrinkling up his little face!
As he cries again for aid;
—And I cannot find the place!

And I cannot find the place
Where his paw is in the snare!
Little One! Oh, Little One!
I am searching everywhere!

1915

BARBARIANS

I pause beside the stream, and hear
The waters talking on the way;
If I had a proper ear
I could tell you what they say!

Yon lovely tree against the sky,
Which the sun first rests upon,
Has a message for my eye;
If I had a proper one!

On the golden heath a wind,
Whispered to me as I stood;
If I had a proper mind
I could answer, so I could!

I am deaf and dumb and blind!
No reply can I invent
When a stream, a tree, a wind,
Asks am I intelligent!

1915

ETCHED IN FROST

The corn is down,
The stooks are gone,
The fields are brown,
And the early dawn
Grows slowly behind
Where the mountains frown,
And a thin white sun
Is shivering down.

There isn't a leaf,
Nor anything green,
To aid belief
That summer has been;
And the puffed-up red-breast
(Ball o' Grief)
Hops at the window
For relief.

The cows are in byre,
The sheep in fold;
The mare and the sire
Are safe from cold;
The hens are sheltered,
In wood and wire,
And the sheep-dog snoozes
Before the fire.

The farmer can grin,
And rub his hands,
For his crops are in
From the resting lands;
And his wheat is stored
In the oaken bin,
And his buxom wife
Makes merry within.

1915

AUTUMN

(1)

It may be on a quiet mountain-top,
Or in a valley folding among hills
You take your path; and often you will stop

To hear the chattering of pleasant rills;
The piping of a wind in branches green;
The murmuring of widely-lifted spray

As the long boughs swing; or hear the twittering
Of drowsy birds, when the great sun is seen
Climbing the steep of darkness to the day.

(2)

The lovely moon trailing a silver dress
By quiet waters! Each living star
Moving apart in holy quietness,

Sphere over golden sphere, moving afar,
These I can see:
And the unquiet zone,

Rolling in snow along the edge of sight:
The world is fair indeed; and I am free
To see its beauty; and to be

In solitude; and quite forget, and quite
Lose out of memory all I have known
But this.

(3)

Straying apart in sad and mournful way;
Alone, or with my heart for company:
Keeping the tone of a dejected day,

And a bewilderment that came to me;
I said—The Spring will never come again,
And there is the end of everything—

Day after day
The sap will ebb away,
From the great tree,

And, when the sap is gone,
All piteously
She'll tumble to the clay:

And we say only—Such, or such a one
Had pleasant shade
But there is end of her—

(4)

And you, and even you, the year
Will drain and dry,
And make to disappear!

Then in my heart there came so wild a stir;
And such great pity and astonishment;
And such a start of fear and woe had I,

That where I went I did not know!
And only this did know,
That you could die!

(5)

I would have liked to sing from fuller throat
To you who sang so well; but here I stay,
Resting the music on a falling note;

And hear it die away, and die away,
With beauty unrehearsed,
And life and love unsung.

For I had clung,
—With what of laughter and of eagerness!—
Unto the hope that I might chance to be

Master of Song! And, singing, be no less
Than those great poets of antiquity,
Who sang of clouds and hills; of stars and clods;

Of trees and streams; and the mind and soul of man;
And chaunted too the universal gods,
And love that is or ever time began;

And did not fail before a theme
Although
It passed the reason.

(6)

I heard a bird sing in the woods to-day
A failing song:
The times had caught on him!

In autumn boughs he tried a wonted lay;
And was abashed to find his music grim
As the crow's song.

Then, when I raised an air
To comfort him,
I wretched was to hear

The crow did croak
And chatter everywhere
Within my ear.

(7)

And so,
Behold!
I am a saddened elf!

And, as a deer
Flies timidly to shade,
I fly to laughter and I hide myself!

And couch me in the coverts that I made
Against those bold ambitions,
And forswear

The palm, the prize, or what of gear instead
A poet gets with his appointed share
Of beer and bread.

(8)

Upon the grass I drop this tuneful reed,
And turn from it aside! And turn from more
That I had fancied to be mine indeed,
Beyond all reclamation. See the door

Set in the boundary wall yawns windily!
It will be shut when I have wandered through!
And open will no more again for me
This side of life, whatever thing I do!

And so good-bye! And so good-night to you!
And farewell all! Behold the lifted hand!
And the long last look upon the view!
And the last glimpse of that most lovely land!

And thus away unto the mundane sphere,
And look not back again nor turn anew,

And hear no more that laughter at the ear!
And sing no more to you.

1916

THE WAVE OF CLIONA

AFTER O'RAHILLY

My heart is withered and my health is gone!
For they, who were not easy put upon,
Masters of mirth, and of fair clemency,
Masters of wealth, and gentle charity,
They are all gone!

Mac Carthy Mor is dead!
Mac Carthy of the Lee is finishèd
Mac Carthy of Kanturk joined clay to clay,
And gat him gone, and bides as deep as they!

Their years, their gentle deeds, their flags are furled!
And deeply down, under the stiffened world,
In oaken chests are kings and princes thrust,
To crumble, day by day, into the dust
A mouth might puff at! Nor is left a trace
Of those who did of grace all that was grace!

O Wave of Cliona, cease thy bellowing!
And let mine ears forget a while to ring
At thy long, lamentable misery!
The great are dead indeed! The great are dead!
And I, in little time, will stoop my head
And put it under, and will be forgot
With them, and be with them, and, thus, be not!

Ease thee! Cease thy long keening! Cry no more!
End is! And here is end! And end is sore!
And to all lamentation be there end!

If I might come on thee, O howling friend!
Knowing that sails were drumming on the sea
Westward to Eire, and that help would be
Trampling for her upon a Spanish deck,
I'd ram thy lamentation down thy neck.

1918

LITTLE THINGS

Little things, that run, and quail,
And die, in silence and despair!

Little things, that fight, and fail,
And fall, on sea, and earth, and air!

All trapped and frightened little things,
The mouse, the coney, hear our prayer!

As we forgive those done to us,
—The lamb, the linnet, and the hare—

Forgive us all our trespasses,
Little creatures, everywhere!

1924

ON A LONELY SPRAY

Under a lonely sky a lonely tree
Is beautiful! All that is loneliness
Is beautiful! A feather, lost at sea;
A staring owl; a moth; a yellow tress
Of seaweed on a rock, is beautiful!

The night-lit moon, wide-wandering in sky!
A blue-bright spark, where ne'er a cloud is up!
A wing, where no wing is, it is so high!
A bee in winter! and a buttercup,
Late blown! are lonely, and are beautiful!

She, whom you saw but once, and saw no more!
That he, who startled you, and went away!
The eye that watched you from a cottage door!
The first leaf, and the last! The break of day!
The mouse, the cuckoo, and the cloud, are beautiful!

For all that is, is lonely! All that may
Will be as lonely as is that you see!
The lonely heart sings on a lonely spray!

The lonely soul swings lonely in the sea;
And all that loneliness is beautiful!

All: all alone: and all without a part
Is beautiful! for beauty is all where!
Where is an eye, is beauty! Where an heart,
Is beauty, brooding out, on empty air,
All that is lonely, and is beautiful!

1925

THE PIT OF BLISS

When I was young
I dared to sing
Of everything,
And anything!
Of joy, and woe, and fate, and God!
Of dreaming cloud, and teeming sod!
Of hill, that thrust an amber spear
Into the sunset! And the sheer
Precipice that shakes the soul
To its black gape—I sang the whole
Of God and Man, nor sought to know
Man, or God, or Joy, or Woe!
And, though an older wight I be,
My soul hath still such Ecstasy
That, on a pulse, I sing and sing
Of Everything, and Anything!

There is a Light
Shines in the head:
It is not gold,
It is not red,
But, as the lightning's blinding light,
It is a stare of silver white
That one surmise might fancy blue!
On that mind-blinding hue I gaze
An instant, and am in a maze
Of thinking—could one call it so?
It is no thinking that I know!
—An hurricane of Knowing, that
Could whelm the soul that was not pat

To flinch, and lose the deadly thing;
—And Sing, and Sing again, and Sing
Of Everything, and Anything!

An Eagle
Whirling up the sky;
Sunblind! Dizzy!
Urging high,
And higher beating yet a wing,
Until he can no longer cling,
Or hold; or do a thing, but fall,
And sink, and whirl, and scream, through all
His dizzy, heaven-hell of Pit,
In mile-a-minute flight from It
That he had dared! From height of height,
So the poet takes his flight
And tumble in the Pit of Bliss!
And, in the roar of that Abyss,
And falling, he will Sing and Sing
Of Everything, and Anything!

What is Knowing?
'Tis to see!
What is Feeling?
'Tis to be!
What is Love? But, more and more,
To See and Be! To be a Pour
And Avalanche of Being, till
Being ceases, and is still
For very motion—What is Joy?
—Being, past all earthly cloy
And intermixture! Being spun
Of itself is Being won
That is Joy—And this is God,
To be That, in cloud and clod!
And, in cloud, and clod, to Sing
Of Everything, and Anything!

1925

CHRISTMAS IN FREELANDS[1]

The Red-Bud, the Kentucky Tree,
Bloomed the spring to life for me
In Freelands; and the Mocking Bird
—Nimble chorister of glee,
Sweet as poet ever heard
In a world of ecstasy—
Sang the summer, and the sun;
Sang the summer in to me.

The spring is gone! The summer gone!
The Cardinal has gone away!
The fire-flies, dancing on the lawn,
—Each a little moon at play—
Are gone, with summer, gone away!
And, where green acres were aglow,
Daisy munches in the snow!

A snowy field! A stable piled
With straw! A donkey's sleepy pow!
A mother beaming on a child!
A manger, and a munching cow!
—These we all remember now—
And airy voices, heard afar!
And three Magicians, and a Star!

Two thousand times of snow declare
That on the Christmas of the year
There is a singing in the air;
And all who listen for it hear
A fairy chime, a seraph strain,
Telling He is born again,
—That all we love is born again.

1925

[1] Freelands is the name of a country estate near Cincinnati, at which Stephens has been a frequent guest. This poem was originally used as a Christmas card.

Siegfried Sassoon

Siegfried Loraine Sassoon, second of the three sons of Alfred and Theresa Thornycroft Sassoon, was born September 8, 1886, at Matfield, Kent. His father, a sculptor, came of a Jewish family of much wealth and influence in both business and politics. His mother's family was also prominent: one brother was a shipbuilder, and she and both her parents were well-known sculptors. Four years before his father's death in 1895, his parents separated, and the children were brought up by their mother.

Until he was nine he had little schooling; then for five years he was taught by tutors and a German governess. In April, 1900, he was sent to The New Beacon, a school at Sevenoaks, and was there until the end of 1901. From January, 1902, till the end of the summer term, 1904, he attended Marlborough, but was absent twice for long periods on account of illness: double pneumonia and a strained heart and ophthalmia. He then went to a "cramming school" for a year to get ready for the University, and in 1905 entered Clare College, Cambridge. Here he started in law, but his poor preparation made him give this up; he then tried history with little better results; and after a year and a half, he left the University. Of this step, he says, "Unmethodical through lack of training and by temperament, I had always been a slow and groping learner, and when confronted by a mass of text-book information I became helpless and unintelligent, and my brain rebelled at being loaded up with knowledge which I felt could be of no possible use to it. If I couldn't be an imaginative writer, I thought, I would rather be a ploughman—or at any rate watch other people ploughing, and write poems about it." [1]

He began writing verse when a child, being encouraged by his

[1] *The Old Century and Seven More Years*, p. 274.

mother; and by the time he was eleven, he had decided to be a poet, and started reading Longfellow, Tennyson, and Shelley as models. His first book—a volume of thirty-six pages—was printed privately and anonymously at Christmas, 1906. He spent the next few years in acquiring the skills of a poet, occasionally issuing a privately-printed, limited edition of his verse, and occupying his spare time with such sports as cricket and fox-hunting.

At the outbreak of World War I he enlisted and became a captain with the Royal Welsh Fusiliers. While attacking in the Hindenburg Line sector in 1917, he was shot in the throat. After recovering, he served in Palestine, and again in France, where he was wounded a second time. For rescuing wounded soldiers under fire, he was awarded the Military Cross; and he later declined the D. S. O. because of a growing sense of the futility of war. His first regularly published volume, *The Old Huntsman* (1917), included poems indicative of his hatred of war; and his next book, *Counter-Attack* (1918), was a bitter indictment of war and those responsible for it.

After the War, he was for a time a journalist, and in 1920 he made a lecture tour in the United States. Although continuing to write poetry, he has given more time in recent years to prose, of which his best works are an autobiography, *The Old Century and Seven More Years* (1938), and a fiction trilogy: *Memoirs of a Fox-Hunting Man* (1928), *Memoirs of an Infantry Officer* (1930), and *Sherstone's Progress* (1936). For *The Fox-Hunting Man* he was awarded the Hawthornden Prize and the James Tate Black Prize as writer of the best book of the year; and in 1930 he received the Benson Medal of the Royal Society of Literature. In 1931 Liverpool University gave him an honorary D. Litt. degree.

He married Hester, daughter of Sir Stephen Gatty, in December, 1933, and they have one son. They live at Heytesbury, Wiltshire.

MORNING GLORY

In this meadow starred with spring
Shepherds kneel before their king.
Mary throned, with dreaming eyes,
Gowned in blue like rain-washed skies,

Lifts her tiny son that he
May behold their courtesy.
And green-smocked children, awed and good,
Bring him blossoms from the wood.

Clear the sunlit steeples chime
Mary's coronation-time.
Loud the happy children quire
To the golden-windowed morn;
While the lord of their desire
Sleeps below the crimson thorn.

1916

THE OLD HUNTSMAN

I've never ceased to curse the day I signed
A seven years' bargain for the Golden Fleece.
'Twas a bad deal all round; and dear enough
It cost me, what with my daft management,
And the mean folk as owed and never paid me,
And backing losers; and the local bucks
Egging me on with whiskies while I bragged
The man I was when huntsman to the Squire.

I'd have been prosperous if I'd took a farm
Of seventy acres, drove my gig and haggled
At Monday markets; now I've squandered all
My savings; nigh three hundred pound I got
As testimonial when I'd grown too stiff
And slow to press a beaten fox.
The Fleece!
'Twas the damned Fleece that wore my Emily out,
The wife of thirty years who served me well;
(Not like this beldam clattering in the kitchen,
That never trims a lamp nor sweeps the floor,
And brings me greasy soup in a foul crock.)

Blast the old harridan! What's fetched her now,
Leaving me in the dark, and short of fire?
And where's my pipe? 'Tis lucky I've a turn
For thinking, and remembering all that's past.
And now's my hour, before I hobble to bed,

To set the works a-wheezing, wind the clock
That keeps the time of life with feeble tick
Behind my bleared old face that stares and wonders.

* * * * *

It's queer how, in the dark, comes back to mind
Some morning of September. We've been digging
In a steep, sandy warren, riddled with holes,
And I've just pulled the terrier out and left
A sharp-nosed cub-face blinking there and snapping,
Then in a moment seen him mobbed and torn
To strips in the baying hurly of the pack.
I picture it so clear: the dusty sunshine
On bracken, and the men with spades, that wipe
Red faces: one tilts up a mug of ale.
And, having stooped to clean my gory hands,
I whistle the jostling beauties out o' the wood.

I'm but a daft old fool! I often wish
The Squire were back again—ah, he was a man!
They don't breed men like him these days; he'd come
For sure, and sit and talk and suck his briar
Till the old wife brings up a dish of tea.

Ay, those were days, when I was serving Squire!
I never knowed such sport as '85,
The winter afore the one that snowed us silly.

* * * * *

Once in a way the parson will drop in
And read a bit o' the Bible, if I'm bad,—
Pray the Good Lord to make my spirit whole
In faith: he leaves some 'baccy on the shelf,
And wonders I don't keep a dog to cheer me,
Because he knows I'm mortal fond of dogs!

I ask you, what's a gent like that to me,
As wouldn't know Elijah if I saw him,
Nor have the wit to keep him on the talk?
'Tis kind of parson to be troubling still
With such as me; but he's a town-bred chap,
Full of his college notions and Christmas hymns.

Religion beats me. I'm amazed at folk
Drinking the gospels in and never scratching
Their heads for questions. When I was a lad
I learned a bit from mother, and never thought
To educate myself for prayers and psalms.
But now I'm old and bald and serious-minded,
With days to sit and ponder. I'd no chance
When young and gay to get the hang of all
This Hell and Heaven: and when the clergy hoick
And holloa from their pulpits, I'm asleep,
However hard I listen; and when they pray
It seems we're all like children sucking sweets
In school, and wondering whether master sees.

I used to dream of Hell when I was first
Promoted to a huntsman's job, and scent
Was rotten, and all the foxes disappeared,
And hounds were short of blood; and officers
From barracks over-rode 'em all day long
On weedy, whistling nags that knocked a hole
In every fence; good sportsmen to a man
And brigadiers by now, but dreadful hard
On a young huntsman keen to show some sport.

Ay, Hell was thick with captains, and I rode
The lumbering brute that's beat in half a mile,
And blunders into every blind old ditch.
Hell was the coldest scenting land I've known,
And both my whips were always lost, and hounds
Would never get their heads down; and a man
On a great yawing chestnut trying to cast 'em
While I was in a corner pounded by
The ugliest hog-backed stile you've clapped your eyes on.
There was an iron-spiked fence round all the coverts,
And civil-spoken keepers I couldn't trust,
And the main earth unstopp'd. The fox I found
Was always a three-legged 'un from a bag
Who reeked of aniseed and wouldn't run.
The farmers were all ploughing their old pasture
And bellowing at me when I rode their beans
To cast for beaten fox, or galloped on
With hounds to a lucky view. I'd lost my voice
Although I shouted fit to burst my guts,
And couldn't blow my horn.

And when I woke,
Emily snored, and barn-cocks started crowing,
And morn was at the window; and I was glad
To be alive because I heard the cry
Of hounds like church-bells chiming on a Sunday,—
Ay, that's the song I'd wish to hear in Heaven!
The cry of hounds was Heaven for me: I know
Parson would call me crazed and wrong to say it,
But where's the use of life and being glad
If God's not in your gladness?

I've no brains
For book-learned studies; but I've heard men say
There's much in print that clergy have to wink at:
Though many I've met were jolly chaps, and rode
To hounds, and walked me puppies; and could pick
Good legs and loins and necks and shoulders, ay,
And feet,—'twas necks and feet I looked at first.

Some hounds I've known were wise as half your saints,
And better hunters. That old dog of the Duke's,
Harlequin; what a dog he was to draw!
And what a note he had, and what a nose
When foxes ran down wind and scent was catchy!
And that light lemon bitch of the Squire's, old Dorcas,—
She were a marvellous hunter, were old Dorcas!
Ay, oft I've thought: "If there were hounds in Heaven,
With God as Master, taking no subscription;
And all His blessèd country farmed by tenants;
And a straight-necked old fox in every gorse!"
But when I came to work it out, I found
There'd be too many huntsmen wanting places,—
Though some I've known might get a job with Nick!

* * * * *

I've come to think of God as something like
The figure of a man the old Duke was
When I was turning hounds to Nimrod King,
Before his Grace was took so bad with gout,
And had to quit the saddle. Tall and spare,
Clean-shaved and grey, with shrewd, kind eyes, that twinkled,
And easy walk; who, when he gave good words,
Gave them whole-hearted; and would never blame
Without just cause. Lord God might be like that,

Sitting alone in a great room of books
Some evening after hunting.

Now I'm tired
With hearkening to the tick-tack on the shelf;
And pondering makes me doubtful.

Riding home
On a moonless night of cloud that feels like frost
Though stars are hidden (hold your feet up, horse!),
And thinking what a task I had to draw
A pack with all those lame 'uns, and the lot
Wanting a rest from all this open weather,—
That's what I'm doing now.

And likely, too,
The frost'll be a long 'un, and the night
One sleep. The parsons say we'll wake to find
A country blinding-white with dazzle of snow.

The naked stars make men feel lonely,—wheeling
And glinting on the puddles in the road.
And then you listen to the wind, and wonder
If folk are quite such bucks as they appear
When dressed by London tailors, looking down
Their boots at covert side, and thinking big.

* * * * *

This world's a funny place to live in. Soon
I'll need to change my country; but I know
'Tis little enough I've understood my life,
And a power of sights I've missed, and foreign marvels.

I used to feel it, riding on spring days
In meadows pied with sun and chasing clouds,
And half forget how I was there to catch
The foxes; lose the angry, eager feeling
A huntsman ought to have, that's out for blood,
And means his hounds to get it!

Now I know
It's God that speaks to us when we're bewitched,
Smelling the hay in June and smiling quiet;

Or when there's been a spell of summer drought,
Lying awake and listening to the rain.

* * * * *

I'd like to be the simpleton I was
In the old days when I was whipping-in
To a little harrier-pack in Worcestershire,
And loved a dairymaid, but never knew it
Until she'd wed another. So I've loved
My life; and when the good years are gone down,
Discover what I've lost.
I never broke
Out of my blundering self into the world,
But let it all go past me, like a man
Half-asleep in a land that's full of wars.

What a grand thing 'twould be if I could go
Back to the kennels now and take my hounds
For summer exercise; be riding out
With forty couple when the quiet skies
Are streaked with sunrise, and the silly birds
Grown hoarse with singing; cobwebs on the furze
Up on the hill, and all the country strange,
With no one stirring; and the horses fresh,
Sniffing the air I'll never breathe again.

* * * * *

You've brought the lamp then, Martha? I've no mind
For newspaper to-night, nor bread and cheese.
Give me the candle, and I'll get to bed.

1917

A WORKING PARTY

Three hours ago he blundered up the trench,
Sliding and poising, groping with his boots;
Sometimes he tripped and lurched against the walls
With hands that pawed the sodden bags of chalk.
He couldn't see the man who walked in front;
Only he heard the drum and rattle of feet
Stepping along the trench-boards,—often splashing
Wretchedly where the sludge was ankle-deep.

Voices would grunt, "Keep to your right,—make way!"
When squeezing past the men from the front-line:
White faces peered, puffing a point of red;
Candles and braziers glinted through the chinks
And curtain-flaps of dug-outs; then the gloom
Swallowed his sense of sight; he stooped and swore
Because a sagging wire had caught his neck.
A flare went up; the shining whiteness spread
And flickered upward, showing nimble rats,
And mounds of glimmering sand-bags, bleached with rain;
Then the slow, silver moment died in dark.
The wind came posting by with chilly gusts
And buffeting at corners, piping thin
And dreary through the crannies; rifle-shots
Would split and crack and sing along the night,
And shells came calmly through the drizzling air
To burst with hollow bang below the hill.

Three hours ago he stumbled up the trench;
Now he will never walk that road again:
He must be carried back, a jolting lump
Beyond all need of tenderness and care;
A nine-stone corpse with nothing more to do.

He was a young man with a meagre wife
And two pale children in a Midland town;
He showed the photograph to all his mates;
And they considered him a decent chap
Who did his work and hadn't much to say,
And always laughed at other people's jokes
Because he hadn't any of his own.

That night when he was busy at his job
Of piling bags along the parapet,
He thought how slow time went, stamping his feet,
And blowing on his fingers, pinched with cold.
He thought of getting back by half-past twelve,
And tot of rum to send him warm to sleep
In draughty dug-out frowsty with the fumes
Of coke, and full of snoring, weary men.

He pushed another bag along the top,
Craning his body outward; then a flare

Gave one white glimpse of No Man's Land and wire;
And as he dropped his head the instant split
His startled life with lead, and all went out.

1917

"THEY"

The Bishop tells us: "When the boys come back
They will not be the same; for they'll have fought
In a just cause: they lead the last attack
On Anti-Christ; their comrade's blood has bought
New right to breed an honorable race.
They have challenged Death and dared him face to face."

"We're none of us the same!" the boys reply.
"For George lost both his legs; and Bill's stone blind;
Poor Jim's shot through the lungs and like to die;
And Bert's gone syphilitic: you'll not find
A chap who's served that hasn't found *some* change."
And the bishop said: "The ways of God are strange!"

1917

THE TROOPS

Dim, gradual thinning of the shapeless gloom
Shudders to drizzling daybreak that reveals
Disconsolate men who stamp their sodden boots
And turn dulled, sunken faces to the sky
Haggard and hopeless. They, who have beaten down
The stale despair of night, must now renew
Their desolation in the truce of dawn,
Murdering the livid hours that grope for peace.

Yet these, who cling to life with stubborn hands,
Can grin through storms of death and find a gap
In the clawed, cruel tangles of his defence.
They march from safety, and the bird-sung joy
Of grass-green thickets, to the land where all
Is ruin, and nothing blossoms but the sky
That hastens over them where they endure
Sad, smoking, flat horizons, reeking woods,
And foundered trench-lines volleying doom for doom.

O my brave brown companions, when your souls
Flock silently away, and the eyeless dead
Shame the wild beast of battle on the ridge,
Death will stand grieving in that field of war
Since your unvanquished hardihood is spent.
And through some mooned Valhalla there will pass
Battalions and battalions, scarred from hell;
The unreturning army that was youth;
The legions who have suffered and are dust.

1918

DREAMERS

Soldiers are citizens of death's grey land,
Drawing no dividend from time's to-morrows.
In the great hour of destiny they stand,
Each with his feuds, and jealousies, and sorrows.
Soldiers are sworn to action; they must win
Some flaming, fatal climax with their lives.
Soldiers are dreamers; when the guns begin
They think of firelit homes, clean beds, and wives.

I see them in foul dug-outs, gnawed by rats,
And in the ruined trenches, lashed with rain,
Dreaming of things they did with balls and bats,
And mocked by hopeless longing to regain
Bank-holidays, and picture shows, and spats,
And going to the office in the train.

1918

PICTURE-SHOW

And still they come and go: and this is all I know—
That from the gloom I watch an endless picture-show,
Where wild or listless faces flicker on their way,
With glad or grievous hearts I'll never understand
Because Time spins so fast, and they've no time to stay
Beyond the moment's gesture of a lifted hand.

And still, between the shadow and the blinding flame,
The brave despair of men flings onward, ever the same
As in those doom-lit years that wait them, and have been . . .
And life is just the picture dancing on a screen.

1919

MEMORY

When I was young my heart and head were light,
And I was gay and feckless as a colt
Out in the fields, with morning in the may,
Wind on the grass, wings in the orchard bloom.
    O thrilling sweet, my joy, when life was free,
    And all the paths led on from hawthorn-time
    Across the carolling meadows into June.

But now my heart is heavy-laden. I sit
Burning my dreams away beside the fire:
For death has made me wise and bitter and strong;
And I am rich in all that I have lost.
    O starshine on the fields of long-ago,
    Bring me the darkness and the nightingale;
    Dim wealds of vanished summer, peace of home,
    And silence; and the faces of my friends.

1919

ON READING THE WAR DIARY OF A DEFUNCT AMBASSADOR

So that's your Diary—that's your private mind
Translated into shirt-sleeved History. That
Is what diplomacy has left behind
For after-ages to peruse, and find
What passed beneath your elegant silk-hat.

You were a fine old gentleman; compact
Of shrewdness, charm, refinement and finesse.
Impeccable in breeding, taste and dress,
No diplomatic quality you lacked—
No tittle of ambassadorial tact.

I can imagine you among "the guns,"
Urbanely peppering partridge, grouse, or pheasant—
Guest of those infinitely privileged ones
Whose lives are padded, petrified, and pleasant.
I visualize you feeding off gold plate
And gossiping on grave affairs of State.

Now you're defunct; your gossip's gravely printed;
The world discovers where you lunched and dined
On such and such a day; and what was hinted
By ministers and generals far behind
The all-important conflict, carnage-tinted.

The world can read the rumors that you gleaned
From various Fronts; the well-known Names you met;
Each conference you attended and convened;
And (at appropriate moments) what you ate.
Thus (if the world's acute) it can derive
Your self, exact, uncensored and alive.

The world will find no pity in your pages;
No exercise of spirit worthy of mention;
Only a public-funeral grief-convention;
And all the circumspection of the ages.
But I, for one, am grateful, overjoyed,
And unindignant that your punctual pen
Should have been so constructively employed
In manifesting to unprivileged men
The visionless officialized fatuity
That once kept Europe safe for Perpetuity.

1926

AN OLD-WORLD EFFECT

While blue-eyed children, goggle-faced and giggling,
Stare, swollen-cheeked (bad-mannered little wretches),
Two Nature-loving ladies dip their brushes,
Glance up, gaze down; with touches broad or niggling,
Remain absorbed in half-completed sketches
Where embryonic apple-blossom flushes
Round a decrepit cottage whence they catch
The ultimate rusticity of thatch.

You ask me why these artists have selected
An unhygienic dwelling as their theme . . .
"Have they no palate for the unexpected,—
No easel for a Cubist housing-scheme?"

A sapless unprolific Past they paint,
Who ramble through the guide-book toward the Quaint.
Meanwhile a blackbird pipes from the vicinity
His free fantasia against virginity.

1926

[IN ME, PAST, PRESENT, FUTURE MEET]

In me, past, present, future meet
To hold long chiding conference.
My lusts usurp the present tense
And strangle Reason in his seat.
My loves leap through the future's fence
To dance with dream-enfranchised feet.

In me the cave-man clasps the seer,
And garlanded Apollo goes
Chanting to Abraham's deaf ear.
In me the tiger sniffs the rose.
Look in my heart, kind friends, and tremble,
Since there your elements assemble.

1927

AT THE GRAVE OF HENRY VAUGHAN

Above the voiceful windings of a river
An old green slab of simply graven stone
Shuns notice, overshadowed by a yew.
Here Vaughan lies dead, whose name flows on for ever
Through pastures of the spirit washed with dew
And starlit with eternities unknown.

Here sleeps the Silurist; the loved physician;
The face that left no portraiture behind;
The skull that housed white angels and had vision
Of daybreak through the gateways of the mind.
Here faith and mercy, wisdom and humility
(Whose influence shall prevail for evermore)
Shine. And this lowly grave tells Heaven's tranquillity.
And here stand I, a suppliant at the door.

1927

AT THE CENOTAPH

I saw the Prince of Darkness, with his Staff,
Standing bare-headed by the Cenotaph:
Unostentatious and respectful, there
He stood, and offered up the following prayer:
"Make them forget, O Lord, what this Memorial
Means; their discredited ideas revive;
Breed new belief that War is purgatorial
Proof of the pride and power of being alive;
Men's biologic urge to readjust
The Map of Europe, Lord of Hosts, increase;
Lift up their hearts in large destructive lust;
And crown their heads with blind vindictive Peace."
The Prince of Darkness to the Cenotaph
Bowed. As he walked away I heard him laugh.

1933

THE ULTIMATE ATROCITY

When the first man who wasn't quite an ape
Felt magnanimity and prayed for more,
The world's redemption stood, in human shape,
With darkness done and betterment before.
From then till now such men have multiplied;
From then till now their task has been the same,
In whom the world's redemption dreamed and died—
To whom the vision of perfection came.

I hear an aeroplane—what years ahead
Who knows?—but if from that machine should fall
The first bacterial bomb, this world might find
That all the aspirations of the dead
Had been betrayed and blotted out, and all
Their deeds denied who hoped for Humankind.

1933

[IT WAS THE LOVE OF LIFE]

It was the love of life, when I was young,
Which led me out in summer to explore
The daybreak world. A bird's first notes were sung

For childhood standing at the garden door.
That loneliness it was which made me wise
When I looked out and saw
Dark trees against the strangely brightening skies
And learnt the love of earth that is my law.

The love of life is my religion still.
Steadfast through rigorous nights, companioned only
By what I am and what I strive to be,—
I seek no mystery now beyond the hill,
And wait no change but to become more lonely,
No freedom till the sleep that sets me free.

1934

[DECEMBER STILLNESS, TEACH ME]

December stillness, teach me through your trees
That loom along the west, one with the land,
The veiled evangel of your mysteries.
While nightfall, sad and spacious, on the down
Deepens, and dusk imbues me where I stand,
With grave diminishings of green and brown,
Speak, roofless Nature, your instinctive words;
And let me learn your secret from the sky,
Following a flock of steadfast-journeying birds
In lone remote migration beating by.
December stillness, crossed by twilight roads,
Teach me to travel far and bear my loads.

1934

VIGILS

Lone heart, learning
By one light burning,
Slow discerning of worldhood's worth;
Soul, awaking
By night and taking
Roads forsaking enchanted earth:
Man, unguided
And self-divided,
Clocked by silence which tells decay;

You that keep
    In a land asleep
One light burning till break of day:
You whose vigil
    Is deed and sigil,
Bond and service of lives afar,—
Seek, in seeing
Your own blind being,
    Peace, remote in the morning star.

1934

C. Day Lewis

Cecil Day Lewis was born April 27, 1904, in Ballintogher, Ireland. He was a son of the Reverend F. C. Day Lewis, an Anglican clergyman, and Kathleen Blake Squires, a descendant of Oliver Goldsmith. When he was three years old his family moved to Nottingham, England, where he grew up. He was precocious, and at the age of six had made his first attempts at authorship. He did his preparatory school work at Sherborne Grammar School in Dorsetshire, where he held a scholarship. In 1923 he went up to Wadham College, Oxford, as an exhibitioner (i.e., on a scholarship), and took his B.A. degree from there in 1927.

After leaving Oxford he taught school: at Summerfields, Oxford, 1927-1928; at Larchfield, Helensburgh, 1928-1930; and in the Junior School at Cheltenham College, 1930-1935. In the latter year, however, he gave up teaching to devote all his time to writing.

He published his first volume of poetry, *Beechen Vigil*, in 1925, while at Oxford, and had his second volume, *Country Comets* (1928), ready for publication when he left the University. Also while at Oxford he was co-editor of *Oxford Poetry* (1927). He has since written, in addition to half a dozen volumes of poetry, *A Hope for Poetry* (1934), an enlightening essay on his own work and that of Auden, Spender, and others; *Noah and the Waters* (1936), a satirical drama in verse; three novels, *The Friendly Tree* (1936), *Starting Point* (1937), and *Child of Misfortune* (1939); some political pamphlets; and, under the pseudonym Nicholas Blake, several detective stories and *Dick Willoughby* (1933), a tale for boys.

In 1928 he married Constance Mary King, and they have two sons. He is now living in Axminster, Devonshire.

[IN HEAVEN, I SUPPOSE, LIE DOWN]

In heaven, I suppose, lie down together
Agonized Pilate and the boa-constrictor
That swallows anything: but we must seize
One horn or the other of our antitheses.
When I consider each independent star
Wearing its world of darkness like a fur
And rubbing shoulders with infinity,
I am content experience should be
More discontinuous than the points pricked
Out by the mazy course of a derelict,
Iceberg, or Flying Dutchman, and the heart
Stationary and passive as a chart.
In such star-frenzy I could boast, betwixt
My yester and my morrow self are fixed
All the birds carolling and all the seas
Groaning from Greenwich to the Antipodes.

But an eccentric hour may come, when systems
Not stars divide the dark; and then life's pistons
Pounding into their secret cylinder
Begin to tickle the most anchorite ear
With hints of mechanisms that include
The man. And once that rhythm arrests the blood,
Who would be satisfied his mind is no
Continent but an archipelago?
They are preposterous paladins and prance
From myth to myth, who take an Agag stance
Upon the needle points of here and now,
Where only angels ought to tread. Allow
One jointure feasible to man, one state
Squared with another—then he can integrate
A million selves and where disorder ruled
Straddle a chaos and beget a world.

Peals of the New Year once for me came tumbling
Out of the narrow night like clusters of humming-
Birds loosed from a black bag, and rose again
Irresponsibly to silence: but now I strain
To follow them and see for miles around
Men square or shrug their shoulders at the sound.

Then I remember the pure and granite hills
Where first I caught an ideal tone that stills,
Like the beloved's breath asleep, all din
Of earth at traffic: silence's first-born,
Carrying over each sensual ravine
To inform the seer and uniform the seen.
So from this ark, this closet of the brain,
The dove emerges and flies back again
With a Messiah sprig of certitude—
Promise of ground below the sprawling flood.

1929

[DESIRE IS A WITCH]

Desire is a witch
And runs against the clock.
It can unstitch
The decent hem
Where space tacks on to time:
It can unlock
Pandora's privacies.

It puffs in these
Top-gallants of the mind,
And away I stand
On the elemental gale
Into an ocean
That the liar Lucian
Had never dared retail.

When my love leans with all
Her shining breast and shoulder,
I know she is older
Than Ararat the hill,
And yet more young
Than the first daffodil
That ever shews a spring.

When her eyes delay
On me, so deep are they
Tunnelled by love, although
You poured Atlantic

In this one and Pacific
In the other, I know
They would not overflow.

Desire clicks back
Like cuckoo into clock;
Leaves me to explain
Eyes that a tear will drown
And a body where youth
Nor age will long remain
To implicate the truth.

It seems that we must call
Anything truth whose well
Is deep enough;
For the essential
Philosopher-stone, desire,
Needs no other proof
Than its own fire.

1929

[IN THE CHAOTIC AGE]

In the chaotic age
  This was enough for me—
Her beauty walked the page
  And it was poetry.

Now that the crust has cooled,
  The floods are kept in pen,
Mountains have got their mould
  And air its regimen.

Nothing of heat remains
  But where the sacred hill
Conserves within her veins
  The fiery principle.

Fire can no longer shake
  Stars from their sockets down;
It burns now but to make
  Vain motions above the town.

This glum canal has lain
  Opaque night after night,
One hour will entertain
  A jubilee of light,

And show that beauty is
  A motion of the mind
By its own dark caprice
  Directed or confined.

1929

[NOW SHE IS LIKE THE WHITE TREE-ROSE]

Now she is like the white tree-rose
That takes a blessing from the sun:
Summer has filled her veins with light,
And her warm heart is washed with noon.

Or as a poplar, ceaselessly
Gives a soft answer to the wind:
Cool on the light her leaves lie sleeping,
Folding a column of sweet sound.

Powder the stars. Forbid the night
To wear those brilliants for a brooch
So soon, dark death, you may close down
The mines that made this beauty rich.

Her thoughts are pleiads, stooping low
O'er glades where nightingale has flown:
And like the luminous night around her
She has at heart a certain dawn.

1931

[LET US NOW PRAISE FAMOUS MEN]

Let us now praise famous men,
Not your earth-shakers, not the dynamiters,
But who in the Home Counties or the Khyber,
Trimming their nails to meet an ill wind,
Facing the Adversary with a clean collar,

Justified the system.
Admire the venerable pile that bred them,
Bones are its foundations,
The pinnacles are stone abstractions,
Whose halls are whispering-galleries designed
To echo voices of the past, dead tongues.
White hopes of England here
Are taught to rule by learning to obey,
Bend over before vested interests,
Kiss the rod, salute the quarter-deck;
Here is no savage discipline
Of peregrine swooping, of fire destroying,
But a civil code; no capital offender
But the cool cad, the man who goes too far.
Ours the curriculum
Neither of building birds nor wasteful waters,
Bound in book not violent in vein:
Here we inoculate with dead ideas
Against blood-epidemics, against
The infection of faith and the excess of life.
Our methods are up to date; we teach
Through head and not by heart,
Language with gramophones and sex with charts,
Prophecy by deduction, prayer by numbers.
For honors see prospectus: those who leave us
Will get a post and pity the poor;
Their eyes glaze at strangeness;
They are never embarrassed, have a word for everything,
Living on credit, dying when the heart stops;
Will wear black armlets and stand a moment in silence
For the passing of an era, at their own funeral.

1933

[LIVE YOU BY LOVE CONFINED]

Live you by love confined,
There is no nearer nearness;
Break not his light bounds,
The stars' and seas' harness:
There is nothing beyond,
We have found the land's end.
We'll take no mortal wound

Who felt him in the furnace,
Drowned in his fierceness,
By his midsummer browned:
Nor ever lose awareness
Of nearness and farness
Who've stood at earth's heart careless
Of suns and storms around,
Who have leant on the hedge of the wind,
On the last ledge of darkness.

We are where love has come
To live: he is that river
Which flows and is the same;
He is not the famous deceiver
Nor early-flowering dream.
Content you. Be at home
In me. There's but one room
Of all the house you may never
Share, deny or enter.
There, as a candle's beam
Stands firm and will not waver
Spire-straight in a close chamber,
As though in shadowy cave a
Stalagmite of flame,
The integral spirit climbs
The dark in light for ever.

1933

[THOUGH WINTER'S BARRICADE DELAYS]

Though winter's barricade delays,
Another season's in the air;
We'll sow the spring in our young days,
Found a Virginia everywhere.

Look where the ranks of crocuses
Their rebel colors will display
Coming with quick fire to redress
The balance of a wintry day.

Those daffodils that from the mould
Drawing a sweet breath soon shall flower,

With a year's labor get their gold
To spend it on a sunny hour.

They from earth's center take their time
And from the sun what love they need:
The proud flower burns away its prime,
Eternity lies in the seed.

Follow the kestrel, south or north;
Strict eye, spontaneous wing can tell
A secret. Where he comes to earth
Is the heart's treasure. Mark it well.

Here he hovers. You're on the scent;
Magnetic mountain is not far,
Across no gulf or continent,
Not where you think but where you are.

Stake out your claim. Go downwards. Bore
Through the tough crust. Oh learn to feel
A way in darkness to good ore.
You are the magnet and the steel.

Out of that dark a new world flowers.
There in the womb, in the rich veins
Are tools, dynamos, bridges, towers,
Your tractors and your travelling-cranes.

1933

[IN THESE OUR WINTER DAYS]

In these our winter days
Death's iron tongue is glib
Numbing with fear all flesh upon
A fiery-hearted globe.

An age once green is buried,
Numbered the hours of light;
Blood-red across the snow our sun
Still trails his faint retreat.

Spring through death's iron guard
Her million blades shall thrust;
Love that was sleeping, not extinct,
Throw off the nightmare crust.

Eyes, though not ours, shall see
Sky-high a signal flame,
The sun returned to power above
A world, but not the same.

1933

BOMBERS

Through the vague morning, the heart preoccupied,
A deep in air buried grain of sound
Starts and grows, as yet unwarning—
The tremor of baited deepsea line.

Swells the seed, and now tight sound-buds
Vibrate, upholding their paean flowers
To the sun. There are bees in sky-bells droning,
Flares of crimson at the heart unfold.

Children look up, and the elms spring-garlanded
Tossing their heads and marked for the axe.
Gallant or woebegone, alike unlucky—
Earth shakes beneath us: we imagine loss.

Black as vermin, crawling in echelon
Beneath the cloud-floor, the bombers come:
The heavy angels, carrying harm in
Their wombs that ache to be rid of death.

This is the seed that grows for ruin,
The iron embryo conceived in fear.
Soon or late its need must be answered
In fear delivered and screeching fire.

Choose between your child and this fatal embryo.
Shall your gilt bear arms, and the children you want
Be condemned to die by the powers you paid for
And haunt the houses you never built?

1938

A HAPPY VIEW

. . . So take a happy view—
This lawn graced with the candle-flames of crocus,
Frail-handed girls under the flowering chestnut,
Or anything will do
That time takes back before it seems untrue:

And, if the truth were told,
You'd count it luck, perceiving in what shallow
Crevices and few crumbling grains of comfort
Man's joy will seed, his cold
And hardy fingers find an eagle's hold.

1938

OVERTURES TO DEATH

1

For us, born into a world
Of fledged, instinctive trees,
Of lengthening days, snowfall at Christmas
And sentried palaces,

You were the one our parents
Could not forget or forgive—
A remittance man, a very very
Distant relative.

We read your name in the family
Bible. It was tabu
At meals and lessons, but in church sometimes
They seemed to be praying for you.

You lived overseas, we gathered:
And often lying safe
In bed we thought of you, hearing the indrawn
Breath of the outcast surf.

Later we heard them saying
You had done well in the War.

And, though you never came home to us,
We saw your name everywhere.

When home grew unsympathetic,
You were all the rage for a while—
The favorite uncle with the blank-cheque-book
And the understanding smile.

Some of us went to look for you
In aeroplanes and fast cars:
Some tried the hospitals, some took to vice,
Others consulted the stars.

But now, sir, that you may be going
To visit us any night,
We watch the french windows, picturing you
In rather a different light.

The house, we perceive, is shabby,
There's dry-rot in the wood:
It's a poor welcome and it won't keep you out
And we wish we had been good.

But there's no time now for spring-cleaning
Or mending the broken lock.
We are here in the shrouded drawing-room till
Your first, your final knock.

2

When all the sky is skimming
And lovers frisk in the hay,
When it's easy forgiving the dead or the living,
He is not so far away.

When love's hands are too hot, too cold,
And justice turns a deaf ear,
When springs congeal and the skies are sealed,
We know that he is near.

Now here was a property, on all sides
Considered quite imposing:
Take a good look round at house and grounds—
The mortgage is foreclosing.

Now Death he is the bailiff
And he sits in our best room
Appraising chintz and ornaments
And the child in the womb.

We were not shysters or loonies,
Our spirit was up to proof:
Simpler far is the reason for our
Notice to quit this roof.

We paid for our lease and rule of life
In hard cash; and one day
The news got through to you-know-who
That we'd ceased to pay our way.

Oh what will happen to our dear sons,
Our dreams of pensioned ease?
They are downed and shredded, for the wind we dreaded
Worries the blossom trees.

Oh Death he is the bailiff
And his men wait outside:
We shall sleep well in our handsome shell
While he auctions away our pride.

3

Sir, I'd not make so bold as to lack all
Respect for one whose prowess in the bed and the battlefield
Have excited (and justly) universal comment.
Nor could I, if I wished—
Who, in the small hours and the talkative
Reception, have felt you ticking within my belly—
Pretend there's any worse ordeal to come.
You and I, my friend, are antagonists
And the fight's framed: for this I blame not you
But the absentee promoter. If I seem to treat
Your titles, stamina, skill with levity,
Call it the rat's bad-loser snarl, the madman
Humoring the two doctors, the point declaring
War on the calm circumference. . . .
  You have appeared to us in many guises—
Pale priest, black camel, the bemedalled sergeant
Of general conscription, a bugbear to affright

Second childhood, or the curtain drawn so deftly
To show that diamond-tiered tree
Evergreen with bliss for all good boys and girls.
You have been called the Leveller: but little
That meant to the aristos you transferred
Straight from one rotten borough to another;
Nor can our state, hollow and cold as theirs,
Much envy the drab democrats of the grave.
Happiest, in our nervous time, who name you
Peace. You are the peace that millions die for.
  If there's a moment's solace, laid like the bloom
Of dew upon our meadows; if honeysuckle
Clings to its sweetened hour, and the appealing
Beauty of flesh makes time falter in his stride;
If anywhere love-lips, flower-flaunt, crimson of cloud-crest
With flames impassioned hold off the pacing shadows—
You can rest indulgent: soon enough
They shall be all, all of your complexion.
  I grant you the last word. But what of these—
The criminal agents of a dying will
Who, frantic with defeat, conspire to force your
Earlier intervention?
It is they, your damned auxiliaries, must answer
For the self-slain in the foodless, fireless room,
For stunted hearts that droop by our olive-green
Canals, the blossom of children untimely shattered
By their crazed, random fire, and the fear like a black frost
Foreshortening our prospect, metallic on our tongues.
If I am too familiar with you, sir,
It is that these have brought you into contempt.
You are in nature. These are most unnatural.
We shall desire your peace in our own time:
But with those, your free-lance and officious gunmen,
Our war is life itself and shall not fail.

4

Forgive us, that we ever thought
You could with innocence be bought,
Or, puffed with queasy power, have tried
Your register to override.

Such diamond-faced and equal laws
Allow no chink or saving clause:

Besotted may-fly, bobbish wren
Count in your books as much as men.

No North-West Passage can be found
To sail those freezing capes around,
Nor no smooth by-pass ever laid
Shall that metropolis evade.

The tampering hand, the jealous eye
That overlooked our infancy—
Forgiven soon, they sank their trust
And our reproach into the dust.

We also, whom a bawdy spring
Tempted to order everything,
Shall shrink beneath your first caress
Into a modest nothingness.

The meshes of the imperious blood,
The wind-flown tower, the poet's word
Can catch no more than a weak sigh
And ghost of immortality.

O lord of leisure, since we know
Your image we shall ne'er outgrow,
Teach us the value of our stay
Lest we insult the living clay.

This clay that binds the roots of man
And firmly foots his flying span—
Only this clay can voice, invest,
Measure and frame our mortal best.

O lord of night, bid us beware
The wistful ghost that speaks us fair:
Once let him in—he clots the veins
And makes a still-birth of our pains.

Now we at last have crossed the line
Where earth's exuberant fields begin,
That green illusion in the sky
Born of our desert years can die.

No longer let predestined need
Cramp our design, or hunger breed
Its windy dreams, or life distil
Rare personal good from common ill.

Lord of us all, now it is true
That we are lords of all but you,
Teach us the order of our day
Lest we deface the honored clay.

5

The sun came out in April,
The hawthorn in May:
We thought the year, like other years,
Would go the Christmas way.

In June we picked the clover,
And sea-shells in July:
There was no silence at the door,
No word from the sky.

A hand came out of August
And flicked his life away:
We had not time to bargain, mope,
Moralize, or pray.

Where he had been, was only
An effigy on a bed
To ask us searching questions or
Hear what we'd left unsaid.

Only that stained parchment
Set out what he had been—
A face we might have learned better,
But now must read unseen.

Thus he resigned his interest
And claims, all in a breath,
Leaving us the long office work
And winding-up of death:

The ordinary anguish,
The stairs, the awkward turn,

The bearers' hats like black mushrooms
Placed upon the lawn.

As a migrant remembers
The sting and warmth of home,
As the fruit bears out the blossom's word,
We remember him.

He loved the sun in April,
The hawthorn in May:
Our tree will not light up for him
Another Christmas Day.

6

It is not you I fear, but the humiliations
You mercifully use to deaden grief—
The downward graph of natural joys,
Imagination's slump, the blunted ear.

I hate this cold and politic self-defence
Of hardening arteries and nerves
Grown dull with time-serving. I see that the heart lives
By self-betrayal, by circumspection is killed.

That boy, whose glance makes heaven open and edges
Each dawning pain with gold, must learn to disbelieve:
The wildfire lust of the eyes will gutter down
To age's dim recalcitrance.

Have we not seen how quick this young girl's thoughts,
Wayward and burning as a charm of goldfinches
Alarmed from thistle-tops, turn into
Spite or a cupboard love or clipped routine?

Nearing the watershed and the difficult passes,
Man wraps up closer against the chill
In his familiar habits; and at the top
Pauses, seeing your kingdom like a net beneath him spread.

Some climbed to this momentous peak of the world
And facing the horizon—that notorious pure woman
Who lures to cheat the last embrace,
Hurled themselves down upon an easier doom.

One the rare air made dizzy renounced
Earth, and the avalanche took him at his word:
One wooed perfection—he's bedded deep in the glacier, perfect
And null, the prince and image of despair.

The best, neither hoarding nor squandering
The radiant flesh and the receptive
Spirit, stepped on together in the rhythm of comrades who
Have found a route on earth's true reckoning based.

They have not known the false humility,
The shamming-dead of the senses beneath your hunter's hand;
But life's green standards they've advanced
To the limit of your salt unyielding zone.

7

For us, born into a still
Unsweetened world, of sparse
Breathing-room, alleys brackish as hell's pit
And heaven-accusing spires,

You were never far nor fable,
Judgement nor happy end:
We have come to think of you, mister, as
Almost the family friend.

Our kiddies play tag with you often
Among the tornado wheels;
Through fevered nights you sit up with them,
You serve their little meals.

You lean with us at street-corners,
We have met you in the mine;
Your eyes are the foundry's glare, you beckon
From the snake-tooth, sly machine.

Low in the flooded engineroom,
High on the yawing steeple—
Wherever we are, we begin to fancy
That we're your chosen people.

They came to us with charity,
They came to us with whips,

They came with chains behind their back
And freedom on their lips:

Castle and field and city—
Ours is a noble land,
Let us work for its fame together, they said;
But we don't quite understand.

For they took the land and the credit,
Took virtue and double-crossed her;
They left us the scrag-end of the luck
And the brunt of their disaster.

And now like horses they fidget
Smelling death in the air:
But we are your chosen people, and
We've little to lose or fear.

When the time comes for a clearance,
When light brims over the hill,
Mister, you can rely on us
To execute your will.

1938

W. H. Auden

Wystan Hugh Auden, youngest of the three sons of George Augustus and Constance Rosalie Bicknell Auden, was born in York on February 21, 1907. His father, whose ancestors were Midland yeomen, was a physician and, from 1908 till his retirement in 1937, was medical officer at the University of Birmingham. His mother, a descendant of a Norman family which settled originally in Somerset, was a daughter of the Reverend R. H. Bicknell of Norfolk. His parents met when his mother was a nurse and his father a young doctor at St. Bartholomew's Hospital, London. Both his grandfathers were Church of England clergymen.

From 1914 to 1920 he was a pupil at a boys private boarding school in Surrey, and from 1920 to 1925 at Gresham's School, Holt, where he specialized in biology. In October, 1925, he went up to Christ Church, Oxford, as an exhibitioner (that is, on a scholarship) in natural science. As an Oxford undergraduate he developed an interest in the drama, and wrote poetry which made him known before he left the University at the end of 1928. He spent the year 1929 in Berlin. After taking his B. A. degree he taught for the next five years at a school for boys, first in Scotland and then near Malvern. During 1935-36 he worked with the Film Unit of the General Post Office, making documentary films.

In 1935 he married Erika Mann, a daughter of Thomas Mann, the novelist. In the summer of 1936 he and Louis MacNeice went to Iceland, and they related their experiences on the trip in *Letters from Iceland* (1937). In 1938, accompanied by Christopher Isherwood, a close friend from the time they were schoolboys together in Surrey, he went to China, where for some months the two traveled about, gathering material for the book, *Journey to a War* (1939), for which Isherwood wrote a prose account of the trip, and Auden contributed a group of pictures and some of his best poetry. The following year Auden took up residence in the United States with the intention of becoming an American citizen. For two years he was a lecturer at the New School for Social Research, New York, and while holding this position he made occasional lecture trips to other parts of the United States. During 1941-42 he held an appointment at the University of Michigan. He was awarded a Guggenheim fellowship for 1942, but gave it up because of the war, and accepted an appointment at Swarthmore College.

Auden at first intended to become a mining engineer, but while at Gresham's School he became aware of a desire to write poetry. At Oxford this interest grew, and the product of his work during these early years he published in his first volume, *Poems*, in 1930. Since then he has edited *The Oxford Book of Light Verse* (1938), has published several volumes of poetry, has collaborated in writing books on Iceland and China, and has written all or part of a number of dramas: *The Dance of Death* (1933), and with Christopher Isherwood, *The Dog Beneath the Skin* (1935), *The Ascent of F6* (1936), and *On the Frontier* (1938), all of which are social and political satires.

[TO THROW AWAY THE KEY] [1]

To throw away the key and walk away
Not abrupt exile, the neighbors asking why,
But following a line with left and right
An altered gradient at another rate
Learns more than maps upon the whitewashed wall
The hand put up to ask; and makes us well
Without confession of the ill. All pasts
Are single old past now, although some posts
Are forwarded, held looking on a new view;
The future shall fulfill a surer vow
Not smiling at queen over the glass rim
Nor making gunpowder in the top room,
Not swooping at the surface still like gulls
But with prolonged drowning shall develop gills.

[1] This lyric appeared as a chorus in the charade, "Paid on Both Sides." It has been taken from the longer work because the author considers it a poem complete in itself.

But there are still to tempt; areas not seen
Because of blizzards or an erring sign
Whose guessed at wonders would be worth alleging,
And lies about the cost of a night's lodging.
Travellers may sleep at inns but not attach,
They sleep one night together, not asked to touch;
Receive no normal welcome, not the pressed lip,
Children to lift, not the assuaging lap.
Crossing the pass descend the growing stream
Too tired to hear except the pulses' strum,
Reach villages to ask for a bed in
Rock shutting out the sky, the old life done.

1930

[WATCH ANY DAY HIS NONCHALANT PAUSES]

Watch any day his nonchalant pauses, see
His dextrous handling of a wrap as he
Steps after into cars, the beggar's envy.

"There is a free one," many say, but err.
He is not that returning conqueror,
Nor ever the poles' circumnavigator.

But poised between shocking falls on razor-edge
Has taught himself this balancing subterfuge
Of the accosting profile, the erect carriage.

The song, the varied action of the blood
Would drown the warning from the iron wood
Would cancel the inertia of the buried:

Travelling by daylight on from house to house
The longest way to the intrinsic peace,
With love's fidelity and with love's weakness.

1930

[TALLER TODAY, WE REMEMBER]

Taller today, we remember similar evenings,
Walking together in the windless orchard
Where the brook runs over the gravel, far from the glacier.

Again in the room with the sofa hiding the grate,
Look down to the river when the rain is over,
See him turn to the window, hearing our last
Of Captain Ferguson.

It is seen how excellent hands have turned to commonness.
One staring too long, went blind in a tower,
One sold all his manors to fight, broke through, and faltered.

Nights come bringing the snow, and the dead howl
Under the headlands in their windy dwelling
Because the Adversary put too easy questions
On lonely roads.

But happy now, though no nearer each other,
We see the farms lighted all along the valley;
Down at the mill-shed the hammering stops
And men go home.

Noises at dawn will bring
Freedom for some, but not this peace
No bird can contradict: passing, but is sufficient now
For something fulfilled this hour, loved or endured.

1930

[THERE ARE SOME BIRDS IN THESE VALLEYS]

There are some birds in these valleys
Who flutter round the careless
With intimate appeal,
By seeming kindness trained to snaring,
They feel no falseness.

Under the spell completely
They circle can serenely,
And in the tricky light
The masked hill has a purer greenness.
Their flight looks fleeter.

But fowlers, O, like foxes,
Lie ambushed in the rushes.
Along the harmless tracks

The madman keeper crawls through brushwood,
Axe under oxter.

Alas, the signal given,
Fingers on trigger tighten.
The real unlucky dove
Must smarting fall away from brightness
Its love from living.

1932

EPILOGUE

"O where are you going?" said reader to rider,
"That valley is fatal when furnaces burn,
Yonder's the midden whose odors will madden,
That gap is the grave where the tall return."

"O do you imagine," said fearer to farer,
"That dusk will delay on your path to the pass,
Your diligent looking discover the lacking
Your footsteps feel from granite to grass?"

"O what was that bird," said horror to hearer,
"Did you see that shape in the twisted trees?
Behind you swiftly the figure comes softly,
The spot on your skin is a shocking disease?"

"Out of this house"—said rider to reader
"Yours never will"—said farer to fearer
"They're looking for you"—said hearer to horror
As he left them there, as he left them there.

1932

[DOOM IS DARK AND DEEPER THAN ANY SEA-DINGLE]

Doom is dark and deeper than any sea-dingle.
Upon what man it fall
In spring, day-wishing flowers appearing,
Avalanche sliding, white snow from rock-face,
That he should leave his house,

No cloud-soft hand can hold him, restraint by women;
But ever that man goes
Through place-keepers, through forest trees,
A stranger to strangers over undried sea,
Houses for fishes, suffocating water,
Or lonely on fell as chat,
By pot-holed becks
A bird stone-haunting, an unquiet bird.

There head falls forward, fatigued at evening,
And dreams of home,
Waving from window, spread of welcome,
Kissing of wife under single sheet;
But waking sees
Bird-flocks nameless to him, through doorway voices
Of new men making another love.

Save him from hostile capture,
From sudden tiger's spring at corner;
Protect his house,
His anxious house where days are counted
From thunderbolt protect,
From gradual ruin spreading like a stain;
Converting number from vague to certain,
Bring joy, bring day of his returning,
Lucky with day approaching, with leaning dawn.

1934

[TO ASK THE HARD QUESTION IS SIMPLE]

To ask the hard question is simple;
Asking at meeting
With the simple glance of acquaintance
To what these go
And how these do:
To ask the hard question is simple,
The simple act of the confused will.
But the answer

Is hard and hard to remember:
On steps or on shore
The ears listening

To words at meeting,
The eyes looking
At the hands helping,
Are never sure
Of what they learn
From how these things are done.
And forgetting to listen or see
Makes forgetting easy;
Only remembering the method of remembering,
Remembering only in another way,
Only the strangely exciting lie,
Afraid
To remember what the fish ignored,
How the bird escaped, or if the sheep obeyed.

Till, losing memory,
Bird, fish, and sheep are ghostly,
And ghosts must do again
What gives them pain.
Cowardice cries
For windy skies,
Coldness for water,
Obedience for a master.

Shall memory restore
The steps and the shore,
The face and the meeting place;
Shall the bird live,
Shall the fish dive,
And sheep obey
In a sheep's way;
Can love remember
The question and the answer,
For love recover
What has been dark and rich and warm all over?

1934.

[NOW THE LEAVES ARE FALLING FAST]

Now the leaves are falling fast,
Nurse's flowers will not last;
Nurses to the graves are gone,
And the prams go rolling on.

Whispering neighbors, left and right,
Pluck us from the real delight;
And the active hands must freeze
Lonely on the separate knees.

Dead in hundreds at the back
Follow wooden in our track,
Arms raised stiffly to reprove
In false attitudes of love.

Starving through the leafless wood
Trolls run scolding for their food;
And the nightingale is dumb,
And the angel will not come.

Cold, impossible, ahead
Lifts the mountain's lovely head
Whose white waterfall could bless
Travellers in their last distress.

1936

[A SHILLING LIFE WILL GIVE YOU]

A shilling life will give you all the facts:
How Father beat him, how he ran away,
What were the struggles of his youth, what acts
Made him the greatest figure of his day:
Of how he fought, fished, hunted, worked all night,
Though giddy, climbed new mountains; named a sea:
Some of the last researchers even write
Love made him weep his pints like you and me.

With all his honors on, he sighed for one
Who, say astonished critics, lived at home;
Did little jobs about the house with skill
And nothing else; could whistle; would sit still
Or potter round the garden; answered some
Of his long marvellous letters but kept none.

1936

[HERE ON THE CROPPED GRASS]

Here on the cropped grass of the narrow ridge I stand,
A fathom of earth, alive in air,
Aloof as an admiral on the old rocks,
    England below me:
Eastward across the Midland plains
An express is leaving for a sailor's country;
Westward is Wales
Where on clear evenings the retired and rich
From the french windows of their sheltered mansions
See the Sugarloaf standing, an upright sentinel
    Over Abergavenny.

When last I stood here I was not alone; happy
Each thought the other, thinking of a crime,
And England to our meditations seemed
    The perfect setting:
But now it has no innocence at all;
It is the isolation and the fear,
    The mood itself;
It is the body of the absent lover,
An image to the would-be hero of the soul,
The little area we are willing to forgive
    Upon conditions.

For private reasons I must have the truth, remember
These years have seen a boom in sorrow;
The presses of idleness issued more despair
    And it was honored,
Gross Hunger took on more hands every month,
Erecting here and everywhere his vast
    Unnecessary workshops;
Europe grew anxious about her health,
Combines tottered, credits froze,
And business shivered in a banker's winter
    While we were kissing.

To-day, no longer occupied like that, I give
The children at the open swimming pool
Lithe in their first and little beauty
    A closer look;

Follow the cramped clerk crooked at his desk,
The guide in shorts pursuing flowers
    In their careers;
A digit of the crowd, would like to know
Them better whom the shops and trams are full of,
The little men and their mothers, not plain but
    Dreadfully ugly.

Deaf to the Welsh wind now, I hear arising
From lanterned gardens sloping to the river
Where saxophones are moaning for a comforter,
    From Gaumont theatres
Where fancy plays on hunger to produce
The noble robber, ideal of boys,
    And from cathedrals,
Luxury liners laden with souls,
Holding to the east their hulls of stone,
The high thin rare continuous worship
    Of the self-absorbed.

Here, which looked north before the Cambrian alignment,
Like the cupped hand of the keen excavator
Busy with bones, the memory uncovers
    The hopes of time;
Of empires stiff in their brocaded glory,
The luscious lateral blossoming of woe
    Scented, profuse;
And of intercalary ages of disorder
When, as they prayed in antres, fell
Upon the noblest in the country night
    Angel assassins.

Small birds above me have the grace of those who founded
The civilization of the delicate olive,
Learning the laws of love and sailing
    On the calm Aegean;
The hawk is the symbol of the rule by thirst,
The central state controlling the canals;
    And the blank sky
Of the womb's utter peace before
The cell, dividing, multiplied desire,
And raised instead of death the image
    Of the reconciler.

And over the Cotswolds now the thunder mutters:
"What little of the truth your seers saw
They dared not tell you plainly but combined
    Assertion and refuge
In the common language of collective lying,
In codes of a bureau, laboratory slang
    And diplomats' French.
The relations of your lovers were, alas, pictorial;
The treasure that you stole, you lost; bad luck
It brought you, but you cannot put it back
    Now with caresses.

"Already behind you your last evening hastens up
And all the customs your society has chosen
Harden themselves into the unbreakable
    Habits of death.
Has not your long affair with death
Of late become increasingly more serious;
    Do you not find
Him growing more attractive every day?
You shall go under and help him with the crops,
Be faithful to him, and to your friends
    Remain indifferent."

And out of the turf the bones of the war continue;
"Know then, cousin, the major cause of our collapse
Was a distortion in the human plastic by luxury produced,

Never higher than in our time were the vital advantages;
To matter entire, to the unbounded vigors of the instrument,
To all logical precision we were the rejoicing heirs.

But pompous, we assumed their power to be our own,
Believed machines to be our hearts' spontaneous fruit,
Taking our premises as shoppers take a tram.

While the disciplined love which alone could have employed
    these engines
Seemed far too difficult and dull, and when hatred promised
An immediate dividend, all of us hated.

Denying the liberty we knew quite well to be our destiny,
It dogged our steps with its accusing shadow
Until in every landscape we saw murder ambushed.

Unable to endure ourselves, we sought relief
In the insouciance of the soldier, the heroic sexual pose
Playing at fathers to impress the little ladies.

Call us not tragic; falseness made farcical our death:
Nor brave; ours was the will of the insane to suffer
By which since we could not live we gladly died:
And now we have gone for ever to our foolish graves."

The Priory clock chimes briefly and I recollect
I am expected to return alive
My will effective and my nerves in order
    To my situation.
"The poetry is in the pity," Wilfred said,
And Kathy in her journal, "To be rooted in life,
    That's what I want."
These moods give no permission to be idle,
For men are changed by what they do;
And through loss and anger the hands of the unlucky
    Love one another.

1936

[FISH IN THE UNRUFFLED LAKES]

Fish in the unruffled lakes
The swarming colors wear,
Swans in the winter air
A white perfection have,
And the great lion walks
Through his innocent grove;
Lion, fish, and swan
Act, and are gone
Upon Time's toppling wave.

We till shadowed days are done,
We must weep and sing
Duty's conscious wrong,
The Devil in the clock,
The Goodness carefully worn
For atonement or for luck;
We must lose our loves,
On each beast and bird that moves
Turn an envious look.

Sighs for folly said and done
Twist our narrow days;
But I must bless, I must praise
That you, my swan, who have
All gifts that to the swan
Impulsive Nature gave,
The majesty and pride,
Last night should add
Your voluntary love.

1936

From LETTER TO LORD BYRON: IV

My passport says I'm five feet and eleven,
  With hazel eyes and fair (it's tow-like) hair,
That I was born in York in 1907,
  With no distinctive markings anywhere.
  Which isn't quite correct. Conspicuous there
On my right cheek appears a large brown mole,
I think I don't dislike it on the whole.

My name occurs in several of the sagas,
  Is common over Iceland still. Down under
Where Das Volk order sausages and lagers
  I ought to be the prize, the living wonder,
  The really pure from any Rassenschander,
In fact I am the great big white barbarian,
The Nordic type, the too too truly Aryan.

In games which mark for beauty out of twenty,
  I'm doing well if my friends give me eight
(When played historically you[1] still score plenty);
  My head looks like an egg upon a plate;
  My nose is not too bad, but isn't straight;
I have no proper eyebrows, and my eyes
Are far too close together to look nice.

Beauty, we're told, is but a painted show,
  But still the public really likes that best;
Beauty of soul should be enough, I know,
  The golden ingot in the plain deal chest.

[1] Lord Byron.

But mine's a rattle in a flannel vest;
I can't think what my It had on Its mind,
To give me flat feet and a big behind.

Apart from lyrics and poetic dramma,
Which Ervine seems more angered by than sad at,
While Sparrow fails to understand their grammar,
I have some harmless hobbies; I'm not bad at
Reading the slower movements, and may add that
Out of my hours of strumming most of them
Pass playing hymn tunes out of A. and M.

Read character from taste. Who seem to me
The great? I know that one as well as you.
"Why, Daunty, Gouty, Shopkeeper, the three
Supreme Old Masters." You must ask me who
Have written just as I'd have liked to do.
I stop to listen and the names I hear
Are those of Firbank, Potter, Carroll, Lear.

Then phantasies? My anima, poor thing,
Must take the dreams my Alter Ego sends her,
And he's a marvellous diver, not a king.
But when I'm sickening for influenza,
I play concertos with my own cadenza;
And as the fever rises find it properer
To sing the love duet from a grand opera.

My vices? I've no wish to go to prison.
I am no Grouper, I will never share
With any prig who thinks he'd like to listen.
At answering letters I am well aware
I'm very slack; I ought to take more care
Over my clothes; my promise always fails
To smoke much less, and not to bite my nails.

I hate pompositas and all authority;
Its air of injured rightness also sends
Me shuddering from the cultured smug minority.
"Perpetual revolution," left-wing friends
Tell me, "in counter-revolution ends.
Your fate will be to linger on outcast
A selfish pink old Liberal to the last."

"No, I am that I am, and those that level
  At my abuses reckon up their own.
I may be straight though they, themselves, are bevel."
  So Shakespeare said, but Shakespeare must have known.
  I daren't say that except when I'm alone,
Must hear in silence till I turn my toes up,
"It's such a pity Wystan never grows up."

So I sit down this fine September morning
  To tell my story. I've another reason.
I've lately had a confidential warning
  That Isherwood is publishing next season
  A book about us all. I call that treason.
I must be quick if I'm to get my oar in
Before his revelations bring the law in.

My father's forbears were all Midland yeomen
  Till royalties from coal mines did them good;
I think they must have been phlegmatic slowmen.
  My mother's ancestors had Norman blood,
  From Somerset I've always understood;
My grandfathers on either side agree
In being clergymen and C. of E.

Father and Mother each was one of seven,
  Though one died young and one was not all there;
Their fathers both went suddenly to Heaven
  While they were still quite small and left them here
  To work on earth with little cash to spare;
A nurse, a rising medico, at Bart's
Both felt the pangs of Cupid's naughty darts.

My home then was professional and "high".
  No gentler father ever lived, I'll lay
All Lombard Street against a shepherd's pie.
  We imitate our loves: well, neighbors say
  I grow more like my mother every day.
I don't like business men. I know a Prot
Will never really kneel, but only squat.

In pleasures of the mind they both delighted;
  The library in the study was enough
To make a better boy than me short-sighted;

Our old cook Ada surely knew her stuff;
My elder brothers did not treat me rough;
We lived at Solihull, a village then;
Those at the gasworks were my favorite men.

My earliest recollection to stay put
Is of a white stone doorstep and a spot
Of pus where father lanced the terrier's foot;
Next, stuffing shag into the coffee pot
Which nearly killed my mother, but did not;
Both psychoanalyst and Christian minister,
Will think these incidents extremely sinister.

With northern myths my little brain was laden,
With deeds of Thor and Loki and such scenes;
My favorite tale was Andersen's *Ice Maiden;*
But better far than any kings or queens
I liked to see and know about machines:
And from my sixth until my sixteenth year
I thought myself a mining engineer.

The mine I always pictured was for lead,
Though copper mines might, *faute de mieux,* be sound.
Today I like a weight upon my bed;
I always travel by the Underground!
For concentration I have always found
A small room best, the curtains drawn, the light on;
Then I can work from nine till tea-time, right on.

I must admit that I was most precocious
(Precocious children rarely grow up good).
My aunts and uncles thought me quite atrocious
For using words more adult than I should;
My first remark at school did all it could
To shake a matron's monumental poise;
"I like to see the various types of boys."

The Great War had begun: but masters' scrutiny
And fists of big boys were the war to us;
It was as harmless as the Indian Mutiny,
A beating from the Head was dangerous.
But once when half the form put down *Bellus,*
We were accused of that most deadly sin,
Wanting the Kaiser and the Huns to win.

The way in which we really were affected
  Was having such a varied lot to teach us.
The best were fighting, as the King expected,
  The remnant either elderly gray creatures,
  Or characters with most peculiar features.
Many were raggable, a few were waxy,
One had to leave abruptly in a taxi.

Surnames I must not write—O Reginald,
  You at least taught us that which fadeth not,
Our earliest visions of the great wide world;
  The beer and biscuits that your favorites got,
  Your tales revealing you a first-class shot,
Your riding breeks, your drama called *The Waves*,
A few of us will carry to our graves.

"Half a lunatic, half a knave." No doubt
  A holy terror to the staff at tea;
A good headmaster must have soon found out
  Your moral character was all at sea;
  I question if you'd got a pass degree:
But little children bless your kind that knocks
Away the edifying stumbling blocks.

How can I thank you? For it only shows
  (Let me ride just this once my hobby-horse),
There're things a good headmaster never knows.
  There must be sober schoolmasters, of course,
  But what a prep school really puts across
Is knowledge of the world we'll soon be lost in:
Today it's more like Dickens than Jane Austen.

I hate the modern trick, to tell the truth,
  Of straightening out the kinks in the young mind,
Our passion for the tender plant of youth,
  Our hatred for all weeds of any kind.
  Slogans are bad: the best that I can find
Is this: "Let each child have that's in our care
As much neurosis as the child can bear."

In this respect, at least, my bad old Adam is
  Pigheadedly against the general trend;
And has no use for all these new academies

Where readers of the better weeklies send
The child they probably did not intend,
To paint a lampshade, marry, or keep pigeons,
Or make a study of the world religions.

Goddess of bossy underlings, Normality!
What murders are committed in thy name!
Totalitarian is thy state Reality,
Reeking of antiseptics and the shame
Of faces that all look and feel the same.
Thy Muse is one unknown to classic histories,
The topping figure of the hockey mistress.

From thy dread Empire not a soul's exempted:
More than the nursemaids pushing prams in parks,
By thee the intellectuals are tempted,
O, to commit the treason of the clerks,
Bewitched by thee to literary sharks.
But I must leave thee to thy office stool,
I must get on now to my public school.

Men had stopped throwing stones at one another,
Butter and Father had come back again;
Gone were the holidays we spent with Mother
In furnished rooms on mountain, moor, and fen;
And gone those summer Sunday evenings, when
Along the seafronts fled a curious noise,
"Eternal Father," sung by three young boys.

Nation spoke Peace, or said she did, with nation;
The sexes tried their best to look the same;
Morals lost value during the inflation,
The great Victorians kindly took the blame;
Visions of Dada to the Post-War came,
Sitting in cafés, nostrils stuffed with bread,
Above the recent and the straight-laced dead.

I've said my say on public schools elsewhere:
Romantic friendship, prefects, bullying,
I shall not deal with, *c'est une autre affaire*.
Those who expect them, will get no such thing,
It is the strictly relevant I sing.
Why should they grumble? They've the Greek Anthology,
And all the spicier bits of Anthropology.

We all grow up the same way, more or less;
  Life is not known to give away her presents;
She only swops. The unself-consciousness
  That children share with animals and peasants
  Sinks in the "stürm und drang" of Adolescence.
Like other boys I lost my taste for sweets,
Discovered sunsets, passion, God, and Keats.

I shall recall a single incident
  No more. I spoke of mining engineering
As the career on which my mind was bent,
  But for some time my fancies had been veering;
  Mirages of the future kept appearing;
Crazes had come and gone in short, sharp gales,
For motor-bikes, photography, and whales.

But indecision broke off with a clean-cut end
  One afternoon in March at half-past three
When walking in a ploughed field with a friend;
  Kicking a little stone, he turned to me
  And said, "Tell me, do you write poetry?"
I never had, and said so, but I knew
That very moment what I wished to do.

Without a bridge passage this leads me straight
  Into the theme marked "Oxford" on my score
From pages twenty-five to twenty-eight.
  Aesthetic trills I'd never heard before
  Rose from the strings, shrill poses from the cor;
The woodwind chattered like a pre-war Russian,
"Art" boomed the brass, and "Life" thumped the percussion.

A raw provincial, my good taste was tardy,
  And Edward Thomas I as yet preferred;
I was still listening to Thomas Hardy
  Putting divinity about a bird;
  But Eliot spoke the still unspoken word;
For gasworks and dried tubers I forsook
The clock at Grantchester, the English rook.

All youth's intolerant certainty was mine as
  I faced life in a double-breasted suit;
I bought and praised but did not read Aquinas,

At the *Criterion's* verdict I was mute,
Though Arnold's I was ready to refute;
And through the quads dogmatic words rang clear,
"Good poetry is classic and austere."

So much for Art. Of course Life had its passions too;
The student's flesh like his imagination
Makes facts fit theories and has fashions too.
We were the tail, a sort of poor relation
To that debauched, eccentric generation
That grew up with their fathers at the War,
And made new glosses on the noun Amor.

Three years passed quickly while the Isis went
Down to the sea for better or for worse;
Then to Berlin, not Carthage, I was sent
With money from my parents in my purse,
And ceased to see the world in terms of verse.
I met a chap called Layard and he fed
New doctrines into my receptive head.

Part came from Lane, and part from D. H. Lawrence;
Gide, though I didn't know it then, gave part.
They taught me to express my deep abhorrence
If I caught anyone preferring Art
To Life and Love and being Pure-in-Heart.
I lived with crooks but seldom was molested;
The Pure-in-Heart can never be arrested.

He's gay; no bludgeonings of chance can spoil it,
The Pure-in-Heart loves all men on a par,
And has no trouble with his private toilet;
The Pure-in-Heart is never ill; catarrh
Would be the yellow streak, the brush of tar;
Determined to be loving and forgiving,
I came back home to try and earn my living.

The only thing you never turned your hand to
Was teaching English in a boarding school.
Today it's a profession that seems grand to
Those whose alternative's an office stool;
For budding authors it's become the rule.
To many an unknown genius postmen bring
Typed notices from Rabbitarse and String.

The Head's M. A., a bishop is a patron,
  The assistant staff is highly qualified;
Health is the care of an experienced matron,
  The arts are taught by ladies from outside;
  The food is wholesome and the grounds are wide;
The aim is training character and poise,
With special coaching for the backward boys.

I found the pay good and had time to spend it,
  Though others may not have the good luck I did:
For you I'd hesitate to recommend it;
  Several have told me that they can't abide it.
  Still, if one tends to get a bit one-sided,
It's pleasant as it's easy to secure
The hero worship of the immature.

More, it's a job, and jobs today are rare:
  All the ideals in the world won't feed us
Although they give our crimes a certain air.
  So barons of the press who know their readers
  Employ to write their more appalling leaders,
Instead of Satan's horned and hideous minions,
Clever young men of liberal opinions.

Which brings me up to nineteen-thirty-five;
  Six months of film work is another story
I can't tell now. But, here I am, alive
  Knowing the true source of that sense of glory
  That still surrounds the England of the Tory,
Come only to the rather tame conclusion
That no man by himself has life's solution.

1937

[O WHO CAN EVER GAZE HIS FILL]

"O who can ever gaze his fill,"
  Farmer and fisherman say,
"On native shore and local hill,
Grudge aching limb or callus on the hand?
Fathers, grandfathers stood upon this land,
And here the pilgrims from our loins shall stand."

So farmer and fisherman say
In their fortunate heyday:
But Death's soft answer drifts across
Empty catch or harvest loss
Or an unlucky May.

The earth is an oyster with nothing inside it
Not to be born is the best for man
The end of toil is a bailiff's order
Throw down the mattock and dance while you can.

"O life's too short for friends who share,"
Travellers think in their hearts,
"The city's common bed, the air,
The mountain bivouac and the bathing beach,
Where incidents draw every day from each
Memorable gesture and witty speech."
So travellers think in their hearts,
Till malice or circumstance parts
Them from their constant humor:
And shyly Death's coercive rumor
In the silence starts.

A friend is the old old tale of Narcissus
Not to be born is the best for man
An active partner in something disgraceful
Change your partner, dance while you can.

"O stretch your hands across the sea,"
The impassioned lover cries,
"Stretch them towards your harm and me.
Our grass is green, and sensual our brief bed,
The stream sings at its foot, and at its head
The mild and vegetarian beasts are fed."
So the impassioned lover cries
Till his storm of pleasure dies:
From the bedpost and the rocks
Death's enticing echo mocks,
And his voice replies.

The greater the love, the more false to its object
Not to be born is the best for man
After the kiss comes the impulse to throttle
Break the embraces, dance while you can.

"I see the guilty world forgiven,"
  Dreamer and drunkard sing,
"The ladders let down out of heaven;
The laurel springing from the martyrs' blood;
The children skipping where the weepers stood;
The lovers natural, and the beasts all good."
  So dreamer and drunkard sing
  Till day their sobriety bring:
  Parrotwise with death's reply
  From whelping fear and nesting lie,
    Woods and their echoes ring.

The desires of the heart are as crooked as corkscrews
  Not to be born is the best for man.
The second best is a formal order
  The dance's pattern, dance while you can.
Dance, dance, for the figure is easy
  The tune is catching and will not stop
Dance till the stars come down with the rafters
  Dance, dance, dance till you drop.

1937

IN TIME OF WAR [1]

So from the years the gifts were showered; each
Ran off with his at once into his life:
Bee took the politics that make a hive,
Fish swam as fish, peach settled into peach.

And were successful at the first endeavor;
The hour of birth their only time at college,
They were content with their precocious knowledge,
And knew their station and were good for ever.

Till finally there came a childish creature
On whom the years could model any feature,
And fake with ease a leopard or a dove;

[1] This is part of a sonnet sequence which was written on a trip to the front lines in China. In these sonnets the references are to man in general, or the race as represented in one individual, rather than to any particular man.

Who by the lightest wind was changed and shaken,
And looked for truth and was continually mistaken,
And envied his few friends and chose his love.

* * * * *

They wondered why the fruit had been forbidden;
It taught them nothing new. They hid their pride,
But did not listen much when they were chidden;
They knew exactly what to do outside.

They left: immediately the memory faded
Of all they'd learnt; they could not understand
The dogs now who, before, had always aided;
The stream was dumb with whom they'd always planned.

They wept and quarrelled: freedom was so wild.
In front, maturity, as he ascended,
Retired like a horizon from the child;

The dangers and the punishments grew greater:
And the way back by angels was defended
Against the poet and the legislator.

* * * * *

He stayed: and was imprisoned in possession.
The seasons stood like guards about his ways,
The mountains chose the mother of his children,
And like a conscience the sun ruled his days.

Beyond him his young cousins in the city
Pursued their rapid and unnatural course,
Believed in nothing but were easy-going,
And treated strangers like a favorite horse.

And he changed little,
But took his color from the earth,
And grew in likeness to his sheep and cattle.

The townsman thought him miserly and simple,
The poet wept and saw in him the truth,
And the oppressor held him up as an example.

* * * * *

His generous bearing was a new invention:
For life was slow; earth needed to be careless:

With horse and sword he drew the girls' attention;
He was the Rich, the Bountiful, the Fearless.

And to the young he came as a salvation;
They needed him to free them from their mothers,
And grew sharp-witted in the long migration,
And round his camp fires learnt all men are brothers.

But suddenly the earth was full: he was not wanted.
And he became the shabby and demented,
And took to drink to screw his nerves to murder;

Or sat in offices and stole,
And spoke approvingly of Law and Order,
And hated life with all his soul.

* * * * *

He watched the stars and noted birds in flight;
The rivers flooded or the Empire fell:
He made predictions and was sometimes right;
His lucky guesses were rewarded well.

And fell in love with Truth before he knew her,
And rode into imaginary lands,
With solitude and fasting hoped to woo her,
And mocked at those who served her with their hands.

But her he never wanted to despise,
But listened always for her voice; and when
She beckoned to him, he obeyed in meekness,

And followed her and looked into her eyes;
Saw there reflected every human weakness,
And saw himself as one of many men.

* * * * *

He was their servant—some say he was blind—
And moved among their faces and their things;
Their feeling gathered in him like a wind
And sang: they cried—"It is a God that sings"—

And worshipped him and set him up apart,
And made him vain, till he mistook for song
The little tremors of his mind and heart
At each domestic wrong.

Songs came no more: he had to make them.
With what precision was each strophe planned,
He hugged his sorrow like a plot of land,

And walked like an assassin through the town,
And looked at men and did not like them,
But trembled if one passed him with a frown.

* * * * *

As a young child the wisest could adore him;
He felt familiar to them like their wives:
The very poor saved up their pennies for him,
And martyrs brought him presents of their lives.

But who could sit and play with him all day?
Their other needs were pressing, work, and bed:
The beautiful stone courts were built where they
Could leave him to be worshipped and well fed.

But he escaped. They were too blind to tell
That it was he who came with them to labor,
And talked and grew up with them like a neighbor:

To fear and greed those courts became a center;
The poor saw there the tyrant's citadel,
And martyrs the lost face of the tormentor.

* * * * *

Far from the heart of culture he was used:
Abandoned by his general and his lice,
Under a padded quilt he closed his eyes
And vanished. He will not be introduced

When this campaign is tidied into books:
No vital knowledge perished in his skull;
His jokes were stale; like wartime, he was dull;
His name is lost forever like his looks.

He neither knew nor chose the Good, but taught us,
And added meaning like a comma, when
He turned to dust in China that our daughters

Be fit to love the earth, and not again
Disgraced before the dogs; that, where are waters,
Mountains and houses, may be also men.

Wandering lost upon the mountains of our choice,
Again and again we sigh for an ancient South,
For the warm nude ages of instinctive poise,
For the taste of joy in the innocent mouth.

Asleep in our huts, how we dream of a part
In the glorious balls of the future; each intricate maze
Has a plan, and the disciplined movements of the heart
Can follow for ever and ever its harmless ways.

We envy streams and houses that are sure:
But we are articled to error; we
Were never nude and calm like a great door,

And never will be perfect like the fountains;
We live in freedom by necessity,
A mountain people dwelling among mountains.

1939

THE CAPITAL

Quarter of pleasures where the rich are always waiting,
Waiting expensively for miracles to happen,
O little restaurant where the lovers eat each other,
Café where exiles have established a malicious village;

You with your charm and your apparatus have abolished
The strictness of winter and the spring's compulsion;
Far from your lights the outraged punitive father,
The dullness of mere obedience here is apparent.

Yet with orchestras and glances, O, you betray us
To belief in our infinite powers; and the innocent
Unobservant offender falls in a moment
Victim to the heart's invisible furies.

In unlighted streets you hide away the appalling;
Factories where lives are made for a temporary use
Like collars or chairs, rooms where the lonely are battered
Slowly like pebbles into fortuitous shapes.

But the sky you illumine, your glow is visible far
Into the dark countryside, the enormous, the frozen,
Where, hinting at the forbidden like a wicked uncle,
Night after night to the farmer's children you beckon.

1940

[THE HOUR-GLASS WHISPERS]

The hour-glass whispers to the lion's paw,
The clock-towers tell the gardens day and night,
How many errors Time has patience for,
How wrong they are in being always right.

Yet Time, however loud its chimes or deep,
However fast its falling torrent flows,
Has never put the lion off his leap
Nor shaken the assurance of the rose.

For they, it seems, care only for success:
While we choose words according to their sound
And judge a problem by its awkwardness;

And Time with us was always popular.
When have we not preferred some going round
To going straight to where we are?

1940

MUSÉE DES BEAUX ARTS

About suffering they were never wrong,
The Old Masters: how well they understood
Its human position; how it takes place
While someone else is eating or opening a window or just
walking dully along;
How, when the aged are reverently, passionately waiting
For the miraculous birth, there always must be
Children who did not specially want it to happen, skating
On a pond at the edge of the wood:
They never forgot
That even the dreadful martyrdom must run its course

Anyhow in a corner, some untidy spot
Where the dogs go on with their doggy life and the torturer's
horse
Scratches its innocent behind on a tree.

In Breughel's *Icarus*, for instance: how everything turns away
Quite leisurely from the disaster; the ploughman may
Have heard the splash, the forsaken cry,
But for him it was not an important failure; the sun shone
As it had to on the white legs disappearing into the green
Water; and the expensive delicate ship that must have seen
Something amazing, a boy falling out of the sky,
Had somewhere to get to and sailed calmly on.

1940

IN MEMORY OF W. B. YEATS

1

He disappeared in the dead of winter:
The brooks were frozen, the air-ports almost deserted,
And snow disfigured the public statues;
The mercury sank in the mouth of the dying day.
O all the instruments agree
The day of his death was a dark cold day.

Far from his illness
The wolves ran on through the evergreen forests,
The peasant river was untempted by the fashionable quays;
By mourning tongues
The death of the poet was kept from his poems.

But for him it was his last afternoon as himself,
An afternoon of nurses and rumors;
The provinces of his body revolted,
The current of his feeling failed: he became his admirers.

Now he is scattered among a hundred cities
And wholly given over to unfamiliar affections;
To find his happiness in another kind of wood
And be punished under a foreign code of conscience.
The words of a dead man
Are modified in the guts of the living.

But in the importance and noise of to-morrow
When the brokers are roaring like beasts on the floor of the
Bourse,
And the poor have the sufferings to which they are fairly accus-
tomed,
And each in the cell of himself is almost convinced of his free-
dom;
A few thousand will think of this day
As one thinks of a day when one did something slightly unusual.

O all the instruments agree
The day of his death was a dark cold day.

2

You were silly like us: your gift survived it all;
The parish of rich women, physical decay,
Yourself; mad Ireland hurt you into poetry.
Now Ireland has her madness and her weather still,
For poetry makes nothing happen: it survives
In the valley of its saying where executives
Would never want to tamper; it flows south
From ranches of isolation and the busy griefs,
Raw towns that we believe and die in; it survives,
A way of happening, a mouth.

3

Earth, receive an honored guest;
William Yeats is laid to rest:
Let the Irish vessel lie
Emptied of its poetry.

Time that is intolerant
Of the brave and innocent,
And indifferent in a week
To a beautiful physique,

Worships language and forgives
Everyone by whom it lives;
Pardons cowardice, conceit,
Lays its honors at their feet.

Time that with this strange excuse
Pardoned Kipling and his views,

And will pardon Paul Claudel,
Pardons him for writing well.

In the nightmare of the dark
All the dogs of Europe bark,
And the living nations wait,
Each sequestered in its hate;

Intellectual disgrace
Stares from every human face,
And the seas of pity lie
Locked and frozen in each eye.

Follow, poet, follow right
To the bottom of the night,
With your unconstraining voice
Still persuade us to rejoice;

With the farming of a verse
Make a vineyard of the curse,
Sing of human unsuccess
In a rapture of distress;

In the deserts of the heart
Let the healing fountain start,
In the prison of his days
Teach the free man how to praise.

1940

[O UNICORN AMONG THE CEDARS] [1]

O Unicorn among the cedars,
To whom no magic charm can lead us,
White childhood moving like a sigh
Through the green woods unharmed in thy
Sophisticated innocence,
To call thy true love to the dance,
O Dove of science and of light,
Upon the branches of the night,
O Ichthus playful in the deep

[1] This lyric is taken at the suggestion of the author from "New Year Letter," III, in *The Double Man* (lines 1651-84).

Sea-lodges that forever keep
Their secret of excitement hidden,
O sudden Wind that blows unbidden,
Parting the quiet reeds, O Voice
Within the labyrinth of choice
Only the passive listener hears,
O Clock and Keeper of the years,
O Source of equity and rest,
Quando non fuerit, non est,[1]
It without image, paradigm
Of matter, motion, number, time,
The grinning gap of Hell, the hill
Of Venus and the stairs of Will,
Disturb our negligence and chill,
Convict our pride of its offence
In all things, even penitence,
Instruct us in the civil art
Of making from the muddled heart
A desert and a city where
The thoughts that have to labor there
May find locality and peace,
And pent-up feelings their release,
Send strength sufficient for our day,
And point our knowledge on its way,
O da quod jubes, Domine.[2]

1941

THE PRESUMPTUOUS [3]

They noticed that virginity was needed
To trap the unicorn in every case,
But not that, of those virgins who succeeded,
A high percentage had an ugly face.

The hero was as daring as they thought him,
But his peculiar boyhood missed them all;
The angel of a broken leg had taught him
The right precautions to avoid a fall.

[1] Since it never was, it doesn't exist (see Origen—*author's note*).

[2] O give what you decree, Lord (see St. Augustine's *Confessions* X—*author's note*).

[3] This and the two sonnets which follow are from a sonnet sequence entitled "The Quest" in *The Double Man*.

So in presumption they set forth alone
On what, for them, was not compulsory:
And stuck halfway to settle in some cave
With desert lions to domesticity;

Or turned aside to be absurdly brave,
And met the ogre and were turned to stone.

1941

VOCATION

Incredulous, he stared at the amused
Official writing down his name among
Those whose request to suffer was refused.

The pen ceased scratching: though he came too late
To join the martyrs, there was still a place
Among the tempters for a caustic tongue

To test the resolution of the young
With tales of the small failings of the great,
And shame the eager with ironic praise.

Though mirrors might be hateful for a while,
Women and books should teach his middle age
The fencing wit of an informal style
To keep the silences at bay and cage
His pacing manias in a worldly smile.

1941

THE USEFUL

The over-logical fell for the witch
Whose argument converted him to stone;
Thieves rapidly absorbed the over-rich;
The over-popular went mad alone,
And kisses brutalized the over-male.

As agents their effectiveness soon ceased;
Yet, in proportion as they seemed to fail,
Their instrumental value was increased
To those still able to obey their wish.

By standing stones the blind can feel their way,
Wild dogs compel the cowardly to fight,
Beggars assist the slow to travel light,
And even madmen manage to convey
Unwelcome truths in lonely gibberish.

1941

Louis MacNeice

Frederick Louis MacNeice was born in Belfast, Ireland, September 12, 1907. He is one of the children of an Anglican clergyman, John Frederick MacNeice, now Bishop of Belfast, and his wife, Elizabeth Margaret Clesham. At the time of Louis' birth, his father was incumbent of Holy Trinity Church, Belfast, but the next year he became incumbent at Carrickfergus, a town ten miles northeast of Belfast, and here Louis spent his early years.

His earliest training was at the hands of a governess, but when he was about eight years old he was sent to school in England, first in Dorsetshire, and then at Marlborough, Wiltshire. He gained a scholarship, paying £100 a year, at Merton College, Oxford, which he entered in the autumn of 1926. He was a brilliant student, and took a first class (highest honors) in the classics in 1930. He was lecturer in classics at the University of Birmingham from 1930 to 1936, and lecturer in Greek at Bedford College for Women from 1936 to 1940. During 1941-42 he held an appointment at Cornell University, Ithaca, New York.

MacNeice wrote verse from very early years, and when at Oxford he was already recognized as having considerable promise as a poet. His first volume, *Blind Fireworks,* was published in 1930, and since then he has written several other volumes, made a translation of the *Agamemnon* of Aeschylus, collaborated with W. H. Auden in writing *Letters from Iceland,* and has done some editing.

In 1930 he married Giovanni Marie Thérèse Babette Ezra, and they had one son. They were divorced in 1936. MacNeice now lives in London.

BIRMINGHAM

Smoke from the train-gulf hid by hoardings blunders upward, the brakes of cars
Pipe as the policeman pivoting round raises his flat hand, bars
With his figure of a monolith Pharaoh the queue of fidgety machines
(Chromium dogs on the bonnet, faces behind the triplex screens),
Behind him the streets run away between the proud glass of shops,
Cubical scent-bottles artificial legs arctic foxes and electric mops,
But beyond this center the slumward vista thins like a diagram:
There, unvisited, are Vulcan's forges who doesn't care a tinker's damn.
Splayed outwards through the suburbs houses, houses for rest
Seducingly rigged by the builder, half-timbered houses with lips pressed
So tightly and eyes staring at the traffic through bleary haws
And only a six-inch grip of the racing earth in their concrete claws;
In these houses men as in a dream pursue the Platonic Forms
With wireless and cairn terriers and gadgets approximating to the fickle norms
And endeavor to find God and score one over the neighbor
By climbing tentatively upward on jerry-built beauty and sweated labor.
The lunch hour: the shops empty, shopgirls' faces relax
Diaphanous as green glass, empty as old almanacs
As incoherent with ticketed gewgaws tiered behind their heads
As the Burne-Jones windows in St. Philip's broken by crawling leads;
Insipid color, patches of emotion, Saturday thrills
(This theatre is sprayed with "June")—the gutter take our old playbills,
Next week-end it is likely in the heart's funfair we shall pull
Strong enough on the handle to get back our money; or at any rate it is possible.
On shining lines the trams like vast sarcophagi move
Into the sky, plum after sunset, merging to duck's egg, barred with mauve
Zeppelin clouds, and Pentecost-like the cars' headlights bud
Out from sideroads and the traffic signals, crème de menthe or bull's blood,

Tell one to stop, the engine gently breathing, or to go on
To where like black pipes of organs in the frayed and fading zone
Of the West the factory chimneys on sullen sentry will all night wait
To call, in the harsh morning, sleep-stupid faces through the daily gate.

1933, 1935

MUSEUMS

Museums offer us, running from among the 'buses,
A centrally heated refuge, parquet floors and sarcophaguses,
Into whose tall fake porches we hurry without a sound
Like a beetle under a brick that lies, useless, on the ground.
Warmed and cajoled by the silence the cowed cypher revives,
Mirrors himself in the cases of pots, paces himself by marble lives,
Makes believe it was he that was the glory that was Rome,
Soft on his cheek the nimbus of other people's martyrdom,
And then returns to the street, his mind an arena where sprawls
Any number of consumptive Keatses and dying Gauls.

1933, 1935

NATURE MORTE

(EVEN SO IT IS NOT SO EASY TO BE DEAD)

As those who are not athletic at breakfast day by day
Employ and enjoy the sinews of others vicariously,
Shielded by the upheld journal from their dream-puncturing wives
And finding in the printed word a multiplication of their lives,
So we whose senses give us things misfelt and misheard
Turn also, for our adjustment, to the pretentious word
Which stabilizes the light on the sun-fondled trees
And, by photographing our ghosts, claims to put us at our ease;
Yet even so, no matter how solid and staid we contrive
Our reconstructions, even a still life is alive
And in your Chardin the appalling unrest of the soul
Exudes from the dried fish and the brown jug and the bowl.

1933, 1935

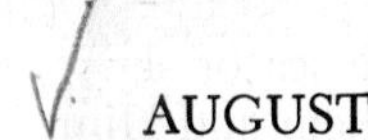

AUGUST

The shutter of time darkening ceaselessly
Has whisked away the foam of may and elder
And I realize how now, as every year before,
Once again the gay months have eluded me.

For the mind, by nature stagey, welds its frame
Tomb-like around each little world of a day;
We jump from picture to picture and cannot follow
The living curve that is breathlessly the same.

While the lawn-mower sings moving up and down
Spirting its little fountain of vivid green,
I, like Poussin, make a still-bound fete of us
Suspending every noise, of insect or machine.

Garlands at a set angle that do not slip,
Theatrically (and as if for ever) grace
You and me and the stone god in the garden
And Time who also is shown with a stone face.

But all this is a dilettante's lie,
Time's face is not stone nor still his wings,
Our mind, being dead, wishes to have time die
For we being ghosts cannot catch hold of things.

1933, 1935

ODE

Tonight is so coarse with chocolate
    The wind blowing from Bournville
That I hanker after the Atlantic
    With a frivolous nostalgia
Like that which film-fans feel
    For their celluloid abstractions
The nifty hero and the deathless blonde
    And find escape by proxy
From the eight-hour day or the wheel
    Of work and bearing children.

If God is boundless as the sea or sky
The eye bounds both of them and Him,
We always have the horizon
Not to swim to but to see:
God is seen with shape and limit
More purple towards the rim,
This segment of His infinite extension
Is all the God of Him for me.

And you too, my love, my limit,
So palpable and your hair shot with red—
I do not want a hundred wives or lives
Any more than I want to be too well-read
Or have money like the sand or ability like the hydra's heads
To flicker the tongues of self-engendering power,
I want a sufficient sample, the exact and framed
Balance of definite masses, the islanded hour.

I would pray for that island; mob mania in the air,
I cannot assume their easy bravery
Drugged with a slogan, chewing the old lie
That parallel lines will meet at infinity;
As I walk on the shore of the regular and rounded sea
I would pray off from my son the love of that infinite
Which is too greedy and too obvious; let his Absolute
Like any four-walled house be put up decently.

Let us turn to homeliness,
Born in the middle of May
Let him accumulate, corroborate while he may
The blessedness of fact
Which lives in the dancing atom and the breathing trees
And everywhere except in the fancy of man
Who daubs his slush on the hawthorn and the may.

Let him have five good senses
The feeling for symmetry
And the sense of the magnet,
His mind deft and unflustered
To change gear easily
And let not the blasphemy
Of dusty words deceive him.

May he hit the golden mean
Which contains the seasonal extreme,
May he riot in the diving sun
And die in the crystal dream,
May his good deeds flung forth
Like boomerangs return
To wear around his neck
As beads of definite worth.

May he pick up daintily
The ambiguous joys,
As a bee in May the blossom of fruit
Cross-fertilize his data and distil
From the drum balalaika fiddle and organ
From sun's gunnery splintering glass
More than the twanging dazzle or the dazzling noise.

To get permanence, to hear the personance
Of all the water-gullies and blackbirds' songs
Drained off or died twenty years back
To make his flesh of them and so renounce the mask
Of the sham soul, the cask bobbing empty
On leaden waves, the veneer the years crack.

To ride two horses at once, a foot on each
Tilting outward on space abstract and packed
With the audience of the dead and the unborn,
To pay his debts to each
To beach his boat so that others can use it
To throw his bread on the waters, the best deposit.

That people are lovable is a strange discovery
And there are many conflicting allegiances;
The pedals of a chance bicycle
Make a gold shower turning in the sun,
Trains leave in all directions on wild rails
And for every act determined on and won
There is a possible world denied and lost.

Do not then turn maudlin or weathercock,
We must cut the throat of the hour
That it may not haunt us because our sentiments
Continued its existence to pollute

Its essence; bottled time turns sour upon the sill.
The children play in the park; the ducklings
Rise and scurry on the water, a car
Changes down, the sandwichmen
Move up and down with the never-changing news.
Do not brood too much on the forking paths.

The leaves dark green on top, light green under, seas of green
Had brought him on full flood, the color laid on in slices
As by a mason's trowel or ice cream in sliders
Bought in dusty streets under the yellow-green beeches,
A little while ago the green was only peppered
But now we gape at a wealthy wave and a tidal tower of green.

Coral azalea and scarlet rhododendron
Syringa and pink horse-chestnut and laburnum
Solid as temples, niched with the song of birds,
Widen the eyes and nostrils, demand homage of words.
And we have to turn from them,
Compose ourselves, fit out an ethic:
Have I anything to hand my son,
Scarab or compass for his journey?

Only so far, so far as I can find, symbols;
No decalogue, no chemical formula;
Unanalyzed scent and noise, the fly on the pane,
The tulips banked on the glass-and-black hearse
A memory of a cock crowing in the dark like a curse
The remembered hypnotism of an aeroplane in June—

Watching the cricket from between
Slabs of green and slabs of blue and slowly ladled clouds
We looked at the sky through straw hats,
The sky was turned into black and white small stars.
Then came, southward as always, the angel
His song like the heat dancing on the gravel
High above the bat-chock and the white umpires
Moving south while the clapping of a run turns chill in echo
And his own drone is whittled to the point of a pin
So that dozing boys fumble the ghost of sound.

But this identical sound the then epitome
Of summer's athletic ease and the smell of cut grass

Will sometime be our augury of war
When these tiny flies like nibs will calmly draw our death
A dipping gradient on the graph of Europe
And over the hairy flatnesses of Russia
This sound when we have died will linger to a wisp
And the endless corn wave tiredly.

Humming and buzzing, the bomber and the fly on the pane
And the telephone wires hung on dead pines,
In Ireland once a string of bright-red haws
Hung, thrown up by children, on those wires:
Not to hang so, O God, between your iron spires!
The town-dweller like a rabbit in a greengrocer's
Who was innocent and integral once
Now, red with slit guts, hangs by the heels
Hangs by the heels gut-open against the fog
Between two spires that are not conscious of him.

Therefore let not my son, halving the truth
Be caught between jagged edges;
And let him not falsify the world
By taking it to pieces;
The marriage of Cause and Effect, Form and Content
Let him not part asunder.
Wisdom for him in the time of tulips
Monastic repose, martial élan,
Then the opening mouth a dragon or a voluptuary—
These moments let him retain like limbs
His time not crippled by flaws of faith or memory.

In the Birmingham Market Hall at this time
There are horseshoe wreaths of mauve stock
Fixed with wire and nailed with pale pink roses
The tribute to a life that ran on standard wheels—
May his life be more than this matter of wheels and wire.

I remember all the houses where parents
Have reared their children to be parents
(Cut box and privet and the parrot's voice)
To be clerks to total the flow of alien money
To be florists to design these wreaths and wedding bouquets.

I cannot draw up any code
    There are too many qualifications

Too many asterisk asides
    Too many crosses in the margin
But as others, forgetting the others,
    Run after the nostrums
Of science art and religion
    So would I mystic and maudlin
Dream of the both real and ideal
    Breakers of ocean.
I must put away this drug.

Must become the migrating bird following felt routes
The comet's superficially casual orbit kept
Not self-abandoning to sky-blind chutes
To climb miles and kiss the miles of foam
For nothing is more proud than humbly to accept
And without soaring or swerving win by ignoring
The endlessly curving sea and so come to one's home.

And so come to one's peace while the yellow waves are roaring.

1934, 1935

VENUS' SPEECH

So you think it is all a matter of love?
And what do you think love is a matter of?
Matter is the word for it.
Atoms—permutations, combinations of atoms.
It's not just a fancy ballet, a *fête champêtre*.
The cycle of life demands to be repeated.
You were made by your parents, you must make in return,
You must make children for Death.
Death is a sculptor, you must quarry him marble,
His chisel will find the shape in the blind block.
What you call love is merely an incident;
Wait till you see the end of it.
There is a city beyond this life, no flesh or blood there,
No food in the shops, no fire in the grates, no smoke from the
    chimneys;
All the people that have ever lived walk there
Renouncing their living,
All the people that have ever loved walk there
Renouncing their loving,

But they do not even think this renunciation
For their brains are solid, of stone,
Their heads and their eyes are of stone,
Being no longer organisms of nature
But final versions of an artist's vision.
For the art of man is supererogation;
Man himself will be a work of art in the end.
Man should not emulate the artist, Death.
Let not man be contriving a frozen beauty;
While he is here and now let him deal in here and now,
Work and fight for meat and love,
Gallant approximation, bravado of defeat.
I am the principle of Unity and Division,
Multiplication by pain,
Spawning of worlds from a discord
Always recurring,
I am the attempt to cover the abyss with grass
And to spangle the grass with flowers
And to put there cattle grazing the grass
And young men picking the flowers,
And to make believe through elaboration of pattern
That life goes on for ever.
Which, thanks to me, is true in a sense.
Which, thanks to me, is true in the world of sense
Though it is not true in the world of precise death,
The world of pure idea, mating statues.
Go to your work, children, the tide is coming in,
The strip of sand is narrow,
You have not much time if you wish to get married,
You have not much time if you wish to build castles.
Blessed are the reckless spendthrifts of vitality
But blessed also are all who last the course,
Blessed are those who endure as a point of etiquette
And blessed are the cynics who carry their cross as a gesture.
Do you remember when you were six years old
The text in the parish church at Christmas,
"Peace on Earth, Goodwill to Men,"
And Christ's lips moving in the stained glass window?
There were no lipreaders present
But I can tell you what he said.
"I come bringing not peace," he said. "I come
Bringing not peace but a sword."
All to their posts. The drum is beating.

Diver, descend. Ploughman, drive your team.
Grapple the bulk of the sea, challenge the flinty soil;
The furrows are there in advance as music is there in the air
Waiting to be realized upon the fiddler's bow.

Chorus

Sleep and wake, sleep and wake,
Sleep to wake but wake to sleep,
And body calling body make
A further body, the insistent task
Of rolling a stone up the steep
Hill of hell, of rolling a stone
Away from the tomb and do not ask
Who comes forth in the dawn alone.

1937

THE SUNLIGHT ON THE GARDEN

The sunlight on the garden
Hardens and grows cold,
We cannot cage the minute
Within its nets of gold;
When all is told
We cannot beg for pardon.

Our freedom as free lances
Advances towards its end;
The earth compels, upon it
Sonnets and birds descend;
And soon, my friend,
We shall have no time for dances.

The sky was good for flying
Defying the church bells
And every evil iron
Siren and what it tells:
The earth compels,
We are dying, Egypt, dying

And not expecting pardon,
Hardened in heart anew,
But glad to have sat under

Thunder and rain with you,
And grateful too
For sunlight on the garden.

1937, 1938

We're on our way out; we're dying

JUNE THUNDER

The Junes were free and full, driving through tiny
Roads, the mudguards brushing the cowparsley,
Through fields of mustard and under boldly embattled
Mays and chestnuts

Or between beeches verdurous and voluptuous
Or where broom and gorse beflagged the chalkland—
All the flare and gusto of the unenduring
Joys of a season

Now returned but I note as more appropriate
To the maturer moods impending thunder
With an indigo sky and the garden hushed except for
The treetops moving.

Then the curtains in my room blow suddenly inward,
The shrubbery rustles, birds fly heavily homeward,
The white flowers fade to nothing on the trees and rain comes
Down like a dropscene.

Now there comes the catharsis, the cleansing downpour
Breaking the blossoms of our overdated fancies
Our old sentimentality and whimsicality
Loves of the morning.

Blackness at half-past eight, the night's precursor,
Clouds like falling masonry and lightning's lavish
Annunciation, the sword of the mad archangel
Flashed from the scabbard.

If only now you would come and dare the crystal
Rampart of rain and the bottomless moat of thunder,
If only now you would come I should be happy
Now if now only.

1937, 1938

LEAVING BARRA

The dazzle on the sea, my darling,
Leads from the western channel
A carpet of brilliance taking
My leave for ever of the island.

I never shall visit that island
Again with its easy tempo—
The seal sunbathing, the circuit
Of gulls on the wing for garbage.

I go to a different garbage
And scuffle for scraps of notice,
Pretend to ignore the stigma
That stains my life and my leisure.

For fretful even in leisure
I fidget for different values,
Restless as a gull and haunted
By a hankering after Atlantis.

I do not know that Atlantis
Unseen and uncomprehended,
Dimly divined but keenly
Felt with a phantom hunger.

If only I could crush the hunger
If only I could lay the phantom
Then I should no doubt be happy
Like a fool or a dog or a buddha.

O the self-abnegation of Buddha
The belief that is disbelieving
The denial of chiaroscuro
Not giving a damn for existence!

But I would cherish existence
Loving the beast and the bubble
Loving the rain and the rainbow,
Considering philosophy alien.

For all the religions are alien
That allege that life is a fiction,
And when we agree in denial
The cock crows in the morning.

If only I could wake in the morning
And find I had learned the solution,
Wake with the knack of knowledge
Who as yet have only an inkling.

Though some facts foster the inkling—
The beauty of the moon and music,
The routine courage of the worker,
The gay endurance of women,

And you who to me among women
Stand for so much that I wish for,
I thank you, my dear, for the example
Of living in tune and moving.

For few are able to keep moving,
They drag and flag in the traffic;
While you are alive beyond question
Like the dazzle on the sea, my darling.

1937, 1938

[AUGUST IS NEARLY OVER] [1]

August is nearly over, the people
  Back from holiday are tanned
With blistered thumbs and a wallet of snaps and a little
  Joie de vivre which is contraband;
Whose stamina is enough to face the annual
  Wait for the annual spree,

[1] This and the three selections which follow are from *Autumn Journal,* a group of poems which form a "record of the author's intellectual and emotional experience" between August and December, 1938. The first of these was written as he was returning from his vacation. The next was written just after the Munich crisis, when the British Prime Minister returned from a meeting with Hitler to declare that there would be "peace in our time." The date of the third is given in the poem. The last, written December 31, 1938, is the conclusion of the *Journal.*

Whose memories are stamped with specks of sunshine
  Like faded *fleurs de lys.*
Now the till and the typewriter call the fingers,
  The workman gathers his tools
For the eight-hour day but after that the solace
  Of films or football pools
Or of the gossip or cuddle, the moments of self-glory
  Or self-indulgence, blinkers on the eyes of doubt,
The blue smoke rising and the brown lace sinking
  In the empty glass of stout.
Most are accepters, born and bred to harness,
  And take things as they come,
But some refusing harness and more who are refused it
  Would pray that another and a better Kingdom come,
Which now is sketched in the air or travestied in slogans
  Written in chalk or tar on stucco or plaster-board
But in time may find its body in men's bodies,
  Its law and order in their hearts' accord,
Where skill will no longer languish nor energy be trammelled
  To competition and graft,
Exploited in subservience but not allegiance
  To an utterly lost and daft
System that gives a few at fancy prices
  Their fancy lives
While ninety-nine in the hundred who never attend the banquet
  Must wash the grease of ages off the knives.
And now the tempter whispers "But you also
  Have the slave-owner's mind,
Would like to sleep on a mattress of easy profits,
  To snap your fingers or a whip and find
Servants or houris ready to wince and flatter
  And build with their degradation your self-esteem;
What you want is not a world of the free in function
  But a niche at the top, the skimmings of the cream."
And I answer that that is largely so for habit makes me
  Think victory for one implies another's defeat,
That freedom means the power to order, and that in order
  To preserve the values dear to the élite
The élite must remain a few. It is so hard to imagine
  A world where the many would have their chance without
A fall in the standard of intellectual living
  And nothing left that the highbrow cared about.
Which fears must be suppressed. There is no reason for thinking

That, if you give a chance to people to think or live,
The arts of thought or life will suffer and become rougher
And not return more than you could ever give.
And now I relapse to sleep, to dreams perhaps and reaction
Where I shall play the gangster or the sheikh,
Kill for the love of killing, make the world my sofa,
Unzip the women and insult the meek.
Which fantasies no doubt are due to my private history,
Matter for the analyst,
But the final cure is not in his past-dissecting fingers
But in a future of action, the will and fist
Of those who abjure the luxury of self-pity,
And prefer to risk a movement without being sure
If movement would be better or worse in a hundred
Years or a thousand when their heart is pure.
None of our hearts are pure, we always have mixed motives,
Are self deceivers, but the worst of all
Deceits is to murmur "Lord, I am not worthy"
And, lying easy, turn your face to the wall.
But may I cure that habit, look up and outwards
And may my feet follow my wider glance
First no doubt to stumble, then to walk with the others
And in the end—with time and luck—to dance.

1938, 1939

[NOW WE ARE BACK TO NORMAL]

Now we are back to normal, now the mind is
Back to the even tenor of the usual day
Skidding no longer across the uneasy camber
Of the nightmare way.
We are safe though others have crashed the railings
Over the river ravine; their wheel-tracks carve the bank
But after the event all we can do is argue
And count the widening ripples where they sank.
October comes with rain whipping around the ankles
In waves of white at night
And filling the raw clay trenches (the parks of London
Are a nasty sight).
In a week I return to work, lecturing, coaching,
As impresario of the Ancient Greeks
Who wore the chiton and lived on fish and olives

And talked philosophy or smut in cliques;
Who believed in youth and did not gloze the unpleasant
Consequences of age;
What is life, one said, or what is pleasant
Once you have turned the page
Of love? The days grow worse, the dice are loaded
Against the living man who pays in tears for breath;
Never to be born was the best, call no man happy
This side death.
Conscious—long before Engels—of necessity
And therein free
They plotted out their life with truism and humor
Between the jealous heaven and the callous sea.
And Pindar sang the garland of wild olive
And Alcibiades lived from hand to mouth
Double-crossing Athens, Persia, Sparta,
And many died in the city of plague, and many of drouth
In Sicilian quarries, and many by the spear and arrow
And many more who told their lies too late
Caught in the eternal factions and reactions
Of the city-state.
And free speech shivered on the pikes of Macedonia
And later on the swords of Rome
And Athens became a mere university city
And the goddess born of the foam
Became the kept hetaera, heroine of Menander,
And the philosopher narrowed his focus, confined
His efforts to putting his own soul in order
And keeping a quiet mind.
And for a thousand years they went on talking,
Making such apt remarks,
A race no longer of heroes but of professors
And crooked business men and secretaries and clerks;
Who turned out dapper little elegiac verses
On the ironies of fate, the transience of all
Affections, carefully shunning an over-statement
But working the dying fall.
The Glory that was Greece: put it in a syllabus, grade it
Page by page
To train the mind or even to point a moral
For the present age:
Models of logic and lucidity, dignity, sanity,
The golden mean between opposing ills

Though there were exceptions of course but only exceptions—
  The bloody Bacchanals on the Thracian hills.
So the humanist in his room with Jacobean panels
  Chewing his pipe and looking on a lazy quad
Chops the Ancient World to turn a sermon
  To the greater glory of God.
But I can do nothing so useful or so simple;
  These dead are dead.
And when I should remember the paragons of Hellas
  I think instead
Of the crooks, the adventurers, the opportunists,
  The careless athletes and the fancy boys,
The hair-splitters, the pedants, the hard-boiled sceptics
  And the Agora and the noise
Of the demagogues and the quacks; and the women pouring
  Libations over graves
And the trimmers at Delphi and the dummies at Sparta and lastly
  I think of the slaves.
And how one can imagine oneself among them
  I do not know;
It was all so unimaginably different
  And all so long ago.

1938, 1939

[THESE DAYS ARE MISTY, INSULATED]

These days are misty, insulated, mute
  Like a faded tapestry and the soft pedal
Is down and the yellow leaves are falling down
  And we hardly have the heart to meddle
Any more with personal ethics or public calls;
  People have not recovered from the crisis,
Their faces are far away, the tone of the words
  Belies their thesis.
For they say that now it is time unequivocally to act,
  To let the pawns be taken,
That criticism, a virtue previously,
  Now can only weaken
And that when we go to Rome
  We must do as the Romans do, cry out together
For bread and circuses; put on your togas now
  For this is Roman weather.

Circuses of death and from the topmost tiers
  A cataract of goggling, roaring faces;
On the arena sand
  Those who are about to die try out their paces.
Now it is night, a cold mist creeps, the night
  Is still and damp and lonely;
Sitting by the fire it is hard to realize
  That the legions wait at the gates and that there is only
A little time for rest though not by rights for rest,
  Rather for whetting the will, for calculating
A compromise between necessity and wish,
  Apprenticed late to learn the trade of hating.
Remember the sergeant barking at bayonet practice
  When you were small;
To kill a dummy you must act a dummy
  Or you cut no ice at all.
Now it is morning again, the 25th of October,
  In a white fog the cars have yellow lights;
The chill creeps up the wrists, the sun is sallow,
  The silent hours grow down like stalactites.
And reading Plato talking about his Forms
  To damn the artist touting round his mirror,
I am glad that I have been left the third best bed
  And live in a world of error.
His world of capital initials, of transcendent
  Ideas is too bleak;
For me there remain to all intents and purposes
  Seven days in the week
And no one Tuesday is another and you destroy it
  If you subtract the difference and relate
It merely to the Form of Tuesday. This is Tuesday
  The 25th of October, 1938.
Aristotle was better who watched the insect breed,
  The natural world develop,
Stressing the function, scrapping the Form in Itself,
  Taking the horse from the shelf and letting it gallop.
Education gives us too many labels
  And clichès, cuts too many Gordian knots;
Trains us to keep the roads nor reconnoitre
  Any of the beauty-spots or danger-spots.
Not that I would rather be a peasant; the Happy Peasant
  Like the Noble Savage is a myth;
I do not envy the self-possession of an elm-tree

Nor the aplomb of a granite monolith.
All that I would like to be is human, having a share
In a civilized, articulate and well-adjusted
Community where the mind is given its due
But the body is not distrusted.
As it is, the so-called humane studies
May lead to cushy jobs
But leave the men who land them spiritually bankrupt
Intellectual snobs.
Not but what I am glad to have my comforts,
Better authentic mammon than a bogus god;
If it were not for Lit. Hum. I might be climbing
A ladder with a hod.
And seven hundred a year
Will pay the rent and the gas and the 'phone and the grocer;
(The Emperor takes his seat beneath the awning,
Those who are about to die . . .) Come, pull the curtains closer.

1938, 1939

[SLEEP SERENE, AVOID THE BACKWARD]

Sleep serene, avoid the backward
Glance; go forward, dreams, and do not halt
(Behind you in the desert stands a token
Of doubt—a pillar of salt).
Sleep, the past, and wake, the future,
And walk out promptly through the open door;
But you, my coward doubts, may go on sleeping,
You need not wake again—not any more.
The New Year comes with bombs, it is too late
To dose the dead with honorable intentions:
If you have honor to spare, employ it on the living;
The dead are dead as 1938.
Sleep to the noise of running water
Tomorrow to be crossed, however deep;
This is no river of the dead or Lethe,
Tonight we sleep
On the banks of Rubicon—the die is cast;
There will be time to audit
The accounts later, there will be sunlight later
And the equation will come out at last.

1938, 1939

PROGNOSIS

Good-bye, Winter,
The days are getting longer,
The tea-leaf in the teacup
Is herald of a stranger.

Will he bring me business
Or will he bring me gladness
Or will he come for cure
Of his own sickness?

With a pedlar's burden
Walking up the garden
Will he come to beg
Or will he come to bargain?

Will he come to pester,
To cringe or to bluster,
A promise in his palm
Or a gun in his holster?

Will his name be John
Or will his name be Jonah
Crying to repent
On the Island of Iona?

Will his name be Jason
Looking for a seaman
Or a mad crusader
Without rhyme or reason?

What will be his message—
War or work or marriage?
News as new as dawn
Or an old adage?

Will he give a champion
Answer to my question
Or will his words be dark
And his ways evasion?

Will his name be Love
And all his talk be crazy?
Or will his name be Death
And his message easy?
Spring 1939, 1940

A TOAST

The slurred and drawled and crooning sounds,
The blurred and suave and sidling smells,
The webs of dew, the bells of buds,
The sun going down in crimson suds—
This is on me and these are yours.

The bland and sculped and urgent beasts,
The here and there and nowhere birds,
The tongues of fire, the words of foam,
The curdling stars in the night's dome—
This is on me and these are yours.

The face and grace and muscle of man,
The balance of his body and mind,
Who keeps a trump behind his brain
Till instinct flicks it out again—
This is on me and these are yours.

The courage of eyes, the craft of hands,
The gay feet, the pulse of hope,
The will that flings a rope—though hard—
To catch the future off its guard—
This is on me and these are yours.

The luck and pluck and plunge of blood,
The wealth and spilth and sport of breath,
And sleep come down like death above
The fever and the peace of love—
This is on me and these are yours.
May 1939, 1940

ENTIRELY

If we could get the hang of it entirely
  It would take too long;
All we know is the splash of words in passing
  And falling twigs of song,
And when we try to eavesdrop on the great
  Presences it is rarely
That by a stroke of luck we can appropriate
  Even a phrase entirely.

If we could find our happiness entirely
  In somebody else's arms
We should not fear the spears of the spring nor the city's
  Yammering fire alarms
But, as it is, the spears each year go through
  Our flesh and almost hourly
Bell or siren banishes the blue
  Eyes of Love entirely.

And if the world were black or white entirely
  And all the charts were plain
Instead of a mad weir of tigerish waters,
  A prism of delight and pain,
We might be surer where we wished to go
  Or again we might be merely
Bored but in brute reality there is no
  Road that is right entirely.

1940, 1940

Stephen Spender

Stephen Harold Spender was born in London, February 28, 1909. He was one of the four children—three sons and a daughter—of Edward Harold Spender, a journalist, novelist, and lecturer, and his wife, Violet Hilda Schuster, who was descended from a family of German Jews.

As a child Spender was interested in painting, but he soon transferred his interest to poetry, and by his nineteenth year he had set up on his own printing press a little pamphlet of verse, *Nine Experiments* (1928). He attended University College School in London, and in October, 1927, he entered University College, Oxford. In the ensuing years he spent much time traveling on the Continent, and he left Oxford in 1931 without taking a degree. In 1936 he married Agnes Marie Pearn, but was later divorced, and in 1941 he made a second marriage. In 1937 he went to Spain to attend the International Writers' Conference, where he made the friendship of the French novelist André Malraux.

Besides several volumes of poetry, Spender has published *The Destructive Element* (1935), a volume of critical essays; *Forward from Liberalism* (1937), a statement of his political views; *The Burning Cactus* (1937), a volume of short stories; *Trial of a Judge* (1938), a poetical drama, which was produced by the Group Theatre in London; *The New Realism* (1939), an essay which was originally given as a lecture before the Association of Writers for Intellectual Liberty; and *The Backward Son* (1940), a novel.

[HE WILL WATCH THE HAWK]

He will watch the hawk with an indifferent eye
Or pitifully;
Nor on those eagles that so feared him, now
Will strain his brow;
Weapons men use, stone, sling and strong-thewed bow
He will not know.

This aristocrat, superb of all instinct,
With death close linked
Had paced the enormous cloud, almost had won
War on the sun;
Till now, like Icarus mid-ocean-drowned,
Hands, wings, are found.

1933

[ROLLED OVER ON EUROPE]

Rolled over on Europe: the sharp dew frozen to stars
Below us: above our heads the night
Frozen again to stars: the stars
In pools between our coats, and that charmed moon:
Ah, what supports? What cross draws out our arms,
Heaves up our bodies towards the wind
And hammers us between the mirrored lights?

Only my body is real: which wolves
Are free to oppress and gnaw. Only this rose
My friend laid on my breast, and these few lines
Written from home, are real.

1933

[NEVER BEING, BUT ALWAYS AT THE EDGE]

Never being, but always at the edge of Being
My head, like Death-mask, is brought into the sun.
The shadow pointing finger across cheek,
I move lips for tasting, I move hands for touching,

But never am nearer than touching
Though the spirit lean outward for seeing.
Observing rose, gold, eyes, an admired landscape,
My senses record the act of wishing
Wishing to be
Rose, gold, landscape or another.
I claim fulfilment in the fact of loving.

1933

[YOUR BODY IS STARS]

Your body is stars whose million glitter here:
I am lost amongst the branches of this sky
Here near my breast, here in my nostrils, here
Where our vast arms like streams of fire lie.

How can this end? My healing fills the night
And hangs its flags in worlds I cannot near.
Our movements range through miles, and when we kiss
The moment widens to enclose long years.

* * * * *

Beholders of the promised dawn of truth
The explorers of immense and simple lines,
Here is our goal, men cried, but it was lost
Amongst the mountain mists and mountain pines.

So with this face of love, whose breathings are
A mystery shadowed on the desert floor:
The promise hangs, this swarm of stars and flowers,
And then there comes the shutting of a door.

1933

[WITHOUT THAT ONCE CLEAR AIM]

Without that once clear aim, the path of flight
To follow for a life-time through white air,
This century chokes me under roots of night
I suffer like history in Dark Ages, where
Truth lies in dungeons, from which drifts no whisper:
We hear of towers long broken off from sight

And tortures and war, in dark and smoky rumor,
But on men's buried lives there falls no light.
Watch me who walk through coiling streets where rain
And fog drown every cry: at corners of day
Road drills explore new areas of pain,
Nor summer nor light may reach down here to play.
The city builds its horror in my brain,
This writing is my only wings away.

1933

[I THINK CONTINUALLY OF THOSE]

I think continually of those who were truly great.
Who, from the womb, remembered the soul's history
Through corridors of light where the hours are suns
Endless and singing. Whose lovely ambition
Was that their lips, still touched with fire,
Should tell of the Spirit clothed from head to foot in song.
And who hoarded from the Spring branches
The desires falling across their bodies like blossoms.

What is precious is never to forget
The essential delight of the blood drawn from ageless springs
Breaking through rocks in worlds before our earth.
Never to deny its pleasure in the morning simple light
Nor its grave evening demand for love.
Never to allow gradually the traffic to smother
With noise and fog the flowering of the spirit.

Near the snow, near the sun, in the highest fields
See how these names are feted by the waving grass
And by the streamers of white cloud
And whispers of wind in the listening sky.
The names of those who in their lives fought for life
Who wore at their hearts the fire's center.
Born of the sun they travelled a short while towards the sun,
And left the vivid air signed with their honor.

1933

THE FUNERAL

Death is another milestone on their way.
With laughter on their lips and with winds blowing round them
They record simply
How this one excelled all others in making driving belts.

This is festivity, it is the time of statistics
When they record what one unit contributed:
They are glad as they lay him back in the earth
And thank him for what he gave them.

They walk home remembering the straining red flags,
And with pennons of song still fluttering through their blood
They speak of the world state
With its towns like brain-centers and its pulsing arteries.

They think how one life hums, revolves and toils,
One cog in a golden and singing hive:
Like spark from fire, its task happily achieved,
It falls away quietly.

No more are they haunted by the individual grief
Nor the crocodile tears of European genius,
The decline of a culture
Mourned by scholars who dream of the ghosts of Greek boys.

1933

THE PYLONS

The secret of these hills was stone, and cottages
Of that stone made,
And crumbling roads
That turned on sudden hidden villages.

Now over these small hills they have built the concrete
That trails black wire:
Pylons, those pillars
Bare like nude, giant girls that have no secret.

The valley with its gilt and evening look
And the green chestnut
Of customary root
Are mocked dry like the parched bed of a brook.

But far above and far as sight endures
Like whips of anger
With lightning's danger
There runs the quick perspective of the future.

This dwarfs our emerald country by its trek
So tall with prophecy:
Dreaming of cities
Where often clouds shall lean their swan-white neck.

1933

[IN RAILWAY HALLS, ON PAVEMENTS]

In railway halls, on pavements near the traffic,
They beg, their eyes made big by empty staring
And only measuring Time, like the blank clock.

No, I shall weave no tracery of pen-ornament
To make them birds upon my singing-tree:
Time merely drives these lives which do not live
As tides push rotten stuff along the shore.

—There is no consolation, no, none
In the curving beauty of that line
Traced on our graphs through history, where the oppressor
Starves and deprives the poor.

Paint here no draped despairs, no saddening clouds
Where the soul rests, proclaims eternity.
But let the wrong cry out as raw as wounds
This Time forgets and never heals, far less transcends.

1933

[NOT PALACES, AN ERA'S CROWN]

Not palaces, an era's crown
Where the mind dwells, intrigues, rests;
The architectural gold-leaved flower
From people ordered like a single mind,
I build. This only what I tell:
It is too late for rare accumulation
For family pride, for beauty's filtered dusts;
I say, stamping the words with emphasis,
Drink from here energy and only energy,
As from the electric charge of a battery,
To will this Time's change.
Eye, gazelle, delicate wanderer,
Drinker of horizon's fluid line;
Ear that suspends on a chord
The spirit drinking timelessness;
Touch, love, all senses,
Leave your gardens, your singing feasts,
Your dreams of suns circling before our sun,
Of heaven after our world.
Instead, watch images of flashing brass
That strike the outward sense, the polished will
Flag of our purpose which the wind engraves.
No spirit seek here rest. But this: No man
Shall hunger: Man shall spend equally.
Our goal which we compel: Man shall be man.

—That program of the antique Satan
Bristling with guns on the indented page
With battleship towering from hilly waves:
For what? Drive of a ruining purpose
Destroying all but its age-long exploiters.
Our program like this, yet opposite,
Death to the killers, bringing light to life.

1933

THE ROOM ABOVE THE SQUARE

The light in the window seemed perpetual
Where you stayed in the high room for me;
It flowered above the trees through leaves
Like my certainty.

The light is fallen and you are hidden
In sunbright peninsulas of the sword:
Torn like leaves through Europe is the peace
Which through me flowed.

Now I climb alone to the dark room
Which hangs above the square
Where among stones and roots the other
Peaceful lovers are.

1939

THE BOMBED HAPPINESS

Children, who extend their smile of crystal,
And their leaping gold embrace,
And wear their happiness as a frank jewel,
Are forced in the mould of the groaning bull
And engraved with lines on the face.

Their harlequin-striped flesh,
Their blood twisted in rivers of song,
Their flashing, trustful emptiness,
Are trampled by an outer heart that pressed
From the sky right through the coral breast
And kissed the heart and burst.

This timed, exploding heart that breaks
The loved and little hearts, is also one
Splintered through the lungs and wombs
And fragments of squares in the sun,
And crushing the floating, sleeping babe
Into a deeper sleep.

Its victoried drumming enters
Above the limbs of bombed laughter
The body of an expanding State
And throbs there and makes it great,
But nothing nothing can recall
Gaiety buried under these dead years,
Sweet jester and young playing fool
Whose toy was human happiness.

1939

TWO KISSES

I wear your kiss like a feather
Laid upon my cheek
And I wander to the quay where the river
Suggests suggests

The dirt off all the streets
And the rotting feet of factories,
But the swans and boats and corks ride
The buoyant running waters
And the eye is carried by a tide

To the far shore and day-green spaces,
And the ear is gently belied
By sounds under dreams under the roar outside.
And then the heart in its white sailing pride

Launches among the swans and the stretched lights
Laid on the water, as on your cheek
The other kiss and my listening
Life, waiting for all your life to speak.

1939

TO A SPANISH POET

(FOR MANUEL ALTOLAGUIRRE)

You stared out of the window on the emptiness
Of a world exploding:
Stones and rubble thrown upwards in a fountain
Blasted sideways by the wind.

Every sensation except loneliness
Was drained out of your mind
By the lack of any motionless object the eye could find.
You were a child again
Who sees for the first time things happen.

Then, stupidly, the sulphur stucco pigeon
Fixed to the gable above your ceiling
Swooped in a curve before the window
Uttering, as it seemed, a coo.
When you smiled,
Everything in the room was shattered;
Only you remained whole
In frozen wonder, as though you stared
At your image in the broken mirror
Where it had always been silverly carried.

Thus I see you
With astonishment whitening in your gaze
Which still retains in the black central irises
Laughing images
Of a man lost in the hills near Malaga
Having got out of his carriage
And spent a week following a partridge;
Or of that broken-hearted general
Who failed to breed a green-eyed bull.

Beyond the violet violence of the news,
The meaningless photographs of the stricken faces,
The weeping from entrails, the vomiting from eyes,
In all the peninsular places,
My imagination reads
The penny fear that you are dead.

Perhaps it is we who are unreal and dead,
We of a world that revolves, dissolves and explodes
While we lay the steadfast corpse under the ground
Just beneath the earth's lid,
And the flowering eyes grow upwards through the grave
As through a rectangular window
Seeing the stars become clear and more clear
In a sky like a sheet of glass,
Beyond these comedies of falling stone.

Your heart looks through the breaking body,
Like axle through the turning wheel,
With eyes of blood.
Unbroken heart,
You stare through my revolving bones
On the transparent rim of the dissolving world
Where all my side is opened
With ribs drawn back like springs to let you enter
And replace my heart that is more living and more cold.

Oh let the violent time
Cut eyes into my limbs
As the sky is pierced with stars that look upon
The map of pain,
For only when the terrible river
Of grief and indignation
Has poured through all my brain
Can I make from lamentation
A world of happiness,
And another constellation,
With your voice that still rejoices
In the center of its night,
As, buried in this night,
The stars burn with their brilliant light.

1939

"The violence of the times we are living in, the necessity of sweeping & general & immediate action tend to dwarf the experience of the individual. Modern poetry is revolutionary because it has has retired ... from the attempt to find satisfaction in the worlds of mythology. It is back in the world which surrounds us."

— Spender

The critics say Spender did not fear his times. He refused to retreat or to isolate himself in his art. He insisted that poetry should reaffirm its power and responsibility, "it" except the world of the airplane & radio, speak to living men about the living age.

"Drink from here energy," Spender insisted, pointing to a world of violent action, "as from the electric charge of a battery."

With energy Spender called for compassion. How could we ever doubt the common heart of humanity, he asked. How could it be "That works, money, interest-building could ever hide the palpable & obvious love of man."

Concern about individual

The American Poets

Edgar Lee Masters

Edgar Lee Masters was born at Garnett, Kansas, August 23, 1869. His father, Hardin Wallace Masters, an attorney, was a descendant of Knottley Masters, who settled in Virginia early in the eighteenth century. His mother, Emma Dexter Masters, was the daughter of a New England minister. When he was a year old his parents moved to Petersburg, Illinois, in the heart of the Lincoln country. From his ninth to his eleventh year he attended a German private school, learning to read and write German with some accuracy. Much of his boyhood, however, was spent on the farm of his grandfather, Davis Masters, a few miles from Petersburg. Here he met many of the kindlier characters of his later poetry and learned much about nature to supplement the knowledge he was already acquiring from books.

In 1880 his family moved to Lewistown, a county seat fifty miles north of Petersburg and five miles from Spoon River. Here at the age of seventeen he completed his high school course. But some years before, he had begun working in his spare time at the office of the Lewistown *News*, setting type, writing news, and corresponding for St. Louis and Chicago newspapers. When he was about fifteen he began writing verse and in 1884 printed one of his poems, "The Minotaur," on the job press of the *News*. The next year he made his first public appearance as an author with the poem, "Zueline," in the Quincy *Herald*. Despite his newspaper and high school work and his writing of verse, he found time between his fifteenth and twentieth years to read Euripides, Seneca, Epictetus, Marcus Aurelius, Shakespeare and other Elizabethan dramatists, Addison, Locke, Goethe, Emerson, Poe, Whitman, and Swinburne.

At his father's request he started when nineteen to study law. But he did not give all his attention to this, for at the same time he was contributing poems to several Illinois newspapers and short stories to two Boston magazines, the *Writer* and the *Waverly Magazine*. He also studied Latin at a small college that was started in Lewistown. In 1889 he entered Knox College, where he studied German, Latin, and Greek; but after a year there he returned home, completed his law studies, and in 1891 was admitted to the bar. Then for a year he assisted his father in his law work, read Virgil, Milton, and Goethe, translated Theocritus, and continued to write poetry.

In the summer of 1892 he went to live in Chicago. There he tried to find a position on a newspaper, but everyone discouraged him; he then applied unsuccessfully at several law offices. After some weeks he became a collector for the Edison Company and retained this job until the following spring, when he formed a partnership and started to practice law. The firm flourished, and for more than twenty years Masters was a successful lawyer. On June 21, 1898, he married Helen Jenkins, daughter of a Chicago attorney; and to them were born three children. He became interested in politics, wrote many political articles for the Chicago press, and served for some years as president of the Jefferson Club. But despite his success as a lawyer and the need of attending to other affairs, he never relinquished the idea of becoming an author. He frequented the Chicago Press Club, where he made many friends among writers, and for some time contributed poems and articles to various newspapers. In 1898 his first volume, *A Book of Verses*, was printed by a Chicago firm, which failed, however, before the book was published. In 1900 he wrote a five-act drama, *Maximilian*, which was published in 1902. Then followed several privately printed works: a poem, *Samson and Delilah* (1903), *The New Star Chamber and Other Essays* (1904), *Blood of the Prophets* (1905), half a dozen plays (1907-1911), *Songs and Sonnets* (1910), and *Songs and Sonnets, Second Series* (1911).

These early books had no wide circulation, and for a while after the last one appeared Masters published only a few articles and poems. But circumstances were conspiring to set him on a new track. He had for years planned a novel dealing with the life of a small community, for it was his idea that the small community was but a cross section of the world at large. Then in 1907 he met William Marion Reedy, publisher of *Reedy's Mirror*, to which he began to contribute. Reedy proved a valuable counselor and sympathetic coach, sending Masters many books and calling his attention to the work of the new schools of poetry in France, to the free verse experiments of Turgenev, and to the *Greek Anthology* and other works by Greek and Latin poets. But for many years before this Masters had been a devoted student of poetry in all its forms. He read Whitman from his youth and wrote a poem on him at his death. He was also a student of Ossian, of Henley, and of the free verse poems of Goethe, Matthew Arnold, and others. Between the work of these authors and the prose translation of the *Greek Anthology* he found the medium for his next book. Thus he had prepared himself for the writing of the *Spoon River Anthology* for years before the so-called poetry revival of 1914 helped to create an audience for his work. Using free verse, but verse that was often metrical and rhythmical, he set to work to depict men and women in a typical community, and thus express life as it was everywhere. It was the idea of the novel long before conceived, carried out in verse and in interrelated interpretations. In May, 1914, he began writing these "epitaphs." They ran in *Reedy's Mirror* from then until January, 1915. Before the series was complete the poems were being quoted and commented upon throughout the country. In April, 1915, they were published in a volume, *Spoon River Anthology*. The book at once became a national best seller, and its author was acclaimed by some critics as the greatest living poet.

Masters now began to devote more time to literature, and in 1923 abandoned altogether the practice of law. In the twenty years following the appearance of the *Spoon River Anthology* he published sixteen volumes of poetry. On the merits of these there has never been the universal agreement that greeted the first Spoon River volume. He himself considers *Domesday Book* (1920), *The Fate of the Jury* (1929), and *Godbey* (1931) as better. Some critics agree with him, and account as equally good *Starved Rock* (1919) and *The New Spoon River* (1924). In 1916 he received the Helen Haire Levinson Poetry Prize.

Besides poetry he has written in late years a number of prose works: the novels *Mitch Miller* (1920), *Children of the Market Place* (1922), *Skeeters Kirby* (1923), *The Nuptial Flight* (1923), *Mirage* (1924), *Kit O'Brien* (1927), and *The Tide of Time* (1937); the biographies, *Lincoln, the Man* (1931), *Vachel Lindsay* (1935), *Whitman* (1937), and *Mark Twain* (1938); a history,

The Tale of Chicago (1933); *Dramatic Duologues* (1934); and *The Sangamon* (1942), in "The Rivers of America" series.

Masters went to Europe in 1906 and again in 1921. In 1925 he made a lecture tour, going as far as the Pacific Coast and reading his poems to many college and university audiences. He was divorced in 1925, and on November 5, 1926, married Ellen Coyne, of Kansas City. By his second marriage he has one son. Since 1923 he has made his home in New York City.

SUPPLICATION

For He knoweth our frame, He remembereth that we are dust.—Psalm ciii, 14

Oh Lord, when all our bones are thrust
  Beyond the gaze of all but Thine;
And these blaspheming tongues are dust
  Which babbled of Thy name divine,
How helpless then to carp or rail
  Against the canons of Thy word;
Wilt Thou, when thus our spirits fail,
  Have mercy, Lord?

Here from this ebon speck that floats
  As but a mote within Thine eye,
Vain sneers and curses from our throats
  Rise to the vault of Thy fair sky:
Yet when this world of ours is still
  Of this all-wondering, tortured horde,
And none is left for Thee to kill—
  Have mercy, Lord!

Thou knowest that our flesh is grass;
  Ah! let our withered souls remain
Like stricken reeds of some morass,
  Bleached, in Thy will, by ceaseless rain.
Have we not had enough of fire,
  Enough of torment and the sword?—
If these accrue from Thy desire—
  Have mercy, Lord!

Dost Thou not see about our feet
  The tangles of our erring thought?

Thou knowest that we run to greet
  High hopes that vanish into naught.
We bleed, we fall, we rise again;
  How can we be of Thee abhorred?
We are Thy breed, we little men—
  Have mercy, Lord!

Wilt Thou then slay for that we slay,
  Wilt Thou deny when we deny?
A thousand years are but a day,
  A little day within Thine eye:
We thirst for love, we yearn for life;
  We lust, wilt Thou the lust record?
We, beaten, fall upon the knife—
  Have mercy, Lord!

Thou givest us youth that turns to age;
  And strength that leaves us while we seek.
Thou pourest the fire of sacred rage
  In costly vessels all too weak.
Great works we planned in hopes that Thou
  Fit wisdom therefor wouldst accord;
Thou wrotest failure on our brow—
  Have mercy, Lord!

1905

DOCTOR MEYERS [1]

No other man, unless it was Doc Hill,
Did more for people in this town than I.
And all the weak, the halt, the improvident
And those who could not pay flocked to me.
I was good-hearted, easy Doctor Meyers.
I was healthy, happy, in comfortable fortune,
Blest with a congenial mate, my children raised,
All wedded, doing well in the world.
And then one night, Minerva, the poetess,
Came to me in her trouble, crying.
I tried to help her out—she died—
They indicted me, the newspapers disgraced me,

[1] This and the twelve poems which follow are from *Spoon River Anthology*.

My wife perished of a broken heart.
And pneumonia finished me.

1915

MRS. MEYERS

He protested all his life long
The newspapers lied about him villainously;
That he was not at fault for Minerva's fall,
But only tried to help her.
Poor soul so sunk in sin he could not see
That even trying to help her, as he called it,
He had broken the law human and divine.
Passers by, an ancient admonition to you:
If your ways would be ways of pleasantness,
And all your pathways peace,
Love God and keep his commandments.

1915

PETIT, THE POET

Seeds in a dry pod, tick, tick, tick,
Tick, tick, tick, like mites in a quarrel—
Faint iambics that the full breeze wakens—
But the pine tree makes a symphony thereof.
Triolets, villanelles, rondels, rondeaus,
Ballades by the score with the same old thought:
The snows and the roses of yesterday are vanished;
And what is love but a rose that fades?
Life all around me here in the village:
Tragedy, comedy, valor, and truth,
Courage, constancy, heroism, failure—
All in the loom, and oh what patterns!
Woodlands, meadows, streams, and rivers—
Blind to all of it all my life long.
Triolets, villanelles, rondels, rondeaus,
Seeds in a dry pod, tick, tick, tick,
Tick, tick, tick, what little iambics,
While Homer and Whitman roared in the pines?

1915

CARL HAMBLIN

The press of the Spoon River *Clarion* was wrecked,
And I was tarred and feathered,
For publishing this on the day the Anarchists were hanged in Chicago:
"I saw a beautiful woman with bandaged eyes
Standing on the steps of a marble temple.
Great multitudes passed in front of her,
Lifting their faces to her imploringly.
In her left hand she held a sword.
She was brandishing the sword,
Sometimes striking a child, again a laborer,
Again a slinking woman, again a lunatic.
In her right hand she held a scale;
Into the scale pieces of gold were tossed
By those who dodged the strokes of the sword.
A man in a black gown read from a manuscript:
'She is no respecter of persons.'
Then a youth wearing a red cap
Leaped to her side and snatched away the bandage.
And lo, the lashes had been eaten away
From the oozy eye-lids;
The eye-balls were seared with a milky mucus;
The madness of a dying soul
Was written on her face—
But the multitude saw why she wore the bandage."

1915

JACOB GODBEY

How did you feel, you libertarians,
Who spent your talents rallying noble reasons
Around the saloon, as if Liberty
Was not to be found anywhere except at the bar
Or at a table, guzzling?
How did you feel, Ben Pantier, and the rest of you,
Who almost stoned me for a tyrant,
Garbed as a moralist,
And as a wry-faced ascetic frowning upon Yorkshire pudding,

Roast beef and ale and good will and rosy cheer—
Things you never saw in a grog-shop in your life?
How did you feel after I was dead and gone,
And your goddess, Liberty, unmasked as a strumpet,
Selling out the streets of Spoon River
To the insolent giants
Who manned the saloons from afar?
Did it occur to you that personal liberty
Is liberty of the mind,
Rather than of the belly?

1915

SETH COMPTON

When I died, the circulating library
Which I built up for Spoon River,
And managed for the good of inquiring minds,
Was sold at auction on the public square,
As if to destroy the last vestige
Of my memory and influence.
For those of you who could not see the virtue
Of knowing Volney's "Ruins" as well as Butler's "Analogy"
And "Faust" as well as "Evangeline,"
Were really the power in the village,
And often you asked me,
"What is the use of knowing the evil in the world?"
I am out of your way now, Spoon River,
Choose your own good and call it good.
For I could never make you see
That no one knows what is good
Who knows not what is evil;
And no one knows what is true
Who knows not what is false.

1915

ANNE RUTLEDGE

Out of me unworthy and unknown
The vibrations of deathless music;
"With malice toward none, with charity for all."
Out of me the forgiveness of millions toward millions,

And the beneficent face of a nation
Shining with justice and truth.
I am Anne Rutledge who sleep beneath these weeds,
Beloved in life of Abraham Lincoln,
Wedded to him, not through union,
But through separation.
Bloom forever, O Republic,
From the dust of my bosom!

1915

LUCINDA MATLOCK

I went to the dances at Chandlerville,
And played snap-out at Winchester.
One time we changed partners,
Driving home in the moonlight of middle June,
And then I found Davis.
We were married and lived together for seventy years,
Enjoying, working, raising the twelve children,
Eight of whom we lost
Ere I had reached the age of sixty.
I spun, I wove, I kept the house, I nursed the sick,
I made the garden, and for holiday
Rambled over the fields where sang the larks,
And by Spoon River gathering many a shell,
And many a flower and medicinal weed—
Shouting to the wooded hills, singing to the green valleys.
At ninety-six I had lived enough, that is all,
And passed to a sweet repose.
What is this I hear of sorrow and weariness,
Anger, discontent, and drooping hopes?
Degenerate sons and daughters,
Life is too strong for you—
It takes life to love Life.

1915

DAVIS MATLOCK

Suppose it is nothing but the hive:
That there are drones and workers
And queens, and nothing but storing honey—

(Material things as well as culture and wisdom)—
For the next generation, this generation never living,
Except as it swarms in the sun-light of youth,
Strengthening its wings on what has been gathered,
And tasting, on the way to the hive
From the clover field, the delicate spoil.
Suppose all this, and suppose the truth:
That the nature of man is greater
Than nature's need in the hive;
And you must bear the burden of life,
As well as the urge from your spirit's excess—
Well, I say to live it out like a god
Sure of immortal life, though you are in doubt,
Is the way to live it.
If that doesn't make God proud of you
Then God is nothing but gravitation,
Or sleep is the golden goal.

1915

THE VILLAGE ATHEIST

Ye young debaters over the doctrine
Of the soul's immortality,
I who lie here was the village atheist,
Talkative, contentious, versed in the arguments
Of the infidels.
But through a long sickness
Coughing myself to death
I read the *Upanishads* and the poetry of Jesus.
And they lighted a torch of hope and intuition
And desire which the Shadow,
Leading me swiftly through the caverns of darkness,
Could not extinguish.
Listen to me, ye who live in the senses
And think through the senses only:
Immortality is not a gift,
Immortality is an achievement;
And only those who strive mightily
Shall possess it.

1915

JAMES GARBER

Do you remember, passer-by, the path
I wore across the lot where now stands the opera house,
Hasting with swift feet to work through many years?
Take its meaning to heart:
You too may walk, after the hills at Miller's Ford
Seem no longer far away;
Long after you see them near at hand,
Beyond four miles of meadow;
And after woman's love is silent,
Saying no more: "I will save you."
And after the faces of friends and kindred
Become as faded photographs, pitifully silent,
Sad for the look which means: "We cannot help you."
And after you no longer reproach mankind
With being in league against your soul's uplifted hands—
Themselves compelled at midnight and at noon
To watch with steadfast eye their destinies;
After you have these understandings, think of me
And of my path, who walked therein and knew
That neither man nor woman, neither toil,
Nor duty, gold nor power
Can ease the longing of the soul,
The loneliness of the soul!

1915

ARLO WILL

Did you ever see an alligator
Come up to the air from the mud,
Staring blindly under the full glare of noon?
Have you seen the stabled horses at night
Tremble and start back at the sight of a lantern?
Have you ever walked in darkness
When an unknown door was open before you
And you stood, it seemed, in the light of a thousand candles
Of delicate wax?
Have you walked with the wind in your ears
And the sunlight about you

And found it suddenly shine with an inner splendor?
Out of the mud many times,
Before many doors of light,
Through many fields of splendor,
Where around your steps a soundless glory scatters
Like new-fallen snow,
Will you go through earth, O strong of soul,
And through unnumbered heavens
To the final flame!

1915

SCHOLFIELD HUXLEY

God! ask me not to record your wonders,
I admit the stars and the suns
And the countless worlds.
But I have measured their distances
And weighed them and discovered their substances.
I have devised wings for the air,
And keels for water,
And horses of iron for the earth.
I have lengthened the vision you gave me a million times,
And the hearing you gave me a million times,
I have leaped over space with speech,
And taken fire for light out of the air.
I have built great cities and bored through the hills,
And bridged majestic waters.
I have written the *Iliad* and *Hamlet;*
And I have explored your mysteries,
And searched for you without ceasing,
And found you again after losing you
In hours of weariness—
And I ask you:
How would you like to create a sun
And the next day have the worms
Slipping in and out between your fingers?

1916

THE MOURNER'S BENCH [1]

They're holding a revival at New Hope Meeting house,
I can't keep from going, I ought to stay away.
For I come home and toss in bed till day,
For thinking of my sin, and the trouble I am in.
I dream I hear the dancers
In the steps and swings,
The quadrilles and the lancers
They danced at Revis Springs.
I lie and think of Charley, Charley, Charley
The Bobtown dandy
Who had his way with me.
And no one is so handy
A dancer as Charley
To *Little Drops of Brandy*,
Or *The Wind that Shakes the Barley*,
Or *Good Mornin', Uncle Johnny, I've Fetched Your Wagon Home*.

And Greenberry Atterberry, who toed it like a pigeon
Has gone and got religion;
He's deserted the dancers, the fiddlers, merry-makers,
And I should do it too.
For Charley, Charley has left me for to roam.
But a woman at the mourner's bench must tell her story true—
What shall I do? What shall I do?

My grandmother told me of Old Peter Cartwright
Who preached hell-fire
And the worm that never dies.
And here's a young preacher at the New Hope Meeting house,
And every one allows, he has old Peter's brows,
And flaming of the eyes,
And the very same way, they say.
Last night he stuck his finger right down in my direction,
And said: "God doesn't care
For your woman's hair.
Jesus wants to know if your soul is fair

[1] In many of his poems Masters portrays the life and problems of the folk of early pioneer days. This is such a poem, and not, as some have supposed, a satire.

As your woman's complexion."
And then I thought he knew—
O what shall I do?

Greenberry Atterberry, weeping and unsteady
Had left his seat already.
He stood at the mourner's bench in great tribulation
And told the congregation:
That fiddling and dancing and tobacco chewin'
Led up to whisky and to woman's ruin—
And I thought he looked at me.
Well, you can stop dancing, and you can stop drinking
And you can leave the quarter-horses at the crooked races.
But a woman, a woman, the people will be thinking
Forever of a woman who confesses her behavior.
And then I couldn't look in the people's faces,
All weeping and singing, *O Gentle Saviour!*

Then the devil said: You wench
You'd cut a pretty figure at the mourner's bench,
Go out and look for Charley,
Go out and look for Charley,
He's down at Leese's Grove.
He has found a fresh love
Go win him back again.
He is dancing on the platform to *The Speckled Hen.*

O Saviour, Saviour, how can I join the mourners,
Face all the scorners?
But how can I hunt Charley at Leese's Grove?
How can I stand the staring, the whispering of things
Down at Revis Springs?
How can I stand the mocking of the fiddle strings?
Charley! Charley!
So it's knowing what's best to do,
Saviour! Saviour!
It's knowing what's best to do!

1916

DESOLATE SCYTHIA

When there are no distances in music,
No far off things suggested of faery forests or celestial heights;
When nothing undiscovered stands back of the written page,
And the landscape contains nothing hidden,
And no alluring spirits of further places;
When no more in eyes shines the light of mystery,
And the thrill of discovered kinships
Has fallen into the familiar recognition
That takes all men and women
As daily associates of an accustomed world,
Then you have come to the uttermost plain of earth
Where lie the rocks of desolate Scythia.

1916

CANTICLE OF THE RACE

SONG OF MEN

How beautiful are the bodies of men—
The agonists!
Their hearts beat deep as a brazen gong
For their strength's behests.
Their arms are lithe as a seasoned thong
In games or tests
When they run or box or swim the long
Sea-waves' crests
With their slender legs, and their hips so strong,
And their rounded chests.

I know a youth who raises his arms
Over his head.
He laughs and stretches and flouts alarms
Of flood or fire.
He springs renewed from a lusty bed
To his youth's desire.
He drowses, for April flames outspread
In his soul's attire.

The strength of men is for husbandry
Of woman's flesh:

Worker, soldier, magistrate
Of city or realm;
Artist, builder, wrestling Fate
Lest it overwhelm
The brood or the race, or the cherished state.
They sing at the helm
When the waters roar and the waves are great,
And the gale is fresh.

There are two miracles, women and men—
Yea, four there be:
A woman's flesh, and the strength of a man,
And God's decree.
And a babe from the womb in a little span
Ere the month be ten.
Their rapturous arms entwine and cling
In the depths of night;
He hunts for her face for his wondering,
And her eyes are bright.
A woman's flesh is soil, but the spring
Is man's delight.

SONG OF WOMEN

How beautiful is the flesh of women—
Their throats, their breasts!
My wonder is a flame which burns,
A flame which rests;
It is a flame which no wind turns,
And a flame which quests.

I know a woman who has red lips,
Like coals which are fanned.
Her throat is tied narcissus, it dips
From her white-rose chin.
Her throat curves like a cloud to the land
Where her breasts begin.
I close my eyes when I put my hand
On her breast's white skin.

The flesh of women is like the sky
When bare is the moon:
Rhythm of backs, hollow of necks,
And sea-shell loins.

I know a woman whose splendors vex
Where the flesh joins—
A slope of light and a circumflex
Of clefts and coigns.
She thrills like the air when silence wrecks
An ended tune.

These are the things not made by hands in the earth:
Water and fire,
The air of heaven, and springs afresh,
And love's desire.
And a thing not made is a woman's flesh,
Sorrow and mirth!
She tightens the strings on the lyric lyre,
And she drips the wine.
Her breasts bud out as pink and nesh
As buds on the vine:
For fire and water and air are flesh,
And love is the shrine.

SONG OF THE HUMAN SPIRIT

How beautiful is the human spirit
In its vase of clay!
It takes no thought of the chary dole
Of the light of day.
It labors and loves, as it were a soul
Whom the gods repay
With length of life, and a golden goal
At the end of the way.

There are souls I know who arch a dome,
And tunnel a hill.
They chisel in marble and fashion in chrome,
And measure the sky.
They find the good and destroy the ill,
And they bend and ply
The laws of nature out of a will
While the fates deny.

I wonder and worship the human spirit
When I behold
Numbers and symbols, and how they reach
Through steel and gold;

A harp, a battle-ship, thought and speech,
And an hour foretold.
It ponders its nature to turn and teach,
And itself to mould.

The human spirit is God, no doubt,
Is flesh made the word:
Jesus, Beethoven and Raphael,
And the souls who heard
Beyond the rim of the world the swell
Of an ocean stirred
By a Power on the waters inscrutable.
There are souls who gird
Their loins in faith that the world is well,
In a faith unblurred.
How beautiful is the human spirit—
The flesh made the word!

1918

MY LIGHT WITH YOURS

I

When the sea has devoured the ships,
And the spires and the towers
Have gone back to the hills.
And all the cities
Are one with the plains again.
And the beauty of bronze,
And the strength of steel
Are blown over silent continents,
As the desert sand is blown—
My dust with yours forever.

II

When folly and wisdom are no more,
And fire is no more,
Because man is no more;
When the dead world slowly spinning
Drifts and falls through the void—
My light with yours
In the Light of Lights forever!

1918

CHRISTMAS AT INDIAN POINT

Who is that calling through the night,
A wail that dies when the wind roars?
We heard it first on Shipley's Hill,
It faded out at Comingoer's.

Along five miles of wintry road
A horseman galloped with a cry,
" 'Twas two o'clock," said Herman Pointer,
"When I heard clattering hoofs go by.

"I flung the winder up to listen;
I heerd him there on Gordon's Ridge;
I heerd the loose boards bump and rattle
When he went over Houghton's Bridge."

Said Roger Ragsdale: "I was doctorin'
A heifer in the barn, and then
My boy says: 'Pap, that's Billy Paris.'
'There,' says my boy, 'it is again.'

"Says I: 'That kain't be Billy Paris,
We seed 'im at the Christmas tree.
It's two o'clock,' says I, 'and Billy
I seed go home with Emily.'

" 'He is too old for galavantin'
Upon a night like this,' says I.
'Well, pap,' says he, 'I know that frosty,
Good-natured huskiness in that cry.'

" 'It kain't be Billy,' says I, swabbin'
The heifer's tongue and mouth with brine,
I never thought—it makes me shiver,
And goose-flesh up and down the spine."

Said Doggie Traylor: "When I heard it
I 'lowed 'twas Pin Hook's rowdy new 'uns.
Them Cashner boys was at the schoolhouse
Drinkin' there at the Christmas doin's."

Said Petė McCue: "I lit a candle
And held it up to the winder pane.
But when I heerd again the holler
'Twere half-way down the Bowman Lane."

Said Andy Ensley: "First I knowed
I thought he'd thump the door away.
I hopped from bed, and says, 'Who is it?'
'O, Emily,' I heard him say.

"And there stood Billy Paris tremblin',
His face so white, he looked so queer.
'O Andy'—and his voice went broken.
'Come in,' says I, 'and have a cheer.'

" 'Sit by the fire,' I kicked the logs up,
'What brings you here?—I would be told.'
Says he, 'My hand just . . . happened near hers,
It teched her hand . . . and it war cold.

" 'We got back from the Christmas doin's
And went to bed, and she was sayin',
(The clock struck ten) "If it keeps snowin'
To-morrow there'll be splendid sleighin'."

" 'My hand teched hers, the clock struck two,
And then I thought I heerd her moan.
It war the wind, I guess, for Emily
War lyin' dead. . . . She's thar alone.'

"I left him then to call my woman
To tell her that her mother died.
When we come back his voice was steady,
The big tears in his eyes was dried.

"He just sot there and quiet like
Talked 'bout the fishin' times they had,
And said for her to die on Christmas
Was somethin' 'bout it made him glad.

"He grew so cam he almost skeered us.
Says he: 'It's a fine Christmas over there.'
Says he: 'She was the lovingest woman
That ever walked this Vale of Care.'

"Says he: 'She allus laughed and sang,
I never heerd her once complain.'
Says he: 'It's not so bad a Christmas
When she can go and have no pain.'

"Says he: 'The Christmas's good for her.'
Says he: . . . 'Not very good for me.'
He hid his face then in his muffler
And sobbed and sobbed, 'O Emily.' "

1918

STARVED ROCK

As a soul from whom companionships subside
The meaningless and onsweeping tide
Of the river hastening, as it would disown
Old ways and places, left this stone
Of sand above the valley, to look down
Miles of the valley, hamlet, village, town.

* * * * *

It is a head-gear of a chief whose head,
Down from the implacable brow,
Waiting is held below
The waters, feather decked
With blossoms blue and red,
With ferns and vines;
Hiding beneath the waters, head erect,
His savage eyes and treacherous designs.

* * * * *

It is a musing memory and memorial
Of geologic ages
Before the floods began to fall;
The cenotaph of sorrows, pilgrimages
Of Marquette and LaSalle.
The eagles and the Indians left it here
In solitude, blown clean
Of kindred things: as an oak whose leaves are sere,
Fly over the valley when the winds are keen,
And nestle where the earth receives
Another generation of exhausted leaves.

* * * * *

Fatigued with age its sleepless eyes look over
Fenced fields of corn and wheat,
Barley and clover.
The lowered pulses of the river beat
Invisibly by shores that stray
In progress and retreat
Past Utica and Ottawa,
And past the meadow where the Illini
Shouted and danced under the autumn moon,
When toddlers and papooses gave a cry,
And dogs were barking for the boon
Of the hunter home again to clamorous tents
Smoking beneath the evening's copper sky.
Later the remnant of the Illini
Climbed up this Rock, to die
Of hunger, thirst, or down its sheer ascents
Rushed on the spears of Pottawatomies,
And found the peace
Where thirst and hunger are unknown.

* * * * *

This is the tragic and the fateful stone
Le Rocher or Starved Rock,
A symbol and a paradigm,
A sphinx of elegy and battle hymn,
Whose lips unlock
Life's secret, which is vanishment, defeat,
In epic dirges for the races
That pass and leave no traces
Before new generations driven in the blast
Of Time and Nature blowing round its head.
Renewing in the Present what the Past
Knew wholly, or in part, so to repeat
Warfare, extermination, old things dead
But brought to life again
In Life's immortal pain.

* * * * *

What Destinies confer,
And laughing mock
LaSalle, his dreamings stir
To wander here, depart
The fortress of Creve Coeur,

Of broken heart,
For this fort of Starved Rock?
After the heart is broken then the cliff
Where vultures flock;
And where below its steeps the savage skiff
Cuts with a pitiless knife the rope let down
For water. From the earth this Indian town
Vanished and on this Rock the Illini
Thirsting, their buckets taken with the knife,
Lay down to die.

* * * * *

This is the land where every generation
Lets down its buckets for the water of Life.
We are the children and the epigone
Of the Illini, the vanished nation.
And this starved scarp of stone
Is now the emblem of our tribulation,
The inverted cup of our insatiable thirst,
The Illini by fate accursed,
This land lost to the Pottawatomies,
They lost the land to us,
Who, baffled and idolatrous,
And thirsting, spurred by hope
Kneel upon aching knees,
And with our eager hands draw up the bucketless rope.

* * * * *

This is the tragic, the symbolic face,
Le Rocher or Starved Rock,
Round which the eternal turtles drink and swim
And serpents green and strange,
As race comes after race,
War after war.
This is the sphinx whose Memnon lips breathe dirges
To empire's wayward star,
And over the race's restless urges,
Whose lips unlock
Life's secret which is vanishment and change.

1919

EPITAPH FOR US

One with the turf, one with the tree
As we are now, you soon shall be,
As you are now, so once were we.

The hundred years we looked upon
Were Goethe and Napoleon.
Now twice a hundred years are gone,

And you gaze back and contemplate,
Lloyd George and Wilson, William's hate,
And Nicholas of the bloody fate;

Us, too, who won the German war,
Who knew less what the strife was for
Than you, now that the conqueror

Lies with the conquered. You will say:
"Here sleep the brave, the grave, the gay,
The wise, the blind, who lost the way."

But for us English, for us French,
Americans who held the trench,
You will not grieve, though the rains drench

The hills and valleys, being these.
Who pities stocks, or pities trees?
Or stones, or meadows, rivers, seas?

We are with nature, we have grown
At one with water, earth, and stone—
Man only is separate and alone,

Earth sundered, left to dream and feel
Illusion still in pain made real,
The hope a mist, but fire the wheel.

But what was love, and what was lust,
Memory, passion, pain or trust,
Returned to clay and blown in dust,

Is nature without memory—
Yet as you are, so once were we,
As we are now, you soon shall be,

Blind fellows of the indifferent stars
Healed of your bruises, of your scars
In love and living, in the wars.

Come to us where the secret lies
Under the riddle of the skies,
Surrender fingers, speech, and eyes.

Sink into nature and become
The mystery that strikes you dumb,
Be clay and end your martyrdom.

Rise up as thought, the secret know.
As passionless as stars bestow
Your glances on the world below,

As a man looks at hand or knee.
What is the turf of you, what the tree?
Earth is a phantom—let it be.

1919

SOUNDS OUT OF SORROW

Of all sounds out of the soul of sorrow
These I would hear no more:
The cry of a new-born child at midnight;
The sound of a closing door,

That hushes the echo of departing feet
When the loneliness of the room
Is haunted with the silence
Of a dead god's tomb;

The songs of robins at the white dawn,
Since I may never see
The eyes they waked in the April
Now gone from me;

Music into whose essence entered
The soul of an hour:—
A face, a voice, the touch of a hand,
The scent of a flower.

1919

NEITHER FAITH NOR BEAUTY CAN REMAIN

Neither faith nor beauty can remain:
Change is our life from hour to hour,
Pain follows after pain,
As ruined flower lies down with ruined flower.

Now you are mine. But in a day to be
Beyond the seas, in cities strange and new
To-day will be a memory
Of a day ephemerally true.

Last night with cheek pressed close to cheek
Through the brief hours we slept.
It must be always so, I heard you speak,
Love found, forever must be kept.

But already we were changed, even as the day
Invisibly transforms its light.
We prayed together then for dawn's delay,
Praying, praying through the night.

Against the change which takes all loveliness,
The truth our desperate hearts would keep,
The memory to be, when comfortless,
Save for the memory we shall yearn for sleep;

Against the sinking flame which no more lights
Our faces, neither any more desired
Through desireless days and nights,
And senses fast expiring and expired.

1919

JAY HAWKINS [1]

Jay walking! Reading the headlines! Struck down
By a fliver and killed while reading
About the man-girl slayer!
For years haunting the news stands,
Waiting for the latest paper from Chicago,
Cursed with the newspaper habit:
Snuffing the powder of monstrous news
Heralding shame and hate and murder:
What dive was raided, what rum was seized;
Who was indicted, and who was lynched;
Who got the rope at the end of the trial;
What governor, officer was accused
Of bribery, graft, or peculation.
Whose picture appeared divorced or caught—
(Were they never noble, did they never achieve,
And so have their pictures printed?)
All about hating, hunting, fighting,
Lying, stealing, lusting, wasting,
Who had been killed, and who had been hanged.
And I ask if life is full of beauty,
And full of nobility and creating,
Why don't they write about it?

1924

MAYOR MARSTON

Every mayor before me, far back as memory ran
Had been denounced as a demagogue dreamer,
Or else as a thief or a crook—
Yet I took the place with a hope,
Intending to beautify, give the people their money's worth,
Make big offenders toe the mark.
As of old *The Ledger* was trying to sell
Its land for a park, but I balked that.
Then I whacked the noses of monstrous swine
Away from the trough. What happened? Well
The crime wave broke—in *The Ledger's* pages!

[1] This and the nine poems which follow are from *The New Spoon River.*

What hold-ups, gamblers, lawless booze,
And places of vice!
The churches began to chatter,
And the courts took a hand against me.
They blackened my name, and the name of the town—
They killed me to get their way.
And this is the bandit game, my friends,
Of what is called democracy!

1924

EURIPIDES ALEXOPOULOS

I had a vision at last:
A divine youth was playing a harp near Trainor's Drug Store.
They listened, passed, conferred on the matter.
They returned and told him to work or get out of town.
He began then to carry coal and sell newspapers,
Playing his harp in the evenings.
The neighbors complained:
He was leading people to idleness, dreams.
He went on playing, emerged to the streets again.
Some tore at him, others hooted him, some praised him;
But he was in need of money, always money.
He put his harp by to work for money . . . no money for
harping!
He took forth his harp again.
The strings were loose, it had to be tuned.
He tuned it and played better than ever.
In the midst of this his money was taken from him.
Shadows had come over him, he was no longer young.
His children were half grown, making voracious demands.
Should he play the harp or work for the children?
Every one said, work for the children.
They must feed and be educated,
And what is this harping after all?
They caught him then and put him to work.
His beard grew long and gray, his eyes were haggard,
He was bent, his hands were thick and dull.
He could neither work now nor play the harp.
Suddenly as he was sitting on a bench in the park
He shed his rags, as the sun sheds clouds.
He rose to the spire of the church,

Stood on one foot,
And spit on the town—
It was Apollo!

1924

LEVY SILVER

Why did I sell you plated silver,
Rhinestones and synthetic rubies?
Why did I sell you gold filled cases?
The question at stake is why did you buy?
I couldn't sell them as real and prosper.
But you could buy and pretend them real,
As part of your game of fooling each other
With fake morality, hollow customs,
And laws compounded of spurious stuff.
The goods I sold matched something in you:
For some of your souls were only plated;
And some of you put yourselves together
To imitate virtues clear and precious:
And some of you were mostly brass
Under a film of gold!

1924

HENRY COGDAL

Bring from Big Creek a huge boulder,
Put it at the head of me,
And bolt upon it a tablet of bronze
With these words:
Here was buried the body of Henry Cogdal,
A private who fell in the war for Wisdom,
And Beauty and Truth.
He strove to be a guide to the creative spirit,
And to uphold the singers and tellers of stories,
Who keep the vision of a nation
Upon the clear realities of life.
At the height of his power and work
He lost his place and means of support
Through a rich manufacturer who bought the newspaper,
And began to popularize it,

And to lower its criticisms
To the level of advertisers and optimists:—
There will come a time when crimes against culture
Will be punished the same as murder!

1924

JULIUS BRINK

Most of you in Spoon River
Were critics of each other, while I was a critic of life.
And you were optimists and believers,
And I a skeptic and pessimist—yes!
But here is my faith in life and death:—
The world was many millions of years
Building itself from mist to soil.
And it took a half a million years
To turn the ape man into a Greek.
So what does it prove to show no progress
Within the time of written records?
If it takes as long to civilize man,
And make his soul stand up with his body
As it took to build the earth, what wonder?
There's time ahead to do it in—
And that was my faith to the last.

1924

D'ARCY SINGER

What is the life of a man,
What is the life of the race,
O friends of Spoon River?
It is that creation out of the spirit of man
Of statuary, pictures, temples, the written page,
Laws and states,
Ideals of Joy and Fellowship.
Humanism, Balance, Beauty.
These are man's creations and creators.
These are the webs of the spider
Woven out of his own body;
These are the combs of the bees
Gathered from life's flowers and architected.
These are the nests of the eagles enduring a century!

1924

LIONEL GRIERSON

How often in our chamber, O adored one,
I woke to see the midnight star, and find you
Warm and sweet as incense, hear your breathing;
Feel the dreaming love of your constant breast.
Then in the throes of death to suffer absence,
And wait for you, and wait for you in vain,
And from our bed—how cold with death and sorrow
To see the star of midnight—what remembrance!
Arielle! Lay your head on this earthen pillow,
Touch my hand of dust with the dust of your hand;
Warm this couch with the passion of your presence;
Sleep by my side forever and give me rest!

1924

ARIELLE GRIERSON

Heartbroken that I could not reach your bed side
In those last hours; heartbroken that death took you,
Soon I came to you, soon to your earthen couch.
Sleep now and rest, I am here. The star of midnight
Over us watches, as once in our chamber of life.
My dust has the April longing to turn and mingle
With yours, which longs for mine.. What flowers shall blossom
With the color of primal passion from such a union!

1924

NATHAN SUFFRIN

Jail would have killed me
Except for my cell mate, Henry Luthinger,
Who had been there often before,
And knew how to soften the walls and bars,
And how to be a friend in jail.
So when they let me out,
I knew at last that life is a prison.
And the best that a man can hope for it
Is a cell mate wise and good!

1924

[NO GRIEF FOR THE GREAT ONES]

[From *Lee*]

No grief for the great ones whose labor is ended,
Who pass from our seeing through doors that are sealed;
Made safe from all danger, by distance defended,
Sepultured in silence they sleep and are healed.

What's a future of bugles, the hills of hereafter,
Where trenches are guarding the captains who sleep?
They dream with the Aprils whose rivulet laughter
Is faint amid grasses on valley and steep.

They have willed you the world, be the trust still evaded
Their rebuke is the quiet, the light of the stars.
They watch as a Truth on a race unpersuaded;
They rule as a Vision that smiles at the wars.

Their realm is dominion of wisdom through living.
They live and they die not through wisdom bequeathed.
They are changed to immortals, relentless, forgiving.
They are swords in the light of eternity sheathed.

1926

[HYMN TO THE SUN]

[From *Ácoma*]

1

House of the Dawn! And of the evening Light,
And of the cloud, and of the mist, the rain,
Heaven! And Spirit mysterious be this rite
Acceptable, who in the Sun again
Rejoices Ácoma! Soul! Sacred Fire,
Which our first fathers, waked by earliest birds,
Emerging from their caves were as a choir
Made dumb for musing music, with no words,
And stood adoring. Then silently descended
From cliffs of sleep to fields, or cropping herds
Of goats along the hills, until was ended
Their labor, and you sank behind the scroll
Of the overshadowing peak. Until was gone
The upward streaming glory to the shoal

Of darkness, where the evening star had drawn
The moth wings of the night—as from a bowl
Of fiery coals a widening glow is sent,
Wherein a silver beetle of irised wing
Suspends itself. Take now our offering,
O Sun, who over heaven spreads the tent
Of clouds and scatters them; and with the snake
Of flame sends rain. With music's instrument,
With dancing steps, and songs, and with the shake
Of rattles, and with leaves of cottonwood
Do we bring worship and incessant song
For earth's fertility, and our daily good,
And for our bodies, beautiful and strong.

2

Come white dawn youths out of you, rising Sun,
With wild verbenas,
With meadow foam, and larkspur; where you run
Fling white azaleas;
Strew ghost flowers for the stars, and whispering bells
Where the lonely hill is;
And heap the heights with thistles, and the dells
With desert lilies:
These for the light, O Sun, which on the rim
Of the mountain quivers,
As milk weeds shiver where the swallows skim
The silver rivers.
Come yellow dawn youths of the Sun, with hands
Of trumpet clustered,
Mescal and desert mallow bound with strands
Of golden mustard.
Tree poppies, phlox, and tulips as the light
Grows red from opal;
Pour on the paleness which has slain the night
Lupine and nopal.
O Sun adored, and Those Above, who draw,
And long have drawn you,
Sire of the thunder, lightning, and our Awe,
The plumed Awanyu,
Health give us, that we may adore you still
With rapt adoring,
With flutes and drums and dances and a will
That serves imploring.

Spire up the smoke bush of the sky, the gift
Of the sea's scions,
Clouds, as the ocotillo when they drift
With dandelions.

3

Forth from the kiva's floor
Our feet restore,
Our hands restore;
And by the laddered entrance
On us pour
Light for the mind, and grain
Of healing, more and more.
Lead us the way to walk
In joy and free of pain,
With songs and happy talk
Lead us to walk
Amid abundant rain.
Silent as flees the hawk,
Silent as feet in pollen by the stream
Pass between stalk and stalk
Of tulips, be our dream
Peace and no brother's harm.
May hate and lust disarm.
Send us the moon, your sister, when
The laughing children sport,
And race among the councils of old men
In the silvered court.
May life be beautiful above us,
And life be beautiful below us;
May you, O Sun, still love us;
And may your splendor show us
The pathway undiminished.
Beauty, O Sun, bestow us,
With beauty be life finished;
Our hearts restore and keep;
Hold death delayed and far;
And lead us out of sleep
As night the star.
I have prayed, O Sun, to bless
Our Ácoma and redress
Our life with loveliness.

1930

THE LOST ORCHARD

Loves and sorrows of those who lose an orchard
Are less seen than the shadow shells
Of butterflies whose wings are tortured
In the perilous escape of rainy dells,
In the ecstatic flight of blinding Junes.
Save for the breath dirge of the wind-rung harebells
They have no words that ever shall be known,
Neither have they speech or tone,
Save the tones when the sun with gold galloons
Trims the blue edges of the air;
And save the quiet which quells
The music of the water drop in the well's
Water far down, where vision swoons.

These are the voices and these alone
Of the lost orchard, and its vague despair.
Branches may gnarl with scale and lift their bare
Paralysis, or the withered crone
Of loneliness breed water sprouts; or frost
Heap the dull turf over the strawberry vines;
Or rust unhinge the gates; or the fallen pear
Waste like the Cretan gold of ruined shrines
In tangled grasses; or the broken share
Be sunk in leaf mould—these are noonday signs
Of the deserted, but not of the orchard that is lost.
Silver secrets speak of the lost orchard, as the shells
Of butterflies escaped whisper the vanished wings;
Or as light shaken from the field of clover tells
Of the zephyr's irised wanderings.

A lost orchard is the memory of a friend
Wronged by life to death, who lies
Lifelike, but with unseeing eyes.
It is music made a ghost, because the end
Of life has come which made the music mean
Eyes that look and lips that thrill.
Music is no breast where wounded souls may lean,
If played when hands it signified are still.
A lost orchard is the road on which we passed
Where a house was with a candle in the night;

And we must go that way still, but at last
The house is by the roadside, but no light.

Over a lost orchard I have strayed
In March when down the wooded ravine
The behemoth wind bellowed to the glade
By the sky-blue water before the rushes were green.
While yet the acorn cups crushed under feet
Against the moss mould, yellow as smoke;
And the lanterns of wild cucumbers quenched by sleet,
And gusts of winter hung by the leafless oak;
When the crow's nest was a splotch of sticks on the sky,
And burnt out torches of feasts the sumach cone.
And I have climbed till the wind was naught but a sigh
Over the stairs of stone and the seat of stone.
And there I have seen the orchard, the apple trees
Patient in loneliness, and forgotten care;
And the grass as heavy as the Sargasso Sea's
Around the trunks, grown like a dead man's hair.
And I have returned in Spring when the nebulae
Of early blossoms whitened before it was June;
And I have seen them merge in their leafy sky
Till they became the light of the full moon.
Warm is the orchard as the stalls of the sun
At midnight, when each budded stem is dewed
With a firefly and the whispering zephyrs run
From leaf to leaf, awaking the dreams that brood
Before the gray woolens of the shadows fall
From the sleeping earth, and the lights of the orchard are wooed
From sea gray to sea green in a carnival
Change of flame, in a dawning many hued.
Till the long winds come, blowing from woodlands over
The glistening water, and meadows beyond the citrine
Sand of the hill that walls the field of clover
Nod their blossoms amid a tide of green.

Angels are never in caverns, nor presences
That speak the will to leave it lingering
About the orchard lost. Nor does the chrysalis
Lie thick in paths of the arisen wing;
Nor butterflies haunt the grasses like innocent
Desires defeated; nor the coverts mourn
With doves; nor are the wild bees rent

From habitations in old trees; nor the forlorn
Grass grow rich bespeaking humble hopes;
Nor corners of giant heliotropes
Droop so memorially; nor the stair of stone
Hold the silence that follows a footfall; nor the sky
Above the stone seat by its emptiness alone
Tell of a face and of a wondering eye;
Nor are flowers without the fruit so richly grown.

The house of the lost orchard is loneliness to the uttermost:
The chimney in the top of the elm tree,
Like the open mouth of a musing ghost
Has nothing but the void of the sky,
And the sequestered flight of the passing cloud,
Though the expectant breeze goes by
To gather smoke from the hearth long disavowed.
And under a brick of the porch the key to the fastened door
Glints out of rust and waits
For those who won the orchard to explore
The rooms and find the unveiled Fates.

Out of the lost orchard is life that needs the orchard no more,
The fence has broken places, and the gates
Swing to the passing wind. But butterflies soar
Over the tree tops to predestined mates.

1935

THE SEVEN CITIES OF AMERICA

How they walled the sea, and felled the woods;
How they baked the lime, and hauled the sand;
How they delved and scooped the earth, and drove the plow
In the old time, building the wall and the tower,
In the beginning of the land, when the great towns arose.

* * * * *

Over Nahant and Marblehead, over Salem and Plymouth
The mists whirl down over the stone walls, and the eternal gulls
Fly forever in a sky haunted by prayers and prophecies of doom.
Here began the gainful lovers of the oar, and the gear of ships
In the days when leviathan was hunted amid the ridges of the sea.
Then as steam became the wings of far-faring keels

More and more did Phorcys gather treasure in his cave by the sea,
Making ready for war, that no breed of men might equal these.
From war the bones of devoured men were reared in reefs
Down which ran the blood of those sacrificed to Trade,
And Boston became a city standing upon these reefs, with spires
Lifted in reverence to the gods which had given her power and
gold.
Nevertheless it is a city haunted by witches with peaked hats,
And glancing green eyes, and on its roofs looking down at the
folk
Are crows which sit with red eyes, sucking their claws.

* * * * *

In Manhattan the Indian welcomed the white man with hands,
And sold him the island for a few pieces of money; and then
The Indian wandered to the North, to the West, ever driven on
And removed, so that his stirred revenge might be prevented.
Then populous streets were laid, and high-roofed houses built,
And the pyramids of man-eating gods lifted ever toward the
clouds.
Here from the first, youth was given wine and love and music
And feasts against the day of stripped coronals, and blows
Urging them to the stone of sacrifice and the excised heart.
Only for a brief day did men sit here on soft fleeces,
Watching the sea and the ships, and playing at bowls.
Abominations were done even on the altars of wisdom,
And frightfulness was born, which turned to stone
The faces of men, and made iron of their hearts,
So that they could guard the caves dug under the towers for the
hoarding of gold.
Now for a long time towers with braziers over the sea have warned
The ships of travelers and have lured them likewise to the shore.

* * * * *

For long years the ships laden with rich wares came out of the sea
And sailed up the Ashley River, along the low sea beaches to docks
Of the plantations where cotton was delivered back for Europe.
Wherefore Charleston throve on low land between two rivers,
And with growing wealth, and pride born of belief that she was
free,
The sons born of the Ashley and the Cooper Rivers enclosed
gardens
With stones and gates of grilled iron and bronze wherein grew

Magnolias and roses under the eaves of noble roofs, which faced
Fort Sumter in the waters of the Bay, looking even then like a ship
Foundered and turned to sand and stone. For hither the gulls from Boston
Came and flew over it against the day when it should be a tomb
For the bones of great defeat in a cause of fading memory.

* * * * *

At the same time the ships came out of the sea, and sailed past swamps
Of live oaks, where the hot steam of the river gladdens the snake
And the alligator, through which the red bird flies, and the mocking bird,
Inhaling the scent of tropic blossoms, sings all day.
By the mouth of the Great River, empire built a city, that ships from the sea,
And ships from the North, bearing furs and grain might enrich these wharves.
So New Orleans arose, a city of balconies, and old courts of stone,
And cathedrals and markets, and the endless spread of low roofs.
Now the balconies are rotting under the shadows of new built towers.
The Great River, that old man of the sea, has forgotten the wharves,
He has forgotten the wharves and the boats spouting fire from pine-knots.
For the Destroyer of cities, who cannot rebuild them as they were,
Having circled the earth with iron ships and wires under the waters,
With soldiers and wings of steel, and Iris-echoes among the clouds,
That Destroyer has taken from New Orleans the joy of wine,
And the tumultuous happiness of sails and side-wheelers and the mixed breeds
That strode the docks, strong of arm, lustful and singing.
For now there are towers with braziers which look down upon the Great River,
And upon the spread of roofs. And the braziers are like the eye of a man-eating giant,
Who searches everywhere for prey and from whom nothing can be hidden.

* * * * *

Where the Onion River like a snake in dog days crawled amid
 weeds,
And skunk-cabbage was drugged to deep sleep by fat mud and
 the flesh of dead fish,
Fort Dearborn stood after the French, once circling the continent
From Quebec to New Orleans, had soldiers in the old days of
 empire.
Here the Indians were cheated of their land and killed, breeding
 revenge.
Here traders came, first in sails, then in steam boats, multiplying
 rapidly.
And soon cabins rose around the stockade by the river of Indian
 canoes,
And on the shore of the Lake of gray waters and the wheeling
 of gulls.
Then came a square mile of roofs, and long rows of columned
 porches
Hemmed with grilled fences, and overlooked by the tower of a
 Court House,
The seat of justice and law. But meanwhile the blood of the
 Indian
Cried from this marshland, this spot of sandy reaches and flat
 water.
The blood of broad-browed cattle cried from this ground, and
 filled the city
And the winds blowing over it with the spirit of Discord and War,
Which gave speed to the wings of crows, making ready to fellow
 with those
Of Plymouth and Marblehead, when fallen men should furnish
 the meat of their bones.
Here then the towers of Chicago arose, founded on spiles
Driven through muck and blood.
For the North Wind kept the hearts of this people revived and
 strong,
So that neither fire nor the waste of war kept back the building
 of towers,
Which spread abroad by the Onion River, and the Lake of gray
 water,
And grew ever higher into the clouds, till their high-lifted braziers
Made light upon the dark dunes far away in midnights of no
 moon,
Where the leafless trees of winter standing loftily on the heaped
 slopes of sand

Could not be seen for the darkness out of the Lake except for the braziers.
Near the city these braziers doubled themselves in the waters of the Lake,
Or were strewn like the phosphor of dead fish to and fro with the sliding waves.
Here are no mountain sides upon which the moon may cast her arrows of silver,
Spilling them amid the roots which bear the thousand-blossomed narcissus.
For this is the Babylon of the hanging gardens, built against the unfriendliness of Earth.
This is Memphis, near the necropolis of countless graves of the dead.
This is Rome of the tiger and the gladiator. And the blood of slaughtered cattle,
And the blood of the despoiled and murdered Indian built this city.

* * * * *

There is a city where the light of drifting mist
Floats out of the Pacific over its hills with many roofs.
Near it are mountain slopes where in the first days of the Spaniard
The creatures of wells and woods, and rivers flowing into the sea
Made the land joyous, as they mingled their voices
With the sound of mission bells, and the shouts of sailors and hunters,
And those who sought the golden fleece, and the sound of the sea
Moving with low thunder upon the reefs of Golden Gate.
Here to this day the mountain sides bloom with poppies, and its valleys
Flourish with apple trees with bright fruit, and with sweet figs,
And olives in bloom with spreading leaves. And even yet the looms of stone
In the bay weave out of the sun-lit air raiment of silver and purple
For the winged breezes to wear when they fly from the breast of the sea
And float over the towers of San Francisco and rest themselves.
By the long ridges of the Olympian Pacific this city of America
Sits enduringly, taking the love and the rage of the iron years.
And golden snooded women stand on the hills of this city
And look at the sea where it stretches far west to Japan.

* * * * *

West of the pasture lands of cattle, and mountains of never failing
snow
The adorers of Dionysus and Christ, the sons of Solomon and
Isaiah
Built their city, and laid the roof of their tabernacle,
And carved the pinnacle of their temple by the blue haze of a
dead sea,
And under the haunted gray-eyed brows of the Wasatch Moun-
tains.
Here the restlessness of poplar leaves makes endless whisperings
By bronze cast as memorials to the miraculous visitation of gulls.
Here the mystery of Cumorah Hill in far New York
And the bewitchment of old Scriptures and Golden Plates
Breathe round the valley of Salt Lake, and with wizardry
Clothe the air, and the blue sky, and the broad spread of roofs,
And even the towers, which have arisen here also, here in the
desert
Where the gulls fly forever up from the still water of the dead
sea.
And when the morning sun springs over the mouse-gray slopes
of the mountains,
And fills the valley with the color of larkspur and the bloom of
desert cactus,
And lifts from the breast of the dead sea wraiths of purple and
gold,
As if they were the departing breath of rock-grown poppies,
then at once
The golden figure of Moroni, standing on the highest pinnacle
of the Temple,
Takes fire and glows, while the ever restless leaves of poplars
By the doors of the Temple whisper their gladness for the light
of dawn.
Thus forever Moroni looks over the Valley and guards it for the
old days.

* * * * *

These are the seven cities of America, which have taken the place
Of the seven cities of Cibola, with their roofs of turquoise
And their doors of gold, wherein stood the bronze skinned Indian
Clothed in the pelt of the deer and the wolf, and with eagle
feathers,
And who welcomed with hands the white man bent on theft
and murder.

These cities old and new were lighted by the sun as he passed
from East to West.
Now wings of fire carry messages of trade and war between the
cities,
For trade and war are as of old. And as of old people rise from
sleep,
They feast, they labor, they wed, they get and they spend,
And children are born to them, as in the seven cities of Cibola.
And all go back to earth as in the seven cities of Cibola, where
now
The dust that eddies about the mesas when the wind rises is the
dust
Of those who worked in turquoise and made arrows and wor-
shipped the Sun.
They too left the cities of Cibola to the care of the iron years,
Friendly to the ever-whispering poplars, and the grass growing
green
From the pasturelands of cattle to the shore of the ever-calling
sea.

1935

E. A. Robinson

Edwin Arlington Robinson was born December 22, 1869, in the village of Head Tide, Maine. His father was Edward Robinson, a descendant of a Scottish carpenter, Gain Robinson, who immigrated to New England at the end of the seventeenth century; and his mother was Mary Palmer Robinson. Edward Robinson was a successful merchant in Head Tide, but when his son was less than a year old he moved to the larger town of Gardiner, Maine, the "Tilbury Town" of the poems. Here Robinson grew up, attending the local school, reading, especially poetry, and eventually trying to write verse himself. He was a dreamy, diffident, but self-sufficient lad, who early discovered that his abilities were not of the sort usually called practical. In about his seventeenth year he became engrossed in the study of English blank verse, translating into that meter as an exercise the whole of Cicero's first oration against Cataline.[1] A few years later he put into English verse the whole of the *Antigone*, using a literal translation supplied him by a friend. About 1889 he realized definitely that "he was doomed, or elected, or sentenced for life, to the writing of poetry"; and although from the first his confidence in his ability was firm he spared his parents and friends the news of his discovery, knowing how the unlikely prospects for his future would worry them. Among others, however, one neighbor, Dr. A. T. Schumann, a skillful and confirmed writer of verse, knew Robinson's secret, and aided him in acquiring mastery over metrical language.

Robinson attended Harvard two years (1891-1893), but then the illness of his father and the straitened circumstances of the family forced him to leave college. From 1893 to 1897 he lived

[1] See "The First Seven Years," *Colophon*, IV, 1930, from which also comes the first two quoted passages in this article.

quietly in Gardiner, practicing his "unaccredited profession" of poet and sending out manuscripts to numerous periodicals. Most of his work was rejected, editors being unwilling to accept for the popular audience verse so original in manner as Robinson's, so that both parents of the poet died without having learned of the occupation their son had chosen.

Convinced finally that editors would not publish his work, Robinson decided to publish it himself; accordingly in 1896 he printed 312 copies of a little volume called *The Torrent and the Night Before*, which carried the notice: "This book is dedicated to any man, woman, or critic who will cut the edges of it. I have done the top." Forty or fifty copies he sent to friends and acquaintances, the others to periodicals to be reviewed and to scholars and known lovers of poetry. A number of those receiving copies wrote Robinson in response; and although the book failed to establish his reputation, the encouragement he received sustained him in his purpose to become a poet.

In 1898 he went to New York City, where he occupied himself chiefly with poetry and at times worked at the incidental task of making a living. He lived frugally, in poorly furnished rooming houses in Yonkers, and on West Twenty-third Street and elsewhere in New York City. For a time he was a checker of materials used in the construction of the new subways. In 1905, however, President Theodore Roosevelt, who had become interested in his poetry, secured a position for him in the New York Customs House, and this job he retained till 1909. In 1911 he discovered the MacDowell Colony, at Peterborough, New Hampshire; and finding its atmosphere congenial, thereafter he customarily spent his summers at the Colony. During most of the year, however, he resided in New York City, living during his later years on East Forty-second Street, in quarters facing the East River. He made one trip abroad—to England in the spring of 1923.

In spite of the noise and confusion of a great city, Robinson was able to remain calm and detached, although he seems to have been disturbed occasionally by the idea that, measured by the standards of matter-of-fact men, he was not successful. He observed all about him shrewdly, discerningly, but he was at heart a bookish man—a devoted reader of Shakespeare, Dickens, the Bible, Thomas Hardy, Cervantes, Melville. As a boy he played the clarinet, and the love of music became one of the passions of his later life. He was fond of folk songs, of the Gilbert and Sullivan operatic scores, of Brahms, Verdi, and Wagner. Wealth, luxuries, and worldly success had little attraction for him; but he set a high value on the good will of his friends; and throughout his career he was sustained by the hope that his poetry would have enduring value.

He was elected a member of the International P. E. N. Club and of the National Institute of Arts and Letters, and in 1929 received a gold medal awarded by the latter body. In 1922 Yale University, and in 1925 Bowdoin College, conferred upon him the honorary degree of Doctor of Literature. Three times—in 1921, 1925, and 1927—he was awarded the Pulitzer Prize for poetry.

During the early days of 1935 he became seriously ill and on January 17 was admitted to the New York Hospital for treatment. There, after an operation for cancer, he died on April 6, 1935. His body was cremated, and the ashes taken to Gardiner for burial.

RICHARD CORY

Whenever Richard Cory went down town,
We people on the pavement looked at him:
He was a gentleman from sole to crown,
Clean favored, and imperially slim.

And he was always quietly arrayed,
And he was always human when he talked;
But still he fluttered pulses when he said,
"Good-morning," and he glittered when he walked.

And he was rich—yes, richer than a king—
And admirably schooled in every grace:
In fine, we thought that he was everything
To make us wish that we were in his place.

So on we worked, and waited for the light,
And went without the meat, and cursed the bread;
And Richard Cory, one calm summer night,
Went home and put a bullet through his head.

1897

CREDO

I cannot find my way: there is no star
In all the shrouded heavens anywhere;
And there is not a whisper in the air
Of any living voice but one so far
That I can hear it only as a bar
Of lost, imperial music, played when fair
And angel fingers wove, and unaware,
Dead leaves to garlands where no roses are.

No, there is not a glimmer, nor a call,
For one that welcomes, welcomes when he fears,
The black and awful chaos of the night;
For through it all—above, beyond it all—
I know the far-sent message of the years,
I feel the coming glory of the Light.

1897

PARTNERSHIP [1]

Yes, you have it; I can see.
Beautiful? . . . Dear, look at me!
Look and let my shame confess
Triumph after weariness.
Beautiful? Ah, yes.

Lift it where the beams are bright;
Hold it where the western light,
Shining in above my bed,
Throws a glory on your head.
Now it is all said.

All there was for me to say
From the first until to-day.

[1] Concerning this poem, the author wrote to the editors as follows: " 'Partnership' was published originally under the title, 'The Wife of Palissy' . . . In a misguided moment I changed it—with some notion, I suppose, of giving the poem a more general application. 'It' is (or was) obviously one of Palissy's porcelains. Now it can be almost anything." Palissy was a French potter of the sixteenth century.

Long denied and long deferred,
Now I say it in one word—
Now; and you have heard.

Life would have its way with us,
And I've called it glorious:
For I know the glory now
And I read it on your brow.
You have shown me how.

I can feel your cheeks all wet,
But your eyes will not forget:
In the frown you cannot hide
I can read where faith and pride
Are not satisfied.

But the word was, two should live:
Two should suffer—and forgive:
By the steep and weary way,
For the glory of the clay,
Two should have their day.

We have toiled and we have wept
For the gift the gods have kept:
Clashing and unreconciled
When we might as well have smiled,
We have played the child.

But the clashing is all past,
And the gift is yours at last.
Lift it—hold it high again! . . .
Did I doubt you now and then?
Well, we are not men.

Never mind; we know the way,—
And I do not need to stay.
Let us have it well confessed:
You to triumph, I to rest.
That will be the best.

1902

THE FIELD OF GLORY

War shook the land where Levi dwelt,
And fired the dismal wrath he felt,
That such a doom was ever wrought
As his, to toil while others fought;
To toil, to dream—and still to dream,
With one day barren as another;
To consummate, as it would seem,
The dry despair of his old mother.

Far off one afternoon began
The sound of man destroying man;
And Levi, sick with nameless rage,
Condemned again his heritage,
And sighed for scars that might have come,
And would, if once he could have sundered
Those harsh, inhering claims of home
That held him while he cursed and wondered.

Another day, and then there came,
Rough, bloody, ribald, hungry, lame,
But yet themselves, to Levi's door,
Two remnants of the day before.
They laughed at him and what he sought;
They jeered him, and his painful acre;
But Levi knew that they had fought,
And left their manners to their Maker.

That night, for the grim widow's ears,
With hopes that hid themselves in fears,
He told of arms, and fiery deeds,
Whereat one leaps the while he reads,
And said he'd be no more a clown,
While others drew the breath of battle.—
The mother looked him up and down,
And laughed—a scant laugh with a rattle.

She told him what she found to tell,
And Levi listened, and heard well
Some admonitions of a voice
That left him no cause to rejoice.—

He sought a friend, and found the stars,
And prayed aloud that they should aid him;
But they said not a word of wars,
Or of a reason why God made him.

And who's of this or that estate
We do not wholly calculate,
When baffling shades that shift and cling
Are not without their glimmering;
When even Levi, tired of faith,
Beloved of none, forgot by many,
Dismissed as an inferior wraith,
Reborn may be as great as any.

1902

THE TOWN DOWN THE RIVER

I

Said the Watcher by the Way
To the young and the unladen,
To the boy and to the maiden,
"God be with you both to-day.
First your song came ringing,
Now you come, you two,—
Knowing naught of what you do,
Or of what your dreams are bringing.

"O you children who go singing
To the Town down the River,
Where the millions cringe and shiver,
Tell me what you know to-day;
Tell me how far you are going,
Tell me how you find your way.
O you children who go dreaming,
Tell me what you dream to-day."

"He is old and we have heard him,"
Said the boy then to the maiden;
"He is old and heavy laden
With a load we throw away.
Care may come to find us,
Age may lay us low;

Still, we seek the light we know,
And the dead we leave behind us.

"Did he think that he would blind us
Into such a small believing
As to live without achieving,
When the lights have led so far?
Let him watch or let him wither,—
Shall he tell us where we are?
We know best who go together,
Downward, onward, and so far."

II

Said the Watcher by the Way
To the fiery folk that hastened,
To the loud and the unchastened,
"You are strong, I see, to-day.
Strength and hope may lead you
To the journey's end,—
Each to be the other's friend
If the Town should fail to need you.

"And are ravens there to feed you
In the Town down the River,
Where the gift appalls the giver
And youth hardens day by day?
O you brave and you unshaken,
Are you truly on your way?
And are sirens in the River,
That you come so far to-day?"

"You are old, and we have listened,"
Said the voice of one who halted;
"You are sage and self-exalted,
But your way is not our way.
You that cannot aid us
Give us words to eat.
Be assured that they are sweet,
And that we are as God made us.

"Not in vain have you delayed us,
Though the River still be calling
Through the twilight that is falling,

And the Town be still so far.
By the whirlwind of your wisdom
Leagues are lifted as leaves are;
But a king without a kingdom
Fails us, who have come so far."

III

Said the Watcher by the Way
To the slower folk who stumbled,
To the weak and the world-humbled,
"Tell me how you fare to-day.
Some with ardor shaken,
All with honor scarred,
Do you falter, finding hard
The far chance that you have taken?

"Or, do you at length awaken
To an antic retribution,
Goading to a new confusion
The drugged hopes of yesterday?
O you poor mad men that hobble,
Will you not return, or stay?
Do you trust, you broken people
To a dawn without the day?"

"You speak well of what you know not,"
Muttered one; and then a second:
"You have begged and you have beckoned,
But you see us on our way.
Who are you to scold us,
Knowing what we know?
Jeremiah, long ago,
Said as much as you have told us.

"As we are, then, you behold us:
Derelicts of all conditions,
Poets, rogues, and sick physicians,
Plodding forward from afar;
Forward now into the darkness
Where the men before us are;
Forward, onward, out of grayness,
To the light that shone so far."

IV

Said the Watcher by the Way
To some aged ones who lingered,
To the shrunken, the claw-fingered,
"So you come for me to-day."—
"Yes, to give you warning;
You are old," one said;
"You have old hairs on your head,
Fit for laurel, not for scorning.

"From the first of early morning
We have toiled along to find you;
We, as others, have maligned you,
But we need your scorn to-day.
By the light that we saw shining,
Let us not be lured alway;
Let us hear no River calling
When to-morrow is to-day."

"But your lanterns are unlighted
And the Town is far before you:
Let us hasten, I implore you,"
Said the Watcher by the Way.
"Long have I waited,
Longer have I known
That the Town would have its own,
And the call be for the fated.

"In the name of all created,
Let us hear no more, my brothers;
Are we older than all others?
Are the planets in our way?"—
"Hark," said one; "I hear the River,
Calling always, night and day."—
"Forward, then! The lights are shining,"
Said the Watcher by the Way.

1910

MINIVER CHEEVY

Miniver Cheevy, child of scorn,
Grew lean while he assailed the seasons;
He wept that he was ever born,
And he had reasons.

Miniver loved the days of old
When swords were bright and steeds were prancing;
The vision of a warrior bold
Would set him dancing.

Miniver sighed for what was not,
And dreamed, and rested from his labors;
He dreamed of Thebes and Camelot,
And Priam's neighbors.

Miniver mourned the ripe renown
That made so many a name so fragrant;
He mourned Romance, now on the town,
And Art, a vagrant.

Miniver loved the Medici,
Albeit he had never seen one;
He would have sinned incessantly
Could he have been one.

Miniver cursed the commonplace
And eyed a khaki suit with loathing;
He missed the mediæval grace
Of iron clothing.

Miniver scorned the gold he sought,
But sore annoyed was he without it;
Miniver thought, and thought, and thought,
And thought about it.

Miniver Cheevy, born too late,
Scratched his head and kept on thinking;
Miniver coughed, and called it fate,
And kept on drinking.

1910

THE PILOT

From the Past and Unavailing
Out of cloudland we are steering:
After groping, after fearing,
Into starlight we come trailing,
And we find the stars are true.
Still, O comrade, what of you?
You are gone, but we are sailing,
And the old ways are all new.

For the Lost and Unreturning
We have drifted, we have waited;
Uncommanded and unrated,
We have tossed and wandered, yearning
For a charm that comes no more
From the old lights by the shore:
We have shamed ourselves in learning
What you knew so long before.

For the Breed of the Far-going
Who are strangers, and all brothers,
May forget no more than others
Who looked seaward with eyes flowing.
But are brothers to bewail
One who fought so foul a gale?
You have won beyond our knowing,
You are gone, but yet we sail.

1910

FOR A DEAD LADY

No more with overflowing light
Shall fill the eyes that now are faded,
Nor shall another's fringe with night
Their woman-hidden world as they did.
No more shall quiver down the days
The flowing wonder of her ways,
Whereof no language may requite
The shifting and the many-shaded.

The grace, divine, definitive,
Clings only as a faint forestalling;
The laugh that love could not forgive
Is hushed, and answers to no calling;
The forehead and the little ears
Have gone where Saturn keeps the years;
The breast where roses could not live
Has done with rising and with falling.

The beauty, shattered by the laws
That have creation in their keeping,
No longer trembles at applause,
Or over children that are sleeping;
And we who delve in beauty's lore
Know all that we have known before
Of what inexorable cause
Makes Time so vicious in his reaping.

1910

FLAMMONDE

The man Flammonde, from God knows where,
With firm address and foreign air,
With news of nations in his talk
And something royal in his walk,
With glint of iron in his eyes,
But never doubt, nor yet surprise,
Appeared, and stayed, and held his head
As one by kings accredited.

Erect, with his alert repose
About him, and about his clothes,
He pictured all tradition hears
Of what we owe to fifty years.
His cleansing heritage of taste
Paraded neither want nor waste;
And what he needed for his fee
To live, he borrowed graciously.

He never told us what he was,
Or what mischance, or other cause,
Had banished him from better days

To play the Prince of Castaways.
Meanwhile he played surpassing well
A part, for most, unplayable;
In fine, one pauses, half afraid
To say for certain that he played.

For that, one may as well forego
Conviction as to yes or no;
Nor can I say just how intense
Would then have been the difference
To several, who, having striven
In vain to get what he was given,
Would see the stranger taken on
By friends not easy to be won.

Moreover, many a malcontent
He soothed and found munificent;
His courtesy beguiled and foiled
Suspicion that his years were soiled;
His mien distinguished any crowd,
His credit strengthened when he bowed;
And women, young and old, were fond
Of looking at the man Flammonde.

There was a woman in our town
On whom the fashion was to frown;
But while our talk renewed the tinge
Of a long-faded scarlet fringe,
The man Flammonde saw none of that,
And what he saw we wondered at—
That none of us, in her distress,
Could hide or find our littleness.

There was a boy that all agreed
Had shut within him the rare seed
Of learning. We could understand,
But none of us could lift a hand.
The man Flammonde appraised the youth,
And told a few of us the truth;
And thereby, for a little gold,
A flowered future was unrolled.

There were two citizens who fought
For years and years, and over nought;

They made life awkward for their friends,
And shortened their own dividends.
The man Flammonde said what was wrong
Should be made right; nor was it long
Before they were again in line,
And had each other in to dine.

And these I mention are but four
Of many out of many more.
So much for them. But what of him—
So firm in every look and limb?
What small satanic sort of kink
Was in his brain? What broken link
Withheld him from the destinies
That came so near to being his?

What was he, when we came to sift
His meaning, and to note the drift
Of incommunicable ways
That make us ponder while we praise?
Why was it that his charm revealed
Somehow the surface of a shield?
What was it that we never caught?
What was he, and what was he not?

How much it was of him we met
We cannot ever know; nor yet
Shall all he gave us quite atone
For what was his, and his alone;
Nor need we now, since he knew best,
Nourish an ethical unrest:
Rarely at once will nature give
The power to be Flammonde and live.

We cannot know how much we learn
From those who never will return,
Until a flash of unforeseen
Remembrance falls on what has been.
We've each a darkening hill to climb;
And this is why, from time to time
In Tilbury Town, we look beyond
Horizons for the man Flammonde.

1916

JOHN GORHAM

"Tell me what you're doing over here, John Gorham,
Sighing hard and seeming to be sorry when you're not;
Make me laugh or let me go now, for long faces in the moon-
light
Are a sign for me to say again a word that you forgot."—

"I'm over here to tell you what the moon already
May have said or maybe shouted ever since a year ago;
I'm over here to tell you what you are, Jane Wayland,
And to make you rather sorry, I should say, for being so."—

"Tell me what you're saying to me now, John Gorham,
Or you'll never see as much of me as ribbons any more;
I'll vanish in as many ways as I have toes and fingers,
And you'll not follow far for one where flocks have been
before."—

"I'm sorry now you never saw the flocks, Jane Wayland,
But you're the one to make of them as many as you need.
And then about the vanishing. It's I who mean to vanish;
And when I'm here no longer you'll be done with me indeed."—

"That's a way to tell me what I am, John Gorham!
How am I to know myself until I make you smile?
Try to look as if the moon were making faces at you,
And a little more as if you meant to stay a little while."—

"You are what it is that over rose-blown gardens
Makes a pretty flutter for a season in the sun;
You are what it is that with a mouse, Jane Wayland,
Catches him and lets him go and eats him up for fun."—

"Sure I never took you for a mouse, John Gorham;
All you say is easy, but so far from being true
That I wish you wouldn't ever be again the one to think so;
For it isn't cats and butterflies that I would be to you."—

"All your little animals are in one picture—
One I've had before me since a year ago to-night;

And the picture where they live will be of you, Jane Wayland,
Till you find a way to kill them or to keep them out of sight."—

"Won't you ever see me as I am, John Gorham,
Leaving out the foolishness and all I never meant?
Somewhere in me there's a woman, if you know the way to find her.
Will you like me any better if I prove it and repent?"—

"I doubt if I shall ever have the time, Jane Wayland;
And I dare say all this moonlight lying round us might as well
Fall for nothing on the shards of broken urns that are forgotten,
As on two that have no longer much of anything to tell."

1916

THE UNFORGIVEN

When he, who is the unforgiven,
Beheld her first, he found her fair:
No promise ever dreamt in heaven
Could then have lured him anywhere
That would have been away from there;
And all his wits had lightly striven,
Foiled with her voice, and eyes, and hair.

There's nothing in the saints and sages
To meet the shafts her glances had,
Or such as hers have had for ages
To blind a man till he be glad,
And humble him till he be mad.
The story would have many pages,
And would be neither good nor bad.

And, having followed, you would find him
Where properly the play begins;
But look for no red light behind him—
No fumes of many-colored sins,
Fanned high by screaming violins.
God knows what good it was to blind him,
Or whether man or woman wins.

And by the same eternal token,
Who knows just how it will all end?—

This drama of hard words unspoken,
This fireside farce, without a friend
Or enemy to comprehend
What augurs when two lives are broken,
And fear finds nothing left to mend.

He stares in vain for what awaits him,
And sees in Love a coin to toss;
He smiles, and her cold hush berates him
Beneath his hard half of the cross;
They wonder why it ever was;
And she, the unforgiving, hates him
More for her lack than for her loss.

He feeds with pride his indecision,
And shrinks from what will not occur,
Bequeathing with infirm derision
His ashes to the days that were,
Before she made him prisoner;
And labors to retrieve the vision
That he must once have had of her.

He waits, and there awaits an ending,
And he knows neither what nor when;
But no magicians are attending
To make him see as he saw then,
And he will never find again
The face that once had been the rending
Of all his purpose among men.

He blames her not, nor does he chide her,
And she has nothing new to say;
If he were Bluebeard he could hide her,
But that's not written in the play,
And there will be no change to-day;
Although, to the serene outsider,
There still would seem to be a way.

1916

BEWICK FINZER

Time was when his half million drew
  The breath of six per cent;
But soon the worm of what-was-not
  Fed hard on his content;
And something crumbled in his brain
  When his half million went.

Time passed, and filled along with his
  The place of many more;
Time came, and hardly one of us
  Had credence to restore,
From what appeared one day, the man
  Whom we had known before.

The broken voice, the withered neck,
  The coat worn out with care,
The cleanliness of indigence,
  The brilliance of despair,
The fond imponderable dreams
  Of affluence,—all were there.

Poor Finzer, with his dreams and schemes,
  Fares hard now in the race,
With heart and eye that have a task
  When he looks in the face
Of one who might so easily
  Have been in Finzer's place.

He comes unfailing for the loan
  We give and then forget;
He comes, and probably for years
  Will he be coming yet,—
Familiar as an old mistake,
  And futile as regret.

1916

THE MAN AGAINST THE SKY

Between me and the sunset, like a dome
Against the glory of a world on fire,
Now burned a sudden hill,
Bleak, round, and high, by flame-lit height made higher,
With nothing on it for the flame to kill
Save one who moved and was alone up there
To loom before the chaos and the glare
As if he were the last god going home
Unto his last desire.

Dark, marvelous, and inscrutable he moved on
Till down the fiery distance he was gone,
Like one of those eternal, remote things
That range across a man's imaginings
When a sure music fills him and he knows
What he may say thereafter to few men,—
The touch of ages having wrought
An echo and a glimpse of what he thought
A phantom or a legend until then;
For whether lighted over ways that save,
Or lured from all repose,
If he go on too far to find a grave,
Mostly alone he goes.

Even he, who stood where I had found him,
On high with fire all round him,
Who moved along the molten west,
And over the round hill's crest
That seemed half ready with him to go down,
Flame-bitten and flame-cleft,
As if there were to be no last thing left
Of a nameless unimaginable town,—
Even he who climbed and vanished may have taken
Down to the perils of a depth not known,
From death defended though by men forsaken,
The bread that every man must eat alone;
He may have walked while others hardly dared
Look on to see him stand where many fell;
And upward out of that, as out of hell,
He may have sung and striven

To mount where more of him shall yet be given,
Bereft of all retreat,
To sevenfold heat,—
As on a day when three in Dura shared
The furnace, and were spared
For glory by that king of Babylon
Who made himself so great that God, who heard,
Covered him with long feathers, like a bird.

Again, he may have gone down easily,
By comfortable altitudes, and found,
As always, underneath him solid ground
Whereon to be sufficient and to stand
Possessed already of the promised land,
Far stretched and fair to see:
A good sight, verily,
And one to make the eyes of her who bore him
Shine glad with hidden tears.
Why question of his ease of who before him,
In one place or another where they left
Their names as far behind them as their bones,
And yet by dint of slaughter, toil and theft,
And shrewdly sharpened stones,
Carved hard the way for his ascendency
Through deserts of lost years?
Why trouble him now who sees and hears
No more than what his innocence requires,
And therefore to no other height aspires
Than one at which he neither quails nor tires?
He may do more by seeing what he sees
Than others eager for iniquities;
He may, by seeing all things for the best,
Incite futurity to do the rest.

Or with an even likelihood,
He may have met with atrabilious eyes
The fires of time on equal terms and passed
Indifferently down, until at last
His only kind of grandeur would have been,
Apparently, in being seen.
He may have had for evil or for good
No argument; he may have had no care
For what without himself went anywhere

To failure or to glory, and least of all
For such a stale, flamboyant miracle;
He may have been the prophet of an art
Immovable to old idolatries;
He may have been a player without a part,
Annoyed that even the sun should have the skies
For such a flaming way to advertise;
He may have been a painter sick at heart
With Nature's toiling for a new surprise;
He may have been a cynic, who now, for all
Of anything divine that his effete
Negation may have tasted,
Saw truth in his own image, rather small,
Forbore to fever the ephemeral,
Found any barren height a good retreat
From any swarming street,
And in the sun saw power superbly wasted;
And when the primitive old-fashioned stars
Came out again to shine on joys and wars
More primitive, and all arrayed for doom,
He may have proved a world a sorry thing
In his imagining,
And life a lighted highway to the tomb.

Or, mounting with infirm unsearching tread,
His hopes to chaos led,
He may have stumbled up there from the past,
And with an aching strangeness viewed the last
Abysmal conflagration of his dreams,—
A flame where nothing seems
To burn but flame itself, by nothing fed;
And while it all went out,
Not even the faint anodyne of doubt
May then have eased a painful going down
From pictured heights of power and lost renown,
Revealed at length to his outlived endeavor
Remote and unapproachable forever;
And at his heart there may have gnawed
Sick memories of a dead faith foiled and flawed
And long dishonored by the living death
Assigned alike by chance
To brutes and hierophants;
And anguish fallen on those he loved around him

May once have dealt the last blow to confound him,
And so have left him as death leaves a child,
Who sees it all too near;
And he who knows no young way to forget
May struggle to the tomb unreconciled.
Whatever suns may rise or set
There may be nothing kinder for him here
Than shafts and agonies;
And under these
He may cry out and stay on horribly;
Or, seeing in death too small a thing to fear,
He may go forward like a stoic Roman
Where pangs and terrors in his pathway lie,—
Or, seizing the swift logic of a woman,
Curse God and die.

Or maybe there, like many another one
Who might have stood aloft and looked ahead,
Black-drawn against wild red,
He may have built, unawed by fiery gules
That in him no commotion stirred,
A living reason out of molecules
Why molecules occurred,
And one for smiling when he might have sighed
Had he seen far enough,
And in the same inevitable stuff
Discovered an odd reason too for pride
In being what he must have been by laws
Infrangible and for no kind of cause.
Deterred by no confusion or surprise
He may have seen with his mechanic eyes
A world without a meaning, and had room,
Alone amid magnificence and doom,
To build himself an airy monument
That should, or fail him in his vague intent,
Outlast an accidental universe—
To call it nothing worse—
Or, by the burrowing guile
Of Time disintegrated and effaced,
Like once-remembered mighty trees go down
To ruin, of which by man may now be traced
No part sufficient even to be rotten,
And in the book of things that are forgotten

Is entered as a thing not quite worth while.
He may have been so great
That satraps would have shivered at his frown,
And all he prized alive may rule a state
No larger than a grave that holds a clown;
He may have been a master of his fate,
And of his atoms—ready as another
In his emergence to exonerate
His father and his mother;
He may have been a captain of a host,
Self-eloquent and ripe for prodigies,
Doomed here to swell by dangerous degrees,
And then give up the ghost.
Nahum's great grasshoppers were such as these,
Sun-scattered and soon lost.

Whatever the dark road he may have taken,
This man who stood on high
And faced alone the sky,
Whatever drove or lured or guided him,—
A vision answering a faith unshaken,
An easy trust assumed of easy trials,
A sick negation born of weak denials,
A crazed abhorrence of an old condition,
A blind attendance on a brief ambition,—
Whatever stayed him or derided him,
His way was even as ours;
And we, with all our wounds and all our powers,
Must each await alone at his own height
Another darkness or another light;
And there, of our poor self dominion reft,
If inference and reason shun
Hell, Heaven, and Oblivion,
May thwarted will (perforce precarious,
But for our conservation better thus)
Have no misgiving left
Of doing yet what here we leave undone?
Or if unto the last of these we cleave,
Believing or protesting we believe
In such an idle and ephemeral
Florescence of the diabolical,—
If, robbed of two fond old enormities,
Our being had no onward auguries,

What then were this great love of ours to say
For launching other lives to voyage again
A little farther into time and pain,
A little faster in a futile chase
For a kingdom and a power and a Race
That would have still in sight
A manifest end of ashes and eternal night?
Is this the music of the toys we shake
So loud,—as if there might be no mistake
Somewhere in our indomitable will?
Are we no greater than the noise we make
Along one blind atomic pilgrimage
Whereon by crass chance billeted we go
Because our brains and bones and cartilage
Will have it so?
If this we say, then let us all be still
About our share in it, and live and die
More quietly thereby.

Where was he going, this man against the sky?
You know not, nor do I.
But this we know, if we know anything:
That we may laugh and fight and sing
And of our transience here make offering
To an orient Word that will not be erased,
Or, save in incommunicable gleams
Too permanent for dreams,
Be found or known.
No tonic and ambitious irritant
Of increase or of want
Has made an otherwise insensate waste
Of ages overthrown
A ruthless, veiled, implacable foretaste
Of other ages that are still to be
Depleted and rewarded variously
Because a few, by fate's economy,
Shall seem to move the world the way it goes;
No soft evangel of equality,
Safe-cradled in a communal repose
That huddles into death and may at last
Be covered well with equatorial snows—
And all for what, the devil only knows—
Will aggregate an inkling to confirm

The credit of a sage or of a worm,
Or tell us why one man in five
Should have a care to stay alive
While in his heart he feels no violence
Laid on his humor and intelligence
When infant Science makes a pleasant face
And waves again that hollow toy, the Race;
No planetary trap where souls are wrought
For nothing but the sake of being caught
And sent again to nothing will attune
Itself to any key of any reason
Why man should hunger through another season
To find out why 'twere better late than soon
To go away and let the sun and moon
And all the silly stars illuminate
A place for creeping things,
And those that root and trumpet and have wings,
And herd and ruminate,
Or dive and flash and poise in rivers and seas,
Or by their loyal tails in lofty trees
Hang screeching lewd victorious derision
Of man's immortal vision.

Shall we, because Eternity records
Too vast an answer for the time-born words
We spell, whereof so many are dead that once
In our capricious lexicons
Were so alive and final, hear no more
The Word itself, the living word
That none alive has ever heard
Or ever spelt,
And few have ever felt
Without the fears and old surrenderings
And terrors that began
When Death let fall a feather from his wings
And humbled the first man?
Because the weight of our humility,
Wherefrom we gain
A little wisdom and much pain,
Falls here too sore and there too tedious,
Are we in anguish or complacency,
Not looking far enough ahead
To see by what mad couriers we are led

Along the roads of the ridiculous,
To pity ourselves and laugh at faith
And while we curse life bear it?
And if we see the soul's dead end in death,
Are we to fear it?
What folly is here that has not yet a name
Unless we say outright that we are liars?
What have we seen beyond our sunset fires
That lights again the way by which we came?
Why pay we such a price, and one we give
So clamoringly, for each racked empty day
That leads one more last human hope away,
As quiet fiends would lead past our crazed eyes
Our children to an unseen sacrifice?
If after all that we have lived and thought,
All comes to Nought,—
If there be nothing after Now,
And we be nothing anyhow,
And we know that,—why live?
'Twere sure but weaklings' vain distress
To suffer dungeons where so many doors
Will open on the cold eternal shores
That look sheer down
To the dark tideless floods of Nothingness
Where all who know may drown.

1916

NEIGHBORS

As often as we thought of her,
    We thought of a gray life
That made a quaint economist
    Of a wolf-haunted wife;
We made the best of all she bore
    That was not ours to bear,
And honored her for wearing things
    That were not things to wear.

There was a distance in her look
    That made us look again;
And if she smiled, we might believe
    That we had looked in vain.

Rarely she came inside our doors,
 And had not long to stay;
And when she left, it seemed somehow
 That she was far away.

At last, when we had all forgot
 That all is here to change,
A shadow on the commonplace
 Was for a moment strange.
Yet there was nothing for surprise,
 Nor much that need be told:
Love, with his gift of pain, had given
 More than one heart could hold.

1920

THE MILL

The miller's wife had waited long,
 The tea was cold, the fire was dead;
And there might yet be nothing wrong
 In how he went and what he said:
"There are no millers any more,"
 Was all that she had heard him say;
And he had lingered at the door
 So long that it seemed yesterday.

Sick with a fear that had no form
 She knew that she was there at last;
And in the mill there was a warm
 And mealy fragrance of the past.
What else there was would only seem
 To say again what he had meant;
And what was hanging from a beam
 Would not have heeded where she went.

And if she thought it followed her,
 She may have reasoned in the dark
That one way of the few there were
 Would hide her and would leave no mark:
Black water, smooth above the weir
 Like starry velvet in the night,
Though ruffled once, would soon appear
 The same as ever to the sight.

1920

TASKER NORCROSS

"Whether all towns and all who live in them—
So long as they be somewhere in this world
That we in our complacency call ours—
Are more or less the same, I leave to you.
I should say less. Whether or not, meanwhile,
We've all two legs—and as for that, we haven't—
There were three kinds of men where I was born:
The good, the not so good, and Tasker Norcross.
Now there are two kinds."

"Meaning, as I divine,
Your friend is dead," I ventured.

Ferguson,
Who talked himself at last out of the world
He censured, and is therefore silent now,
Agreed indifferently: "My friends are dead—
Or most of them."

"Remember one that isn't,"
I said, protesting. "Honor him for his ears;
Treasure him also for his understanding."
Ferguson sighed, and then talked on again:
"You have an overgrown alacrity
For saying nothing much and hearing less;
And I've a thankless wonder, at the start,
How much it is to you that I shall tell
What I have now to say of Tasker Norcross,
And how much to the air that is around you.
But given a patience that is not averse
To the slow tragedies of haunted men—
Horrors, in fact, if you've a skilful eye
To know them at their firesides, or out walking,—"

"Horrors," I said, "are my necessity;
And I would have them, for their best effect,
Always out walking."

Ferguson frowned at me:
"The wisest of us are not those who laugh

Before they know. Most of us never know—
Or the long toil of our mortality
Would not be done. Most of us never know—
And there you have a reason to believe
In God, if you may have no other. Norcross,
Or so I gather of his infirmity,
Was given to know more than he should have known,
And only God knows why. See for yourself
An old house full of ghosts of ancestors,
Who did their best, or worst, and having done it,
Died honorably; and each with a distinction
That hardly would have been for him that had it,
Had honor failed him wholly as a friend.
Honor that is a friend begets a friend.
Whether or not we love him, still we have him;
And we must live somehow by what we have,
Or then we die. If you say chemistry,
Then you must have your molecules in motion,
And in their right abundance. Failing either,
You have not long to dance. Failing a friend,
A genius, or a madness, or a faith
Larger than desperation, you are here
For as much longer than you like as may be.
Imagining now, by way of an example,
Myself a more or less remembered phantom—
Again, I should say less—how many times
A day should I come back to you? No answer.
Forgive me when I seem a little careless,
But we must have examples, or be lucid
Without them; and I question your adherence
To such an undramatic narrative
As this of mine, without the personal hook."

"A time is given in Ecclesiastes
For divers works," I told him. "Is there one
For saying nothing in return for nothing?
If not, there should be." I could feel his eyes,
And they were like two cold inquiring points
Of a sharp metal. When I looked again,
To see them shine, the cold that I had felt
Was gone to make way for a smouldering
Of lonely fire that I, as I knew then,
Could never quench with kindness or with lies.

I should have done whatever there was to do
For Ferguson, yet I could not have mourned
In honesty for once around the clock
The loss of him, for my sake or for his,
Try as I might; nor would his ghost approve,
Had I the power and the unthinking will
To make him tread again without an aim
The road that was behind him—and without
The faith, or friend, or genius, or the madness
That he contended was imperative.

After a silence that had been too long,
"It may be quite as well we don't," he said;
"As well, I mean, that we don't always say it.
You know best what I mean, and I suppose
You might have said it better. What was that?
Incorrigible? Am I incorrigible?
Well, it's a word; and a word has its use,
Or, like a man, it will soon have a grave.
It's a good word enough. Incorrigible,
May be, for all I know, the word for Norcross.
See for yourself that house of his again
That he called home: An old house, painted white,
Square as a box, and chillier than a tomb
To look at or to live in. There were trees—
Too many of them, if such a thing may be—
Before it and around it. Down in front
There was a road, a railroad, and a river;
Then there were hills behind it, and more trees.
The thing would fairly stare at you through trees,
Like a pale inmate out of a barred window
With a green shade half down; and I dare say
People who passed have said: 'There's where he lives.
We know him, but we do not seem to know
That we remember any good of him,
Or any evil that is interesting.
There you have all we know and all we care.'
They might have said it in all sorts of ways;
And then, if they perceived a cat, they might
Or might not have remembered what they said.
The cat might have a personality—
And maybe the same one the Lord left out
Of Tasker Norcross, who, for lack of it,

Saw the same sun go down year after year;
All which at last was my discovery.
And only mine, so far as evidence
Enlightens one more darkness. You have known
All round you, all your days, men who are nothing—
Nothing, I mean, so far as time tells yet
Of any other need it has of them
Than to make sextons hardy—but no less
Are to themselves incalculably something,
And therefore to be cherished. God, you see,
Being sorry for them in their fashioning,
Indemnified them with a quaint esteem
Of self, and with illusions long as life.
You know them well, and you have smiled at them;
And they, in their serenity, may have had
Their time to smile at you. Blessed are they
That see themselves for what they never were
Or were to be, and are, for their defect,
At ease with mirrors and the dim remarks
That pass their tranquil ears."
"Come, come," said I;
"There may be names in your compendium
That we are not yet all on fire for shouting.
Skin most of us of our mediocrity,
We should have nothing then that we could scratch.
The picture smarts. Cover it, if you please,
And do so rather gently. Now for Norcross."

Ferguson closed his eyes in resignation,
While a dead sigh came out of him. "Good God!"
He said, and said it only half aloud,
As if he knew no longer now, nor cared,
If one were there to listen: "Have I said nothing—
Nothing at all—of Norcross? Do you mean
To patronize him till his name becomes
A toy made out of letters? If a name
Is all you need, arrange an honest column
Of all the people you have ever known
That you have never liked. You'll have enough;
And you'll have mine, moreover. No, not yet.
If I assume too many privileges,
I pay, and I alone, for their assumption;
By which, if I assume a darker knowledge

Of Norcross than another, let the weight
Of my injustice aggravate the load
That is not on your shoulders. When I came
To know this fellow Norcross in his house,
I found him as I found him in the street—
No more, no less; indifferent, but no better.
'Worse' were not quite the word: he was not bad;
He was not . . . well, he was not anything.
Has your invention ever entertained
The picture of a dusty worm so dry
That even the early bird would shake his head
And fly on farther for another breakfast?"

"But why forget the fortune of the worm,"
I said, "if in the dryness you deplore
Salvation centered and endured? Your Norcross
May have been one for many to have envied."

"Salvation? Fortune? Would the worm say that?
He might; and therefore I dismiss the worm
With all dry things but one. Figures away,
Do you begin to see this man a little?
Do you begin to see him in the air,
With all the vacant horrors of his outline
For you to fill with more than it will hold?
If so, you needn't crown yourself at once
With epic laurel if you seem to fill it.
Horrors, I say, for in the fires and forks
Of a new hell—if one were not enough—
I doubt if a new horror would have held him
With a malignant ingenuity
More to be feared than his before he died.
You smile, as if in doubt. Well, smile again.
Now come into his house, along with me:
The four square sombre things that you see first
Around you are four walls that go as high
As to the ceiling. Norcross knew them well,
And he knew others like them. Fasten to that
With all the claws of your intelligence;
And hold the man before you in his house
As if he were a white rat in a box,
And one that knew himself to be no other.

I tell you twice that he knew all about it,
That you may not forget the worst of all
Our tragedies begin with what we know.
Could Norcross only not have known, I wonder
How many would have blessed and envied him!
Could he have had the usual eye for spots
On others, and for none upon himself,
I smile to ponder on the carriages
That might as well as not have clogged the town
In honor of his end. For there was gold,
You see, though all he needed was a little,
And what he gave said nothing of who gave it.
He would have given it all if in return
There might have been a more sufficient face
To greet him when he shaved. Though you insist
It is the dower, and always, of our degree
Not to be cursed with such invidious insight,
Remember that you stand, you and your fancy,
Now in his house; and since we are together,
See for yourself and tell me what you see.
Tell me the best you see. Make a slight noise
Of recognition when you find a book
That you would not as lief read upside down
As otherwise, for example. If there you fail,
Observe the walls and lead me to the place,
Where you are led. If there you meet a picture
That holds you near it for a longer time
Than you are sorry, you may call it yours,
And hang it in the dark of your remembrance,
Where Norcross never sees. How can he see
That has no eyes to see? And as for music,
He paid with empty wonder for the pangs
Of his infrequent forced endurance of it;
And having had no pleasure, paid no more
For needless immolation, or for the sight
Of those who heard what he was never to hear.
To see them listening was itself enough
To make him suffer; and to watch worn eyes,
On other days, of strangers who forgot
Their sorrows and their failures and themselves
Before a few mysterious odds and ends
Of marble carted from the Parthenon—
And all for seeing what he was never to see,

Because it was alive and he was dead,—
Here was a wonder that was more profound
Than any that was in fiddles and brass horns.

"He knew, and in his knowledge there was death.
He knew there was a region all around him
That lay outside man's havoc and affairs,
And yet was not all hostile to their tumult,
Where poets would have served and honored him,
And saved him, had there been anything to save.
But there was nothing, and his tethered range
Was only a small desert. Kings of song
Are not for thrones in deserts. Towers of sound
And flowers of sense are but a waste of heaven
Where there is none to know them from the rocks
And sand-grass of his own monotony
That makes earth less than earth. He could see that,
And he could see no more. The captured light
That may have been or not, for all he cared,
The song that is in sculpture was not his,
But only, to his God-forgotten eyes,
One more immortal nonsense in a world
Where all was mortal, or had best be so,
And so be done with. 'Art,' he would have said,
'Is not life, and must therefore be a lie';
And with a few profundities like that
He would have controverted and dismissed
The benefit of the Greeks. He had heard of them,
As he had heard of his aspiring soul—
Never to the perceptible advantage,
In his esteem, of either. 'Faith,' he said,
Or would have said if he had thought of it,
'Lives in the same house with Philosophy,
Where the two feed on scraps and are forlorn
As orphans after war.' He could see stars,
On a clear night, but he had not an eye
To see beyond them. He could hear spoken words,
But had no ear for silence when alone.
He could eat food of which he knew the savor,
But had no palate for the Bread of Life,
That human desperation, to his thinking,
Made famous long ago, having no other.
Now do you see? Do you begin to see?"

I told him that I did begin to see;
And I was nearer than I should have been
To laughing at his malign inclusiveness,
When I considered that, with all our speed,
We are not laughing yet at funerals.
I see him now as I could see him then,
And I see now that it was good for me,
As it was good for him, that I was quiet;
For Time's eye was on Ferguson, and the shaft
Of its inquiring hesitancy had touched him,
Or so I chose to fancy more than once
Before he told of Norcross. When the word
Of his release (he would have called it so)
Made half an inch of news, there were no tears
That are recorded. Women there may have been
To wish him back, though I should say, not knowing,
The few there were to mourn were not for love,
And were not lovely. Nothing of them, at least,
Was in the meagre legend that I gathered
Years after, when a chance of travel took me
So near the region of his nativity
That a few miles of leisure brought me there;
For there I found a friendly citizen
Who led me to his house among the trees
That were above a railroad and a river.
Square as a box and chillier than a tomb
It was indeed, to look at or to live in—
All which had I been told. "Ferguson died,"
The stranger said, "and then there was an auction.
I live here, but I've never yet been warm.
Remember him? Yes, I remember him.
I knew him—as a man may know a tree—
For twenty years. He may have held himself
A little high when he was here, but now . . .
Yes, I remember Ferguson. Oh, yes."

Others, I found, remembered Ferguson,
But none of them had heard of Tasker Norcross.

1920

DISCOVERY

We told of him as one who should have soared
And seen for us the devastating light
Whereof there is not either day or night,
And shared with us the glamor of the Word
That fell once upon Amos to record
For men at ease in Zion, when the sight
Of ills obscured aggrieved him and the might
Of Hamath was a warning of the Lord.

Assured somehow that he would make us wise,
Our pleasure was to wait; and our surprise
Was hard when we confessed the dry return
Of his regret. For we were still to learn
That earth has not a school where we may go
For wisdom, or for more than we may know.

1920

FIRELIGHT

Ten years together without yet a cloud,
They seek each other's eyes at intervals
Of gratefulness to firelight and four walls
For love's obliteration of the crowd.
Serenely and perennially endowed
And bowered as few may be, their joy recalls
No snake, no sword; and over them there falls
The blessing of what neither says aloud.

Wiser for silence, they were not so glad
Were she to read the graven tale of lines
On the wan face of one somewhere alone;
Nor were they more content could he have had
Her thoughts a moment since of one who shines
Apart, and would be hers if he had known.

1920

MR. FLOOD'S PARTY

Old Eben Flood, climbing alone one night
Over the hill between the town below
And the forsaken upland hermitage
That held as much as he should ever know
On earth again of home, paused warily.
The road was his with not a native near;
And Eben, having leisure, said aloud,
For no man else in Tilbury Town to hear:

"Well, Mr. Flood, we have the harvest moon
Again, and we may not have many more;
The bird is on the wing, the poet says,
And you and I have said it here before.
Drink to the bird." He raised up to the light
The jug that he had gone so far to fill,
And answered huskily: "Well, Mr. Flood,
Since you propose it, I believe I will."

Alone, as if enduring to the end
A valiant armor of scarred hopes outworn,
He stood there in the middle of the road
Like Roland's ghost winding a silent horn.
Below him, in the town among the trees,
Where friends of other days had honored him,
A phantom salutation of the dead
Rang thinly till old Eben's eyes were dim.

Then, as a mother lays her sleeping child
Down tenderly, fearing it may awake,
He set the jug down slowly at his feet
With trembling care, knowing that most things break;
And only when assured that on firm earth
It stood, as the uncertain lives of men
Assuredly did not, he paced away,
And with his hand extended paused again:

"Well, Mr. Flood, we have not met like this
In a long time; and many a change has come
To both of us, I fear, since last it was

We had a drop together. Welcome home!"
Convivially returning with himself,
Again he raised the jug up to the light;
And with an acquiescent quaver said:
"Well, Mr. Flood, if you insist, I might.

"Only a very little, Mr. Flood—
For auld lang syne. No more, sir; that will do."
So, for the time, apparently it did,
And Eben evidently thought so too;
For soon amid the silver loneliness
Of night he lifted up his voice and sang,
Secure, with only two moons listening,
Until the whole harmonious landscape rang—

"For auld lang syne." The weary throat gave out,
The last word wavered; and the song being done,
He raised again the jug regretfully
And shook his head, and was again alone.
There was not much that was ahead of him,
And there was nothing in the town below—
Where strangers would have shut the many doors
That many friends had opened long ago.

1921

KARMA

Christmas was in the air and all was well
With him, but for a few confusing flaws
In divers of God's images. Because
A friend of his would neither buy nor sell,
Was he to answer for the axe that fell?
He pondered; and the reason for it was,
Partly, a slowly freezing Santa Claus
Upon the corner, with his beard and bell.

Acknowledging an improvident surprise,
He magnified a fancy that he wished
The friend whom he had wrecked were here again.
Not sure of that, he found a compromise;
And from the fulness of his heart he fished
A dime for Jesus who had died for men.

1925

WHY HE WAS THERE

Much as he left it when he went from us
Here was the room again where he had been
So long that something of him should be seen,
Or felt—and so it was. Incredulous,
I turned about, loath to be greeted thus,
And there he was in his old chair, serene
As ever, and as laconic and as lean
As when he lived, and as cadaverous.

Calm as he was of old when we were young,
He sat there gazing at the pallid flame
Before him. "And how far will this go on?"
I thought. He felt the failure of my tongue,
And smiled: "I was not here until you came;
And I shall not be here when you are gone."

1925

Amy Lowell

Amy Lowell, youngest of the five children of Augustus and Katherine Bigelow Lawrence Lowell, was born February 9, 1874, in Brookline, Massachusetts. Her father was a descendant of Percival Lowell, a merchant of Bristol, who came to New England in 1639. To the family belonged many persons of importance: among them, Francis Cabot Lowell, who founded the city of Lowell in 1822; John Lowell, founder of the Lowell Institute in Boston; and James Russell Lowell, diplomat and man of letters, who was a cousin of Amy Lowell's grandfather. Among her immediate family were Abbott Lawrence Lowell, a brother, who was President of Harvard University; another brother, Percival Lowell, who established the Lowell Observatory at Harvard and at Flagstaff, Arizona; and a sister, Mrs. T. J. Bowlker, the founder and president of the Women's Municipal League in Boston. Her mother's family was also noted, her maternal grandfather, Abbott Lawrence, being at one time Minister to the Court of St. James's.

As a child, Amy Lowell had the advantages of wealth and the care of a mother who was an accomplished musician and linguist. At the age of eight she was taken on a European tour extending over six months, during which she travelled over England and much of the Continent. The mental excitement and nervous strain caused by this tour resulted in a collapse from which she did not completely recover for two or three years. Nevertheless she was able, several months later, to travel across the United States, for her first visit to California—and the only other extended journey during her girlhood. She attended private schools, acquired an interest in gardening and in domestic animals, and for recreation played tennis and rode horseback. After the completion of her schooling, and the death of her mother in 1895, she travelled abroad again, spending six months on the Continent in 1896, and travelling up the Nile Valley in 1898. Again, however, the excitement of travel brought on a nervous breakdown, so that for her health's sake she spent the winter of 1898-1899 on a fruit ranch in California. Upon the death of her father in 1900, she purchased Sevenels, the family residence in Brookline, and for a while devoted herself to educational and library work in the interest of her native city.

At the age of thirteen she began to write verse, and in 1888 she appeared as author of a volume of stories, *Dream Drops*. Not until 1902, however, did she decide definitely upon a literary career. After that decision she began a period of apprenticeship as poet which lasted for eight years, during which she read the great poets, studied the technique of verse-writing, and filled many sheets of paper with her own composition. In 1911 she made a translation of Alfred de Musset's *Caprice* and took part in the performance of it by amateurs in Boston. Her first published poem appeared in the *Atlantic Monthly* for August, 1910; and two years later she issued her first volume of poems, *A Dome of Many-Coloured Glass*. Thereafter, to the end of her life, her writings appeared regularly, both in magazines and between the covers of books.

In the early years of her apprenticeship, she spent her time between the home in Brookline and a summer residence in Dublin, New Hampshire; but presently she was again in Europe. She passed the summer of 1905 in England, and during the winter and spring of 1908 was in Greece and Turkey. In 1913, and again in 1914, she returned to England, on the first of these visits meeting Ezra Pound. Through him she became associated with the Imagists and in this way was led to identify herself actively with the unconventional, experimental poets of the day. From 1915 to the end of her life she was an energetic, enthusiastic, and influential defender of the "New Poetry"; by means of her book reviews, readings, and lectures she helped greatly to popularize the work of the poets of her generation.

She was Phi Beta Kappa poet at Tufts College in 1918, and at Columbia University in 1920. In the latter year Baylor University gave her the degree of Doctor of Literature. She lectured at the Brooklyn Institute of Arts and Sciences during 1917-1919, at Yale University on the Francis Bergen Foundation in 1921, and at Brown University in the same year on the Marshall Woods Lectureship. In 1923 she received the Levinson Prize, offered by *Poetry: A Magazine of Verse*; and in 1926 her posthumously published volume, *What's O'Clock*, was awarded the Pulitzer Prize for poetry.

Shortly after the appearance of *John Keats*, on which she had labored with devotion for several years, she completed plans for a trip to England, during the course of which she was to have lectured at several universities—Oxford and Cambridge, among them. On the eve of this proposed journey, however, she was stricken with paralysis, and died without regaining consciousness—on May 12, 1925. Her body was cremated, and the ashes buried in the family plot in Mt. Auburn Cemetery, Cambridge.

A GIFT

See! I give myself to you, Beloved!
My words are little jars
For you to take and put upon a shelf.
Their shapes are quaint and beautiful,
And they have many pleasant colors and lustres
To recommend them.
Also the scent from them fills the room
With sweetness of flowers and crushed grasses.

When I shall have given you the last one,
You will have the whole of me,
But I shall be dead.

1914

THE SHADOW

Paul Jannes was working very late,
For this watch must be done by eight
To-morrow or the Cardinal
Would certainly be vexed. Of all
His customers the old prelate
Was the most important, for his state
Descended to his watches and rings,
And he gave his mistresses many things
To make them forget his age and smile

When he paid visits, and they could while
The time away with a diamond locket
Exceedingly well. So they picked his pocket,
And he paid in jewels for his slobbering kisses.
This watch was made to buy him blisses
From an Austrian countess on her way
Home, and she meant to start next day.
Paul worked by the pointed, tulip-flame
Of a tallow candle, and became
So absorbed, that his old clock made him wince
Striking the hour a moment since.
Its echo, only half apprehended,
Lingered about the room. He ended
Screwing the little rubies in,
Setting the wheels to lock and spin,
Curling the infinitesimal springs,
Fixing the filigree hands. Chippings
Of precious stones lay strewn about.
The table before him was a rout
Of splashes and sparks of colored light.
There was yellow gold in sheets, and quite
A heap of emeralds, and steel.
Here was a gem, there was a wheel.
And glasses lay like limpid lakes
Shining and still, and there were flakes
Of silver, and shavings of pearl,
And little wires all awhirl
With the light of the candle. He took the watch
And wound its hands about to match
The time, then glanced up to take the hour
From the hanging clock.
Good, Merciful Power!
How came that shadow on the wall,
No woman was in the room! His tall
Chiffonier stood gaunt behind
His chair. His old cloak, rabbit-lined,
Hung from a peg. The door was closed.
Just for a moment he must have dozed.
He looked again, and saw it plain.
The silhouette made a blue-black stain
On the opposite wall, and it never wavered
Even when the candle quavered
Under his panting breath. What made

That beautiful, dreadful thing, that shade
Of something so lovely, so exquisite,
Cast from a substance which the sight
Had not been tutored to perceive?
Paul brushed his eyes across his sleeve.

Clear-cut, the Shadow on the wall
Gleamed black, and never moved at all.

Paul's watches were like amulets,
Wrought into patterns and rosettes;
The cases were all set with stones,
And wreathing lines, and shining zones.
He knew the beauty in a curve,
And the Shadow tortured every nerve
With its perfect rhythm of outline
Cutting the whitewashed wall. So fine
Was the neck he knew he could have spanned
It about with the fingers of one hand.
The chin rose to a mouth he guessed,
But could not see, the lips were pressed
Loosely together, the edges close,
And the proud and delicate line of the nose
Melted into a brow, and there
Broke into undulant waves of hair.
The lady was edged with the stamp of race.
A singular vision in such a place.

He moved the candle to the tall
Chiffonier; the Shadow stayed on the wall.
He threw his cloak upon a chair,
And still the lady's face was there.
From every corner of the room
He saw, in the patch of light, the gloom
That was the lady. Her violet bloom
Was almost brighter than that which came
From his candle's tulip-flame.
He set the filigree hands; he laid
The watch in the case which he had made;
He put on his rabbit cloak, and snuffed
His candle out. The room seemed stuffed
With darkness. Softly he crossed the floor,
And let himself out through the door.

The sun was flashing from every pin
And wheel, when Paul let himself in.
The whitewashed walls were hot with light.
The room was the core of a chrysolite,
Burning and shimmering with fiery might.
The sun was so bright that no shadow could fall
From the furniture upon the wall.
Paul sighed as he looked at the empty space
Where a glare usurped the lady's place.
He settled himself to his work, but his mind
Wandered, and he would wake to find
His hand suspended, his eyes grown dim,
And nothing advanced beyond the rim
Of his dreaming. The Cardinal sent to pay
For his watch, which had purchased so fine a day.
But Paul could hardly touch the gold,
It seemed the price of his Shadow, sold.
With the first twilight he struck a match
And watched the little blue stars hatch
Into an egg of perfect flame.
He lit his candle, and almost in shame
At his eagerness, lifted his eyes.
The Shadow was there, and its precise
Outline etched the cold, white wall.
The young man swore, "By God! You, Paul,
There's something the matter with your brain.
Go home now and sleep off the strain."

The next day was a storm; the rain
Whispered and scratched at the window-pane.
A grey and shadowless morning filled
The little shop. The watches, chilled,
Were dead and sparkless as burnt-out coals.
The gems lay on the table like shoals
Of stranded shells, their colors faded,
Mere heaps of stone, dull and degraded.
Paul's head was heavy, his hands obeyed
No orders, for his fancy strayed.
His work became a simple round
Of watches repaired and watches wound.
The slanting ribbons of the rain
Broke themselves on the window-pane,
But Paul saw the silver lines in vain.

Only when the candle was lit
And on the wall just opposite
He watched again the coming of IT,
Could he trace a line for the joy of his soul
And over his hands regain control.

Paul lingered late in his shop that night
And the designs which his delight
Sketched on paper seemed to be
A tribute offered wistfully
To the beautiful shadow of her who came
And hovered over his candle flame.
In the morning he selected all
His perfect jacinths. One large opal
Hung like a milky, rainbow moon
In the centre, and blown in loose festoon
The red stones quivered on silver threads
To the outer edge, where a single, fine
Band of mother-of-pearl the line
Completed. On the other side,
The creamy porcelain of the face
Bore diamond hours, and no lace
Of cotton or silk could ever be
Tossed into being more airily
Than the filmy golden hands; the time
Seemed to tick away in rhyme.
When, at dusk, the Shadow grew
Upon the wall, Paul's work was through.
Holding the watch, he spoke to her:
"Lady, Beautiful Shadow, stir
Into one brief sign of being.
Turn your eyes this way, and seeing
This watch, made from those sweet curves
Where your hair from your forehead swerves,
Accept the gift which I have wrought
With your fairness in my thought.
Grant me this, and I shall be
Honored overwhelmingly."

The Shadow rested black and still,
And the wind sighed over the window-sill.
Paul put the despised watch away
And laid out before him his array

Of stones and metals, and when the morning
Struck the stones to their best adorning,
He chose the brightest, and this new watch
Was so light and thin it seemed to catch
The sunlight's nothingness, and its gleam.
Topazes ran in a foamy stream
Over the cover; the hands were studded
With garnets, and seemed red roses, budded.
The face was of crystal, and engraved
Upon it the figures flashed and waved
With zircons, and beryls, and amethysts.
It took a week to make, and his trysts
At night with the Shadow were his alone.
Paul swore not to speak till his task was done.
The night that the jewel was worthy to give,
Paul watched the long hours of daylight live
To the faintest streak; then lit his light,
And sharp against the wall's pure white
The outline of the Shadow started
Into form. His burning-hearted
Words so long imprisoned swelled
To tumbling speech. Like one compelled,
He told the lady all his love,
And holding out the watch above
His head, he knelt, imploring some
Littlest sign.
                    The Shadow was dumb.

Weeks passed, Paul worked in fevered haste,
And everything he made he placed
Before his lady. The Shadow kept
Its perfect passiveness. Paul wept.
He wooed her with the work of his hands,
He waited for those dear commands
She never gave. No word, no motion,
Eased the ache of his devotion.
His days passed in a strain of toil,
His nights burnt up in a seething coil.
Seasons shot by; uncognisant
He worked. The Shadow came to haunt
Even his days. Sometimes quite plain
He saw on the wall the blackberry stain

Of his lady's picture. No sun was bright
Enough to dazzle that from his sight.

There were moments when he groaned to see
His life spilled out so uselessly,
Begging for boons the Shade refused,
His finest workmanship abused,
The iridescent bubbles he blew
Into lovely existence, poor and few
In the shadowed eyes. Then he would curse
Himself and her! The Universe!
And more, the beauty he could not make,
And give her, for her comfort's sake!
He would beat his weary, empty hands
Upon the table, would hold up strands
Of silver and gold, and ask her why
She scorned the best which he could buy.
He would pray as to some high-niched saint,
That she would cure him of the taint
Of failure. He would clutch the wall
With his bleeding fingers, if she should fall
He could catch, and hold her, and make her live!
With sobs he would ask her to forgive
All he had done. And broken, spent,
He would call himself impertinent;
Presumptuous; a tradesman; a nothing; driven
To madness by the sight of Heaven.
At other times he would take the things
He had made, and winding them on strings,
Hang garlands before her, and burn perfumes,
Chanting strangely, while the fumes
Wreathed and blotted the shadow face,
As with a cloudy, nacreous lace.
There were days when he wooed as a lover, sighed
In tenderness, spoke to his bride,
Urged her to patience, said his skill
Should break the spell. A man's sworn will
Could compass life, even that, he knew.
By Christ's Blood! He would prove it true!

The edge of the Shadow never blurred.
The lips of the Shadow never stirred.

He would climb on chairs to reach her lips,
And pat her hair with his finger-tips.
But instead of young, warm flesh returning
His warmth, the wall was cold and burning
Like stinging ice, and his passion, chilled,
Lay in his heart like some dead thing killed
At the moment of birth. Then, deadly sick,
He would lie in a swoon for hours, while thick
Phantasmagoria crowded his brain,
And his body shrieked in the clutch of pain.
The crisis passed, he would wake and smile
With a vacant joy, half-imbecile
And quite confused, not being certain
Why he was suffering; a curtain
Fallen over the tortured mind beguiled
His sorrow. Like a little child
He would play with his watches and gems, with glee
Calling the Shadow to look and see
How the spots on the ceiling danced prettily
When he flashed his stones. "Mother, the green
Has slid so cunningly in between
The blue and the yellow. Oh, please look down!"
Then, with a pitiful, puzzled frown,
He would get up slowly from his play
And walk round the room, feeling his way
From table to chair, from chair to door,
Stepping over the cracks in the floor,
Till reaching the table again, her face
Would bring recollection, and no solace
Could balm his hurt till unconsciousness
Stifled him and his great distress.

One morning he threw the street door wide
On coming in, and his vigorous stride
Made the tools on his table rattle and jump.
In his hands he carried a new-burst clump
Of laurel blossoms, whose smooth-barked stalks
Were pliant with sap. As a husband talks
To the wife he left an hour ago,
Paul spoke to the Shadow. "Dear, you know
To-day the calendar calls it spring,
And I woke this morning gathering
Asphodels, in my dreams, for you.

So I rushed out to see what flowers blew
Their pink-and-purple-scented souls
Across the town-wind's dusty scrolls,
And made the approach to the Market Square
A garden with smells and sunny air.
I feel so well and happy to-day,
I think I shall take a holiday.
And to-night we will have a little treat.
I am going to bring you something to eat!"
He looked at the Shadow anxiously.
It was quite grave and silent. He
Shut the outer door and came
And leant against the window-frame.
"Dearest," he said, "we live apart
Although I bear you in my heart.
We look out each from a different world.
At any moment we may be hurled
Asunder. They follow their orbits, we
Obey their laws entirely.
Now you must come, or I go there,
Unless we are willing to live the flare
Of a lighted instant and have it gone."

A bee in the laurels began to drone.
A loosened petal fluttered prone.

"Man grows by eating; if you eat
You will be filled with our life; sweet
Will be our planet in your mouth.
If not, I must parch in death's wide drouth
Until I gain to where you are,
And give you myself in whatever star
May happen. O You Beloved of Me!
Is it not ordered cleverly?"

The Shadow, bloomed like a plum, and clear,
Hung in the sunlight. It did not hear.

Paul slipped away as the dusk began
To dim the little shop. He ran
To the nearest inn, and chose with care
As much as his thin purse could bear.
As rapt-souled monks watch over the baking

Of the sacred wafer, and through the making
Of the holy wine whisper secret prayers
That God will bless this labor of theirs;
So Paul, in a sober ecstasy,
Purchased the best which he could buy.
Returning, he brushed his tools aside,
And laid across the table a wide
Napkin. He put a glass and plate
On either side, in duplicate.
Over the lady's, excellent
With loveliness, the laurels bent.
In the centre the white-flaked pastry stood,
And beside it the wine flask. Red as blood
Was the wine which should bring the lustihood
Of human life to his lady's veins.
When all was ready, all which pertains
To a simple meal was there, with eyes
Lit by the joy of his great emprise,
He reverently bade her come,
And forsake for him her distant home.
He put meat on her plate and filled her glass,
And waited what should come to pass.

The Shadow lay quietly on the wall.
From the street outside came a watchman's call:
"A cloudy night. Rain beginning to fall."

And still he waited. The clock's slow tick
Knocked on the silence. Paul turned sick.
He filled his own glass full of wine;
From his pocket he took a paper. The twine
Was knotted, and he searched a knife
From his jumbled tools. The cord of life
Snapped as he cut the little string.
He knew that he must do the thing
He feared. He shook powder into the wine,
And holding it up so the candle's shine
Sparked a ruby through its heart,
He drank it. "Dear, never apart
Again! You have said it was mine to do.
It is done, and I am come to you!"

Paul Jannes let the empty wine-glass fall,
And held out his arms. The insentient wall

Stared down at him with its cold, white glare
Unstained! The Shadow was not there!
Paul clutched and tore at his tightening throat.
He felt the veins in his body bloat,
And the hot blood run like fire and stones
Along the sides of his cracking bones.
But he laughed as he staggered towards the door,
And he laughed aloud as he sank on the floor.

The Coroner took the body away,
And the watches were sold that Saturday.
The Auctioneer said one could seldom buy
Such watches, and the prices were high.

1914

PATTERNS

I walk down the garden paths,
And all the daffodils
Are blowing, and the bright blue squills.
I walk down the patterned garden paths
In my stiff, brocaded gown.
With my powdered hair and jewelled fan,
I too am a rare
Pattern. As I wander down
The garden paths.

My dress is richly figured,
And the train
Makes a pink and silver stain
On the gravel, and the thrift
Of the borders.
Just a plate of current fashion,
Tripping by in high-heeled, ribboned shoes.
Not a softness anywhere about me,
Only whalebone and brocade.
And I sink on a seat in the shade
Of a lime tree. For my passion
Wars against the stiff brocade.
The daffodils and squills
Flutter in the breeze
As they please.

And I weep;
For the lime tree is in blossom
And one small flower has dropped upon my bosom.

And the plashing of waterdrops
In the marble fountain
Comes down the garden paths.
The dripping never stops.
Underneath my stiffened gown
Is the softness of a woman bathing in a marble basin,
A basin in the midst of hedges grown
So thick, she cannot see her lover hiding,
But she guesses he is near,
And the sliding of the water
Seems the stroking of a dear
Hand upon her.
What is summer in a fine brocaded gown!
I should like to see it lying in a heap upon the ground.
All the pink and silver crumpled up on the ground.

I would be the pink and silver as I ran along the paths,
And he would stumble after,
Bewildered by my laughter.
I should see the sun flashing from his sword-hilt and the
    buckles on his shoes.
I would choose
To lead him in a maze along the patterned paths,
A bright and laughing maze for my heavy-booted lover.
Till he caught me in the shade,
And the buttons of his waistcoat bruised my body as he
    clasped me,
Aching, melting, unafraid.
With the shadows of the leaves and the sundrops,
And the plopping of the waterdrops,
All about us in the open afternoon—
I am very like to swoon
With the weight of this brocade,
For the sun sifts through the shade.

Underneath the fallen blossom
In my bosom,
Is a letter I have hid.
It was brought to me this morning by a rider from the Duke.

"Madam, we regret to inform you that Lord Hartwell
Died in action Thursday se'nnight."
As I read it in the white, morning sunlight,
The letters squirmed like snakes.
"Any answer, Madam," said my footman.
"No," I told him.
"See that the messenger takes some refreshment.
No, no answer."
And I walked into the garden,
Up and down the patterned paths,
In my stiff, correct brocade.
The blue and yellow flowers stood up proudly in the sun,
Each one.
I stood upright too,
Held rigid to the pattern
By the stiffness of my gown.
Up and down I walked,
Up and down.

In a month he would have been my husband.
In a month, here, underneath this lime,
We would have broke the pattern;
He for me, and I for him,
He as Colonel, I as Lady,
On this shady seat.
He had a whim
That sunlight carried blessing.
And I answered, "It shall be as you have said."
Now he is dead.

In summer and in winter I shall walk
Up and down
The patterned garden paths
In my stiff, brocaded gown.
The squills and daffodils
Will give place to pillared roses, and to asters, and to snow.
I shall go
Up and down,
In my gown.
Gorgeously arrayed,
Boned and stayed.
And the softness of my body will be guarded from embrace
By each button, hook, and lace.

For the man who should loose me is dead,
Fighting with the Duke in Flanders,
In a pattern called a war.
Christ! What are patterns for?

1916

THE DINNER-PARTY

FISH

"So . . ." they said,
With their wine-glasses delicately poised,
Mocking at the thing they cannot understand.
"So . . ." they said again,
Amused and insolent.
The silver on the table glittered,
And the red wine in the glasses
Seemed the blood I had wasted
In a foolish cause.

GAME

The gentleman with the grey-and-black whiskers
Sneered languidly over his quail.
Then my heart flew up and labored,
And I burst from my own holding
And hurled myself forward.
With straight blows I beat upon him,
Furiously, with red-hot anger, I thrust against him.
But my weapon slithered over his polished surface,
And I recoiled upon myself,
Panting.

DRAWING-ROOM

In a dress all softness and half-tones,
Indolent and half-reclined,
She lay upon a couch,
With the firelight reflected in her jewels.
But her eyes had no reflection,
They swam in a grey smoke,
The smoke of smoldering ashes,
The smoke of her cindered heart.

COFFEE

They sat in a circle with their coffee-cups.
One dropped in a lump of sugar,
One stirred with a spoon.
I saw them as a circle of ghosts
Sipping blackness out of beautiful china,
And mildly protesting against my coarseness
In being alive.

TALK

They took dead men's souls
And pinned them on their breasts for ornament;
Their cuff-links and tiaras
Were gems dug from a grave;
They were ghouls battening on exhumed thoughts;
And I took a green liqueur from a servant
So that he might come near me
And give me the comfort of a living thing.

ELEVEN O'CLOCK

The front door was hard and heavy,
It shut behind me on the house of ghosts.
I flattened my feet on the pavement
To feel it solid under me;
I ran my hand along the railings
And shook them,
And pressed their pointed bars
Into my palms.
The hurt of it reassured me,
And I did it again and again
Until they were bruised.
When I woke in the night
I laughed to find them aching,
For only living flesh can suffer.

1916

MADONNA OF THE EVENING FLOWERS

All day long I have been working,
Now I am tired.
I call: "Where are you?"

But there is only the oak-tree rustling in the wind.
The house is very quiet,
The sun shines in on your books,
On your scissors and thimble just put down,
But you are not there.
Suddenly I am lonely:
Where are you?
I go about searching.

Then I see you,
Standing under a spire of pale blue larkspur,
With a basket of roses on your arm.
You are cool, like silver,
And you smile.
I think the Canterbury bells are playing little tunes.

You tell me that the peonies need spraying,
That the columbines have overrun all bounds,
That the pyrus japonica should be cut back and rounded.
You tell me these things.
But I look at you, heart of silver,
White heart-flame of polished silver,
Burning beneath the blue steeples of the larkspur,
And I long to kneel instantly at your feet,
While all about us peal the loud, sweet *Te Deums* of the Canterbury bells.

1919

A DECADE

When you came, you were like red wine and honey,
And the taste of you burnt my mouth with its sweetness.
Now you are like morning bread,
Smooth and pleasant.
I hardly taste you at all for I know your savor,
But I am completely nourished.

1919

FRIMAIRE

Dearest, we are like two flowers
Blooming last in a yellowing garden,
A purple aster flower and a red one
Standing alone in a withered desolation.

The garden plants are shattered and seeded,
One brittle leaf scrapes against another,
Fiddling echoes of a rush of petals.
Now only you and I nodding together.

Many were with us; they have all faded.
Only we are purple and crimson,
Only we in the dew-clear mornings,
Smarten into color as the sun rises.

When I scarcely see you in the flat moonlight,
And later when my cold roots tighten,
I am anxious for the morning,
I cannot rest in fear of what may happen.

You or I—and I am a coward.
Surely frost should take the crimson.
Purple is a finer color,
Very splendid in isolation.

So we nod above the broken
Stems of flowers almost rotted.
Many mornings there cannot be now
For us both. Ah, Dear, I love you!

1919

APPULDURCOMBE PARK

I am a woman, sick for passion,
Sitting under the golden beech-trees.
I am a woman, sick for passion,
Crumbling the beech leaves to powder in my fingers.
The servants say: "Yes, my Lady," and "No, my Lady."
And all day long my husband calls me

From his invalid chair:
"Mary, Mary, where are you, Mary? I want you."
Why does he want me?
When I come, he only pats my hand
And asks me to settle his cushions.
Poor little beech leaves,
Slowly falling,
Crumbling,
In the great park.
But there are many golden beech leaves
And I am alone.

I am a woman, sick for passion,
Walking between rows of painted tulips.
Parrot flowers, toucan-feathered flowers,
How bright you are!
You hurt me with your colors;
Your reds and yellows lance at me like flames.
Oh, I am sick—sick—
And your darting loveliness hurts my heart.
You burn me with your parrot-tongues.
Flame!
Flame!
My husband taps on the window with his stick:
"Mary, come in. I want you. You will take cold."

I am a woman, sick for passion,
Gazing at a white moon hanging over tall lilies.
The lilies sway and darken,
And a wind ruffles my hair.
There is a scrape of gravel behind me.
A red coat crashes scarlet against the lilies.
"Cousin-Captain!
I thought you were playing piquet with Sir Kenelm."
"Piquet, Dear Heart! And such a moon!"
Your red coat chokes me, Cousin-Captain.
Blood-color, your coat:
I am sick—sick—for your heart.
Keep away from me, Cousin-Captain.
Your scarlet coat dazzles and confuses me.
O heart of red blood, what shall I do!
Even the lilies blow for the bee.
Does your heart beat so loud, Beloved?

No, it is the tower-clock chiming eleven.
I must go in and give my husband his posset.
I hear him calling:
"Mary, where are you? I want you."

I am a woman, sick for passion,
Waiting in the long, black room for the funeral procession to pass.
I sent a messenger to town last night.
When will you come?
Under my black dress a rose is blooming.
A rose?—a heart?—it rustles for you with open petals.
Come quickly, Dear,
For the corridors are full of noises.
In this fading light I hear whispers,
And the steady, stealthy purr of the wind.
What keeps you, Cousin-Captain? . . .
What was that?
"Mary, I want you."
Nonsense, he is dead,
Buried by now.
Oh, I am sick of these long, cold corridors!
Sick—for what?
Why do you not come?

I am a woman, sick—sick—
Sick of the touch of cold paper,
Poisoned with the bitterness of ink.
Snowflakes hiss, and scratch the windows.
"Mary, where are you?"
That voice is like water in my ears;
I cannot empty them.
He wanted me, my husband,
But these stone parlors do not want me.
You do not want me either, Cousin-Captain.
Your coat lied;
Only your white sword spoke the truth.
"Mary! Mary!"
Will nothing stop the white snow
Sifting,
Sifting?
Will nothing stop that voice,
Drifting through the wide, dark halls?
The tower-clock strikes eleven dully, stifled with snow.

Softly over the still snow,
Softly over the lonely park,
Softly . . .
Yes, I have only my slippers, but I shall not take cold.
A little dish of posset.
Do the dead eat?
I have done it so long,
So strangely long.

1919

FOUR SIDES TO A HOUSE

Peter, Peter, along the ground,
Is it wind I hear, or your shoes' sound?
Peter, Peter, across the air,
Do dead leaves fall, or is it your hair?
Peter, Peter, North and South,
They have stopped your mouth
With water, Peter.

The long road runs, and the long road runs,
    Who comes over the long road, Peter?
Who knocks at the door in the cold twilight,
And begs a heap of straw for the night,
And a bit of a sup, and a bit of a bite—
    Do you know the face, Peter?

He lays him down on the floor and sleeps.
    Must you wind the clock, Peter?
It will strike and strike the dark night through.
He will sleep past one, he will sleep past two,
But when it strikes three what will he do?
    He will rise and kill you, Peter.

He will open the door to one without.
    Do you hear that voice, Peter?
Two men prying and poking about,
Is it here, is it there, is it in, is it out?
Cover his staring eyes with a clout.
    But you're dead, dead, Peter.

They have ripped up the boards, they have pried up the stones,
    They have found your gold, dead Peter.

Ripe, red coins to itch a thief's hand,
But you drip ripe red on the floor's white sand,
You burn their eyes like a firebrand.
    They must quench you, Peter.

It is dark in the North, it is dark in the South.
    The wind blows your white hair, Peter.
One at your feet and one at your head.
A soft bed, a smooth bed,
Scarcely a splash, you sink like lead.
    Sweet water in your well, Peter.

Along the road and along the road,
    The next house, Peter.
Four-square to the bright and the shade of the moon.
The North winds shuffle, the South winds croon,
Water with white hair over-strewn.
    The door, the door, Peter!
Water seeps under the door.

They have risen up in the morning grey.
    What will they give to Peter?
The sorrel horse with the tail of gold,
Fastest pacer ever was foaled.
Shoot him, skin him, blanch his bones,
Nail up his skull with a silver nail
Over the door; it will not fail.
No ghostly thing can ever prevail
    Against a horse's skull, Peter.

Over the lilacs, gazing down,
    Is a window, Peter.
The North winds call, and the South winds cry.
Silver white hair in a bitter blowing,
Eel-green water washing by,
A red mouth floating and flowing.
    Do you come, Peter?

They rose as the last star sank and set.
    One more for Peter.
They slew the black mare at the flush of the sun,
And nailed her skull to the window-stone.
In the light of the moon how white it shone—
    And your breathing mouth, Peter!

Around the house, and around the house,
With a wind that is North, and a wind that is South,
    Peter, Peter.
Mud and ooze and a dead man's wrist
Wrenching the shutters apart, like mist
The mud and the ooze and the dead man twist.
    They are praying, Peter.

Three in stable a week ago.
    This is the last, Peter.
"My strawberry roan in the morning clear,
Lady heart and attentive ear,
Foot like a kitten, nose like a deer,
But the fear! The fear!"
    Three skulls, Peter.

The sun goes down, and the night draws in.
    Toward the hills, Peter.
What lies so stiff on the hill-room floor,
When the gusty wind claps to the door?
They have paid three horses and two men more.
    Gather your gold, Peter.

Softly, softly, along the ground
Lest your shoes sound,
Gently, gently, across the air
Lest it stream, your hair.
North and South
For your aching mouth.
But the moon is old, Peter,
And death is long, and the well is deep.
Can you sleep, sleep, Peter?

1921

PURPLE GRACKLES

The grackles have come.
The smoothness of the morning is puckered with their incessant
    chatter.
A sociable lot, these purple grackles,
Thousands of them strung across a long run of wind,
Thousands of them beating the air-ways with quick wing-jerks,

Spinning down the currents of the South.
Every year they come;
My garden is a place of solace and recreation evidently,
For they always pass a day with me.
With high good nature they tell me what I do not want to hear.
The grackles have come.

I am persuaded that grackles are birds;
But when they are settled in the trees,
I am inclined to declare them fruits
And the trees turned hybrid blackberry vines.
Blackness shining and bulging under leaves,
Does not that mean blackberries, I ask you?
Nonsense! The grackles have come.

Nonchalant highwaymen, pickpockets, second-story burglars,
Stealing away my little hope of summer.
There is no stealthy robbing in this.
Who ever heard such a gabble of thieves' talk!
It seems they delight in unmasking my poor pretence.
Yes, now I see that the hydrangea blooms are rusty;
That the hearts of the golden glow are ripening to lustreless seeds;
That the garden is dahlia-colored,
Flaming with its last over-hot hues;
That the sun is pale as a lemon too small to fill the picking-ring.
I did not see this yesterday,
But to-day the grackles have come.

They drop out of the trees
And strut in companies over the lawn,
Tired of flying, no doubt;
A grand parade to limber legs and give wings a rest.
I should build a great fish-pond for them,
Since it is evident that a bird-bath, meant to accommodate two
    goldfinches at most,
Is slight hospitality for these hordes.
Scarcely one can get in,
They all peck and scrabble so,
Crowding, pushing, chasing one another up the bank with spread
    wings.
"Are we ducks, you, owner of such inadequate comforts,
That you offer us lily-tanks where one must swim or drown,
Not stand and splash like a gentleman?"

I feel the reproach keenly, seeing them perch on the edges of
the tanks, trying the depth with a chary foot,
And hardly able to get their wings under water in the bird-bath.
But there are resources I had not considered,
If I am bravely ruled out of count.
What is that thudding against the eaves just beyond my window?
What is that spray of water blowing past my face?
Two—three—grackles bathing in the gutter,
The gutter providentially choked with leaves.
I pray they think I put the leaves there on purpose;
I would be supposed thoughtful and welcoming
To all guests, even thieves.
But considering that they are going South and I am not,
I wish they would bathe more quietly;
It is unmannerly to flaunt one's good fortune.

They rate me of no consequence,
But they might reflect that it is my gutter.
I know their opinion of me,
Because one is drying himself on the window-sill
Not two feet from my hand.
His purple neck is sleek with water,
And the fellow preens his feathers for all the world as if I were
a fountain statue.
If it were not for the window,
I am convinced he would light on my head.
Tyrian-feathered freebooter,
Appropriating my delightful gutter with so extravagant an ease,
You are as cool a pirate as ever scuttled a ship,
And are you not scuttling my summer with every peck of your
sharp bill?

But there is a cloud over the beech-tree,
A quenching cloud for lemon-livered suns.
The grackles are all swinging in the tree-tops,
And the wind is coming up, mind you.
That boom and reach is no summer gale;
I know that wind;
It blows the equinox over seeds and scatters them;
It rips petals from petals, and tears off half-turned leaves.
There is rain on the back of that wind.
Now I would keep the grackles,
I would plead with them not to leave me.

I grant their coming, but I would not have them go.
It is a milestone, this passing of grackles.
A day of them, and it is a year gone by.
There is magic in this and terror,
But I only stare stupidly out of the window.
The grackles have come.

Come! Yes, they surely came.
But they have gone.
A moment ago the oak was full of them;
They are not there now.
Not a speck of a black wing,
Not an eye-peep of a purple head.
The grackles have gone.
And I watch an autumn storm
Stripping the garden,
Shouting black rain challenges
To an old, limp summer
Laid down to die in the flower-beds.

1925

THE DAY THAT WAS THAT DAY

The wind rose, and the wind fell,
And the day that was that day
Floated under a high Heaven.

"Home! Home! Home!"
Sang a robin in a spice-bush.
"Sun on a roof-tree! Sun on a roof-tree!"
Rang thin clouds
In a chord of silver across a placid sky.

Rachel Gibbs stepped up the path
To pass the time of day
With Haywood Green's Minnie.
My, ef she ain't shut th' door!
An' all th' breeze this side th' house too.
She must like to stew.
"Minnie,
Minnie,
You ain't gone out, have yer?

I'll skin my knuckles ef I knock agin.
I wonder did she lock th' door—
Well, I never!
Have you gone hard o' hearin'?
Have you—
Minnie, child, what's th' matter?
Why do you look like that?
What you doin'?
Speak, I tell yer,
What you hidin' that cup fer?
God A'mighty, girl, what you doin' with wood-alcohol
In a drinkin'-cup?
Here, give it ter me,
An' I'll set it on th' table.
Set down, Minnie, dear,
Set right here in th' rocker
An' tell me
What ails yer to be wantin'
To drink stuff like that?
There, there, you poor lamb,
Don't look so scared.
Jest tell me all about it,
An' ease your heart.
Minnie, I'll have to shake yer
Ef you don't stop starin'
In that dretful way.
Poor Dear,
You just lay your head up agin me
An' let me soothe yer.
Poor little thing.
Poor little thing."

"Don't, don't, Rachel,
I can't bear it.
I'm a wicked woman,
But I jest couldn't stand no more."

"No more o' what?
Ain't yer Pa good to yer?
What's come over yer, Minnie?
My! I'm jest as sorry as I can be."

"Oh, it ain't nothin' like that.
An' don't be so good to me,

You'll make me want to cry agin,
An' I can't cry.
I'm all dried up,
An' it's like squeezin' my heart sick
To want to cry, an' can't."

"But what is it?
Ain't yer never goin' ter tell me?"

"Why ther' ain't nothin' to tell
'Cept that I'm tired."

"Now, look-a-here, Minnie,
No one don't drink poison jest 'cause they're tired."

"I didn't drink it, as it happens."

"No, you didn't, 'cause I come in an' stopped yer.
But I'm mighty afeered you would have.
Lord, it makes me shudder!"

"I guess yer right,
I would have.
An' I wish you'd ha' let me be.
Now it's all to do over agin,
An' I don't know as I'll git th' courage
A second time.
I guess you ain't never been right down tired, Rachel."

"Well, never to th' poison point, no, I haven't,
But what's gone wrong to wear yer out so?"

"The cat's sick."

"Minnie Green, was you takin' poison
'Cause you got a sick cat?
That's down-right foolishness."

"Yes, it does sound so.
But I couldn't face nussin' her.
Look here, Rachel,
I may be foolish, or mad, or jest plain bad,
But I couldn't stan' another thing.

I'm all fretted now
An' more's one too many.
I can't go on!
Oh, God! I can't go on!
I ain't got no more'n most women,
I know that,
But I fuss a lot more.
There's al'ays th' same things
Goin' roun' like th' spokes to a cart-wheel,
Ef one ain't a-top it's another,
An' th' next comin' up all th' time.
It's breakfast, an' dinner, an' supper,
Every day.
An' th' same dishes to wash.
I hate them dishes.
I smashed a plate yesterday
'Cause I couldn't bear to see it
Settin' on th' sink waitin' fer me.
An' when I go up to make father's bed
I git seasick
Thinkin' I'll have to see that old check spread agin.
I've settled it,
An' twitched it this way an' that,
For thirty year,
An' I hate th' sight o' th' thing.
Sometimes I've set an hour on th' stair
Ruther'n go in an' touch it.
Oh, my God! Why couldn't yer let me be?
Why'd you have to come interferin'?
Why?
Why?"

"Thank th' Everlastin' Mercy I did!
But, Minnie, how long's this been goin' on?
I never had no idea anythin' was wrong."

"I don't know.
For ever an' ever, I guess.
Rachel, you can't think how hard it is fer me
To set one foot after th' other sometimes.
I hate lookin' out th' winder,
I'm so tired o' seein' th' path to th' barn.
An' I can't hardly bear

To hear father talkin' to th' horses.
He loves 'em.
But I don't love nothin'
'Cept th' cat,
An' cats is cold things to cling to,
An' now mine's sick!"

"Don't take on so, Minnie.
She'll get well.
There, you rest awhile,
You can tell me afterwards."

A wind rose, and a wind fell,
And the day that was that day
Hung against a turning sun.

The robin sang "Home! Home! Home!"
In an up-and-down scale of small, bright notes.
The clouds rang silver arpeggios
Stretched across a pleasant sky.

"I wish I loved somethin', Rachel."

"Bless your heart, Child, don't you love yer father?"

"I suppose so. But he don't mean nothin' ter me.
He don't say nothin' I want ter hear.
My ears is achin' to hear words,
Words like what's written in books,
Words that would make me all bright like a spring day.
I lay awake nights
Thinkin' o' hearin' things,
An' seein' things.
I'm awful tired o' these hills,
They crowd in so.
Seems sometimes ef I could see th' ocean,
Or a real big city,
'Twould help.
Kind o' lay my eyes out straight fer a while;
Everythin's so short here
My eyes feels pushed in,
An' it hurts 'em.
I love laylocks,

But I git so tired o' watchin'
Th' leaves come an' th' flowers
Every year th' same,
I'd like to root 'em up.
I've set an' set in th' kitchen evenin's
Awful late,
Fer not bein' able to git up an' light th' lamp
To go ter bed.
I'm all lead somehow.
I guess ef anybody did say anythin'
I'd be deaf
Jest with listenin' so long.
I'm plumb tired out."

"Look-a-here, Minnie,
Why don't you go away
Fer a spell?"

"Me go away!
Oh, no, I couldn't never do that.
I couldn't go no place.
I can't hardly git over to Dicksville
Fer my week with Aunt Abby now.
I'm all wrong away from home.
I can't do nothin'!
Nothin' at all.
I'm so awful tired."

"Minnie, did you ever love anybody?
Any man, I mean?"

"No, Rachel, I never did.
I know that sounds queer, but it's a fact.
I've tried to think I did,
But 'twarn't true.
I hadn't hardly no time fer men-folks,
Mother was sick so long,
An' then ther' was father.
I never was much account with 'em anyway,
But I s'pose I might ha' had one
Ef I'd fixed my mind so.
But I al'ays waited.
An' now I'm through waitin',

I'm through waitin' fer anythin', Rachel.
It's jest go, go, go,
With never no end,
And nothin' done that ain't to do over agin.
Ther' now it's six o'clock,
An' I must be gittin' supper.
You needn't move that cup, Rachel.
I ain't a-goin' to touch it.
I'll jest keep on now till th' Lord takes me,
An' I only hope he'll do it soon."

The robin flew down from the spice-bush
And pecked about for worms.
The clouds were brazen trumpets
Tumbled along the edge of an apple-colored sky.
The shadow of the house
Fell across the path to the barn,
Confusing it with the grass and the daisies.

A wind rose, and a wind fell,
And the day that was that day
Vanished in the darkness.

1926

THORN PIECE

Cliffs,
Cliffs,
And a twisted sea
Beating under a freezing moon.
Why should I,
Sitting peaceful and warm,
Cut my heart on so sharp a tune?

Liquid lapping of seething fire
Eating the heart of an old beech-tree.
Crack of icicles under the eaves,
Dog-wind whining eerily.

The oaks are red, and the asters flame,
And the sun is warm on bark and stones.
There's a Hunter's Moon abroad to-night—
The twigs are snapping like brittle bones.

You carry a lantern of rose-green glass,
Your dress is red as a Cardinal's cloak.
I kneel at the trace of your feet on the grass,
But when I would sing you a song, I choke.

Choke for the fragile careless years
We have scattered so easily from our hands.
They flutter like leaves through an autumn sun,
One by one, one by one.

I have lived in a place,
I shall die in a place,
I have no craving for distant lands.
But a place is nothing, not even space,
Unless at its heart a figure stands

Swinging a rose-green lantern for me.
I fear the fall of a rose-green gate,
And the cry of a cliff-driven, haunted sea,
And the crackle of ice while I wait—wait!

Your face is flowers and singing sun,
Your hands are the cool of waters falling.
If the rose-green bars should drop between
Would you know that I was calling?

For the stars I see in that sky are black.
The kind earth holds me and laughs in my ear.
I have nothing to do with the planet's track,
I only want you, my Dear.

Beyond is a glaze, but here is fire,
And love to comfort, and speech to bind,
And the common things of morning and evening,
And the light of your lantern I always find.

One or the other—then let it be me,
For I fear the whirl of the cliff-wrung sea,
And the biting night. You smile at my fears,
But the years—years—
Like leaves falling.

1927

Robert Frost

Robert Lee Frost was born in San Francisco, March 26, 1875. He was a descendant of Nicholas Frost, who in 1634 came from Plymouth to New England, where the Frost family had since lived. His father, William Prescott Frost, after attending Harvard, went to teach in Lewiston, Pennsylvania. There he met and married Belle Moody, also a teacher, who at the age of fifteen had come to America from Edinburgh, Scotland. Although too young to take part in the Civil War, William Frost had favored the South, and being still an ardent State rights man, and thus out of sympathy with his New England neighbors, he decided to try his fortunes in the West. Going to San Francisco, he obtained work on a Democratic newspaper, the *Bulletin*. Soon after his wife joined him, she gave birth to a son, who was named for the Southern general. For the next ten years William Frost was active in newspaper work and politics, but in 1885 he died of tuberculosis; and his widow, now without means of support, went to Lawrence, Massachusetts, to live with her husband's father.

Robert's early education was poor, but in Lawrence he progressed rapidly, and upon his graduation from high school in 1893 he was valedictorian of his class. In the autumn he entered Dartmouth, but after a few months he dropped out and returned to Lawrence, where he worked in turn as bobbin boy in a mill, as Latin teacher in a school his mother was conducting, and as reporter on the Lawrence *Sentinel*. When in high school he had fallen in love with Elinor Miriam White, the daughter of a retired Universalist clergyman, and after she completed her education at St. Lawrence University, they were married on December 28, 1895. In 1897 Frost moved his family to Cambridge and entered Harvard, where he was a student for two years, specializing in Latin and Greek. He then withdrew from college, and after working for a while in a shoe factory and again on a newspaper, he moved to a farm which his grandfather bought for him near Derry, New Hampshire. He farmed, rather unprofitably, till 1905, when he became a teacher of English in the Pinkerton Academy, Derry. He held this position till 1911, when he went, with the principal of the academy, to the New Hampshire State Normal School, Plymouth. Here during the year 1911-1912 he taught psychology.

From boyhood Frost had been writing verse. In 1894 he sold a poem to the *Independent* for $15, and later disposed of others to the *Forum* and the *Youth's Companion*. American editors were generally unreceptive to his work, however, and in September, 1912, having sold his farm, he decided to go to England, where poetry at the time was receiving more attention. He settled at Beaconsfield, Buckinghamshire, and in the next two years had two volumes of poetry published. In 1914 he moved to Hertfordshire, where he had as neighbors Wilfrid Gibson, Lascelles Abercrombie, and Edward Thomas. Because of the war, however, he returned home in March, 1915, and settled on a farm near Franconia, New Hampshire. In 1916 he went to Amherst to teach English, and though he was often on leave of absence, he was connected with this college till 1938. For two years, 1921-1923, he was Poet in Residence at the University of Michigan, and in 1925-1926 he was there as Fellow in Letters. In 1935-1936 he was Charles Eliot Norton Professor of Poetry at Harvard, and since 1939 he has been Ralph Waldo Emerson Fellow there.

Frost has received many honors. Twice, in 1916 and in 1936, he was Phi Beta Kappa poet at Harvard; in 1922 he was named Poet Laureate of Vermont; in 1917 and in 1922 he was awarded poetry prizes by *Poetry*, and he won the Pulitzer Prize for poetry three times—in 1924, 1931, and 1937. He was the first recipient, in 1931, of the Russell Loines Memorial Poetry Prize, awarded by the National Institute of Arts and Letters; and he is a member of the American Philosophical Society, of the International P. E. N. Club, and of the American Academy of Arts and Letters. He has been given many honorary degrees: M.A. by Amherst (1917) and the University of Michigan (1922); L.H.D. by the University of Vermont (1923), Wesleyan University (1931), and St. Lawrence University (1936); Litt.D. by Yale (1923), Middlebury (1924), Bowdoin (1926), New Hampshire State University (1930), Columbia (1932), Williams (1932), Dartmouth (1933), Bates (1936), the University of Pennsylvania (1936), Harvard (1937), the University of Colorado (1939), and Princeton (1941).

In 1920 Frost bought a farm at South Shaftsbury, Vermont, where for some years he lived with his wife and four children when he was not engaged in academic work. But since the death of his wife in 1938 he has lived more in town. In addition to his teaching and writing, he has done much lecturing.

RELUCTANCE

Out through the fields and the woods
  And over the walls I have wended;
I have climbed the hills of view
  And looked at the world, and descended;
I have come by the highway home,
  And lo, it is ended.

The leaves are all dead on the ground,
  Save those that the oak is keeping
To ravel them one by one
  And let them go scraping and creeping
Out over the crusted snow,
  When others are sleeping.

And the dead leaves lie huddled and still,
  No longer blown hither and thither;
The last lone aster is gone;
  The flowers of the witch-hazel wither;
The heart is still aching to seek,
  But the feet question "Whither?"

Ah, when to the heart of man
  Was it ever less than a treason
To go with the drift of things,
  To yield with a grace to reason,
And bow and accept the end
  Of a love or a season?

1913

THE PASTURE

I'm going out to clean the pasture spring;
I'll only stop to rake the leaves away
(And wait to watch the water clear, I may):
I sha'n't be gone long.—You come too.

I'm going out to fetch the little calf
That's standing by the mother. It's so young,
It totters when she licks it with her tongue.
I sha'n't be gone long.—You come too.

1914

MENDING WALL

Something there is that doesn't love a wall,
That sends the frozen-ground-swell under it,
And spills the upper boulders in the sun;
And makes gaps even two can pass abreast.
The work of hunters is another thing:
I have come after them and made repair
Where they have left not one stone on a stone,
But they would have the rabbit out of hiding,
To please the yelping dogs. The gaps I mean,
No one has seen them made or heard them made,
But at spring mending-time we find them there.
I let my neighbor know beyond the hill;
And on a day we meet to walk the line
And set the wall between us once again.
We keep the wall between us as we go.
To each the boulders that have fallen to each.
And some are loaves and some so nearly balls
We have to use a spell to make them balance:
"Stay where you are until our backs are turned!"
We wear our fingers rough with handling them.
Oh, just another kind of out-door game,
One on a side. It comes to little more:
There where it is we do not need the wall:
He is all pine and I am apple orchard.
My apple trees will never get across
And eat the cones under his pines, I tell him.

He only says, "Good fences make good neighbors."
Spring is the mischief in me, and I wonder
If I could put a notion in his head:
"*Why* do they make good neighbors? Isn't it
Where there are cows? But here there are no cows.
Before I built a wall I'd ask to know
What I was walling in or walling out,
And to whom I was like to give offence.
Something there is that doesn't love a wall,
That wants it down." I could say "Elves" to him,
But it's not elves exactly, and I'd rather
He said it for himself. I see him there
Bringing a stone grasped firmly by the top
In each hand, like an old-stone savage armed.
He moves in darkness as it seems to me,
Not of woods only and the shade of trees.
He will not go behind his father's saying,
And he likes having thought of it so well
He says again, "Good fences make good neighbors."

1914

THE DEATH OF THE HIRED MAN

Mary sat musing on the lamp-flame at the table
Waiting for Warren. When she heard his step,
She ran on tip-toe down the darkened passage
To meet him in the doorway with the news
And put him on his guard. "Silas is back."
She pushed him outward with her through the door
And shut it after her. "Be kind," she said.
She took the market things from Warren's arms
And set them on the porch, then drew him down
To sit beside her on the wooden steps.

"When was I ever anything but kind to him?
But I'll not have the fellow back," he said.
"I told him so last haying, didn't I?
'If he left then,' I said, 'that ended it.'
What good is he? Who else will harbor him
At his age for the little he can do?
What help he is there's no depending on.
Off he goes always when I need him most.

'He thinks he ought to earn a little pay,
Enough at least to buy tobacco with,
So he won't have to beg and be beholden.'
'All right,' I say, 'I can't afford to pay
Any fixed wages, though I wish I could.'
'Someone else can.' 'Then someone else will have to.'
I shouldn't mind his bettering himself
If that was what it was. You can be certain,
When he begins like that, there's someone at him
Trying to coax him off with pocket-money,—
In haying time, when any help is scarce.
In winter he comes back to us. I'm done."

"Sh! not so loud: he'll hear you," Mary said.

"I want him to: he'll have to soon or late."

"He's worn out. He's asleep beside the stove.
When I came up from Rowe's I found him here,
Huddled against the barn-door fast asleep,
A miserable sight, and frightening, too—
You needn't smile—I didn't recognize him—
I wasn't looking for him—and he's changed.
Wait till you see."

"Where did you say he'd been?"

"He didn't say. I dragged him to the house,
And gave him tea and tried to make him smoke.
I tried to make him talk about his travels.
Nothing would do: he just kept nodding off."

"What did he say? Did he say anything?"

"But little."

"Anything? Mary, confess
He said he'd come to ditch the meadow for me."

"Warren!"

"But did he? I just want to know."

"Of course he did. What would you have him say?
Surely you wouldn't grudge the poor old man

Some humble way to save his self-respect.
He added, if you really care to know,
He meant to clear the upper pasture, too.
That sounds like something you have heard before?
Warren, I wish you could have heard the way
He jumbled everything. I stopped to look
Two or three times—he made me feel so queer—
To see if he was talking in his sleep.
He ran on Harold Wilson—you remember—
The boy you had in haying four years since.
He's finished school, and teaching in his college.
Silas declares you'll have to get him back.
He says they two will make a team for work:
Between them they will lay this farm as smooth!
The way he mixed that in with other things.
He thinks young Wilson a likely lad, though daft
On education—you know how they fought
All through July under the blazing sun,
Silas up on the cart to build the load,
Harold along beside to pitch it on."

"Yes, I took care to keep well out of earshot."

"Well, those days trouble Silas like a dream.
You wouldn't think they would. How some things linger!
Harold's young college boy's assurance piqued him.
After so many years he still keeps finding
Good arguments he sees he might have used.
I sympathize. I know just how it feels
To think of the right thing to say too late.
Harold's associated in his mind with Latin.
He asked me what I thought of Harold's saying
He studied Latin like the violin
Because he liked it—that an argument!
He said he couldn't make the boy believe
He could find water with a hazel prong—
Which showed how much good school had ever done him.
He wanted to go over that. But most of all
He thinks if he could have another chance
To teach him how to build a load of hay—"

"I know, that's Silas' one accomplishment.
He bundles every forkful in its place,

And tags and numbers it for future reference,
So he can find and easily dislodge it
In the unloading. Silas does that well.
He takes it out in bunches like big birds' nests.
You never see him standing on the hay
He's trying to lift, straining to lift himself."

"He thinks if he could teach him that, he'd be
Some good perhaps to someone in the world.
He hates to see a boy the fool of books.
Poor Silas, so concerned for other folk,
And nothing to look backward to with pride,
And nothing to look forward to with hope,
So now and never any different."

Part of a moon was falling down the west,
Dragging the whole sky with it to the hills.
Its light poured softly in her lap. She saw
And spread her apron to it. She put out her hand
Among the harp-like morning-glory strings,
Taut with the dew from garden bed to eaves,
As if she played unheard the tenderness
That wrought on him beside her in the night.
"Warren," she said, "he has come home to die:
You needn't be afraid he'll leave you this time."

"Home," he mocked gently.

"Yes, what else but home?
It all depends on what you mean by home.
Of course he's nothing to us, any more
Than was the hound that came a stranger to us
Out of the woods, worn out upon the trail."

"Home is the place where, when you have to go there,
They have to take you in."

"I should have called it
Something you somehow haven't to deserve."

Warren leaned out and took a step or two,
Picked up a little stick, and brought it back
And broke it in his hand and tossed it by.

"Silas has better claim on us you think
Than on his brother? Thirteen little miles
As the road winds would bring him to his door.
Silas has walked that far no doubt to-day.
Why didn't he go there? His brother's rich,
A somebody—director in the bank."

"He never told us that."

"We know it though."

"I think his brother ought to help, of course.
I'll see to that if there is need. He ought of right
To take him in, and might be willing to—
He may be better than appearances.
But have some pity on Silas. Do you think
If he'd had any pride in claiming kin
Or anything he looked for from his brother,
He'd keep so still about him all this time?"

"I wonder what's between them."

"I can tell you.
Silas is what he is—we wouldn't mind him—
But just the kind that kinsfolk can't abide.
He never did a thing so very bad.
He don't know why he isn't quite as good
As anyone. He won't be made ashamed
To please his brother, worthless though he is."

"*I* can't think Si ever hurt anyone."

"No, but he hurt my heart the way he lay
And rolled his old head on that sharp-edged chair-back.
He wouldn't let me put him on the lounge.
You must go in and see what you can do.
I made the bed up for him there to-night.
You'll be surprised at him—how much he's broken.
His working days are done; I'm sure of it."

"I'd not be in a hurry to say that."

"I haven't been. Go, look, see for yourself,
But, Warren, please remember how it is:

He's come to help you ditch the meadow.
He has a plan. You mustn't laugh at him.
He may not speak of it, and then he may.
I'll sit and see if that small sailing cloud
Will hit or miss the moon."

It hit the moon.
Then there were three there, making a dim row,
The moon, the little silver cloud, and she.
Warren returned—too soon, it seemed to her,
Slipped to her side, caught up her hand and waited.
"Warren," she questioned.

"Dead," was all he answered.
1914

THE ROAD NOT TAKEN

Two roads diverged in a yellow wood,
And sorry I could not travel both
And be one traveler, long I stood
And looked down one as far as I could
To where it bent in the undergrowth;

Then took the other, as just as fair,
And having perhaps the better claim,
Because it was grassy and wanted wear;
Though as for that the passing there
Had worn them really about the same,

And both that morning equally lay
In leaves no step had trodden black.
Oh, I kept the first for another day!
Yet knowing how way leads on to way,
I doubted if I should ever come back.

I shall be telling this with a sigh
Somewhere ages and ages hence:
Two roads diverged in a wood, and I—
I took the one less traveled by,
And that has made all the difference.
1916

A PATCH OF OLD SNOW

There's a patch of old snow in a corner
  That I should have guessed
Was a blow-away paper the rain
  Had brought to rest.

It is speckled with grime as if
  Small print overspread it,
The news of a day I've forgotten—
  If I ever read it.

1916

BIRCHES

When I see birches bend to left and right
Across the lines of straighter darker trees,
I like to think some boy's been swinging them.
But swinging doesn't bend them down to stay.
Ice-storms do that. Often you must have seen them
Loaded with ice a sunny winter morning
After a rain. They click upon themselves
As the breeze rises, and turn many-colored
As the stir cracks and crazes their enamel.
Soon the sun's warmth makes them shed crystal shells
Shattering and avalanching on the snow-crust—
Such heaps of broken glass to sweep away
You'd think the inner dome of heaven had fallen.
They are dragged to the withered bracken by the load,
And they seem not to break; though once they are bowed
So low for long, they never right themselves:
You may see their trunks arching in the woods
Years afterwards, trailing their leaves on the ground
Like girls on hands and knees that throw their hair
Before them over their heads to dry in the sun.
But I was going to say when Truth broke in
With all her matter-of-fact about the ice-storm
(Now am I free to be poetical?)
I should prefer to have some boy bend them
As he went out and in to fetch the cows—
Some boy too far from town to learn baseball,

Whose only play was what he found himself,
Summer or winter, and could play alone.
One by one he subdued his father's trees
By riding them down over and over again
Until he took the stiffness out of them,
And not one but hung limp, not one was left
For him to conquer. He learned all there was
To learn about not launching out too soon
And so not carrying the tree away
Clear to the ground. He always kept his poise
To the top branches, climbing carefully
With the same pains you use to fill a cup
Up to the brim, and even above the brim.
Then he flung outward, feet first, with a swish,
Kicking his way down through the air to the ground.
So was I once myself a swinger of birches.
And so I dream of going back to be.
It's when I'm weary of considerations,
And life is too much like a pathless wood
Where your face burns and tickles with the cobwebs
Broken across it, and one eye is weeping
From a twig's having lashed across it open.
I'd like to get away from earth awhile
And then come back to it and begin over.
May no fate willfully misunderstand me
And half grant what I wish and snatch me away
Not to return. Earth's the right place for love:
I don't know where it's likely to go better.
I'd like to go by climbing a birch tree,
And climb black branches up a snow-white trunk
Toward heaven, till the tree could bear no more,
But dipped its top and set me down again.
That would be good both going and coming back.
One could do worse than be a swinger of birches.

1916

THE HILL WIFE

LONELINESS

(Her Word)

One ought not to have to care
  So much as you and I
Care when the birds come round the house
  To seem to say good-bye;

Or care so much when they come back
  With whatever it is they sing;
The truth being we are as much
  Too glad for the one thing

As we are too sad for the other here—
  With birds that fill their breasts
But with each other and themselves
  And their built or driven nests.

HOUSE FEAR

Always—I tell you this they learned—
Always at night when they returned
To the lonely house from far away
To lamps unlighted and fire gone gray
They learned to rattle the lock and key
To give whatever might chance to be
Warning and time to be off in flight:
And preferring the out- to the in-door night,
They learned to leave the house-door wide
Until they had lit the lamp inside.

THE SMILE

(Her Word)

I didn't like the way he went away.
That smile! It never came of being gay.
Still he smiled—did you see him?—I was sure!
Perhaps because we gave him only bread
And the wretch knew from that that we were poor.
Perhaps because he let us give instead

Of seizing from us as he might have seized.
Perhaps he mocked at us for being wed,
Or being very young (and he was pleased
To have a vision of us old and dead).
I wonder how far down the road he's got.
He's watching from the woods as like as not.

THE OFT-REPEATED DREAM

She had no saying dark enough
  For the dark pine that kept
Forever trying the window-latch
  Of the room where they slept.

The tireless but ineffectual hands
  That with every futile pass
Made the great tree seem as a little bird
  Before the mystery of glass!

It never had been inside the room,
  And only one of the two
Was afraid in an oft-repeated dream
  Of what the tree might do.

THE IMPULSE

It was too lonely for her there,
  And too wild,
And since there were but two of them,
  And no child,

And work was little in the house,
  She was free,
And followed where he furrowed field,
  Or felled tree.

She rested on a log and tossed
  The fresh chips,
With a song only to herself
  On her lips.

And once she went to break a bough
  Of black alder.
She strayed so far she scarcely heard
  When he called her—

And didn't answer—didn't speak—
  Or return.
She stood, and then she ran and hid
  In the fern.

He never found her, though he looked
  Everywhere,
And he asked at her mother's house
  Was she there.

Sudden and swift and light as that
  The ties gave,
And he learned of finalities
  Besides the grave.

1916

THE SOUND OF THE TREES

I wonder about the trees.
Why do we wish to bear
Forever the noise of these
More than another noise
So close to our dwelling place?
We suffer them by the day
Till we lose all measure of pace,
And fixity in our joys,
And acquire a listening air.
They are that that talks of going
But never gets away;
And that talks no less for knowing,
As it grows wiser and older,
That now it means to stay.
My feet tug at the floor
And my head sways to my shoulder
Sometimes when I watch trees sway,
From the window or the door.
I shall set forth for somewhere,
I shall make the reckless choice
Some day when they are in voice
And tossing so as to scare
The white clouds over them on.
I shall have less to say,
But I shall be gone.

1916

THE STAR-SPLITTER

"You know Orion always comes up sideways.
Throwing a leg up over our fence of mountains,
And rising on his hands, he looks in on me
Busy outdoors by lantern-light with something
I should have done by daylight, and indeed,
After the ground is frozen, I should have done
Before it froze, and a gust flings a handful
Of waste leaves at my smoky lantern chimney
To make fun of my way of doing things,
Or else fun of Orion's having caught me.
Has a man, I should like to ask, no rights
These forces are obliged to pay respect to?"
So Brad McLaughlin mingled reckless talk
Of heavenly stars with hugger-mugger farming,
Till having failed at hugger-mugger farming,
He burned his house down for the fire insurance
And spent the proceeds on a telescope
To satisfy a life-long curiosity
About our place among the infinities.

"What do you want with one of those blame things?"
I asked him well beforehand. "Don't you get one!"
"Don't call it blamed; there isn't anything
More blameless in the sense of being less
A weapon in our human fight," he said.
"I'll have one if I sell my farm to buy it."
There where he moved the rocks to plow the ground
And plowed between the rocks he couldn't move
Few farms changed hands; so rather than spend years
Trying to sell his farm and then not selling,
He burned his house down for the fire insurance
And bought the telescope with what it came to.
He had been heard to say by several:
"The best thing that we're put here for's to see;
The strongest thing that's given us to see with's
A telescope. Someone in every town
Seems to me owes it to the town to keep one.
In Littleton it may as well be me."
After such loose talk it was no surprise
When he did what he did and burned his house down.

Mean laughter went about the town that day
To let him know we weren't the least imposed on,
And he could wait—we'd see to him to-morrow.
But the first thing next morning we reflected
If one by one we counted people out
For the least sin, it wouldn't take us long
To get so we had no one left to live with.
For to be social is to be forgiving.
Our thief, the one who does our stealing from us,
We don't cut off from coming to church suppers,
But what we miss we go to him and ask for.
He promptly gives it back, that is if still
Uneaten, unworn out, or undisposed of.
It wouldn't do to be too hard on Brad
About his telescope. Beyond the age
Of being given one's gift for Christmas,
He had to take the best way he knew how
To find himself in one. Well, all we said was
He took a strange thing to be roguish over.
Some sympathy was wasted on the house,
A good old-timer dating back along;
But a house isn't sentient; the house
Didn't feel anything. And if it did,
Why not regard it as a sacrifice,
And an old-fashioned sacrifice by fire,
Instead of a new-fashioned one at auction?

Out of a house and so out of a farm
At one stroke (of a match), Brad had to turn
To earn a living on the Concord railroad,
As under-ticket-agent at a station
Where his job, when he wasn't selling tickets,
Was setting out up track and down, not plants
As on a farm, but planets, evening stars
That varied in their hue from red to green.

He got a good glass for six hundred dollars.
His new job gave him leisure for star-gazing.
Often he bid me come and have a look
Up the brass barrel, velvet black inside,
At a star quaking in the other end.
I recollect a night of broken clouds
And underfoot snow melted down to ice,

And melting further in the wind to mud.
Bradford and I had out the telescope.
We spread our two legs as we spread its three,
Pointed our thoughts the way we pointed it,
And standing at our leisure till the day broke,
Said some of the best things we ever said.
That telescope was christened the Star-splitter,
Because it didn't do a thing but split
A star in two or three the way you split
A globule of quicksilver in your hand
With one stroke of your finger in the middle.
It's a star-splitter if there ever was one
And ought to do some good if splitting stars
'S a thing to be compared with splitting wood.

We've looked and looked, but after all where are we?
Do we know any better where we are,
And how it stands between the night to-night
And a man with a smoky lantern-chimney?
How different from the way it ever stood?

1923

FIRE AND ICE

Some say the world will end in fire,
Some say in ice.
From what I've tasted of desire
I hold with those who favor fire.
But if it had to perish twice,
I think I know enough of hate
To say that for destruction ice
Is also great
And would suffice.

1923

DUST OF SNOW

The way a crow
Shook down on me
The dust of snow
From a hemlock tree

Has given my heart
A change of mood
And saved some part
Of a day I had rued.

1923

STOPPING BY WOODS ON A SNOWY EVENING

Whose woods these are I think I know.
His house is in the village though;
He will not see me stopping here
To watch his woods fill up with snow.

My little horse must think it queer
To stop without a farmhouse near
Between the woods and frozen lake
The darkest evening of the year.

He gives his harness bells a shake
To ask if there is some mistake.
The only other sound's the sweep
Of easy wind and downy flake.

The woods are lovely, dark and deep.
But I have promises to keep,
And miles to go before I sleep,
And miles to go before I sleep.

1923

THE ONSET

Always the same, when on a fated night
At last the gathered snow lets down as white
As may be in dark woods, and with a song
It shall not make again all winter long
Of hissing on the yet uncovered ground,
I almost stumble looking up and round,
As one who overtaken by the end
Gives up his errand, and lets death descend
Upon him where he is, with nothing done
To evil, no important triumph won,
More than if life had never been begun.

Yet all the precedent is on my side:
I know that winter death has never tried
The earth but it has failed: the snow may heap
In long storms an undrifted four feet deep
As measured against maple, birch, and oak,
It cannot check the peeper's silver croak;
And I shall see the snow all go down hill
In water of a slender April rill
That flashes tail through last year's withered brake
And dead weeds, like a disappearing snake.
Nothing will be left white but here a birch,
And there a clump of houses with a church.

1923

GOOD-BYE AND KEEP COLD

This saying good-bye on the edge of the dark
And cold to an orchard so young in the bark
Reminds me of all that can happen to harm
An orchard away at the end of the farm
All winter, cut off by a hill from the house.
I don't want it girdled by rabbit and mouse,
I don't want it dreamily nibbled for browse
By deer, and I don't want it budded by grouse.
(If certain it wouldn't be idle to call
I'd summon grouse, rabbit, and deer to the wall
And warn them away with a stick for a gun.)
I don't want it stirred by the heat of the sun.
(We made it secure against being, I hope,
By setting it out on a northerly slope.)
No orchard's the worse for the wintriest storm;
But one thing about it, it mustn't get warm.
"How often already you've had to be told,
Keep cold, young orchard. Good-bye and keep cold.
Dread fifty above more than fifty below."
I have to be gone for a season or so.
My business awhile is with different trees,
Less carefully nourished, less fruitful than these,
And such as is done to their wood with an axe—
Maples and birches and tamaracks.
I wish I could promise to lie in the night
And think of an orchard's arboreal plight

When slowly (and nobody comes with a light)
Its heart sinks lower under the sod.
But something has to be left to God.

1923

ACCEPTANCE

When the spent sun throws up its rays on cloud
And goes down burning into the gulf below,
No voice in nature is heard to cry aloud
At what has happened. Birds, at least, must know
It is the change to darkness in the sky.
Murmuring something quiet in its breast,
One bird begins to close a faded eye;
Or overtaken too far from its nest,
Hurrying low above the grove, some waif
Swoops just in time to his remembered tree.
At most he thinks or twitters softly, "Safe!
Now let the night be dark for all of me.
Let the night be too dark for me to see
Into the future. Let what will be, be."

1928

A MINOR BIRD

I have wished a bird would fly away,
And not sing by my house all day;

Have clapped my hands at him from the door
When it seemed as if I could bear no more.

The fault must partly have been in me;
The bird was not to blame for his key.

And of course there must be something wrong
In wanting to silence any song.

1928

ACQUAINTED WITH THE NIGHT

I have been one acquainted with the night.
I have walked out in rain—and back in rain.
I have outwalked the furthest city light.

I have looked down the saddest city lane.
I have passed by the watchman on his beat
And dropped my eyes, unwilling to explain.

I have stood still and stopped the sound of feet
When far away an interrupted cry
Came over houses from another street,

But not to call me back or say good-bye;
And further still at an unearthly height,
One luminary clock against the sky

Proclaimed the time was neither wrong nor right.
I have been one acquainted with the night.

1928

THE INVESTMENT

Over back where they speak of life as staying
("You couldn't call it living, for it ain't"),
There was an old, old house renewed with paint,
And in it a piano loudly playing.

Out in the ploughed ground in the cold a digger,
Among unearthed potatoes standing still
Was counting winter dinners, one a hill,
With half an ear to the piano's vigor.

All that piano and new paint back there,
Was it some money suddenly come into?
Or some extravagance young love had been to?
Or old love on an impulse not to care—

Not to sink under being man and wife,
But get some color and music out of life?

1928

THE ARMFUL

For every parcel I stoop down to seize,
I lose some other off my arms and knees,
And the whole pile is slipping, bottles, buns,
Extremes too hard to comprehend at once,
Yet nothing I should care to leave behind.
With all I have to hold with, hand and mind
And heart if need be, I will do my best
To keep their building balanced at my breast.
I crouch down to prevent them as they fall;
Then sit down in the middle of them all.
I had to drop the armful in the road
And try to stack them in a better load.

1928

ON LOOKING UP BY CHANCE AT THE CONSTELLATIONS

You'll wait a long, long time for anything much
To happen in heaven beyond the floats of cloud
And the Northern Lights that run like tingling nerves.
The sun and moon get crossed, but they never touch,
Nor strike out fire from each other, nor crash out loud.
The planets seem to interfere in their curves,
But nothing ever happens, no harm is done.
We may as well go patiently on with our life,
And look elsewhere than to stars and moon and sun
For the shocks and changes we need to keep us sane.
It is true the longest drouth will end in rain,
The longest peace in China will end in strife.
Still it wouldn't reward the watcher to stay awake
In hopes of seeing the calm of heaven break
On his particular time and personal sight.
That calm seems certainly safe to last tonight.

1928

TWO TRAMPS IN MUD TIME

Out of the mud two strangers came
And caught me splitting wood in the yard.
And one of them put me off my aim
By hailing cheerily "Hit them hard!"
I knew pretty well why he dropped behind
And let the other go on a way.
I knew pretty well what he had in mind:
He wanted to take my job for pay.

Good blocks of beech it was I split,
As large around as the chopping block;
And every piece I squarely hit
Fell splinterless as a cloven rock.
The blows that a life of self-control
Spares to strike for the common good
That day, giving a loose to my soul,
I spent on the unimportant wood.

The sun was warm but the wind was chill.
You know how it is with an April day
When the sun is out and the wind is still,
You're one month on in the middle of May.
But if you so much as dare to speak,
A cloud comes over the sunlit arch,
A wind comes off a frozen peak,
And you're two months back in the middle of March.

A bluebird comes tenderly up to alight
And fronts the wind to unruffle a plume,
His song so pitched as not to excite
A single flower as yet to bloom.
It is snowing a flake: and he half knew
Winter was only playing possum.
Except in color he isn't blue,
But he wouldn't advise a thing to blossom.

The water for which we may have to look
In summertime with a witching-wand,
In every wheelrut's now a brook,
In every print of a hoof a pond.

Be glad of water, but don't forget
The lurking frost in the earth beneath
That will steal forth after the sun is set
And show on the water its crystal teeth.

The time when most I loved my task
These two must make me love it more
By coming with what they came to ask.
You'd think I never had felt before
The weight of an ax-head poised aloft,
The grip on earth of outspread feet,
The life of muscles rocking soft
And smooth and moist in vernal heat.

Out of the woods two hulking tramps
(From sleeping God knows where last night,
But not long since in the lumber camps).
They thought all chopping was theirs of right.
Men of the woods and lumberjacks,
They judged me by their appropriate tool.
Except as a fellow handled an ax,
They had no way of knowing a fool.

Nothing on either side was said.
They knew they had but to stay their stay
And all their logic would fill my head:
As that I had no right to play
With what was another man's work for gain.
My right might be love but theirs was need.
And where the two exist in twain
Theirs was the better right—agreed.

But yield who will to their separation,
My object in living is to unite
My avocation and my vocation
As my two eyes make one in sight.
Only where love and need are one,
And the work is play for mortal stakes,
Is the deed ever really done
For Heaven and the future's sakes.

1936

ON THE HEART'S BEGINNING TO CLOUD THE MIND

Something I saw or thought I saw
In the desert at midnight in Utah,
Looking out of my lower berth
At moonlit sky and moonlit earth.
The sky had here and there a star;
The earth had a single light afar,
A flickering, human pathetic light,
That was maintained against the night,
It seemed to me, by the people there,
With a God-forsaken brute despair.
It would flutter and fall in half an hour
Like the last petal off a flower.
But my heart was beginning to cloud my mind.
I knew a tale of a better kind.
That far light flickers because of trees.
The people can burn it as long as they please:
And when their interests in it end,
They can leave it to someone else to tend.
Come back that way a summer hence,
I should find it no more no less intense.
I pass, but scarcely pass no doubt,
When one will say "Let us put it out."
The other without demur agrees.
They can keep it burning as long as they please;
They can put it out whenever they please.
One looks out last from the darkened room
At the shiny desert with spots of gloom
That might be people and are but cedar,
Have no purpose, have no leader,
Have never made the first move to assemble,
And so are nothing to make her tremble.
She can think of places that are not thus
Without indulging a "Not for us!"
Life is not so sinister-grave.
Matter of fact has made them brave.
He is husband, she is wife.
She fears not him, they fear not life.
They know where another light has been,
And more than one to theirs akin,
But earlier out for bed tonight,
So lost on me in my surface flight.

This I saw when waking late,
Going by at a railroad rate,
Looking through wreaths of engine smoke
Far into the lives of other folk.

1936

DESERT PLACES

Snow falling and night falling fast oh fast
In a field I looked into going past,
And the ground almost covered smooth in snow,
But a few weeds and stubble showing last.

The woods around it have it—it is theirs.
All animals are smothered in their lairs.
I am too absent-spirited to count;
The loneliness includes me unawares.

And lonely as it is that loneliness
Will be more lonely ere it will be less—
A blanker whiteness of benighted snow
With no expression, nothing to express.

They cannot scare me with their empty spaces
Between stars—on stars where no human race is.
I have it in me so much nearer home
To scare myself with my own desert places.

1936

THE STRONG ARE SAYING NOTHING

The soil now gets a rumpling soft and damp,
And small regard to the future of any weed.
The final flat of the hoe's approval stamp
Is reserved for the bed of a few selected seed.

There is seldom more than a man to a harrowed piece.
Men work alone, their lots plowed far apart,
One stringing a chain of seed in an open crease,
And another stumbling after a halting cart.

To the fresh and black of the squares of early mould
The leafless bloom of a plum is fresh and white;
Though there's more than a doubt if the weather is not too cold
For the bees to come and serve its beauty aright.

Wind goes from farm to farm in wave on wave,
But carries no cry of what is hoped to be.
There may be little or much beyond the grave,
But the strong are saying nothing until they see.

1936

THERE ARE ROUGHLY ZONES

We sit indoors and talk of the cold outside.
And every gust that gathers strength and heaves
Is a threat to the house. But the house has long been tried.
We think of the tree. If it never again has leaves,
We'll know, we say, that this was the night it died.
It is very far north, we admit, to have brought the peach.
What comes over a man, is it soul or mind—
That to no limits and bounds he can stay confined?
You would say his ambition was to extend the reach
Clear to the Arctic of every living kind.
Why is his nature forever so hard to teach
That though there is no fixed line between wrong and right,
There are roughly zones whose laws must be obeyed.
There is nothing much we can do for the tree tonight,
But we can't help feeling more than a little betrayed
That the northwest wind should rise to such a height
Just when the cold went down so many below.
The tree has no leaves and may never have them again.
We must wait till some months hence in the spring to know.
But if it is destined never again to grow,
It can blame this limitless trait in the hearts of men.

1936

Carl Sandburg

Carl Sandburg was born in Galesburg, Illinois, January 6, 1878. His parents, August and Clara Anderson Sandburg, were Swedish immigrants with but little education. Sandburg's father was named August Johnson, but as there were several other August Johnsons in the railroad construction crew with which he worked, in consequence of which the pay envelopes sometimes became mixed, he changed his name to Sandburg. During the poet's youth, his father worked in the railroad blacksmith shops at Galesburg.

Sandburg attended the public schools in Galesburg, but as soon as he was old enough he also worked at various jobs—as driver of a milk wagon, porter in a barber shop, sceneshifter in a theatre, and truck operator at a brick kiln. At seventeen he went west, riding freight cars and blind baggage. There among other jobs he pitched wheat in the Kansas wheatfields, washed dishes in hotels in Kansas City, Omaha, and Denver, and worked as carpenter's helper in Kansas. Returning to Galesburg, he worked for a while at his old job of delivering milk, and then started what, but for the Spanish-American war, might have been his regular occupation —the trade of house painter. But with the outbreak of the war, Sandburg enlisted in Company C of the Sixth Illinois Infantry, and was sent to Puerto Rico, where he served for eight months. In the army he met a student from Lombard College, Galesburg, who so aroused his interest in college that when the war was ended and Sandburg was mustered out, he took the hundred-dollar bonus he was given and entered Lombard as a special student.

He attended the college from 1898 to 1902, making his way by working as janitor of the gymnasium, ringing the college bell, and tutoring. In college he was captain of the basketball team, and editor of both the college monthly magazine and the college annual. There, too, he came into contact with Philip Green Wright, one of the teachers of the college, and became a member of the Poor Writers' Club, which Wright organized, and the members of which read and criticized one another's prose and verse.

After leaving college, Sandburg travelled for a while, selling films for Underwood and Underwood. In 1907-1908 he was a district organizer for the Social-Democrat party of Wisconsin. Next he did newspaper work in Milwaukee, and there on June 15, 1908, he married Lillian Steichen. From 1910 to 1912 he was secretary to Emil Seidel, the first Socialist mayor of Milwaukee. Going to Chicago, he was associated for a while with the magazine *System*, and then assisted N. D. Cochran in the experiment of running a newspaper, the *Daybook*, without advertising. When this journal ceased publication in 1917, Sandburg joined the staff of the Chicago *Daily News*. In 1918 he travelled in Norway and Sweden as a reporter for the Newspaper Enterprise Association. After returning from this trip, he again joined the staff of the *Daily News*, continuing as editorial writer for this newspaper for several years.

Sandburg's first volume, a paper-bound pamphlet entitled *In Reckless Ecstasy*, was issued privately in 1904. It was not until 1914, however, that he received any recognition as a poet. In that year *Poetry: A Magazine of Verse* published a number of his poems, including "Chicago," for which he received the Levinson Prize. In 1916 *Chicago Poems* appeared, followed by *Cornhuskers* (1918), *Smoke and Steel* (1920), *Slabs of the Sunburnt West* (1922), *Good Morning, America* (1928), and *The People, Yes* (1936). In 1927 he published a collection of ballads he had gathered over a period of several years, *The American Songbag*. In 1922 and 1923, respectively, he published the children's books *Rootabaga Stories* and *Rootabaga Pigeons*. In 1926 came his first work on Lincoln, *The Prairie Years*, and later (with Paul M. Angle) *Mary Lincoln, Wife and Widow* (1932) and *Abraham Lincoln: The War Years* (1939). For the latter he was awarded a Pulitzer Prize.

In 1919 and again in 1921 Sandburg shared half of the award of the Poetry Society of America. In 1928 he was the Phi Beta Kappa poet at Harvard. He has been given many honorary degrees: Litt.D. by Lombard (1928), Knox (1929), Northwestern (1931), New

York University (1940), Yale (1940), and Harvard (1940); and LL.D. by Rollins (1940).

He is a member of the American Academy of Arts and Letters; and in 1934 he was a special lecturer at the University of Hawaii. He has been conspicuously successful as an interpreter of his own work. For a number of years he has travelled across the United States, lecturing, reading his own poems, singing folk songs, studying local customs, and collecting local ballads. More recently he has added to his activities reading and speaking over the radio.

Sandburg lives near Harbert, Michigan, on a bluff overlooking Lake Michigan. He is the father of three daughters.

CHICAGO

Hog Butcher for the World,
Tool Maker, Stacker of Wheat,
Player with Railroads and the Nation's
  Freight Handler;
Stormy, husky, brawling,
City of the Big Shoulders:

They tell me you are wicked and I believe them, for I have seen
  your painted women under the gas lamps luring the farm
  boys.
And they tell me you are crooked and I answer: Yes, it is true
  I have seen the gunman kill and go free to kill again.
And they tell me you are brutal and my reply is: On the faces of
  women and children I have seen the marks of wanton hunger.
And having answered so I turn once more to those who sneer
  at this my city, and I give them back the sneer and say to
  them:
Come and show me another city with lifted head singing so proud
  to be alive and coarse and strong and cunning.
Flinging magnetic curses amid the toil of piling job on job, here
  is a tall bold slugger set vivid against the little soft cities;
Fierce as a dog with tongue lapping for action, cunning as a savage
  pitted against the wilderness,
    Bareheaded,
    Shoveling,
    Wrecking,
    Planning,
    Building, breaking, rebuilding,

Under the smoke, dust all over his mouth, laughing with white teeth,
Under the terrible burden of destiny laughing as a young man laughs,
Laughing even as an ignorant fighter laughs who has never lost a battle,
Bragging and laughing that under his wrist is the pulse, and under his ribs the heart of the people,
Laughing!
Laughing the stormy, husky, brawling laughter of Youth, half-naked, sweating, proud to be Hog Butcher, Tool Maker, Stacker of Wheat, Player with Railroads and Freight Handler to the Nation.

1916

LOST

Desolate and lone
All night long on the lake
Where fog trails and mist creeps,
The whistle of a boat
Calls and cries unendingly,
Like some lost child
In tears and trouble
Hunting the harbor's breast
And the harbor's eyes.

1916

AT A WINDOW

Give me hunger,
O you gods that sit and give
The world its orders.
Give me hunger, pain and want,
Shut me out with shame and failure
From your doors of gold and fame,
Give me your shabbiest, weariest hunger!

But leave me a little love,
A voice to speak to me in the day end,

A hand to touch me in the dark room
Breaking the long loneliness.
In the dusk of day-shapes
Blurring the sunset,
One little wandering, western star
Thrust out from the changing shores of shadow.
Let me go to the window,
Watch there the day-shapes of dusk
And wait and know the coming
Of a little love.

1916

MONOTONE

The monotone of the rain is beautiful,
And the sudden rise and slow relapse
Of the long multitudinous rain.

The sun on the hills is beautiful,
Or a captured sunset sea-flung,
Bannered with fire and gold.

A face I know is beautiful—
With fire and gold of sky and sea,
And the peace of long warm rain.

1916

PRAIRIE

I was born on the prairie and the milk of its wheat, the red of its clover, the eyes of its women, gave me a song and a slogan.

Here the water went down, the icebergs slid with gravel, the gaps and the valleys hissed, and the black loam came, and the yellow sandy loam.
Here between the sheds of the Rocky Mountains and the Appalachians, here now a morning star fixes a fire sign over the timber claims and cow pastures, the corn belt, the cotton belt, the cattle ranches.
Here the gray geese go five hundred miles and back with a wind under their wings honking the cry for a new home.
Here I know I will hanker after nothing so much as one more

sunrise or a sky moon of fire doubled to a river moon of water.

The prairie sings to me in the forenoon and I know in the night I rest easy in the prairie arms, on the prairie heart.

* * * * *

After the sunburn of the day
handling a pitchfork at a hayrack,
after the eggs and biscuit and coffee,
the pearl-gray haystacks
in the gloaming
are cool prayers
to the harvest hands.

In the city among the walls the overland passenger train is choked and the pistons hiss and the wheels curse.
On the prairie the overland flits on phantom wheels and the sky and the soil between them muffle the pistons and cheer the wheels.

* * * * *

I am here when the cities are gone.
I am here before the cities come.
I nourished the lonely men on horses.
I will keep the laughing men who ride iron.
I am dust of men.

The running water babbled to the deer, the cottontail, the gopher.
You came in wagons, making streets and schools,
Kin of the ax and rifie, kin of the plow and horse,
Singing *Yankee Doodle, Old Dan Tucker, Turkey in the Straw,*
You in the coonskin cap at a log house door hearing a lone wolf howl,
You at a sod house door reading the blizzards and chinooks let loose from Medicine Hat,
I am dust of your dust, as I am brother and mother
To the copper faces, the worker in flint and clay,
The singing women and their sons a thousand years ago
Marching single file the timber and the plain.

I hold the dust of these amid changing stars.
I last while old wars are fought, while peace broods motherlike,

While new wars arise and the fresh killings of young men.
I fed the boys who went to France in great dark days.
Appomattox is a beautiful word to me and so is Valley Forge and the Marne and Verdun,
I who have seen the red births, and the red deaths
Of sons and daughters, I take peace or war, I say nothing and wait.

Have you seen a red sunset drip over one of my cornfields, the shore of night stars, the wave lines of dawn up a wheat valley?
Have you heard my threshing crews yelling in the chaff of a strawpile and the running wheat of the wagonboards, my cornhuskers, my harvest hands hauling crops, singing dreams of women, worlds, horizons?

* * * * *

Rivers cut a path on flat lands.
The mountains stand up.
The salt oceans press in
And push on the coast lines.
The sun, the wind, bring rain
And I know what the rainbow writes across the east or west in a half-circle:
A love-letter pledge to come again.

* * * * *

Towns on the Soo Line,
Towns on the Big Muddy,
Laugh at each other for cubs
And tease as children.

Omaha and Kansas City, Minneapolis and St. Paul, sisters in a house together, throwing slang, growing up.
Towns in the Ozarks, Dakota wheat towns, Wichita, Peoria, Buffalo, sisters throwing slang, growing up.

* * * * *

Out of prairie-brown grass crossed with a streamer of wigwam smoke—out of a smoke pillar, a blue promise—out of wild ducks woven in greens and purples—
Here I saw a city rise and say to the peoples round world: Listen, I am strong, I know what I want.
Out of log houses and stumps—canoes stripped from tree-sides—flatboats coaxed with an ax from the timber claims—in the

years when the red and the white men met—the houses and streets rose.

A thousand red men cried and went away to new places for corn and women: a million white men came and put up skyscrapers, threw out rails and wires, feelers to the salt sea: now the smokestacks bite the skyline with stub teeth.

In an early year the call of a wild duck woven in greens and purples: now the riveter's chatter, the police patrol, the song-whistle of the steamboat.

To a man across a thousand years I offer a handshake.
I say to him: Brother, make the story short, for the stretch of a thousand years is short.

* * * * *

What brothers these in the dark?
What eaves of skyscrapers against a smoke moon?
These chimneys shaking on the lumber shanties
When the coal boats plow by on the river—
The hunched shoulders of the grain elevators—
The flame sprockets of the sheet steel mills
And the men in the rolling mills with their shirts off
Playing their flesh arms against the twisting wrists of steel:
what brothers these
in the dark
of a thousand years?

* * * * *

A headlight searches a snowstorm.
A funnel of white light shoots from over the pilot of the Poineer Limited crossing Wisconsin.

In the morning hours, in the dawn,
The sun puts out the stars of the sky
And the headlight of the Limited train.

The fireman waves his hand to a country school teacher on a bobsled.
A boy, yellow hair, red scarf and mittens, on the bobsled, in his lunch box a pork chop sandwich and a V of gooseberry pie.

The horses fathom a snow to their knees.
Snow hats are on the rolling prairie hills.
The Mississippi bluffs wear snow hats.

* * * * *

Keep your hogs on changing corn and mashes of grain,
O farmerman.
Cram their insides till they waddle on short legs
Under the drums of bellies, hams of fat.
Kill your hogs with a knife slit under the ear.
Hack them with cleavers.
Hang them with hooks in the hind legs.

* * * * *

A wagonload of radishes on a summer morning.
Sprinkles of dew on the crimson-purple balls.
The farmer on the seat dangles the reins on the rumps of dapple-gray horses.
The farmer's daughter with a basket of eggs dreams of a new hat to wear to the county fair.

* * * * *

On the left- and right-hand side of the road,
Marching corn—
I saw it knee high weeks ago—now it is head high—tassels of red silk creep at the ends of the ears.

* * * * *

I am the prairie, mother of men, waiting.
They are mine, the threshing crews eating beefsteak, the farmboys driving steers to the railroad cattle pens.
They are mine, the crowds of people at a Fourth of July basket picnic, listening to a lawyer read the Declaration of Independence, watching the pinwheels and Roman candles at night, the young men and women two by two hunting the bypaths and kissing bridges.
They are mine, the horses looking over a fence in the frost of late October, saying good-morning to the horses hauling wagons of rutabaga to market.
They are mine, the old zigzag rail fences, the new barb wire.

* * * * *

The cornhuskers wear leather on their hands.
There is no let-up to the wind.
Blue bandannas are knotted at the ruddy chins.

Falltime and winter apples take on the smolder of the five-o'clock
November sunset: falltime, leaves, bonfires, stubble, the old things go, and the earth is grizzled.
The land and the people hold memories, even among the anthills and the angleworms, among the toads and woodroaches —among gravestone writings rubbed out by the rain—they keep old things that never grow old.

The frost loosens corn husks.
The sun, the rain, the wind
loosen corn husks.
The men and women are helpers.
They are all cornhuskers together.
I see them late in the western evening
in a smoke-red dust.

* * * * *

The phantom of a yellow rooster flaunting a scarlet comb, on top of a dung pile crying hallelujah to the streaks of daylight,
The phantom of an old hunting dog nosing in the underbrush for muskrats, barking at a coon in a treetop at midnight, chewing a bone, chasing his tail round a corncrib,
The phantom of an old workhorse taking the steel point of a plow across a forty-acre field in spring, hitched to a harrow in summer, hitched to a wagon among cornshocks in fall,
These phantoms come into the talk and wonder of people on the front porch of a farmhouse late summer nights.
"The shapes that are gone are here," said an old man with a cob pipe in his teeth one night in Kansas with a hot wind on the alfalfa.

* * * * *

Look at six eggs
In a mockingbird's nest.

Listen to six mockingbirds
Flinging follies of O-be-joyful
Over the marshes and uplands.

Look at songs
Hidden in eggs.

* * * * *

When the morning sun is on the trumpet-vine blossoms, sing at the kitchen pans: *Shout All Over God's Heaven.*
When the rain slants on the potato hills and the sun plays a silver shaft on the last shower, sing to the bush at the backyard fence: *Mighty Lak a Rose.*
When the icy sleet pounds on the storm windows and the house lifts to a great breath, sing for the outside hills: *The Ole Sheep Done Know the Road, the Young Lambs Must Find the Way.*

* * * * *

Spring slips back with a girl face calling always: "Any new songs for me? Any new songs?"

O prairie girl, be lonely, singing, dreaming, waiting—your lover comes—your child comes—the years creep with toes of April rain on new-turned sod.
O prairie girl, whoever leaves you only crimson poppies to talk with, whoever puts a good-by kiss on your lips and never comes back—
There is a song deep as the falltime red haws, long as the layer of black loam we go to, the shine of the morning star over the corn belt, the wave line of dawn up a wheat valley.

* * * * *

O prairie mother, I am one of your boys.
I have loved the prairie as a man with a heart shot full of pain over love.
Here I know I will hanker after nothing so much as one more sunrise or a sky moon of fire doubled to a river moon of water.

* * * * *

I speak of new cities and new people.
I tell you the past is a bucket of ashes.
I tell you yesterday is a wind gone down,
a sun dropped in the west.
I tell you there is nothing in the world
only an ocean of to-morrows,
a sky of to-morrows.

I am a brother of the cornhuskers who say
at sundown:
To-morrow is a day.

1918

CABOOSE THOUGHTS

It's going to come out all right—do you know?
The sun, the birds, the grass—they know.
They get along—and we'll get along.

Some days will be rainy and you will sit waiting
And the letter you wait for won't come,
And I will sit watching the sky tear off gray and gray
And the letter I wait for won't come.

There will be ac-ci-dents.
I know ac-ci-dents are coming.
Smash-ups, signals wrong, washouts, trestles rotten,
Red and yellow ac-ci-dents.
But somehow and somewhere the end of the run
The train gets put together again
And the caboose and the green tail lights
Fade down the right of way like a new white hope.

I never heard a mockingbird in Kentucky
Spilling its heart in the morning.

I never saw the snow on Chimborazo.
It's a high white Mexican hat, I hear.

I never had supper with Abe Lincoln,
Nor a dish of soup with Jim Hill.

But I've been around.
I know some of the boys here who can go a little.
I know girls good for a burst of speed any time.

I heard Williams and Walker
Before Walker died in the bughouse.

I knew a mandolin player
Working in a barber shop in an Indiana town,
And he thought he had a million dollars.

I knew a hotel girl in Des Moines.
She had eyes; I saw her and said to myself

The sun rises and the sun sets in her eyes.
I was her steady and her heart went pit-a-pat.
We took away the money for a prize waltz at a Brotherhood
    dance.
She had eyes; she was safe as the bridge over the Mississippi at
    Burlington; I married her.

Last summer we took the cushions going west.
Pike's Peak is a big old stone, believe me.
It's fastened down; something you can count on.

It's going to come out all right—do you know?
The sun, the birds, the grass—they know.
They get along—and we'll get along.

1918

LOAM

In the loam we sleep,
In the cool moist loam,
To the lull of years that pass
And the break of stars,

From the loam, then,
The soft warm loam,
  We rise:
To shape of rose leaf,
Of face and shoulder.

  We stand, then,
  To a whiff of life,
Lifted to the silver of the sun
Over and out of the loam
  A day.

1918

PRAYERS OF STEEL

Lay me on an anvil, O God.
Beat me and hammer me into a crowbar.
Let me pry loose old walls.
Let me lift and loosen old foundations.

Lay me on an anvil, O God.
Beat me and hammer me into a steel spike.
Drive me into the girders that hold a skyscraper together.
Take red-hot rivets and fasten me into the central girders.
Let me be the great nail holding a skyscraper through blue nights into white stars.

1918

COOL TOMBS

When Abraham Lincoln was shoveled into the tombs, he forgot the copperheads and the assassin . . . in the dust, in the cool tombs.

And Ulysses Grant lost all thought of con men and Wall Street, cash and collateral turned ashes . . . in the dust, in the cool tombs.

Pocahontas' body, lovely as a poplar, sweet as a red haw in November or a pawpaw in May, did she wonder? does she remember? . . . in the dust, in the cool tombs?

Take any streetful of people buying clothes and groceries, cheering a hero or throwing confetti and blowing tin horns . . . tell me if the lovers are losers . . . tell me if any get more than the lovers . . . in the dust . . . in the cool tombs.

1918

HOUSE

Two Swede families live downstairs and an Irish policeman upstairs, and an old soldier, Uncle Joe.
Two Swede boys go upstairs and see Joe. His wife is dead, his only son is dead, and his two daughters in Missouri and Texas don't want him around.
The boys and Uncle Joe crack walnuts with a hammer on the bottom of a flatiron while the January wind howls and the zero air weaves laces on the window glass.
Joe tells the Swede boys all about Chickamauga and Chattanooga, how the Union soldiers crept in rain somewhere a dark night and ran forward and killed many Rebels, took flags, held a hill, and won a victory told about in the histories in school.

Joe takes a piece of carpenter's chalk, draws lines on the floor and piles stove wood to show where six regiments were slaughtered climbing a slope.
"Here they went" and "Here they went," says Joe, and the January wind howls and the zero air weaves laces on the window glass.
The two Swede boys go downstairs with a big blur of guns, men, and hills in their heads. They eat herring and potatoes and tell the family war is a wonder and soldiers are a wonder.
One breaks out with a cry at supper: I wish we had a war now and I could be a soldier.

1918

RED-HEADED RESTAURANT CASHIER

Shake back your hair, O red-headed girl.
Let go your laughter and keep your two proud freckles on your chin.
Somewhere is a man looking for a red-headed girl and some day maybe he will look into your eyes for a restaurant cashier and find a lover, maybe.
Around and around go ten thousand men hunting a red-headed girl with two freckles on her chin.
I have seen them hunting, hunting.
Shake back your hair; let go your laughter.

1920

THE HANGMAN AT HOME

What does the hangman think about
When he goes home at night from work?
When he sits down with his wife and
Children for a cup of coffee and a
Plate of ham and eggs, do they ask
Him if it was a good day's work
And everything went well, or do they
Stay off some topics and talk about
The weather, baseball, politics
And the comic strips in the papers
And the movies? Do they look at his
Hands when he reaches for the coffee

Or the ham and eggs? If the little
Ones say, Daddy, play horse, here's
A rope—does he answer like a joke:
I seen enough rope for to-day?
Or does his face light up like a
Bonfire of joy and does he say:
It's a good and dandy world we live
In. And if a white face moon looks
In through a window where a baby girl
Sleeps and the moon gleams mix with
Baby ears and baby hair—the hangman—
How does he act then? It must be easy
For him. Anything is easy for a hangman,
I guess.

1920

DEATH SNIPS PROUD MEN

Death is stronger than all the governments because the governments are men and men die and then death laughs: Now you see 'em, now you don't.

Death is stronger than all proud men and so death snips proud men on the nose, throws a pair of dice and says: Read 'em and weep.

Death sends a radiogram every day: When I want you I'll drop in —and then one day he comes with a master-key and lets himself in and says: We'll go now.

Death is a nurse mother with big arms: 'Twon't hurt you at all; it's your time now; you just need a long sleep, child; what have you had anyhow better than sleep?

1920

LOSERS

If I should pass the tomb of Jonah
I would stop there and sit for awhile;
Because I was swallowed one time deep in the dark
And came out alive after all.

If I pass the burial spot of Nero
I shall say to the wind, "Well, well!"—
I who have fiddled in a world on fire,
I who have done so many stunts not worth doing.

I am looking for the grave of Sinbad too.
I want to shake his ghost-hand and say,
"Neither of us died very early, did we?"

And the last sleeping-place of Nebuchadnezzar—
When I arrive there I shall tell the wind:
"You ate grass; I have eaten crow—
Who is better off now or next year?"

Jack Cade, John Brown, Jesse James,
There too I could sit down and stop for awhile.
I think I could tell their headstones:
"God, let me remember all good losers."

I could ask people to throw ashes on their heads
In the name of that sergeant at Belleau Woods,
Walking into the drumfires, calling his men,
"Come on, you . . . Do you want to live forever?"

1920

STARS, SONGS, FACES

Gather the stars if you wish it so.
Gather the songs and keep them.
Gather the faces of women.
Gather for keeping years and years.
        And then . . .
Loosen your hands, let go and say good-by,
    Let the stars and songs go.
    Let the faces and years go.
    Loosen your hands and say good-by.

1920

HELGA

The wishes on this child's mouth
Came like snow on marsh cranberries;
The tamarack kept something for her;
The wind is ready to help her shoes.
The north has loved her; she will be
A grandmother feeding geese on frosty
Mornings; she will understand
Early snow on the cranberries
Better and better then.

1920

SANDHILL PEOPLE

I took away three pictures.
One was a white gull forming a half-mile arch from the pines toward Waukegan.
One was a whistle in the little sandhills, a bird crying either to the sunset gone or the dusk come.
One was three spotted waterbirds, zigzagging, cutting scrolls and jags, writing a bird Sanscrit of wing points, half over the sand, half over the water, a half-love for the sea, a half-love for the land.

I took away three thoughts.
One was a thing my people call "love," a shut-in river hunting the sea, breaking white falls between tall clefts of hill country.
One was a thing my people call "silence," the wind running over the butter faced sand-flowers, running over the sea, and never heard of again.
One was a thing my people call "death," neither a whistle in the little sandhills, nor a bird Sanscrit of wing points, yet a coat all the stars and seas have worn, yet a face the beach wears between sunset and dusk.

1920

MIST FORMS

The sheets of night mist travel a long valley.
I know why you came at sundown in a scarf mist.

What was it we touched asking nothing and asking all?
How many times can death come and pay back what we saw?

In the oath of the sod, the lips that swore,
In the oath of night mist, nothing and all,
A riddle is here no man tells, no woman.

1920

NIGHT STUFF

Listen a while, the moon is a lovely woman, a lonely woman, lost in a silver dress, lost in a circus rider's silver dress.

Listen a while, the lake by night is a lonely woman, a lovely woman, circled with birches and pines mixing their green and white among stars shattered in spray clear nights.

I know the moon and the lake have twisted the roots under my heart the same as a lonely woman, a lovely woman, in a silver dress, in a circus rider's silver dress.

1920

FOR YOU

The peace of great doors be for you.
Wait at the knobs, at the panel oblongs.
Wait for the great hinges.

The peace of great churches be for you,
Where the players of loft pipe organs
Practice old lovely fragments, alone.

The peace of great books be for you,
Stains of pressed clover leaves on pages,
Bleach of the light of years held in leather.

The peace of great prairies be for you.
Listen among windplayers in cornfields,
The wind learning over its oldest music.

The peace of great seas be for you.
Wait on a hook of land, a rock footing
For you, wait in the salt wash.

The peace of great mountains be for you,
The sleep and the eyesight of eagles,
Sheet mist shadows and the long look across.

The peace of great hearts be for you,
Valves of the blood of the sun,
Pumps of the strongest wants we cry.

The peace of great silhouettes be for you,
Shadow dancers alive in your blood now,
Alive and crying, "Let us out, let us out."

The peace of great changes be for you.
Whisper, Oh beginners in the hills.
Tumble, Oh cubs—to-morrow belongs to you.

The peace of great loves be for you.
Rain, soak these roots; wind, shatter the dry rot.
Bars of sunlight, grips of the earth, hug these.

The peace of great ghosts be for you,
Phantoms of night-gray eyes, ready to go
To the fog-star dumps, to the fire-white doors.

Yes, the peace of great phantoms be for you,
Phantom iron men, mothers of bronze,
Keepers of the lean clean breeds.

1920

WASHINGTON MONUMENT BY NIGHT

I

The stone goes straight.
A lean swimmer dives into night sky,
Into half-moon mist.

II

Two trees are coal black.
This is a great white ghost between.
It is cool to look at.
Strong men, strong women, come here.

III

Eight years is a long time
To be fighting all the time.

IV

The republic is a dream.
Nothing happens unless first a dream.

V

The wind bit hard at Valley Forge one Christmas.
Soldiers tied rags on their feet.
Red footprints wrote on the snow . . .
. . . and stone shoots into stars here
. . . into half-moon mist to-night.

VI

Tongues wrangled dark at a man.
He buttoned his overcoat and stood alone.
In a snowstorm, red hollyberries, thoughts, he stood alone.

VII

Women said: He is lonely
. . . fighting . . . fighting . . . eight years . . .

VIII

The name of an iron man goes over the world.
It takes a long time to forget an iron man.

IX

. . . .
. . . .

1922

EXPLANATIONS OF LOVE

There is a place where love begins and a place where love ends.

There is a touch of two hands that foils all dictionaries.

There is a look of eyes fierce as a big Bethlehem open hearth furnace or a little green-fire acetylene torch.

There are single careless bywords portentous as a big bend in the Mississippi River.

Hands, eyes, bywords—out of these love makes battlegrounds and workshops.

There is a pair of shoes love wears and the coming is a mystery.

There is a warning love sends and the cost of it is never written till long afterward.

There are explanations of love in all languages and not one found wiser than this:

There is a place where love begins and a place where love ends —and love asks nothing.

1928

[THE PEOPLE, YES—]

[Section 29 of *The People, Yes*]

The people, yes—
Born with bones and heart fused in deep and violent secrets
Mixed from a bowl of sky blue dreams and sea slime facts—
A seething of saints and sinners, toilers, loafers, oxen, apes
In a womb of superstition, faith, genius, crime, sacrifice—
The one and only source of armies, navies, work-gangs,
The living flowing breath of the history of nations,
Of the little Family of Man hugging the little ball of Earth,
And a long hall of mirrors, straight, convex and concave,
Moving and endless with scrolls of the living,

Shimmering with phantoms flung from the past,
Shot over with lights of babies to come, not yet here.

The honorable orators, the gazettes of thunder,
The tycoons, big shots and dictators,
Flicker in the mirrors a few moments
And fade through the glass of death
For discussion in an autocracy of worms
While the rootholds of the earth nourish the majestic people
And the new generations with names never heard of
Plow deep in broken drums and shoot craps for old crowns,
Shouting unimagined shibboleths and slogans,
Tracing their heels in moth-eaten insignia of bawdy leaders—
Piling revolt on revolt across night valleys,
Letting loose insurrections, uprisings, strikes,
Marches, mass-meetings, banners, declared resolves,
Plodding in a somnambulism of fog and rain
Till a given moment exploded by long-prepared events—
Then again the overthrow of an old order
And the trials of another new authority
And death and taxes, crops and droughts,
Chinch bugs, grasshoppers, corn borers, boll weevils,
Top soil farms blown away in a dust and wind,
Inexorable rains carrying off rich loam,
And mortgages, house rent, groceries,
Jobs, pay cuts, layoffs, relief
And passion and poverty and crime
And the paradoxes not yet resolved
Of the shrewd and elusive proverbs,
The have-you-heard yarns,
The listen-to-this anecdote
Made by the people out of the roots of the earth,
Out of dirt, barns, workshops, time-tables,
Out of lumberjack payday jamborees,
Out of joybells and headaches the day after,
Out of births, weddings, accidents,
Out of wars, laws, promises, betrayals,
Out of mists of the lost and anonymous,
Out of plain living, early rising and spare belongings.

1936

Vachel Lindsay

Nicholas Vachel Lindsay, one of the six children of Dr. Vachel T. and Catherine Frazee Lindsay, was born November 10, 1879, in Springfield, Illinois. He was of Scotch descent, with some admixture of English, Welsh, and Spanish. His immediate forebears, on both sides, were Southerners. The Lindsay household was religious, yet in it also prevailed an interest in artistic and cultural matters. Dr. Lindsay, a thrifty and practical man, was fond of reading and of singing to his children and telling them stories, particularly the tales of Uncle Remus. More important, Mrs. Lindsay maintained an active interest in works of art; and through her the tastes of her son were largely shaped.

Because of an illness as a baby Lindsay was not sent to school for his first instruction, but was taught to read by his mother—from a volume of Grimm's *Fairy Tales*. Like the other children of the household, he was required to memorize a passage from the Bible daily. He early discovered the beauty of Poe's verse, read Rawlinson's *History of Egypt* and Stanley's *Darkest Africa*, and pored over Gustave Doré's illustrations of the *Inferno* and *Paradise Lost*. Apparently his parents early decided that he should adopt the profession of his father, that of physician. They gave him, as they did all their children, the best education within their means. After a brief period in a private school he was sent to one of the grade schools of Springfield, then to the high school, where he distinguished himself by writing verse and reading Shakespeare impressively. In the fall of 1897 he matriculated at Hiram College, Ohio, but his record as a student at that institution was not satisfactory. A growing desire to go his own way, to give expression to ideas now taking hold of him, made Lindsay chafe under the routine of college life; and despite the objection of his family, he left the college at the end of three years and went to Chicago for training at the Art Institute.

From 1900 to 1904 he lived in Chicago, studying drawing and writing much verse, which editors invariably refused to print. In 1904 he left the city to seek further instruction in the Chase School in New York City. Here he spent most of the next four years, working at his drawings, visiting the Metropolitan Museum, attending exhibits, haunting galleries, and supporting himself in the meantime by lecturing to art classes at a West Side Y. M. C. A. As time passed without his being able to establish himself by means of his paintings and drawings, he turned more and more to the writing of verse, seeing in this, as in his pictures, the possibilities of effecting a cultural revolution—of making America a more beautiful and civilized country and Americans a happier people. In 1906 he tramped from Florida to Tennessee, making the first of several walking tours over parts of the country in the interests of what he called "the Gospel of Beauty." On this, as on his other trips, he traded pamphlets containing his verse and drawings for food and shelter, and talked and read to all who showed an interest in what he had to say. His parents were displeased at his assumption of the rôle of beggar and in order to induce him to abandon his plan offered to take him on a trip to Europe. The summer of 1906, therefore, the three spent abroad, visiting together the great art galleries of England and the Continent. In 1908 Lindsay made another "poetic pilgrimage" among the people, this time into New Jersey and Pennsylvania.

In 1909 he returned to Springfield, but his homecoming was not a happy one. He was now almost thirty years old, and he had settled down to no steady occupation. His parents were disappointed in him, and failed to understand the dreams of a more beautiful America—and in particular of a more beautiful Springfield—which now motivated his conduct. Still less did the citizens of the city understand him. He came to be regarded as a crank, and his efforts on behalf of civic reform and his proposal to bring poetry home to the hearts of the people as visionary. He organized groups in the city for the purpose of discussing literature; he worked to have elected to office commissioners who seemed to desire a better Springfield; he issued what he called *War Bulletins*, pamphlets containing his writings and drawings, directed against the Philistine elements of the city; and from time to time he lectured in central Illinois in support of the Anti-Saloon League. At length, in 1912, after wearying of the combat with his fellow townsmen, he set out on another tramping tour through Missouri, Kansas, Colorado, and into New Mexico. On the way west he found new literary material and wrote much new verse; and after the trip had come to an end he began the composition of one poem—"General William Booth Enters into Heaven"—which was to bring him, for the first time, to the attention of the public.

In January, 1913, this poem was printed in *Poetry: A Magazine of Verse*; and later in the same year appeared his first important volume, *General William Booth Enters into Heaven and Other Poems*. His reputation was now quickly established. Within a few years he was known to readers throughout the country, and he entered upon a busy career, publishing seven or eight volumes of verse as well as several volumes of prose—among them being *The Art of the Moving Picture* (1915) and *The Golden Book of Springfield* (1920). By 1920 he had become a successful and popular lecturer on poetry and reader of his own work. For several seasons his readings were the most fashionable literary events of the time; and he was so constantly in demand, and his popularity was so great, that he was deceived into believing that a great poetic renaissance had appeared. He failed to see that many of those who applauded him were interested, not in poetry, but in his showmanship. His booming voice, his dynamic personality, the enthusiasm he brought to the interpretations of his poems won him a success which was encouraging but which did not last when time brought new literary fashions.

In the summer of 1920 he visited England, appearing before audiences at the English universities and in London. For three semesters, in 1923-1924, he conducted classes in literature at Gulf Park College, in Mississippi. From there he went to Spokane, Washington, where in 1925 he married Elizabeth Conner and where for three years he lived. In 1929, however, he returned to Springfield. His last days were saddened by the realization that his creative powers had waned and his popularity declined. Physically and mentally ill, harassed by debts and the sense of defeat, he committed suicide on December 5, 1931, in the house in which he had lived as a boy. He was survived by his wife and two children, a son and a daughter. His body was buried in Oak Park Cemetery, Springfield.

I HEARD IMMANUEL SINGING

The poem shows the Master with his work done, singing to free his heart in Heaven.

This poem is intended to be half said, half sung, very softly, to the well-known tune:

> *"Last night I lay a-sleeping,*
> *There came a dream so fair,*
> *I stood in Old Jerusalem*
> *Beside the temple there,"—etc.*

Yet this tune is not to be fitted on, arbitrarily. It is here given to suggest the manner of handling rather than determine it.

I heard Immanuel singing *To be sung.*
Within his own good lands;
I saw him bend above his harp.
I watched his wandering hands
Lost amid the harp-strings;
Sweet, sweet I heard him play.
His wounds were altogether healed.
Old things had passed away.

All things were new, but music.
The blood of David ran
Within the Son of David,
Our God, the Son of Man.
He was ruddy like a shepherd.
His bold young face, how fair.
Apollo of the silver bow
Had not such flowing hair.

I saw Immanuel singing *To be read very softly, but in spirited response.*
On a tree-girdled hill.
The glad remembering branches
Dimly echoed still
The grand new song proclaiming
The Lamb that had been slain.
New-built, the Holy City
Gleamed in the murmuring plain.

The crowning hours were over.
The pageants all were past.
Within the many mansions
The hosts, grown still at last,
In homes of holy mystery
Slept long by crooning springs
Or waked to peaceful glory,
A universe of Kings.

He left his people happy.
He wandered free to sigh
Alone in lowly friendship
With the green grass and the sky.
He murmured ancient music
His red heart burned to sing
Because his perfect conquest
Had grown a weary thing.

To be sung.

No chant of gilded triumph—
His lonely song was made
Of Art's deliberate freedom;
Of minor chords arrayed
In soft and shadowy colors
That once were radiant flowers:—
The Rose of Sharon, bleeding
In Olive-shadowed bowers:—

And all the other roses
In the songs of East and West
Of love and war and worshipping,
And every shield and crest
Of thistle or of lotus
Or sacred lily wrought
In creeds and psalms and palaces
And temples of white thought:—

All these he sang, half-smiling
And weeping as he smiled,
Laughing, talking to his harp
As to a new-born child:—
As though the arts forgotten
But bloomed to prophecy
These careless, fearless harp-strings,
New-crying in the sky.

To be read very softly, yet in spirited response.

"When this his hour of sorrow *To be sung.*
For flowers and Arts of men
Has passed in ghostly music,"
I asked my wild heart then—
What will he sing to-morrow,
What wonder, all his own
Alone, set free, rejoicing
With a green hill for his throne?
What will he sing to-morrow,
What wonder all his own
Alone, set free, rejoicing,
With a green hill for his throne?

1906, 1909

PROLOGUE TO "RHYMES TO BE TRADED FOR BREAD"

Even the shrewd and bitter,
Gnarled by the old world's greed,
Cherished the stranger softly
Seeing his utter need.
Shelter and patient hearing,
These were their gifts to him,
To the minstrel chanting, begging,
As the sunset-fire grew dim.
The rich said, "You are welcome."
Yea, even the rich were good.
How strange that in their feasting
His songs were understood!
The doors of the poor were open,
The poor who had wandered too,
Who slept with never a roof-tree
Under the wind and dew.
The minds of the poor were open,
There dark mistrust was dead:
They loved his wizard stories,
They bought his rhymes with bread.

Those were his days of glory,
Of faith in his fellow-men.
Therefore, to-day the singer
Turns beggar once again.

1912

GENERAL WILLIAM BOOTH ENTERS INTO HEAVEN

(To be sung to the tune of "The Blood of the Lamb" with indicated instrument.)

I

(Bass drum beaten loudly.)
Booth led boldly with his big bass drum—
(Are you washed in the blood of the Lamb?)
The Saints smiled gravely and they said: "He's come."
(Are you washed in the blood of the Lamb?)
Walking lepers followed, rank on rank,
Lurching bravos from the ditches dank,
Drabs from the alleyways and drug fiends pale—
Minds still passion-ridden, soul-powers frail:—
Vermin-eaten saints with moldy breath,
Unwashed legions with the ways of Death—
(Are you washed in the blood of the Lamb?)

(Banjos.)
Every slum had sent its half-a-score
The round world over. (Booth had groaned for more.)
Every banner that the wide world flies
Bloomed with glory and transcendent dyes.
Big-voiced lasses made their banjos bang;
Tranced, fanatical they shrieked and sang:—
"Are you washed in the blood of the Lamb?"
Hallelujah! It was queer to see
Bull-necked convicts with that land make free.
Loons with trumpets blowed a blare, blare, blare
On, on upward thro' the golden air!
(Are you washed in the blood of the Lamb?)

II

(Bass drum slower and softer.)
Booth died blind and still by faith he trod,
Eyes still dazzled by the ways of God.
Booth led boldly, and he looked the chief,
Eagle countenance in sharp relief,
Beard a-flying, air of high command
Unabated in that holy land.

(*Sweet flute music.*)
Jesus came from out the court-house door,
Stretched his hands above the passing poor.
Booth saw not, but led his queer ones there
Round and round the mighty court-house square.
Then, in an instant all that blear review
Marched on spotless, clad in raiment new.
The lame were straightened, withered limbs uncurled
And blind eyes opened on a new, sweet world.

(*Bass drum louder.*)
Drabs and vixens in a flash made whole!
Gone was the weasel-head, the snout, the jowl!
Sages and sibyls now, and athletes clean,
Rulers of empires, and of forests green!

(*Grand chorus of all instruments. Tambourines to the foreground.*)
The hosts were sandalled, and their wings were fire!
(Are you washed in the blood of the Lamb?)
But their noise played havoc with the angel-choir.
(Are you washed in the blood of the Lamb?)
Oh, shout Salvation! It was good to see
Kings and Princes by the Lamb set free.
The banjos rattled and the tambourines
Jing-jing-jingled in the hands of Queens.

(*Reverently sung, no instruments.*)
And when Booth halted by the curb for prayer
He saw his Master thro' the flag-filled air.
Christ came gently with a robe and crown
For Booth the soldier, while the throng knelt down.
He saw King Jesus. They were face to face,
And he knelt a-weeping in that holy place.
Are you washed in the blood of the Lamb?

1913

THE GAMBLERS

Life's a jail where men have common lot.
Gaunt the one who has, and who has not.
All our treasures neither less nor more,
Bread alone comes through the guarded door.
Cards are foolish in this jail, I think,
Yet they play for shoes, for drabs and drink.
She, my lawless, sharp-tongued gypsy maid,
Will not scorn with me this jail-bird trade,
Pets some fox-eyed boy who turns the trick,
Though he win a button or a stick,
Pencil, garter, ribbon, corset-lace—
His the glory, *mine* is the disgrace.

Sweet, I'd rather lose than win despite
Love of hearty words and maids polite.
"Love's a gamble," say you. I deny.
Love's a gift. I love you till I die.
Gamblers fight like rats. I will not play.
All I ever had I gave away.
All I ever coveted was peace
Such as comes if we have jail release.
Cards are puzzles, though the prize be gold;
Cards help not the bread that tastes of mold;
Cards dye not your hair to black more deep;
Cards make not the children cease to weep.

Scorned, I sit with half-shut eyes all day—
Watch the cataract of sunshine play
Down the wall, and dance upon the floor.
Sun, come down and break the dungeon door!
Of such gold dust could I make a key,—
Turn the bolt—how soon we would be free!
Over borders we would hurry on
Safe by sunrise farms, and springs of dawn,
Wash our wounds and jail stains there at last,
Azure rivers flowing, flowing past.
God has great estates just past the line,
Green farms for all, and meat and corn and wine.

1913

THE EAGLE THAT IS FORGOTTEN

JOHN P. ALTGELD. BORN DECEMBER 30, 1847; DIED MARCH 12, 1902.

Sleep softly . . . eagle forgotten . . . under the stone.
Time has its way with you there, and the clay has its own.

"We have buried him now," thought your foes, and in secret
 rejoiced.
They made a brave show of their mourning, their hatred unvoiced.
They had snarled at you, barked at you, foamed at you day after
 day.
Now you were ended. They praised you, . . . and laid you away.

The others that mourned you in silence and terror and truth,
The widow bereft of her crust, and the boy without youth,
The mocked and the scorned and the wounded, the lame and
 the poor
That should have remembered forever, . . . remember no more.

Where are those lovers of yours, on what name do they call,
The lost, that in armies wept over your funeral pall?
They call on the names of a hundred high-valiant ones;
A hundred white eagles have risen the sons of your sons;
The zeal in their wings is a zeal that your dreaming began,
The valor that wore out your soul in the service of man.

Sleep softly, . . . eagle forgotten, . . . under the stone,
Time has its way with you there, and the clay has its own.
Sleep on, O brave-hearted, O wise man, that kindled the flame—
To live in mankind is far more than to live in a name,
To live in mankind, far, far more . . . than to live in a name.

1913

A NET TO SNARE THE MOONLIGHT

(WHAT THE MAN OF FAITH SAID)

The dew, the rain and moonlight
All prove our Father's mind.
The dew, the rain and moonlight
Descend to bless mankind.

Come, let us see that all men
Have land to catch the rain,
Have grass to snare the spheres of dew,
And fields spread for the grain.

Yea, we would give to each poor man
Ripe wheat and poppies red,—
A peaceful place at evening
With the stars just overhead:

A net to snare the moonlight,
A sod spread to the sun,
A place of toil by daytime,
Of dreams when toil is done.

1913

THE CONGO

A STUDY OF THE NEGRO RACE

I. THEIR BASIC SAVAGERY

Fat black bucks in a wine-barrel room,
Barrel-house kings, with feet unstable,
Sagged and reeled and pounded on the table,
Pounded on the table,
Beat an empty barrel with the handle of a broom,
Hard as they were able,
Boom, boom, BOOM,
With a silk unbrella and the handle of a broom,
Boomlay, boomlay, boomlay, BOOM.
THEN I had religion, THEN I had a vision.
I could not turn from their revel in derision.

A deep rolling bass.

THEN I SAW THE CONGO, CREEPING THROUGH THE BLACK,
CUTTING THROUGH THE FOREST WITH A GOLDEN TRACK.

More deliberate. Solemnly chanted.

Then along that riverbank
A thousand miles
Tattooed cannibals danced in files;
Then I heard the boom of the blood-lust song
And a thigh-bone beating on a tin-pan gong.
And "BLOOD" screamed the whistles and the fifes of the warriors,

A rapidly piling climax of speed and racket.

"Blood" screamed the skull-faced, lean witch-doctors,
"Whirl ye the deadly voo-doo rattle,
Harry the uplands,
Steal all the cattle,
Rattle-rattle, rattle-rattle,
Bing.
Boomlay, boomlay, boomlay, BOOM,"
A roaring, epic, rag-time tune
From the mouth of the Congo
To the Mountains of the Moon.
Death is an Elephant,
Torch-eyed and horrible,
Foam-flanked and terrible.
Boom, steal the pygmies,
Boom, kill the Arabs,
Boom, kill the white men,
Hoo, HOO, HOO.
Listen to the yell of Leopold's ghost
Burning in Hell for his hand-maimed host.
Hear how the demons chuckle and yell
Cutting his hands off, down in Hell.
Listen to the creepy proclamation,
Blown through the lairs of the forest-nation,
Blown past the white-ants' hill of clay,
Blown past the marsh where the butterflies play:
"Be careful what you do,
Or Mumbo-Jumbo, God of the Congo,
And all of the other
Gods of the Congo,
Mumbo-Jumbo will hoo-doo you,
Mumbo-Jumbo will hoo-doo you,
Mumbo-Jumbo will hoo-doo you."

With a philosophic pause.

Shrilly and with a heavily accented metre.

Like the wind in the chimney.

All the "o" sounds very golden. Heavy accents very heavy. Light accents very light. Last line whispered.

II. THEIR IRREPRESSIBLE HIGH SPIRITS

Wild crap-shooters with a whoop and a call
Danced the juba in their gambling hall
And laughed fit to kill, and shook the town,
And guyed the policemen and laughed them down
With a boomlay, boomlay, boomlay, BOOM.
THEN I SAW THE CONGO, CREEPING THROUGH THE BLACK,

Rather shrill and high.

Read exactly as in first section.

CUTTING THROUGH THE FOREST WITH A GOLDEN
TRACK.
A negro fairyland swung into view,
A minstrel river
Where dreams come true.
The ebony palace soared on high
Through the blossoming trees to the evening sky.
The inlaid porches and casements shone
With gold and ivory and elephant-bone.
And the black crowd laughed till their sides were sore
At the baboon butler in the agate door,
And the well-known tunes of the parrot band
That trilled on the bushes of that magic land.

Lay emphasis on the delicate ideas. Keep as light-footed as possible.

A troupe of skull-faced witch-men came
Through the agate doorway in suits of flame,
Yea, long-tailed coats with a gold-leaf crust
And hats that were covered with diamond-dust.
And the crowd in the court gave a whoop and a call
And danced the juba from wall to wall.
But the witch-men suddenly stilled the throng
With a stern cold glare, and a stern old song:—
"Mumbo-Jumbo will hoo-doo you." . . .
Just then from the doorway, as fat as shotes,
Came the cake-walk princes in their long
red coats,
Canes with a brilliant lacquer shine,
And tall silk hats that were red as wine.
And they pranced with their butterfly partners
there,
Coal-black maidens with pearls in their hair,
Knee-skirts trimmed with the jassamine sweet,
And bells on their ankles and little black feet.
And the couples railed at the chant and the frown
Of the witch-men lean, and laughed them down.
(Oh, rare was the revel, and well worth while
That made those glowering witch-men smile.)

With pomposity.

With a great deliberation and ghostliness.

With overwhelming assurance, good cheer, and pomp.

With growing speed and sharply marked dance-rhythm.

The cake-walk royalty then began
To walk for a cake that was tall as a man
To the tune of "Boomlay, boomlay, BOOM,"
While the witch-men laughed, with a sinister air,
And sang with the scalawags prancing there:—

"Walk with care, walk with care,
Or Mumbo-Jumbo, God of the Congo,
And all of the other Gods of the Congo,
Mumbo-Jumbo will hoo-doo you.
Beware, beware, walk with care,
Boomlay, boomlay, boomlay, boom.
Boomlay, boomlay, boomlay, boom.
Boomlay, boomlay, boomlay, boom.
Boomlay, boomlay, boomlay,
Boom."

With a touch of negro dialect, and as rapidly as possible toward the end.

(Oh, rare was the revel, and well worth while
That made those glowering witch-men smile.)

Slow philosophic calm.

III. THE HOPE OF THEIR RELIGION

A good old negro in the slums of the town
Preached at a sister for her velvet gown.
Howled at a brother for his low-down ways,
His prowling, guzzling, sneak-thief days.
Beat on the Bible till he wore it out
Starting the jubilee revival shout.
And some had visions, as they stood on chairs,
And sang of Jacob, and the golden stairs,
And they all repented, a thousand strong,
From their stupor and savagery and sin and wrong,
And slammed with their hymn books till they shook
the room
With "Glory, glory, glory,"
And "Boom, boom, BOOM."

Heavy bass. With a literal imitation of camp-meeting racket, and trance.

THEN I SAW THE CONGO, CREEPING THROUGH THE
BLACK,
CUTTING THROUGH THE JUNGLE WITH A GOLDEN
TRACK.
And the gray sky opened like a new-rent veil
And showed the Apostles with their coats of mail.
In bright white steel they were seated round
And their fire-eyes watched where the Congo
wound
And the twelve Apostles, from their thrones on
high,
Thrilled all the forest with their heavenly cry:—

Exactly as in the first section. Begin with terror and power, end with joy.

"Mumbo-Jumbo will die in the jungle;
Never again will he hoo-doo you,
Never again will he hoo-doo you."

Sung to the tune of "Hark, ten thousand harps and voices."

Then along that river, a thousand miles,
The vine-snared trees fell down in files.
Pioneer angels cleared the way
For a Congo paradise, for babes at play,
For sacred capitals, for temples clean.
Gone were the skull-faced witch-men lean.
There, where the wild ghost-gods had wailed
A million boats of the angels sailed
With oars of silver, and prows of blue
And silken pennants that the sun shone through.
'Twas a land transfigured, 'twas a new creation.
Oh, a singing wind swept the negro nation
And on through the backwoods clearing flew:—
"Mumbo-Jumbo is dead in the jungle.
Never again will he hoo-doo you.
Never again will he hoo-doo you."

With growing deliberation and joy.

In a rather high key—as delicately as possible.

To the tune of "Hark, ten thousand harps and voices."

Redeemed were the forests, the beasts and the men,
And only the vulture dared again
By the far, lone mountains of the moon
To cry, in the silence, the Congo tune:—
"Mumbo-Jumbo will hoo-doo you,
Mumbo-Jumbo will hoo-doo you,
Mumbo . . . Jumbo . . . will . . . hoo-doo
. . . you."

Dying down into a penetrating, terrified whisper.

1914

THE LEADEN-EYED

Let not young souls be smothered out before
They do quaint deeds and fully flaunt their pride.
It is the world's one crime its babes grow dull,
Its poor are ox-like, limp and leaden-eyed.

Not that they starve, but starve so dreamlessly,
Not that they sow, but that they seldom reap,
Not that they serve, but have no gods to serve,
Not that they die, but that they die like sheep.

1914

THE MOUSE THAT GNAWED THE OAK-TREE DOWN

The mouse that gnawed the oak-tree down
Began his task in early life.
He kept so busy with his teeth
He had no time to take a wife.

He gnawed and gnawed through sun and rain
When the ambitious fit was on,
Then rested in the sawdust till
A month of idleness had gone.

He did not move about to hunt
The coteries of mousie-men.
He was a snail-paced, stupid thing
Until he cared to gnaw again.

The mouse that gnawed the oak-tree down,
When that tough foe was at his feet—
Found in the stump no angel-cake
Nor buttered bread, nor cheese nor meat—

The forest-roof let in the sky.
"This light is worth the work," said he.
"I'll make this ancient swamp more light."
And started on another tree.

1914

THE MOON'S THE NORTH WIND'S COOKY

(WHAT THE LITTLE GIRL SAID)

The Moon's the North Wind's cooky.
He bites it, day by day,
Until there's but a rim of scraps
That crumble all away.

The South Wind is a baker.
He kneads clouds in his den,
And bakes a crisp new moon *that . . . greedy*
North . . . Wind . . . eats . . . again!

1914

ALADDIN AND THE JINN

"Bring me soft song," said Aladdin.
"This tailor-shop sings not at all.
Chant me a word of the twilight,
Of roses that mourn in the fall.
Bring me a song like hashish
That will comfort the stale and the sad,
For I would be mending my spirit,
Forgetting these days that are bad,
Forgetting companions too shallow,
Their quarrels and arguments thin,
Forgetting the shouting Muezzin:"—
"I AM YOUR SLAVE," said the Jinn.

"Bring me old wines," said Aladdin.
"I have been a starved pauper too long.
Serve them in vessels of jade and of shell,
Serve them with fruit and with song:—
Wines of pre-Adamite Sultans
Digged from beneath the black seas:—
New-gathered dew from the heavens
Dripped down from Heaven's sweet trees,
Cups from the angels' pale tables
That will make me both handsome and wise,
For I have beheld her, the princess,
Firelight and starlight her eyes.
Pauper I am, I would woo her.
And—let me drink wine, to begin,
Though the Koran expressly forbids it."
"I AM YOUR SLAVE," said the Jinn.

"Plan me a dome," said Aladdin,
"That is drawn like the dawn of the MOON,
When the sphere seems to rest on the mountains,
Half-hidden, yet full-risen soon.
Build me a dome," said Aladdin,
"That shall cause all young lovers to sigh,
The fullness of life and of beauty,
Peace beyond peace to the eye—
A palace of foam and of opal,
Pure moonlight without and within,

Where I may enthrone my sweet lady."
"I AM YOUR SLAVE," said the Jinn.

1914

THE UNPARDONABLE SIN

This is the sin against the Holy Ghost:—
To speak of bloody power as right divine,
And call on God to guard each vile chief's house,
And for such chiefs, turn men to wolves and swine:—

To go forth killing in White Mercy's name,
Making the trenches stink with spattered brains,
Tearing the nerves and arteries apart,
Sowing with flesh the unreaped golden plains.

In any Church's name, to sack fair towns,
And turn each home into a screaming sty,
To make the little children fugitive,
And have their mothers for a quick death cry,—

This is the sin against the Holy Ghost:
This is the sin no purging can atone:—
To send forth rapine in the name of Christ:—
To set the face, and make the heart a stone.

1914

THE CHINESE NIGHTINGALE

(A SONG IN CHINESE TAPESTRIES)

"How, how," he said. "Friend Chang," I said,
"San Francisco sleeps as the dead—
Ended license, lust and play:
Why do you iron the night away?
Your big clock speaks with a deadly sound,
With a tick and a wail till dawn comes round.
While the monster shadows glower and creep,
What can be better for man than sleep?"

"I will tell you a secret," Chang replied;
"My breast with vision is satisfied,

And I see green trees and fluttering wings,
And my deathless bird from Shanghai sings."
Then he lit five firecrackers in a pan.
"Pop, pop," said the firecrackers, "cra-cra-crack."
He lit a joss stick long and black.
Then the proud gray joss in the corner stirred;
On his wrist appeared a gray small bird,
And this was the song of the gray small bird:
"Where is the princess, loved forever,
Who made Chang first of the kings of men?"

And the joss in the corner stirred again;
And the carved dog, curled in his arms, awoke,
Barked forth a smoke-cloud that whirled and broke.
It piled in a maze round the ironing-place,
And there on the snowy table wide
Stood a Chinese lady of high degree,
With a scornful, witching, tea-rose face. . . .
Yet she put away all form and pride,
And laid her glimmering veil aside
With a childlike smile for Chang and for me.

The walls fell back, night was aflower,
The table gleamed in a moonlit bower,
While Chang, with a countenance carved of stone,
Ironed and ironed, all alone.
And thus she sang to the busy man Chang:
"Have you forgotten . . .
Deep in the ages, long, long ago,
I was your sweetheart, there on the sand—
Storm-worn beach of the Chinese land?
We sold our grain in the peacock town—
Built on the edge of the sea-sands brown—
Built on the edge of the sea-sands brown. . . .

When all the world was drinking blood
From the skulls of men and bulls
And all the world had swords and clubs of stone,
We drank our tea in China beneath the sacred spice-trees,
And heard the curled waves of the harbor moan.
And this gray bird, in Love's first spring,
With a bright-bronze breast and a bronze-brown wing,
Captured the world with his carolling.

Do you remember, ages after,
At last the world we were born to own?
You were the heir of the yellow throne—
The world was the field of the Chinese man
And we were the pride of the Sons of Han?
We copied deep books and we carved in jade,
And wove blue silks in the mulberry shade. . . ."

"I remember, I remember
That Spring came on forever,
That Spring came on forever,"
Said the Chinese nightingale.

My heart was filled with marvel and dream,
Though I saw the western street-lamps gleam,
Though dawn was bringing the western day,
Though Chang was a laundryman ironing away. . . .
Mingled there with the streets and alleys,
The railroad-yard and the clock-tower bright,
Demon clouds crossed ancient valleys;
Across wide lotus-ponds of light
I marked a giant firefly's flight.

And the lady, rosy-red,
Flourished her fan, her shimmering fan,
Stretched her hand toward Chang, and said:
"Do you remember,
Ages after,
Our palace of heart-red stone?
Do you remember
The little doll-faced children
With their lanterns full of moon-fire,
That came from all the empire
Honoring the throne?—
The loveliest fête and carnival
Our world had ever known?
The sages sat about us
With their heads bowed in their beards,
With proper meditation on the sight.
Confucius was not born;
We lived in those great days
Confucius later said were lived aright. . . .
And this gray bird, on that day of spring,

With a bright-bronze breast, and a bronze-brown wing,
Captured the world with his carolling.
Late at night his tune was spent.
Peasants,
Sages,
Children,
Homeward went,
And then the bronze bird sang for you and me.
We walked alone. Our hearts were high and free.
I had a silvery name, I had a silvery name,
I had a silvery name—do you remember
The name you cried beside the tumbling sea?"

Chang turned not to the lady slim—
He bent to his work, ironing away;
But she was arch, and knowing and glowing,
For the bird on his shoulder spoke for him.

"Darling . . . darling . . . darling . . . darling . . ."
Said the Chinese nightingale.

The great gray joss on the rustic shelf,
Rakish and shrewd, with his collar awry,
Sang impolitely, as though by himself,
Drowning with his bellowing the nightingale's cry:
"Back through a hundred, hundred years
Hear the waves as they climb the piers,
Hear the howl of the silver seas,
Hear the thunder.
Hear the gongs of holy China,
How the waves and tunes combine
In a rhythmic clashing wonder,
Incantation old and fine:
    'Dragons, dragons, Chinese dragons,
    Red firecrackers, and green firecrackers
    And dragons, dragons, Chinese dragons.'"

Then the lady, rosy-red,
Turned to her lover Chang and said:
"Dare you forget that turquoise dawn
When we stood in our mist-hung velvet lawn,
And worked a spell this great joss taught
Till a God of the Dragons was charmed and caught?

From the flag high over our palace home
He flew to our feet in rainbow-foam—
A king of beauty and tempest and thunder
Panting to tear our sorrows asunder.
A dragon of fair adventure and wonder.
We mounted the back of that royal slave
With thoughts of desire that were noble and grave.
We swam down the shore to the dragon-mountains,
We whirled to the peaks and the fiery fountains.
To our secret ivory house we were borne.
We looked down the wonderful wing-filled regions
Where the dragons darted in glimmering legions.
Right by my breast the nightingale sang;
The old rhymes rang in the sunlit mist
That we this hour regain—
Song-fire for the brain.
When my hands and my hair and my feet you kissed,
When you cried for your heart's new pain,
What was my name in the dragon-mist,
In the rings of rainbowed rain?"

"Sorrow and love, glory and love,"
Said the Chinese nightingale.
"Sorrow and love, glory and love,"
Said the Chinese nightingale.

And now the joss broke in with his song:
"Dying ember, bird of Chang,
Soul of Chang, do you remember?—
Ere you returned to the shining harbor
There were pirates by ten thousand
Descended on the town
In vessels mountain-high and red and brown,
Moon-ships that climbed the storms and cut the skies.
On their prows were painted terrible bright eyes.
But I was then a wizard and a scholar and a priest;
I stood upon the sand;
With lifted hand I looked upon them
And sunk their vessels with my wizard eyes,
And the stately lacquer-gate made safe again.
Deep, deep below the bay, the seaweed, and the spray,
Embalmed in amber every pirate lies,
Embalmed in amber every pirate lies."

Then this did the noble lady say:
"Bird, do you dream of our home-coming day
When you flew like a courier on before
From the dragon-peak to our palace-door,
And we drove the steed in your singing path—
The ramping dragon of laughter and wrath:
And found our city all aglow,
And knighted this joss that decked it so?
There were golden fishes in the purple river
And silver fishes and rainbow fishes.
There were golden junks in the laughing river,
And silver junks and rainbow junks:
There were golden lilies by the bay and river,
And silver lilies and tiger-lilies,
And tinkling wind-bells in the gardens of the town
By the black-lacquer gate
Where walked in state
The kind king Chang
And his sweetheart mate. . . .
With his flag-born dragon
And his crown of pearl . . . and . . . jade,
And his nightingale reigning in the mulberry shade,
And sailors and soldiers on the sea-sands brown,
And priests who bowed them down to your song—
By the city called Han, the peacock town,
By the city called Han, the nightingale town,
The nightingale town."

Then sang the bird, so strangely gay,
Fluttering, fluttering, ghostly and gray,
A vague, unravelling, final tune,
Like a long unwinding silk cocoon;
Sang as though for the soul of him
Who ironed away in that bower dim:—
        "I have forgotten
        Your dragons great,
        Merry and mad and friendly and bold.
Dim is your proud lost palace-gate.
I vaguely know
There were heroes of old,
Troubles more than the heart could hold,
There were wolves in the woods
Yet lambs in the fold,

Nests in the top of the almond tree. . . .
The evergreen tree . . . and the mulberry tree . . .
Life and hurry and joy forgotten,
Years on years I but half-remember . . .
Man is a torch, then ashes soon,
May and June, then dead December,
Dead December, then again June.
Who shall end my dream's confusion?
Life is a loom, weaving illusion . . .
I remember, I remember
There were ghostly veils and laces . . .
In the shadowy bowery places . . .
With lovers' ardent faces
Bending to one another,
Speaking each his part.
They infinitely echo
In the red cave of my heart.
'Sweetheart, sweetheart, sweetheart,'
They said to one another.
They spoke, I think, of perils past.
They spoke, I think, of peace at last.
One thing I remember:
Spring came on forever,
Spring came on forever,"
Said the Chinese nightingale.

1917

THE BRONCHO THAT WOULD NOT BE BROKEN

A little colt—broncho, loaned to the farm
To be broken in time without fury or harm,
Yet black crows flew past you, shouting alarm,
Calling "Beware," with lugubrious singing . . .
The butterflies there in the bush were romancing,
The smell of the grass caught your soul in a trance,
So why be a-fearing the spurs and the traces,
O broncho that would not be broken of dancing?

You were born with the pride of the lords great and olden
Who danced, through the ages, in corridors golden.
In all the wide farm-place the person most human.
You spoke out so plainly with squealing and capering,

With whinnying, snorting, contorting and prancing,
As you dodged your pursuers, looking askance,
With Greek-footed figures, and Parthenon paces,
O broncho that would not be broken of dancing.

The grasshoppers cheered. "Keep whirling," they said.
The insolent sparrows called from the shed,
"If men will not laugh, make them wish they were dead."
But arch were your thoughts, all malice displacing,
Though the horse-killers came, with snake-whips advancing.
You bantered and cantered away your last chance.
And they scourged you, with Hell in their speech and their faces,
O broncho that would not be broken of dancing.

"Nobody cares for you," rattled the crows,
As you dragged the whole reaper, next day, down the rows.
The three mules held back, yet you danced on your toes.
You pulled like a racer, and kept the mules chasing.
You tangled the harness with bright eyes side-glancing,
While the drunk driver bled you—a pole for a lance—
And the giant mules bit at you—keeping their places,
O broncho that would not be broken of dancing.

In that last afternoon your boyish heart broke.
The hot wind came down like a sledge-hammer stroke.
The blood-sucking flies to a rare feast awoke.
And they searched out your wounds, your death-warrant tracing.
And the merciful men, their religion enhancing,
Stopped the red reaper, to give you a chance.
Then you died on the prairie, and scorned all disgraces,
O broncho that would not be broken of dancing.

1917

DANIEL

Darius the Mede was a king and a wonder. *Beginning with a strain of "Dixie."*
His eye was proud, and his voice was thunder.
He kept bad lions in a monstrous den.
He fed up the lions on Christian men.

Daniel was the chief hired man of the land. *With a touch of*
He stirred up the music in the palace band.

He whitewashed the cellar. He shovelled in the coal.
And Daniel kept a-praying:—"Lord save my soul."
Daniel kept a-praying:—"Lord save my soul."
Daniel kept a-praying:—"Lord save my soul."

"Alexander's Ragtime Band."

Daniel was the butler, swagger and swell.
He ran up stairs. He answered the bell.
And *he* would let in whoever came a-calling:—
Saints so holy, scamps so appalling.
"Old man Ahab leaves his card.
Elisha and the bears are a-waiting in the yard.
Here comes Pharaoh and his snakes a-calling.
Here comes Cain and his wife a-calling.
Shadrach, Meshach and Abednego for tea.
Here comes Jonah and the whale,
And the *Sea!*
Here comes St. Peter and his fishing pole.
Here comes Judas and his silver a-calling.
Here comes old Beelzebub a-calling."
And Daniel kept a-praying:—"Lord save my soul."
Daniel kept a-praying:—"Lord save my soul."
Daniel kept a-praying:—"Lord save my soul."

His sweetheart and his mother were Christian and meek.
They washed and ironed for Darius every week.
One Thursday he met them at the door:—
Paid them as usual, but acted sore.

He said:—"Your Daniel is a dead little pigeon.
He's a good hard worker, but he talks religion."
And he showed them Daniel in the lions' cage.
Daniel standing quietly, the lions in a rage.
His good old mother cried:—
"Lord save him."
And Daniel's tender sweetheart cried:—
"Lord save him."

And she was a golden lily in the dew.
And she was as sweet as an apple on the tree,
And she was as fine as a melon in the corn-field,
Gliding and lovely as a ship on the sea,
Gliding and lovely as a ship on the sea.

This to be repeated three times, very softly and slowly.

And she prayed to the Lord:—
"Send Gabriel. Send Gabriel."

King Darius said to the lions:—
"Bite Daniel. Bite Daniel.
Bite him. Bite him. Bite him!"

Thus roared the lions:—
"We want Daniel, Daniel, Daniel,
We want Daniel, Daniel, Daniel."

Here the audience roars with the leader.

And Daniel did not frown,
Daniel did not cry.
He kept on looking at the sky.
And the Lord said to Gabriel:—
"Go chain the lions down.
Go chain the lions down.
Go chain the lions down.
Go chain the lions down."

The audience sings this with the leader, to the old negro tune.

And *Gabriel* chained the lions,
And *Gabriel* chained the lions,
And *Gabriel* chained the lions,
And Daniel got out of the den,
And Daniel got out of the den,
And Daniel got out of the den.
And Darius said:—"You're a Christian child,"
Darius said:—"You're a Christian child,"
Darius said:—"You're a Christian child,"
And gave him his job again,
And gave him his job again,
And gave him his job again.

1920

MY LADY IS COMPARED TO A YOUNG TREE

When I see a young tree
In its white beginning,
With white leaves
And white buds
Barely tipped with green,
In the April weather,

In the weeping sunshine—
Then I see my lady,
My democratic queen,
Standing free and equal
With the youngest woodland sapling
Swaying, singing in the wind,
Delicate and white:
Soul so near to blossom,
Fragile, strong as death;
A kiss from far-off Eden,
A flash of Judgment's trumpet—
April's breath.

1920

WHEN THE MISSISSIPPI FLOWED IN INDIANA

INSCRIBED TO BRUCE CAMPBELL, WHO READ "TOM SAWYER" WITH ME IN THE OLD HOUSE.

Beneath Time's roaring cannon
Many walls fall down.
But though the guns break every stone,
Level every town:—
Within our Grandma's old front hall
Some wonders flourish yet:—
The Pavement of Verona,
Where stands young Juliet;
The roof of Blue-beard's palace,
And Kubla Khan's wild ground;
The cave of young Aladdin,
Where the jewel-flowers were found;
And the garden of old Sparta
Where little Helen played;
The grotto of Miranda
That Prospero arrayed;
And the cave, by the Mississippi,
Where Becky Thatcher strayed.

On that Indiana stairway
Gleams Cinderella's shoe.
Upon that mighty mountainside
Walks Snow-white in the dew.
Upon that grassy hillside

Trips shining Nicolette:—
That stairway of remembrance
Time's cannon will not get—
That chattering slope of glory
Our little cousins made,
That hill by the Mississippi
Where Becky Thatcher strayed.

Spring beauties on that cliffside,
Love in the air,
While the soul's deep Mississippi
Sweeps on, forever fair.
And he who enters in the cave,
Nothing shall make afraid,
The cave by the Mississippi
Where Tom and Becky strayed.

1920

THE COMET OF GOING-TO-THE-SUN

On the mountain peak, called "Going-to-the-Sun,"
A comet stopped to drink from a cool spring
And like a spirit-harp began to sing
To us, then hurried on to reach the sun.
We called him "Homer's soul," and "Milton's wing."
The harp-sound stayed, though he went up and on.
It turned to thunder, when he had quite gone—
And yet was like a soft voice of the sea,
And every whispering root and every blade of grass
And every tree
In the whole world, and brought thoughts of old songs
That blind men sang ten thousand years ago,
And all the springtime hearts of every nation know.

1923

RAIN

Each storm-soaked flower has a beautiful eye.
And this is the voice of the stone-cold sky:
"Only boys keep their cheeks dry.
Only boys are afraid to cry.

Men thank God for tears,
Alone with the memory of their dead,
Alone with lost years."

1926

NANCY HANKS, MOTHER OF ABRAHAM LINCOLN

Out of the eater came forth meat; and out of the strong came forth sweetness.—Judges XIV, 14.

A sweet girl graduate, lean as a fawn,
The very whimsy of time,
Read her class poem Commencement Day—
A trembling filigree rhyme.

The pansy that blooms on the window sill,
Blooms in exactly the proper place;
And she nodded just like a pansy there,
And her poem was all about bowers and showers,
Sugary streamlet and mossy rill,
All about daisies on dale and hill—
And she was the mother of Buffalo Bill.

Another girl, a cloud-drift sort,
Dreamlit, moonlit, marble-white,
Light-footed saint on the pilgrim shore,
The best since New England fairies began,
Was the mother of Barnum, the circus man.

A girl from Missouri, snippy and vain,
As frothy a miss as any you know,
A wren, a toy, a pink silk bow,
The belle of the choir, she drove insane
Missouri deacons and all the sleek,
Her utter tomfoolery made men weak,
Till they could not stand and they could not speak.
Oh, queen of fifteen and sixteen,
Missouri sweetened beneath her reign—
And she was the mother of bad Mark Twain.

Not always are lions born of lions,
Roosevelt sprang from a palace of lace;
On the other hand is the dizzy truth:

Not always is beauty born of beauty.
Some treasures wait in a hidden place.
All over the world were thousands of belles
In far-off eighteen hundred and nine,
Girls of fifteen, girls of twenty,
Their mammas dressed them up a-plenty—
Each garter was bright, each stocking fine,
But for all their innocent devices,
Their cheeks of fruit and their eyes of wine,
And each voluptuous design,
And all soft glories that we trace
In Europe's palaces of lace,
A girl who slept in dust and sorrow,
Nancy Hanks, in a lost log cabin,
Nancy Hanks had the loveliest face!

1926

Sara Teasdale

Sara Teasdale, the youngest child of John Warren and Mary Elizabeth Willard Teasdale, was born in St. Louis, Missouri, August 8, 1884. She came of an old and distinguished American family, one ancestor, Major Simon Willard, being the founder of Concord, Massachusetts. Her ancestors on both sides fought in the Revolutionary War, and both emigrated west about the middle of the nineteenth century. Her maternal grandfather owned steamboats on the Mississippi River; her paternal grandfather was a Baptist minister.

As a child she was not strong; consequently she received her earliest education at home. Later, however, she attended Hosmer Hall, a private school for girls, from which she was graduated in 1903. Ill health prevented her from attending a university, but through the habit of wide reading, which she had formed in childhood, she continued her education. In 1905 she went abroad, and spent some time in Europe, Egypt, and Palestine; and in 1912 she spent a summer in Italy and Switzerland. She also travelled a great deal in the United States, and lived several winters in California and Arizona. On December 19, 1914, she married Ernst B. Filsinger, of St. Louis, an authority on international trade; but they were divorced in 1929. From 1916 to the end of her life she maintained a permanent residence in New York City.

Her interest in poetry began early, being first awakened through the reading of Christina Rossetti. While at school she made translations in verse from Heine and other German poets. After graduation she continued to write, and with some of her friends issued in manuscript a monthly magazine, the *Potter's Wheel*, which was limited to one copy a month. In it from time to time her early work appeared. Her first recognition came in 1907 with the acceptance by *Reedy's Mirror* of her poem "Guenevere." In the same year she published her first volume, *Sonnets to Duse and Other Poems*. Subsequently six other books of verse by her appeared, one of them, *Strange Victory* (1933), being posthumously published. She also edited *The Answering Voice* (1917), containing a hundred love lyrics by women, and *Rainbow Gold* (1922), a volume of poems for children.

In 1916 her group of poems, "Songs out of Sorrow," won the prize offered by the Poetry Society of America; and in 1918 she was awarded the Pulitzer Prize for *Love Songs* (1917).

In the summer of 1932 she went to England for material for a biography of Christina Rossetti, and while in London became ill with pneumonia. Returning to the United States in September, she continued in bad health; and on the morning of January 29, 1933, she was found dead in her apartment on lower Fifth Avenue. Her body was cremated and the ashes buried in the family plot in a cemetery in St. Louis.

FAULTS

They came to tell your faults to me,
They named them over one by one;
I laughed aloud when they were done,
I knew them all so well before;—
Oh, they were blind, too blind to see
Your faults had made me love you more.

1907

THE WAYFARER

Love entered in my heart one day,
  A sad, unwelcome guest;
But when he begged that he might stay,
  I let him wait and rest.

He broke my sleep with sorrowing,
  And shook my dreams with tears,
And when my heart was fain to sing,
  He stilled its joy with fears.

But now that he has gone his way,
I miss the old sweet pain,
And sometimes in the night I pray,
That he may come again.

1907

THE SONG FOR COLIN

I sang a song at dusking time
Beneath the evening star,
And Terence left his latest rhyme
To answer from afar.

Pierrot laid down his lute to weep,
And sighed, "She sings for me."
But Colin slept a careless sleep
Beneath an apple tree.

1911

BURIED LOVE

I have come to bury Love
Beneath a tree,
In the forest tall and black
Where none can see.

I shall put no flowers at his head,
Nor stone at his feet,
For the mouth I loved so much
Was bittersweet.

I shall go no more to his grave,
For the woods are cold.
I shall gather as much of joy
As my hands can hold.

I shall stay all day in the sun
Where the wide winds blow,—
But oh, I shall cry at night
When none will know.

1911

PIERROT

Pierrot stands in the garden
  Beneath a waning moon,
And on his lute he fashions
  A fragile silver tune.

Pierrot plays in the garden,
  He thinks he plays for me,
But I am quite forgotten
  Under the cherry tree.

Pierrot plays in the garden,
  And all the roses know
That Pierrot loves his music,—
  But I love Pierrot.

1911

THE KISS

I hoped that he would love me,
  And he has kissed my mouth,
But I am like a stricken bird
  That cannot reach the south.

For though I know he loves me,
  To-night my heart is sad;
His kiss was not so wonderful
  As all the dreams I had.

1911

THE METROPOLITAN TOWER

We walked together in the dusk
  To watch the tower grow dimly white,
And saw it lift against the sky
  Its flower of amber light.

You talked of half a hundred things,
  I kept each hurried word you said;

And when at last the hour was full,
  I saw the light turn red.

You did not know the time had come,
  You did not see the sudden flower,
Nor know that in my heart Love's birth
  Was reckoned from that hour.

1911

CENTRAL PARK AT DUSK

Buildings above the leafless trees
  Loom high as castles in a dream,
While one by one the lamps come out
  To thread the twilight with a gleam.

There is no sign of leaf or bud,
  A hush is over everything—
Silent as women wait for love,
  The world is waiting for the spring.

1911

THE PRAYER

My answered prayer came up to me,
And in the silence thus spake he:
"O you who prayed for me to come,
Your greeting is but cold and dumb."

My heart made answer: "You are fair,
But I have prayed too long to care.
Why came you not when all was new,
And I had died for joy of you."

1915

SPRING NIGHT

The park is filled with night and fog,
  The veils are drawn about the world,
The drowsy lights along the paths
  Are dim and pearled.

Gold and gleaming the empty streets,
  Gold and gleaming the misty lake,
The mirrored lights like sunken swords,
  Glimmer and shake.

Oh, is it not enough to be
Here with this beauty over me?
My throat should ache with praise, and I
Should kneel in joy beneath the sky.
Oh, beauty are you not enough?
Why am I crying after love,
With youth, a singing voice and eyes
To take earth's wonder with surprise?
Why have I put off my pride,
Why am I unsatisfied,
I for whom the pensive night
Binds her cloudy hair with light,
I for whom all beauty burns
Like incense in a million urns?
Oh, beauty, are you not enough?
Why am I crying after love?

1915

COME

Come, when the pale moon like a petal
  Floats in the pearly dusk of spring,
Come with arms outstretched to take me,
  Come with lips pursed up to cling.

Come, for life is a frail moth flying,
  Caught in the web of the years that pass,
And soon we two, so warm and eager,
  Will be as the gray stones in the grass.

1915

I SHALL NOT CARE

When I am dead and over me bright April
  Shakes out her rain-drenched hair,
Though you should lean above me broken-hearted,
  I shall not care.

I shall have peace, as leafy trees are peaceful
  When rain bends down the bough,
And I shall be more silent and cold-hearted
  Than you are now.

1915

LONGING

I am not sorry for my soul
  That it must go unsatisfied,
For it can live a thousand times;
  Eternity is deep and wide.

I am not sorry for my soul,
  But oh, my body that must go
Back to a little drift of dust
  Without the joy it longed to know.

1915

THE INN OF EARTH

I came to the crowded Inn of Earth,
  And called for a cup of wine,
But the Host went by with averted eye
  From a thirst as keen as mine.

Then I sat down with weariness
  And asked a bit of bread,
But the Host went by with averted eye
  And never a word he said.

While always from the outer night
  The waiting souls came in
With stifled cries of sharp surprise
  At all the light and din.

"Then give me a bed to sleep," I said,
  "For midnight comes apace"—
But the Host went by with averted eye
  And I never saw his face.

"Since there is neither food nor rest,
  I go where I fared before"—
But the Host went by with averted eye
  And barred the outer door.

1915

THOUGHTS

When I can make my thoughts come forth
  To walk like ladies up and down,
Each one puts on before the glass
  Her most becoming hat and gown.

But oh, the shy and eager thoughts
  That hide and will not get them dressed,
Why is it that they always seem
  So much more lovely than the rest?

1915

"I AM NOT YOURS"

I am not yours, not lost in you,
  Not lost, although I long to be
Lost as a candle lit at noon,
  Lost as a snow-flake in the sea.

You love me, and I find you still
  A spirit beautiful and bright,
Yet I am I, who long to be
  Lost as a light is lost in light.

Oh, plunge me deep in love—put out
  My senses, leave me deaf and blind,
Swept by the tempest of your love,
  A taper in a rushing wind.

1915

NIGHT SONG AT AMALFI

I asked the heaven of stars
  What I should give my love—
It answered me with silence,
  Silence above.

I asked the darkened sea
  Down where the fishers go—
It answered me with silence,
  Silence below.

Oh, I could give him weeping,
  Or I could give him song—
But how can I give silence,
  My whole life long?

1915

SONG AT CAPRI

When beauty grows too great to bear
  How shall I ease me of its ache,
For beauty more than bitterness
  Makes the heart break.

Now while I watch the dreaming sea
  With isles like flowers against her breast,
Only one voice in all the world
  Could give me rest.

1915

TO E.

I have remembered beauty in the night;
  Against black silences I waked to see
  A shower of sunlight over Italy
And green Ravello dreaming on her height;
I have remembered music in the dark,
  The clean swift brightness of a fugue of Bach's,
  And running water singing on the rocks
When once in English woods I heard a lark.

But all remembered beauty is no more
Than a vague prelude to the thought of you—
You are the rarest soul I ever knew,
Lover of beauty, knightliest and best;
My thoughts seek you as waves that seek the shore,
And when I think of you, I am at rest.

1917

BARTER

Life has loveliness to sell,
All beautiful and splendid things,
Blue waves whitened on a cliff,
Soaring fire that sways and sings,
And children's faces looking up,
Holding wonder like a cup.

Life has loveliness to sell,
Music like a curve of gold,
Scent of pine trees in the rain,
Eyes that love you, arms that hold,
And for your spirit's still delight,
Holy thoughts that star the night.

Spend all you have for loveliness,
Buy it and never count the cost;
For one white singing hour of peace
Count many a year of strife well lost,
And for a breath of ecstasy
Give all you have been, or could be.

1917

MASTERY

I would not have a god come in
To shield me suddenly from sin,
And set my house of life to rights;
Nor angels with bright burning wings
Ordering my earthly thoughts and things;
Rather my own frail guttering lights

Wind blown and nearly beaten out;
Rather the terror of the nights
And long, sick groping after doubt:
Rather be lost than let my soul
Slip vaguely from my own control—
Of my own spirit let me be
In sole though feeble mastery.

1917

BECAUSE

Oh, because you never tried
To bow my will or break my pride,
And nothing of the cave-man made
You want to keep me half afraid,
Nor ever with a conquering air
You thought to draw me unaware—
'Take me, for I love you more
Than I ever loved before.

And since the body's maidenhood
Alone were neither rare nor good
Unless with it I gave to you
A spirit still untrammeled, too,
Take my dreams and take my mind
That were masterless as wind;
And "Master!" I shall say to you
Since you never asked me to.

1917

DOUBT

My soul lives in my body's house,
  And you have both the house and her—
But sometimes she is less your own
  Than a wild, gay adventurer;
A restless and an eager wraith,
  How can I tell what she will do—
Oh, I am sure of my body's faith,
  But what if my soul broke faith with you?

1917

THE LAMP

If I can bear your love like a lamp before me,
When I go down the long steep Road of Darkness,
I shall not fear the everlasting shadows,
Nor cry in terror.

If I can find out God, then I shall find Him;
If none can find Him, then I shall sleep soundly,
Knowing how well on earth your love sufficed me,
A lamp in darkness.

1917

BLUE SQUILLS

How many million Aprils came
Before I ever knew
How white a cherry bough could be,
A bed of squills, how blue!

And many a dancing April
When life is done with me,
Will lift the blue flame of the flower
And the white flame of the tree.

Oh, burn me with your beauty, then,
Oh, hurt me, tree and flower,
Lest in the end death try to take
Even this glistening hour.

O shaken flowers, O shimmering trees,
O sunlit white and blue,
Wound me, that I, through endless sleep,
May bear the scar of you.

1920

"I HAVE LOVED HOURS AT SEA"

I have loved hours at sea, gray cities,
  The fragile secret of a flower,
Music, the making of a poem
  That gave me heaven for an hour;

First stars above a snowy hill,
  Voices of people kindly and wise,
And the great look of love, long hidden,
  Found at last in meeting eyes.

I have loved much and been loved deeply—
  Oh, when my spirit's fire burns low,
Leave me the darkness and the stillness;
  I shall be tired and glad to go.

1920

THE VOICE

Atoms as old as stars,
Mutation on mutation,
Millions and millions of cells
Dividing, yet still the same,
From air and changing earth,
From ancient Eastern rivers,
From turquoise tropic seas,
Unto myself I came.

My spirit like my flesh
Sprang from a thousand sources,
From cave-man, hunter and shepherd,
From Karnak, Cyprus, Rome;
The living thoughts in me
Spring from dead men and women,
Forgotten time out of mind
And many as bubbles of foam.

Here for a moment's space
Into the light out of darkness,
I come and they come with me,

Finding words with my breath;
From the wisdom of many life-times
I hear them cry: "Forever
Seek for Beauty; she only
Fights with man against Death!"

1920

"THERE WILL COME SOFT RAINS"

WAR TIME

There will come soft rains and the smell of the ground,
And swallows circling with their shimmering sound;

And frogs in the pools singing at night,
And wild plum-trees in tremulous white;

Robins will wear their feathery fire
Whistling their whims on a low fence-wire;

And not one will know of the war, not one
Will care at last when it is done.

Not one would mind, neither bird nor tree,
If mankind perished utterly;

And Spring herself, when she woke at dawn,
Would scarcely know that we were gone.

1920

THE UNCHANGING

Sun-swept beaches with a light wind blowing
  From the immense blue circle of the sea,
And the soft thunder where long waves whiten—
  These were the same for Sappho as for me.

Two thousand years—much has gone by forever;
  Change takes the gods and ships and speech of men—
But here on the beaches that time passes over
  The heart aches now as then.

1920

IF DEATH IS KIND

Perhaps if Death is kind, and there can be returning,
  We will come back to earth some fragrant night,
And take these lanes to find the sea, and bending
  Breathe the same honeysuckle, low and white.

We will come down at night to these resounding beaches
  And the long gentle thunder of the sea,
Here for a single hour in the wide starlight
  We shall be happy, for the dead are free.

1920

THE LONG HILL

I must have passed the crest a while ago
  And now I am going down—
Strange to have crossed the crest and not to know,
  But the brambles were always catching the hem of my gown.

All the morning I thought how proud I should be
  To stand there straight as a queen,
Wrapped in the wind and the sun with the world under me—
  But the air was dull; there was little I could have seen.

It was nearly level along the beaten track
  And the brambles caught in my gown—
But it's no use now to think of turning back,
  The rest of the way will be only going down.

1920

SEPTEMBER DAY

(PONT DE NEUILLY)

The Seine flows out of the mist
  And into the mist again;
The trees lean over the water,
  The small leaves fall like rain.

The leaves fall patiently;
  Nothing remembers or grieves;
The river takes to the sea
  The yellow drift of the leaves.

Milky and cold is the air,
  The leaves float with the stream,
The river comes out of a sleep
  And goes away in a dream.

1926

THE FOUNTAIN

Fountain, fountain, what do you say
  Singing at night alone?
"It is enough to rise and fall
  Here in my basin of stone."

But are you content as you seem to be
So near the freedom and rush of the sea?
  "I have listened all night to its laboring sound,
  It heaves and sags, as the moon runs round;
Ocean and fountain, shadow and tree,
Nothing escapes, nothing is free."

1926

DAY'S ENDING

(TUCSON)

Aloof as aged kings,
Wearing like them the purple,
The mountains ring the mesa
Crowned with a dusky light;
Many a time I watched
That coming-on of darkness
Till stars burned through the heavens
Intolerably bright.

It was not long I lived there,
But I became a woman
Under those vehement stars,

For it was there I heard
For the first time my spirit
Forging an iron rule for me,
As though with slow cold hammers
Beating out word by word:

"Only yourself can heal you;
Only yourself can lead you;
The road is heavy going
And ends where no man knows;
Take love when love is given,
But never think to find it
A sure escape from sorrow
Or a complete repose."

1926

"I HAVE SEEN THE SPRING"

Nothing is new; I have seen the spring too often;
There have been other plum-trees white as this one
Like a silvery cloud tethered beside the road;
I have been waked from sleep too many times
By birds at dawn boasting their love is beautiful.
The grass-blades gleam in the wind, nothing is changed.
Nothing is lost; it is all as it used to be;
Unopened lilacs are still as deep a purple;
The boughs of the elm are dancing still in a veil of tiny leaves;
Nothing is lost but a few years from my life.

1926

WINTER NIGHT SONG

Will you come as of old with singing,
  And shall I hear as of old?
Shall I rush to open the window
  In spite of the arrowy cold?

Ah no, my dear, ah no,
  I shall sit by the fire reading,
Though you sing half the night in the snow
  I shall not be heeding.

Though your voice remembers the forest,
  The warm green light and the birds,
Though you gather the sea in your singing
  And pour its sound into words,

Even so, my dear, even so,
  I shall not heed you at all;
Though your shoulders are white with snow,
  Though you strain your voice to a call,
I shall drowse and the fire will drowse,
  The draught will be cold on the floor,
The clock running down,
  Snow banking the door.

1926

THE FLIGHT

We are two eagles
Flying together
Under the heavens,
Over the mountains,
Stretched on the wind.
Sunlight heartens us,
Blind snow baffles us,
Clouds wheel after us
Ravelled and thinned.

We are like eagles,
But when Death harries us,
Human and humbled
When one of us goes,
Let the other follow,
Let the flight be ended,
Let the fire blacken,
Let the book close.

1926

MOON'S ENDING

Moon, worn thin to the width of a quill,
In the dawn clouds flying,
How good to go, light into light, and still
Giving light, dying.

1933

TRUCE

Take heart, for now the battle is half over,
  We have not shamed our sires;
Pride, the lone pennon, ravelled by the storm-wind
  Stands in the sunset fires.

It may be, with the coming-on of evening
  We shall be granted unassailed repose,
And what is left of dusk will be less darkness
  Than luminous air, on which the crescent glows.

1933

TO THE SEA

Bitter and beautiful, sing no more;
Scarf of spindrift strewn on the shore,
Burn no more in the noon-day light,
Let there be night for me, let there be night.

On the restless beaches I used to range
The two that I loved have walked with me—
I saw them change and my own heart change—
I cannot face the unchanging sea.

1933

Elinor Wylie

Elinor Morton Hoyt was born in Somerville, New Jersey, September 7, 1885. She was the eldest of the five children of Henry Martyn Hoyt, a banker and lawyer, and Anne MacMichael Hoyt. When she was about two years old, her parents moved to Rosemont, a suburb of Philadelphia, where she first attended school. In 1897 her father became Assistant Attorney General and afterwards Solicitor General, and the family moved to Washington. There she attended Mrs. Flint's school (later known as the Holton Arms School), from which she was graduated in 1903. The same year she went to Europe with her grandfather.

In her twentieth year she married Philip Hichborn, the son of an admiral, and they had one son; but four years later she eloped with Horace Wylie, who was also married. They went to England, and as Mr. and Mrs. Waring lived in Burley, Thruxton, and Puttenham, out-of-the-way towns in southern England, or travelled in France. Finally they bought a house at Witley, near Godalming; but in 1916 the war forced them to return to America. Her husband had died some years before, and Wylie, who had been refused a divorce by his wife, was also free at last to marry; they went through the wedding ceremony, therefore, and afterwards went to live in Washington.

Mrs. Wylie had begun writing poetry when at school, but she had not published any of this early work. In 1912 her mother, when on a visit to her in England, had paid to have a small volume of her poetry, *Incidental Numbers*, printed in an edition of sixty copies. In 1916 some of her poems were accepted by *Poetry* and the *Century*. In Washington she met many writers, among whom were Sinclair Lewis, who urged her to write prose, and William Rose Benét, who helped her find a publisher. Her first volume to appear regularly, *Nets to Catch the Wind,* was published in 1921, and two years later she published a novel, *Jennifer Lorn.*

In 1923 she divorced Wylie to marry William Rose Benét, and thereafter she lived in New York, though with frequent long stays in England. She became poetry editor of *Vanity Fair,* and continued to write both poetry and fiction. In the last five years of her life, in addition to three more volumes of poetry, she published three novels—*The Venetian Glass Nephew* (1925), *The Orphan Angel* (1927), a novel about the poet Shelley, and *Mr. Hodge and Mr. Hazard* (1928). While staying at a country house near Henley, England, in the summer of 1928, she fell down stairs and fractured a vertebra. In October she had a slight stroke, followed shortly by another, which paralyzed one side of her face. In December she returned to New York, and there on December 16, 1928, she died suddenly—just as she had finished preparing her last volume of poetry for the publisher.

THE EAGLE AND THE MOLE

Avoid the reeking herd,
Shun the polluted flock,
Live like that stoic bird,
The eagle of the rock.

The huddled warmth of crowds
Begets and fosters hate;
He keeps, above the clouds,
His cliff inviolate.

When flocks are folded warm,
And herds to shelter run,
He sails above the storm,
He stares into the sun.

If in the eagle's track
Your sinews cannot leap,
Avoid the lathered pack,
Turn from the steaming sheep.

If you would keep your soul
From spotted sight or sound,
Live like the velvet mole;
Go burrow underground.

And there hold intercourse
With roots of trees and stones,
With rivers at their source,
And disembodied bones.

1921

A PROUD LADY

Hate in the world's hand
Can carve and set its seal
Like the strong blast of sand
Which cuts into steel.

I have seen how the finger of hate
Can mar and mold
Faces burned passionate
And frozen cold.

Sorrowful faces worn
As stone with rain,
Faces writhing with scorn
And sullen with pain.

But you have a proud face
Which the world cannot harm,
You have turned the pain to a grace
And the scorn to a charm.

You have taken the arrows and slings
Which prick and bruise
And fashioned them into wings
For the heels of your shoes.

From the world's hand which tries
To tear you apart
You have stolen the falcon's eyes
And the lion's heart.

What has it done, this world,
With hard finger tips,
But sweetly chiseled and curled
Your inscrutable lips?

1921

THE TORTOISE IN ETERNITY

Within my house of patterned horn
I sleep in such a bed
As men may keep before they're born
And after they are dead.

Sticks and stones may break their bones,
And words may make them bleed;
There is not one of them who owns
An armor to his need.

Tougher than hide or lozenged bark,
Snow-storm and thunder proof,
And quick with sun, and thick with dark,
Is this my darling roof.

Men's troubled dreams of death and birth
Pulse mother-o'-pearl to black;
I bear the rainbow bubble Earth
Square on my scornful back.

1921

VELVET SHOES

Let us walk in the white snow
  In a soundless space;
With footsteps quiet and slow,
  At a tranquil pace,
  Under veils of white lace.

I shall go shod in silk,
  And you in wool,
White as a white cow's milk,
  More beautiful
  Than the breast of a gull.

We shall walk through the still town
  In a windless peace;
We shall step upon white down,
  Upon silver fleece,
  Upon softer than these.

We shall walk in velvet shoes:
  Wherever we go
Silence will fall like dews
  On white silence below.
  We shall walk in the snow.

1921

EPITAPH

For this she starred her eyes with salt
And scooped her temples thin,
Until her face shone pure of fault
From the forehead to the chin.

In coldest crucibles of pain
Her shrinking flesh was fired
And smoothed into a finer grain
To make it more desired.

Pain left her lips more clear than glass;
It colored and cooled her hand.
She lay a field of scented grass
Yielded as pasture land.

For this her loveliness was curved
And carved as silver is:
For this she was brave: but she deserved
A better grave than this.

1923

LET NO CHARITABLE HOPE

Now let no charitable hope
Confuse my mind with images
Of eagle and of antelope:
I am in nature none of these.

I was, being human, born alone;
I am, being woman, hard beset;
I live by squeezing from a stone
The little nourishment I get.

In masks outrageous and austere
The years go by in single file;
But none has merited my fear,
And none has quite escaped my smile.

1923

COLD-BLOODED CREATURES

Man, the egregious egoist
(In mystery the twig is bent),
Imagines, by some mental twist,
That he alone is sentient

Of the intolerable load
Which on all living creatures lies,
Nor stoops to pity in the toad
The speechless sorrow of its eyes.

He asks no questions of the snake,
Nor plumbs the phosphorescent gloom
Where lidless fishes, broad awake,
Swim staring at a night-mare doom.

1923

LAST SUPPER

Now that the shutter of the dusk
  Begins to tremble in its groove,
I am constrained to strip the husk
  From everything I truly love.

So short a time remains to taste
  The ivory pulp, the seven pips,
My heart is happy without haste
  With revelation at its lips.

So calm a beauty shapes the core,
So grave a blossom frames the stem,
In this last minute and no more
My eyes alone shall eat of them.
1928

[WHAT OTHER NAME HAD HALF EXPRESSED]

What other name had half expressed the whole
Of that incomparable and touching grace
Which spells the shape of danger in your face?
It is the very pattern of your soul;
The eagle's home, above the moon's control,
Above the seas, the high precipitate place;
The stairway cut from planetary space;
The crystal steps which climb a steeper goal.

The shadow of its light is only this:
That all your beauty is the work of wars
Between the upper and the nether stars;
Its symmetry is perfect and severe
Because the barbarous force of agonies
Broke it, and mended it, and made it clear.
1929

["CHILDREN AND DOGS ARE SUBJECT"]

"Children and dogs are subject to my power,"
You said, and smiled, and I beside you smiled,
Perceiving my unwisdom of a child,
My courage of a wolf new-taught to cower:
Upon the grass, beneath the falling flower,
I saw my spirit silent and beguiled
Standing at gaze; a brute no longer wild;
An infant wearied by the difficult hour.

And am I not your child who has come home?
And am I not your hound for faithfulness?
Put forth your hand, put forth your hand to bless
A creature stricken timorous and dumb,

Who now regards you with a lover's eyes
And knows that you are merciful and wise.

1929

[NOW AM I ORSON TO YOUR VALENTINE]

Now am I Orson to your Valentine
Forever, and I choose it shall be so;
For how should the uncivil briar grow
Germane in nature to the noble vine?
The savage should be servant to the fine;
The falcon fly superior to the crow;
O dear my lord, believe me that I know
How far your virtues have outnumbered mine.

And you have levied final tribute now—
Your chivalry demanding the pretence—
You have constrained your vassal to avow
That we are equals, lest a violence
Be suffered by our love, and so I must
Deny the intrinsic difference in our dust.

1929

[WHEN I PERCEIVE THE SABLE]

When I perceive the sable of your hair
Silvered, and deep within those caverns are
Your eyesockets, a double-imaged star,
And your fine substance fretted down by care,
Then do I marvel that a woman dare
Prattle of mortal matters near and far
To one so wounded in demonic war
Against some prince of Sirius or Altair.

How is it possible that this hand of clay,
Though white as porcelain, can contrive a touch
So delicate it shall not hurt too much?
What voice can my invention find to say
So soft, precise, and scrupulous a word
You shall not take it for another sword?

1929

HYMN TO EARTH

Farewell, incomparable element,
Whence man arose, where he shall not return;
And hail, imperfect urn
Of his last ashes, and his firstborn fruit;
Farewell, the long pursuit,
And all the adventures of his discontent;
The voyages which sent
His heart averse from home:
Metal of clay, permit him that he come
To thy slow-burning fire as to a hearth;
Accept him as a particle of earth.

Fire, being divided from the other three,
It lives removed, or secret at the core;
Most subtle of the four,
When air flies not, nor water flows,
It disembodied goes,
Being light, elixir of the first decree,
More volatile than he;
With strength and power to pass
Through space, where never his least atom was:
He has no part in it, save as his eyes
Have drawn its emanation from the skies.

A wingless creature heavier than air,
He is rejected of its quintessence;
Coming and going hence,
In the twin minutes of his birth and death,
He may inhale as breath,
As breath relinquish heaven's atmosphere,
Yet in it have no share,
Nor can survive therein
Where its outer edge is filtered pure and thin:
It doth but lend its crystal to his lungs
For his early crying, and his final songs.

The element of water has denied
Its child; it is no more his element;
It never will relent;
Its silver harvests are more sparsely given

Than the rewards of heaven,
And he shall drink cold comfort at its side:
The water is too wide:
The seamew and the gull
Feather a nest made soft and pitiful
Upon its foam; he has not any part
In the long swell of sorrow at its heart.

Hail and farewell, beloved element,
Whence he departed, and his parent once;
See where thy spirit runs
Which for so long hath had the moon to wife;
Shall this support his life
Until the arches of the waves he bent
And grow shallow and spent?
Wisely it cast him forth
With his dead weight of burdens nothing worth,
Leaving him, for the universal years,
A little seawater to make his tears.

Hail, element of earth, receive thy own,
And cherish, at thy charitable breast,
This man, this mongrel beast:
He plows the sand, and, at his hardest need,
He sows himself for seed;
He plows the furrow, and in this lies down
Before the corn is grown;
Between the apple bloom
And the ripe apple is sufficient room
In time, and matter, to consume his love
And make him parcel of a cypress grove.

Receive him as thy lover for an hour
Who will not weary, by a longer stay,
The kind embrace of clay;
Even within thine arms he is dispersed
To nothing, as at first;
The air flings downward from its four-quartered tower
Him whom the flames devour;
At the full tide, at the flood,
The sea is mingled with his salty blood:
The traveller dust, although the dust be vile,
Sleeps as thy lover for a little while.

1929

[HOW MANY FAULTS]

How many faults you might accuse me of
Are truth, and by my truthfulness admitted!
A fool, perhaps, how many caps had fitted,
How many motleys clothed me like a glove.
Thriftless of gold and prodigal of love;
Fanatical in pride, and feather-witted
In the world's business; if your tongue had spitted
Such frailties, they were possible to prove.

But you have hit the invulnerable joint
In this poor armor patched from desperate fears;
This is the breastplate that you cannot pierce,
That turns and breaks your most malicious point;
This strict ascetic habit of control
That industry has woven for my soul.

1932

Ezra Pound

Ezra Loomis Pound was born October 30, 1885, at Hailey, Idaho, but grew up in Pennsylvania, where he was taken by his family at the age of eighteen months. His parents, Homer Loomis Pound and Isabel Weston Pound, were descendants of early English settlers in New England; and his mother was distantly related to Longfellow.

For two years Pound was an undergraduate at the University of Pennsylvania; but in 1903 he went to Hamilton College, from which he received the A.B. degree two years later. In the fall of 1905 he returned to the University of Pennsylvania on a fellowship in the Romance languages, receiving his A.M. degree in June, 1906. He then went to Europe in search of further material for a dissertation on Lope de Vega, and during 1906-1907 travelled in Spain, Italy, and southern France. Returning to America in the fall of 1907, he was for four months an instructor in Romance languages at Wabash College, but he proved to be too Europeanized to meet the requirements of the position and was soon on his way across the Atlantic again. He landed at Gibraltar, and for the next few years lived in Italy, France, and England; chiefly, however, in London.

While in Venice in 1908 he issued his first little volume of verse, *A Lume Spento*, and in the following year he published in London *Personae* and *Exultations*, which first showed him as an original force in the literary world. He soon became one of the most influential, as well as one of the most energetic, of living men of letters. He lectured on art, occupied himself with translations, led in a number of literary movements, discovered and encouraged young authors who showed originality and talent. He pointed out the importance of the sculptor Gaudier-Brzeska and the musician, Antheil. Through his efforts, moreover, the Imagist poets emerged as a group in 1913. He helped to popularize the literature of China and Japan in the English-speaking world. During the years when there was great opposition to the "new poetry," he was one of its most untiring champions. And along with all these occupations, he continued to write poetry of his own and occasionally to issue a volume of prose. He contributed to the *Fortnightly Review*, the *Dial*, the *Egoist*, *Poetry: A Magazine of Verse*, and numerous other periodicals, and from 1917 to 1919 he was London editor of the *Little Review*. In 1927 he was awarded the cash prize given by the *Dial* for distinguished service to American literature.

Pound's interests have been wide and varied. In *How to Read* (1931) and *A B C of Reading* (1934) he gave his theories of literary interpretation; and in *A B C of Economics* (1932), *Jefferson and/or Mussolini* (1935), and *Social Credit* (1935) he expressed his views on political and economic matters. His economic theories also furnished the principal theme for his most ambitious poetical work, the *Cantos*, at which he worked for more than twenty years, and which he published in parts. In the *Cantos*, among other things, he ascribes the ills of society to the system of private credit, and as a cure for these ills he advocates a social state in which the owning and lending of money is a state function. In developing his ideas he draws his illustrations principally from three periods and countries: ancient China, Italy in the time of the Medici, and the early days of the American republic.

He returned to the United States for a visit in the spring of 1939, his first in eighteen years. While he was here, his Alma Mater, Hamilton College, gave him a Litt. D. degree. His disapproval of American universities and colleges, however, as well as of American institutions in general, was as pronounced as earlier; and he attracted considerable attention as the result of condemnatory remarks on what he saw and because of his favorable comments on Fascism.

In 1914 he married Dorothy Shakespear, who had been a student in a class in Romance literature which he taught at the Polytechnic Institute in London. They have no children. In 1924 he settled in Rapallo, Italy, where he now lives.

THE TREE

I stood still and was a tree amid the wood,
Knowing the truth of things unseen before;
Of Daphne and the laurel bow
And that god-feasting couple old
That grew elm-oak amid the wold.
'Twas not until the gods had been
Kindly entreated, and been brought within
Unto the hearth of their heart's home
That they might do this wonder thing;
Nathless I have been a tree amid the wood
And many a new thing understood
That was rank folly to my head before.
1908

NIGHT LITANY

O Dieu, purifiez nos cœurs!
Purifiez nos cœurs!

Yea, the lines hast thou laid unto me
in pleasant places,
And the beauty of this thy Venice
hast thou shown unto me
Until is its loveliness become unto me
a thing of tears.

O God, what great kindness
have we done in times past
and forgotten it,
That thou givest this wonder unto us,
O God of waters?

O God of the night,
What great sorrow
Cometh unto us,
That thou thus repayest us
Before the time of its coming?

O God of silence,
Purifiez nos cœurs,
Purifiez nos cœurs,
For we have seen
The glory of the shadow of the
likeness of thine handmaid,

Yea, the glory of the shadow
of thy Beauty hath walked
Upon the shadow of the waters
in this thy Venice.
And before the holiness
Of the shadow of thy handmaid
Have I hidden mine eyes,
O God of waters.

O God of silence,
Purifiez nos cœurs,
Purifiez nos cœurs,
O God of waters,
make clean our hearts within us
And our lips to show forth thy praise,
For I have seen the
Shadow of this thy Venice
Floating upon the waters,
And thy stars
Have seen this thing; out of their far courses
Have they seen this thing,
O God of waters;
Even as are thy stars
Silent unto us in their far-coursing,
Even so is mine heart
become silent within me.

Purifiez nos cœurs,
O God of the silence,
Purifiez nos cœurs,
O God of waters.

1909

BALLAD OF THE GOODLY FERE [1]

Simon Zelotes speaketh it somewhile after the Crucifixion.

Ha' we lost the goodliest fere o' all
For the priests and the gallows tree?
Aye lover he was of brawny men,
O' ships and the open sea.

When they came wi' a host to take Our Man
His smile was good to see;
"First let these go!" quo' our Goodly Fere,
"Or I'll see ye damned," says he.

Aye, he sent us out through the crossed high spears,
And the scorn of his laugh rang free;
"Why took ye not me when I walked about
Alone in the town?" says he.

Oh, we drunk his "Hale" in the good red wine
When we last made company;
No capon priest was the Goodly Fere
But a man o' men was he.

I ha' seen him drive a hundred men
Wi' a bundle o' cords swung free,
That they took the high and holy house
For their pawn and treasury.

They'll no' get him a' in a book I think,
Though they write it cunningly;
No mouse of the scrolls was the Goodly Fere
But aye loved the open sea.

If they think they ha' snared our Goodly Fere
They are fools to the last degree.
"I'll go to the feast," quo' our Goodly Fere,
"Though I go to the gallows tree."

"Ye ha' seen me heal the lame and blind,
And wake the dead," says he;

[1] Fere = mate, companion.

"Ye shall see one thing to master all:
'Tis how a brave man dies on the tree."

A son of God was the Goodly Fere
That bade us his brothers be.
I ha' seen him cow a thousand men.
I have seen him upon the tree.

He cried no cry when they drave the nails
And the blood gushed hot and free;
The hounds of the crimson sky gave tongue
But never a cry cried he.

I ha' seen him cow a thousand men
On the hills o' Galilee;
They whined as he walked out calm between,
Wi' his eyes like the grey o' the sea,

Like the sea that brooks no voyaging
With the winds unleashed and free,
Like the sea that he cowed at Genseret
Wi' twey words spoke' suddently.

A master of men was the Goodly Fere,
A mate of the wind and sea;
If they think they ha' slain our Goodly Fere
They are fools eternally.

I ha' seen him eat o' the honey-comb
Sin' they nailed him to the tree.

1909

THE EYES

Rest, Master, for we be a-weary, weary
And would feel the fingers of the wind
Upon these lids that lie over us
Sodden and lead-heavy.

Rest, brother, for lo! the dawn is without!
The yellow flame paleth
And the wax runs low.

Free us, for without be goodly colors,
Green of the wood-moss and flower colors,
And coolness beneath the trees.

Free us, for we perish
In this ever-flowing monotony
Of ugly print marks, black
Upon white parchment.

Free us, for there is one
Whose smile more availeth
Than all the age-old knowledge of thy books:
And we would look thereon.

1909

HISTRION

No man hath dared to write this thing as yet,
And yet I know, how that the souls of all men great
At times pass through us,
And we are melted into them, and are not
Save reflexions of their souls.
Thus am I Dante for a space and am
One François Villon, ballad-lord and thief,
Or am such holy ones I may not write,
Lest blasphemy be writ against my name;
This for an instant and the flame is gone.

'Tis as in midmost us there glows a sphere
Translucent, molten gold, that is the "I,"
And into this some form projects itself:
Christus, or John, or eke the Florentine;
And as the clear space is not if a form's
Imposed thereon,
So cease we from all being for the time,
And these, the Masters of the Soul, live on.

1909

AN IMMORALITY

Sing we for love and idleness,
Naught else is worth the having.

Though I have been in many a land,
There is naught else in living.

And I would rather have my sweet,
Though rose-leaves die of grieving,

Than do high deeds in Hungary
To pass all men's believing.

1912

A VIRGINAL

No, no! Go from me. I have left her lately.
I will not spoil my sheath with lesser brightness,
For my surrounding air hath a new lightness;
Slight are her arms, yet they have bound me straitly
And left me cloaked as with a gauze of æther;
As with sweet leaves: as with a subtle clearness.
Oh, I have picked up magic in her nearness
To sheathe me half in half the things that sheathe her.

No, no! Go from me. I have still the flavor,
Soft as spring wind that's come from birchen bowers.
Green come the shoots, aye April in the branches,
As winter's wound with her sleight hand she staunches,
Hath of the trees a likeness of the savor:
As white their bark, so white this lady's hours.

1912

DANCE FIGURE

FOR THE MARRIAGE IN CANA OF GALILEE.

Dark-eyed,
O woman of my dreams,
Ivory-sandaled,

There is none like thee among the dancers,
None with swift feet.

I have not found thee in the tents,
In the broken darkness.
I have not found thee at the well-head
Among the women with pitchers.

Thine arms are as a young sapling under the bark;
Thy face as a river with lights.

White as an almond are thy shoulders;
As new almonds stripped from the husk.
They guard thee not with eunuchs;
Not with bars of copper.

Gilt, turquoise and silver are in the place of thy rest.
A brown robe, with threads of gold woven in patterns, hast
thou gathered about thee,
O Nathat-Ikanaie, "Tree-at-the-river."

As a rillet among the sedge are thy hands upon me;
Thy fingers a frosted stream.

Thy maidens are white like pebbles;
Their music about thee!

There is none like thee among the dancers;
None with swift feet.

1916

THE STUDY IN ÆSTHETICS

The very small children in patched clothing,
Being smitten with an unusual wisdom,
Stopped in their play as she passed them
And cried up from their cobbles:
Guarda! Ahi, guarda! ch' è be'a! [1]

[1] Look! Ah, look! That's beautiful!

But three years after this
I heard the young Dante, whose last name I do not know—
For there are, in Sirmione, twenty-eight young Dantes and
    thirty-four Catulli;
And there had been a great catch of sardines,
And his elders
Were packing them in the great wooden boxes
For the market in Brescia, and he
Leapt about, snatching at the bright fish
And getting in both of their ways;
And in vain they commanded him to *sta fermo!* [1]
And when they would not let him arrange
The fish in the boxes
He stroked those which were already arranged,
Murmuring for his own satisfaction
This identical phrase:
    Ch' è be'a.

And at this I was mildly abashed.

1916

ENVOI (1919)

Go, dumb-born book,
Tell her that sang me once that song of Lawes:
Hadst thou but song
As thou hast subjects known,
Then were there cause in thee that should condone
Even my faults that heavy upon me lie,
And build her glories their longevity.

Tell her that sheds
Such treasure in the air,
Recking naught else but that her graces give
Life to the moment,
I would bid them live
As roses might, in magic amber laid,
Red overwrought with orange and all made
One substance and one color
Braving time.

[1] Stand still.

Tell her that goes
With song upon her lips
But sings not out the song, nor knows
The maker of it, some other mouth
May be as fair as hers,
Might, in new ages, gain her worshippers
When our two dusts with Waller's shall be laid,
Siftings on siftings in oblivion,
Till change hath broken down
All things save Beauty alone.

1920

CANTO XXI

"Keep the peace, Borso!" Where are we?
"Keep on with the business,
That's made me,
"And the res publica didn't.
When I was broke, and a poor kid,
They all knew me, all of these *cittadini*,[1]
And they all of them cut me dead, della gloria."
Intestate, 1429, leaving 178,221 florins *di sugello*,[2]
As is said in Cosimo's red leather note book. Di sugello.
And "with his credit emptied Venice of money"—
That was Cosimo—
"And Naples, and made them accept his peace."
And he caught the young boy Ficino
And had him taught the Greek language;
"With two ells of red cloth per person
I will make you," Cosimo speaking, "as many
Honest citizens as you desire."
Col credito suo . . .
Napoli e Venezia di danari . . .
Costretti . . . Napoli e Venezia . . . a quella pace . . .[3]
Or another time . . . oh well, pass it.
And Piero called in the credits,
(Diotisalvi was back of that)
And firms failed as far off as Avignon,
And Piero was like to be murdered,

[1] Citizens.

[2] I.e., sterling (bearing the crest).

[3] With his credit . . . Naples and Venice of money . . . constrained . . . to that peace.

And young Lauro came down ahead of him, in the road,
And said: Yes, father is coming.

Intestate, '69, in December, leaving me 237,989 florins,
As you will find in my big green account book
In carta di capretto;[1]
And from '34 when I count it, to last year,
We paid out 600,000 and over,
That was for building, taxes and charity.
Nic Uzano saw us coming. Against it, honest,
And warned 'em. They'd have murdered him,
And would Cosimo, but he bribed 'em;
And they did in Giuliano. E difficile,
A Firenze difficile viver ricco
Senza aver lo stato.
"E non avendo stato Piccinino
Doveva temerlo qualunque era in stato";[2]
And "that man sweated blood to put through that railway";
"Could you," wrote Mr. Jefferson,
"Find me a gardener
Who can play the french horn?
The bounds of American fortune
Will not admit the indulgence of a domestic band of
Musicians, yet I have thought that a passion for music
Might be reconciled with that economy which we are
Obliged to observe. I retain among my domestic servants
A gardener, a weaver, a cabinet-maker, and a stone-cutter,
To which I would add a vigneron.[3] In a country like yours
(id est Burgundy) where music is cultivated and
Practiced by every class of men, I suppose there might
Be found persons of these trades who could perform on
The french horn, clarionet, or hautboy and bassoon, so
That one might have a band of two french horns, two
Clarionets, two hautboys and a bassoon, without enlarging
Their domestic expenses. A certainty of employment for
Half a dozen years
(*affatigandose per suo piacer o non*)[4]

[1] In goat skin binding.

[2] It is difficult; it's hard to live in Florence and be rich without having power. "And Piccinino not having any power had to fear whoever was in power."

[3] Vineyard keeper.

[4] Wearing himself out for his own pleasure or not.

And at the end of that time, to find them, if they
Choose, a conveyance to their own country, might induce
Them to come here on reasonable wages. Without meaning to
Give you trouble, perhaps it might be practicable for you
In your ordinary intercourse with your people to find out
Such men disposed to come to America. Sobriety and good
Nature would be desirable parts of their characters."
June 1778 Montecello

And in July I went up to Milan for Duke Galeaz
To sponsor his infant in baptism,
Albeit were others more worthy,
And took his wife a gold collar holding a diamond
That cost about 3000 ducats, on which account
That signor Galeaz Sforza Visconti has wished me
To stand sponsor to all of his children.

Another war without glory, and another peace without quiet.

And the Sultan sent him an assassin, his brother;
And the Soldan of Egypt, a lion;
And he begat one pope and one son and four daughters,
And an University, Pisa; (Lauro Medici)
And nearly went broke in his business,
And bought land in Siena and Pisa,
And made peace by his own talk in Naples.
And there was grass on the floor of the temple,
Or where the floor of it might have been;
Gold fades in the gloom,
Under the blue-black roof, Placidia's,
Of the exarchate; and we sit here
By the arena, *les gradins*[1] . . .
And the palazzo, baseless, hangs there in the dawn
With low mist over the tide-mark;
And floats there nel tramonto[2]
With gold mist over the tide-mark.
The tesserae of the floor, and the patterns.
Fools making new shambles;
night over green ocean,
And the dry black of the night.
Night of the golden tiger,
And the dry flame in the air,
Voices of the procession,

[1] Steps. [2] In the sunset.

Faint now, from below us,
And the sea with tin flash in the sun-dazzle,
Like dark wine in the shadows.
"Wind between the sea and the mountains"
The tree-spheres half dark against sea
half clear against sunset,
The sun's keel freighted with cloud,
And after that hour, dry darkness
Floating flame in the air, gonads in organdy,
Dry flamelet, a petal borne in the wind.
Gignetei kalon.[1]
Impenetrable as the ignorance of old women.
In the dawn, as the fleet coming in after Actium,
Shore to the eastward, and altered,
And the old man sweeping leaves:
"Damned to you Midas, Midas lacking a Pan!"
And now in the valley,
Valley under the day's edge:
"Grow with the Pines of Ise;
As the Nile swells with Inopos.
As the Nile falls with Inopos."
Phoibos, turris eburnea,[2]
ivory against cobalt,
And the boughs cut on the air,
The leaves cut on the air,
The hounds on the green slope by the hill,
water still black in the shadow.
In the crisp air,
the discontinuous gods;
Pallas, young owl in the cup of her hand,
And, by night, the stag runs, and the leopard,
Owl-eye amid pine boughs.
Moon on the palm-leaf,
confusion;
Confusion, source of renewals;
Yellow wing, pale in the moon shaft,
Green wing, pale in the moon shaft,
Pomegranate, pale in the moon shaft,
White horn, pale in the moon shaft, and Titania
By the drinking hole,
steps, cut in the basalt.
Danced there Athame, danced, and there Phaethusa

[1] It becomes beautiful.
[2] Bright, ivory tower.

With color in the vein,
Strong as with blood-drink, once,
With color in the vein,
Red in the smoke-faint throat. Dis caught her up.

And the old man went on there
beating his mule with an asphodel.

1928

John Gould Fletcher

John Gould Fletcher was born January 3, 1886, at Little Rock, Arkansas. His father was Scotch-Irish, and came of pioneer stock, the family having lived in Tennessee from pre-Revolutionary days until the early nineteenth century, when the poet's grandfather moved westward across the Mississippi River. John Gould Fletcher, Sr., enlisted in the Southern army at the beginning of the Civil War, was made captain after the battle of Shiloh, and served with distinction until he was wounded at the battle of Murfreesboro. He had little formal education, but possessed excellent business sense, and as cotton buyer and owner of a general store in Little Rock was able to amass considerable wealth. In 1877 he married Adolphine Krause, a talented woman of Danish and German descent, her father having come from Denmark in 1839 and her mother from Hanover in 1835.

When Fletcher was four years old, he moved with his parents and two sisters into a large square white house of Colonial design, and this became the background of his childhood. His mother began his training herself, but when he was seven, teachers were employed to instruct him in Latin and German. From 1896 to 1899 he attended a private school, and from 1899 to 1902 a public high school in Little Rock; then for a year he was a pupil in Phillips Academy, Andover. In 1903 he entered Harvard, remaining there until his senior year, when he came into a small competence through the death of his father; whereupon he left college and moved to Boston to devote all his time to writing.

In August, 1908, he sailed for Europe, and going first to Italy, lived in Venice till November, and in Rome till the following May, when he went to England. Finding London a congenial place in which to work, he settled there at Adelphi Terrace. In

1910 he went for a while to Paris, where he read much French literature. Soon, however, he was back in London, working hard. In 1913 he published in rapid succession five volumes of poetry, but these brought him little recognition. His first book to receive much attention was *Irradiations—Sand and Spray* (1915), for which Amy Lowell secured an American publisher. It was written in free verse, and indicated that Fletcher had definitely renounced the conventional forms of poetry. About this time he became identified with the Imagist group, and has since been an ardent advocate of the newer poetic forms.

He came back to the United States in November, 1914, and after short stays in New York and Little Rock, settled in Boston, where, except for a summer in northern Michigan and trips to the West, he lived till May, 1916, when he returned to England. He revisited America in 1920, 1923, and 1926, travelling from coast to coast, lecturing and gathering material for such typically American works as *Breakers and Granite* (1921).

On July 5, 1916, Fletcher married Florence Emily Arbuthnot, of England. He lived in London till March, 1933, when he returned to Arkansas to make his home. Early in 1936 he obtained a divorce from his first wife, and on January 18, 1936, married Charlie May Hogue, of Arkansas. The University of Arkansas awarded him the honorary degree of LL.D. in 1933; and in 1939 he received the Pulitzer Prize for his *Selected Poems* (1938).

Fletcher's work falls into four periods. In the first (1909-1914) he was influenced by the French Symbolists and Ezra Pound; in the second (1914-1920) the chief influence on him was Amy Lowell; in the third (1920-1930) he was attracted to T. S. Eliot; and it is only since 1930 that he feels he has achieved his own individual way of writing, made up of all the influences he has felt. This eclectism, he feels, is characteristic of the modern poet. "In times gone by," he says, "when the poets had a common stock of stylistic devices and subjects to draw upon, it was not necessary to read so widely or so deeply as now. The modern poet is less sure of his own knowledge or of his skill than the poet of old. But he commands a wider range, and his technical effects often go deeper. It is better for him to have read one hundred poets rather than one."

THE CAGED EAGLE

He sits upon his perch in the far evening:
  Motionless, watching twilight fade away.
His wings he never rustles, he never makes a sound,
  He waits until the night devours the day.

And then he shuts his eyes, still poised deliberate
  Upon his perch, nor moves throughout the night;
He dreams, before the morning brings him waking,
  That bars have vanished 'twixt him and the light.

He sits upon his perch in the fresh morning:
  Interrogating silently the sky.
No eyelid moves, no feather, as I watch him:—
  I also know the bars more strong than I!

1913

IRRADIATIONS: XVIII

Blue, brown, blue: sky, sand, sea:
I swell to your immensity.
I will run over the endless beach,
I will shout to the breaking spray,
I will touch the sky with my fingers.
My happiness is like this sand:
I let it run out of my hand.

1915

THE GROUNDSWELL

(*Marcia Funebre*)

With heavy doleful clamor, hour on hour, and day on day,
The muddy groundswell lifts and breaks and falls and slides away.

The cold and naked wind runs shivering over the sands,
Salt are its eyes, open its mouth, its brow wet, blue its hands.

It finds naught but a starving gull whose wings trail at its side,
And the dull battered wreckage, grey jetsam of the tide.

The lifeless chilly slaty sky with no blue hope is lit,
A rusty waddling steamer plants a smudge of smoke on it.

Stupidly stand the factory chimneys staring over all,
The grey grows ever denser, and soon the night will fall:

The wind runs sobbing over the beach and touches with its hands
Straw, chaff, old bottles, broken crates, the litter of the sands.

Sometimes the bloated carcase of a dog or fish is found,
Sometimes the rumpled feathers of a sea-gull shot or drowned.

Last year it was an unknown man who came up from the sea,
There is his grave hard by the dunes under a stunted tree.

With heavy doleful clamor, hour on hour, and day on day,
The muddy groundswell lifts and breaks and falls and slides away.

1915

SNOW AT SEA

(*Andante*)

Silently fell
The snow on the waters
In the grey dusk
Of the winter evening:
Swirling and falling,
Sucked into the oily
Blue-black surface
Of the sea.

We pounded on slowly;
From our bows sheeted
A shuddering mass of heavy foam:
Night closed about us,
But ere we were darkened,
We saw close in
A great gaunt schooner
Beating to southward.

Silently fell
The snow on the waters,

As we pounded north
In the winter evening.
1915

BLUE SYMPHONY[1]

I

The darkness rolls upward.
The thick darkness carries with it
Rain and a ravel of cloud.
The sun comes forth upon earth.

Palely the dawn
Leaves me facing timidly
Old gardens sunken:
And in the walks is water.

Sombre wreck—autumnal leaves;
Shadowy roofs
In the blue mist,
And a willow-branch that is broken.

Oh, old pagodas of my soul, how you glittered across
green trees!

Blue and cool:
Blue, tremulously,
Blow faint puffs of smoke
Across sombre pools.
The damp green smell of rotted wood;
And a heron that cries from out the water.

[1] "I have called my works 'Symphonies,' when they are really dramas of the soul, and hence, in them I have used color for verity, for ornament, for drama, for its inherent beauty, and for intensifying the form of the emotion that each of these poems is intended to evoke.

"Let us take an artist, a young man at the outset of his career. His years of searching, of fumbling, of other men's influence, are coming to an end. Sure of himself, he yet sees that he will spend all his life pursuing a vision of beauty which will elude him at the very last. This is the first symphony, which I have called the 'Blue,' because blue suggests to me depth, mystery, and distance. . . .

"So he passes to the 'White Symphony,' the central poem of this series, in which I have sought to describe the artist's struggle to attain unutterable and superhuman perfection. This struggle goes on from the midsummer of his life to midwinter. The end of it is stated in the poem."—Preface to *Goblins and Pagodas* (1916), pp. xx-xxi.

II

Through the upland meadows
I go alone.
For I dreamed of someone last night
Who is waiting for me.

Flower and blossom, tell me, do you know of her?

Have the rocks hidden her voice?
They are very blue and still.

Long upward road that is leading me,
Light-hearted I quit you,
For the long loose ripples of the meadow-grass
Invite me to dance upon them.

Quivering grass
Daintily poised
For her foot's tripping.

Oh, blown clouds, could I only race up like you,
Oh, the last slopes that are sun-drenched and steep!

Look, the sky!
Across black valleys
Rise blue-white aloft
Jagged unwrinkled mountains, ranges of death.

Solitude. Silence.

III

One chuckles by the brook for me:
One rages under the stone.
One makes a spout of his mouth,
One whispers—one is gone.

One over there on the water
Spreads cold ripples
For me
Enticingly.

The vast dark trees
Flow like blue veils
Of tears
Into the water.

Sour sprites,
Moaning and chuckling,
What have you hidden from me?

"In the palace of the blue stone she lies forever
Bound hand and foot."

Was it the wind
That rattled the reeds together?

Dry reeds,
A faint shiver in the grasses.

IV

On the left hand there is a temple:
And a palace on the right-hand side.
Foot passengers in scarlet
Pass over the glittering tide.

Under the bridge
The old river flows
Low and monotonous
Day after day.

I have heard and have seen
All the news that has been:
Autumn's gold and spring's green!

Now in my palace
I see foot passengers
Crossing the river:
Pilgrims of autumn
In the afternoons.

Lotus pools:
Petals in the water.
These are my dreams.
For me silks are outspread.
I take my ease, unthinking.

V

And now the lowest pine-branch
Is drawn across the disk of the sun.
Old friends who will forget me soon,
I must go on,
Towards those blue death-mountains
I have forgot so long.

In the marsh grasses
There lies forever
My last treasure,
With the hopes of my heart.

The ice is glazing over,
Torn lanterns flutter,
On the leaves is snow.

In the frosty evening
Toll the old bell for me
Once, in the sleepy temple.

Perhaps my soul will hear.

Afterglow:
Before the stars peep
I shall creep out into darkness.
1913, 1916

WHITE SYMPHONY

I

Forlorn and white,
Whorls of purity about a golden chalice,
Immense the peonies
Flare and shatter their petals over my face.

They slowly turn paler,
They seem to be melting like blue-grey flakes of ice,
Thin greyish shivers
Fluctuating mid the dark green lance-thrust of the leaves.

Like snowballs tossed,
Like soft white butterflies,
The peonies poise in the twilight.
And their narcotic insinuating perfume
Draws me into them
Shivering with the coolness,
Aching with the void.
They kiss the blue chalice of my dreams
Like a gesture seen for an instant and then lost forever.

* * * * *

Outwards the petals
Thrust to embrace me,
Pale daggers of coldness
Run through my aching breast.

Outwards, still outwards,
Till on the brink of twilight
They swirl downwards silently,
Flurry of snow in the void.

Outwards, still outwards,
Till the blue walls are hidden,
And in the blinding white radiance
Of a whirlpool of clouds, I awake.

* * * * *

Like spraying rockets
My peonies shower
Their glories on the night.

Wavering perfumes,
Drift about the garden;
Shadows of the moonlight,
Drift and ripple over the dew-gemmed leaves.

Soar, crash, and sparkle,
Shoal of stars drifting
Like silver fishes,
Through the black sluggish boughs.

Towards the impossible,
Towards the inaccessible,

Towards the ultimate,
Towards the silence,
Towards the eternal,
These blossoms go.

The peonies spring like rockets in the twilight,
And out of them all I rise.

II

Downwards through the blue abyss it slides,
The white snow-water of my dreams,
Downwards crashing from slippery rock
Into the boiling chasm:
In which no eye dare look, for it is the chasm of death.

Upwards from the blue abyss it rises,
The chill water-mist of my dreams;
Upwards to greyish weeping pines,
And to skies of autumn ever about my heart,
It is blue at the beginning,
And blue-white against the grey-greenness;
It wavers in the upper air,
Catching unconscious sparkles, a rainbow-glint of sunlight,
And fading in the sad depths of the sky.

Outwards rush the strong pale clouds,
Outwards and ever outwards;
The blue-grey clouds indistinguishable one from another:
Nervous, sinewy, tossing their arms and brandishing,
Till on the blue serrations of the horizon
They drench with their black rain a great peak of changless snow.

* * * * *

As evening came on, I climbed the tower,
To gaze upon the city far beneath:
I was not weary of day; but in the evening
A white mist assembled and gathered over the earth
And blotted it from sight.

But to escape:
To chase with the golden clouds galloping over the horizon:
Arrows of the northwest wind
Singing amid them,
Ruffling up my hair!

As evening came on the distance altered,
Pale wavering reflections rose from out the city,
Like sighs or the beckoning of half-invisible hands.
Monotonously and sluggishly they crept upwards
A river that had spent itself in some chasm,
And dwindled and foamed at last at my weary feet.

Autumn! Golden fountains,
And the winds neighing
Amid the monotonous hills:
Desolation of the old gods,
Rain that lifts and rain that moves away;
In the green-black torrent
Scarlet leaves.

It was now perfectly evening:
And the tower loomed like a gaunt peak in mid-air
Above the city: its base was utterly lost.
It was slowly coming on to rain,
And the immense columns of white mist
Wavered and broke before the faint-hurled spears.

I will descend the mountains like a shepherd,
And in the folds of tumultuous misty cities,
I will put all my thoughts, all my old thoughts, safely to sleep.
For it is already autumn,
O whiteness of the pale southwestern sky!
O wavering dream that was not mine to keep!

* * * * *

In midnight, in mournful moonlight,
By paths I could not trace,
I walked in the white garden;
Each flower had a white face.
Their perfume intoxicated me: thus I began my dream.

I was alone; I had no one to guide me,
But the moon was like the sun:
It stooped and kissed each waxen petal,
One after one.

Green and white was that garden: diamond rain hung in the
    branches;
You will not believe it!

In the morning, at the dayspring,
I wakened, shivering; lo,
The white garden that blossomed at my feet
Was a garden hidden in snow.

It was my sorrow to see that all this was a dream.

III

Blue, clogged with purple,
Mists uncoil themselves:
Sparkling to the horizon,
I see the snow alone.

In the deep blue chasm,
Boats sleep under gold thatch;
Icicle-like trees fret
Faintly rose-touched sky.

Under their heaped snow-eaves,
Leaden houses shiver.
Through thin blue crevasses
Trickles an icy stream.

The pines groan white-laden,
The waves shiver, struck by the wind;
Beyond from treeless horizons,
Broken snow-peaks crawl to the sea.

* * * * *

Wearily the snow glares,
Through the grey silence, day after day,
Mocking the colorless, cloudless sky
With the reflection of death.

There is no smoke through the pine tops,
No strong red boatmen in pale green reeds,
No herons to flicker an instant,
No lanterns to glow with gay ray.

No sails beat up to the harbor,
With creaking cordage and sailors' song.
Somnolent, bare-poled, indifferent,
They sleep, and the city sleeps.

Mid-winter about them casts
Its dreary fortifications:
Each day is a gaunt grey rock,
And death is the last of them all.

* * * * *

Over the sluggish snow,
Drifts now a pallid weak shower of bloom;
Boredom of fresh creation,
Death-weariness of old returns.

White, white blossom,
Fall of the shattered cups day on day:
Is there anything here that is not ancient,
That has not bloomed a thousand years ago?

Under the glare of the white-hot day,
Under the restless wind-rakes of the winter,
White blossom or white snow scattered,
And beneath them, dark, the graves.

Dark graves never changing,
White dream drifting, never changing above them:
O that the white scroll of heaven might be rolled up,
And the naked red lightning thrust at the smouldering earth!

1914, 1916

A WOMAN STANDING BY A GATE WITH AN UMBRELLA

Late summer changes to autumn:
Chrysanthemums are scattered
Behind the palings.

Gold and vermilion
The afternoon.

I wait here dreaming of vermilion sunsets:
In my heart is a half fear of the chill autumn rain.

1918

A WOMAN IN WINTER COSTUME

She is like the great rains
That fall over the earth in winter-time.

Wave on wave her heavy robes collapse
In green torrents
Lashed with slaty foam.

Downward the sun strikes amid them
And enkindles a lone flower;
A violet iris standing yet in seething pools of grey.

1918

CHANGING LOVE

My love for her at first was like the smoke that drifts
Across the marshes
From burning woods.

But, after she had gone,
It was like the lotus that lifts up
Its heart shaped buds from the dim waters.

1918

A LIFE

Her life was like a swiftly rushing stream
Green and scarlet,
Falling into darkness.

The seasons passed for her,
Like pale iris wilting,
Or peonies flying to ribbons before the storm-gusts.
The sombre pine-tops waited until the seasons had passed.

Then in her heart they grew
The snows of changeless winter
Stirred by the bitter winds of unsatisfied desire.

1918

MUTABILITY

The wind shakes the mists,
Making them quiver
With faint drum-tones of thunder.

Out of the crane-haunted mists of autumn,
Blue and brown
Rolls the moon.

There was a city living here long ago;
Of all that city
There is only one stone left half-buried in the marsh,
With characters upon it which no one now can read.

1918

EVENING SKY

The sky spreads out its poor array
Of tattered flags,
Saffron and rose
Over the weary huddle of housetops
Smoking their evening pipes in silence.

1918

FUGITIVE BEAUTY

As the fish that leaps from the river,
As the dropping of a November leaf at twilight,
As the faint flicker of lightning down the southern sky,
So I saw beauty, far away.

1918

FAITH

The dark clouds gather around my path, they bar me in every
way,
Every way but westward, where is the great sun's death;
But I do not fear those great dark clouds, nor the tragic death
of a day;

My heart beats fully and steadily; faith is new-born with each
breath,
Faith in that part of me which was not mine, which was given
to me to use,
Which shall live on though all the suns fall dead into the night;
Faith in a love which rules all things: for though I fall and lose,
I shall live on for ever, for I have held with the light.

1918

IN THE OPEN AIR

It is only in the open air
That our love can be given to us:
We must be free each instant,
And over our heads see the sky.
The roystering cry of the vagabond wind
Wakens the gipsy song in our hearts;
The sun on the black horizon
Is the camp-fire at which we may sleep.

I am the wind,
And you are the slender birch for me;
Over the hilltops I shall seek you;
You will wait drooping at last.
You caress me with eager fingers;
I breathe into your entangled boughs:
In the sunlight we laugh together,
And breathe side by side in the night.

Golden clouds we have seen racing
Full-bellied up the blue waveless sky;
All of our hearts have soared on to them
Like skylarks striving in flight.
We have taken the old green earth
For our great lawless adventure,
And seen in the white-thorn blossoming
The pale smile of the Crucified.

It is only in the open air
That our love may be given to us;
No house may for long time hold us,
Love does not dwell in houses.

Freely over the pathless earth
Rove our two hearts together:
Joy and song in the morning,
At nightfall kisses and sleep.

1918

EBB-TIDE

Ebb-tide at ending of the sea,
Which wrecked our castles on the sands;
We drift apart mysteriously,
With empty eyes, with open hands,
Knowing not what could make us so,
Not able to check the current's might;
The force that set our hearts aglow,
Now dwindling down to endless night.

It is as if we never met:
Was't I who loved, and I who lost?
Were yours the lips on which I set
That kiss which, lit with passion, cost
Half life, half reason? Now, alas,
The vision fades, the glory's gone,
The image shatters with the glass,
The empty frame is all I own.

Ebb-tide, the dying of the sea;
A weedy stretch of gloomy beach
Torn by the gale—and, mystery,
A wave that sparkles out of reach.
All we have left is rubbish now,
Mere wrecks of glory, lifeless, wet;
The chalice spoilt, the broken vow,
Bury them together, let's forget!

The year is whirling withered leaves;
The last one falls soon—when 'tis gone,
No matter who suffers or who grieves,
Time blows a truce, our love is done.
The dream of summer far-off stands;
Its hours are spent beyond recall,
Only the dull and lifeless sands,
And darkness rising as we fall.

Ebb-tide, the waning of the light;
I cannot hope, I cannot weep.
Only at middle of the night
Shall rise the dream that conquers sleep;
And that, too, fails soon, like false light.
We could not keep love, 'twas too fair;
Within each empty heart to-night
Only the ashes of despair!

Perhaps the tide will rise once more;
Perhaps ere death will call us in,
We'll hear again its fading roar,
But then too old, too cold to win.
The sparkling glimmering mystery
That swept us on, is gone from sight.
Ebb-tide at ending of the sea,
My love, my lost, good-night, good-night.

1918

SKYSCRAPERS

What are these, angels or demons,
Or steel and stone?
Soaring, alert,
Striped with diversified windows,
These sweep aloft
And the multitude crane their necks to them:—
Are they angels, or demons,
Or stone?

If the grey sapless people,
Moving along the street, thought them angels,
They too would be beautiful,
Erect and laughing to the sky for joy.
If as demons they feared them,
They would smite with fierce hatred
These brown haughty foreheads:
They would not suffer them to hold the sun in trust.

What are they, then, angels, or demons,
Or stone?

Deaf sightless towers
Unendowed yet with life;
Soaring vast effort
Spent in the sky till it breaks there.
You men of my country
Who shaped these proud visions,
You have yet to find godhead
Not here, but in the human heart.

1921

DOWN THE MISSISSIPPI

EMBARKATION

Dull masses of dense green,
The forests range their sombre platforms;
Between them silently, like a spirit,
The river finds its own mysterious path.

Loosely the river sways out, backward, forward,
Always fretting the outer side;
Shunning the invisible focus of each crescent,
Seeking to spread into shining loops over fields.

Like an enormous serpent, dilating, uncoiling,
Displaying a broad scaly back of earth-smeared gold;
Swaying out sinuously between the dull motionless forests,
As molten metal might glide down the lip of a vase of dark
bronze;

It goes, while the steamboat drifting out upon it,
Seems now to be floating not only outwards but upwards;
In the flight of a petal detached and gradually moving skyward
Above the pink explosion of the calyx of the dawn.

HEAT

As if the sun had trodden down the sky,
Until no more it holds living air, but only humid vapor,
Heat pressing upon earth with irresistible languor,
Turns all the solid forest into half-liquid smudge.

The heavy clouds like cargo-boats strain slowly against its current;
And the flickering of the haze is like the thunder of ten thousand
paddles

Against the heavy wall of the horizon, pale-blue and utterly
windless,
Whereon the sun hangs motionless, a brassy disc of flame.

FULL MOON

Flinging its arc of silver bubbles, quickly shifts the moon
From side to side of us as we go down its path;
I sit on the deck at midnight and watch it slipping and sliding,
Under my tilted chair, like a thin film of spilt water.

It is weaving a river of light to take the place of this river;
A river where we shall drift all night, then come to rest in its
shallows;
And then I shall wake from my drowsiness and look down from
some dim treetop
Over white lakes of cotton, like moonfields on every side.

THE MOON'S ORCHESTRA

When the moon lights up
Its dull red campfire through the trees;
And floats out, like a white balloon,
Into the blue cup of the night, borne by a casual breeze;
The moon-orchestra then begins to stir.
Jiggle of fiddles commence their crazy dance in the darkness.
Crickets churr
Against the stark reiteration of the rusty flutes which frogs
Puff at from rotted logs
In the swamp.
And then the moon begins her dance of frozen pomp
Over the lightly quivering floor of the flat and mournful river.
Her white feet slightly twist and swirl.
She is a mad girl
In an old unlit ballroom
Whose walls, half-guessed at through the gloom,
Are hung with the rusty crape of stark black cypress
Which show, through gaps and tatters, red stains half hidden
away.

THE STEVEDORES

Frieze of warm bronze that glides with catlike movements
Over the gangplank poised and yet awaiting,
The sinewy thudding rhythm of forty shuffling feet
Falling like muffled drumbeats on the stillness.

O roll the cotton down,
Roll, roll the cotton down,
From the further side of Jordan,
O roll the cotton down!

And the river waits.
The river listens,
Chuckling little banjo-notes that break with a flop on the stillness;
And by the low dark shed that holds the heavy freights,
Two lonely cypress trees stand up and point with stiffened fingers
Far southward where a single chimney stands out aloof in the sky.

NIGHT LANDING

After the whistle's roar has bellowed and shuddered,
Shaking the sleeping town and the somnolent river,
The deep toned floating of the pilot's bell
Suddenly warns the engines.

They stop like heartbeats that abruptly stop;
The shore glides to us, in a wide low curve.

And then—supreme revelation of the river—
The tackle is loosed—the long gangplank swings outwards—
And poised at the end of it, half-naked beneath the searchlight,
A blue-black negro with gleaming teeth waits for his chance to
leap.

THE SILENCE

There is a silence I carry about with me always;
A silence perpetual, for it is self-created;
A silence of heat, of water, of unchecked fruitfulness
Through which each year the heavy harvests bloom and burst
and fall.

Deep, matted green silence of my South,
Often within the push and scorn of great cities,
I have seen that mile-wide waste of water swaying out to you,
And on its current glimmering, I am going to the sea.

There is a silence I have achieved: I have walked beyond its
threshold;
I know it is without horizons, boundless, fathomless, perfect.

And some day maybe, far away,
I will curl up in it at last and sleep an endless sleep.
Aug. 20-27, 1915, 1921

THE GRAND CANYON OF THE COLORADO

I

I have seen that which is mysterious,
Aloof, divided, silent;
Something not of this earth.

Suddenly the endless dark green piney uplands
Stopped.
Yellow, red, grey-green, purple-black chasms fell swiftly below
each other.

On the other side,
Strong-built, arose
Towers whose durable terraces were hammered from red sand-
stone,
Purple granite, and gold.

Beyond
A golden wall,
Aloof, inscrutable.

It was hidden
Behind layers of white silence.
No voice might reach it;
It was not of this earth.

II

When the free thunder-spirit
Had built and carved these terraced walls,
Completing his task of ages,
He wrote upon them
In dark invisible words,
"It is finished."

Silent and windless,
The forever completed

Is never broken but by clouds.
Sometimes dark eagles slow-sailing
Rise out of it, like spirits,
Wheeling away.

Now in the steady glare,
Some will moves darkly,
Driving the clouds, piling them,
Shaping masses of shadow
That move slowly forward
Over the array of towers.

Yet still behind them,
Unscarred, unaltered,
The work stands finished.
Without a cry of protest, for protest is uncompletion,
Moulded and fashioned forever in durable ageless stone,
And on every surface is written
In strong invisible words:
"It is finished."

III

Should I by chance deserve some last reward from earth,—
The rewards of earth are usually unwholesome;—
One single thing I would ask for,
Burn my body here.

Kindle the pyre
Upon this jutting point:
Dry aromatic juniper,
Lean flame, blue smoke,
Ashes and dust.

The winds would drift the ash
Outwards across the canyon,
To the rose-purple rim of the desert
Beyond the red-barred towers.

The rabbits in the morning
Would come and snuff at the embers,
While the chasm, rekindling,
Would build up its silent poem of color to the sun.

IV

Shadows of clouds
March across the canyon,
Shadows of blue hands passing
Over a curtain of flame.

Clutching, staggering, upstriking,
Darting in blue-black fury,
To where the pinnacles, green and orange,
Await.

The winds are battling and striving to break them;
Thin lightnings spit and flicker;
The peaks seem a dance of scarlet demons
Flitting amid the shadows.

Grey rain-curtains wave afar off;
Wisps of vapor curl and vanish:
The sun throws soft shafts of golden light
Over rose-buttressed palisades.

Now the clouds are a lazy procession:
Blue balloons bobbing solemnly
Over black-dappled walls:

Where rise sharp-fretted, golden-roofed cathedrals
Exultantly, and split the sky with light.

Aug., 1915, 1921

MEXICAN QUARTER

By an alley lined with tumble-down shacks,
And street-lamps askew, half-sputtering,
Feebly glimmering on gutters choked with filth and dogs
Scratching their mangy backs:
Half-naked children are running about,
Women puff cigarettes in black doorways,
Crickets are crying.
Men slouch sullenly
Into the shadows:
Behind a hedge of cactus,

The smell of a dead horse
Mingles with the smell of tortillas frying.

And a girl in a black lace shawl
Sits in a rickety chair by the square of an unglazed window,
And sees the explosion of the stars
Softly poised on a velvet sky,
And she is humming to herself:—
"Stars, if I could reach you,
(You are so very clear that it seems as if I could reach you)
I would give you all to the Madonna's image,
On the grey-plastered altar behind the paper flowers,
So that Juan would come back to me,
And we could live again those lazy burning hours,
Forgetting the tap of my fan and my sharp words.
And I would only keep four of you,
Those two blue-white ones overhead,
To hang in my ears;
And those two orange ones yonder,
To fasten on my shoe-buckles."

A little further along the street
A man sits stringing a brown guitar.
The smoke of his cigarette curls 'round his head,
And he too is humming, but other words:
"Think not that at your window I wait;
New love is better, the old is turned to hate.
Fate! Fate! All things pass away;
Life is forever, youth is for a day.
Love again if you may
Before the stars are blown out of the sky,
And the crickets die!
Babylon and Samarkand
Are mud walls in a waste of sand."

1921

LINCOLN

I

Like a gaunt, scraggly pine
Which lifts its head above the mournful sandhills;
And patiently, through dull years of bitter silence,
Untended and uncared for, starts to grow.

Ungainly, laboring, huge,
The wind of the north has twisted and gnarled its branches;
Yet in the heat of mid-summer days, when thunder clouds ring
    the horizon,
A nation of men shall rest beneath its shade.

And it shall protect them all,
Hold everyone safe there, watching aloof in silence;
Until at last, one mad stray bolt from the zenith
Shall strike it in an instant down to earth.

II

There was a darkness in this man; an immense and hollow
    darkness,
Of which we may not speak, nor share with him nor enter;
A darkness through which strong roots stretched downwards
    into the earth,
Towards old things;

Towards the herdman-kings who walked the earth and spoke
    with God,
Towards the wanderers who sought for they knew not what, and
    found their goal at last;
Towards the men who waited, only waited patiently when all
    seemed lost,
Many bitter winters of defeat;

Down to the granite of patience,
These roots swept, knotted fibrous roots, prying, piercing, seeking,
And drew from the living rock and the living waters about it,
The red sap to carry upwards to the sun.

Not proud, but humble,
Only to serve and pass on, to endure to the end through service,
For the axe is laid at the roots of the trees, and all that brings
    not forth good fruit
Shall be cut down on the day to come and cast into the fire.

III

There is a silence abroad in the land to-day,
And in the hearts of men, a deep and anxious silence;
And, because we are still at last, those bronze lips slowly open,
Those hollow and weary eyes take on a gleam of light.

Slowly a patient, firm-syllabled voice cuts through the endless
silence,
Like laboring oxen that drag a plough through the chaos of
rude clay-fields,
"I went forward as the light goes forward in early spring,
But there were also many things which I left behind.

"Tombs that were quiet;
One, of a mother, whose brief light went out in the darkness,
One of a loved one, the snow on whose grave is long falling,
One only of a child, but it was mine.

"Have you forgotten your graves? Go, question them in anguish,
Listen long to their unstirred lips. From your hostages to silence
Learn there is no life without death, no dawn without sunsetting,
No victory but to him who has given all."

The clamor of cannon dies down, the furnace-mouth of the
battle is silent,
The midwinter sun dips and descends, the earth takes on afresh
its bright colors.
But he whom we mocked and obeyed not, he whom we scorned
and mistrusted,
He has descended, like a god, to his rest.

Over the uproar of cities,
Over the million intricate threads of life weaving and crossing,
In the midst of problems we know not, tangling, perplexing,
ensnaring,
Rises one white tomb alone.

Beam over it, stars,
Wrap it 'round, stripes—stripes red for the pain that he bore
for you—
Enfold it forever, O flag, rent, soiled, but repaired through
your anguish;
Long as you keep him there safe, the nations shall bow to
your law.

Strew over him flowers:
Blue forget-me-nots from the north and the bright pink arbutus
From the east, and from the west rich orange blossom,
But from the heart of the land take the passion-flower;

Rayed, violet, dim,
With the nails that pierced, the cross that he bore and the circlet,
And beside it there lay also one lonely snow-white magnolia,
Bitter for remembrance of the healing which has passed.

1916, 1921

LOST CORNER

Sound that the whippoorwill sobbed adown the mountain
Amid the twisted oaks, the pines uprising;
Lost Corner where the wagons came to rest,
Because a spring gushed out beneath the stone,
Or because men were weary of their going
Back of beyond: the hills still hold some secrets.
There are some memories that the trees have taken;
Holloa them how you will, they will not soon come home.

Here time has stopped, and nothing ever changes;
Speech too has stopped with time; the hills and valleys,
Ridge beyond wooded ridge, have ceased to wait
A future, having never known a past:
Even the Indians never walked this country
Where lazily like smoke the frosty morning
Curls low mist-shapes around the dry creek-bottoms
That clasp the paintless shacks and will not let them go.

Back of beyond—Lost Corner—far off hiding
From the loud locomotive bell and whistle
That roars through clayey cuts, or over trestles
That look to where the mountains stand so far
In purple darkness that their shapes seem only
Another world than this, too far to reckon.
What trail amid the hickories hides your chimneys?
I think no guide will ever show that way.

Here time is not, or cancels out; and space is
A mere vague string of sounds; gone over yonder;
Maybe; behind that ridge; out of that valley;
Further along the creek; and still so far to go:
Only the deer knows, or the mountain-holly
Has shown the path to these who found the prospect
More sweet than any gain; these stringy figures
That seem as speechless as their sandy clay.

Sleep on the husk-filled mattress, let the evening
Rouse ague in your bones, or go and scrabble
With the thin hoe about the paintless cabin;
Get skeered at night; or watch for days unchanging
The corn hang withered in the sizzling heat
Of mid-July; and then perhaps you'll tell me
Why should you, stripped of all but earth, still value
Life more than death? Is there much left to make
A fuss about? The sky's still there, the mountain;
The slow and gangling walk 'twixt birth and death;
Misery in the flesh—heaven over yonder,
And something else unsaid no one need know.

Lost Corner—lost to all but a dark freedom—
Some day we all must find you ere we go.

1936

Hilda Doolittle (H. D.)

Hilda Doolittle, usually referred to by the pseudonym "H. D.," was born in Bethlehem, Pennsylvania, September 10, 1886. Her father, Charles L. Doolittle, was Professor of Mathematics and Astronomy at Lehigh University; and her mother was his second wife, Helen Wolle Doolittle. In her ninth year the family moved to Philadelphia, where her father became director of the Flower Astronomical Observatory at the University of Pennsylvania, a position he held until 1912, when he retired.

In Bethlehem she attended one of the public schools, and in Philadelphia she became a student in the Gordon School, where she remained until 1902. Then she went to the Friends' Central School to prepare for admission to Bryn Mawr College, which she entered in 1904. Her scholastic record was not brilliant, although while in the college she studied literature appreciatively and continued her efforts, begun when a child, to learn to write. Among other subjects she acquired an interest in the Latin lyric poets, translating from their work. In her sophomore year, however, illness forced her to leave college.

Soon after leaving Bryn Mawr she began to write short stories, and some of these, designed for children, were published in a Presbyterian paper in Philadelphia. In 1911 she went abroad, intending to stay only for the summer; but after completing a journey through Italy and France and reaching London, she became interested in the literary activities in England and decided to remain there. In London she met Ezra Pound, whom she had previously known in Philadelphia, and showed him some verse she had written. It pleased him, and he sent it to *Poetry: A Magazine of Verse*, where, in the issue for January, 1913, it made its appearance—her first poetry to be published. She now joined the

Imagists, and soon became a leading member of that group. Her first volume of poetry, *Sea Garden,* was published in 1916.

Another member of the Imagist group was the English poet Richard Aldington. Their interest in Greek and Latin poetry brought them together, and on October 18, 1913, they were married. They had one child, a daughter, but at the close of World War I, in which Aldington served, they separated. She eventually settled in a small town in Switzerland, where she lived until the second World War. She then returned to London, where she now lives.

Of all the Imagists she has remained most faithful to the creed announced in the early days of the movement. In addition to her poetry she has written several plays, a novel, *Hedylus* (1928), and a short prose work, *Hedgehog* (1937). She has made one trip to the United States—in 1920—since first going abroad in 1911.

SEA ROSE

Rose, harsh rose,
marred and with stint of petals,
meagre flower, thin,
sparse of leaf,

more precious
than a wet rose
single on a stem—
you are caught in the drift.

Stunted, with small leaf,
you are flung on the sand,
you are lifted
in the crisp sand
that drives in the wind.

Can the spice-rose
drip such acrid fragrance
hardened in a leaf?

1916

EVENING

The light passes
from ridge to ridge,
from flower to flower—
the hypaticas, wide-spread
under the light
grow faint—
the petals reach inward,
the blue tips bend
toward the bluer heart
and the flowers are lost.

The cornel-buds are still white,
but shadows dart
from the cornel-roots—
black creeps from root to root,
each leaf
cuts another leaf on the grass,
shadow seeks shadow,
then both leaf
and leaf-shadow are lost.

1916

SEA GODS

I

They say there is no hope—
sand—drift—rocks—rubble of the sea—
the broken hulk of a ship,
hung with shreds of rope,
pallid under the cracked pitch.

They say there is no hope
to conjure you—
no whip of the tongue to anger you—
no hate of words
you must rise to refute.

They say you are twisted by the sea,
you are cut apart

by wave-break upon wave-break,
that you are misshapen by the sharp rocks,
broken by the rasp and after-rasp.

That you are cut, torn, mangled,
torn by the stress and beat,
no stronger than the strips of sand
along your ragged beach.

II

But we bring violets,
great masses—single, sweet,
wood-violets, stream-violets,
violets from a wet marsh.

Violets in clumps from hills,
tufts with earth at the roots,
violets tugged from rocks,
blue violets, moss, cliff, river-violets.

Yellow violets' gold,
burnt with a rare tint—
violets like red ash
among tufts of grass.

We bring deep-purple
bird-foot violets.

We bring the hyacinth-violet,
sweet, bare, chill to the touch—
And violets whiter than the in-rush
of your own white surf.

III

For you will come,
you will yet haunt men in ships,
you will trail across the fringe of strait
and circle the jagged rocks.

You will trail across the rocks
and wash them with your salt,
you will curl between sand-hills—

you will thunder along the cliff—
break—retreat—get fresh strength—
gather and pour weight upon the beach.

You will draw back,
and the ripple on the sand-shelf
will be witness of your track.
O privet-white, you will paint
the lintel of wet sand with froth.

You will bring myrrh-bark
and drift laurel-wood from hot coasts!
when you hurl high—high—
we will answer with a shout.

For you will come,
you will come,
you will answer our taut hearts,
you will break the lie of men's thoughts,
and cherish and shelter us.

1916

CITIES

Can we believe—by an effort
comfort our hearts:
it is not waste, all this,
not placed here in disgust,
street after street,
each patterned alike,
no grace to lighten
a single house of the hundred
crowded into one garden-space.

Crowded—can we believe,
not in utter disgust,
in ironical play—
but the maker of cities grew faint
with the beauty of temple
and space before temple,
arch upon perfect arch,
of pillars and corridors that led out

to strange court-yards and porches
where sun-light stamped
hyacinth-shadows
black on the pavement.

That the maker of cities grew faint
with the splendor of palaces,
paused while the incense-flowers
from the incense-trees
dropped on the marble-walk,
thought anew, fashioned this—
street after street alike.

For alas,
he had crowded the city so full
that men could not grasp beauty,
beauty was over them,
through them, about them,
no crevice unpacked with the honey,
rare, measureless.

So he built a new city,
ah, can we believe, not ironically,
but for new splendor,
constructed new people
to lift through slow growth
to a beauty unrivalled yet—
and created new cells,
hideous first, hideous now—
spread larvæ across them,
not honey but seething life;

And in these dark cells,
packed street after street,
souls live, hideous yet—
O disfigured, defaced,
with no trace of the beauty
men once held so light.

Can we think a few old cells
were left—we are left—
grains of honey,

old dust of stray pollen
dull on our torn wings,
we are left to recall the old streets?

Is our task the less sweet
that the larvæ still sleep in their cells?
Or crawl out to attack our frail strength:
You are useless. We live.
We await great events.
We are spread through this earth.
We protect our strong race.
You are useless.
Your cells take the place
of our young future strength.

Though they sleep or wake to torment
and wish to displace our old cells—
thin rare gold—
that their larvæ grow fat—
is our task the less sweet?

Though we wander about,
find no honey of flowers in this waste,
is our task the less sweet—
who recall the old splendor,
await the new beauty of cities?

The city is peopled
with spirits, not ghosts, O my love:

Though they crowded between
and usurped the kiss of my mouth
their breath was your gift,
their beauty, your life.

1916

[WHERE LOVE IS KING]

[From *Hymen*]

Where love is king,
Ah, there is little need
To dance and sing,

With bridal-torch to flare
Amber and scatter light
Across the purple air,
To sing and dance
To flute-note and to reed.

Where love is come
(Ah, love is come indeed!)
Our limbs are numb
Before his fiery need;
With all their glad
Rapture of speech unsaid,
Before his fiery lips
Our lips are mute and dumb.

Ah, sound of reed,
Ah, flute and trumpet wail,
Ah, joy decreed—
The fringes of her veil
Are seared and white;
Across the flare of light,
Blinded the torches fail.
(Ah, love is come indeed!)

1921

CUCKOO SONG

Ah, bird,
our love is never spent
with your clear note,
nor satiate our soul;
not song, not wail, not hurt,
but just a call summons us
with its simple top-note
and soft fall;

not to some rarer heaven
of lilies over-tall,
nor tuberose set against
some sun-lit wall,
but to a gracious
cedar-palace hall;

not marble set with purple
hung with roses and tall
sweet lilies—such
as the nightingale
would summon for us
with her wail—
(surely only unhappiness
could thrill
such a rich madrigal!)
not she, the nightingale
can fill our souls
with such a wistful joy as this:

nor, bird, so sweet
was ever a swallow note—
not hers, so perfect
with the wing of lazuli
and bright breast—
nor yet the oriole
filling with melody
from her fiery throat
some island-orchard
in a purple sea.

Ah, dear, ah, gentle bird,
you spread warm length
of crimson wool
and tinted woven stuff
for us to rest upon,
nor numb with ecstasy
nor drown with death:

only you soothe, make still
the throbbing of our brain:
so through her forest trees,
when all her hope was gone
and all her pain,
Calypso heard your call—
across the gathering drift
of burning cedar-wood,
across the low-set bed
of wandering parsley and violet,
when all her hope was dead.

1921

WASH OF COLD RIVER

Wash of cold river
in a glacial land,
Ionian water,
chill, snow-ribbed sand,
drift of rare flowers,
clear, with delicate shell-
like leaf enclosing
frozen lily-leaf,
camellia texture,
colder than a rose;

wind-flower
that keeps the breath
of the north-wind—
these and none other;

intimate thoughts and kind
reach out to share
the treasure of my mind,
intimate hands and dear
draw garden-ward and sea-ward
all the sheer rapture
that I would take
to mould a clear
and frigid statue;

rare, of pure texture,
beautiful space and line,
marble to grace
your inaccessible shrine.

1924

HELIODORA

He and I sought together,
over the spattered table,
rhymes and flowers,
gifts for a name.

He said, among others,
I will bring
(and the phrase was just and good,
but not as good as mine,)
"the narcissus that loves the rain."

We strove for a name,
while the light of the lamps burnt thin
and the outer dawn came in,
a ghost, the last at the feast
or the first,
to sit within
with the two that remained
to quibble in flowers and verse
over a girl's name.

He said, "the rain, loving,"
I said, "the narcissus, drunk,
drunk with the rain."

Yet I had lost
for he said,
"the rose, the lover's gift,
is loved of love,"
he said it,
"loved of love";
I waited, even as he spoke,
to see the room filled with a light,
as when in winter
the embers catch in a wind
when a room is dank;
so it would be filled, I thought,
our room with a light
when he said
(and he said it first,)
"the rose, the lover's delight,
is loved of love,"
but the light was the same.

Then he caught,
seeing the fire in my eyes,
my fire, my fever, perhaps,
for he leaned

with the purple wine
stained on his sleeve,
and said this:
"did you ever think
a girl's mouth
caught in a kiss,
is a lily that laughs?"

I had not.
I saw it now
as men must see it forever afterwards;
no poet could write again,
"the red-lily,
a girl's laugh caught in a kiss";
it was his to pour in the vat
from which all poets dip and quaff,
for poets are brothers in this.

So I saw the fire in his eyes,
it was almost my fire,
(he was younger,)
I saw the face so white,
my heart beat,
it was almost my phrase;
I said, "surprise the muses,
take them by surprise;
it is late,
rather it is dawn-rise,
those ladies sleep, the nine,
our own king's mistresses."

A name to rhyme,
flowers to bring to a name,
what was one girl faint and shy,
with eyes like the myrtle,
(I said: "her underlids
are rather like myrtle,")
to vie with the nine?

Let him take the name,
he had the rhymes,
"the rose, loved of love,
the lily, a mouth that laughs,"

he had the gift,
"the scented crocus,
the purple hyacinth,"
what was one girl to the nine?

He said:
"I will make her a wreath";
he said:
"I will write it thus:

I will bring you the lily that laughs.
I will twine
with soft narcissus, the myrtle,
sweet crocus, white violet,
the purple hyacinth, and last,
the rose, loved-of-love,
that these may drip on your hair
the less soft flowers,
may mingle sweet with the sweet
of Heliodora's locks,
myrrh-curled."

(He wrote myrrh-curled,
I think, the first.)

I said:
"they sleep, the nine,"
when he shouted swift and passionate:
"*that* for the nine!
above the hills
the sun is about to wake,
and to-day white violets
shine beside white lilies
adrift on the mountain side;
to-day the narcissus opens
that loves the rain."

I watched him to the door,
catching his robe
as the wine-bowl crashed to the floor,
spilling a few wet lees,
(ah, his purple hyacinth!)
I saw him out of the door,

I thought:
There will never be a poet
in all the centuries after this,
who will dare write,
after my friend's verse,
"a girl's mouth
is a lily kissed."

1924

FRAGMENT THIRTY-SIX

I know not what to do: my mind is divided.—Sappho.

I know not what to do,
my mind is reft:
is song's gift best?
is love's gift loveliest?
I know not what to do,
now sleep has pressed
weight on your eyelids.

Shall I break your rest,
devouring, eager?
is love's gift best?
nay, song's the loveliest:
yet were you lost,
what rapture
could I take from song?
what song were left?

I know not what to do:
to turn and slake
the rage that burns,
with my breath burn
and trouble your cool breath?
so shall I turn and take
snow in my arms?
(is love's gift best?)
yet flake on flake
of snow were comfortless,
did you lie wondering,
wakened yet unawake.

Shall I turn and take
comfortless snow within my arms?
press lips to lips
that answer not,
press lips to flesh
that shudders not nor breaks?

Is love's gift best?
shall I turn and slake
all the wild longing?
O I am eager for you!
as the Pleiads shake
white light in whiter water
so shall I take you?

My mind is quite divided,
my minds hesitate,
so perfect matched,
I know not what to do:
each strives with each
as two white wrestlers
standing for a match,
ready to turn and clutch
yet never shake muscle nor nerve nor tendon;
so my mind waits
to grapple with my mind,
yet I lie quiet,
I would seem at rest.

I know not what to do:
strain upon strain,
sound surging upon sound
makes my brain blind;
as a wave-line may wait to fall
yet (waiting for its falling)
still the wind may take
from off its crest,
white flake on flake of foam,
that rises,
seeming to dart and pulse
and rend the light,
so my mind hesitates
above the passion

quivering yet to break,
so my mind hesitates
above my mind,
listening to song's delight.

I know not what to do:
will the sound break,
rending the night
with rift on rift of rose
and scattered light?
will the sound break at last
as the wave hesitant,
or will the whole night pass
and I lie listening awake?

1924

LETHE

Nor skin nor hide nor fleece
  Shall cover you,
Nor curtain of crimson nor fine
Shelter of cedar-wood be over you,
  Nor the fir-tree
  Nor the pine.

Nor sight of whin nor gorse
  Nor river-yew,
Nor fragrance of flowering bush,
Nor wailing of reed-bird to waken you,
  Nor of linnet,
  Nor of thrush.

Nor word nor touch nor sight
  Of lover; you
Shall long through the night but for this:
The roll of the full tide to cover you
  Without question,
  Without kiss.

1924

Robinson Jeffers

John Robinson Jeffers was born in Pittsburgh, Pennsylvania, January 10, 1887, the elder of the two sons of William Hamilton Jeffers and his wife, Annie Robinson Tuttle Jeffers. On his mother's side he was descended from English settlers of pre-Revolutionary stock, on his father's side from Irish and Scotch people who had lived in America for a generation. The father was a learned man, a linguist and teacher of theology, who gave his son a thorough training in the classical languages and encouraged him in the effort to write. Jeffers had other early advantages: he was enabled to travel widely over Europe while still a boy and received good training in schools both abroad and at home. From his twelfth to his fifteenth year he lived in Europe, attending schools in Switzerland and Germany and going on walking trips with his father during the summer months. In his fifteenth year, however, he was brought back to the United States, and his college training began. After he had finished one year's study at the University of Western Pennsylvania, the family moved to California, and in 1903 he entered Occidental College. He received the A.B. degree from this college in 1905, at the age of eighteen, and later spent three years in desultory study at the University of Southern California, the University of Zurich, and the University of Washington. At the last named institution he was enrolled for a year in the School of Forestry, and at the University of Southern California he was a medical student. The acquaintance with scientific fields which he gained while in the medical school and his reading of Freud and Jung had much effect on his thinking.

Jeffers first became seriously interested in poetry at the age of fourteen or fifteen, when his father presented him with a copy of the poetry of Dante Gabriel Rossetti. In December, 1903, his first published verse appeared in the *Aurora*, an undergraduate magazine at Occidental College; and the *Youth's Companion*, in June, 1904, contained the first poetry for which he was paid. During his years as a graduate student, ostensibly preparing himself for a profession, he held steadily to one interest, poetry, and harbored the desire to devote all his time to cultivating this interest. Good fortune presently enabled him to have his wish. In 1912 he received from John F. Robinson, a banker of Pittsburgh, and a cousin of his maternal grandfather, a legacy which made him financially independent. Forthwith he began the literary career which he has since followed. In December, 1912, he had printed at his own expense five hundred copies of a volume of verse, *Flagons and Apples*, and in 1916 appeared his second book of poems, *Californians*. Not until 1924, however, did he publish another book—*Tamar and Other Poems*, which brought his name into prominence among critics and students of poetry. Since then he has written more voluminously and published more steadily.

While a student at the University of Southern California he became acquainted with Mrs. Una Call Kuster, a fellow-student who was interested in literature. She encouraged him in the effort to write poetry, and after her husband had given her a divorce Jeffers married her—on August 2, 1913. A year later, in August, 1914, they settled at Carmel, California; and there, on a bluff a hundred feet from the Pacific Ocean, Jeffers built a stone house—Tor House—later erecting with his own hands a stone tower in which he has done much of his writing.

Jeffers is self-sufficient, and although not a recluse avoids crowds and the attention of strangers whenever possible, leaving to his wife the practical management of the household and the carrying out of business arrangements with the outside world. The poet's only children are twin boys, Donnan Call and Garth Sherwood, born in 1916. The family made an extended trip through Ireland and Great Britain in 1929, and another in 1937. Other trips have taken them by automobile to New Mexico, Wyoming, and other parts of the United States. In 1937 Occidental College awarded Jeffers the honorary degree of LL.D., and in 1939 the University of Southern California that of L. H. D.

SHINE, PERISHING REPUBLIC

While this America settles in the mould of its vulgarity, heavily thickening to empire,
And protest, only a bubble in the molten mass, pops and sighs out, and the mass hardens,

I sadly smiling remember that the flower fades to make fruit, the fruit rots to make earth.
Out of the mother; and through the spring exultances, ripeness and decadence; and home to the mother.

You making haste haste on decay: not blameworthy; life is good, be it stubbornly long or suddenly
A mortal splendor: meteors are not needed less than mountains: shine, perishing republic.

But for my children, I would have them keep their distance from the thickening center; corruption
Never has been compulsory, when the cities lie at the monster's feet there are left the mountains.

And boys, be in nothing so moderate as in love of man, a clever servant, insufferable master.
There is the trap that catches noblest spirits, that caught—they say—God, when he walked on earth.

1925

JOY

Though joy is better than sorrow, joy is not great;
Peace is great, strength is great.
Not for joy the stars burn, not for joy the vulture
Spreads her gray sails on the air
Over the mountain; not for joy the worn mountain
Stands, while years like water
Trench his long sides. "I am neither mountain nor bird
Nor star; and I seek joy."
The weakness of your breed: yet at length quietness
Will cover those wistful eyes.

1925

GALE IN APRIL

Intense and terrible beauty, how has our race with the frail naked nerves,
So little a craft swum down from its far launching?
Why now, only because the northwest blows and the headed grass billows,
Great seas jagging the west and on the granite
Blanching, the vessel is brimmed, this dancing play of the world is too much passion.
A gale in April so overfilling the spirit,
Though his ribs were thick as the earth's, arches of mountain, how shall one dare to live,
Though his blood were like the earth's rivers and his flesh iron,
How shall one dare to live? One is born strong, how do the weak endure it?
The strong lean upon death as on a rock,
After eighty years there is shelter and the naked nerves shall be covered with deep quietness,
O beauty of things go on, go on, O torture
Of intense joy I have lasted out my time, I have thanked God and finished,
Roots of millennial trees fold me in the darkness,
Northwest wind shake their tops, not to the root, not to the root, I have passed
From beauty to the other beauty, peace, the night splendor.

1925

HURT HAWKS

I

The broken pillar of the wing jags from the clotted shoulder,
The wing trails like a banner in defeat,
No more to use the sky forever but live with famine
And pain a few days: cat nor coyote
Will shorten the week of waiting for death, there is game without talons.
He stands under the oak-bush and waits
The lame feet of salvation; at night he remembers freedom
And flies in a dream, the dawns ruin it.

He is strong and pain is worse to the strong, incapacity is worse.
The curs of the day come and torment him
At distance, no one but death the redeemer will humble that
head,
The intrepid readiness, the terrible eyes.
The wild God of the world is sometimes merciful to those
That ask mercy, not often to the arrogant.
You do not know him, you communal people, or you have
forgotten him;
Intemperate and savage, the hawk remembers him;
Beautiful and wild, the hawks, and men that are dying, remember
him.

II

I'd sooner, except the penalties, kill a man than a hawk; but the
great redtail
Had nothing left but unable misery
From the bone too shattered for mending, the wing that
trailed under his talons when he moved.
We had fed him six weeks, I gave him freedom,
He wandered over the foreland hill and returned in the evening,
asking for death,
Not like a beggar, still eyed with the old
Implacable arrogance. I gave him the lead gift in the twilight.
What fell was relaxed,
Owl-downy, soft feminine feathers; but what
Soared: the fierce rush: the night-herons by the flooded river
cried fear at its rising
Before it was quite unsheathed from reality.

1928

MEDITATION ON SAVIOURS

I

When I considered it too closely, when I wore it like an
element and smelt it like water,
Life is become less lovely, the net nearer than the skin, a little
troublesome, a little terrible.

I pledged myself awhile ago not to seek refuge, neither in
death nor in a walled garden,

In lies nor gated loyalties, nor in the gates of contempt, that
easily lock the world out of doors.

Here on the rock it is great and beautiful, here on the foam-wet
granite sea-fang it is easy to praise
Life and water and the shining stones: but whose cattle are the
herds of the people that one should love them?

If they were yours, then you might take a cattle-breeder's
delight in the herds of the future. Not yours.
Where the power ends let love, before it sours to jealousy.
Leave the joys of government to Caesar.

Who is born when the world wanes, when the brave soul of
the world falls on decay in the flesh increasing
Comes one with a great level mind, sufficient vision, sufficient
blindness, and clemency for love.

This is the breath of rottenness I smelt; from the world waiting,
stalled between storms, decaying a little,
Bitterly afraid to be hurt, but knowing it cannot draw the
saviour Caesar but out of the blood-bath.

The apes of Christ lift up their hands to praise love: but
wisdom without love is the present saviour,
Power without hatred, mind like a many-bladed machine
subduing the world with deep indifference.

The apes of Christ itch for a sickness they have never known;
words and the little envies will hardly
Measure against that blinding fire behind the tragic eyes they
have never dared to confront.

II

Point Lobos lies over the hollowed water like a humped whale
swimming to shoal; Point Lobos
Was wounded with that fire; the hills at Point Sur endured it;
the palace at Thebes; the hill Calvary.

Out of incestuous love power and then ruin. A man forcing the
imaginations of men,
Possessing with love and power the people: a man defiling his
own household with impious desire.

King Oedipus reeling blinded from the palace doorway, red
    tears pouring from the torn pits
Under the forehead; and the young Jew writhing on the domed
    hill in the earthquake, against the eclipse

Frightfully uplifted for having turned inward to love the people:—
    that root was so sweet Oh, dreadful agonist?—
I saw the same pierced feet, that walked in the same crime to
    its expiation; I heard the same cry.

A bad mountain to build your world on. Am I another keeper
    of the people, that on my own shore,
On the gray rock, by the grooved mass of the ocean, the sicknesses
    I left behind me concern me?

Here where the surf has come incredible ways out of the splendid
    west, over the deeps
Light nor life sounds forever; here where enormous sundowns
    flower and burn through color to quietness;

Then the ecstasy of the stars is present? As for the people, I have
    found my rock, let them find theirs.
Let them lie down at Caesar's feet and be saved; and he in his
    time reap their daggers of gratitude.

III

Yet I am the one made pledges against the refuge contempt, that
    easily locks the world out of doors.
This people as much as the sea-granite is part of the God from
    whom I desire not to be fugitive.

I see them: they are always crying. The shored Pacific makes
    perpetual music, and the stone mountains
Their music of silence, the stars blow long pipings of light: the
    people are always crying in their hearts.

One need not pity; certainly one must not love. But who has
    seen peace, if he should tell them where peace
Lives in the world . . . they would be powerless to understand;
    and he is not willing to be reinvolved.

IV

How should one caught in the stone of his own person dare
tell the people anything but relative to that?
But if a man could hold in his mind all the conditions at once,
of man and woman, of civilized

And barbarous, of sick and well, of happy and under torture, of
living and dead, of human and not
Human, and dimly all the human future:—what should persuade
him to speak? And what could his words change?

The mountain ahead of the world is not forming but fixed. But
the man's words would be fixed also,
Part of that mountain, under equal compulsion; under the same
present compulsion in the iron consistency.

And nobody sees good or evil but out of a brain a hundred centuries quieted, some desert
Prophet's, a man humped like a camel, gone mad between the
mud-walled village and the mountain sepulchres.

V

Broad wagons before sunrise bring food into the city from the
open farms, and the people are fed.
They import and they consume reality. Before sunrise a hawk
in the desert made them their thoughts.

VI

Here is an anxious people, rank with suppressed bloodthirstiness.
Among the mild and unwarlike
Gautama needed but live greatly and be heard, Confucius needed
but live greatly and be heard.

This people has not outgrown blood-sacrifice, one must writhe
on the high cross to catch at their memories;
The price is known. I have quieted love; for love of the people
I would not do it. For power I would do it.

—But that stands against reason: what is power to a dead man,
dead under torture?—What is power to a man
Living, after the flesh is content? Reason is never a root, neither
of act nor desire.

For power living I would never do it; they are not delightful to
touch, one wants to be separate. For power
After the nerves are put away underground, to lighten the abstract
unborn children toward peace . . .

A man might have paid anguish indeed. Except he had found
the standing sea-rock that even this last
Temptation breaks on; quieter than death but lovelier; peace that
quiets the desire even of praising it.

VII

Yet look: are they not pitiable? No: if they lived forever they
would be pitiable:
But a huge gift reserved quite overwhelms them at the end; they
are able then to be still and not cry.

And having touched a little of the beauty and seen a little of
the beauty of things, magically grow
Across the funeral fire or the hidden stench of burial themselves
into the beauty they admired,

Themselves into the God, themselves into the sacred steep
unconsciousness they used to mimic
Asleep between lamp's death and dawn, while the last drunkard
stumbled homeward down the dark street.

They are not to be pitied but very fortunate; they need no saviour,
salvation comes and takes them by force,
It gathers them into the great kingdoms of dust and stone, the
blown storms, the stream's-end ocean.

With this advantage over their granite grave-marks, of having
realized the petulant human consciousness
Before, and then the greatness, the peace: drunk from both pitchers: these to be pitied? These not fortunate?

But while he lives let each man make his health in his mind, to
love the coast opposite humanity
And so be freed of love, laying it like bread on the waters; it is
worst turned inward, it is best shot farthest.

Love, the mad wine of good and evil, the saint's and murderer's,
the mote in the eye that makes its object

Shine the sun black; the trap in which it is better to catch the
inhuman God than the hunter's own image.

1928

FIRE ON THE HILLS

The deer were bounding like blown leaves
Under the smoke in front of the roaring wave of the brushfire;
I thought of the smaller lives that were caught.
Beauty is not always lovely; the fire was beautiful, the terror
Of the deer was beautiful; and when I returned
Down the black slopes after the fire had gone by, an eagle
Was perched on the jag of a burnt pine,
Insolent and gorged, cloaked in the folded storms of his shoulders.
He had come from far off for the good hunting
With fire for his beater to drive the game; the sky was merciless
Blue, and the hills merciless black,
The sombre-feathered great bird sleepily merciless between them.
I thought, painfully, but the whole mind,
The destruction that brings an eagle from heaven is better than
mercy.

1932

MARGRAVE

On the small marble-paved platform
On the turret on the head of the tower,
Watching the night deepen.
I feel the rock-edge of the continent
Reel eastward with me below the broad stars,
I lean on the broad worn stones of the parapet top
And the stones and my hands that touch them reel eastward.
The inland mountains go down and new lights
Glow over the sinking east rim of the earth.
The dark ocean comes up,
And reddens the western stars with its fog-breath
And hides them with its mounded darkness.

The earth was the world and man was its measure, but our minds
have looked
Through the little mock-dome of heaven the telescope-slotted observatory eye-ball, there space and multitude came in

And the earth is a particle of dust by a sand-grain sun, lost in a nameless cove of the shores of a continent.
Galaxy on galaxy, innumerable swirls of innumerable stars, endured as it were forever and humanity
Came into being, its two or three million years are a moment, in a moment it will certainly cease out from being.
And galaxy on galaxy endure after that as it were forever . . . But man is conscious,
He brings the world to focus in a feeling brain,
In a net of nerves catches the splendor of things,
Breaks the somnambulism of nature . . . His distinction perhaps,
Hardly his advantage. To slaver for contemptible pleasures
And scream with pain are hardly an advantage.
Consciousness? The learned astronomer
Analyzing the light of most remote star-swirls
Has found them—or a trick of distance deludes his prism—
All at incredible speeds fleeing outward from ours.
I thought, no doubt they are fleeing the contagion
Of consciousness that infects this corner of space.

For often I have heard the hard rocks I handled
Groan, because lichen and time and water dissolve them,
And they have to travel down the strange falling scale
Of soil and plants and the flesh of beasts to become
The bodies of men; they murmur at their fate
In the hollows of windless nights, they'd rather be anything
Than human flesh played on by pain and joy,
They pray for annihilation sooner, but annihilation's
Not in the book yet.

So, I thought, the rumor
Of human consciousness has gone abroad in the world,
The sane uninfected far-outer universes
Flee it in a panic of escape, as men flee the plague
Taking a city: for look at the fruits of consciousness:
As in young Walter Margrave when he'd been sentenced for murder: he was thinking when they brought him back
To the cell in jail, "I've only a moment to arrange my thoughts, I must think quickly, I must think clearly,
And settle the world in my mind before I kick off," but to feel the curious eyes of his fellow-prisoners
And the wry-mouthed guard's and so forth torment him through the steel bars put his mind in a stupor, he could only

Sit frowning, ostentatiously unafraid. "But I can control my mind, their eyes can't touch my will.
One against all. What use is will at this end of everything? A kind of nausea is the chief feeling . . .
In my stomach and throat . . . but in my head pride: I fought a good fight and they can't break me; alone, unbroken,
Against a hundred and twenty-three million people. They are going to kill the best brain perhaps in the world,
That might have made such discoveries in science
As would set the world centuries ahead, for I had the mind and the power. Boo, it's their loss. Blind fools,
Killing their best." When his mind forgot the eyes it made rapid capricious pictures instead of words,
But not of the medical school and the laboratories, its late intense interest; not at all of his crime; glimpses
Of the coast-range at home; the V of a westward canyon with the vibrating
Blue line of the ocean strung sharp across it; that domed hill up the valley, two cows like specks on the summit
And a beautiful-colored jungle of poison-oak at the foot; his sister half naked washing her hair,
"My dirty sister," whose example and her lovers had kept him chaste by revulsion; the reed-grown mouth of the river
And the sand-bar against the stinging splendor of the sea . . . and anguish behind all the pictures
(He began to consider his own mind again) "like a wall they hang on." Hang. The anguish came forward, an actual
Knife between two heart-beats, the organ stopped and then raced. He experimented awhile with his heart,
Making in his mind a picture of a man hanged, pretending to himself it was to happen next moment,
Trying to observe whether the beat suspended—"suspended," he thought—in systole or in diastole.
The effect soon failed; the anguish remained. "Ah my slack lawyer, damn him, let slip chance after chance.
Scared traitor." Then broken pictures of the scenes in court, the jury, the judge, the idlers, and not one face
But bleak with hatred. "But I met their eyes, one against all." Suddenly his mind became incapable
Of making pictures or words, but still wildly active, striking in all directions like a snake in a fire,
Finding nothing but the fiery element of its own anguish. He got up and felt the guard's eyes and sat down,

Turned side-face, resting his chin on his fist, frowning and trembling. He saw clearly in his mind the little
Adrenal glands perched on the red-brown kidneys, as if all his doomed tissues became transparent,
Pouring in these passions their violent secretion
Into his blood-stream, raising the tension unbearably. And the thyroids; tension, tension. A long course of that
Should work grave changes. "If they tortured a man like a laboratory dog for discovery: there'd be value gained: but by process
Of law for vengeance, because his glands and his brain have made him act in another than common manner:
You incredible breed of asses!" He smiled self-consciously in open scorn of the people, the guard at the door
To observe that smile—"my God, do I care about the turnkey's opinion?"—suddenly his mind again
Was lashing like a burnt snake. Then it was torpid for a while. This continued for months.

His father had come to visit him, he saw the ruinous white-haired head
Through two steel wickets under the bluish electric light that seemed to peel the skin from the face.
Walter said cheerfully too loudly, "Hullo. You look like a skull." The shaven sunk jaws in answer chewed
Inaudible words. Walter with an edge of pleasure thought "Once he was stronger than I! I used to admire
This poor old man's strength when I was a child," and said "Buck up, old fellow, it will soon be over. Here's nothing
To cry for. Do you think I'm afraid to die? It's good people that fear death, people with the soft streak
Of goodness in them fear death: but I, you know, am a monster, don't you read the papers? Caught at last:
I fought a hundred and twenty-three million people. How's Hazel? How's the farm? I could get out of this scrape
By playing dementia, but I refuse to, there's not an alienist living
Could catch me out. I'm the king of Spain dying for the world. I've been persecuted since I was born
By a secret sect, they stuck pins into me
And fed me regular doses of poison for a certain reason. Why do you pretend that you're my father?
God is. . . . Believe me, I could get by with it.
But I refuse."

Old Margrave looked timidly at the two guards listening, and drew his brown tremulous hand
Across his eyes below the white hair. "I thought of going to try to see the governor, Walter."
"That's it!" "Don't hope for anything, Walter, they tell me that there's no hope. They say that I shan't even
Be allowed to see him." "By God," the young man said trembling, "you can if you want to. Never believe that lawyer.
If I'd had Dorking: but you couldn't afford him. Poor men have no right to breed sons. I'd not be here
If you'd had money to put me through college. Tell the governor
I know he won't pardon, but he can commute the sentence to life imprisonment. Then I can read and study,
I can help the penitentiary doctor, I can do something to help humanity. Tell him it's madness
To throw such a brain as mine into the garbage. Don't deny my guilt but tell him my reasons.
I kidnapped the little girl to get money to finish my medical education. What's one child's life
Against a career like mine that might have saved
Thousands of children? Say I'd isolated the organism of infantile paralysis: I'd have done more:
But that alone would save thousands of children. I was merciful; she died quietly; tell him that.
It was only pithing a little white frog.
Don't you think you can make him understand? I'm not a criminal: I judge differently from others. I wasn't
Afraid to think for myself. All I did
Was for money for my education, to help humanity. And tell him if I've done wrong—what's wrong?—I've paid for it
With frightful suffering: the more developed the brain the greater the agony. He won't admit that. Oh God,
These brains the size of a pea! To be juried
And strangled by a hundred and twenty-three million peas. Go down on your knees to him. You owe me that: you'd no right
To breed, you're poor.
But you itched for a woman, you had to fetch me out of the happy hill of not-being. Pfah, to hug a woman
And make this I. That's the evil in the world, that letter. I—I— Tell the governor
That I'm not afraid of dying, that I laugh at death. No, no, we'll laugh in private. Tell him I'm crazy.

I've come to that: after being the only sane mind among a hundred and twenty-three million peas.
Anything, anything . . ."

He had let his nerves go wild on purpose, to edge on the old man to action, now at last
Escaping utterly out of control they stumbled into a bog of thick sobs. The guards pulled him up
And walked him away as if he were half insensible. He was not insensible, but more acutely aware
Than ever in his life before of all that touched him, and of shame and anguish.

You would be wise, you far stars,
To flee with the speed of light this infection.
For here the good sane invulnerable material
And nature of things more and more grows alive and cries.
The rock and water grow human, the bitter weed
Of consciousness catches the sun, it clings to the near stars,
Even the nearer portion of the universal God
Seems to become conscious, yearns and rejoices
And suffers: I believe this hurt will be healed
Some age of time after mankind has died,
Then the sun will say "What ailed me a moment?" and resume
The old soulless triumph, and the iron and stone earth
With confident inorganic glory obliterate
Her ruins and fossils, like that incredible unfading red rose
Of desert in Arizona glowing life to scorn,
And grind the chalky emptied seed-shells of consciousness
The bare skulls of the dead to powder; after some million
Courses around the sun her sadness may pass:
But why should you worlds of the virgin distance
Endure to survive what it were better to escape.

I also am not innocent
Of contagion, but have spread my spirit on the deep world.
I have gotten sons and sent the fire wider.
I have planted trees, they also feel while they live.
I have humanized the ancient sea-sculptured cliff
And the ocean's wreckage of rock
Into a house and a tower,
Hastening the sure decay of granite with my hammer,
Its hard dust will make soft flesh;

And have widened in my idleness
The disastrous personality of life with poems,
That are pleasant enough in the breeding but go bitterly at last
To envy oblivion and the early deaths of nobler
Verse, and much nobler flesh;
And I have projected my spirit
Behind the superb sufficient forehead of nature
To gift the inhuman God with this rankling consciousness.

But who is our judge? It is likely the enormous
Beauty of the world requires for completion our ghostly increment,
It has to dream, and dream badly, a moment of its night.

On the little stone-belted platform
On the turret on the head of the tower,
Between the stars and the earth,
And the ocean and the continent.
One ship's light shines and eclipses
Very far out, behind the high waves on the hill of water.
In the east under the Hyades and rising Orion
Are many cities and multitudes of people,
But westward a long way they are few enough.
It is fortunate to look westward as to look upward.
In the south the dark river-mouth pool mirrors a star
That stands over Margrave's farmhouse. The old man has lost it, he isn't there any more. He went down to the river-mouth
Last December, when recent rains had opened the stream and the salmon were running. Fishermen very solemnly
Stood all along the low sand like herons, and sea-lions offshore in the rolling waves with deep wet voices
Coughed at each other; the sea air is hoarse with their voices that time of year. Margrave had rambled since noon
Among the little folds of the seaward field that he had forgotten to plow and was trying to sell
Though he used to love it, but everything was lost now. He lay awhile on his face in the rotting stubble and random
Unsown green blades, then he got up and drifted over the ridge to the river-mouth sands, unaimed,
Pale and gap-eyed, as the day moon a clear morning, opposite the sun. He noticed with surprise the many
Fishermen like herons in the shallows and along the sands; and then that his girl Hazel was with him: who'd feared

What he might do to himself and had come to watch him when
he lay face down in the field. "I know what they're doing,"
He said slyly, "Hazel, they're fishing! I guess they don't know,"
He whispered, "about our trouble. Oh no, don't tell them." She
said, "Don't go down, father, your face would tell them.
Sit here on the edge of grass, watch the brown river meet the
blue sea. Do look: that boy's caught something.
How the line cuts the water and the small wheel sings." "If I'd
been rich,"
Old Margrave answered, "they'd have fixed the hook for . . .
Walter . . . with some other bait. It sticks in my mind that
. . . Walter
Blames me too much." "Look," Hazel said, "he's landing it now.
Oh, it's a big one." "I dreamed about fishing,
Some time ago," he answered, "but we were the fish. I saw the
people all running reaching for prizes
That dangled on long lines from the sky. A lovely girl or a sack
of money or a case of whiskey,
Or fake things like reputation, hackle-feathers and a hook. A man
would reach up and grab and the line
Jerked, then you knew by his face that the hook was in him,
wherever he went. Often they're played for half
A lifetime before they're landed: others, like . . . my son . . .
pulled up short. Oh, Oh,
It's not a dream." He said gently, "He wanted money for his
education, but you poor girl
Wanted boy friends, now you've got a round belly. That's the
hook. I wanted children and got
Walter and you. Hm? Hooked twice is too much. Let's walk."
"Not that way: let's go up home, daddy.
It makes you unhappy to see them fishing." "No," he answered,
"nothing can. I have it in my pocket." She walked behind
him,
Hiding herself, ashamed of her visible pregnancy and her brother's
fate; but when the old man stumbled
And wavered on the slope she went beside him to support him,
her right hand under his elbow, and wreathed his body
With the other arm.

The clear brown river ran eagerly
through the sand-hill, undercutting its banks,
That slid in masses; tall waves walked very slowly up stream from
the sea, and stood

Stationary in the throat of the channel before they dissolved. The rock the children call Red-cap stood
High and naked among the fishermen, the orange lichen on its head. At the sea-end of the sand
Two boys and a man had rifles instead of rods, they meant to punish the salmon-devouring sea-lions
Because the fish were fewer than last year; whenever a sleek brown head with the big questioning eyes
Broke sea they fired. Margrave had heard the shots but taken no notice, but when he walked by the stream
He saw a swimmer look up from the water and its round dark eye
Suddenly burst red blood before it went down. He cried out and twisted himself from Hazel's hand
And ran like a squirrel along the stream-bank. "I'll not allow it!" He snatched at a rifle. "Why should my lad
Be hanged for killing and all you others go free?" He wrestled feebly to gain the rifle, the sand-bank
Slid under his feet, he slipped and lay face down in the running stream and was hauled astrand. Then Hazel
Came running heavily, and when he was able to walk she led him away. The sea-beast, blinded but a painful
Vain gleam, starved long before it could die; old Margrave still lives. Death's like a little gay child that runs
The world around with the keys of salvation in his foolish fingers, lends them at random where they're not wanted,
But often withholds them where most required.

Margrave's son at this time
Had only four days to wait, but death now appeared so dreadful to him that to speak of his thoughts and the abject
Horror, would be to insult humanity more than it deserves. At last the jerked hemp snapped the neck sideways
And bruised the cable of nerves that threads the bone rings; the intolerably strained consciousness in a moment changed.
It was strangely cut in two parts at the noose, the head's
Consciousness from the body's; both were set free and flamed; the head's with flashing paradisal light
Like the wild birth of a star, but crying in bewilderment and suddenly extinguished; the body's with a sharp emotion
Of satisfied love, a wave of hard warmth and joy, that ebbed cold on darkness. After a time of darkness
The dreams that follow upon death came and subsided, like fibrillar twitchings

Of the nerves unorganizing themselves; and some of the small
    dreams were delightful and some, slight miseries,
But nothing intense; then consciousness wandered home from the
    cell to the molecule, was utterly dissolved and changed;
Peace was the end of the play, so far as concerns humanity. Oh
    beautiful capricious little saviour,
Death, the gay child with the gipsy eyes, to avoid you for a time
    I think is virtuous, to fear you is insane.

On the little stone-girdled platform
Over the earth and the ocean
I seem to have stood a long time and watched the stars pass.
They also shall perish I believe.
Here to-day, gone to-morrow, desperate wee galaxies
Scattering themselves and shining their substance away
Like a passionate thought. It is very well ordered.

1932

STILL THE MIND SMILES

Still the mind smiles at its own rebellions,
Knowing all the while that civilization and the other evils
That make humanity ridiculous, remain
Beautiful in the whole fabric, excesses that balance each other
Like the paired wings of a flying bird.
Misery and riches, civilization and squalid savagery,
Mass war and the odor of unmanly peace:
Tragic flourishes above and below the normal of life.
In order to value this fretful time
It is necessary to remember our norm, the unaltered passions,
The same-colored wings of imagination,
That the crowd clips, in lonely places new-grown; the unchanged
Lives of herdsmen and mountain farms,
Where men are few, and few tools, a few weapons, and their
    dawns are beautiful.
From here for normal one sees both ways,
And listens to the splendor of God, the exact poet, the sonorous
Antistrophe of desolation to the strophe multitude.

1933

CRUMBS OR THE LOAF

If one should tell them what's clearly seen
They'd not understand; if they understood they would not believe;
If they understood and believed they'd say,
"Hater of men, annihilating with a sterile enormous
Splendor our lives: where are our lives?"
A little chilled perhaps, but not hurt. But it's quite true
The invulnerable love is not bought for nothing.
It is better no doubt to give crumbs than the loaf; make fables again,
Tell people not to fear death, toughen
Their bones if possible with bitter fables not to fear life.
—And one's own, not to have pity too much;
For it seems compassion sticks longer than the other colors, in this bleaching cloth.

1933

LIFE FROM THE LIFELESS

Spirits and illusions have died,
The naked mind lives
In the beauty of inanimate things.

Flowers wither, grass fades, trees wilt,
The forest is burnt;
The rock is not burnt.

The deer starve, the winter birds
Die on their twigs and lie
In the blue dawns in the snow.

Men suffer want and become
Curiously ignoble; as prosperity
Made them curiously vile.

But look how noble the world is,
The lonely-flowing waters, the secret-
Keeping stones, the flowing sky.

1935

GRAY WEATHER

It is true that, older than man and ages to outlast him, the Pacific surf
Still cheerfully pounds the worn granite drum;
But there's no storm; and the birds are still, no song; no kind of excess;
Nothing that shines, nothing is dark;
There is neither joy nor grief nor a person, the sun's tooth sheathed in cloud,
And life has no more desires than a stone.
The stormy conditions of time and change are all abrogated, the essential
Violences of survival, pleasure,
Love, wrath and pain, and the curious desire of knowing, all perfectly suspended.
In the cloudy light, in the timeless quietness,
One explores deeper than the nerves or heart of nature, the womb or soul,
To the bone, the careless white bone, the excellence.

1935

THE PURSE-SEINE

Our sardine fishermen work at night in the dark of the moon; daylight or moonlight
They could not tell where to spread the net, unable to see the phosphorescence of the shoals of fish.
They work northward from Monterey, coasting Santa Cruz; off New Year's Point or off Pigeon Point
The look-out man will see some lakes of milk-color light on the sea's night-purple; he points, and the helmsman
Turns the dark prow, the motorboat circles the gleaming shoal and drifts out her seine-net. They close the circle
And purse the bottom of the net, then with great labor haul it in.

I cannot tell you
How beautiful the scene is, and a little terrible, then, when the crowded fish
Know they are caught, and wildly beat from one wall to the other of their closing destiny the phosphorescent

Water to a pool of flame, each beautiful slender body sheeted with flame, like a live rocket
A comet's tail wake of clear yellow flame; while outside the narrowing
Floats and cordage of the net great sea-lions come up to watch, sighing in the dark; the vast walls of night
Stand erect to the stars.

Lately I was looking from a night mountain-top
On a wide city, the colored splendor, galaxies of light: how could I help but recall the seine-net
Gathering the luminous fish? I cannot tell you how beautiful the city appeared, and a little terrible.
I thought, We have geared the machines and locked all together into interdependence; we have built the great cities; now
There is no escape. We have gathered vast populations incapable of free survival, insulated
From the strong earth, each person in himself helpless, on all dependent. The circle is closed, and the net
Is being hauled in. They hardly feel the cords drawing, yet they shine already. The inevitable mass-disasters
Will not come in our time nor in our children's, but we and our children
Must watch the net draw narrower, government take all powers—or revolution, and the new government
Take more than all, add to kept bodies kept souls—or anarchy, the mass-disasters.

These things are Progress;
Do you marvel our verse is troubled or frowning, while it keeps its reason? Or it lets go, lets the mood flow
In the manner of the recent young men into mere hysteria, splintered gleams, crackled laughter. But they are quite wrong.
There is no reason for amazement: surely one always knew that cultures decay, and life's end is death.

1937

THE ANSWER

Then what is the answer?—Not to be deluded by dreams.
To know that great civilizations have broken down into violence, and their tyrants come, many times before.

When open violence appears, to avoid it with honor or choose the least ugly faction; these evils are essential.
To keep one's own integrity, be merciful and uncorrupted and not wish for evil; and not be duped
By dreams of universal justice or happiness. These dreams will not be fulfilled.
To know this, and to know that however ugly the parts appear the whole remains beautiful. A severed hand
Is an ugly thing, and man dissevered from the earth and stars and his history . . . for contemplation or in fact . . .
Often appears atrociously ugly. Integrity is wholeness, the greatest beauty is
Organic wholeness, the wholeness of life and things, the divine beauty of the universe. Love that, not man
Apart from that, or else you will share man's pitiful confusions, or drown in despair when his days darken.

1937

NOVA

That Nova was a moderate star like our good sun; it stored no doubt a little more than it spent
Of heat and energy until the increasing tension came to the trigger-point
Of a new chemistry; then what was already flaming found a new manner of flaming ten-thousandfold
More brightly for a brief time; what was a pin-point fleck on a sensitive plate at the great telescope's
Eye-piece now shouts down the steep night to the naked eye, a nine-day super-star.

It is likely our moderate
Father the sun will some time put off his nature for a similar glory. The earth would share it; these tall
Green trees would become a moment's torches and vanish, the oceans would explode into invisible steam,
The ships and the great whales fall through them like flaming meteors into the emptied abysm, the six mile
Hollows of the Pacific sea-bed might smoke for a moment. Then the earth would be like the pale proud moon,
Nothing but vitrified sand and rock would be left on earth. This is a probable death-passion

For the sun's planets; we have no knowledge to assure us it may not happen at any moment of time.

Meanwhile the sun shines wisely and warm, trees flutter green in the wind, girls take their clothes off
To bathe in the cold ocean or to hunt love; they stand laughing in the white foam, they have beautiful
Shoulders and thighs, they are beautiful animals, all life is beautiful. We cannot be sure of life for one moment;
We can, by force and self-discipline, by many refusals and a few assertions, in the teeth of fortune assure ourselves
Freedom and integrity in life or integrity in death. And we know that the enormous invulnerable beauty of things
Is the face of God, to live gladly in its presence, and die without grief or fear knowing it survives us.

1937

WATCH THE LIGHTS FADE

Gray steel, cloud-shadow-stained,
The ocean takes the last lights of evening.
Loud is the voice and the foam lead-color,
And flood-tide devours the sands.

Here stand, like an old stone,
And watch the lights fade and hear the sea's voice.
Hate and despair take Europe and Asia,
And the sea-wind blows cold.

Night comes: night will claim all.
The world is not changed, only more naked:
The strong struggle for power, and the weak
Warm their poor hearts with hate.

Night comes: come into the house,
Try around the dial for a late news-cast.
These others are America's voices: naïve and
Powerful, spurious, doom-touched.

How soon? Four years or forty?
Why should an old stone pick at the future?
Stand on your shore, old stone, be still while the
Sea-wind salts your head white.

1941

THE BLOODY SIRE

It is not bad. Let them play.
Let the guns bark and the bombing-plane
Speak his prodigious blasphemies.
It is not bad, it is high time,
Stark violence is still the sire of all the world's values.

What but the wolf's tooth whittled so fine
The fleet limbs of the antelope?
What but fear winged the birds, and hunger
Jeweled with such eyes the great goshawk's head?
Violence has been the sire of all the world's values.

Who would remember Helen's face
Lacking the terrible halo of spears?
Who formed Christ but Herod and Caesar,
The cruel and bloody victories of Caesar?
Violence, the bloody sire of all the world's values.

Never weep, let them play,
Old violence is not too old to beget new values.

1941

John Crowe Ransom

John Crowe Ransom was born in Pulaski, Tennessee, April 30, 1888. He was the son of James Ransom, a Methodist preacher, who had married Ella Crowe. He received the B.A. degree from Vanderbilt University in 1909, and having won a Rhodes Scholarship, he attended Oxford from 1910 to 1913. Upon his return to the United States he became a member of the English Department at Vanderbilt, a position he held from 1914 to 1937 with the exception of two years, 1917-1919, when he served as an officer of Field Artillery in the first World War. Since 1937 he has been at Kenyon College, Gambier, Ohio, as professor of English and editor of the *Kenyon Review*.

Ransom wrote his first poetry in 1916; and in 1919 his first volume, *Poems about God*, was published. In 1922 he helped found the *Fugitive*, a poetry magazine in which a group of Southern writers first gave expression to views by which they became known as agrarian distributionists. The chief tenet of this group, of which Ransom was a leading member, was that men should live according to the cultural tradition of their own region. Besides publishing several volumes of poetry, Ransom has been a frequent contributor to magazines, has edited textbooks, and has written a volume of criticism, *The World's Body* (1938). He spent a year, 1931-1932, in England as a Guggenheim Fellow.

On December 20, 1920, he married Robb Reavill. They have three children—two sons and a daughter.

BELLS FOR JOHN WHITESIDES' DAUGHTER

There was such speed in her little body,
And such lightness in her footfall,
It is no wonder that her brown study
Astonishes us all.

Her wars were bruited in our high window.
We looked among orchard trees and beyond,
Where she took arms against her shadow,
Or harried unto the pond

The lazy geese, like a snow cloud
Dripping their snow on the green grass,
Tricking and stopping, sleepy and proud,
Who cried in goose, Alas,

For the tireless heart within the little
Lady with rod that made them rise
From their noon apple dreams, and scuttle
Goose-fashion under the skies!

But now go the bells, and we are ready;
In one house we are sternly stopped
To say we are vexed at her brown study,
Lying so primly propped.

1924

HERE LIES A LADY

Here lies a lady of beauty and high degree.
Of chills and fever she died, of fever and chills,
The delight of her husband, her aunts, an infant of three,
And of medicos marvelling sweetly on her ills.

For either she burned, and her confident eyes would blaze,
And her fingers fly in a manner to puzzle their heads—
What was she making? Why, nothing; she sat in a maze
Of old scraps of laces, snipped into curious shreds—

Or this would pass, and the light of her fire decline
Till she lay discouraged and cold as a thin stalk white and blown,
And would not open her eyes, to kisses, to wine;
The sixth of these states was her last; the cold settled down.

Sweet ladies, long may ye bloom, and toughly I hope ye may thole,
But was she not lucky? In flowers and lace and mourning,
In love and great honor we bade God rest her soul
After six little spaces of chill, and six of burning.

1924

MISS EUPHEMIA

Out of her house she crept,
Which was her winter's gaol,
Hearing the rumor that now
Was the birds' common tale—
Birds for all the ladies,
And husbands at church-door—
In fine, a spring was promised
As fifty years before.

A phase of green and tender
Was on the mortal clay,
But white upon her stick went
Miss Euphemia,
To count up all her tulips
That celebrated March,
Out of the frore escaping
To the blue upper arch.

Into her house she fled,
Buffeted back to prison,
And sought the very great-chair
From which she had arisen;
Down sat in her whiteness—
Bitter how she laughed—
Opening doors to March, yet
Quaking in his draught.

Nor scarcely can she, dwindling,
Throw down a bridge of dream
For a broken lady's traverse,
Neat-footing on the beam;
She had too much of winter,
And all her ways were lost,
And she sits with us only
Till next Pentecost.

1924

EMILY HARDCASTLE, SPINSTER

We shall come to-morrow morning, who were not to have her
    love;
We shall bring no face of envy, but a gift of praise and lilies
To the stately ceremonial we are not the heroes of.

Let the sisters now attend her, who are red-eyed, who are wroth;
They were younger, she was finer, for they wearied of the waiting
And they married them to merchants, being unbelievers both.

I was dapper when I dangled in my pepper-and-salt;
We were only local beauties, and we beautifully trusted
If the proud one had to tarry we would take her by default.

But right across her threshold has the Grizzled Baron come;
Let them wrap her as a princess, who would patter down a
    stairway
Where the foreigner may take her for his gloomy halidom.

1924

INLAND CITY

She lies far inland, and no stick nor stone of her
Ever has looked on the sounding sea,
And how should she speak of her swift barks and roadways
And white sloops crowding to lift and be free?

"Ye towers and steeples, and belfries and crosses,
Toll for the doomed ships passing to sea.
But ye walls and gateposts, and ye halls and gardens,
Moor in my little boats vigilantly!"

1924

BLUE GIRLS

Twirling your blue skirts, travelling the sward
Under the towers of your seminary,
Go listen to your teachers old and contrary
Without believing a word.

Tie the white fillets then about your lustrous hair
And think no more of what will come to pass
Than bluebirds that go walking on the grass
And chattering on the air.

Practise your beauty, blue girls, before it fail;
And I will cry with my loud lips and publish
Beauty which all our power shall never establish,
It is so frail.

For I could tell you a story which is true;
I know a lady with a terrible tongue,
Blear eyes fallen from blue,
All her perfections tarnished—and yet it is not long
Since she was lovelier than any of you.

1927

SOMEWHERE IS SUCH A KINGDOM

The famous kingdom of the birds
Has a sweet tongue and liquid words,—
The red-birds polish their notes
In their easy practised throats,—
Smooth as orators are the thrushes
Of the airy city of the bushes,—
And God reward the fierce cock wrens
Who have such suavity with their hens.

To me this has its worth
As I sit upon the earth
Lacking my winter and quiet hearth.
For I go up into a nook
With a mind burdened, or a book,
And hear no strife or quarreling
As the birds and their wives sing.

Or, so it has been today.
Yet I cannot therefore say
If the red-bird, wren, or thrush
Know when to speak and when to hush;
Though their manifest education
Be a right enunciation

And their chief excellence
A verbal elegance,
I cannot say if the wind never blows,
Nor how it sometimes goes.

This I know, that if they wrangle
Their words inevitably will jangle.

If they be hateful as men
They will be harsh as we have been.
When they go to pecking
You will soon hear shrieking,
And they who will have the law,
How those will jaw!
Girls that dream unlawful dreams
Will waken full of their own screams,
And boys that get too arrant
Will have rows with a parent,—
And when friend falls out with friend,
All songs must have quick end.

Have they not claws like knives?
Have not these gentlemen wives?

But when they croak and fleer and swear,
My dull heart I must take elsewhere;
For I will see if God has made
Otherwhere another shade
Where the men or beasts or birds
Exchange few words and pleasant words.
And dare I think it is absurd
If no such beast were, no such bird?

1927

THE EQUILIBRISTS

Full of her long white arms and milky skin
He had a thousand times remembered sin.
Alone in the press of people travelled he,
Minding her jacinth and myrrh and ivory.

Mouth he remembered: the quaint orifice
From which came heat that flamed upon the kiss,
Till cold words came down spiral from the head,
Grey doves from the officious tower illsped.

Body: it was a white field ready for love.
On her body's field, with the gaunt tower above,
The lilies grew, beseeching him to take,
If he would pluck and wear them, bruise and break.

Eyes talking: Never mind the cruel words,
Embrace my flowers but not embrace the swords.
But what they said, the doves came straightway flying
And unsaid: Honor, Honor, they came crying.

Importunate her doves. Too pure, too wise,
Clambering on his shoulder, saying, Arise,
Leave me now, and never let us meet,
Eternal distance now command thy feet.

Predicament indeed, which thus discovers
Honor among thieves, Honor between lovers.
O such a little word is Honor, they feel!
But the grey word is between them cold as steel.

At length I saw these lovers fully were come
Into their torture of equilibrium:
Dreadfully had forsworn each other, and yet
They were bound each to each, and they did not forget.

And rigid as two painful stars, and twirled
About the clustered night their prison world,
They burned with fierce love always to come near,
But Honor beat them back and kept them clear.

Ah, the strict lovers, they are ruined now!
I cried in anger. But with puddled brow
Devising for those gibbeted and brave
Came I descanting: Man, what would you have?

For spin your period out, and draw your breath,
A kinder saeculum begins with Death.
Would you ascend to Heaven and bodiless dwell?
Or take your bodies honorless to Hell?

In Heaven you have heard no marriage is,
No white flesh tinder to your lecheries,
Your male and female tissue sweetly shaped
Sublimed away, and furious blood escaped.

Great lovers lie in Hell, the stubborn ones
Infatuate of the flesh upon the bones;
Stuprate, they rend each other when they kiss;
The pieces kiss again—no end to this.

But still I watched them spinning, orbited nice.
Their flames were not more radiant than their ice.
I dug in the quiet earth and wrought the tomb
And made these lines to memorize their doom:—

Equilibrists lie here; stranger, tread light;
Close, but untouching in each other's sight;
Mouldered the lips and ashy the tall skull,
Let them lie perilous and beautiful.

1927

T. S. Eliot

Thomas Stearns Eliot was born in St. Louis, Missouri, September 26, 1888. He was the youngest of the seven children of Henry Ware Eliot and Charlotte Chauncy Stearns Eliot, both of whom were descended from old New England families. His father, a prominent business man of St. Louis, was a son of the Reverend William Greenleaf Eliot, who had settled in St. Louis after leaving Harvard, had established the first Unitarian church in St. Louis, and had helped found Washington University, of which he was afterwards Chancellor.

Eliot secured his early training at the Smith Academy, a department of Washington University, and at Milton. In 1906 he entered Harvard and in three years completed the work required for the A.B. degree. While an undergraduate he was editor of the *Harvard Advocate*, in which appeared several of his poems. Entering the graduate school as a student of philosophy, he continued at Harvard, and in 1910 received from there the A.M. degree. The next year he spent at the Sorbonne, in Paris, studying philosophy and French literature, particularly poetry; then returning to Harvard he resumed his graduate work, supplementing the study of philosophy with the study of ancient languages, including Sanskrit. He pursued these studies for three years, and in 1913-1914 he was an assistant in the Department of Philosophy. Receiving a travelling fellowship for 1914-1915, he went abroad—first to Germany, where he spent part of the summer before the outbreak of World War I, then to England, where he continued the study of philosophy at Merton College, Oxford.

In the spring of 1915 Eliot married an Englishwoman, Vivienne Haigh. During the year in England he also made a number of congenial literary friendships. As a result of his marriage and these literary contacts he decided to settle in England, and since that time he has resided in London. After leaving Oxford he taught for a year or so at the Highgate School, near London, then changed his occupation to banking, and for several years worked as a clerk in Lloyds Bank, Ltd. Meanwhile he had begun to write for several British and American periodicals, and as time passed he was more and more drawn to literary work. Finally he resigned from Lloyds to devote all his time to writing and editing. From 1917 to 1919 he was assistant editor of the *Egoist*, and in 1923 he became editor of the quarterly review, the *Criterion*. He later joined the publishing firm of Faber & Faber, Ltd., of which he is now a director. In 1927 he became a British subject, and at about the same time he embraced the faith of the High Church party of the Anglican Church.

Save for his contributions to the *Harvard Advocate* in his undergraduate days, Eliot's first poems were published in 1915 in *Poetry: A Magazine of Verse*, of which Ezra Pound was foreign editor, and in the *Catholic Anthology*, which Pound edited. Thereafter he contributed to a number of magazines, and in 1917 appeared his first slender volume of poetry, followed by one or two others as slender. This work brought him into general notice and won him the admiration of numerous critics and of many of his fellow poets. His reputation was already well established before the publication, in the *Dial* in 1922, of his noted poem, *The Waste Land*, for which he received the *Dial* award of two thousand dollars. Although at no time a prolific poet, Eliot has written less poetry in recent years than formerly. The number of his critical works has grown, however, and these have exerted considerable influence on contemporary literature. With such works as *The Sacred Wood* (1920), *For Lancelot Andrewes* (1928), *John Dryden* (1932), *Selected Essays* (1932), and some later volumes, he has established himself as one of the strongest forces in the literary world.

In 1926 Eliot was Clark Lecturer in Trinity College, Cambridge. In 1932 he returned to the United States for a long visit, and during 1932-1933 he was the Charles Eliot Norton Professor of Poetry at Harvard. In 1933 he gave the Page-Barbour lectures at the University of Virginia and also lectured at several other universities. He holds the honorary degree of Litt.D. from the universities of Columbia, Cambridge, Bristol, Leeds, and Edinburgh, and he is an honorary Fellow of Magdalen College, Oxford.

Called arrow collar man of modern poetry

THE LOVE SONG OF J. ALFRED PRUFROCK

S'io credesse che mia risposta fosse
A persona che mai tornasse al mondo,
Questa fiamma staria senza piu scosse.
Ma perciocche giammai di questo fondo
Non torno vivo alcun, s'i'odo il vero,
Senza tema d'infamia ti rispondo.[1]

Let us go then, you and I,
When the evening is spread out against the sky
Like a patient etherised upon a table;
Let us go, through certain half-deserted streets,
The muttering retreats
Of restless nights in one-night cheap hotels
And sawdust restaurants with oyster-shells:
Streets that follow like a tedious argument
Of insidious intent
To lead you to an overwhelming question . . .
Oh, do not ask, "What is it?"
Let us go and make our visit.

In the room the women come and go
Talking of Michelangelo.

The yellow fog that rubs its back upon the window-panes,
The yellow smoke that rubs its muzzle on the window-panes
Licked its tongue into the corners of the evening,
Lingered upon the pools that stand in drains,
Let fall upon its back the soot that falls from chimneys,
Slipped by the terrace, made a sudden leap,
And seeing that it was a soft October night,
Curled once about the house, and fell asleep.

[1] If I believed that my answer might belong
To anyone who ever returned to the world,
This flame would leap no more.
But since, however, from these depths
No one ever returns alive, if I know the truth,
Then without fear of infamy I answer you.
Dante, *Inferno*, xxvii, 61-66.

And indeed there will be time
For the yellow smoke that slides along the street,
Rubbing its back upon the window-panes;
There will be time, there will be time
To prepare a face to meet the faces that you meet;
There will be time to murder and create,
And time for all the works and days of hands
That lift and drop a question on your plate;
Time for you and time for me,
And time yet for a hundred indecisions,
And for a hundred visions and revisions,
Before the taking of a toast and tea.

In the room the women come and go
Talking of Michelangelo.

And indeed there will be time
To wonder, "Do I dare?" and, "Do I dare?"
Time to turn back and descend the stair,
With a bald spot in the middle of my hair—
(They will say: "How his hair is growing thin!")
My morning coat, my collar mounting firmly to the chin,
My necktie rich and modest, but asserted by a simple pin—
(They will say: "But how his arms and legs are thin!")
Do I dare
Disturb the universe?
In a minute there is time
For decisions and revisions which a minute will reverse.

For I have known them all already, known them all:
Have known the evenings, mornings, afternoons,
I have measured out my life with coffee spoons;
I know the voices dying with a dying fall
Beneath the music from a farther room.
  So how should I presume?

And I have known the eyes already, known them all—
The eyes that fix you in a formulated phrase,
And when I am formulated, sprawling on a pin,
When I am pinned and wriggling on the wall,
Then how should I begin
To spit out all the butt-ends of my days and ways?
  And how should I presume?

And I have known the arms already, known them all—
Arms that are braceleted and white and bare
(But in the lamplight, downed with light brown hair!)
Is it perfume from a dress
That makes me so digress?
Arms that lie along a table, or wrap about a shawl.
  And should I then presume?
  And how should I begin?

* * * * *

Shall I say, I have gone at dusk through narrow streets
And watched the smoke that rises from the pipes
Of lonely men in shirt-sleeves, leaning out of windows? . . .

I should have been a pair of ragged claws
Scuttling across the floors of silent seas.

* * * * *

And the afternoon, the evening, sleeps so peacefully!
Smoothed by long fingers,
Asleep . . . tired . . . or it malingers,
Stretched on the floor, here beside you and me.
Should I, after tea and cakes and ices,
Have the strength to force the moment to its crisis?
But though I have wept and fasted, wept and prayed,
Though I have seen my head (grown slightly bald) brought in
    upon a platter,
I am no prophet—and here's no great matter;
I have seen the moment of my greatness flicker,
And I have seen the eternal Footman hold my coat, and snicker,
And in short, I was afraid.

And would it have been worth it, after all,
After the cups, the marmalade, the tea,
Among the porcelain, among some talk of you and me,
Would it have been worth while,
To have bitten off the matter with a smile,
To have squeezed the universe into a ball
To roll it toward some overwhelming question,
To say: "I am Lazarus, come from the dead,
Come back to tell you all, I shall tell you all"—
If one, settling a pillow by her head,
  Should say: "That is not what I meant at all;
  That is not it, at all."

And would it have been worth it, after all,
Would it have been worth while,
After the sunsets and the dooryards and the sprinkled streets,
After the novels, after the teacups, after the skirts that trail along
the floor—
And this, and so much more?—
It is impossible to say just what I mean!
But as if a magic lantern threw the nerves in patterns on a screen:
Would it have been worth while
If one, settling a pillow or throwing off a shawl,
And turning toward the window, should say:
"That is not it at all,
That is not what I meant, at all."

* * * * *

No! I am not Prince Hamlet, nor was meant to be;
Am an attendant lord, one that will do
To swell a progress, start a scene or two,
Advise the prince; no doubt, an easy tool,
Deferential, glad to be of use,
Politic, cautious, and meticulous;
Full of high sentence, but a bit obtuse;
At times, indeed, almost ridiculous—
Almost, at times, the Fool.

I grow old . . . I grow old . . .
I shall wear the bottoms of my trousers rolled.

Shall I part my hair behind? Do I dare to eat a peach?
I shall wear white flannel trousers, and walk upon the beach.
I have heard the mermaids singing, each to each.

I do not think that they will sing to me.

I have seen them riding seaward on the waves
Combing the white hair of the waves blown back
When the wind blows the water white and black.

We have lingered in the chambers of the sea
By sea-girls wreathed with seaweed red and brown
Till human voices wake us, and we drown.

1917

MORNING AT THE WINDOW

They are rattling breakfast plates in basement kitchens,
And along the trampled edges of the street
I am aware of the damp souls of housemaids
Sprouting despondently at area gates.

The brown waves of fog toss up to me
Twisted faces from the bottom of the street,
And tear from a passer-by with muddy skirts
An aimless smile that hovers in the air
And vanishes along the level of the roofs.

1917

LA FIGLIA CHE PIANGE[1]

O quam te memorem virgo . . .

Stand on the highest pavement of the stair—
Lean on a garden urn—
Weave, weave the sunlight in your hair—
Clasp your flowers to you with a pained surprise—
Fling them to the ground and turn
With a fugitive resentment in your eyes:
But weave, weave the sunlight in your hair.

So I would have had him leave,
So I would have had her stand and grieve,
So he would have left
As the soul leaves the body torn and bruised,
As the mind deserts the body it has used.
I should find
Some way incomparably light and deft,
Some way we both should understand,
Simple and faithless as a smile and shake of the hand.

She turned away, but with the autumn weather
Compelled my imagination many days,
Many days and many hours:
Her hair over her arms and her arms full of flowers.

1 The girl who laments. The quotation under the title—O, what shall I call you, girl?—is from Virgil's *Aeneid*, I, 327.

And I wonder how they should have been together!
I should have lost a gesture and a pose.
Sometimes these cogitations still amaze
The troubled midnight and the noon's repose.

1917

GERONTION

Thou hast nor youth nor age
But as it were an after dinner sleep
Dreaming of both.

Here I am, an old man in a dry month,
Being read to by a boy, waiting for rain.
I was neither at the hot gates
Nor fought in the warm rain
Nor knee deep in the salt marsh, heaving a cutlass,
Bitten by flies, fought.
My house is a decayed house,
And the jew squats on the window sill, the owner,
Spawned in some estaminet of Antwerp,
Blistered in Brussels, patched and peeled in London.
The goat coughs at night in the field overhead;
Rocks, moss, stonecrop, iron, merds.
The woman keeps the kitchen, makes tea,
Sneezes at evening, poking the peevish gutter.
I an old man,
A dull head among windy spaces.

Signs are taken for wonders. "We would see a sign!"
The word within a word, unable to speak a word,
Swaddled with darkness. In the juvescence of the year
Came Christ the tiger

In depraved May, dogwood and chestnut, flowering judas,
To be eaten, to be divided, to be drunk
Among whispers; by Mr. Silvero
With caressing hands, at Limoges
Who walked all night in the next room:

By Hakagawa, bowing among the Titians;
By Madame de Tornquist, in the dark room
Shifting the candles; Fräulein von Kulp

Who turned in the hall, one hand on the door.
    Vacant shuttles
Weave the wind. I have no ghosts,
An old man in a draughty house
Under a windy knob.

After such knowledge, what forgiveness? Think now
History has many cunning passages, contrived corridors
And issues, deceives with whispering ambitions,
Guides us by vanities. Think now
She gives when our attention is distracted
And what she gives, gives with such supple confusions
That the giving famishes the craving. Gives too late
What's not believed in, or if still believed,
In memory only, reconsidered passion. Gives too soon
Into weak hands, what's thought can be dispensed with
Till the refusal propagates a fear. Think
Neither fear nor courage saves us. Unnatural vices
Are fathered by our heroism. Virtues
Are forced upon us by our impudent crimes.
These tears are shaken from the wrath-bearing tree.

The tiger springs in the new year. Us he devours.
    Think at last
We have not reached conclusion, when I
Stiffen in a rented house. Think at last
I have not made this show purposelessly
And it is not by any concitation
Of the backward devils.
I would meet you upon this honestly.
I that was near your heart was removed therefrom
To lose beauty in terror, terror in inquisition.
I have lost my passion: why should I need to keep it
Since what is kept must be adulterated?
I have lost my sight, smell, hearing, taste, and touch:
How should I use them for your closer contact?

These with a thousand small deliberations
Protract the profit of their chilled delirium,
Excite the membrane, when the sense has cooled,
With pungent sauces, multiply variety
In a wilderness of mirrors. What will the spider do,
Suspend its operations, will the weevil

Delay? De Bailhache, Fresca, Mrs. Cammel, whirled
Beyond the circuit of the shuddering Bear
In fractured atoms. Gull against the wind, in the windy straits
Of Belle Isle, or running on the Horn,
White feathers in the snow, the Gulf claims,
And an old man driven by the Trades
To a sleepy corner.
                                        Tenants of the house,
Thoughts of a dry brain in a dry season.

1920

THE HIPPOPOTAMUS

Similiter et omnes revereantur Diaconos, ut mandatum Jesu Christi; et Episcopum, ut Jesum Christum, existentem filium Patris; Presbyteros autem, ut concilium Dei et conjunctionem Apostolorum. Sine his Ecclesia non vocatur; de quibus suadeo vos sic habeo.—S. Ignatii ad Trallianos.[1]

And when this epistle is read among you, cause that it *be read also in the church of the Laodiceans.*

The broad-backed hippopotamus
Rests on his belly in the mud;
Although he seems so firm to us
He is merely flesh and blood.

Flesh and blood is weak and frail,
Susceptible to nervous shock;
While the True Church can never fail
For it is based upon a rock.

The hippo's feeble steps may err
In compassing material ends,
While the True Church need never stir
To gather in its dividends.

The 'potamus can never reach
The mango on the mango-tree;

[1] Likewise let everyone revere the Deacons, according to the orders of Jesus Christ; and the Bishop, as ordained by Jesus Christ, the living son of the Father; likewise the Priests, according to the dictates of God and the injunction of the Apostles. For without these the church does not exist; which I urge upon you as I have (done).

But fruits of pomegranate and peach
Refresh the Church from over sea.

At mating time the hippo's voice
Betrays inflexions hoarse and odd,
But every week we hear rejoice
The Church, at being one with God.

The hippopotamus's day
Is passed in sleep; at night he hunts;
God works in a mysterious way—
The Church can sleep and feed at once.

I saw the 'potamus take wing
Ascending from the damp savannas,
And quiring angels round him sing
The praise of God, in loud hosannas.

Blood of the Lamb shall wash him clean
And him shall heavenly arms enfold,
Among the saints he shall be seen
Performing on a harp of gold.

He shall be washed as white as snow,
By all the martyr'd virgins kist,
While the True Church remains below
Wrapt in the old miasmal mist.

1920

WHISPERS OF IMMORTALITY

Webster was much possessed by death
And saw the skull beneath the skin;
And breastless creatures under ground
Leaned backward with a lipless grin.

Daffodil bulbs instead of balls
Stared from the sockets of the eyes!
He knew that thought clings round dead limbs
Tightening its lusts and luxuries.

Donne, I suppose, was such another
Who found no substitute for sense;

To seize and clutch and penetrate,
Expert beyond experience,

He knew the anguish of the marrow
The ague of the skeleton;
No contact possible to flesh
Allayed the fever of the bone.

* * * * *

Grishkin is nice: her Russian eye
Is underlined for emphasis;
Uncorseted, her friendly bust
Gives promise of pneumatic bliss.

The couched Brazilian jaguar
Compels the scampering marmoset
With subtle effluence of cat;
Grishkin has a maisonette;

The sleek Brazilian jaguar
Does not in its arboreal gloom
Distil so rank a feline smell
As Grishkin in a drawing-room.

And even the Abstract Entities
Circumambulate her charm;
But our lot crawls between dry ribs
To keep our metaphysics warm.

1920

SWEENEY AMONG THE NIGHTINGALES

ὤμοι, πέπληγμαι καιρίαν πληγὴν ἔσω.[1]

Apeneck Sweeney spreads his knees
Letting his arms hang down to laugh,
The zebra stripes along his jaw
Swelling to maculate giraffe.

[1] Woe's me! I'm stricken a mortal blow within.—Aeschylus, *Agamemnon*, 1343.

The circles of the stormy moon
Slide westward toward the River Plate,
Death and the Raven drift above
And Sweeney guards the hornèd gate.

Gloomy Orion and the Dog
Are veiled; and hushed the shrunken seas;
The person in the Spanish cape
Tries to sit on Sweeney's knees

Slips and pulls the table cloth
Overturns a coffee-cup,
Reorganized upon the floor
She yawns and draws a stocking up;

The silent man in mocha brown
Sprawls at the window-sill and gapes;
The waiter brings in oranges
Bananas figs and hothouse grapes;

The silent vertebrate in brown
Contracts and concentrates, withdraws;
Rachel *née* Rabinovitch
Tears at the grapes with murderous paws;

She and the lady in the cape
Are suspect, thought to be in league;
Therefore the man with heavy eyes
Declines the gambit, shows fatigue,

Leaves the room and reappears
Outside the window, leaning in,
Branches of wistaria
Circumscribe a golden grin;

The host with someone indistinct
Converses at the door apart,
The nightingales are singing near
The Convent of the Sacred Heart,

And sang within the bloody wood
When Agamemnon cried aloud,
And let their liquid siftings fall
To stain the stiff dishonored shroud.

1920

THE HOLLOW MEN

A penny for the Old Guy

I

We are the hollow men
We are the stuffed men
Leaning together
Headpiece filled with straw. Alas!
Our dried voices, when
We whisper together
Are quiet and meaningless
As wind in dry grass
Or rats' feet over broken glass
In our dry cellar.

Shape without form, shade without color,
Paralyzed force, gesture without motion;

Those who have crossed
With direct eyes, to death's other Kingdom
Remember us—if at all—not as lost
Violent souls, but only
As the hollow men
The stuffed men.

II

Eyes I dare not meet in dreams
In death's dream kingdom
These do not appear:
There, the eyes are
Sunlight on a broken column
There, is a tree swinging
And voices are
In the wind's singing
More distant and more solemn
Than a fading star.

Let me be no nearer
In death's dream kingdom
Let me also wear
Such deliberate disguises

Rat's skin, crowskin, crossed staves
In a field
Behaving as the wind behaves
No nearer—

Not that final meeting
In the twilight kingdom.

III

This is the dead land
This is cactus land
Here the stone images
Are raised, here they receive
The supplication of a dead man's hand
Under the twinkle of a fading star.

Is it like this
In death's other kingdom
Waking alone
At the hour when we are
Trembling with tenderness
Lips that would kiss
Form prayers to broken stone.

IV

The eyes are not here
There are no eyes here
In this valley of dying stars
In this hollow valley
This broken jaw of our lost kingdoms

In this last of meeting places
We grope together
And avoid speech
Gathered on this beach of the tumid river

Sightless, unless
The eyes reappear
As the perpetual star
Multifoliate rose
Of death's twilight kingdom
The hope only
Of empty men.

V

Here we go round the prickly pear
Prickly pear prickly pear
Here we go round the prickly pear
At five o'clock in the morning.

Between the idea
And the reality
Between the motion
And the act
Falls the Shadow
For Thine is the Kingdom

Between the conception
And the creation
Between the emotion
And the response
Falls the Shadow
Life is very long

Between the desire
And the spasm
Between the potency
And the existence
Between the essence
And the descent
Falls the Shadow
For Thine is the Kingdom

For Thine is
Life is
For Thine is the

This is the way the world ends
This is the way the world ends
This is the way the world ends
Not with a bang but a whimper.

1925

JOURNEY OF THE MAGI

"A cold coming we had of it,
Just the worst time of the year
For a journey, and such a long journey:
The ways deep and the weather sharp,
The very dead of winter."
And the camels galled, sore-footed, refractory,
Lying down in the melting snow
There were times we regretted
The summer palaces on slopes, the terraces,
And the silken girls bringing sherbet.
Then the camel men cursing and grumbling
And running away, and wanting their liquor and women,
And the night-fires going out, and the lack of shelters,
And the cities hostile and the towns unfriendly
And the villages dirty and charging high prices:
A hard time we had of it.
At the end we preferred to travel all night,
Sleeping in snatches,
With the voices singing in our ears, saying
That this was all folly.

Then at dawn we came down to a temperate valley,
Wet, below the snow line, smelling of vegetation;
With a running stream and a water-mill beating the darkness,
And three trees on the low sky,
And an old white horse galloped away in the meadow.
Then we came to a tavern with vine-leaves over the lintel,
Six hands at an open door dicing for pieces of silver,
And feet kicking the empty wine-skins.
But there was no information, and so we continued
And arrived at evening, not a moment too soon
Finding the place; it was (you may say) satisfactory.

All this was a long time ago, I remember,
And I would do it again, but set down
This set down
This: were we led all that way for
Birth or Death? There was a Birth, certainly,
We had evidence and no doubt. I had seen birth and death,
But had thought they were different; this Birth was

Hard and bitter agony for us, like Death, our death.
We returned to our places, these Kingdoms,
But no longer at ease here, in the old dispensation,
With an alien people clutching their gods.
I should be glad of another death.

1927

ANIMULA[1]

"Issues from the hand of God, the simple soul"
To a flat world of changing lights and noise,
To light, dark, dry or damp, chilly or warm;
Moving between the legs of tables and of chairs,
Rising or falling, grasping at kisses and toys,
Advancing boldly, sudden to take alarm,
Retreating to the corner of arm and knee,
Eager to be reassured, taking pleasure
In the fragrant brilliance of the Christmas tree,
Pleasure in the wind, the sunlight and the sea;
Studies the sunlit pattern on the floor
And running stags around a silver tray;
Confounds the actual and the fanciful,
Content with playing-cards and kings and queens,
What the fairies do and what the servants say.
The heavy burden of the growing soul
Perplexes and offends more, day by day;
Week by week, offends and perplexes more
With the imperatives of "is and seems"
And may and may not, desire and control.
The pain of living and the drug of dreams
Curl up the small soul in the window seat
Behind the *Encyclopædia Britannica.*
Issues from the hand of time the simple soul
Irresolute and selfish, misshapen, lame,
Unable to fare forward or retreat,
Fearing the warm reality, the offered good,
Denying the importunity of the blood,
Shadow of its own shadows, spectre in its own gloom,
Leaving disordered papers in a dusty room;
Living first in the silence after the viaticum.

[1] Small soul.

Pray for Guiterriez, avid of speed and power,
For Boudin, blown to pieces,
For this one who made a great fortune,
And that one who went his own way.
Pray for Floret, by the boarhound slain between the yew trees,
Pray for us now and at the hour of our birth.

1929

ASH WEDNESDAY

I

Because I do not hope to turn again
Because I do not hope
Because I do not hope to turn
Desiring this man's gift and that man's scope
I no longer strive to strive towards such things
(Why should the aged eagle stretch its wings?)
Why should I mourn
The vanished power of the usual reign?

Because I do not hope to know again
The infirm glory of the positive hour
Because I do not think
Because I know I shall not know
The one veritable transitory power
Because I cannot drink
There, where trees flower, and springs flow, for there is nothing again

Because I know that time is always time
And place is always and only place
And what is actual is actual only for one time
And only for one place
I rejoice that things are as they are and
I renounce the blessed face
And renounce the voice
Because I cannot hope to turn again
Consequently I rejoice, having to construct something
Upon which to rejoice

And pray to God to have mercy upon us
And I pray that I may forget

These matters that with myself I too much discuss
Too much explain
Because I do not hope to turn again
Let these words answer
For what is done, not to be done again
May the judgment not be too heavy upon us

Because these wings are no longer wings to fly
But merely vans to beat the air
The air which is now thoroughly small and dry
Smaller and dryer than the will
Teach us to care and not to care
Teach us to sit still.

Pray for us sinners now and at the hour of our death
Pray for us now and and at the hour of our death.

II

Lady, three white leopards sat under a juniper-tree
In the cool of the day, having fed to satiety
On my legs my heart my liver and that which had been contained
In the hollow round of my skull. And God said
Shall these bones live? shall these
Bones live? And that which had been contained
In the bones (which were already dry) said chirping:
Because of the goodness of this Lady
And because of her loveliness, and because
She honors the Virgin in meditation,
We shine with brightness. And I who am here dissembled
Proffer my deeds to oblivion, and my love
To the posterity of the desert and the fruit of the gourd.
It is this which recovers
My guts the strings of my eyes and the indigestible portions
Which the leopards reject. The Lady is withdrawn
In a white gown, to contemplation, in a white gown.
Let the whiteness of bones atone to forgetfulness.
There is no life in them. As I am forgotten
And would be forgotten, so I would forget
Thus devoted, concentrated in purpose. And God said
Prophesy to the wind, to the wind only for only
The wind will listen. And the bones sang chirping
With the burden of the grasshopper, saying

Lady of silences
Calm and distressed
Torn and most whole
Rose of memory
Rose of forgetfulness
Exhausted and life-giving
Worried reposeful
The single Rose
Is now the Garden
Where all loves end
Terminate torment
Of love unsatisfied
The greater torment
Of love satisfied
End of the endless
Journey to no end
Conclusion of all that
Is inconclusible
Speech without word and
Word of no speech
Grace to the Mother
For the Garden
Where all love ends.

Under a juniper-tree the bones sang, scattered and shining
We are glad to be scattered, we did little good to each other,
Under a tree in the cool of the day, with the blessing of sand,
Forgetting themselves and each other, united
In the quiet of the desert. This is the land which ye
Shall divide by lot. And neither division nor unity
Matters. This is the land. We have our inheritance.

III

At the first turning of the second stair
I turned and saw below
The same shape twisted on the banister
Under the vapor in the fetid air
Struggling with the devil of the stairs who wears
The deceitful face of hope and of despair.

At the second turning of the second stair
I left them twisting, turning below;
There were no more faces and the stair was dark,

Damp, jaggèd, like an old man's mouth drivelling, beyond
repair,
Or the toothed gullet of an agèd shark.

At the first turning of the third stair
Was a slotted window bellied like the fig's fruit
And beyond the hawthorn blossom and a pasture scene
The broadbacked figure drest in blue and green
Enchanted the maytime with an antique flute.
Blown hair is sweet, brown hair over the mouth blown,
Lilac and brown hair;
Distraction, music of the flute, stops and steps of the mind over
the third stair,
Fading, fading; strength beyond hope and despair
Climbing the third stair.

Lord, I am not worthy
Lord, I am not worthy

but speak the word only.

IV

Who walked between the violet and the violet
Who walked between
The various ranks of varied green
Going in white and blue, in Mary's color,
Talking of trivial things
In ignorance and in knowledge of eternal dolor
Who moved among the others as they walked,
Who then made strong the fountains and made fresh the springs

Made cool the dry rock and made firm the sand
In blue of larkspur, blue of Mary's color,
Sovvegna vos [1]

Here are the years that walk between, bearing
Away the fiddles and the flutes, restoring
One who moves in the time between sleep and waking, wearing

White light folded, sheathed about her, folded.
The new years walk, restoring
Through a bright cloud of tears, the years, restoring

[1] Be ye mindful.

With a new verse the ancient rhyme. Redeem
The time. Redeem
The unread vision in the higher dream
While jewelled unicorns draw by the gilded hearse.

The silent sister veiled in white and blue
Between the yews, behind the garden god,
Whose flute is breathless, bent her head and signed but spoke
no word

But the fountain sprang up and the bird sang down
Redeem the time, redeem the dream
The token of the word unheard, unspoken

Till the wind shake a thousand whispers from the yew

And after this our exile

V

If the lost word is lost, if the spent word is spent
If the unheard, unspoken
Word is unspoken, unheard;
Still is the unspoken word, the Word unheard,
The Word without a word, the Word within
The world and for the world;
And the light shone in darkness and
Against the Word the unstilled world still whirled
About the centre of the silent Word.

O my people, what have I done unto thee.

Where shall the word be found, where will the word
Resound? Not here, there is not enough silence
Not on the sea or on the islands, not
On the mainland, in the desert or the rain land,
For those who walk in darkness
Both in the day time and in the night time
The right time and the right place are not here
No place of grace for those who avoid the face
No time to rejoice for those who walk among noise and deny
the voice

Will the veiled sister pray for
Those who walk in darkness, who chose thee and oppose thee,

Those who are torn on the horn between season and season,
time and time, between
Hour and hour, word and word, power and power, those who wait
In darkness? Will the veiled sister pray
For children at the gate
Who will not go away and cannot pray:
Pray for those who chose and oppose

O my people, what have I done unto thee.

Will the veiled sister between the slender
Yew trees pray for those who offend her
And are terrified and cannot surrender
And affirm before the world and deny between the rocks
In the last desert between the last blue rocks
The desert in the garden the garden in the desert
Of drouth, spitting from the mouth the withered apple-seed.

O my people.

VI

Although I do not hope to turn again
Although I do not hope
Although I do not hope to turn

Wavering between the profit and the loss
In this brief transit where the dreams cross
The dreamcrossed twilight between birth and dying
(Bless me father) though I do not wish to wish these things
From the wide window towards the granite shore
The white sails still fly seaward, seaward flying
Unbroken wings

And the lost heart stiffens and rejoices
In the lost lilac and the lost sea voices
And the weak spirit quickens to rebel
For the bent golden-rod and the lost sea smell
Quickens to recover
The cry of quail and the whirling plover
And the blind eye creates
The empty forms between the ivory gates
And smell renews the salt savor of the sandy earth

This is the time of tension between dying and birth
The place of solitude where three dreams cross

Between blue rocks
But when the voices shaken from the yew-tree drift away
Let the other yew be shaken and reply.

Blessèd sister, holy mother, spirit of the fountain, spirit of the
    garden,
Suffer us not to mock ourselves with falsehood
Teach us to care and not to care
Teach us to sit still
Even among these rocks,
Our peace in His will
And even among these rocks
Sister, mother
And spirit of the river, spirit of the sea,
Suffer me not to be separated

And let my cry come unto Thee.

1930

MARINA

Quis hic locus, quae regio, quae mundi plaga? [1]

What seas what shores what grey rocks and what islands
What water lapping the bow
And scent of pine and the woodthrush singing through the fog
What images return
O my daughter.

Those who sharpen the tooth of the dog, meaning
Death
Those who glitter with the glory of the humming-bird, meaning
Death
Those who sit in the stye of contentment, meaning
Death
Those who suffer the ecstasy of the animals, meaning
Death

Are become unsubstantial, reduced by a wind,
A breath of pine, and the woodsong fog
By this grace dissolved in place

[1] What is this place, this territory, this region of the world? Marina is the name of the daughter of Pericles in Shakespeare's play of that title; she was separated in infancy from her father, who found her many years later.

What is this face, less clear and clearer
The pulse in the arm, less strong and stronger—
Given or lent? more distant than stars and nearer than the eye

Whispers and small laughter between leaves and hurrying feet
Under sleep, where all the waters meet.

Bowsprit cracked with ice and paint cracked with heat.
I made this, I have forgotten
And remember.
The rigging weak and the canvas rotten
Between one June and another September.
Made this unknowing, half conscious, unknown, my own.
The garboard strake leaks, the seams need caulking.
This form, this face, this life
Living to live in a world of time beyond me; let me
Resign my life for this life, my speech for that unspoken,
The awakened, lips parted, the hope, the new ships.

What seas what shores what granite islands towards my timbers
And woodthrush calling through the fog
My daughter.

1930

Eliot only reports and criticizes
poets should do more than this
really great poets bring order out of the
chaos of life

Eliot is an intellectual: he is not a poet of feeling

Heady "Makes people out of love with poetry"
Clever
Cynical
Ununderstandable
befoggable
unmusical

Conrad Aiken

Conrad Potter Aiken, eldest of the three sons of William Ford Aiken and Anna Potter Aiken, was born at Savannah, Georgia, on August 5, 1889. Both his parents were descended from old and prominent New England families. His father, a graduate of the Harvard Medical School, established a practice in Savannah, where he enjoyed a high reputation as physician and surgeon.

Aiken secured his early education in the Savannah public schools. From the first he evinced an interest in poetry, and at nine began to write verse. In his eleventh year, his father, while temporarily deranged, killed his wife and himself. As a result of this tragedy Aiken went to live with a great aunt in New Bedford, Massachusetts. For the next seven years he attended the Middlesex School. In 1907 he entered Harvard. While an undergraduate he wrote verse and prose for the *Harvard Monthly* and the *Harvard Advocate* and was President of the *Advocate* and class poet. In his senior year he ranked high enough in scholarship to enjoy the privilege of irregular class attendance, but when he absented himself from classes for ten days to write a poem, the authorities thought he was using his privilege too freely and placed him on probation. Considering this treatment unjust, he left college and went abroad for six months, but returned the following autumn and finished with the class of 1912. In his senior year he became engaged to Jessie McDonald, of Montreal. They were married on August 25, 1912, and spent the next year in England, France, and Italy. After that Aiken lived in Cambridge, Boston, and South Yarmouth, Massachusetts. He made frequent trips to Europe, however, and in 1923 settled at Winchelsea, on the Sussex coast. Some months later he bought a house at Rye, within a block or two of Henry James's old home, and until the outbreak of the second

World War had lived there except for two short visits to the United States in 1925 and 1933 and a lengthier one from 1927 to 1930. During the latter stay, he taught for a year, 1927-1928, at Harvard.

In 1914 appeared his first volume, *Earth Triumphant and Other Tales in Verse,* and since then he has published more than a dozen volumes of poetry. From 1917 to 1919 he was an editor of the *Dial,* for which he wrote many critical articles. The best of these he published in a book, *Scepticisms* (1919). He has also written a number of prose works, among them several volumes of short stories and several novels, *Bring! Bring! and Other Stories* (1925), *Costumes by Eros* (1928), *Among the Lost People* (1934), *Blue Voyage* (1927), *Great Circle* (1933), *King Coffin* (1935) and *Conversation* (1940). He has edited several collections of poetry and a selection of the poems of Emily Dickinson, and is a frequent contributor to such magazines as the *New Yorker, Esquire,* and the *Atlantic Monthly.*

In 1930 he received the Pulitzer Prize for poetry and was the first recipient, in the same year, of the Shelley Memorial Award. During the year 1934-1935 he held a Guggenheim Fellowship.

Aiken and his wife were divorced in 1929, and in 1930 he was married to Clarice Mary Lorenz, from whom he was also divorced —in April, 1938. Later in the same year he was married to the painter, Mary Augusta Hoover, of Boston. They now live in Massachusetts.

[MUSIC I HEARD WITH YOU]

Music I heard with you was more than music,
And bread I broke with you was more than bread;
Now that I am without you, all is desolate;
All that was once so beautiful is dead.

Your hands once touched this table and this silver,
And I have seen your fingers hold this glass.
These things do not remember you, belovèd,—
And yet your touch upon them will not pass.

For it was in my heart you moved among them,
And blessed them with your hands and with your eyes;

poems remind you of A. E. Housman

And in my heart they will remember always,—
They knew you once, O beautiful and wise.

1916

He is very much interested in the psychology of things around him

[DEAD CLEOPATRA LIES IN A CRYSTAL CASKET]

could be like "Nobody loses all the time", by E. E. Cummings

Dead Cleopatra lies in a crystal casket,
Wrapped and spiced by the cunningest of hands.
Around her neck they have put a golden necklace,
Her tatbebs, it is said, are worn with sands.

Dead Cleopatra was once revered in Egypt,
Warm-eyed she was, this princess of the South.
Now she is very old and dry and faded,
With black bitumen they have sealed up her mouth.

he doesn't like Egyptian method of mummifying

Grave-robbers pulled the gold rings from her fingers,
Despite the holy symbols across her breast;
They scared the bats that quietly whirled above her.
Poor lady! she would have been long since at rest,

If she had not been wrapped and spiced so shrewdly,
Preserved, obscene, to mock black flights of years. . . .
What would her lover have said,—had he foreseen it?
Had he been moved to ecstasy,—or tears?

O sweet clean earth, from whom the green blade cometh!
When we are dead, my best belovèd and I,
Close well above us, that we may rest forever,
Sending up grass and blossoms to the sky.

beauty coming from dead bodies

1916

[ALL LOVELY THINGS WILL HAVE AN ENDING]

perfect example of Aiken's philosophy

All lovely things will have an ending,
All lovely things will fade and die,
And youth, that's now so bravely spending,
Will beg a penny by and by.

Fine ladies all are soon forgotten,
And goldenrod is dust when dead,
The sweetest flesh and flowers are rotten
And cobwebs tent the brightest head.

Come back, true love! Sweet youth, return!—
But time goes on, and will, unheeding,
Though hands will reach, and eyes will yearn,
And the wild days set true hearts bleeding.

Come back, true love! Sweet youth, remain!—
But goldenrod and daisies wither,
And over them blows autumn rain,
They pass, they pass, and know not whither.

1916

NOCTURNE OF REMEMBERED SPRING

I

Moonlight silvers the tops of trees,
Moonlight whitens the lilac-shadowed wall;
And through the evening fall,
Clearly, as if through enchanted seas,
Footsteps passing, an infinite distance away,
In another world and another day.
Moonlight turns the purple lilacs blue,
Moonlight leaves the fountain hoar and old,
And the boughs of elms grow green and cold.
Our footsteps echo on gleaming stones,
The leaves are stirred to a jargon of muted tones.
This is the night we have kept, you say:
This is the moonlight night that never will die.
Let us return there, let us return, you and I,—
Through the grey streets our memories retain
Let us go back again.

II

Mist goes up from the river to dim the stars,
The river is black and cold; so let us dance
To flare of horns, and clang of cymbals, and drums;
And strew the glimmering floor with roses,
And remember, while rich music yawns and closes,

With a luxury of pain, how silence comes.
Yes, we loved each other, long ago;
We moved like wind to a music's ebb and flow.
At a phrase from violins you closed your eyes,
And smiled, and let me lead you . . . how young we were!
Your hair, upon that music, seemed to stir.
Let us return there, let us return, you and I;
Through changeless streets our memories retain
Let us go back again.

III

Mist goes up from rain-steeped earth, and clings
Ghostly with lamplight among drenched maple trees.
We walk in silence and see how the lamplight flings
Fans of shadow upon it . . . the music's mournful pleas
Die out behind us, the door is closed at last,
A net of silver silence is softly cast
Over our thought . . . slowly we walk,
Quietly, with delicious pause, we talk,
Of foolish trivial things; of life and death,
Time, and forgetfulness, and dust and truth;
Lilacs and youth.
You laugh, I hear the after-taken breath,
You darken your eyes, and turn away your head
At something I have said—
Some intuition that flew too deep,
And struck a plangent chord. To-night, to-night,
You will remember it as you fall asleep,
Your dream will suddenly blossom with sharp delight,
Good-night! you say.
The leaves of the lilac dip and sway;
The purple spikes of bloom
Nod their sweetness upon us, lift again,
Your white face turns, I am caught with pain,—
And silence descends, and dripping of dew from eaves
And jewelled points of leaves.

IV

I walk in a pleasure of sorrow along the street
And try to remember you; slow drops patter;
Water upon the lilacs has made them sweet;
I brush them with my sleeve, the cool drops scatter;

And suddenly I laugh . . . and stand and listen
As if another had laughed . . . a gust
Rustles the leaves, the wet spikes glisten;
And it seems as though it were you who had shaken the bough,
And spilled the fragrance—I pursue your face again,
It grows more vague and lovely, it eludes me now.
I remember that you are gone, and drown in pain.
Something there was I said to you, I recall,
Something,—just as the music seemed to fall,—
That made you laugh, and burns me still with pleasure.
What were the words—the words like dripping fire?
I remember them now, and in sweet leisure
Rehearse the scene, more exquisite than before,
And you more beautiful, and I more wise.
Lilacs and spring, and night, and your clear eyes,
And you, in white, by the darkness of a door:
These things, like voices weaving to richest music,
Flow and fall in the cool night of my mind,
I pursue your ghost among green leaves that are ghostly,
I pursue you, but cannot find.
And suddenly, with a pang that is sweetest of all,
I become aware that I cannot remember you;
The ghost I knew
Has silently plunged in shadows, shadows that stream and fall.

V

Let us go in and dance once more
On the dream's glimmering floor,
Beneath the balcony festooned with roses.
Let us go in and dance once more.
The door behind us closes
Against an evening purple with stars and mist.
Let us go in and keep our tryst
With music and white roses, and spin around
In swirls of sound.
Do you foresee me, married and grown old?
And you, who smile about you at this room,
Is it foretold
That you must step from tumult into gloom,
Forget me, love another?
No, you are Cleopatra, fiercely young,
Laughing upon the topmost stair of night;
Roses upon the desert must be flung;

Above us, light by light,
Weaves the delirious darkness, petals fall,
And music breaks in waves on the pillared wall;
And you are Cleopatra, and do not care.
And so, in memory, you will always be—
Young and foolish, a thing of dream and mist;
And so, perhaps, when all is disillusioned,
And eternal spring returns once more,
Bringing a ghost of lovelier springs remembered,
You will remember me.

VI

Yet when we meet we seem in silence to say,
Pretending serene forgetfulness of our youth,
"Do you remember . . . but then why should you remember! . . .
Do you remember, a certain day,
Or evening rather,—spring evening long ago,—
We talked of death, and love, and time, and truth . . .
And said such wise things, things that amused us so . . . ?
How foolish we were, who thought ourselves so wise!"—
And then we laugh, with shadows in our eyes.

1917

[MORNING SONG OF SENLIN]

It is morning, Senlin says, and in the morning
When the light drips through the shutters like the dew,
I arise, I face the sunrise,
And do the things my fathers learned to do.
Stars in the purple dusk above the rooftops
Pale in a saffron mist and seem to die,
And I myself on a swiftly tilting planet
Stand before a glass and tie my tie.

Vine leaves tap my window,
Dew-drops sing to the garden stones,
The robin chirps in the chinaberry tree
Repeating three clear tones.

It is morning. I stand by the mirror
And tie my tie once more.
While waves far off in a pale rose twilight

Crash on a white sand shore.
I stand by a mirror and comb my hair:
How small and white my face!—
The green earth tilts through a sphere of air
And bathes in a flame of space.

There are houses hanging above the stars
And stars hung under a sea . . .
And a sun far off in a shell of silence
Dapples my walls for me . . .

It is morning, Senlin says, and in the morning
Should I not pause in the light to remember god?
Upright and firm I stand on a star unstable,
He is immense and lonely as a cloud.
I will dedicate this moment before my mirror
To him alone; for him I will comb my hair.
Accept these humble offerings, cloud of silence!
I will think of you as I descend the stair.

Vine leaves tap my window,
The snail-track shines on the stones,
Dew-drops flash from the chinaberry tree
Repeating two clear tones.

It is morning, I awake from a bed of silence,
Shining I rise from the starless waters of sleep.
The walls are about me still as in the evening,
I am the same, and the same name still I keep.

The earth revolves with me, yet makes no motion,
The stars pale silently in a coral sky.
In a whistling void I stand before my mirror,
Unconcerned, and tie my tie.

There are horses neighing on far-off hills
Tossing their long white manes,
And mountains flash in the rose-white dusk,
Their shoulders black with rains . . .
It is morning. I stand by the mirror
And surprise my soul once more;
The blue air rushes above my ceiling,
There are suns beneath my floor . . .

. . . It is morning, Senlin says, I ascend from darkness
And depart on the winds of space for I know not where,
My watch is wound, a key is in my pocket,
And the sky is darkened as I descend the stair.
There are shadows across the windows, clouds in heaven,
And a god among the stars; and I will go
Thinking of him as I might think of daybreak
And humming a tune I know . . .

Vine leaves tap at the window,
Dew-drops sing to the garden stones,
The robin chirps in the chinaberry tree
Repeating three clear tones.

1918

VARIATIONS: XII

Wind, wind, wind in the old trees,
Whispering prophecies all night long . . .
What do the grey leaves sing to the wind,
What do they say in their whispered song?

We were all young once, and green as the sea,
We all loved beauty, the maiden of white.
But now we are old. O wind, have mercy
And let us remember our youth this night!

The wind is persuasive, it turns through the trees
And sighs of a miracle under its breath . . .
Beauty the dream will die with the dreamer,
None shall have mercy, but all shall have death.

1918

PORTRAIT OF ONE DEAD

This is the house. On one side there is darkness,
On one side there is light.
Into the darkness you may lift your lanterns—
Oh, any number—it will still be night.
And here are echoing stairs to lead you downward
To long sonorous halls.

And here is spring forever at these windows,
With roses on the walls.

This is her room. On one side there is music—
On one side not a sound.
At one step she could move from love to silence,
Feel myriad darkness coiling round.
And here are balconies from which she heard you,
Your steady footsteps on the stair.
And here the glass in which she saw your shadow
As she unbound her hair.

Here is the room—with ghostly walls dissolving—
The twilight room in which she called you "lover";
And the floorless room in which she called you "friend."
So many times, in doubt, she ran between them!—
Through windy corridors of darkening end.

Here she could stand with one dim light above her
And hear far music, like a sea in caverns,
Murmur away at hollowed walls of stone.
And here, in a roofless room where it was raining,
She bore the patient sorrow of rain alone.

Your words were walls which suddenly froze around her.
Your words were windows,—large enough for moonlight,
Too small to let her through.
Your letters—fragrant cloisters faint with music.
The music that assuaged her there was you.

How many times she heard your step ascending
Yet never saw your face!
She heard them turn again, ring slowly fainter,
Till silence swept the place.
Why had you gone? . . . The door, perhaps, mistaken . . .
You would go elsewhere. The deep walls were shaken.

A certain rose-leaf—sent without intention—
Became, with time, a woven web of fire—
She wore it, and was warm.
A certain hurried glance, let fall at parting,
Became, with time, the flashings of a storm.

Yet, there was nothing asked, no hint to tell you
Of secret idols carved in secret chambers
From all you did and said.
Nothing was done, until at last she knew you.
Nothing was known, till, somehow, she was dead.

How did she die?—You say, she died of poison.
Simple and swift. And much to be regretted.
You did not see her pass
So many thousand times from light to darkness,
Pausing so many times before her glass;

You did not see how many times she hurried
To lean from certain windows, vainly hoping,
Passionate still for beauty, remembered spring.
You did not know how long she clung to music,
You did not hear her sing.

Did she, then, make the choice, and step out bravely
From sound to silence,—close, herself, those windows?
Or was it true, instead,
That darkness moved,—for once,—and so possessed her? . . .
We'll never know, you say, for she is dead.

1920

PALIMPSEST: A DECEITFUL PORTRAIT

Well, as you say, we live for small horizons:
We move in crowds, we flow and talk together,
Seeing so many eyes and hands and faces,
So many mouths, and all with secret meanings,—
Yet know so little of them; only seeing
The small bright circle of our consciousness,
Beyond which lies the dark. Some few we know,—
Or think we know. . . . Once, on a sun-bright morning,
I walked in a certain hallway, trying to find
A certain door: I found one, tried it, opened,
And there in a spacious chamber, brightly lighted,
A hundred men played music, loudly, swiftly,
While one tall woman sent her voice above them
In powerful sweetness. . . . Closing then the door

I heard it die behind me, fade to whisper,—
And walked in a quiet hallway as before.
Just such a glimpse, as through that opened door,
Is all we know of those we call our friends. . . .
We hear a sudden music, see a playing
Of ordered thoughts—and all again is silence.
The music, we suppose, (as in ourselves)
Goes on forever there, behind shut doors,—
As it continues after our departure,
So, we divine, it played before we came . . .
What do you know of me, or I of you? . . .
Little enough. . . . We set these doors ajar
Only for chosen movements of the music:
This passage, (so I think—yet this is guesswork)
Will please him,—it is in a strain he fancies,—
More brilliant, though, than his; and while he likes it
He will be piqued . . . He looks at me bewildered
And thinks (to judge from self—this too is guesswork)
The music strangely subtle, deep in meaning,
Perplexed with implications; he suspects me
Of hidden riches, unexpected wisdom. . . .
Or else I let him hear a lyric passage,—
Simple and clear; and all the while he listens
I make pretense to think my doors are closed.
This too bewilders him. He eyes me sidelong
Wondering "Is he such a fool as this?
Or only mocking?"—There I let it end. . . .
Sometimes, of course, and when we least suspect it—
When we pursue our thoughts with too much passion,
Talking with too great zeal—our doors fly open
Without intention; and the hungry watcher
Stares at the feast, carries away our secrets,
And laughs . . . but this, for many counts, is seldom.
And for the most part we vouchsafe our friends,
Our lovers too, only such few clear notes
As we shall deem them likely to admire:
"Praise me for this" we say, or "laugh at this,"
Or "marvel at my candor" . . . all the while
Withholding what's most precious to ourselves,—
Some sinister depth of lust or fear or hatred,
The sombre note that gives the chord its power;
Or a white loveliness—if such we know—
Too much like fire to speak of without shame.

Well, this being so, and we who know it being
So curious about those well-locked houses,
The minds of those we know,—to enter softly,
And steal from floor to floor up shadowy stairways,
From room to quiet room, from wall to wall,
Breathing deliberately the very air,
Pressing our hands and nerves against warm darkness
To learn what ghosts are there,—
Suppose for once I set my doors wide open
And bid you in. . . . Suppose I try to tell you
The secrets of this house, and how I live here;
Suppose I tell you who I am, in fact. . . .
Deceiving you—as far as I may know it—
Only so much as I deceive myself.

If you are clever you already see me
As one who moves forever in a cloud
Of warm bright vanity: a luminous cloud
Which falls on all things with a quivering magic,
Changing such outlines as a light may change,
Brightening what lies dark to me, concealing
Those things that will not change . . . I walk sustained
In a world of things that flatter me: a sky
Just as I would have had it; trees and grass
Just as I would have shaped and colored them;
Pigeons and clouds and sun and whirling shadows,
And stars that brightening climb through mist at nightfall,—
In some deep way I am aware these praise me:
Where they are beautiful, or hint of beauty,
They point, somehow, to me. . . . This water says,—
Shimmering at the sky, or undulating
In broken, gleaming parodies of clouds,
Rippled in blue, or sending from cool depths
To meet the falling leaf the leaf's clear image,—
This water says, there is some secret in you
Akin to my clear beauty, beauty swaying
To mirror beauty, silently responsive
To all that circles you. This bare tree says,—
Austere and stark and leafless, split with frost,
Resonant in the wind, with rigid branches
Flung out against the sky,—this tall tree says,
There is some cold austerity in you,
A frozen strength, with long roots gnarled on rocks,

Fertile and deep; you bide your time, are patient,
Serene in silence, bare to outward seeming,
Concealing what reserves of power and beauty!
What teeming Aprils!—chorus of leaves on leaves!
These houses say, such walls in walls as ours,
Such streets of walls, solid and smooth of surface,
Such hills and cities of walls, walls upon walls;
Motionless in the sun, or dark with rain;
Walls pierced with windows, where the light may enter;
Walls windowless where darkness is desired;
Towers and labyrinths and domes and chambers,—
Amazing deep recesses, dark on dark,—
All these are like the walls which shape your spirit:
You move, are warm, within them, laugh within them,
Proud of their depth and strength; or sally from them,
When you are bold, to blow great horns at the world. . . .
This deep cool room, with shadowed walls and ceiling,
Tranquil and cloistral, fragrant of my mind,
This cool room says,—just such a room have you,
It waits you always at the tops of stairways,
Withdrawn, remote, familiar to your uses,
Where you may cease pretence and be yourself. . . .
And this embroidery, hanging on this wall,
Hung there forever,—these so soundless glidings
Of dragons golden-scaled, sheer birds of azure,
Coilings of leaves in pale vermilion, griffins
Drawing their rainbow wings through involutions
Of mauve chrysanthemums and lotus flowers,—
This goblin wood where someone cries enchantment,—
This says, just such an involuted beauty
Of thought and coiling thought, dream linked with dream,
Image to image gliding, wreathing fires,
Soundlessly cries enchantment in your mind:
You need but sit and close your eyes a moment
To see these deep designs unfold themselves.

And so, all things discern me, name me, praise me—
I walk in a world of silent voices, praising;
And in this world you see me like a wraith
Blown softly here and there, on silent winds.
"Praise me"—I say; and look, not in a glass,
But in your eyes, to see my image there—
Or in your mind; you smile, I am contented;

You look at me with interest unfeigned,
And listen—I am pleased; or else, alone,
I watch thin bubbles veering brightly upward
From unknown depths,—my silver thoughts ascending;
Saying now this, now that, hinting of all things,—
Dreams, and desires, velleities, regrets,
Faint ghosts of memory, strange recognitions,—
But all with one deep meaning: this is I,
This is the glistening secret holy I,
This silver-wingèd wonder, insubstantial,
This singing ghost. . . . And hearing, I am warmed.

* * * * *

You see me moving, then, as one who moves
Forever at the centre of his circle:
A circle filled with light. And into it
Come bulging shapes from darkness, loom gigantic,
Or huddle in dark again. . . . A clock ticks clearly,
A gas-jet steadily whirs, light streams across me;
Two church bells, with alternate beat, strike nine;
And through these things my pencil pushes softly
To weave grey webs of lines on this clear page.
Snow falls and melts; the eaves make liquid music;
Black wheel-tracks line the snow-touched street; I turn
And look one instant at the half-dark gardens,
Where skeleton elm-trees reach with frozen gesture
Above unsteady lamps,—with black boughs flung
Against a luminous snow-filled grey-gold sky.
"Beauty!" I cry. . . . My feet move on, and take me
Between dark walls, with orange squares for windows.
Beauty; beheld like someone half-forgotten,
Remembered, with slow pang, as one neglected . . .
Well, I am frustrate; life has beaten me,
The thing I strongly seized has turned to darkness,
And darkness rides my heart. . . . These skeleton elm-trees—
Leaning against that grey-gold snow filled sky—
Beauty! they say, and at the edge of darkness
Extend vain arms in a frozen gesture of protest . . .
A clock ticks softly; a gas-jet steadily whirs:
The pencil meets its shadow upon clear paper,
Voices are raised, a door is slammed. The lovers,
Murmuring in an adjacent room, grow silent,
The eaves make liquid music. . . . Hours have passed,

And nothing changes, and everything is changed.
Exultation is dead, Beauty is harlot, —
And walks the streets. The thing I strongly seized
Has turned to darkness, and darkness rides my heart.
If you could solve this darkness you would have me.
This causeless melancholy that comes with rain,
Or on such days as this when large wet snowflakes
Drop heavily, with rain . . . whence rises this?
Well, so-and-so, this morning when I saw him,
Seemed much preoccupied, and would not smile;
And you, I saw too much; and you, too little;
And the word I chose for you, the golden word,
The word that should have struck so deep in purpose,
And set so many doors of wish wide open,
You let it fall, and would not stoop for it,
And smiled at me, and would not let me guess
Whether you saw it fall. . . . These things, together,
With other things, still slighter, wove to music,
And this in time drew up dark memories;
And there I stand. This music breaks and bleeds me,
Turning all frustrate dreams to chords and discords,
Faces and griefs, and words, and sunlit evenings,
And chains self-forged that will not break nor lengthen,
And cries that none can answer, few will hear.
Have these things meaning? Or would you see more clearly
If I should say "My second wife grows tedious,
Or, like gay tulip, keeps no perfumed secret"?
Or "One day dies eventless as another,
Leaving the seeker still unsatisfied,
And more convinced life yields no satisfaction"?
Or "seek too hard, the sight at length grows callous,
And beauty shines in vain"?—

These things you ask for,
These you shall have. . . . So, talking with my first wife,
At the dark end of evening, when she leaned
And smiled at me, with blue eyes weaving webs
Of finest fire, revolving me in scarlet,—
Calling to mind remote and small successions
Of countless other evenings ending so,—
I smiled, and met her kiss, and wished her dead;
Dead of a sudden sickness, or by my hands
Savagely killed; I saw her in her coffin,

I saw her coffin borne downstairs with trouble,
I saw myself alone there, palely watching,
Wearing a masque of grief so deeply acted
That grief itself possessed me. Time would pass,
And I should meet this girl,—my second wife—
And drop the masque of grief for one of passion.
Forward we move to meet, half hesitating,
We drown in each other's eyes, we laugh, we talk,
Looking now here, now there, faintly pretending
We do not hear the powerful pulsing prelude
Roaring beneath our words . . . The time approaches.
We lean unbalanced. The mute last glance between us,
Profoundly searching, opening, asking, yielding,
Is steadily met: our two lives draw together . . .
. . . "What are you thinking of?" . . . My first wife's voice
Scattered these ghosts. "Oh, nothing—nothing much—
Just wondering where we'd be two years from now,
And what we might be doing . . ." And then remorse
Turned sharply in my mind to sudden pity,
And pity to echoed love. And one more evening
Drew to the usual end of sleep and silence.

And, as it is with this, so too with all things.
The pages of our lives are blurred palimpsest;
New lines are wreathed on old lines half-erased,
And those on older still; and so forever.
The old shines through the new, and colors it.
What's new? What's old? All things have double meanings,—
All things return. I write a line with passion
(Or touch a woman's hand, or plumb a doctrine)
Only to find the same thing, done before,—
Only to know the same thing comes to-morrow. . . .
This curious riddled dream I dreamed last night,—
Six years ago I dreamed it just as now;
The same man stooped to me; we rose from darkness,
And broke the accustomed order of our days,
And struck for the morning world, and warmth, and freedom. . . .
What does it mean? Why is this hint repeated?
What darkness does it spring from, seek to end?

You see me, then, pass up and down these stairways,
Now through a beam of light, and now through shadow,—
Pursuing silent ends. No rest there is,—

No more for me than you. I move here always,
From quiet room to room, from wall to wall,
Searching and plotting, weaving a web of days.
This is my house, and now, perhaps, you know me. . . .
Yet I confess, for all my best intentions,
Once more I have deceived you. . . . I withhold
The one thing precious, the one dark thing that guides me;
And I have spread two snares for you, of lies.

1920

TETÉLESTAI[1]

I

How shall we praise the magnificence of the dead,
The great man humbled, the haughty brought to dust?
Is there a horn we should not blow as proudly
For the meanest of us all, who creeps his days,
Guarding his heart from blows, to die obscurely?
I am no king, have laid no kingdoms waste,
Taken no princes captive, led no triumphs
Of weeping women through long walls of trumpets;
Say rather, I am no one, or an atom;
Say rather, two great gods, in a vault of starlight,
Play ponderingly at chess, and at the game's end
One of the pieces, shaken, falls to the floor
And runs to the darkest corner; and that piece
Forgotten there, left motionless, is I. . . .
Say that I have no name, no gifts, no power,
Am only one of millions, mostly silent;
One who came with eyes and hands and a heart,
Looked on beauty, and loved it, and then left it.
Say that the fates of time and space obscured me,
Led me a thousand ways to pain, bemused me,
Wrapped me in ugliness; and like great spiders
Dispatched me at their leisure. . . . Well, what then?
Should I not hear, as I lie down in dust,
The horns of glory blowing above my burial?

II

Morning and evening opened and closed above me:
Houses were built above me; trees let fall

[1] It is finished.

Yellowing leaves upon me, hands of ghosts;
Rain has showered its arrows of silver upon me
Seeking my heart; winds have roared and tossed me;
Music in long blue waves of sound has borne me
A helpless weed to shores of unthought silence;
Time, above me, within me, crashed its gongs
Of terrible warning, sifting the dust of death;
And here I lie. Blow now your horns of glory
Harshly over my flesh, you trees, you waters!
You stars and suns, Canopus, Deneb, Rigel,
Let me, as I lie down, here in this dust,
Hear, far off, your whispered salutation!
Roar now above my decaying flesh, you winds,
Whirl out your earth-scents over this body, tell me
Of ferns and stagnant pools, wild roses, hillsides!
Anoint me, rain, let crash your silver arrows
On this hard flesh! I am the one who named you,
I lived in you, and now I die in you.
I your son, your daughter, treader of music,
Lie broken, conquered . . . Let me not fall in silence.

III

I, the restless one; the circler of circles;
Herdsman and roper of stars, who could not capture
The secret of self; I who was tyrant to weaklings,
Striker of children; destroyer of women; corrupter
Of innocent dreamers, and laugher at beauty; I,
Too easily brought to tears and weakness by music,
Baffled and broken by love, the helpless beholder
Of the war in my heart of desire with desire, the struggle
Of hatred with love, terror with hunger; I
Who laughed without knowing the cause of my laughter, who grew
Without wishing to grow, a servant to my own body;
Loved without reason the laughter and flesh of a woman,
Enduring such torments to find her! I who at last
Grow weaker, struggle more feebly, relent in my purpose,
Choose for my triumph an easier end, look backward
At earlier conquests; or, caught in the web, cry out
In a sudden and empty despair, "Tetélestai!"
Pity me, now! I, who was arrogant, beg you!
Tell me, as I lie down, that I was courageous.

Blow horns of victory now, as I reel and am vanquished.
Shatter the sky with trumpets above my grave.

IV

. . . Look! this flesh how it crumbles to dust and is blown!
These bones, how they grind in the granite of frost and are nothing!
This skull, how it yawns for a flicker of time in the darkness,
Yet laughs not and sees not! It is crushed by a hammer of sunlight,
And the hands are destroyed. . . . Press down through the leaves of the jasmine,
Dig through the interlaced roots—nevermore will you find me;
I was no better than dust, yet you cannot replace me. . . .
Take the soft dust in your hand—does it stir: does it sing?
Has it lips and a heart? Does it open its eyes to the sun?
Does it run, does it dream, does it burn with a secret, or tremble
In terror of death? Or ache with tremendous decisions? . . .
Listen! . . . It says: "I lean by the river. The willows
Are yellowed with bud. White clouds roar up from the south
And darken the ripples; but they cannot darken my heart,
Nor the face like a star in my heart! . . . Rain falls on the water
And pelts it, and rings it with silver. The willow trees glisten,
The sparrows chirp under the eaves; but the face in my heart
In a secret of music. . . . I wait in the rain and am silent."
Listen again! . . . It says: "I have worked, I am tired,
The pencil dulls in my hand: I see through the window
Walls upon walls of windows with faces behind them,
Smoke floating up to the sky, an ascension of sea-gulls.
I am tired. I have struggled in vain, my decision was fruitless,
Why then do I wait? with darkness, so easy, at hand! . . .
But to-morrow, perhaps . . . I will wait and endure till to-morrow!" . . .
Or again: "It is dark. The decision is made. I am vanquished
By terror of life. The walls mount slowly about me
In coldness. I had not the courage. I was forsaken.
I cried out, was answered by silence . . . Tetélestai! . . ."

V

Hear how it babbles!—Blow the dust out of your hand,
With its voices and visions, tread on it, forget it, turn homeward
With dreams in your brain. . . . This, then, is the humble, the nameless,—

The lover, the husband and father, the struggler with shadows,
The one who went down under shoutings of chaos, the weakling
Who cried his "forsaken!" like Christ on the darkening hill-
    top! . . .
This, then, is the one who implores, as he dwindles to silence,
A fanfare of glory . . . And which of us dares to deny him?

1918, 1925

PRIAPUS AND THE POOL

IV

This is the shape of the leaf, and this of the flower,
And this the pale bole of the tree
Which watches its bough in a pool of unwavering water
In a land we never shall see.

The thrush on the bough is silent, the dew falls softly,
In the evening is hardly a sound.
And the three beautiful pilgrims who come here together
Touch lightly the dust of the ground,

Touch it with feet that trouble the dust but as wings do,
Come shyly together, are still,
Like dancers who wait, in a pause of the music, for music
The exquisite silence to fill.

This is the thought of the first, and this of the second,
And this the grave thought of the third:
"Linger we thus for a moment, palely expectant,
And silence will end, and the bird

"Sing the pure phrase, sweet phrase, clear phrase in the twilight
To fill the blue bell of the world;
And we, who on music so leaflike have drifted together,
Leaflike apart shall be whirled

"Into what but the beauty of silence, silence forever?" . . .
. . . This is the shape of the tree,
And the flower, and the leaf, and the three pale beautiful pilgrims:
This is what you are to me.

IX

There is nothing moving there, in that desert of silence,
Nothing living there, not even a blade of grass.
The morning there is as silent as the evening;
The nights and days with an equal horror pass.

Nothing moving except the cold, slow shadow
Thrown on sand by a boulder, or by the cliff
Whose rock not even a lichen comes to cover,
To hide—from what?—time's ancient hieroglyph.

The sun, at noon, sings like a flaming cymbal
Above that waste: but the waste makes no reply.
In all that desolation of rock and gravel
There is no water, no answer to the sky.

Sometimes, perhaps, from other lands more happy,
A faint wind, slow, exhausted, ventures there,
And loses itself in silence, like a music.
And then—who knows?—beneath that alien air,

Which moves mysteriously as memory over
Forlorn abysms and peaks of stone and sand,
Ghosts of delight awake for a shining moment,
And all is troubled, and that desolate land

Remembers grass and flowers, and birds that sang there
Their miracles of song in lovely trees,
And waters that poured, or stood, in dreaming azure,
Praising the sky. Perhaps once more it sees

The rose, the moon, the pool, in the blue evening,
And knows that silence in which one bird will sing
Slowly and sleepily his praise of gardens.
Perhaps once more, for a moment, it remembers spring.

XV

There was an island in the sea
That out of immortal chaos reared
Towers of topaz, trees of pearl,
For maidens adored and warriors feared.

Long ago it sank in the sea;
And now, a thousand fathoms deep,
Sea-worms above it whirl their lamps,
Crabs on the pale mosaic creep.

Voyagers over that haunted sea
Hear from the waters under the keel
A sound that is not wave or foam;
Nor do they only hear, but feel

The timbers quiver, as eerily comes
Up from the dark an elfin singing
Of voices happy as none can be,
And bells an ethereal anthem ringing.

Thereafter, where they go or come,
They will be silent; they have heard
Out of the infinite of the soul
An incommunicable word;

Thereafter, they are as lovers who
Over an infinite brightness lean:
"It is Atlantis!" all their speech;
"To lost Atlantis have we been."

1920-21, 1925

KING BORBORIGMI

You say you heard King Borborigmi laugh?
Say how it was. Some heavenly body moved him?
The moon laughed first? Dark earth put up a finger
Of honeysuckle, through his moonlit window,
And tickled him?
—King Borborigmi laughed
Alone, walking alone in an empty room,
Thinking, and yet not thinking, seeing, yet blind.
One hand was on his chin, feeling the beard
That razors could not stay; the other groped;
For it was dark, and in the dark were chairs;
Midnight, or almost midnight; Aldebaran
Hanging among the dews.

—King Borborigmi
Laughed once or twice at nothing, just as midnight
Released a flock of bells?

—Not this alone;
Not bells in flight toward Aldebaran;
Nor the immitigable beard; nor dews
Heavily pattering on the pent-house roof;
Nor chairs in shadow which his foot disturbed.
Yet it was all of these, and more: the air
Twirling the curtain where a red moth hung:
The one bell flying later than the others
Into the starstrung silence: the garden breaking
To let a thousand seedlings have their way:
An eye-tooth aching, and the pendulum
That heavily ticked upon the leftward swing.

—These trifles woke the laughter of a king?

—Much less than these, and more! He softly stepped
Among the webby world, and felt it shudder.
Under the earth—a strand or two of web—
He saw his father's bones, fallen apart,
The jawbone sunken and the skull caved in.
Among his mother's bones a cactus rooted,
And two moles crept, and ants held carnival.
Above the obscene tomb an aloe blossomed;
Dew glistened on the marble. This he saw,
And at the selfsame moment heard the cook
Wind the alarm-clock in her bedroom, yawn,
And creak the bed. And it was then, surprised,
He touched a chair, and laughed, and twitched the curtain,—
And the moth flew out.

—Alas, poor Borborigmi,
That it should be so little, and so sorry
A thing to make him laugh!

—Young Borborigmi,
Saw more than this. The infinite octopus
With eyes of chaos and long arms of stars,
And belly of void and darkness, became clear
About him, and he saw himself embraced
And swept along a vein, with chairs and teeth,
Houses and bones and gardens, cooks and clocks;

The midnight bell, a snoring cook, and he,
Mingled and flowed like atoms.

—It was this
That made him laugh—to see himself as one
Corpuscle in the infinite octopus? . . .
And was this all, old fool, old turner of leaves? . . .

—Alone, thinking alone in an empty room
Where moonlight and the mouse were met together,
And pulse and clock together ticked, and dew
Made contrapuntal patter, Borborigmi
Fathomed in his own viscera the world,
Went downward, sounding like a diver, holding
His peakèd nose; and when he came up, laughed.
These things and others saw. But last of all
Ultimate or penultimate, he saw
The one thing that undid him!

—What was this?
The one grotesquer thing among grotesques?
Carrion, offal, or the toothbrush ready
For carnal fangs? Cancer, that grasps the heart,
Or fungus, whitely swelling in the brain?
Some gargoyle of the thought?

—King Borborigmi,
Twitching the curtain as the last bell flew
Melodious to Aldebaran, beheld
The moth fly also. Downward dropped it softly
Among dropped petals, white. And there one rose
Was open in the moonlight! Dew was on it;
The bat, with ragged wing, cavorting, sidling,
Snapped there a sleeping bee—

—And crunched the moth? . . .
—It was the rose in moonlight, crimson, yet
Blanched by the moon; the bee asleep; the bat
And fallen moth—but most the guileless rose,
Guileless! . . . King Borborigmi struck his foot
Against a chair, and saw the guileless rose
Joining himself (King Bubblegut), and all
Those others—the immitigable beard;

Razors and teeth; his mother's bones; the tomb:
The yawning cook; the clock; the dew; the bells
Bursting upward like bubbles—; all so swept
Along one vein of the infinite octopus
With eyes of chaos and long arms of stars
And belly of void and darkness. It was then
He laughed; as he would never laugh again.
For he saw everything; and, in the centre
Of corrupt change, one guileless rose; and laughed
For puzzlement and sorrow.

—Ah, poor man,
Poor Borborigmi, young, to be so wise!

—Wise? No. For what he laughed at was just this:
That to see all, to know all, is to rot.
So went to bed; and slept; is sleeping still,
If none has waked him.

—Dead? King Borborigmi
Is dead? Died laughing? Sleeps a dreamless sleep
Till cook's alarm clock wakes him?

—Sleeps like Hamlet,
King of infinite space in a walnut shell—
But has bad dreams; I fear he has bad dreams.

1924, 1925

THE WEDDING

At noon, Tithonus, withered by his singing,
Climbing the oatstalk with his hairy legs,
Met grey Arachne, poisoned and shrunk down
By her own beauty; pride had shrivelled both.
In the white web—where seven flies hung wrapped—
She heard his footstep; hurried to him; bound him;
Enshrouded him in silk; then poisoned him.
Twice shrieked Tithonus, feebly; then was still.
Arachne loved him. Did he love Arachne?
She watched him with red eyes, venomous sparks,
And the furred claws outspread . . . "O sweet Tithonus!
Darling! Be kind, and sing that song again!

Shake the bright web again with that deep fiddling!
Are you much poisoned? sleeping? do you dream?
Darling Tithonus!"

And Tithonus, weakly
Moving one hairy shin against the other
Within the silken sack, contrived to fiddle
A little tune, half-hearted: "Shrewd Arachne!
Whom pride in beauty withered to this shape
As pride in singing shrivelled me to mine—
Unwrap me, let me go—and let me limp,
With what poor strength your venom leaves me, down
This oatstalk, and away."

Arachne, angry,
Stung him again, twirling him with rough paws,
The red eyes keen. "What! you would dare to leave me?
Unkind Tithonus! Sooner I'll kill and eat you
Than let you go. But sing that tune again—
So plaintive was it!"

And Tithonus faintly
Moved the poor fiddles, which were growing cold,
And sang: "Arachne, goddess envied of gods,
Beauty's eclipse eclipsed by angry beauty,
Have pity, do not ask the withered heart
To sing too long for you! My strength goes out,
Too late we meet for love. O be content
With friendship, which the noon sun once may kindle
To give one flash of passion, like a dewdrop,
Before it goes! . . . Be reasonable, Arachne!"

Arachne heard the song grow weaker, dwindle
To first a rustle, and then half a rustle,
And last a tick, so small no ear could hear it
Save hers, a spider's ear. And her small heart,
(Rusted away, like his, to a pinch of dust,)
Gleamed once, like his, and died. She clasped him tightly
And sunk her fangs in him. Tithonus dead,
She slept awhile, her last sensation gone;
Woke from the nap, forgetting him; and ate him.

1925

AT A CONCERT OF MUSIC

Be still, while the music rises about us; the deep enchantment
Towers, like a forest of singing leaves and birds,
Built, for an instant, by the heart's troubled beating,
Beyond all power of words.

And while you are listening, silent, I escape you;
And I run by a secret path through that dark wood
To another time, long past, and another woman,
And another mood.

Then, too, the music's cold algebra of enchantment
Wrought all about us a bird-voice-haunted grove;
Then, too, I escaped, as now, to an earlier moment,
And a brighter love.

Alas! Can I never have peace in the shining instant?
The hard bright crystal of being, in time and space?
Must I always touch, in the moment, an earlier moment,
And an earlier face?

Absolve me. I would adore you, had I the secret,
With all this music's power, for yourself alone;
I would try to answer, in the world's chaotic symphony,
Your one clear tone;

But alas, alas, being everything you are nothing—
The history of all my life is in your face;
And all I can know is an earlier, more haunted moment,
And a happier place.

1930

[WATCH LONG ENOUGH, AND YOU WILL SEE]

Watch long enough, and you will see the leaf
Fall from the bough. Without a sound it falls:
And soundless meets the grass. . . . And so you have
A bare bough, and a dead leaf in dead grass.
Something has come and gone. And that is all.

But what were all the tumults in this action?
What wars of atoms in the twig, what ruins,
Fiery and disastrous, in the leaf?
Timeless the tumult was, but gave no sign.
Only, the leaf fell, and the bough is bare.

This is the world: there is no more than this.
The unseen and disastrous prelude, shaking
The trivial act from the terrific action.
Speak: and the ghosts of change, past and to come,
Throng the brief word. The maelstrom has us all.

1931

[KEEP IN THE HEART THE JOURNAL]

Keep in the heart the journal nature keeps;
Mark down the limp nasturtium leaf with frost;
See that the hawthorn bough is ice-embossed,
And that the snail, in season, has his grief;
Design the winter on the window pane;
Admit pale sun through cobwebs left from autumn;
Remember summer when the flies are stilled;
Remember spring, when the cold spider sleeps.

Such diary, too, set down as this: the heart
Beat twice or thrice this day for no good reason;
For friends and sweethearts dead before their season;
For wisdom come too late, and come to naught.
Put down "the hand that shakes," "the eye that glazes";
The "step that falters betwixt thence and hence";
Observe that hips and haws burn brightest red
When the North Pole and sun are most apart.

Note that the moon is here, as cold as ever,
With ages on her face, and ice and snow;
Such as the freezing mind alone can know,
When loves and hates are only twigs that shiver.
Add in a postscript that the rain is over,
The wind from southwest backing to the south,
Disasters all forgotten, hurts forgiven;
And that the North Star, altered, shines forever.

Then say: I was a part of nature's plan;
Knew her cold heart, for I was consciousness;
Came first to hate her, and at last to bless;
Believed in her; doubted; believed again.
My love the lichen had such roots as I,—
The snowflake was my father; I return,
After this interval of faith and question,
To nature's heart, in pain, as I began.

1931

[BEND AS THE BOW BENDS]

Bend as the bow bends, and let fly the shaft,
the strong cord loose its word as light as flame;
speak without cunning, love, as without craft,
careless of answer, as of shame or blame.
This to be known, that love is love, despite
knowledge or ignorance, truth, untruth, despair;
careless of all things, if that love be bright,
careless of hate and fate, careless of care.
Spring the word as it must, the leaf or flower,
broken or bruised, yet let it, broken, speak
of time transcending this too transient hour,
and space that finds the beating heart too weak.
Thus, and thus only, will our tempest come
by continents of snow to find a home.

1940

[SNOWFLAKE ON ASPHODEL]

Snowflake on asphodel, clear ice on rose,
frost over thistledown, the instant death
that speaks Time's judgment, turning verse to prose,
or withering June to blackness in a breath—
icicle, cheek by jowl with goldenrod,
and on the purple aster silver rime,
a web of death, bright as the web of god,
spun on these simple themes and schemes by time:
snowflake on asphodel—how clear, how bright
the blue burns through the melting star! how brave

the dying flower, and the snow how light
that on the dying flower makes his grave!
Snow's death on dying flower, yet both immortal—
love, these are you and I—enter this portal.

1940

these things will go on and one
pays great tribute to love
thru eyes of love all things are immortal.
themes are always nostalgic; all lovely
things must have an ending
old style; ideas are new — contemporary

Edna St. Vincent Millay

Edna St. Vincent Millay, a daughter of Henry Tolman Millay and Cora Buzzelle Millay, was born February 22, 1892, at Rockland, Maine. She spent her childhood in Maine, attending schools at Rockland and Camden. At the age of fourteen she already showed promise as a poet. In 1912 she submitted "Renascence" in a competition by Mitchell Kennerley, publisher of *The Lyric Year*, an anthology. Although failing to win a prize, her poem was placed first by one of the judges, and attracted considerable notice among critics.

For a short time she attended Barnard College, and then transferred to Vassar from which she was graduated in 1917. While in college she also wrote, and acted in, two plays, *The Princess Marries the Page* and *Two Slatterns and a King*. After graduation she went to New York City, and settled in a tiny room in Greenwich Village, with the intention of winning recognition as a poet. In the same year she published her first volume, *Renascence*.

She lived in poverty in New York, and to eke out her meager income from writing she turned her hand to other work. For a while she was connected with the Provincetown Players, acting in a number of comedies, and having some of her own plays produced; and eventually she obtained a minor part in a Theatre Guild production. The small income from this source she supplemented by translating songs and writing short stories (which were published under the pseudonym Nancy Boyd), and thus she was able to exist. In 1920, *Poetry: A Magazine of Verse* awarded her a cash prize, and in 1922 she won the Pulitzer Prize for Poetry, which enabled her to make her first trip to Europe. On July 19, 1923, she married Eugen Jan Boissevain, a New York business man.

Besides several volumes of lyric poetry, Miss Millay has written a number of plays, a volume of short stories, *Distressing Dialogues*, and the libretto for Deems Taylor's opera, *The King's Henchman* (1927), which was produced at the Metropolitan Opera House, New York, on February 17, 1927. In recent years she has done considerable lecturing, including some by radio. With the start of the second World War she became active in working for aid to Britain.

In 1931 she was awarded the Helen Haire Levinson Prize by *Poetry: A Magazine of Verse*. She has received the honorary degrees of Litt.D. from Tufts College (1925), the Russell Sage College and the University of Wisconsin (1933), and Colby College (1937), and of L.H.D. from New York University (1940); and in 1940 she was elected to membership in the American Academy of Arts and Letters.

For sometime after her marriage she lived in the old section of New York City, and afterwards in the Berkshire Hills. Her home is now in Austerlitz, N. Y.

RENASCENCE

All I could see from where I stood
Was three long mountains and a wood;
I turned and looked the other way,
And saw three islands in a bay.
So with my eyes I traced the line
Of the horizon, thin and fine,
Straight around till I was come
Back to where I'd started from;
And all I saw from where I stood
Was three long mountains and a wood.
Over these things I could not see:
These were the things that bounded me;
And I could touch them with my hand,
Almost, I thought, from where I stand.
And all at once things seemed so small
My breath came short, and scarce at all.
But, sure, the sky is big, I said;
Miles and miles above my head;
So here upon my back I'll lie

And look my fill into the sky.
And so I looked, and, after all,
The sky was not so very tall.
The sky, I said, must somewhere stop,
And—sure enough!—I see the top!
The sky, I thought, is not so grand;
I 'most could touch it with my hand!
And reaching up my hand to try,
I screamed to feel it touch the sky.
I screamed, and—lo!—Infinity
Came down and settled over me;
Forced back my scream into my chest,
Bent back my arm upon my breast,
And, pressing of the Undefined
The definition on my mind,
Held up before my eyes a glass
Through which my shrinking sight did pass
Until it seemed I must behold
Immensity made manifold;
Whispered to me a word whose sound
Deafened the air for worlds around,
And brought unmuffled to my ears
The gossiping of friendly spheres,
The creaking of the tented sky,
The ticking of Eternity.
I saw and heard and knew at last
The How and Why of all things, past,
And present, and forevermore.
The Universe, cleft to the core,
Lay open to my probing sense
That, sick'ning, I would fain pluck thence
But could not,—nay! But needs must suck
At the great wound, and could not pluck
My lips away till I had drawn
All venom out.—Ah, fearful pawn!
For my omniscience paid I toll
In infinite remorse of soul.
All sin was of my sinning, all
Atoning mine, and mine the gall
Of all regret. Mine was the weight
Of every brooded wrong, the hate
That stood behind each envious thrust,
Mine every greed, mine every lust.

And all the while for every grief,
Each suffering, I craved relief
With individual desire,—
Craved all in vain! And felt fierce fire
About a thousand people crawl;
Perished with each,—then mourned for all!
A man was starving in Capri;
He moved his eyes and looked at me;
I felt his gaze, I heard his moan,
And knew his hunger as my own.
I saw at sea a great fog-bank
Between two ships that struck and sank;
A thousand screams the heavens smote;
And every scream tore through my throat.
No hurt I did not feel, no death
That was not mine; mine each last breath
That, crying, met an answering cry
From the compassion that was I.
All suffering mine, and mine its rod;
Mine, pity like the pity of God.
Ah, awful weight! Infinity
Pressed down upon the finite Me!
My anguished spirit, like a bird,
Beating against my lips I heard;
Yet lay the weight so close about
There was no room for it without.
And so beneath the weight lay I
And suffered death, but could not die.

Long had I lain thus, craving death,
When quietly the earth beneath
Gave way, and inch by inch, so great
At last had grown the crushing weight,
Into the earth I sank till I
Full six feet under ground did lie,
And sank no more,—there is no weight
Can follow here, however great.
From off my breast I felt it roll,
And as it went my tortured soul
Burst forth and fled in such a gust
That all about me swirled the dust.

Deep in the earth I rested now;
Cool is its hand upon the brow

And soft its breast beneath the head
Of one who is so gladly dead.
And all at once, and over all
The pitying rain began to fall;
I lay and heard each pattering hoof
Upon my lowly, thatchèd roof,
And seemed to love the sound far more
Than ever I had done before.
For rain it hath a friendly sound
To one who's six feet under ground;
And scarce the friendly voice or face:
A grave is such a quiet place.

The rain, I said, is kind to come
And speak to me in my new home.
I would I were alive again
To kiss the fingers of the rain,
To drink into my eyes the shine
Of every slanting silver line,
To catch the freshened, fragrant breeze
From drenched and dripping apple-trees.
For soon the shower will be done,
And then the broad face of the sun
Will laugh above the rain-soaked earth
Until the world with answering mirth
Shakes joyously, and each round drop
Rolls, twinkling, from its grass-blade top.
How can I bear it; buried here,
While overhead the sky grows clear
And blue again after the storm?
O, multi-colored, multiform,
Belovèd beauty over me,
That I shall never, never see
Again! Spring-silver, autumn-gold,
That I shall never more behold!
Sleeping your myriad magics through,
Close-sepulchred away from you!
O God, I cried, give me new birth,
And put me back upon the earth!
Upset each cloud's gigantic gourd
And let the heavy rain, down-poured
In one big torrent, set me free,
Washing my grave away from me!

I ceased; and through the breathless hush
That answered me, the far-off rush
Of herald wings came whispering
Like music down the vibrant string
Of my ascending prayer, and—crash!
Before the wild wind's whistling lash
The startled storm-clouds reared on high
And plunged in terror down the sky,
And the big rain in one black wave
Fell from the sky and struck my grave.
I know not how such things can be;
I only know there came to me
A fragrance such as never clings
To aught save happy living things;
A sound as of some joyous elf
Singing sweet songs to please himself,
And, through and over everything,
A sense of glad awakening.
The grass, a-tiptoe at my ear,
Whispering to me I could hear;
I felt the rain's cool finger-tips
Brushed tenderly across my lips,
Laid gently on my sealèd sight,
And all at once the heavy night
Fell from my eyes and I could see,—
A drenched and dripping apple-tree,
A last long line of silver rain,
A sky grown clear and blue again.
And as I looked a quickening gust
Of wind blew up to me and thrust
Into my face a miracle
Of orchard-breath, and with the smell,—
I know not how such things can be!—
I breathed my soul back into me.

Ah! Up then from the ground sprang I
And hailed the earth with such a cry
As is not heard save from a man
Who has been dead, and lives again.
About the trees my arms I wound;
Like one gone mad I hugged the ground;
I raised my quivering arms on high;
I laughed and laughed into the sky,

Till at my throat a strangling sob
Caught fiercely, and a great heart-throb
Sent instant tears into my eyes;
O God, I cried, no dark disguise
Can e'er hereafter hide from me
Thy radiant identity!
Thou canst not move across the grass
But my quick eyes will see Thee pass,
Nor speak, however silently,
But my hushed voice will answer Thee.
I know the path that tells Thy way
Through the cool eve of every day;
God, I can push the grass apart
And lay my finger on Thy heart!

The world stands out on either side
No wider than the heart is wide;
Above the world is stretched the sky,—
No higher than the soul is high.
The heart can push the sea and land
Farther away on either hand;
The soul can split the sky in two,
And let the face of God shine through.
But East and West will pinch the heart
That can not keep them pushed apart;
And he whose soul is flat—the sky
Will cave in on him by and by.

1917

GOD'S WORLD

O World, I cannot hold thee close enough!
  Thy winds, thy wide grey skies!
  Thy mists, that roll and rise!
Thy woods, this autumn day, that ache and sag
And all but cry with color! That gaunt crag
To crush! To lift the lean of that black bluff!
World, World, I cannot get thee close enough!

Long have I known a glory in it all,
  But never knew I this;
  Here such a passion is

As stretcheth me apart,—Lord, I do fear
Thou'st made the world too beautiful this year;
My soul is all but out of me,—let fall
No burning leaf; prithee, let no bird call.

1917

[THOU ART NOT LOVELIER THAN LILACS]

Thou are not lovelier than lilacs,—no,
Nor honeysuckle; thou art not more fair
Than small white single poppies,—I can bear
Thy beauty; though I bend before thee, though
From left to right, not knowing where to go,
I turn my troubled eyes, nor here nor there
Find any refuge from thee, yet I swear
So has it been with mist,—with moonlight so.

Like him who day by day unto his draught
Of delicate poison adds him one drop more
Till he may drink unharmed the death of ten,
Even so, inured to beauty, who have quaffed
Each hour more deeply than the hour before,
I drink—and live—what has destroyed some men.

1917

THE PHILOSOPHER

And what are you that, missing you,
  I should be kept awake
As many nights as there are days
  With weeping for your sake?

And what are you that, missing you,
  As many days as crawl
I should be listening to the wind
  And looking at the wall?

I know a man that's a braver man
  And twenty men as kind,
And what are you, that you should be
  The one man in my mind?

Yet women's ways are witless ways,
As any sage will tell,—
And what am I, that I should love
So wisely and so well?

1920

[OH, THINK NOT I AM FAITHFUL TO A VOW!]

Oh, think not I am faithful to a vow!
Faithless am I save to love's self alone.
Were you not lovely I would leave you now:
After the feet of beauty fly my own.
Were you not still my hunger's rarest food,
And water ever to my wildest thirst,
I would desert you—think not but I would!—
And seek another as I sought you first.
But you are mobile as the veering air,
And all your charms more changeful than the tide,
Wherefore to be inconstant is no care:
I have but to continue at your side.
So wanton, light and false, my love, are you,
I am most faithless when I most am true.

1920

ELEGY BEFORE DEATH

There will be rose and rhododendron
When you are dead and under ground;
Still will be heard from white syringas
Heavy with bees, a sunny sound;

Still will the tamaracks be raining
After the rain has ceased, and still
Will there be robins in the stubble,
Brown sheep upon the warm green hill.

Spring will not ail nor autumn falter;
Nothing will know that you are gone,
Saving alone some sullen plough-land
None but yourself sets foot upon;

Saving the may-weed and the pig-weed
  Nothing will know that you are dead,—
These, and perhaps a useless wagon
  Standing beside some tumbled shed.

Oh, there will pass with your great passing
  Little of beauty not your own,—
Only the light from common water,
  Only the grace from simple stone!

1921

SONG OF A SECOND APRIL

April this year, not otherwise
  Than April of a year ago,
Is full of whispers, full of sighs,
  Of dazzling mud and dingy snow;
  Hepaticas that pleased you so
Are here again, and butterflies.

There rings a hammering all day,
  And shingles lie about the doors;
In orchards near and far away
  The grey wood-pecker taps and bores;
  And men are merry at their chores,
And children earnest at their play.

The larger streams run still and deep,
  Noisy and swift the small brooks run;
Among the mullein stalks the sheep
  Go up the hillside in the sun,
  Pensively,—only you are gone,
You that alone I cared to keep.

1921

[I KNOW I AM BUT SUMMER TO YOUR HEART]

I know I am but summer to your heart,
And not the full four seasons of the year;
And you must welcome from another part
Such noble moods as are not mine, my dear.

No gracious weight of golden fruits to sell
Have I, nor any wise and wintry thing;
And I have loved you all too long and well
To carry still the high sweet breast of Spring.
Wherefore I say: O love, as summer goes,
I must be gone, steal forth with silent drums,
That you may hail anew the bird and rose
When I come back to you, as summer comes.
Else will you seek, at some not distant time,
Even your summer in another clime.

1923

[EUCLID ALONE HAS LOOKED ON BEAUTY]

Euclid alone has looked on Beauty bare.
Let all who prate of Beauty hold their peace,
And lay them prone upon the earth and cease
To ponder on themselves, the while they stare
At nothing, intricately drawn nowhere
In shapes of shifting lineage; let geese
Gabble and hiss, but heroes seek release
From dusty bondage into luminous air.

O blinding hour, O holy, terrible day,
When first the shaft into his vision shone
Of light anatomized! Euclid alone
Has looked on Beauty bare. Fortunate they
Who, though once only and then but far away,
Have heard her massive sandal set on stone.

1923

THE ANGUISH

I would to God I were quenched and fed
As in my youth
From the flask of song, and the good bread
Of beauty richer than truth.

The anguish of the world is on my tongue.
My bowl is filled to the brim with it; there is more than I can eat.
Happy are the toothless old and the toothless young,
That cannot rend this meat.

1928

TO JESUS ON HIS BIRTHDAY

For this your mother sweated in the cold,
For this you bled upon the bitter tree:
A yard of tinsel ribbon bought and sold;
A paper wreath; a day at home for me.
The merry bells ring out, the people kneel;
Up goes the man of God before the crowd;
With voice of honey and with eyes of steel
He drones your humble gospel to the proud.
Nobody listens. Less than the wind that blows
Are all your words to us you died to save.
O Prince of Peace! O Sharon's dewy Rose!
How mute you lie within your vaulted grave.
  The stone the angel rolled away with tears
  Is back upon your mouth these thousand years.

1928

[NOT IN A SILVER CASKET COOL WITH PEARLS]

Not in a silver casket cool with pearls
Or rich with red corundum or with blue,
Locked, and the key withheld, as other girls
Have given their loves, I give my love to you;
Not in a lovers'-knot, not in a ring
Worked in such fashion, and the legend plain—
Semper fidelis, where a secret spring
Kennels a drop of mischief for the brain:
Love in the open hand, no thing but that,
Ungemmed, unhidden, wishing not to hurt,
As one should bring you cowslips in a hat
Swung from the hand, or apples in her skirt,
  I bring you, calling out as children do:
  "Look what I have!—And these are all for you."

1931

[LOVE IS NOT ALL]

Love is not all; it is not meat nor drink
Nor slumber nor a roof against the rain,
Nor yet a floating spar to men that sink
And rise and sink and rise and sink again;
Love can not fill the thickened lung with breath,
Nor clean the blood, nor set the fractured bone;
Yet many a man is making friends with death
Even as I speak, for lack of love alone.
It well may be that in a difficult hour,
Pinned down by pain and moaning for release,
Or nagged by want past resolution's power,
I might be driven to sell your love for peace,
  Or trade the memory of this night for food.
  It well may be. I do not think I would.

1931

ON THE WIDE HEATH

On the wide heath at evening overtaken,
  When the fast-reddening sun
Drops, and against the sky the looming bracken
  Waves, and the day is done,

Though no unfriendly nostril snuffs his bone,
  Though English wolves be dead,
The fox abroad on errands of his own,
  The adder gone to bed,

The weary traveler from his aching hip
  Lengthens his long stride;
Though Home be but a humming on his lip,
  No happiness, no pride,

He does not drop him under the yellow whin
  To sleep the darkness through;
Home to the yellow light that shines within
  The kitchen of a loud shrew,

Home over stones and sand, through stagnant water
  He goes, mile after mile
Home to a wordless poaching son and a daughter
  With a disdainful smile,

Home to the worn reproach, the disagreeing,
  The shelter, the stale air; content to be
Pecked at, confined, encroached upon,—it being
  Too lonely, to be free.

1934

MY SPIRIT, SORE FROM MARCHING

My spirit, sore from marching
  Toward that receding west
Where Pity shall be governor,
  With Wisdom for his guest:

Lie down beside these waters
  That bubble from the spring;
Hear in the desert silence
  The desert sparrow sing;

Draw from the shapeless moment
  Such pattern as you can;
And cleave henceforth to Beauty;
  Expect no more from man.

Man, with his ready answer,
  His sad and hearty word,
For every cause in limbo,
  For every debt deferred,

For every pledge forgotten,
  His eloquent and grim
Deep empty gaze upon you,—
  Expect no more from him.

From cool and aimless Beauty
  Your bread and comfort take,
Beauty, that made no promise
  And has no word to break;

Have eyes for Beauty only,
  That has no eyes for you;
Follow her struck pavilion,
  Halt with her retinue;

Catch from the board of Beauty
  Such careless crumbs as fall.
Here's hope for priest and layman;
  Here's heresy for all.

1934

Archibald MacLeish

Archibald MacLeish was born May 7, 1892, in Glencoe, Illinois, a suburb of Chicago, in a large house overlooking Lake Michigan. His father, Andrew MacLeish, a Scotch Presbyterian, was one of the early settlers in Chicago; and his mother, Martha Hillard MacLeish, came from Connecticut and belonged to an old seagoing New England family. He attended the local schools and the Hotchkiss School, Lakeview, Connecticut, passing to Yale University in 1911. At Yale he made an excellent record in studies and athletics, was chairman of the editorial board of the literary magazine, and did much writing. After receiving the A.B. degree in 1915, he entered the Harvard Law School, where he made an even better scholastic record, leading the class during his last year. In the meantime, on June 23, 1916, he married Ada Hitchcock of Farmington, Connecticut, and in 1917 the first of their four children was born. He interrupted his studies to enter the army, and served as a captain of artillery in the World War. While he was in France his first volume of verse, *Tower of Ivory* (1917), was published. After the war, he completed his law course, taught for a year at Harvard, and was then employed in the law offices of Choate, Hall and Stuart of Boston.

Increasingly, however, the desire to give all his time to poetry grew on him, and in 1923 he decided to gratify that desire. Going with his family to Europe, he lived in Paris for a time, spent a summer in Normandy, made a tour of the Mediterranean countries, and journeyed through Persia. He studied the work of Laforgue, Rimbaud, Léon Paul Fargue, Paul Valéry, Ezra Pound, and T. S. Eliot, and produced new work of his own. In 1924 appeared the first volume belonging to this period, *The Happy Marriage and Other Poems*.

MacLeish returned from Europe in 1928 and lived for a time on a farm in New England. In 1929 he made an extended trip through Mexico to gather literary material, travelling over the route taken by Cortez. He also did reviewing and editorial work in New York, and in 1935 his verse play, *Panic*, was produced there. His plays for the radio, broadcast during 1937 and 1938, were widely discussed as significant experiments, testing the possibilities of a new artistic medium.

During the second term of 1936-37 he held the appointment of Visiting Member of the Faculty at Princeton. In 1938 Harvard made him Curator of the Neiman Foundation for Journalists, which position he held until 1939, when he was appointed Librarian of the Library of Congress.

He has received honorary degrees from Tufts College (M.A., 1932), Colby College (Litt.D., 1938), Wesleyan University (Litt.D., 1939), Yale (Litt.D., 1939), Johns Hopkins (LL.D., 1940), and Union College (D.C.L., 1941). In 1929 he was awarded the John Reed Memorial Prize by *Poetry*, and in 1932 he received the Shelley Memorial Award. He now lives in Washington, D. C.

THE TOO-LATE BORN

We too, we too, descending once again
The hills of our own land, we too have heard
Far off—Ah, *que ce cor a longue haleine* [1]—
The horn of Roland in the passages of Spain,
The first, the second blast, the failing third,
And with the third turned back and climbed once more
The steep road southward, and heard faint the sound
Of swords, of horses, the disastrous war,
And crossed the dark defile at last, and found
At Roncevaux upon the darkening plain
The dead against the dead and on the silent ground
The silent slain—

1926

[1] Ah, how far that horn reverberates!

LE SECRET HUMAIN

It was not God that told us. We knew
Before, long before, long, long ago.
We knew that tonight—or tomorrow—. We know
Still—tomorrow. It is true that we know.

The incredulous surprise
In the faces of the dead, in dead eyes:
There was something still to happen—
There was someone that was always going to come.

And the eyes of those that sleep,
The puzzled eyes:
There are promises the silence does not keep—
And the dark has no replies.

Ah, we know
As the wind blows,
Not to the south, the north,
Not to, not ever to, but toward.

We know beyond the doors we press and open,
Beyond the smell of breakfast in the hall,
Beyond the soggy towel and the soap—
Wait! We shall know all.

We that sit and think and talk,
We that lie awake till late,
We that walk beside the river:
We can wait—O we can wait!

1926

EINSTEIN

Standing between the sun and moon preserves
A certain secrecy. Or seems to keep
Something inviolate if only that
His father was an ape.

Sweet music makes
All of his walls sound hollow and he hears
Sighs in the paneling and underfoot
Melancholy voices. So there is a door
Behind the seamless arras and within
A living something:—but no door that will
Admit the sunlight nor no windows where
The mirror moon can penetrate his bones
With cold deflection. He is small and tight
And solidly contracted into space
Opaque and perpendicular which blots
Earth with its shadow. And he terminates
In shoes which bearing up against the sphere
Attract his concentration,

Einstein upon a public bench Wednesday the ninth contemplates finity

for he ends
If there why then no farther, as, beyond
Extensively the universe itself,
Or chronologically the two dates
Original and ultimate of time,

Nor could Jehovah and the million stars
Staring within their solitudes of light,
Nor all night's constellations be contained
Between his boundaries,
nor could the sun
Receive him nor his groping roots run down
Into the loam and steaming sink of time
Where coils the middle serpent and the ooze
Breeds maggots.
But it seems assured he ends
Precisely at his shoes in proof whereof
He can revolve in orbits opposite
The orbit of the earth and so refuse
All planetary converse. And he wears
Cloths that distinguish him from what is not
His own circumference, as first a coat
Shaped to his back or modeled in reverse
Of the surrounding cosmos and below
Trousers preserving his detachment from
The revolutions of the stars.

Einstein descends the Hartmannsweilerstrasse

His hands

And face go naked and alone converse
With what encloses him, as rough and smooth
And sound and silence and the intervals
Of rippling ether and the swarming motes
Clouding a privy: move to them and make
Shadows that mirror them within his skull
In perpendiculars and curves and planes
And bodiless significances blurred
As figures undersea and images
Patterned from eddies of the air.
Which are
Perhaps not shadows but the thing itself
And may be understood.

Einstein provisionally before a mirror accepts the hypothesis of subjective reality

Decorticate
The petals of the enfolding world and leave
A world in reason which is in himself
And has his own dimensions. Here do trees
Adorn the hillside and hillsides enrich
The hazy marches of the sky and skies
Kindle and char to ashes in the wind,
And winds blow toward him from the verge, and suns
Rise on his dawn and on his dusk go down
And moons prolong his shadow. And he moves
Here as within a garden in a close
And where he moves the bubble of the world
Takes center and there circle round his head
Like golden flies in summer the gold stars.

. . . rejects it

Disintegrates.
For suddenly he feels
The planet plunge beneath him, and a flare
Falls from the upper darkness to the dark
And awful shadows loom across the sky
That have no life from him and suns go out
And livid as a drowned man's face the moon
Floats to the lapsing surface of the night
And sinks discolored under.
So he knows
Less than a world and must communicate
Beyond his knowledge.

Einstein unsuccessfully after lunch attempts to enter, essaying synthesis with what's not he, the Bernese Oberland

Outstretched on the earth
He plunges both his arms into the swirl
Of what surrounds him but the yielding grass
Excludes his finger tips and the soft soil
Will not endure confusion with his hands
Nor will the air receive him nor the light
Dissolve their difference but recoiling turns
Back from his touch. By which denial he can
Crawl on the earth and sense the opposing sun
But not make answer to them.
Put out leaves
And let the old remembering wind think through
A green intelligence or under sea
Float out long filaments of amber in
The numb and wordless revery of tides.

In autumn the black branches dripping rain
Bruise his uncovered bones and in the spring
His swollen tips are gorged with aching blood
That bursts the laurel.
But although they seize
His sense he has no name for them, no word
To give them meaning and no utterance
For what they say. Feel the new summer's sun
Crawl up the warmed relaxing hide of earth
And weep for his lost youth, his childhood home
And a wide water on an inland shore!
Or to the night's mute asking in the blood
Give back a girl's name and three notes together!

He cannot think the smell of after rain
Nor close his thought around the long smooth lag
And falter of a wind, nor bring to mind
Dusk and the whippoorwill.

Einstein dissolved in violins invades the molecular structure of F. P. Paepke's Sommergarten. Is repulsed

But violins
Split out of trees and strung to tone can sing
Strange nameless words that image to the ear
What has no waiting image in the brain.
She plays in darkness and the droning wood
Dissolves to reverberations of a world

Beating in waves against him till his sense
Trembles to rhythm and his naked brain
Feels without utterance in form the flesh
Of dumb and incommunicable earth,
And knows at once, and without knowledge how,
The stroke of the blunt rain, and blind receives
The sun.
When he a moment occupies
The hollow of himself and like an air
Pervades all other.
But the violin
Presses its dry insistence through the dream
That swims above it, shivering its speech
Back to a rhythm that becomes again
Music and vaguely ravels into sound.

To Einstein asking at the gate of stone none opens

So then there is no speech that can resolve
Their texture to clear thought and enter them.

The Virgin of Chartres whose bleaching bones still wear
The sapphires of her glory knew a word—
That now is three round letters like the three
Round empty staring punctures in a skull.
And there were words in Rome once and one time
Words at Eleusis.
Now there are no words
Nor names to name them and they will not speak
But grope against his groping touch and throw
The long unmeaning shadows of themselves
Across his shadow and resist his sense.

Einstein hearing behind the wall of the Grand Hôtel du Nord the stars discovers the Back Stair

Why then if they resist destroy them. Dumb
Yet speak them in their elements. Whole,
Break them to reason.
He lies upon his bed
Exerting on Arcturus and the moon
Forces proportional inversely to
The squares of their remoteness and conceives
The universe.
Atomic.

He can count
Ocean in atoms and weigh out the air
In multiples of one and subdivide
Light to its numbers.
If they will not speak
Let them be silent in their particles.
Let them be dead and he will lie among
Their dust and cipher them—undo the signs
Of their unreal identities and free
The pure and single factor of all sums—
Solve them to unity.
Democritus
Scooped handfuls out of stones and like the sea
Let earth run through his fingers. Well, he too,
He can achieve obliquity and learn
The cold distortion of the winter's sun
That breaks the surfaces of summer.

Einstein on the terrasse of The Acacias forces the secret door

Stands
Facing the world upon a windy slope
And with his mind relaxes the stiff forms
Of all he sees until the heavy hills
Impend like rushing water and the earth
Hangs on the steep and momentary crest
Of overflowing ruin.
Overflow!
Sweep over into movement and dissolve
All differences in the indifferent flux!
Crumble to eddyings of dust and drown
In change the thing that changes!
There begins
A vague unquiet in the fallow ground,
A seething in the grass, a bubbling swirl
Over the surface of the fields that spreads
Around him gathering until the green
Boils and under frothy loam the rocks
Ferment and simmer and like thinning smoke
The trees melt into nothing.
Still he stands
Watching the vortex widen and involve
In swirling dissolution the whole earth
And circle through the skies till swaying time

Collapses crumpling into dark the stars
And motion ceases and the sifting world
Opens beneath.
When he shall feel infuse
His flesh with the rent body of all else
And spin within his opening brain the motes
Of suns and worlds and spaces.

Einstein enters

Like a foam
His flesh is withered and his shriveling
And ashy bones are scattered on the dark.
But still the dark denies him. Still withstands
The dust his penetration and flings back
Himself to answer him.
Which seems to keep
Something inviolate. A living something.

1926

THE FARM

Why do you listen, trees?
Why do you wait?
Why do you fumble at the breeze—
Gesticulate
With hopeless fluttering hands—
Stare down the vanished road beyond the gate
That now no longer stands?
Why do you wait—
Trees—
Why do you listen, trees?

(1750)

Ephraim Cross drives up the trail
From Worcester. Hepsibah goes pale
At sumac feathers in the pines.
The wooden wagon grunts and whines.
Blunt oxen leaning outward lurch
Over the boulders. Pine to birch
The hills change color. In the west
Wachusett humps a stubborn crest.
Ephraim takes the promised land,
Earth, rock and rubble, in his hand.

(1800)

Young sugar maples in a row
Flap awkward leaves. Ripe acres blow
In failing ripples to the blue
Of hemlocks. Ephraim's house stands true
Above the troubling of a brook.
Ephraim's gravestones seem to look
West of the Berkshires and still west.
Hepsibah's stones turn back compressed
And bitter silence toward the sea.
Between, her sons sleep patiently.

(1871)

A blind door yawing to the snow
Questions them in. They knock and go
Through the old bedroom to the back.
The kitchen door swings out a crack
Framing Aunt Aggie in her chair—
Dead as a haddock—ragged hair
Scrawled over on her shriveled eyes.
Since Monday morning, they surmise:
Last of her name she was, and best
Be lyin' up there with the rest.

(1923)

Plummets of moonlight thinning through
Deep fathoms of the dark renew
Moments of vision and deflect
Smooth images the eyes expect
To images the brain perceives.
Choked in a pine wood chafe the leaves
Of aged maples, but the moon
Remembers; and its shadows strewn
Sidelong and slantingly restore
Ephraim's trees about his door.

Why do you listen, trees?
Why do you wait?
Why do you fumble at the breeze—
Gesticulate
With hopeless fluttering hands—
Stare down the vanished road beyond the gate

That now no longer stands?
Why do you wait, trees?
Why do you listen, trees?

1926

ELEVEN

And summer mornings the mute child, rebellious,
Stupid, hating the words, the meanings, hating
The Think now, Think, the O but Think! would leave
On tiptoe the three chairs on the verandah
And crossing tree by tree the empty lawn
Push back the shed door and upon the sill
Stand pressing out the sunlight from his eyes
And enter and with outstretched fingers feel
The grindstone and behind it the bare wall
And turn and in the corner on the cool
Hard earth sit listening. And one by one,
Out of the dazzled shadow in the room
The shapes would gather, the brown plowshare, spades,
Mattocks, the polished helves of picks, a scythe
Hung from the rafters, shovels, slender tines
Glinting across the curve of sickles—shapes
Older than men were, the wise tools, the iron
Friendly with earth. And sit there quiet, breathing
The harsh dry smell of withered bulbs, the faint
Odor of dung, the silence. And outside
Beyond the half-shut door the blind leaves
And the corn moving. And at noon would come,
Up from the garden, his hard crooked hands
Gentle with earth, his knees still earth-stained, smelling
Of sun, of summer, the old gardener, like
A priest, like an interpreter, and bend
Over his baskets.
And they would not speak:
They would say nothing. And the child would sit there
Happy as though he had no name, as though
He had been no one: like a leaf, a stem,
Like a root growing—

1926

"NOT MARBLE NOR THE GILDED MONUMENTS"[1]

The praisers of women in their proud and beautiful poems
Naming the grave mouth and the hair and the eyes
Boasted those they loved should be forever remembered
These were lies

The words sound but the face in the Istrian sun is forgotten
The poet speaks but to her dead ears no more
The sleek throat is gone—and the breast that was troubled to listen
Shadow from door

Therefore I will not praise your knees nor your fine walking
Telling you men shall remember your name as long
As lips move or breath is spent or the iron of English
Rings from a tongue

I shall say you were young and your arms straight and your mouth scarlet
I shall say you will die and none will remember you
Your arms change and none remember the swish of your garments
Nor the click of your shoe

Not with my hand's strength not with difficult labor
Springing the obstinate words to the bones of your breast
And the stubborn line to your young stride and the breath to your breathing
And the beat to your haste
Shall I prevail on the hearts of unborn men to remember

(What is a dead girl but a shadowy ghost
Or a dead man's voice but a distant and vain affirmation
Like dream words most)

Therefore I will not speak of the undying glory of women
I will say you were young and straight and your skin fair
And you stood in the door and the sun was a shadow of leaves on your shoulders
And a leaf on your hair

[1] The first line of Shakespeare's fifty-fifth sonnet.

I will not speak of the famous beauty of dead women
I will say the shape of a leaf lay once on your hair
Till the world ends and the eyes are out and the mouths broken
Look! It is there!

1930

YOU, ANDREW MARVELL [1]

And here face down beneath the sun
And here upon earth's noonward height
To feel the always coming on
The always rising of the night

To feel creep up the curving east
The earthy chill of dusk and slow
Upon those under lands the vast
And ever climbing shadow grow

And strange at Ecbatan the trees
Take leaf by leaf the evening strange
The flooding dark about their knees
The mountains over Persia change

And now at Kermanshah the gate
Dark empty and the withered grass
And through the twilight now the late
Few travelers in the westward pass

And Baghdad darken and the bridge
Across the silent river gone
And through Arabia the edge
Of evening widen and steal on

And deepen on Palmyra's street
The wheel rut in the ruined stone
And Lebanon fade out and Crete
High through the clouds and overblown

[1] In connection with this poem, the reader is meant to consider Andrew Marvell's "To His Coy Mistress," especially the lines beginning "But at my back I always hear."

And over Sicily the air
Still flashing with the landward gulls
And loom and slowly disappear
The sails above the shadowy hulls

And Spain go under and the shore
Of Africa the gilded sand
And evening vanish and no more
The low pale light across that land

Nor now the long light on the sea

And here face downward in the sun
To feel how swift how secretly
The shadow of the night comes on . . .

1930

SALUTE

O sun! Instigator of cocks!
Thou . . .

Quickener! Maker of sound in the leaves
and of running
Stir over the curve of the earth like the ripple of
Scarlet under the skin of the lizard
Hunter!
Starter of westward birds!

Be heard
Sun on our mountains! Oh be now
Loud with us! Wakener let the wings
Descend of dawn on our roof-trees! Bring
Bees now! Let the cicadas sing
In the heat on the gummed trunks of the pine!
Make now the winds! Take thou the orchards!

(We that have heard the beat of our hearts in the silence
And the count of the clock all night at our listening ears)
Be near!
Shake the branches of day on our roofs!
Oh
Be over us!

1930

IMMORTAL AUTUMN

I speak this poem now with grave and level voice
In praise of autumn of the far-horn-winding fall
I praise the flower-barren fields the clouds the tall
Unanswering branches where the wind makes sullen noise

I praise the fall it is the human season
                                        now
No more the foreign sun does meddle at our earth
Enforce the green and bring the fallow land to birth
Nor winter yet weigh all with silence the pine bough

But now in autumn with the black and outcast crows
Share we the spacious world the whispering year is gone
There is more room to live now the once secret dawn
Comes late by daylight and the dark unguarded goes

Between the mutinous brave burning of the leaves
And winter's covering of our hearts with his deep snow
We are alone there are no evening birds we know
The naked moon the tame stars circle at our eaves

It is the human season on this sterile air
Do words outcarry breath the sound goes on and on
I hear a dead man's cry from autumn long since gone

I cry to you beyond upon this bitter air.

1930

REPROACH TO DEAD POETS

You who have spoken words in the earth
You who have broken the silence
                                        utterers
Sayers in all lands to all peoples
Writers in candle soot on the skins
Of rams for those who come after you
                                        voices
Echoed at night in the arched doors

And at noon in the shadow of fig trees
Hear me
                                        Were there not
Words
    Were there not words to tell with
    Were there not leaf sounds in the mouths
Of women from over-sea and a call
Of birds on the lips of the children of strangers
Were there not words in all languages
In many tongues the same thing differently
The name cried out Thalassa the sea
The Sea
The sun and moon character representing
Brightness the night sound of the wind for
Always for ever and ever the verb
Created after the speech of crickets
            Were there not words to tell with
                                        to tell
What lands these are
                                What are these
Lights through the night leaves and these voices
Crying among us as winds rise

Or whence of what race we are that dwell with them

Were there not words to tell with
                                        you that have told
The kings' names and the hills remembered for battles

1930

MEN

(ON A PHRASE OF APOLLINAIRE)

Our history is grave noble and tragic
We trusted the look of the sun on the green leaves
We built our towns of stone with enduring ornaments
We worked the hard flint for basins of water

We believed in the feel of the earth under us
We planted corn grapes apple-trees rhubarb
Nevertheless we knew others had died
Everything we have done has been faithful and dangerous

We believed in the promises made by the brows of women
We begot children at night in the warm wool
We comforted those who wept in fear on our shoulders
Those who comforted us had themselves vanished

We fought at the dikes in the bright sun for the pride of it
We beat drums and marched with music and laughter
We were drunk and lay with our fine dreams in the straw
We saw the stars through the hair of lewd women

Our history is grave noble and tragic
Many of us have died and are not remembered
Many cities are gone and their channels broken
We have lived a long time in this land and with honor

1930

EPISTLE TO BE LEFT IN THE EARTH

. . . It is colder now
there are many stars
we are drifting
North by the Great Bear
the leaves are falling
The water is stone in the scooped rocks
to southward
Red sun grey air
the crows are
Slow on their crooked wings
the jays have left us
Long since we passed the flares of Orion
Each man believes in his heart he will die
Many have written last thoughts and last letters
None know if our deaths are now or forever
None know if this wandering earth will be found

We lie down and the snow covers our garments
I pray you
you (if any open this writing)
Make in your mouths the words that were our names
I will tell you all we have learned
I will tell you everything
The earth is round
there are springs under the orchards

The loam cuts with a blunt knife
beware of
Elms in thunder
the lights in the sky are stars
We think they do not see
we think also
The trees do not know nor the leaves of the grasses
hear us
The birds too are ignorant
Do not listen
Do not stand at dark in the open windows
We before you have heard this
they are voices
They are not words at all but the wind rising
Also none among us has seen God
(. . . We have thought often
The flaws of sun in the late and driving weather
Pointed to one tree but it was not so)
As for the nights I warn you the nights are dangerous
The wind changes at night and the dreams come

It is very cold
there are strange stars near Arcturus

Voices are crying an unknown name in the sky

1930

LINES FOR AN INTERMENT

Now it is fifteen years you have lain in the meadow:
The boards at your face have gone through: the earth is
Packed down and the sound of the rain is fainter:
The roots of the first grass are dead:

It's a long time to lie in the earth with your honor:
The world, Soldier, the world has been moving on:

The girls wouldn't look at you twice in the cloth cap:
Six years old they were when it happened:

It bores them even in books: "Soissons besieged!"
As for the gents they have joined the American Legion:

Belts and a brass band and the ladies' auxiliaries:
The Californians march in the OD silk:

We are all acting again like civilized beings:
People mention it at tea . . .

The Facts of Life we have learned are Economic:
You were deceived by the detonations of bombs:

You thought of courage and death when you thought of warfare:
Hadn't they taught you the fine words were unfortunate?

Now that we understand we judge without bias:
We feel of course for those who had to die:

Women have written us novels of great passion
Proving the useless death of the dead was a tragedy:

Nevertheless it is foolish to chew gall:
The foremost writers on both sides have apologized:

The Germans are back in the Midi with cropped hair:
The English are drinking the better beer in Bavaria:

You can rest now in the rain in the Belgian meadow—
Now that it's all explained away and forgotten:
Now that the earth is hard and the wood rots:

Now you are dead . . .

1933

PONY ROCK

FOR THE MEMORY OF H. T. C.

One who has loved the hills and died, a man
Intimate with them—how their profiles fade
Large out of evening or through veils of rain
Vanish and reappear or how the sad
Long look of moonlight troubles their blind stones—
One who has loved them does not utterly,
Letting his fingers loosen and the green
Ebb from his eyeballs, close his eyes and go:

But other men long after he is dead
Seeing those hills will catch their breath and stare
As one who reading in a book some word
That calls joy back but can recall not where—
Only the crazy sweetness in the head—
Will stare at the black print till the page is blurred.

1933

AMERICA WAS PROMISES

Who is the voyager in these leaves?
Who is the traveler in this journey
Deciphers the revolving night: receives
The signal from the light returning?

America was promises to whom?

East were the
Dead kings and the remembered sepulchres:
West was the grass.
The groves of the oaks were at evening.

Eastward are the nights where we have slept.

And we move on: we move down:
With the first light we push forward:
We descend from the past as a wandering people from mountains.
We cross into the day to be discovered.
The dead are left where they fall—at dark
At night late under the coverlets.
We mark the place with the shape of our teeth on our fingers.
The room is left as it was: the love
Who is the traveler in these leaves these
Annual waters and beside the doors
Jonquils: then the rose: the eaves
Heaping the thunder up: the mornings
Opening on like great valleys
Never till now approached: the familiar trees
Far off: distant with the future:
The hollyhocks beyond the afternoons:
The butterflies over the ripening fruit on the balconies:
And all beautiful
All before us

America was always promises.
From the first voyage and the first ship there were promises—
"the tropic bird which does not sleep at sea"
"the great mass of dark heavy clouds which is a sign"
"the drizzle of rain without wind which is a sure sign"
"the whale which is an indication"
"the stick appearing to be carved with iron"
"the stalk loaded with roseberries"
"and all these signs were from the west"
"and all night heard birds passing"

Who is the voyager on these coasts?
Who is the traveler in these waters
Expects the future as a shore: foresees
Like Indies to the west the ending—he
The rumor of the surf intends?

America was promises—to whom?

Jefferson knew:
Declared it before God and before history:
Declares it still in the remembering tomb.
The promises were Man's: the land was his—
Man endowed by his Creator:
Earnest in love: perfectible by reason:
Just and perceiving justice: his natural nature
Clear and sweet at the source as springs in trees are.
It was Man the promise contemplated.
The times had chosen Man: no other:
Bloom on his face of every future:
Brother of stars and of all travelers:
Brother of time and of all mysteries:
Brother of grass also: of fruit trees.
It was Man who had been promised: who should have.
Man was to ride from the Tidewater: over the Gap:
West and South with the water: taking the book with him:
Taking the wheat seed: corn seed: pip of apple:
Building liberty a farmyard wide:
Breeding for useful labor: for good looks:
For husbandry: humanity: for pride—
Practising self-respect and common decency.

And Man turned into men in Philadelphia
Practising prudence on a long-term lease:
Building liberty to fit the parlor:
Bred for crystal on the frontroom shelves:
Just and perceiving justice by the dollar:
Patriotic with the bonds at par
(And their children's children brag of their deeds for the
    Colonies).
Man rode up from the Tidewater: over the Gap:
Turned into men: turned into two-day settlers:
Lawyers with the land-grants in their caps:
Coon-skin voters wanting theirs and getting it.

Turned the promises to capital: invested it.

America was always promises:
"the wheel like a sun as big as a cart wheel
    with many sorts of pictures on it
    the whole of fine gold"

"twenty golden ducks
    beautifully worked and very natural looking
    and some like dogs of the kind they keep"

And they waved us west from the dunes: they cried out
Colua! Colua!
Mexico! Mexico! . . . Colua!

America was promises to whom?

Old Man Adams knew. He told us—
An aristocracy of compound interest
Hereditary through the common stock!
We'd have one sure before the mare was older.
"The first want of every man was his dinner:
The second his girl." Kings were by the pocket.
Wealth made blood made wealth made blood made wealthy.
Enlightened selfishness gave lasting light.
Winners bred grandsons: losers only bred!

And the Aristocracy of politic selfishness
Bought the land up: bought the towns: the sites:
The goods: the government: the people. Bled them.
Sold them. Kept the profit. Lost itself.

The Aristocracy of Wealth and Talents
Turned its talents into wealth and lost them.
Turned enlightened selfishness to wealth.
Turned self-interest into bankbooks: balanced them.
Bred out: bred to fools; to hostlers:
Card sharps: well dressed women: dancefloor doublers.
The Aristocracy of Wealth and Talents
Sold its talents: bought the public notice:
Drank in public: went to bed in public:
Patronized the arts in public: pall'd with
Public authors public beauties: posed in
Public postures for the public page.
The Aristocracy of Wealth and Talents
Withered of talent and ashamed of wealth
Bred to sonsinlaw: insane relations:
Girls with open secrets: sailors' Galahads:
Prurient virgins with the tales to tell:
Women with dead wombs and living wishes.

The Aristocracy of Wealth and Talents
Moved out: settled on the Continent:
Sat beside the water at Rapallo:
Died in a rented house: unwept: unhonored.

And the child says I see the lightning on you.

The weed between the railroad tracks
Tasting of sweat: tasting of poverty:
The bitter and pure taste where the hawk hovers:
Native as the deer bone in the sand

O my America for whom?

For whom the promises? For whom the river
"It flows west! Look at the ripple of it!"
The grass "So that it was wonderful to see
And endless without end with wind wonderful!"
The Great Lakes: landless as oceans: their beaches
Coarse sand: clean gravel: pebbles:
Their bluffs smelling of sunflowers: smelling of surf:
Of fresh water: of wild sunflowers . . . wilderness.
For whom the evening mountains on the sky:
The night wind from the west: the moon descending?

Tom Paine knew.
Tom Paine knew the People.
The promises were spoken to the People.
History was voyages toward the People.
Americas were landfalls of the People.
Stars and expectations were the signals of the People.

Whatever was truly built the People had built it.
Whatever was taken down they had taken down.
Whatever was worn they had worn—ax-handles: fiddle-bows:
Sills of doorways: names for children: for mountains.
Whatever was long forgotten they had forgotten—
Fame of the great: names of the rich and their mottos.
The People had the promises: they'd keep them.
They waited their time in the world: they had wise sayings.
They counted out their time by day to day.
They counted it out day after day into history.
They had time and to spare in the spill of their big fists.
They had all the time there was like a handful of wheat seed.
When the time came they would speak and the rest would listen.

And the time came and the People did not speak.

The time came: the time comes: the speakers
Come and these who speak are not the People.

These who speak with gunstocks at the doors:
These the coarse ambitious priest
Leads by the bloody fingers forward:
These who reach with stiffened arm to touch
What none who took dared touch before:
These who touch the truth are not the People.

These the savage fables of the time
Lick at the fingers as a bitch will waked at morning:
These who teach the lie are not the People.

The time came: the time comes

Comes and to whom? To these? Was it for these
The surf was secret on the new-found shore?
Was it for these the branch was on the water?—
These whom all the years were toward
The golden images the clouds the mountains?

Never before: never in any summer:
Never were days so generous: stars so mild:
Even in old men's talk or in books or remembering
Far back in a gone childhood
Or farther still to the light where Homer wanders—
The air all lucid with the solemn blue
That hills take at the distance beyond change . . .
That time takes also at the distances.

Never were there promises as now:
Never was green deeper: earth warmer:
Light more beautiful to see: the sound of
Water lovelier: the many forms of
Leaves: stones: clouds: beasts: shadows
Clearer more admirable or the faces
More like answering faces or the hands
Quicker: more brotherly:
                                                the aching taste of
Time more salt upon the tongue: more human
Never in any summer: and to whom?

At dusk: by street lights: in the rooms we ask this.

We do not ask for Truth now from John Adams.
We do not ask for Tongues from Thomas Jefferson.
We do not ask for Justice from Tom Paine.
We ask for answers.

And there is an answer.

There is Spain Austria Poland China Bohemia.
There are dead men in the pits in all those countries.
Their mouths are silent but they speak. They say
"The promises are theirs who take them."

Listen! Brothers! Generation!
Listen! You have heard these words. Believe it!
Believe the promises are theirs who take them!

Believe unless we take them for ourselves
Others will take them for the use of others!
Believe unless we take them for ourselves
All of us: one here: another there:

Men not Man: people not the People:
Hands: mouths: arms: eyes: not syllables—
Believe unless we take them for ourselves
Others will take them: not for us: for others!

Believe unless we take them for ourselves
Now: soon: by the clock: before tomorrow:
Others will take them: not for now: for longer!

Listen! Brothers! Generation!
Companions of leaves: of the sun: of the slow evenings:
Companions of the many days: of all of them:
Listen! Believe the speaking dead! Believe
The journey is our journey. O believe
The signals were to us: the signs: the birds by
Night: the breaking surf.

Believe

America is promises to
Take!
America is promises to
Us
To take them
Brutally
With love but
Take them.

O believe this!

1939

His world was dreary, but look to the future - you can do something for the world, but hurry up about it.

E. E. Cummings

Edward Estlin Cummings, the son of Edward and Rebecca Clarke Cummings, was born in Cambridge, Massachusetts, October 14, 1894. His father once taught at Harvard, and from 1905 till his death in 1926 he was pastor of the South Congregational Church, Boston.

Cummings was educated at Harvard; he received the A.B. degree in 1915 and the M.A. degree in 1916. In 1917 he enlisted in an ambulance unit and drove an ambulance in France for six months; then through an error by French officials he was arrested and imprisoned for three months, an experience which he treated in a prose work, *The Enormous Room* (1922). After his release he returned home and enlisted as a private in the army, but was not sent back to France before the war ended.

He is both an artist and poet, and since 1920 he has devoted all his time to the two arts. In 1920 and again in 1931 he lived for a time in Paris, and he has travelled in other parts of Europe. In 1923 his first volume of poetry, *Tulips and Chimneys*, was published; and in 1925 he received the *Dial* Award for distinguished service to American literature. Since then he has published seven books of poetry; a play, *him* (1927); a book of paintings and drawings, CIOPW (1931)—the initials standing for charcoal, ink, oil, pencil, and water color; and a prose narrative, *eimi* (1933), about a trip he made to Russia.

He married Ann Barton in 1929, but they were later divorced.

What first strikes a reader of his poetry is the eccentric arrangement of much of it on the page and the peculiarity of his punctuation and use of capitals. Though the latter is perhaps merely an idiosyncrasy, the former derives from his belief that since poetry is now rarely read aloud, the poet owes it to his reader to indicate his meaning by the typography of his verse. It is not these eccentricities of style, however, but the high lyrical quality of much of his poetry that gives him a place among important contemporary poets.

[ALL IN GREEN WENT MY LOVE RIDING]

All in green went my love riding
on a great horse of gold
into the silver dawn.

four lean hounds crouched low and smiling
the merry deer ran before.

Fleeter be they than dappled dreams
the swift sweet deer
the red rare deer.

Four red roebuck at a white water
the cruel bugle sang before.

Horn at hip went my love riding
riding the echo down
into the silver dawn.

four lean hounds crouched low and smiling
the level meadows ran before.

Softer be they than slippered sleep
the lean lithe deer
the fleet flown deer.

Four fleet does at a gold valley
the famished arrow sang before.

Bow at belt went my love riding
riding the mountain down
into the silver dawn.

four lean hounds crouched low and smiling
the sheer peaks ran before.

Paler be they than daunting death
the sleek slim deer
the tall tense deer.

Four tall stags at a green mountain
the lucky hunter sang before.

All in green went my love riding
on a great horse of gold
into the silver dawn.

four lean hounds crouched low and smiling
my heart fell dead before.

1923

[THE HOURS RISE UP PUTTING OFF STARS]

the hours rise up putting off stars and it is
dawn
into the street of the sky light walks scattering poems

on earth a candle is
extinguished   the city
wakes
with a song upon her
mouth having death in her eyes

and it is dawn
the world
goes forth to murder dreams. . . .

i see in the street where strong
men are digging bread
and i see the brutal faces of
people contented hideous hopeless cruel happy

and it is day,

in the mirror
i see a frail
man
dreaming

dreams
dreams in the mirror

and it
is dusk   on earth
a candle is lighted
and it is dark.
the people are in their houses
the frail man is in his bed
the city

sleeps with death upon her mouth having a song in her eyes
the hours descend,
putting on stars. . . .

in the street of the sky night walks scattering poems

1923

[WHEN GOD LETS MY BODY BE]

when god lets my body be

From each brave eye shall sprout a tree
fruit that dangles therefrom

the purpled world will dance upon
Between my lips which did sing

a rose shall beget the spring
that maidens whom passion wastes

will lay between their little breasts
My strong fingers beneath the snow

Into strenuous birds shall go
my love walking in the grass

their wings will touch with her face
and all the while shall my heart be

With the bulge and nuzzle of the sea

1923

[IN JUST-SPRING WHEN THE WORLD]

in Just-
spring when the world is mud-
luscious the little
lame balloonman

whistles far and wee

and eddieandbill come
running from marbles and
piracies and it's
spring

when the world is puddle-wonderful

the queer
old balloonman whistles
far and wee
and bettyandisbel come dancing

from hop-scotch and jump-rope and

it's
spring
and
the
goat-footed

balloonMan whistles
far
and
wee

1923

[NOBODY LOSES ALL THE TIME]

nobody loses all the time

i had an uncle named
Sol who was a born failure and
nearly everybody said he should have gone

into vaudeville perhaps because my Uncle Sol could
sing McCann He Was A Diver on Xmas Eve like Hell Itself which
may or may not account for the fact that my Uncle

Sol indulged in that possibly most inexcusable
of all to use a highfalootin phrase
luxuries that is or to
wit farming and be
it needlessly
added

my Uncle Sol's farm
failed because the chickens
ate the vegetables so
my Uncle Sol had a
chicken farm till the
skunks ate the chickens when

my Uncle Sol
had a skunk farm but
the skunks caught cold and
died and so
my Uncle Sol imitated the
skunks in a subtle manner

or by drowning himself in the watertank
but somebody who'd given my Uncle Sol a Victor
Victrola and records while he lived presented to
him upon the auspicious occasion of his decease a
scrumptious not to mention splendiferous funeral with
tall boys in black gloves and flowers and everything and

i remember we all cried like the Missouri
when my Uncle Sol's coffin lurched because
somebody pressed a button
(and down went
my Uncle
Sol

and started a worm farm)

1926

[IT IS SO LONG SINCE MY HEART]

it is so long since my heart has been with yours

shut by our mingling arms through
a darkness where new lights begin and
increase,
since your mind has walked into
my kiss as a stranger
into the streets and colors of a town—

that i have perhaps forgotten
how, always (from
these hurrying crudities
of blood and flesh) Love
coins His most gradual gesture,

and whittles life to eternity

—after which our separating selves become museums
filled with skilfully stuffed memories

1926

[IF I HAVE MADE, MY LADY]

if i have made, my lady, intricate
imperfect various things chiefly which wrong
your eyes (frailer than most deep dreams are frail)
songs less firm than your body's whitest song
upon my mind—if i have failed to snare
the glance too shy—if through my singing slips
the very skillful strangeness of your smile
the keen primeval silence of your hair

—let the world say "his most wise music stole
nothing from death"—

you only will create
(who are so perfectly alive) my shame:
lady through whose profound and fragile lips
the sweet small clumsy feet of April came

into the ragged meadow of my soul.

1926

[IF YOU CAN'T EAT]

If you can't eat you got to

smoke and we aint got
nothing to smoke:come on kid

let's go to sleep
if you can't smoke you got to

Sing and we aint got

nothing to sing;come on kid
let's go to sleep

if you can't sing you got to
die and we aint got

Nothing to die,come on kid

let's go to sleep
if you can't die you got to

dream and we aint got
nothing to dream(come on kid

Let's go to sleep)

1940

[A PRETTY A DAY]

a pretty a day
(and every fades)
is here and away
(but born are maids
to flower an hour
in all,all)

o yes to flower
until so blithe
a doer a wooer

some limber and lithe
some very fine mower
a tall;tall

some jerry so very
(and nellie and fan)
some handsomest harry
(and sally and nan
they tremble and cower
so pale:pale)

for betty was born
to never say nay
but lucy could learn
and lily could pray
and fewer were shyer
than doll. doll

1940

[AS FREEDOM IS A BREAKFASTFOOD]

as freedom is a breakfastfood
or truth can live with right and wrong
or molehills are from mountains made
—long enough and just so long
will being pay the rent of seem
and genius please the talentgang
and water most encourage flame

as hatracks into peachtrees grow
or hopes dance best on bald men's hair
and every finger is a toe
and any courage is a fear
—long enough and just so long
will the impure think all things pure
and hornets wail by children stung

or as the seeing are the blind
and robins never welcome spring
nor flatfolk prove their world is round
nor dingsters die at break of dong
and common's rare and millstones float
—long enough and just so long
tomorrow will not be too late

worms are the words but joy's the voice
down shall go which and up come who
breasts will be breasts thighs will be thighs
deeds cannot dream what dreams can do
—time is a tree(this life one leaf)
but love is the sky and i am for you
just so long and long enough

1940

[ANYONE LIVED IN A PRETTY HOW TOWN]

anyone lived in a pretty how town
(with up so floating many bells down)
spring summer autumn winter
he sang his didn't he danced his did.

Women and men(both little and small)
cared for anyone not at all
they sowed their isn't they reaped their same
sun moon stars rain

children guessed(but only a few
and down they forgot as up they grew
autumn winter spring summer)
that noone loved him more by more

when by now and tree by leaf
she laughed his joy she cried his grief
bird by snow and stir by still
anyone's any was all to her

someones married their everyones
laughed their cryings and did their dance
(sleep wake hope and then)they
said their nevers they slept their dream

stars rain sun moon
(and only the snow can begin to explain
how children are apt to forget to remember
with up so floating many bells down)

one day anyone died i guess
(and noone stooped to kiss his face)
busy folk buried them side by side
little by little and was by was

all by all and deep by deep
and more by more they dream their sleep
noone and anyone earth by april
wish by spirit and if by yes.

Women and men(both dong and ding)
summer autumn winter spring
reaped their sowing and went their came
sun moon stars rain

1940

[MY FATHER MOVED THROUGH DOOMS OF LOVE]

my father moved through dooms of love
through sames of am through haves of give,
singing each morning out of each night
my father moved through depths of height

this motionless forgetful where
turned at his glance to shining here;
that if(so timid air is firm)
under his eyes would stir and squirm

newly as from unburied which
floats the first who,his april touch
drove sleeping selves to swarm their fates
woke dreamers to their ghostly roots

and should some why completely weep
my father's fingers brought her sleep:
vainly no smallest voice might cry
for he could feel the mountains grow.

Lifting the valleys of the sea
my father moved through griefs of joy;
praising a forehead called the moon
singing desire into begin

joy was his song and joy so pure
a heart of star by him could steer
and pure so now and now so yes
the wrists of twilight would rejoice

keen as midsummer's keen beyond
conceiving mind of sun will stand,
so strictly(over utmost him
so hugely)stood my father's dream

his flesh was flesh his blood was blood:
no hungry man but wished him food;
no cripple wouldn't creep one mile
uphill to only see him smile.

Scorning the pomp of must and shall
my father moved through dooms of feel;
his anger was as right as rain
his pity was as green as grain

septembering arms of year extend
less humbly wealth to foe and friend
than he to foolish and to wise
offered immeasurable is

proudly and(by octobering flame
beckoned)as earth will downward climb,
so naked for immortal work
his shoulders marched against the dark

his sorrow was as true as bread:
no liar looked him in the head;
if every friend became his foe
he'd laugh and build a world with snow.

My father moved through theys of we,
singing each new leaf out of each tree
(and every child was sure that spring
danced when she heard my father sing)

then let men kill which cannot share,
let blood and flesh be mud and mire,
scheming imagine,passion willed,
freedom a drug that's bought and sold

giving to steal and cruel kind,
a heart to fear,to doubt a mind,
to differ a disease of same,
conform the pinnacle of am

though dull were all we taste as bright,
bitter all utterly things sweet,
maggoty minus and dumb death
all we inherit,all bequeath

and nothing quite so least as truth
—i say though hate were why men breathe—
because my father lived his soul
love is the whole and more than all

1940

[I AM SO GLAD]

i am so glad and very
merely my fourth will cure
the laziest self of weary
the hugest sea of shore

so far your nearness reaches
a lucky fifth of you
turns people into eachs
and cowards into grow

our can'ts were born to happen
our mosts have died in more
our twentieth will open
wide a wide open door

we are so both and oneful
night cannot be so sky
sky cannot be so sunful
i am through you so i

1940

[LOVE IS THE EVERY ONLY GOD]

love is the every only god

who spoke this earth so glad and big
even a thing all small and sad
man,may his mighty briefness dig

for love beginning means return
seas who could sing so deep and strong

one queerying wave will whitely yearn
from each last shore and home come young

so truly perfectly the skies
by merciful love whispered were,
completes its brightness with your eyes

any illimitable star

1940

Horace Gregory

Horace Victor Gregory, the son of Henry Bolton and Anna Catherine Henkel Gregory, was born in Milwaukee, Wisconsin, April 10, 1898. He was enrolled in some classes at the Milwaukee School of Fine Arts from 1913 to 1916, and received his preparatory training for college at the German-English Academy, Milwaukee, which he attended from 1914 to 1919 except for an interlude when he served with the army in France. In the autumn of 1919 he entered the University of Wisconsin, from which institution he received the B.A. degree in 1923. From the time of his graduation from college till 1934, he devoted himself to writing, and contributed to such magazines as the *Atlantic Monthly*, *Hound and Horn*, the *Nation*, the *New Republic*, and *Poetry*. Since 1934 he has been a lecturer on poetry and critical theory at Sarah Lawrence College, Bronxville, New York.

In 1928 he was awarded the Lyric Prize and in 1934 the Helen Haire Levinson Prize by *Poetry*. His first volume of poetry, *Chelsea Rooming House*, was published in 1930; and this was followed by *No Retreat* (1933), *Chorus for Survival* (1935), and *Poems 1930-1940* (1941). He has made a translation of the poems of Catullus (1931) and has written a critical study of D. H. Lawrence, *Pilgrim of the Apocalypse* (1933).

On August 21, 1925, he married the poet Marya Zaturenska, who had immigrated to the United States from Russia, and whom he met at the University of Wisconsin, which she also attended. They have two children, a daughter born in 1927 and a son born in 1932. Their home is in New York City.

LONGFACE MAHONEY DISCUSSES HEAVEN

If someone said, *Escape.*
Let's get away from here,
you'd see snow mountains thrown
against the sky,
cold, and you'd draw your breath and feel
air like cold water going through your veins,
but you'd be free, up so high,
or you'd see a row of girls dancing on a beach
with tropic trees and a warm moon
and warm air floating under your clothes
and through your hair.
Then you'd think of heaven
where there's peace, away from here
and you'd go someplace unreal
where everybody goes after something happens,
set up in the air, safe, a room in a hotel.
A brass bed, military hair brushes,
a couple of coats, trousers, maybe a dress
on a chair or draped on the floor.
This room is not on earth, feel the air,
warm like heaven and far away.

This is a place
where marriage nights are kept
and sometimes here you say Hello
to a neat girl with you
and sometimes she laughs
because she thinks it's funny to be sitting here
for no reason at all, except, perhaps,
she likes to see how strong you are
and the color of your eyes.
Maybe this isn't heaven but near
to something like it,
more like love coming up in elevators
and nothing to think about, except, O God,
you love her now and it makes no difference
if it isn't spring. All seasons are warm
in the warm air
and the brass bed is always there.

If you've done something
and the cops get you afterwards, you
can't remember the place again,
away from cops and streets—
it's all unreal—
the warm air, a dream
that couldn't save you now.
No one would care
to hear about it,
it would be heaven
far away, dark and no music,
not even a girl there.

1930

NO COCK CROWS AT MORNING

There is no cock crowing in our bedroom,
waking good morning startled by his cries:
the great bird has vanished in a fiery dream,
his clamorous wings are shut
and his rolling golden eye
has gone blind
and his radiant comb is a laurel of ashes.

Listen, there is no cock crowing
(Somebody murdered someone else's wife
and left a pool of blood in the subway,
crying his matins out of Gothic type,
shouting the resurrection and the life,
rising in vapors from an invisible flame,
sloughing his shirt and trousers
in an electric chair).

There is no cock crowing,
but there is a phantom bird walking
through prison walls, walking through streets and houses,
silent, invulnerable, walking over the dead—
ever the martyrs and the wrongdoers
there is no cock crowing.

1930

O MORS AETERNA

Be for a little while eternal,
singing with all the songs in your body
but making no sound.

The Rose of Sharon singing in an old city
was eternal suddenly
for a little while.

And the mountains fell away
and the city sank into earth again
and the voices of dead men came from the ground
crying, Incest and poverty and murder
(all in the many dead years
that had sent them into the earth)
but now rising, crying against the world
and mortal sun and moon and stars,
against life and the masters
in purple victories, clothed with iron wars.

For a little while
the Rose of Sharon sang eternally
until the city came around her again
and there was no sound.

1930

CYMBALUM MUNDI

Regret, return, do not return, retreat,
the mouthpiece siren at my ear
speaks from a million faces in the street
shouting,
We are alive and do not die,
not die, give us the power
not to die but to return
at each imperishable hour.
Enter the winding, top-flight floor,
lean from its door with naked, private eye
until a searchlight gains
an iron terrace and a broken stair
downward to midnight city of the plains.

Will someone close the door, padlock retreat
in quiet air?
until stilled eyes discern
the pale, bright shadow of the greenwood deer,
the silver arrow in the sun to follow
always the dawn tomorrow, in sleep to hear
lost echoes of the horn
return tympanum deep.
Do not regret retreat
in memory that strikes through tissue, vein
to wake again new limbs, new eyes, new voices:
Vita Nuova! *every lip rejoices.*

As light shifts in a dream, so these sounds carry
their alternate replies of joy and fear,
again I wake with siren at my ear,
Give us the power before we fail, descend
into day's end, year's end, each hour's
darkening in the sun
to call retreat
down mirrored halls
through passageway and street
in places where all faces seem the same,

until at last all voices are one voice,
even the face unseen,
electric smile candescent in the sky:
Give me the power
to stay in no retreat and not to die.

1933

[HOMAGE TO] COLUMBUS

Columbus is remembered by young men
walking the world at night in street-walled prison:
Where is my country? Why do I return
at midnight to a moonlit, inland ocean
whose waves beat as a heart beats in my side?

Is the return to these receding shores
the end of earth, fallen to deep sea traffic,
the end of all things?

Even the cities that coil upward
from sumach bush and sand flow into grass:
roofs, towers mingling
with roots and the bodies of men who died in wars
against the masters.
Columbus who believed his own miracles,
conquered his India, oceans, mermaids, golden savages—
where was his country?
Only a small stone room at night
where a man walks over the world and seasons merge
in darkness. And time echoes time saying: Columbus no more,
no more Columbus. He is a vanished cloud in the sky
where stars move toward the sun.
All that is his
is where his bones lie.

1933

EMERSON: LAST DAYS AT CONCORD

Enter America at Concord's bridge,
true marriage of the east and west, Brahma
whose lips nurse at my veins.

Where was the green brass canon
sunken in churchyards after the shots were fired?
Listen, the world is sleeping and the noise
coils in thunder where Dover's beach
shall wake no more
and the Indian ocean
pours its blood into the sun when evening's tide
uncovers bones upon the shore.

Cut me a frock coat, for the oversoul
lies naked: parts, limbs exposed
within a broken coffin. O light that stirs in dust
as eastwind darkens nightfall into rain.

Where are your lips, hands, Brahma?
What was the name, your name or mine?

Come, friend,
we shall walk in the west orchard drinking russet wine,
kiss daisies where the transcendental tree

(look how the death worm feeds upon its roots)
shelters our love and fiery blossoms fall in Plato's vineyard.
I have rolled the world in my brain, have seen its heroes diminish,
saw oceans, continents dissolve in sunlight
on Concord window sills:

Are you my friend?
then here's my secret; I have forgotten
all friends and the words that joined my lips to theirs.
Better to keep faith
and believe
no one. Better to be a patriot disowning
this land. Give back America to sunlight, wind and rain;
set sail for India from Concord's bridge,
leap to the quarter-deck where our Columbus
once more commands his ships.
Is that a storm in the sky?
And are these apples ripe? I grew this orchard to be a paradise
this side of Eden.

1933

SALVOS FOR RANDOLPH BOURNE

O bitterness never spoken, the death mask etched in silver,
the dark limbs rolled in lead where the shallow grave conceals
despair: the image of a large head, forward, devouring
the collarbone. No general in brass over it and no
conquering angel kneels.

This was the end:
there were no firing squads,
no City Hall Nathan Hale with a bronze cord at his throat
speaking of lives and his country where a hundred million lives
rose, wavered, shattered like an invisible sea coiling
against a rock (no longer there) but sunken
into a shore line of weeds and sand.

Only a small room and a million words to be written before midnight
against poverty and idiot death like the gray face of Emerson
fading in New England winter twilight; the hard face vanishing

in snow, the passionately soft words issuing from the mouth.
Listen to the rock, the oracle no longer there!

To be the last American, an embryo coiled in a test tube,
to be a fixed and paralytic smile cocked upward to the clouds,
to see friends and enemies depart (around the corner)
their sticks and smart fedoras bright in sunlight,
to be or not to be Hamlet, the Prince of Wales,
or last week's *New Republic;*
to be death delicately walking betwen chimney pots on Eighth
    Street,
possibly this is best to be
                                        or not to be.

1933

TO MY GENERATION (1919-1933)

The return after ten years: New York, Chicago, Madison.

Entrain airport: New York, Chicago, west
piercing the sunset's firmament where day
breaks midnight into stars before the dawn:
Superior, Lake Erie, Michigan:
seawind but no saltsea in this lake spray
clear eyes and nostrils: drink our health: the sand
our shores.
                    Stop signals home again!

Awake at morning, Spring coiled in the body
and at the narrow window slit in stone,
skylight and sun.
                              Tilt the horizon down,
ride windward through Wisconsin miles of corn,
grazing the shallow valley and long plains.

The University of Wisconsin: 1919.

Here was the campus of our heart, my friends,
Plato's green-treed republic of the air:
see what miraculous fruit its branches bear,
oceans of maple spray, green-harbored, flowing
against the sky: and from these shores Greek towers . . .

See how the white dome trembles in the sun,
dissolves at noon three thousand years away
where the antique nightingale engraved in bronze

still sways unheard forever, now entwined
within the steel crescendos of the wind.

The indecisive peace after war which lasted until 1929.

This peace was ours: the troopship disembarked,
the drink, the laughter beyond death,
death fallen behind each cross on a low hill,
behind each eye that found no peace at home:
Drive homeward angels from Versailles
from graves that opened under no man's land;
these faces were the looks, the glances,
the shadows of old friends,
the bodies of those unslain, exiled from war.
Are these alive,
but now returned, furloughs of exile signed
from all green ports on earth?
                                        The birth certificate of love
declared obscene: Faith of no Faith, Our Father,
do not destroy this faithlessness to friend
or enemy, lest we perish to no end.

Alternate speeches: individual lovers walking in the shadow of Lucretius.

Measure the atoms of our soul, O Roman
death's astronomer Lucretius.

                                        Spires of light ascend
discarnate memories: the four years spanned
by the quick, sinewy shadow of his hand:

    (And in this shadow where she stood,
    light in her hair!
    The limbs reveal undress that virgins wear
    to meet the bridegroom on the wedding stair,
    do not unsay her testament, O love:

    "Live for this hour and we who die today
    kiss lips that bloom forever underground."

    And did you call me by his name who died
    naked, Parian attitudes of death
    entwined your limbs and his: kiss and restore
    his body's heat in mine, this earth his grave:
    sleepless, his blood drives home
    Niagaras in our veins)

O Mors Aeterna,
lean from the fiery ramparts of world's end,
time's end and love's last image scrolled
in quicksilver across the mind—descend
voice of a million tongues, your elegies
(some say that suicide usurped his blood)
resound no more. . . .

Mount stairways to the sun!
We have survived your heritage, these years
consuming time toward death too swift for tears.

The valediction.

The course of empire westward to Cathay
rides in the east: the circle breaks in fire:
these charred remains of what we were expire
(O incandescent speed!), the hands, lips, eyes
anonymous. Rise, *atque vale*, rise:
another generation shall disown
these years in darkness, each to four winds blown
(the deeds are obsolete as Helen's war). . . .

Good-bye, when voices greet another spring,
forgive our ashes and destroy the urn:
unwind the clock, empty the seasons down
rivers of memory—do not return!

1933

From CHORUS FOR SURVIVAL

I

Tell us that love
returns,
O Hymen, sing
In every hour that burns
After the midnight hour
In darkness here.
Wake with thy song
The antique smiling year,
Always thy axis turning to restore
The Greek dawn breaking
On Aegean seas.

Break here
The silent wave upon the shore
In dreams to darkness-driven memories;
Wake with thy song,
Tell us to wake and sing—
Midnight and starlight night are always long
For the impatient young.
Open gray skies and fling
Thy yellow veil, the sun,
down city streets
Where tireless seasons run,
Speed here October, our retarded spring,
Daylight and green
Live forests blossoming:
The wave-washed rock in embers glowing red,
Wake even here,
till climbing overhead,
Window and cornice on steel branches bear
Fire of morning from another spring.

Wake with thy song
time-darkened waters
That have not reached their end
Westward to India, passage through storm,
Bearing the image of a Grecian bride,
Eyes like cornflowers staring at our side,
The blue flame lighting darkness in the shade
Of trees knee-deep in grass
At summer's tide . . .
Only our lips recall
That she was beautiful:
the pure
Alcestis memory of a kiss:
the violet-
Scented breast, the virginal
Breathing light in sunlit air;
Handclasp remembers hand,
quick limbs enthrall
Entwining limbs, the nervous, flexible,
Growing green grape vine,
until the blood
Flows into sleep and blood is wine.

This is thy memory, America,
The tenuous marriage of disunited blood,
Captain and slave one bed,
in dust until the wind
Stirs dust to life again . . .
and walking here,
Conquered and conqueror
(The apple blossoms white in midnight hair).

Wake with thy song
Even in death (they sleep like death)
Men in the wilderness
(The night is long),
breaking through forests of a foreign land,
Sell and move on, *We have no heritage,*
This place no name;
Westward we follow to an unknown star
And shall not come again the way we came.

Tell us that love
returns
After the midnight hour
In darkness here,
Season of iron cities against the sky,
The cold room where I write my signature
Toward my survival in the waning year:
Winter and frost, each day revolves to night,
The longer night that brings a short tomorrow
Of middle-age in dark, divided faces,
In faces that I know too well, my own
Face staring likeness in the mirror
Beyond the hour of death or hope or doom;
When doors swing wide upon an empty room,
Window and door open to empty air
Echo in darkness of the lost frontier.

Wake with thy song
the voices
Of men who cannot sleep:
We count our losses
In decimals of time, the ten per cent
Of what we hope: To let:
the naked bed, the folding chair,

Space for the body motionless in air,
Permit survival if we stand alone.
Voiceless we smile; we are not violent.

And from these places
On the abyss of loss,
                                        the steel-edged towers
Pierce the moon, the sun:
Look where Atlantis leaves forgotten traces,
Empire of empty houses under seas.

This is thy heritage, America,
Scaffold of iron deep in stone.
                                                        Destroy the ruins,
This is the place; wreck here and build again.

Tell us that love
                                    returns,
Not soft nor kind,
But like a crystal turning in the mind,
Light where the body is:
                                              thy limbs are fire
Walking alive among the ancient trees,
The ruined town, cathedral wall, church spire.

Say love, though always young,
Remembers these . . .
                                            place, house we entered
And shall not return . . .
                                                Spirit that outlives time
To join our hands in love,
                                               do you remember
Serpent and dove, the wild rose and the thorn,
Blossom and leaf in secret flowering
Read in a book of broken prophecies?

Wake with thy song
                                        (I speak a difficult and treacherous tongue
That was not made for wedding song or carol;
Measure my dwindling shadow on the wall,
Wait for the silence when my lips are gone
That say:
                    Though night is long, this bitter hour wakes
And is not sterile).

Wake here
                    Atlantis under hard blue skies,
Thy Indian Summer bride is like the spring
Roof-tree in light
                              thy blossoming
In fire to love returns.

III

Poet and friend, how many times have I
wished to forget your image at the door,
told you:
                Get out before we starve,
before the house rots and my days are gone,
the more we talk, the more's undone.

"Loaf and invite the soul," the deer that strays
into my hands, the silver beast
with children's eyes, feed it once more;
count this day lost, say all my years are emptied,
a paragraph in old newspaper files:
My arms embracing hero, heroine,
whose love, whose death; whose race won and whose cheers?
All set in type and each bright face forgotten.

We have been poor together,
hating each other,
breaking our hopes, our lives,
and know that terror waits at each street corner:
gain, loss, sweepstake or ruin at day's end.
Exit before we sleep—not death, but living
with no name,
the mind gone and the smile returning, Yes.
Where did I put my hat? Always the same.

Meet X, the scientist, exploding ions
in basement quiet, sane: measures electron
B, the steady hand arrives at no decision:
"Wait! for the day's too short, and night's too long;
wait for the square root of the heart of X
in physics, metaphysics, Einstein, Marx,
somewhere the calibration is concealed,
the perfect temperature, until the glass
breaks, I begin. . . ."

X, tired, relaxed, does not commit himself
(even to death) "See how I wake each morning
to hope (it is not easy) to survive."

Hear Y, the Communist at Union Square,
Lenin's great hand against the sky, the lips declaiming:
"Down, metaphysics down; up heart, up fire
to burn old doubt and fear.
Pay as you enter to the house of gold,
and through this door glide parasite millionaire,
poet and engineer: check body, soul
with overcoat and stick,
the delicate laboratory brains of men
are all subzero here."
Where steady hands
arrive at no decision, doubt answers doubt:
"Did Henry go insane, did John divorce,
did someone pick my pockets?"
You hear them crying:
"They pick my pockets
Of silver and gold
a year's rent, furniture,
insurance, Ph.D., moonlight and yachts,
and horseback riding in the park
and a young face with blue wide staring eyes,
gone, like time gone."

And each man separates,
as you and I break handclasp, turn
remembering unpaid debts, unanswered letters,
the lighted clock above an empty square
waits for the hour of strike,
strike Monday morning,
"They gave me murder when I asked for bread,
now, guns and battleships."
Yes and goodnight,
they shall not find me dead,
turn with me as I go
between the fire and the bright winter's cold.

IX

Will someone tell me where Fort Dearborn fell,
Chicago river's end?

The place is gone,
history without memory, trying to remember
something not seen at all
but is a sound at night of the wave breaking,
distant the echo of that waterfall.

Turn to the prairie over the Mormon's Trail,
landmark diminished tombstone on the hill,
someone died there and his son's sons died poor,
yet land (increasing earth) grew over them,
and ruined house, stone wall, rotted roof pine
lie buried under acres flowing green
in the flood-tide of corn.

And the familiar names we knew are gone,
not even the forgotten dead rest here,
as though invisible lips stirred heart to saying:
"Too soon stone over us and iron against the sun,
these walls are not our tomb, nor this our home,
nor tall winged city, clipped in steel, our room;
our address has moved west two hundred years,
exile from peace our heritage and war
flows under earth we have not made our own,
nor last year's drought our will, nor seed our sowing;
through this dark hour (in a time like yours)
forever ours, yet always we return
to walk toward morning and new seasons growing."

XIV

Ask no return for love that's given
embracing mistress, wife or friend,
ask no return:
on this deep earth or in pale heaven,
awake and spend
hands, lips, and eyes in love,
in darkness burn,
the limbs entwined until the soul ascend.

Ask no return of seasons gone:
the fire of autumn and the first hour of spring,
the short bough blossoming
through city windows when night's done,
when fears adjourn
backward in memory where all loves end

in self again, again the inward tree
growing against the heart
and no heart free.
From love that sleeps behind each eye
in double symmetry
                                        ask no return,
even in enmity, look! I shall take your hand;
nor can our limbs disjoin in separate ways again,
walking, even at night on foreign land
through houses open to the wind, through cold and rain,
waking alive, meet, kiss and understand.

1935

Hart Crane

Harold Hart Crane was born July 21, 1899, at Garretsville, Ohio. He was the only child of Stephen A. Crane, a merchant and candy manufacturer, and his wife, Grace Edna Hart, of Chicago. Both parents were descendants of old New England families, and the immediate families on both sides were substantial business folk in the neighborhood of Cleveland.

As a child he delighted in color, but as he grew older he transferred his interest to poetry. He was extraordinarily sensitive: for hours after the slightest discipline he was likely to be nauseated and ill; and after a quarrel his body would break out in great red blotches, and he would have all the manifestations of severe illness. Yet no one in the family seemed aware of his delicately balanced nervous system, for he was constantly involved in the growing tension between his parents, which arose shortly after their marriage, and which grew into quarrels and threats of separation, and finally into an open break between them. Nor did he receive at school the discipline and sympathy he needed. He took little interest in any study except English; and after he entered high school, in 1913, his attendance was interrupted to allow his going on an extended trip with his mother to the family plantation on an island south of Cuba. He made another trip with his mother (to California and British Columbia) in 1916. On their return his parents were divorced, and he dropped out of school for good. For a short time he was a clerk in a picture store, and then he went to New York, where he hoped to find work and to make his name as a poet.

He had been writing verse from his twelfth year, and in 1915 he had his first poem published—in *Bruno's Bohemia*, a Greenwich Village magazine. This led him to declare his intention of becoming a poet, and his father, alarmed and worried at this decision, sought advice from Mrs. William Vaughn Moody. She counseled moderation in dealing with the boy, and getting in touch with him, she gave him encouragement and advice.

In New York he was joined shortly by his mother, who persuaded him to start tutoring for entrance to Columbia, but he soon gave this up and sought work. Since he had supported his mother in his parents' quarrel, his father refused him any help unless he would work in the family business. Crane, therefore, struggled to survive in New York on the pittance he was able to earn and what small sums his mother could give him; but in May, 1918, being desperately in need, he returned to Cleveland. He worked in turn in a munitions factory, as a riveter in a shipyard, and as a reporter on the Cleveland *Plain Dealer*. Another attempt to gain a foothold in New York also failed, and obsessed by poverty and worry, finally in November, 1918, he went to work for his father. He was given the most menial tasks to do, possibly with the idea of having the nonsense about poetry knocked out of his head, but he bore this discipline with reasonable tranquillity till April, 1921, when some petty effort of his father's to discipline him led to a violent quarrel and to his quitting the candy business forever.

For some months his search for work was unfruitful, and he had to rely for support on his mother; then he found a job with an advertising agency and worked there for fifteen months before resigning to try his luck again in New York. From March, 1923, when he took up residence in New York, till shortly before his death, his life became a succession of attempts to resolve his two opposed needs: to make a living and to find time to write. He was maladjusted; times were bad; and whatever job he found soon proved so distasteful that he gave it up. He accepted what help his mother could give him, or borrowed money from his friends or was cared for by them. Meanwhile, intoxication and sex aberrations so weakened his faculties that the effort to create became a burden, and for the first time he began to doubt his own abilities. Then towards the end of 1925 the banker Otto Kahn assisted him with a loan of $2,000, which for a while relieved his financial troubles; and a stay at his mother's plantation on the Isle of Pines renewed his creative faculties. But a hurricane destroyed his house, and he returned to New York to the old round of dissipations and frustrations. In December, 1928, having inherited some money from his grandmother, he went to Europe for six months. In 1930 he received the Helen Haire Levinson Prize from *Poetry*, and the next year he was awarded a Guggenheim Fellowship. Since this Fellowship required him to live outside the United States, he chose to go to Mexico for the year. While he was away, his father died, leaving him well provided for; then came word that the estate was being sued, making it necessary that he return home. He had accomplished nothing till shortly before he left Mexico, when he wrote "The Broken Tower" and sent it off to his friends. Though they recognized this poem as in his best vein, they did not write him at once, and he left Mexico believing the poem a failure and that as a poet he was finished. On the way home he committed suicide by jumping overboard as his ship sailed along the Florida coast on April 26, 1932.

Crane earned his first money for his poetry in January, 1921, when the *Dial* paid him $10 for "My Grandmother's Love Letters." His first volume, *White Buildings*, was published in 1926, and *The Bridge*, the best part of which he had written on the Isle of Pines, in 1930. He made a few dollars by writing articles and reviews, but his total direct earnings from his writings amounted to no more than a few hundred dollars.

Before he died his hair was entirely white, and though his brown eyes were still fine, his face showed the effect of his long dissipations. When he was sober he was charming and thoughtful, but towards the end his manner when he was drunk was such as to indicate symptoms of insanity.

MY GRANDMOTHER'S LOVE LETTERS

There are no stars to-night
But those of memory.
Yet how much room for memory there is
In the loose girdle of soft rain.

There is even room enough
For the letters of my mother's mother,
Elizabeth,
That have been pressed so long
Into a corner of the roof
That they are brown and soft,
And liable to melt as snow.

Over the greatness of such space
Steps must be gentle.
It is all hung by an invisible white hair.
It trembles as birch limbs webbing the air.

And I ask myself:

"Are your fingers long enough to play
Old keys that are but echoes:
Is the silence strong enough
To carry back the music to its source
And back to you again
As though to her?"

Yet I would lead my grandmother by the hand
Through much of what she would not understand;
And so I stumble. And the rain continues on the roof
With such a sound of gently pitying laughter.

1926

PRAISE FOR AN URN

IN MEMORIAM: ERNEST NELSON

It was a kind and northern face
That mingled in such exile guise
The everlasting eyes of Pierrot
And, of Gargantua, the laughter.

His thoughts, delivered to me
From the white coverlet and pillow,
I see now, were inheritances—
Delicate riders of the storm.

The slant moon on the slanting hill
Once moved us toward presentiments
Of what the dead keep, living still,
And such assessments of the soul

As, perched in the crematory lobby,
The insistent clock commented on,
Touching as well upon our praise
Of glories proper to the time.

Still, having in mind gold hair,
I cannot see that broken brow
And miss the dry sound of bees
Stretching across a lucid space.

Scatter these well-meant idioms
Into the smoky spring that fills
The suburbs, where they will be lost.
They are no trophies of the sun.

1926

CHAPLINESQUE

We make our meek adjustments,
Contented with such random consolations
As the wind deposits
In slithered and too ample pockets.

For we can still love the world, who find
A famished kitten on the step, and know
Recesses for it from the fury of the street,
Or warm torn elbow coverts.

We will sidestep, and to the final smirk
Dally the doom of that inevitable thumb
That slowly chafes its puckered index toward us,
Facing the dull squint with what innocence
And what surprise!

And yet these fine collapses are not lies
More than the pirouettes of any pliant cane;
Our obsequies are, in a way, no enterprise.
We can evade you, and all else but the heart:
What blame to us if the heart live on.

The game enforces smirks; but we have seen
The moon in lonely alleys make
A grail of laughter of an empty ash can,
And through all sound of gaiety and quest
Have heard a kitten in the wilderness.

1926

NORTH LABRADOR

A land of leaning ice
Hugged by plaster-grey arches of sky,
Flings itself silently
Into eternity.

"Has no one come here to win you,
Or left you with the faintest blush
Upon your glittering breasts?
Have you no memories, O Darkly Bright?"

Cold-hushed, there is only the shifting of moments
That journey toward no Spring—
No birth, no death, no time nor sun
In answer.

1926

From VOYAGES

I

Above the fresh ruffles of the surf
Bright striped urchins flay each other with sand.
They have contrived a conquest for shell shucks,
And their fingers crumble fragments of baked weed
Gaily digging and scattering.

And in answer to their treble interjections
The sun beats lightning on the waves,
The waves fold thunder on the sand;
And could they hear me I would tell them:

O brilliant kids, frisk with your dog,
Fondle your shells and sticks, bleached
By time and the elements; but there is a line
You must not cross nor ever trust beyond it
Spry cordage of your bodies to caresses
Too lichen-faithful from too wide a breast.
The bottom of the sea is cruel.

V

Meticulous, past midnight in clear rime,
Infrangible and lonely, smooth as though cast
Together in one merciless white blade—
The bay estuaries fleck the hard sky limits.

—As if too brittle or too clear to touch!
The cables of our sleep so swiftly filed,
Already hang, shred ends from remembered stars.
One frozen tractless smile . . . What words
Can strangle this deaf moonlight? For we

Are overtaken. Now no cry, no sword
Can fasten or deflect this tidal wedge,
Slow tyranny of moonlight, moonlight loved
And changed . . . "There's

Nothing like this in the world," you say,
Knowing I cannot touch your hand and look
Too, into that godless cleft of sky
Where nothing turns but dead sands flashing.

"—And never to quite understand!" No,
In all the argosy of your bright hair I dreamed
Nothing so flagless as this piracy.

But now
Draw in your head, alone and too tall here.
Your eyes already in the slant of drifting foam;
Your breath sealed by the ghosts I do not know:
Draw in your head and sleep the long way home.

VI

Where icy and bright dungeons lift
Of swimmers their lost morning eyes,
And ocean rivers, churning, shift
Green borders under stranger skies,

Steadily as a shell secretes
Its beating leagues of monotone,
Or as many waters trough the sun's
Red kelson past the cape's wet stone;

O rivers mingling toward the sky
And harbor of the phœnix' breast—
My eyes pressed black against the prow,
—Thy derelict and blinded guest

Waiting, afire, what name, unspoke,
I cannot claim: let thy waves rear
More savage than the death of kings,
Some splintered garland for the seer.

Beyond siroccos harvesting
The solstice thunders, crept away,
Like a cliff swinging or a sail
Flung into April's inmost day—

Creation's blithe and petalled word
To the lounged goddess when she rose
Conceding dialogue with eyes
That smile unsearchable repose—

Still fervid covenant, Belle Isle,
—Unfolded floating dais before
Which rainbows twine continual hair—
Belle Isle, white echo of the oar!

The imaged Word, it is, that holds
Hushed willows anchored in its glow.
It is the unbetrayable reply
Whose accent no farewell can know.

1926

TO BROOKLYN BRIDGE

How many dawns, chill from his rippling rest
The seagull's wings shall dip and pivot him,
Shedding white rings of tumult, building high
Over the chained bay waters Liberty—

Then, with inviolate curve, forsake our eyes
As apparitional as sails that cross
Some page of figures to be filed away;
—Till elevators drop us from our day . . .

I think of cinemas, panoramic sleights
With multitudes bent toward some flashing scene
Never disclosed, but hastened to again,
Foretold to other eyes on the same screen;

And Thee, across the harbor, silver-paced
As though the sun took step of thee, yet left
Some motion ever unspent in thy stride,—
Implicitly thy freedom staying thee!

Out of some subway scuttle, cell or loft
A bedlamite speeds to thy parapets,
Tilting there momently, shrill shirt ballooning,
A jest falls from the speechless caravan.

Down Wall, from girder into street noon leaks,
A rip-tooth of the sky's acetylene;
All afternoon the cloud-flown derricks turn . . .
Thy cables breathe the North Atlantic still.

And obscure as that heaven of the Jews,
Thy guerdon . . . Accolade thou dost bestow
Of anonymity time cannot raise:
Vibrant reprieve and pardon thou dost show.

O harp and altar, of the fury fused,
(How could mere toil align thy choiring strings!)
Terrific threshold of the prophet's pledge,
Prayer of pariah, and the lover's cry,—

Again the traffic lights that skim thy swift
Unfractioned idiom, immaculate sigh of stars,
Beading thy path—condense eternity:
And we have seen night lifted in thine arms.

Under thy shadow by the piers I waited;
Only in darkness is thy shadow clear.
The City's fiery parcels all undone,
Already snow submerges an iron year . . .

O Sleepless as the river under thee,
Vaulting the sea, the prairies' dreaming sod,
Unto us lowliest sometime sweep, descend
And of the curveship lend a myth to God.

1930

KEY WEST

Here has my salient faith annealed me.
Out of the valley, past the ample crib
To skies impartial, that do not disown me
Nor claim me, either, by Adam's spine—nor rib.

The oar plash, and the meteorite's white arch
Concur with wrist and bicep. In the moon
That now has sunk I strike a single march
To heaven or hades—to an equally frugal noon.

Because these millions reap a dead conclusion
Need I presume the same fruit of my bone
As draws them towards a doubly mocked confusion
Of apish nightmares into steel-strung stone?

O, steel and stone! But gold was, scarcity before.
And here is water, and a little wind. . . .
There is no breath of friends and no more shore
Where gold has not been sold and conscience tinned.

1933

ROYAL PALM

FOR GRACE HART CRANE

Green rustlings, more than regal charities
Drift coolly from that tower of whispered light.
Amid the noontide's blazed asperities
I watched the sun's most gracious anchorite

Climb up as by communings, year on year
Uneaten of the earth or aught earth holds,
And the grey trunk, that's elephantine, rear
Its frondings sighing in ætherial folds.

Forever fruitless, and beyond that yield
Of sweat the jungle presses with hot love
And tendril till our deathward breath is sealed—
It grazes the horizons, launched above

Mortality—ascending emerald-bright,
A fountain at salute, a crown in view—
Unshackled, casual of its azured height
As though it soared suchwise through heaven too.

1933

THE HURRICANE

Lo, Lord, Thou ridest!
Lord, Lord, Thy swifting heart

Naught stayeth, naught now bideth
But's smithereened apart!

Ay! Scripture flee'th stone!
Milk-bright, Thy chisel wind

Rescindeth flesh from bone
To quivering whittlings thinned—

Swept—whistling straw! Battered,
Lord, e'en boulders now out-leap

Rock sockets, levin-lathered!
Nor, Lord, may worm out-deep

Thy drum's gambade, its plunge abscond!
Lord God, while summits crashing

Whip sea-kelp screaming on blond
Sky-seethe, high heaven dashing—

Thou ridest to the door, Lord!
Thou bidest wall nor floor, Lord!

1933

TO EMILY DICKINSON

You who desired so much—in vain to ask—
Yet fed your hunger like an endless task,
Dared dignify the labor, bless the quest—
Achieved that stillness ultimately best,

Being, of all, least sought for: Emily, hear!
O sweet, dead Silencer, most suddenly clear
When singing that Eternity possessed
And plundered momently in every breast;

—Truly no flower yet withers in your hand,
The harvest you descried and understand
Needs more than wit to gather, love to bind.
Some reconcilement of remotest mind—

Leaves Ormus rubyless, and Ophir chill.
Else tears heap all within one clay-cold hill.

1933

THE PHANTOM BARK

So dream thy sails, O phantom bark
That I thy drowned man may speak again
Perhaps as once Will Collins spoke the lark,
And leave me half a-dream upon the main.

For who shall lift head up to funnel smoke,
And who trick back the leisured winds again
As they were fought—and wooed? They now but stoke
Their vanity, and dream no land in vain.

Of old there was a promise, and thy sails
Have kept no faith but wind, the cold stream
—The hot fickle wind, the breath of males
Imprisoned never, no not soot or rain.

1933

OLD SONG

Thine absence overflows the rose,—
From every petal gleam
Such words as it were vain to close,
Such tears as crowd the dream

So eyes that mind thee fair and gone,
Bemused at waking, spend

On skies that gild thy remote dawn
  More hopes than here attend.

The burden on the rose will fade
  Sped in the spectrum's kiss.
But here the thorn in sharpened shade
  Weathers all loneliness.

1933

called "inverted Sandburg" - is pessimistic, plays down American people

Kenneth Fearing

Kenneth Flexner Fearing was born in Oak Park, Illinois, July 28, 1902. After his graduation from high school, he attended the University of Illinois, and from there transferred to the University of Wisconsin as a junior in 1922. He was graduated in 1924, and in that year was awarded the William F. Vilas Prize for Essays.

After graduation he worked as salesman, millhand, free-lance writer, and newspaper reporter. For a time he was a writer for the Chicago *Herald and Examiner*, and he also wrote for the pulp magazines. He finally gravitated to New York, where for a while he taught poetry at the League of American Writers, and contributed book reviews and poems to the *New Masses*, the *Nation*, the *New Republic*, the *New Yorker*, and *Poetry: a Magazine of Verse*. In 1940 he was awarded the Guarantors Prize by *Poetry*. He was also twice awarded a Guggenheim Fellowship.

His first book of poems, *Angel Arms*, was published in 1929, and he has since published *Poems* (1935), *Dead Reckoning* (1938), and *Collected Poems* (1940). He has also written a novel, *The Hospital* (1939), based on events during twenty-four hours at St. Vincent's Hospital, where his wife is a social worker; and two mystery tales—*Dagger of the Mind* (1941) and *Clark Gifford's Body* (1942).

In 1933 he married Rachel Meltzer, and they have one son, Bruce. For some years he has resided in New York City.

CULTURAL NOTES

Professor Burke's symphony, "Colorado Vistas,"
In four movements,
I Mountains, II Canyons, III Dusk, IV Dawn,

Was played recently by the Philharmonic.
Snapshots of the localities described in music were passed around and the audience checked for accuracy.
All O.K.
After the performance Maurice Epstein, 29, tuberculosis, stoker on the S.S. *Tarboy*, rose to his feet and shouted,
"He's crazy, them artists are all crazy,
I can prove it by Max Nordau. They poison the minds of young girls."
Otto Svoboda, 500 Avenue A, butcher, Pole, husband, philosopher, argued in rebuttal,
"Shut your trap, you.
The question is, does the symphony fit in with Karl Marx?"

At the Friday evening meeting of the Browning Writing League,
Mrs. Whittamore Ralston-Beckett,
Traveler, lecturer, novelist, critic, poet, playwright, editor, mother, idealist,
Fascinated her audience with a brief talk, whimsical and caustic,
Appealing to the younger generation to take a brighter, happier, more sunny and less morbid view of life's eternal fundamentals.
Mrs. Ralston-Beckett quoted Sir Henry Parke-Bennett: "O Beauty," she said,
"Take your fingers off my throat, take your elbow out of my eye,
Take your sorrow off my sorrow,
Take your hat, take your gloves, take your feet down off the table,
Take your beauty off my beauty, and go."
In the open discussion that followed, Maurice Epstein, 29, tuberculosis, stoker on the S.S. *Tarboy*, arose and queried the speaker,
"Is it true, as certain scientists assert, that them artists are all of them crazy?"
A Mr. Otto Svoboda present spoke in reply,
"Shut your trap, you. The question is, what about Karl Marx?"

1929

EVENING SONG

Go to sleep, McKade;
Fold up the day, it was a bright scarf;
Put it away;
Take yourself apart like a house of cards.

It is time to be a gray mouse under a tall building;
Go there; go there now.
Look at the huge nails; run behind the pipes;
Scamper in the walls;
Crawl toward the beckoning girl, her breasts are warm.
But here is a dead man. A lunatic?
Kill him with your pistol. Creep past him to the girl.

Sleep, McKade;
Throw one arm across the bed; wind your watch;
You are a gentleman, and important;
Yawn; go to sleep.

The continent, turning from the sun, is dark and quiet;
Your ticker waits for tomorrow morning,
And you are alive now;
It will be a long time before they put McKade under the sod.
Sometime, but not now.
Sometime, though. Sometime, for certain.

Take apart your brain,
Close the mouths in it that have been hungry, they are fed for
 a while,
Go to sleep, you are a gentleman, McKade, alive and sane, a
 gentleman of position.
Tip your hat to the lady;
Speak to the mayor;
You are a friend of the mayor's, are you not?
True, a friend of the mayor's.
And you met the Queen of Rumania? True.

Then go to sleep;
Be a dog sleeping in the old sun;
Be an animal dreaming in the old sun, beside a Roman road;
Be a dog lying in the meadow, watching soldiers pass;

Follow the girl who beckons to you;
Run from the man with the dagger; it can split your bones;
Be terrified of strangers, and the sea, and of great height;
Forget it, then; curl up and dream in the old sun that warms
    Manhattan.
Sleep, McKade.
Yawn. Go to sleep.

1929

RESURRECTION

You will remember the kisses, real or imagined;
You will remember the faces that were before you, and the words
    exchanged;
You will remember the minute crowded with meaning, the moment of pain, the aimless hour;
You will remember the cities, and the plains, and the mountains,
    and the sea,

And recall the friendly voice of the killer, or the voice of the
    priest, inhumanly sweet;
Recall the triumphant smile of the duped;
You will not forget compassion that glittered in the eyes of the
    money-lender, refusing you, not forget the purpose that lay
    beneath the merchant's warmth;
You will not forget the voice of the bought magistrate quivering
    in horror through the courtroom above prostitute and pimp,
The majesty of the statesman at the microphone, the sober majesty of the listening clerk,
The face of the fool, radiant on newspaper and screen;

You will remember hope that crawled up the bar-room tap and
    spoke through the confident speech of the lost,
Happiness clearly displayed on the glaring billboards,
Love casually revealed in the magazines and novels, or stated in
    the trembling limbs of ancient millionaires;
You will remember the triumph easily defined by the rebel
    messiah, by the breadloaf in the hand of the ghetto wife,
    by the inscription on the patriot tomb;
You will remember your laughter that rose with the steam from
    the carcass on the street
In hatred and pity exactly matched.

These are the things that will return to you,
To mingle with the days and nights, with the sound of motors and the sun's warmth,
With fatigue and desire,
As you work, and sleep, and talk, and laugh, and die.

1935

NO CREDIT

Whether dinner was pleasant, with the windows lit by gunfire, and no one disagreed; or whether, later, we argued in the park, and there was a touch of vomit-gas in the evening air;
Whether we found a greater, deeper, more perfect love, by courtesy of Camels, over NBC; whether the comics amused us, or the newspapers carried a hunger death and a White House prayer for mother's day;
Whether the bills were paid or not, whether or not we had our doubts, whether we spoke our minds at Joe's, and the receipt said "Not Returnable," and the cash-register rang up "No Sale,"
Whether the truth was then, or later, or whether the best had already gone—

Nevertheless, we know; as every turn is measured; as every unavoidable risk is known;
As nevertheless, the flesh grows old, dies, dies in its only life, is gone;
The reflection goes from the mirror; as the shadow, of even a rebel, is gone from the wall;
As nevertheless, the current is thrown and the wheels revolve; and nevertheless, as the word is spoken and the wheat grows tall and the ships sail on—

None but the fool is paid in full; none but the broker, none but the scab is certain of profit;
The sheriff alone may attend a third degree in formal attire; alone, the academy artists multiply in dignity as trooper's bayonet guards the door;
Only Steve, the side-show robot, knows content; only Steve, the mechanical man in love with a photo-electric beam, remains aloof; only Steve, who sits and smokes or stands in salute, is secure;

Steve, whose shoebutton eyes are blind to terror, whose painted ears are deaf to appeal, whose welded breast will never be slashed by bullets, whose armature soul can hold no fear.

1935

LULLABY

Wide as this night, old as this night is old and young as it is young, still as this, strange as this;
Filled as this night is filled with the light of a moon as gray;
Dark as these trees, heavy as this scented air from the fields, warm as this hand;
As warm, as strong;

Is the night that wraps all the huts of the south and folds the empty barns of the west;
Is the wind that fans the roadside fire;
Are the trees that line the country estates, tall as the lynch trees, as straight, as black;
Is the moon that lights the mining towns, dim as the light upon tenement roofs, gray upon the hands at the bars of Moabit, cold as the bars of the Tombs.

1935

TWENTIETH-CENTURY BLUES

What do you call it, bobsled champion, and you, too, Olympic roller-coaster ace,
High-diving queen, what is the word,
Number one man on the Saturday poker squad, motion-picture star incognito as a home girl, life of the party or you, the serious type, what is it, what is it,

When it's just like a fever shooting up and up and up but there are no chills and there is no fever,
Just exactly like a song, like a knockout, like a dream, like a book,

What is the word, when you know that all the lights of all the cities of all the world are burning bright as day, and you know that some time they all go out for you,
Or your taxi rolls and rolls through streets made of velvet, what

is the feeling, what is the feeling when the radio never ends, but the hour, the swift, the electric, the invisible hour does not stop and does not turn,
What does it mean, when the get-away money burns in dollars big as moons, but where is there to go that's just exactly right,
What have you won, plunger, when the 20-to-1 comes in; what have you won, salesman, when the dotted line is signed; irresistible lover, when her eyelids flutter shut at last, what have you really, finally won;
And what is gone soldier, soldier, step-and-a-half marine who saw the whole world; hot-tip addict, what is always just missed; picker of crumbs, how much has been lost, denied, what are all the things destroyed,
Question mark, question mark, question mark, question mark,
And you, fantasy Frank, and dreamworld Dora and hallucination Harold, and delusion Dick, and nightmare Ned,

What is it, how do you say it, what does it mean, what's the word,
That miracle thing, the thing that can't be so, quote, unquote, but just the same it's true,
That third-rail, million-volt exclamation mark, that ditto, ditto, ditto,
That stop, stop, go.

1935

MEMO

Is there still any shadow there, on the rainwet window of the coffee pot,
Between the haberdasher's and the pinball arcade,
There, where we stood one night in the warm, fine rain, and smoked and laughed and talked.

Is there now any sound at all,
Other than the sound of tires, and motors, and hurrying feet,
Is there on tonight's damp, heelpocked pavement somewhere the mark of a certain toe, an especial nail, or the butt of a particular dropped cigarette?—

(There must be, there has to be, no heart could beat if this were not so,

That was an hour, a glittering hour, an important hour in a tremendous year)

Where we talked for a while of life and love, of logic and the senses, of you and of me, character and fate, pain, revolution, victory and death,

Is there tonight any shadow, at all,
Other than the shadows that stop for a moment and then hurry past the windows blurred by the same warm, slow, still rain?

1938

DEVIL'S DREAM

But it could never be true;
How could it ever happen, if it never did before, and it's not so now?

But suppose that the face behind those steel prison bars—
Why do you dream about a face lying cold in the trenches streaked with rain and dirt and blood?
Is it the very same face seen so often in the mirror?
Just as though it could be true—

But what if it is, what if it is, what if it is, what if the thing that cannot happen really happens just the same,
Suppose the fever goes a hundred, then a hundred and one,
What if Holy Savings Trust goes from 98 to 88 to 78 to 68, then drops down to 28 and 8 and out of sight,
And the fever shoots a hundred two, a hundred three, a hundred four, then a hundred five and out?

But now there's only the wind and the sky and sunlight and the clouds,
With everyday people walking and talking as they always have before along the everyday street,
Doing ordinary things with ordinary faces and ordinary voices in the ordinary way,
Just as they always will—

Then why does it feel like a bomb, why does it feel like a target,
Like standing on the gallows with the trap about to drop,

Why does it feel like a thunderbolt the second before it strikes,
why does it feel like a tight-rope walk high over hell?

Because it is not, will not, never could be true
That the whole wide, bright, green, warm, calm world goes:
CRASH.

1938

TOMORROW

Now that the others are gone, all of them, forever,
And they have your answer, and you have theirs, and the decision is made,
And the river of minutes between you widens to a tide of hours, a flood of days, a gulf of years and a sea of silence;

If, now, there are any questions you would like to ask of the shapes that still move and speak inaudibly in the empty room,
If there are any different arrangements you would like to suggest,

Make them to the riverboats, whose echoing whistle will be a clear reply,
Speak to the seagulls, their effortless flight will provide any answer you may wish to hear,
Ask the corner chestnut vendor, ask the tireless hammer and pulse of the subway,
Speak to the family on the illuminated billboard, forever friendly, or to the wind, or to the sign that sways and creaks above the stationer's door.

1938

REQUIEM

Will they stop,
Will they stand there for a moment, perhaps before some shop where you have gone so many times
(Stand with the same blue sky above them and the stones, so often walked, beneath)

Will it be a day like this—
As though there could be such a day again—

And will their own concerns still be about the same,
And will the feeling still be this that you have felt so many times,
Will they meet and stop and speak, one perplexed and one aloof,

Saying: Have you heard,
Have you heard,
Have you heard about the death?

Yes, choosing the words, tragic, yes, a shock,
One who had so much of this, they will say, a life so filled with that,
Then will one say that the days are growing crisp again, the other that the leaves are turning,
And will they say good-bye, good-bye, you must look me up some time, good-bye,
Then turn and go, each of them thinking, and yet, and yet,

Each feeling, if it were I, instead, would that be all,
Each wondering, suddenly alone, if that is all, in fact—

And will that be all?
On a day like this, with motors streaming through the fresh parks, the streets alive with casual people,
And everywhere, on all of it, the brightness of the sun.

1938

AD

WANTED: Men;
Millions of men are WANTED AT ONCE in a big new field;
NEW, TREMENDOUS, THRILLING, GREAT.

If you've ever been a figure in the chamber of horrors,
If you've ever escaped from a psychiatric ward,
If you thrill at the thought of throwing poison into wells, have heavenly visions of people, by the thousands, dying in flames—

YOU ARE THE VERY MAN WE WANT
We mean business and our business is YOU
WANTED: A race of brand-new men.

Apply: Middle Europe;
No skill needed;
No ambition required; no brains wanted and no character allowed;

TAKE A PERMANENT JOB IN THE COMING PROFESSION
Wages: DEATH.

1938

PACT

It is written in the skyline of the city (you have seen it, that bold and accurate inscription), where the gray and gold and soot-black roofs project against the rising or the setting sun,
It is written in the ranges of the farthest mountains, and written by the lightning bolt,
Written, too, in the winding rivers of the prairies, and in the strangely familiar effigies of the clouds,

That there will be other days and remoter times, by far, than these, still more prodigious people and still less credible events,
When there will be a haze, as there is today, not quite blue and not quite purple, upon the river, a green mist upon the valley below, as now,

And we will build, upon that day, another hope (because these cities are young and strong),
And we will raise another dream (because these hills and fields are rich and green),

And we will fight for all of this again, and if need be again,
And on that day, and in that place, we will try again, and this time we shall win.

1940

HOMAGE

They said to him, "It is a very good thing that you have done, yes, both good and great, proving this other passage to the Indies. Marvelous," they said. "Very. But where, Señor, is the gold?"

They said: "We like it, we admire it very much, don't misunderstand us, in fact we think it's almost great. But isn't there, well, a little too much of this Prince of Denmark? After all, there is no one quite like you in your lighter vein."
"Astonishing," they said. "Who would have thought you had it in you, Orville?" They said, "Wilbur, this machine of yours is amazing, if it works, and perhaps some day we can use it to distribute eggs, or to advertise."

And they were good people, too. Decent people.
They did not beat their wives. They went to church. And they kept the law.

1940

ANY MAN'S ADVICE TO HIS SON

If you have lost the radio beam, then guide yourself by the sun or the stars.
(By the North Star at night, and in daytime by the compass and the sun.)
Should the sky be overcast and there are neither stars nor a sun, then steer by dead reckoning.
If the wind and direction and speed are not known, then trust to your wits and your luck.

Do you follow me? Do you understand? Or is this too difficult to learn?
But you must and you will, it is important that you do,
Because there may be troubles even greater than these that I have said.

Because, remember this: Trust no man fully.
Remember: If you must shoot at another man squeeze, do not jerk the trigger. Otherwise you may miss and die, yourself, at the hand of some other man's son.
And remember: In all this world there is nothing so easily squandered, or once gone, so completely lost as life.

I tell you this because I remember you when you were small,
And because I remember all your monstrous infant boasts and lies,

And the way you smiled, and how you ran and climbed, as no one else quite did, and how you fell and were bruised,
And because there is no other person, anywhere on earth, who remembers these things as clearly as I do now.

1940

A LA CARTE

Some take to liquor, some turn to prayer,
Many prefer to dance, others to gamble, and a few resort to gas or the gun.
(Some are lucky, and some are not.)

Name your choice, any selection from one to twenty-five:
Music from Harlem? A Viennese waltz on the slot-machine phonograph at Jack's Bar & Grill? Or a Brahms Concerto over WXV?
(Many like it wild, others sweet.)

Champagne for supper, murder for breakfast, romance for lunch and terror for tea,
This is not the first time, nor will it be the last time the world has gone to hell.
(Some can take it, and some cannot.)

1940

PAY-OFF

Do you, now, as the news becomes known,
And you have the telegram still in your hand, here in the familiar room where there is no sound but the ticking of the clock,
Or there on the street, where you see the first headlines, and it is true this time, really true, actual as the green and red of the traffic lights, as real as the fruit vendor's rhythmic cry,

Do you recall any being other than this, before your world suddenly shook and settled to this new, strange axis upon which it will turn, now, always while you live?
Does it seem possible, now, you were ever bored? Or drunk and confident? Or sober and afraid?
Will the sound of the clock ever fade, or the voice of the vendor sometime stop?

1940

Bibliographies

The English and Irish Poets

THOMAS HARDY

A. POETICAL WORKS

Wessex Poems and Other Verses. With 30 Illustrations by the Author. N. Y. and London: Harper & Brothers. 1898. xi, 228 pp.

Poems of the Past and the Present. [N. Y. and London: Harper & Brothers, 1902.] xi, 260 pp.

The Dynasts. A Drama of the Napoleonic Wars, in Three Parts, Nineteen Acts, & One Hundred and Thirty Scenes. Part First. London: Macmillan & Co., Ltd.; N. Y.: The Macmillan Co., 1904. xxii, 228 pp. Part Second. London: Macmillan & Co., Ltd.; N. Y.: The Macmillan Co., 1906. xiii [304] pp. Part Third. London: Macmillan & Co., Ltd., 1908. xiii, 356 pp.

The Pocket Thomas Hardy: Being Selections from the Wessex Novels and Poems of Thomas Hardy. Made by A. H. Hyatt. London: Chatto & Windus, 1906. 312 pp.

Time's Laughingstocks and Other Verses. London: Macmillan & Co., Ltd., 1909. x [208] pp.

Satires of Circumstance: Lyrics and Reveries, with Miscellaneous Pieces. London: Macmillan & Co., Ltd., 1914. ix, 230 pp.

Song of the Soldiers. [Privately printed for Clement Shorter, London, 1914. 8 pp.] (12 copies.)

Before Marching and After. [Privately printed for Clement Shorter, London, 1915.] (25 copies.)

The Oxen. [Privately printed, 1915. 4 pp.]

Selected Poems. [Golden Treasury Series.] London: Macmillan & Co., Ltd., 1916. ix, 214 pp. (Also N. Y.: The Macmillan Co., 1927.) (The same, Edited with an Introduction by G. M. Young. N. Y.: The Macmillan Co., 1940. 204 pp.)

Domicilium. [Privately printed for Clement Shorter at the Chiswick Press. London, 1916. 7 pp.] (25 copies.)

In Time of "The Breaking of Nations." [Privately printed for Clement Shorter, London, 1916. 8 pp.] (25 copies.)

To Shakespeare after Three Hundred Years. [Privately printed for Florence Emily Hardy at the Chiswick Press. London, 1916. 6 pp.] (50 copies.)

When I Weekly Knew. [Privately printed for Florence Emily Hardy, London, 1916. 5 pp.] (25 copies.)

Moments of Vision and Miscellaneous Verses. London: Macmillan & Co., Ltd., 1917. xi, 256 pp.

The Fiddler's Story. A Jingle on the Times. [Privately printed for Florence Emily Hardy at the Chiswick Press, London, 1917. 8 pp.] (25 copies.)

A Call to National Service. An Appeal to America. Cry of the Homeless. [Privately printed for Florence Emily Hardy at the Chiswick Press, London, 1917. 8 pp.] (25 copies.)

England to Germany. The Pity of It. I Met a Man. A New Year's Eve in War Time. [Privately printed for Florence Emily Hardy at the Chiswick Press, London, 1917.] (25 copies.)

Jezreel. The Master and the Leaves. [Privately printed for Florence Emily Hardy at the Chiswick Press, London, 1919.] (25 copies.)

Collected Poems. London: Macmillan & Co., Ltd., 1919. xx, 521 pp. (New edition, London: Macmillan & Co., Ltd., 1928. 840 pp. Another new edition, London: Macmillan & Co., Ltd., 1932. xxxi, 917 pp. New Complete American Edition, N. Y.: The Macmillan Co., 1926. 818 pp. *Collected Poems* (1919) the same as Volume One of *The Poetical Works of Thomas Hardy*, London: Macmillan & Co., 1919, the second volume being *The Dynasts*, London: Macmillan & Co., Ltd., 1921. xxi, 525 pp.).

"And There Was a Great Calm." [Privately printed for Florence Emily Hardy at the Chiswick Press, London, 1920?] (25 copies.)

Selected Poems. With Portrait and Title-Page Design Engraved on the Wood by William Nicholson. London: P. Lee Warner, 1921. 154 pp.

Late Lyrics and Earlier, with Many Other Verses. London: Macmillan & Co., Ltd., 1922. xxiv, 288 pp.

Haunting Fingers. Voices from Things Growing. [Privately printed for Florence Emily Hardy at the Chiswick Press, London, 1922.] (25 copies.)

The Famous Tragedy of the Queen of Cornwall at Tintagel in Lyonnesse. A New Version of an Old Story. Arranged as a Play for Mummers. In One Act. Requiring No Theatre or Scenery. London: Macmillan & Co., Ltd., 1923. [77 pp.] (Also N. Y.: The Macmillan Co., 1923.)

Compassion. An Ode in Celebration of the Centenary of the Royal Society for the Prevention of Cruelty to Animals. [Privately printed for A. J. A. Symons, London, 1924.] (50 copies.)

Human Shows; Far Phantasies; Songs, and Trifles. London: Macmillan & Co., Ltd., 1925. x, 279 pp. (Also N. Y.: The Macmillan Co., 1925.)

Yuletide in a Younger World. Drawings by Albert Rutherston. [Ariel Poems, No. 1.] London: Faber & Gwyer [1927. 4 pp.]

Winter Words in Various Moods and Metres. London: Macmillan & Co., Ltd., 1928. xi, 202 pp. (Also N. Y.: The Macmillan Co., 1928. 184 pp.)

B. SELECTED REFERENCES

ABERCROMBIE, LASCELLES. *Thomas Hardy. A Critical Study.* London. Martin Secker, 1912. [225 pp.]

CHEW, SAMUEL C. *Thomas Hardy. Poet and Novelist* [Bryn Mawr Notes and Monographs. III.] Bryn Mawr: Bryn Mawr College: N. Y., London [etc.]: Longmans, Green & Co., 1921. 257 pp. (Revised edition, N. Y.: Alfred A. Knopf, 1928.)

HARDY, FLORENCE EMILY. *The Early Life of Thomas Hardy, 1840-1891. . . .* London: Macmillan & Co., Ltd., 1928. 328 pp. (Also N. Y.: The Macmillan Co., 1928. 327 pp.)

HARDY, FLORENCE EMILY. *The Later Years of Thomas Hardy, 1892-1928.* London: Macmillan & Co., Ltd., 1930. 289 pp. (Also N. Y.: The Macmillan Co., 1930. xi, 289 pp.)

HOLLAND, CLIVE [*pseud.*] *Thomas Hardy. The Man, His Works, and the Land of Wessex.* London: Herbert Jenkins, Ltd., 1933. 320 pp.

JOHNSON, LIONEL. *The Art of Thomas Hardy.* [New Edition.] To Which Is Added a Chapter on the Poetry by J. E. Barton and a Bibliography by John Lane together with a New Portrait by Vernon Hill and the Etched Portrait by William Strang. London: John Lane, 1923. 357 pp.

MACDOWALL, ARTHUR S. *Thomas Hardy. A Critical Study.* London: Faber & Faber, Ltd. [1931]. [284 pp.]

A *Thomas Hardy Dictionary.* The Characters and Scenes of the Novels and Poems Alphabetically Arranged and Described. By F. Outwin Saxelby. London: George Routledge & Sons, Ltd.; N. Y.: E. P. Dutton & Co.; Toronto: Musson Book Co., Ltd., 1911. 238 pp.

WEBER, CARL J. *Centennial Bibliography of Hardiana.* Waterville, Maine: Colby College Library, 1942. 276 pp.

GERARD MANLEY HOPKINS

A. POETICAL WORKS

Poems, Now First Published. Edited with Notes by Robert Bridges. London: Oxford University Press, 1919. 124 pp. (A second edition, with additional poems and an introduction by Charles Williams, appeared in 1930.)

See also the early poems published in *The Note-Books and Papers of Gerard Manley Hopkins,* listed below.

B. SELECTED REFERENCES

Abbott, Claude C., editor. *The Letters of Gerard Manley Hopkins to Robert Bridges.* London: Oxford University Press, 1935. 322 pp.

Abbott, Claude C., editor. *The Correspondence of Gerard Manley Hopkins and Richard Watson Dixon.* London: Oxford University Press, 1935. 192 pp.

Abbott, Claude C., editor. *Further Letters of Gerard Manley Hopkins, Including His Correspondence with Coventry Patmore.* London: Oxford University Press, 1938. 298 pp.

House, Humphrey, editor. *The Note-Books and Papers of Gerard Manley Hopkins.* London: Oxford University Press, 1937. 474 pp.

Lahey, G. F. *Gerard Manley Hopkins.* London: Oxford University Press, 1930. 172 pp.

Phare, Elsie Elizabeth [Mrs. Austin Duncan-Jones]. *The Poetry of Gerard Manley Hopkins.* Cambridge: Cambridge University Press, 1933. 150 pp.

ROBERT BRIDGES

A. POETICAL WORKS

Poems. London: B. M. Pickering, 1873. 125 pp.

The Growth of Love. A Poem in Twenty-Four Sonnets. London: E. Bumpus, 1876. 28 pp. (22 copies.) (Enlarged ed. Oxford: H. Daniel, 1889. [79 pp.])

Carmen Elegiacum. London: Edward Bumpus, 1876.

Poems. By the Author of "The Growth of Love." London: E. Bumpus, 1879. 51 pp.

Poems. By the Author of "The Growth of Love." [Third Series.] London: E. Bumpus, 1880. 27 pp.

Prometheus the Firegiver. Oxford: H. Daniel, 1883. 72 pp. (100 copies.)

Poems. Oxford: Printed at the Private Press of H. Daniel, 1884. 52 pp.

Eight Plays. [*Nero I*. (1885), *Palicio* (1890), *Return of Ulysses* (1890), *Christian Captives* (1890), *Achilles in Scyros* (1890), *Humours of the Court* (1893), *Feast of Bacchus* (1894), *Nero II*. (1894). London: George Bell & Sons; E. Bumpus, 1885-94.] 264 pp. (Each play published separately.)

Eros & Psyche . . . [Translated from the Latin of Apuleius.] London: George Bell & Sons [1885]. 158 pp. (Rev. ed., 1894.)

The Feast of Bacchus. Oxford: H. Daniel, 1889. 96 pp.

The Shorter Poems of Robert Bridges. London: George Bell & Sons, 1890. 91 pp. (Enlarged ed., Oxford: Clarendon Press, 1931. 234 pp.)

Eden. An Oratorio . . . Set to Music by C. V. Stanford. London: George Bell & Sons, 1891. 40 pp.

Achilles in Scyros. London: George Bell & Sons, 1892. 68 pp.

Founders Day. A Secular Ode on the Ninth Jubilee of Eton College. Oxford: H. Daniel [1893]. 7 pp.

The Humours of the Court, a Comedy, and Other Poems. N. Y.: The Macmillan Co.; London: George Bell & Sons, 1893. v, 185 pp. (100 copies.)

Ode for the Bicentenary Commemoration of Henry Purcell. With Other Poems and a Preface on the Musical Setting of Poetry. [E. Mathews' Shilling Garland, No. 2. London: E. Mathews, 1896.] 43 pp.

Poetical Works. [6 vols.] London: Smith, Elder & Co., 1898-1905. (The only vol. containing new poems is Vol. II, 1899.)

Now in Wintry Delights. Oxford: H. Daniel, 1903. 23 pp.

Peace Ode Written on the Conclusion of the Three Years' War. [Oxford: H. Daniel, 1903. 8 pp.]

Demeter, a Mask. Oxford: Clarendon Press, 1905. 67 pp.

An Invitation to the Pageant: Ode. [*The Oxford Pageant Book*, pp. 13-15.] Oxford: Horace Hart, 1907.

Poetical Works of Robert Bridges. Excluding the Eight Dramas. London: H. Froude, Oxford University Press, 1912. 472 pp. (New edition, six volumes, Oxford: Oxford University Press, 1930.)

Poems Written in the Year 1913. [Privately printed by St. John Hornby, Ashendene Press, Chelsea, 1914.] 20 pp. (91 copies.)

Ode on the Tercentenary Commemoration of Shakespeare. [Privately printed, 1916.] 4 pp.

Lord Kitchener. [Privately printed for Clement Shorter, London, 1916. 8 pp.] (20 copies.)

Ibant Obscuri: an Experiment in the Classical Hexameter. Oxford: Clarendon Press, 1916. 158 pp.

Britannia Victrix. London: Oxford University Press, 1918. [4 pp.]

October and Other Poems, with Occasional Verses on the War. London: William Heinemann, 1920. xii, 63 pp. (Also N. Y.: Alfred A. Knopf, 1920.)

Poor Poll. [Privately printed at the Oxford University Press, 1923.] 4 pp.

The Tapestry. London: [privately printed], 1925. 43 pp. (150 copies.)

New Verse. Written in 1921 . . . with the Other Poems of That Year and a Few Earlier Pieces. Oxford: Clarendon Press, 1925. viii [89] pp.

The Testament of Beauty. Oxford: Clarendon Press, 1929. 154 pp. (250 copies. Also N. Y.: Oxford University Press, 1930. 183 pp.)

On Receiving Trivia from the Author. [Privately printed at the Mill House Press, 1930. 4 pp.]

Verses Written for Mrs. Daniel. Oxford: Clarendon Press, 1932. 19 pp. (300 copies.)

Selected Poems. London: Faber & Faber, Ltd., 1941. 90 pp.

B. SELECTED REFERENCES

DAVIDSON, EDWARD. *Some Modern Poets* (N. Y., 1928), pp. 79-111.

DE SELINCOURT, ERNEST. *Oxford Lectures on Poetry* (Oxford, 1934), pp. 207-256.

ELTON, OLIVER. *Robert Bridges and The Testament of Beauty.* [Eng. Assn. Pamphlets, No. 83.] London: Oxford University Press, 1932. 15 pp.

GUÉRARD, ALBERT, Jr. *Robert Bridges.* Cambridge: Harvard University Press, 1942. xvi, 332 pp.

HUGHES, MABEL L. V. *Everyman's Testament of Beauty.* London: Student Christian Movement Press, 1932. 188 pp.

KELSHALL, T. M. *Robert Bridges (Poet Laureate).* London: Robert Scott, [1924]. 93 pp.

MCKAY, GEORGE L. *A Bibliography of Robert Bridges.* N. Y.: Columbia University Press, 1933. 215 pp.

SMITH, NOWELL C. *Notes on "The Testament of Beauty."* London: Oxford University Press, 1931. 94 pp.

A. E. HOUSMAN

A. POETICAL WORKS

A Shropshire Lad. London: Kegan Paul & Co., 1896. vii, 96 pp. (A number of subsequent editions, both in England and America. Authorized American Edition, N. Y.: Henry Holt & Co., 1922.)

Last Poems. London: Grant Richards, Ltd., 1922. [79 pp.] (Also N. Y.: Henry Holt & Co., 1922.)

More Poems. [Selected by Laurence Housman.] London: J. Cape, 1936. xiii, 73 pp. (Also N. Y.: Alfred A. Knopf.)

Collected Poems. London: J. Cape, 1939. 264 pp. (Also N. Y.: Henry Holt & Co.)

B. SELECTED REFERENCES

EHRSAM, T. G. *A Bibliography of Alfred Edward Housman.* Boston: F. W. Faxon, 1941. 44 pp.

GARROD, H. W. *The Profession of Poetry* (Oxford, 1929), pp. 211-224.

GOW, A. S. F. *A. E. Housman: A Sketch.* N. Y.: The Macmillan Co., 1936. 137 pp.

HOUSMAN, A. E. *The Name and Nature of Poetry.* Cambridge: Cambridge University Press, 1933. 50 pp.

HOUSMAN, LAURENCE. *The Unexpected Years.* Indianapolis: The Bobbs-Merrill Co., 1936. vii, 338 pp. (An autobiography, but much about the family and A. E. H.)

HOUSMAN, LAURENCE. *A. E. Housman: Some Poems, Some Letters, and A Personal Memoir.* London: J. Cape, 1937. 286 pp.

HYDER, C. K. & PADEN, W. D. *A Concordance to the Poems of A. E. Housman.* Lawrence, Kans.: University of Kansas Press, 1940. 133 pp.

RICHARDS, GRANT. *Housman, 1897-1936.* N. Y.: Oxford University Press, 1942. 493 pp.

SYMONS, KATHERINE, *et al. Alfred Edward Housman:* Recollections . . . Bromsgrove: Bromsgrove School, 1936. 60 pp.

WITHERS, PERCY. *A Buried Life.* London: Jonathan Cape, 1940. 133 pp.

W. B. YEATS

A. POETICAL WORKS

Mosada. A Dramatic Poem. Dublin: Sealy, Bryers & Walker, 1886. 12 pp.

The Wanderings of Oisin and Other Poems. London: K. Paul, Trench & Co., 1889. 156 pp.

The Countess Kathleen: an Irish Drama; and Various Legends and Lyrics. [Cameo Series.] London: T. Fisher Unwin, 1892. 141 pp. (Also Boston: Roberts Brothers, 1893.)

The Land of Heart's Desire. London: T. F. Unwin; Chicago: Stone & Kimball, 1894. 43 pp.

Poems. London: T. F. Unwin; Boston: Copeland & Day, 1895. xi [286 pp.] (A number of later editions of *Poems* published by T. F. Unwin.)

The Wind among the Reeds. London: Elkin Mathews, 1899. vii, 108 pp.

The Shadowy Waters. London: Hodder & Stoughton, 1900. 57 pp. (Also N. Y.: Dodd, Mead & Co., 1901.)

In the Seven Woods. Being Poems Chiefly of the Irish Heroic Age. N. Y.: The Macmillan Co.; London: Macmillan & Co., Ltd., 1903. 87 pp. (Also Dundrum: Dun Emer Press, 1903. 63 pp.)

The King's Threshold. A Play in Verse. N. Y.: [Printed for private circulation, N. Y.: University Press], 1904, 58 pp.

The King's Threshold: and On Baile's Strand. Being Volume Three of Plays for an Irish Theatre. London: A. H. Bullen, 1904. 117 pp.

Poems, 1899-1905. London: A. H. Bullen; Dublin: Maunsel & Co., Ltd., 1906. xv [280] pp.

The Poetical Works of William B. Yeats. In Two Volumes. N. Y.: The Macmillan Co.; London: Macmillan & Co., Ltd., 1906-7.

Deirdre. Being Volume Five of Plays for an Irish Theatre. London: A. H. Bullen; Dublin; Maunsel & Co., Ltd., 1907. [48 pp.]

The Golden Helmet. N. Y.: J. Quinn, 1908. 32 pp.

The Collected Works in Verse and Prose. (8 vols.) Stratford-on-Avon: Shakespeare Head Press, 1908. (Vol. I, *Poems Lyrical and Narrative*, viii, 244 pp.; II, *Plays*, vi, 258 pp.; III, *Plays*, vi, 239 pp.; IV, *Plays in Prose*, vi, 247 pp.; V, *Prose*, x, 261 pp.; VI, *Prose*, vi, 266 pp.; VII, *Prose*, vi, 299 pp.; VIII, *Prose and Bibliography*, vi, 287 pp.)

The Green Helmet and Other Poems. Churchtown, Dundrum: Cuala Press, 1910. 33 pp. (Also N. Y.: The Macmillan Co., 1912. 91 pp.)

Poems Written in Discouragement. [Dundrum, Ireland: Cuala Press, 1913.]

A Selection from the Love Poetry of William Butler Yeats. Dundrum: Cuala Press, 1913. [30 pp.] (400 copies.)

Responsibilities: Poems and a Play. Churchtown, Dundrum, Ireland: Cuala Press, 1914. viii [81 pp.].

Lyric Poems. N. Y.: The Macmillan Co., 1916. 338 pp.

Dramatic Poems. N. Y.: The Macmillan Co., 1916. 478 pp.

Easter, 1916. [Privately printed by Clement Shorter, 1916.] 5 pp. (25 copies.)

Eight Poems. Transcribed by Edward Pay. London: Morland Press, Ltd. [1916. 20 pp.]

Responsibilities and Other Poems. London: Macmillan & Co., Ltd., 1916. vii, 188 pp. (Also N. Y.: The Macmillan Co., 1916.)

The Wild Swans at Coole, Other Verses and a Play in Verse. Churchtown, Dundrum: Cuala Press, 1917. [47 pp.]

Nine Poems. [Privately printed by Clement Shorter, 1918. 15 pp.] (25 copies.)

Two Plays for Dancers. [Churchtown, Dundrum]: Cuala Press, 1919. 38 pp.

The Wild Swans at Coole. London: Macmillan & Co., Ltd., 1919. xi, 114 pp. (Also N. Y.: The Macmillan Co., 1919. [115 pp.])

Michael Robartes and the Dancer. Churchtown, Dundrum: Cuala Press, 1920. [35 pp.]

Four Plays for Dancers. London: Macmillan & Co., Ltd., 1921. xi, 138 pp.

Selected Poems. N. Y.: The Macmillan Co., 1921. 308 pp.

Later Poems. London: Macmillan & Co., Ltd., 1922. xiii, 363 pp. (Also N. Y.: The Macmillan Co., 1924.)

Plays in Prose and Verse. Written for an Irish Theatre, and Generally with the Help of a Friend. London: Macmillan & Co., Ltd., 1922. ix, 447 pp. (Also N. Y.: The Macmillan Co., 1924.)

Seven Poems and a Fragment. Dundrum: Ireland: Cuala Press, 1922. 24 pp.

Plays and Controversies. London: Macmillan & Co., Ltd., 1923. ix, 461 pp. (Both prose and verse.)

The Cat and the Moon and Certain Poems. Dublin: Cuala Press, 1924. 41 pp. (500 copies.)

The Lake Isle of Innisfree. . . . [With facsimile in Yeats's handwriting. San Francisco: J. H. Nash, 1924. 8 pp.]

Early Poems and Stories. London: Macmillan & Co., Ltd., 1925. x, 528 pp. (Also N. Y.: The Macmillan Co., 1925.)

October Blast. Dublin: Cuala Press, 1927. [25 pp.]

The Tower. London: Macmillan & Co., Ltd., 1928. vi, 110 pp. (Also N. Y.: The Macmillan Co., 1928.)

Selected Poems, Lyrical and Narrative. London: Macmillan & Co., Ltd., 1929. x, 202 pp.

Three Things. [Ariel Poems, No. 18.] London: Faber & Faber, Ltd., 1929. 4 pp.

The Winding Stair. N. Y.: Fountain Press, 1929. 25 pp. (Also N. Y.: Random House, Inc., 1929. 40 pp.)

Words for Music Perhaps, and Other Poems. Dublin: Cuala Press, 1932. [42 pp.]

The Winding Stair and Other Poems. London: Macmillan & Co., Ltd., 1933. ix, 101 pp.

The Collected Poems of W. B. Yeats. London: Macmillan & Co., Ltd., 1933. xvi, 474 pp. (Also N. Y.: The Macmillan Co., 1933. 478 pp.)

The King of the Great Clock Tower. Commentaries and Poems. Dublin: Cuala Press, 1934. 46 pp. (Also N. Y.: The Macmillan Co., 1935.)

The Herne's Egg and Other Plays. N. Y.: The Macmillan Co., 1938. 136 pp.

New Poems. Dublin: Cuala Press, 1938. [47] pp. (450 copies.)

Last Poems and Plays. N. Y.: The Macmillan Co., 1940. 126 pp.

B. SELECTED REFERENCES

BAX, CLIFFORD (Ed.). *Florence Farr, Bernard Shaw, W. B. Yeats: Letters.* N. Y.: Dodd, Mead & Co., 1942. 96 pp.

HONE, JOSEPH. *Life of W. B. Yeats.* N. Y.: The Macmillan Co., 1942. 520 pp.

MACNEICE, LOUIS. *The Poetry of W. B. Yeats.* London: Oxford University Press, 1941. 242 pp.

MASEFIELD, JOHN. *Some Memories of W. B. Yeats.* N. Y.: The Macmillan Co., 1940. 35 pp.

MOORE, GEORGE. *Hail and Farewell.* [3 vols. I. *Ave.* II. *Salve.* III. *Vale.*] N. Y.: D. Appleton & Co., 1912-14. (Much information on Yeats in the three volumes.)

POLLOCK, J. H. *William Butler Yeats.* [Noted Irish Lives.] London: Gerald Duckworth & Co., Ltd., 1935. 112 pp.

REID, FORREST. *W. B. Yeats. A Critical Study.* N. Y.: Dodd, Mead & Co., 1915. [258 pp.]

SYMONS, A. J. A. *A Bibliography of the First Editions of Books by William Butler Yeats.* London: First Edition Club, 1924. 46 pp.

WILSON, EDMUND. *Axel's Castle* (N. Y., 1931), pp. 26-64.

YEATS, W. B. *Autobiography.* [*Reveries over Childhood and Youth; The Trembling of the Veil; Dramatis Personæ.*] N. Y.: The Macmillan Co., 1938. 479 pp.

YEATS, W. B. *Letters on Poetry to Dorothy Wellesley.* London: Oxford University Press, 1940. 216 pp.

RUDYARD KIPLING

A. POETICAL WORKS

Schoolboy Lyrics. [Privately printed, Lahore, India, 1881. 46 pp.]

Echoes. By Two Writers [Kipling and his sister Beatrice]. [Privately printed, Lahore, India, 1884. 72 pp.]

Quartette. The Christmas Annual of the Civil and Military Gazette. By Four Anglo-Indian Writers [i.e., Kipling and his father, mother, and sister]. [Prose and verse by Kipling.] [Privately printed, Lahore, India, 1885. 126 pp.]

Departmental Ditties and Other Verses. Calcutta: Thacker, Spink & Co., 1886. 64 pp.

Barrack-Room Ballads and Other Verses. London: Methuen & Co., 1892. 208 pp.

The Seven Seas. London: Methuen & Co., 1896. 230 pp.

White Horses. [Printed for private circulation, London, 1897, 10 pp.]

The Dipsy Chanty and Other Selected Poems. Aurora, N. Y.: Elbert Hubbard, 1899. 96 pp.

Recessional and Other Poems. [Privately published, London, 1899. 38 pp.]

With Number Three. Surgical & Medical and New Poems. Santiago, Chile: Hume & Co., 1900. 172 pp.

Pan in Vermont. London: Methuen & Co., 1902. 8 pp.

The Five Nations. London: Methuen & Co., 1903. 216 pp.

The Muse among the Motors. London: Carmelite House, 1904. 8 pp.

Rewards and Fairies. [Prose and Verse.] London: Macmillan & Co., Ltd., 1910. 338 pp.

Three Poems. Oxford: The Clarendon Press, 1911. 8 pp.

Collected Verse. London: Hodder & Stoughton, 1912. 480 pp.

Songs from Books. N. Y.: Doubleday, Page & Co., 1912. 250 pp.

A Song of the English. London: Hodder & Stoughton, 1913. 92 pp.

The Neutral. N. Y.: Doubleday, Page & Co., 1916. 8 pp.

A Nativity. N. Y.: Doubleday, Page & Co., 1917. 8 pp.

"*The Holy War*." N. Y.: Doubleday, Page & Co., 1917. 8 pp.

Twenty Poems from Rudyard Kipling. London: Methuen & Co., 1918. 40 pp.

The Years Between. London: Methuen & Co., Ltd., 1919. 160 pp.

Rudyard Kipling's Verse. Inclusive Edition. London: Hodder & Stoughton, 1919. 3 vols. (Reissued in 1929.)

The Novels, Tales and Poems of Rudyard Kipling. Edition de Luxe. London: Macmillan & Co., Ltd., 1920. 31 vols. (Reissued in 1937-39 in 35 vols.)

Songs for Youth. [From the *Collected Poems* of Rudyard Kipling.] N. Y.: Doubleday, Doran & Co., Inc., 1925. 225 pp.

Sixty Poems. London: Hodder & Stoughton, 1939. 189 pp.

Rudyard Kipling's Verse. Definitive Edition. London: Hodder & Stoughton, 1940. 852 pp. (Also N. Y.: Doubleday, Doran & Co., Inc., 1940.)

Choice of Kipling's Verse; made by T. S. Eliot [with an essay on Kipling by Eliot]. London: Faber & Faber, Inc., 1941. 306 pp.

B. SELECTED REFERENCES

Beresford, George C. *Schooldays with Kipling*. N. Y.: G. P. Putnam's Sons, 1936. 270 pp.

Durand, Ralph. *A Handbook of the Poetry of Rudyard Kipling*. N. Y.: Doubleday, Page & Co., 1914. 386 pp.

Hopkins, R. Thurston. *Rudyard Kipling*. A Character Study, Life, Writings and Literary Landmarks. London: Simpkin, Marshall Hamilton, Kent & Co., Ltd., 1921. (Rev. ed.) 251 pp.

Kipling, Rudyard. *Something of Myself, for My Friends Known and Unknown*. N. Y.: Doubleday, Doran & Co., 1937. 252 pp.

LIVINGSTON, F. V. *A Bibliography of the Works of Rudyard Kipling.* N. Y.: E. H. Wells & Co., 1927. (A supplementary issue appeared in 1938.)

MARTINDELL, E. W. *A Bibliography of the Works of Rudyard Kipling.* A New Edition much Enlarged. London: John Lane, 1923. 224 pp.

SHANKS, E. B. *Rudyard Kipling. A Study in Literature and Political Ideas.* London: Macmillan & Co., Ltd., 1940. 276 pp.

G. W. RUSSELL (A. E.)

A. POETICAL WORKS

Homeward, Songs by the Way. Dublin: Whaley, 1894. xiv, 52 pp. (Also London: John Lane, 1894. 64 pp. Also Portland, Me.: Thomas B. Mosher, 1895. 87 pp.)

The Earth Breath and Other Poems. N. Y. and London: John Lane, 1897. [94 pp.]

The Nuts of Knowledge, Lyrical Poems Old and New. [Dundrum, Ireland: Dun Emer Press, 1903. 32 pp.]

The Divine Vision and Other Poems. London: Macmillan & Co., Ltd.; N. Y.: The Macmillan Co., 1904. xiv [96] pp.

By Still Waters. Lyrical Poems Old and New. Dundrum, Ireland: Dun Emer Press, 1906. [33 pp.]

Collected Poems. London: Macmillan & Co., Ltd., 1913. xv, 275 pp. (Enlarged edition, London: Macmillan & Co., Ltd., 1926. xviii, 373 pp.)

Gods of War and Other Poems. [Dundrum, Ireland: Cuala Press, 1915.]

Salutation: A Poem on the Irish Rebellion of 1916. [Privately Printed for Clement Shorter, London, 1917.] 10 pp. (25 copies.)

The Interpreters. London: Macmillan & Co., Ltd., 1922. viii, 180 pp. (Also N. Y.: The Macmillan Co., 1923.) (Prose with some verse included.)

Voices of the Stones. London: Macmillan & Co., Ltd., 1925. 61 pp. (Also N. Y.: The Macmillan Co., 1925.)

Midsummer Eve. N. Y.: Random House, Inc., 1928. 25 pp. (450 copies.)

The Dark Weeping. [Ariel Poems, No. 19.] London: Faber & Faber, Ltd., 1929. 13 pp.

Enchantment and Other Poems. N. Y.: The Fountain Press; London: Macmillan & Co., Ltd., 1930. 34 pp. (542 copies.)

Vale and Other Poems. London: Macmillan & Co., Ltd., 1931. viii, 56 pp.

The House of the Titans and Other Poems. London: Macmillan & Co., Ltd., 1934. 82 pp.

Selected Poems. N. Y.: The Macmillan Co., 1935. xiii [198] pp.

B. SELECTED REFERENCES

Figgis, Darrell. *Æ* (George W. Russell). *A Study of a Man and a Nation.* [Irishmen of To-day.] Dublin and London: Maunsel & Co., Ltd., 1916. 159 pp.

Magee, W. K. *Memoir of A. E., George William Russell.* N. Y.: The Macmillan Co., 1937. 291 pp. (Pseud., John Eglinton.)

Moore, George. *Hail and Farewell.* [3 vols. I. *Ave.* II. *Salve.* III. *Vale.*] N. Y.: D. Appleton & Co., 1912-14. (Much information on Russell in the three volumes.)

[Russell, G. W.] *A E's Letters to Mínanlábáin.* N. Y.: The Macmillan Co., 1937. 102 pp.

[Russell, G. W.] *Some Passages from the Letters of A. E. to W. B. Yeats.* Dublin: Cuala Press, 1936. 63 pp.

[Russell, G. W.] *Song and Its Fountains.* London: Macmillan & Co., Ltd., 1932. 133 pp.

W. H. DAVIES

A. POETICAL WORKS

The Soul's Destroyer and Other Poems. [London: Farmhouse, Marshalsea Road, S. E.: Printed for the Author by Watts & Co., 1905. 108 pp.]

New Poems. London: Elkin Mathews, 1907. 75 pp. (New rev. ed., London: J. Cape, 1922. 67 pp.)

Nature Poems and Others. London: A. C. Fifield, 1908. 62 pp.

Farewell to Poesy and Other Pieces. London: A. C. Fifield, 1910. 60 pp. (Also London: J. Cape, 1921.)

Songs of Joy and Others. London: A. C. Fifield, 1911. 94 pp. (Also Boston: B. Humphries, 1937. 94 pp.)

Foliage. Various Poems. London: Elkin Mathews, 1913. 63 pp. (New rev. ed., London: J. Cape, 1922.)

The Bird of Paradise and Other Poems. London: Methuen & Co. [1914.] 86 pp. (Reissued by J. Cape, London, 1926.)

Child Lovers and Other Poems. London: A. C. Fifield, 1916. 29 pp.

Collected Poems. With a Portrait in Collotype from a Pencil Sketch by Will Rothenstein, and Facsimile of Author's Script. London: A. C. Fifield [1916]. 160 pp. (Also N. Y.: Alfred A. Knopf, 1916.)

Raptures. A Book of Poems. [London: William Beaumont, 1918.] 39 pp. (22 copies.) (Larger edition of *Raptures* issued as *Forty New Poems*, London: A. C. Fifield, 1918. 53 pp.)

The Song of Life and Other Poems. With a Frontispiece from a Portrait by Laura Knight. London: A. C. Fifield, 1920. 61 pp.

The Captive Lion & Other Poems. New Haven: Yale University Press, 1921. 99 pp.

The Hour of Magic and Other Poems. Decorated by William Nicholson. N. Y.: Harper & Brothers, 1922. 34 pp. (Also London: J. Cape [1922].)

Collected Poems: First Series. London: J. Cape [1923]. 160 pp. (Also N. Y.: Harper & Bros., 1923.)

Collected Poems: Second Series. London: J. Cape [1923]. 157 pp. (Also N. Y.: Harper & Bros., 1923.)

Selected Poems. Decorated with Woodcuts by Stephen Bone. London: J. Cape [1923]. 76 pp. (Also N. Y.: Harcourt, Brace & Co., 1925.)

True Travellers. A Tramp's Opera in Three Acts. With Decorations by William Nicholson. London: J. Cape [1923]. 52 pp. (Prose, with songs included.)

Secrets. London: J. Cape [1924]. 48 pp. (Also N. Y.: Harcourt, Brace & Co. [1924].)

A Poet's Alphabet. [With Decorations by Dora M. Batty.] London: J. Cape. [1925]. 63 pp.

The Song of Love. [With Decorations by Dora M. Batty.] London: J. Cape [1926]. 61 pp.

A Poet's Calendar. London: J. Cape [1927]. 61 pp.

Collected Poems. London: J. Cape, 1928. xx, 399 pp. (Also N. Y.: Peter Smith, 1929.)

Forty-nine Poems. . . . Selected and Illustrated by Jacynth Parsons. London: Medici Society, 1928. 58 pp.

Moss and Feathers. [Ariel Poems, No. 10.] London: Faber & Gwyer, Ltd. [1928]. [4 pp.]

Selected Poems. . . . Arranged by Edward Garnett. Newtown: Gregynog Press, 1928. vii, 91 pp.

Ambition, and Other Poems. London: J. Cape, 1929. 32 pp.

In Winter. [Privately printed: Fylton Armstrong, 1931. 8 pp.]

Poems, 1930-31. London: J. Cape, 1932. 48 pp. (Also N. Y.: Peter Smith, 1932.)

The Lover's Song Book. Newtown: Gregynog Press, 1933. 30 pp.

My Birds. London: J. Cape, 1933. [128 pp.] (Also N. Y.: Peter Smith, 1933.) (Prose but with original poems interspersed.)

My Garden. London: J. Cape, 1933. [127 pp.] (Also N. Y.: Peter Smith, 1933.) (Prose but with original poems interspersed.)

The Poems of W. H. Davies. London: J. Cape, 1934. 475 pp. (Also N. Y.: Oxford University Press, 1935.)

Love Poems. London: J. Cape, 1935. 60 pp. (Also N. Y.: Oxford University Press, 1935.)

The Birth of Song: Poems 1935-36. London: J. Cape, 1936. 32 pp. (Also N. Y.: Oxford University Press, 1936. 32 pp.)

The Loneliest Mountain and Other Poems. London: J. Cape, 1939. 32 pp.

Poems: 1940. London: J. Cape, 1940. 525 pp.

Common Joy. Selected Poems. London: Faber & Faber, Ltd., 1941. 80 pp.

B. SELECTED REFERENCES

DAVIES, W. H. *The Autobiography of a Super-Tramp.* With a Preface by Bernard Shaw. London: A. C. Fifield, 1908. 295 pp.

DAVIES, W. H. *Later Days.* London: J. Cape, Ltd. [1925]. 223 pp.

MOULT, THOMAS. *W. H. Davies.* [Modern Writers and Playwrights.] London: Thornton Butterworth, Ltd., 1934. [150 pp.]

RALPH HODGSON

POETICAL WORKS

The Last Blackbird and Other Lines. London: George Allen, 1907. viii, 96 pp. (Also N. Y.: The Macmillan Co., 1917.)

The Bull. London: Printed by A. T. Stevens for Flying Fame, 1913. 20 pp.

Eve, and Other Poems. London: Printed by A. T. Stevens for Flying Fame, 1913. 24 pp.

The Mystery and Other Poems. London: Printed by A. T. Stevens for Flying Fame, 1913. 20 pp.

The Song of Honour. London: Printed by A. T. Stevens for Flying Fame, 1913. 24 pp.

Poems. London: Macmillan & Co., Ltd., 1917. viii, 70 pp. (Also N. Y.: The Macmillan Co., 1917. 64 pp.)

Silver Wedding and Other Poems. Minerva, Ohio: Boerner Printing Co., 1941. 20 pp.

The Muse and the Mastiff. Minerva, Ohio: Boerner Printing Co., 1942. 20 pp.

WALTER DE LA MARE

A. POETICAL WORKS

Songs of Childhood. By Walter Ramal [Pseud.] With Frontispiece. London: Longmans, Green & Co., 1902. 106 pp.

Poems. London: John Murray, 1906. 127 pp.

The Listeners and Other Poems. London: Constable & Co., Ltd., 1912. ix. 92 pp. (Also N. Y.: Henry Holt & Co., 1916.)

A Child's Day. A Book of Rhymes. . . . To Pictures by Carine and Will Cadby. London: Constable & Co., Ltd., 1912. 57 pp. (Also N. Y.: E. P. Dutton & Co., 1912.)

Peacock Pie. A Book of Rhymes. London: Constable & Co., Ltd., 1913. viii, 122 pp. (Also N. Y.: Henry Holt & Co., 1917.)

The Sunken Garden and Other Poems. [Limited Edition. London: Beaumont Press, 1917]. 40 pp.

Motley and Other Poems. London: Constable & Co., 1918. viii, 75 pp. (Also N. Y.: Henry Holt & Co., 1918.)

Flora. A Book of Drawings by Pamela Bianco. With Illustrative Poems by Walter de la Mare. London: William Heinemann [1919]. 45 pp.

Poems: 1901 to 1918. [2 vols.] London: Constable & Co., Ltd. [1920]. 251, 250 pp. (Published as *Collected Poems: 1901-1918.* [2 vols.] N. Y.: Henry Holt & Co., 1920.)

Crossings. A Fairy Play. With Music by C. Armstrong Gibbs. [London: Beaumont Press, 1921.] 132 pp. (Also N. Y.: Alfred A. Knopf, 1923.) (Prose text with lyrics included.)

Story and Rhyme. A Selection from the Writings of Walter de la Mare. Chosen by the Author. [King's Treasuries of Literature.] London: J. M. Dent & Co. [1921]. 160 pp.

The Veil and Other Poems. London: Constable & Co., Ltd. [1921]. xii [92 pp.] (Also N. Y.: Henry Holt & Co., 1922.)

Down-adown-Derry. A Book of Fairy Poems. With Illustrations by Dorothy P. Lathrop. London: Constable & Co., Ltd. [1922]. 193 pp. (Also N. Y.: Henry Holt & Co. [1922].)

Thus Her Tale. A Poem. Designs by William Ogilvie. Edinburgh: Porpoise Press, 1923. 8 pp.

Ding Dong Bell. London: Selwyn & Blount, Ltd., 1924. ix, 76 pp. (Also N. Y.: Alfred A. Knopf, 1924.) (Prose and verse.)

A Ballad of Christmas. Decorated by Alec Buckles. London: Selwyn & Blount [1924]. 8 pp.

Before Dawn. Decorated by Alec Buckles. London: Selwyn & Blount, 1924. 8 pp. (Reprinted from *The Veil.*)

Alone. Wood Engravings by Blair Hughes-Stanton. [Ariel Poems, No. 4.] London: Faber & Gwyer, 1927. [4 pp.]

Selected Poems. N. Y.: Henry Holt & Co. [1927]. 120 pp.

Stuff and Nonsense, and So On. With Woodcuts by Bold. London: Constable & Co., Ltd., 1927. xi, 110 pp. (275 copies.) (Also N. Y.: Henry Holt & Co., [1927].)

The Captive and Other Poems. N. Y.: The Bowling Green Press, 1928. 19 pp. (600 copies.)

Self to Self. [Ariel Poems, No. 11.] London: Faber & Gwyer, [1928]. 4 pp.

A Snowdrop. [Ariel Poems, No. 20.] London: Faber & Faber, Ltd., 1929. 4 pp.

Poems for Children. London: Constable & Co., Ltd. [1930]. xxxiii, 264 pp. (Also N. Y.: Henry Holt & Co., 1930.)

News. . . . With Drawings by Barnett Freedman. [Ariel Poems. No. 31.] London: Faber & Faber, Ltd., 1930. 6 pp.

To Lucy. [Ariel Poems, No. 33.] London: Faber & Faber, Ltd., 1931. 4 pp.

Old Rhymes and New. London: Constable & Co., Ltd., 1932. 2 vols. 52, 60 pp.

The Fleeting and Other Poems. London: Constable & Co., Ltd., 1933. xi, 179 pp. (Also N. Y.: Alfred A. Knopf, Inc., 1933.)

Poems 1919 to 1934. N. Y.: Henry Holt & Co., [1936.] xiv, 379 pp.

This Year, Next Year. [Verse by de la Mare; pictures by Howard Jones.] N. Y.: Henry Holt & Co., 1937.

Memory and Other Poems. N. Y.: Henry Holt & Co., 1938. 92 pp.

Collected Poems. N. Y.: Henry Holt & Co., 1941. 327 pp.

Bells and Grass. A Book of Rhymes. London: Faber & Faber, Ltd., 1941. 154 pp. (Children's verse.)

B. SELECTED REFERENCES

de la Mare, Walter. *Poetry in Prose.* [Wharton Lecture on English Poetry, British Academy.] London: Oxford University Press, 1936. 85 pp.

Mégroz, R. L. *Walter de la Mare: A Biographical and Critical Study.* London: Hodder & Stoughton, 1924. 303 pp.

Reid, Forrest. *Walter de la Mare. A Critical Study.* London: Faber & Faber, Ltd., 1929. 256 pp.

JOHN MASEFIELD

A. POETICAL WORKS

Salt-Water Ballads. London: Grant Richards, 1902. xv, 112 pp. (Also N. Y.: The Macmillan Co., 1913.)

Ballads. [Vigo Cabinet Series, No. 13.] London: Elkin Mathews, 1903. 56 pp. (Second ed., rev. and enlarged, London: E. Mathews, 1910. 62 pp.)

Verse in: Jack B. Yeats. *A Little Fleet.* London: Elkin Mathews [1909. 28 pp.]

Ballads and Poems. London: Elkin Mathews, 1910. 100 pp.

The Everlasting Mercy. London: Sidgwick & Jackson, Ltd., 1911. [96 pp.]

The Widow in the Bye Street. London: Sidgwick & Jackson, Ltd., 1912. [104 pp.]

The Everlasting Mercy and The Widow in the Bye Street. N. Y.: The Macmillan Co., 1912. 230 pp.

The Story of a Round-House and Other Poems. N. Y.: The Macmillan Co., 1912. 324 pp.

The Daffodil Fields. London: William Heinemann, 1913. [112 pp.] (Also N. Y.: The Macmillan Co., 1913.)

Dauber. A Poem. London: William Heinemann, Ltd., 1913. [98 pp.]

Philip the King and Other Poems. With a Portrait by William Strang. London: William Heinemann, 1914. [120 pp.] (Also N. Y.: The Macmillan Co., 1914.)

The Faithful. A Tragedy in Three Acts. London: William Heinemann,

1915. ix, 131 pp. (Also N. Y.: The Macmillan Co., 1915.) (Prose with a few lyrics.)

Good Friday and Other Poems. N. Y.: The Macmillan Co., 1916. 131 pp. (Also a later, limited ed. Letchworth: Garden City Press, Ltd., 1916. [80 pp.]. Also London: W. Heinemann, 1917. vii, 78 pp.)

Salt-Water Poems and Ballads. Illustrated by Chas. Pears. N. Y.: The Macmillan Co., 1916. 163 pp.

Sonnets and Poems. Letchworth: Garden City Press, Ltd., 1916. 51 pp. (A different edition, Lollingdon, Cholsey, Berkshire: John Masefield, 1916.)

Lollingdon Downs and Other Poems. N. Y.: The Macmillan Co., 1917. 53 pp.

Lollingdon Downs and Other Poems, with Sonnets. London: William Heinemann, 1917. [93 pp.]

The Cold Cotswolds. [Reprinted from *The Cambridge Magazine.*] Cambridge: Express Printing Works [1917. 4 pp.]

Poems by John Masefield. Selected by Henry Seidel Canby, Frederick Erastus Pierce, Willard Higley Durham. [Published with the consent of Mr. Masefield.] N. Y.: The Macmillan Co., 1917. 313 pp.

Rosas. N. Y.: The Macmillan Co., 1918. 65 pp.

A Poem and Two Plays. London: William Heinemann, 1919. v, 151 pp.

Reynard the Fox, or The Ghost Heath Run. London: William Heinemann, 1919. 124 pp. (Also N. Y.: The Macmillan Co., 1919.)

Enslaved and Other Poems. London: William Heinemann [1920. 125 pp.] (Also N. Y.: The Macmillan Co., 1920.)

Right Royal. London: William Heinemann, 1920. 120 pp. (Also N. Y.: The Macmillan Co., 1920.)

King Cole. With Drawings in Black and White by Judith Masefield. London: William Heinemann, 1921. 53 pp. (Also N. Y.: The Macmillan Co., 1921. 87 pp.)

The Dream. Illustrated by Judith Masefield. London: William Heinemann, 1922. 13 pp. (Also N. Y.: The Macmillan Co., 1922.)

Esther. A Tragedy. Adapted and Partially Translated from the French of Jean Racine. London: William Heinemann, 1922. 68 pp.

Berenice. . . . Tr. from the French of Jean Racine. London: William Heinemann, 1922. 61 pp.

Esther and Berenice. Two Plays. [Adapted and translated from the French of Racine.] N. Y.: The Macmillan Co., 1922. 205 pp.

Selected Poems. London: William Heinemann, 1922. viii. 244 pp. (Also N. Y.: The Macmillan Co., 1923.) (Rev. and enlarged ed., N. Y.: Macmillan, 1938. 271 pp.)

Dauber: The Daffodil Fields. N. Y.: The Macmillan Co., 1923. 163 pp.

The Collected Poems of John Masefield. London: William Heinemann, Ltd., 1923. ix, 784 pp. (Same, rev. and enlarged ed., London: William Heinemann, 1932. xi, 957 pp.)

The Dream and Other Poems. Illustrated by Judith Masefield. N. Y.: The Macmillan Co., 1923. 63 pp.

King Cole and Other Poems. London: William Heinemann, Ltd. [1923]. 93 pp. (Also N. Y.: The Macmillan Co., 1923.)

A King's Daughter. A Tragedy in Verse. London: William Heinemann, 1923. 127 pp. (Also N. Y.: The Macmillan Co., 1923.)

Philip the King; Good Friday, a Play in Verse; Lollingdon Downs and Other Poems, with Sonnets. N. Y.: The Macmillan Co., 1923. 277 pp.

Poems. [2 vols.] N. Y.: The Macmillan Co., 1925. 446, 291 pp. (Enlarged ed., 1929. 446, 438 pp.)

Verse Plays. N. Y.: The Macmillan Co., 1925. 313 pp.

The Trial of Jesus. London: William Heinemann, Ltd. [1925]. 101 pp. (Prose with some verse included.)

Tristan and Isolt. A Play in Verse. London: William Heinemann, Ltd. [1927]. 135 pp. (Also N. Y.: The Macmillan Co., 1927.)

The Coming of Christ. London: William Heinemann, Ltd., 1928. vi, 48 pp. (Also N. Y.: The Macmillan Co., 1928. 57 pp.)

Midsummer Night and Other Tales in Verse. London: William Heinemann, Ltd., 1928. 207 pp. (Also N. Y.: The Macmillan Co., 1928. 164 pp.)

Easter. A Play for Singers. London: William Heinemann, Ltd., 1929. viii, 14 pp. (Also N. Y.: The Macmillan Co., 1929.)

South and East. London: Medici Society, 1929. 30 pp. (Also N. Y.: The Macmillan Co., 1929.)

The Wanderer of Liverpool. London: William Heinemann, Ltd., 1930. viii, 119 pp. (Also N. Y.: The Macmillan Co., 1930.) (In prose and verse.)

Minnie Maylow's Story and Other Tales and Scenes. London: William Heinemann, Ltd., 1931. 194 pp. (Also N. Y.: The Macmillan Co., 1931.)

A Tale of Troy. London: William Heinemann, Ltd., 1932. 57 pp. (Also N. Y.: The Macmillan Co., 1932.)

End and Beginning. London: William Heinemann, Ltd., 1933. [vii], 50 pp. (Also N. Y.: The Macmillan Co., 1933.)

Poems. Complete Edition, with Recent Poems. N. Y.: The Macmillan Co., 1935. 2 vols. 433, 673 pp.

Letter from Pontus and Other Verse. N. Y.: The Macmillan Co., 1936. vii, 118 pp.

Lines on the Tercentenary of Harvard University. N. Y.: The Macmillan Co., 1937. 12 pp.

Country Scene. [Verse by Masefield; pictures by Edward Seago.] N. Y.: The Macmillan Co., 1937. 98 pp.

Tribute to Ballet. [Verse by Masefield; pictures by Edward Seago.] N. Y.: The Macmillan Co., 1938. 72 pp.

Some Verses to Some Germans. N. Y.: The Macmillan Co., 1939. 10 pp.

Some Memories of W. B. Yeats. N. Y.: The Macmillan Co., 1940. 35 pp. (Contains some poetry.)

Gautama the Enlightened. N. Y.: The Macmillan Co., 1941. 58 pp.

Natalie Maisie and Pavilastukay. Two Tales in Verse. N. Y.: The Macmillan Co., 1942. 69 pp.

B. SELECTED REFERENCES

BIGGANE, CECIL. *John Masefield. A Study.* Cambridge: W. Heffer & Sons., Ltd., 1924. 53 pp.

HAMILTON, W. H. *John Masefield. A Critical Study.* London: George Allen & Unwin, Ltd.; N. Y.: The Macmillan Co. [1922]. 155 pp.

MASEFIELD, JOHN. *In the Mill.* N. Y.: The Macmillan Co., 1941. 158 pp. (Autobiography.)

MASON, JOHN EDWARD. *John Masefield.* [Makers of Literature.] Exeter, Eng.: A. Wheaton & Co., Ltd., 1939. 55 pp.

SIMMONS, CHARLES N. *A Bibliography of John Masefield.* N. Y.: Columbia University Press, 1930. xi, 173 pp.

THOMAS, GILBERT. *John Masefield.* [Modern Writers Series.] London: Thornton Butterworth, Ltd., 1932. 261 pp.

WILFRID GIBSON

POETICAL WORKS

Urlyn the Harper and Other Song. [Vigo Cabinet Series No. 7.] London: Elkin Mathews, 1902. 64 pp.

The Queen's Vigil and Other Song. [Vigo Cabinet Series No. 9.] London: Elkin Mathews, 1902. 64 pp.

The Golden Helm and Other Verse. London: Elkin Mathews, 1903. 132 pp.

The Nets of Love. [Vigo Cabinet Series No. 28.] London: Elkin Mathews, 1905. 58 pp.

On the Threshold. [Cranleigh, Surrey: Samurai Press, 1907.] 33 pp.

The Stonefolds. [Cranleigh, Surrey: Samurai Press, 1907.] 32 pp. (Another ed., London: Elkin Mathews, 1916. 65 pp.)

The Web of Life. A Book of Poems. [Cranleigh, Surrey: Samurai Press, 1908.] 111 pp.

Akra the Slave. London: Elkin Mathews, 1910. [42 pp.]

Daily Bread. London: Elkin Mathews, 1910. 3 vols. 63, 63, 63 pp. (Also N. Y.: The Macmillan Co., 1912. Another ed., rewritten, London: Elkin Mathews, 1923. 118 pp.)

Mates and Other Dramatic Poems. London: Elkin Mathews, 1910.

Fires. London: Elkin Mathews, 1912. 3 vols. 64, 46, 45 pp. (Also N. Y.: The Macmillan Co., 1912. 175 pp. Another ed., London: Elkin Mathews, 1915. 143 pp.)

Womenkind. A Play in One Act. London: D. Nutt, 1912. 24 pp. (Also N. Y.: The Macmillan Co., 1912.)

Borderlands. London: Elkin Mathews, 1914. 64 pp.

Thoroughfares. London: Elkin Mathews, 1914. 48 pp.

Borderlands and Thoroughfares. N. Y.: The Macmillan Co., 1914. 195 pp.

Battle. London: Elkin Mathews, 1915. 45 pp. (Also N. Y.: The Macmillan Co., 1915. 54 pp.)

Battle and Other Poems. N. Y.: The Macmillan Co., 1916. 198 pp.

Friends. London: Elkin Mathews, 1916. 37 pp.

Poems (1904-1917). N. Y.: The Macmillan Co., 1917. 552 pp.

Livelihood: Dramatic Reveries. London: Macmillan & Co., Ltd., 1917. xii, 135 pp. (Also N. Y.: The Macmillan Co., 1917. 119 pp.)

Whin. London: Macmillan & Co., Ltd., 1918. [59 pp.]

Hill-Tracks. With Portrait. N. Y.: The Macmillan Co., 1918. 65 pp. (Same as *Whin.*)

Neighbors. London: Macmillan & Co., Ltd., 1920. xi, 170 pp. (Also N. Y.: The Macmillan Co., 1920. 169 pp.)

Home. A Book of Poems. [London: William Beaumont, 1920.] 41 pp. (295 copies.)

Krindlesyke. London: Macmillan & Co., Ltd., 1922. ix [140] pp.

Kestrel Edge and Other Plays. London: Macmillan & Co., Ltd., 1924. v, 150 pp.

I Heard a Sailor. London: Macmillan & Co., Ltd., 1925. x, 133 pp.

Collected Poems. 1905-1925. London: Macmillan & Co., Ltd., 1926. 791 pp.

Sixty-Three Poems. Selected for Use in Schools and Colleges by E. A. Parker. With a Critical Introduction. London: Macmillan & Co., Ltd., 1926. vii, 148 pp.

The Early Whistler. Drawings by John Nash. [Ariel Poems, No. 6.] London: Faber & Gwyer, Ltd., 1927. [4 pp.]

The Golden Room and Other Poems. London: Macmillan & Co., Ltd., 1928. xiv, 173 pp. (Also N. Y.: The Macmillan Co., 1928.)

Hazards. London: Macmillan & Co., Ltd., 1930. xi, 99 pp. (Also N. Y.: The Macmillan Co., 1930.)

Highland Dawn. Bradford: Beamsley House, 1932. [20] pp.

Islands (Poems 1930-1932). London: Macmillan & Co., Ltd., 1932. x, 85 pp. (Also N. Y.: The Macmillan Co., 1932.)

Fuel. London: Macmillan & Co., Ltd., 1934. vi [154] pp. (Also N. Y.: The Macmillan Co., 1934.)

Coming and Going. London: Oxford University Press, 1938. 83 pp.

The Alert. N. Y.: Oxford University Press, 1942. 41 pp.

HAROLD MONRO

POETICAL WORKS

Poems. [Vigo Cabinet Series.] London: Elkin Mathews, 1906. [64 pp.]

Judas. Cranleigh, Surrey: Samurai Press, 1907. 31 pp. (Also London: S. Low, Marston & Co., Ltd. [1912]. 31 pp.)

Before Dawn (Poems and Impressions). London: Constable & Co., Ltd., 1911. 144 pp.

Children of Love. London: Poetry Bookshop, 1914. 31 pp.

Trees. London: Poetry Bookshop, 1916. [15 pp.]

Strange Meetings. London: Poetry Bookshop, 1917. 63 pp.

Real Property. London: Poetry Bookshop, 1922. 63 pp.

The Earth for Sale. London: Chatto & Windus, 1928. [64 pp.]

The Winter Solstice. [Ariel Poems, No. 13.] London: Faber & Gwyer, Ltd. [1928]. 4 pp.

Elm Angel. [Ariel Poems, No. 26.] London: Faber & Faber, Ltd., 1930. 4 pp.

The Collected Poems of Harold Monro. Edited by Alida Monro. With a Biographical Sketch by F. S. Flint and a Critical Note by T. S. Eliot. London: Cobden-Sanderson, 1933. xx, 217 pp.

ALFRED NOYES

A. POETICAL WORKS

The Loom of Years. London: Grant Richards, 1902. 115 pp.

The Flower of Old Japan: A Dim Strange Tale for All Ages. London: Grant Richards, 1903. ix, 90 pp.

Poems. Edinburgh and London: W. Blackwood & Sons, 1904. xi, 236 pp.

The Forest of Wild Thyme. A Tale for Children under Ninety. Edinburgh and London: W. Blackwood & Sons, 1905. x, 99 pp.

Drake. An English Epic. Books I-III. Edinburgh and London: W. Blackwood & Sons, 1906. 173 pp.

Poems. With an Introduction by Hamilton W. Mabie. N. Y.: The Macmillan Co.; London: Macmillan & Co., Ltd., 1906. 193 pp.

The Flower of Old Japan and Other Poems. N. Y.: The Macmillan Co., 1907. 175 pp.

Forty Singing Seamen and Other Poems. Edinburgh and London: W. Blackwood & Sons, 1907. viii, 175 pp.

Drake. An English Epic. Books IV-XII. Edinburgh and London: W. Blackwood & Sons, 1908. 324 pp. (Also N. Y.: Frederick A. Stokes Co., [1909].)

The Golden Hynde and Other Poems. N. Y.: The Macmillan Co., 1908. 185 pp.

The Enchanted Island and Other Poems. Edinburgh and London: W. Blackwood & Sons, 1909. viii, 209 pp. (Also N. Y.: Frederick A. Stokes Co. [1910].)

Collected Poems. Edinburgh and London: W. Blackwood & Sons, 1910. 2 vols. 344, 374 pp. (Another volume, Edinburgh and London: W. Blackwood & Sons, 1927. 312 pp. Also *Collected Poems,* N. Y.: Frederick A. Stokes Co. [1913-20]. 3 vols. 426, 451, 315 pp. *Collected Poems,* 4 vols., Edinburgh: W. Blackwood & Sons, 1934.)

The Prayer for Peace. Cleveland, Ohio: [Printed for private distribution], 1911. 12 pp.

Sherwood, or Robin Hood and the Three Kings. A Play in Five Acts. N. Y.: Frederick A. Stokes Co. [1911. 225 pp.]

The Carol of the Fir Tree. London: Burns & Oates, Ltd., 1912. 19 pp.

Peace Poems. N. Y.: Frederick A. Stokes Co., 1913. [3 pp.]

Tales of the Mermaid Tavern. Edinburgh and London: W. Blackwood & Sons, 1913. [216 pp.] (Also N. Y.: Frederick A. Stokes Co., 1913.)

Two Christmas Poems. With a Drawing by Walter A. Heller. . . . Cleveland, Ohio [1913. 11 pp.]

The Wine-Press. A Tale of War. Edinburgh and London: W. Blackwood & Sons, 1913. xiv, 95 pp. (Also N. Y.: Frederick A. Stokes Co. [1913].)

Rada. A Drama of War in One Act. N. Y.: Frederick A. Stokes Co., 1914. 31 pp.

The Searchlights. London: Methuen & Co. [1914. 4 pp.]

A Belgian Christmas Eve. Being *Rada* Rewritten and Enlarged as an Episode of the Great War. With Four Illustrations. N. Y.: Frederick A. Stokes Co., 1915. 71 pp. (Also London: Methuen & Co., Ltd., 1915.)

The Lord of Misrule and Other Poems. With Frontispiece in Colours by Spencer Baird Nichols. N. Y.: Frederick A. Stokes Co., [1915]. 184 pp.

A Salute from the Fleet and Other Poems. London: Methuen & Co., Ltd., 1915. vii [208] pp.

Songs of the Trawlers. [London: privately printed, 1916.] 11 pp. (25 copies.)

Open Boats. Edinburgh and London: W. Blackwood & Sons, 1917. 136 pp. (Prose with several poems.)

The New Morning. Poems. N. Y.: Frederick A. Stokes Co. [1919]. 172 pp.

The Elfin Artist and Other Poems. Edinburgh and London: W. Blackwood & Sons, 1920. x, 195 pp. (Also N. Y.: Frederick A. Stokes Co. [1920].)

Selected Verse, *including a Victory Dance and Other Poems Old and New.* Edinburgh and London: W. Blackwood & Sons, 1921. [92] pp.

The Torch Bearers. Edinburgh and London: W. Blackwood & Sons, 1922. ix, 281 pp. (Published as *Watchers of the Sky,* N. Y.: Frederick A. Stokes Co. [1922].)

Songs of Shadow-of-a-Leaf and Other Poems. Edinburgh and London: W. Blackwood & Sons, 1924. x, 127 pp.

The Torch-Bearers. Volume II: The Book of Earth. Edinburgh and London: W. Blackwood & Sons, 1925. vii, 375 pp. (Also N. Y.: Frederick A. Stokes Co., 1925. 328 pp.)

Dick Turpin's Ride and Other Poems. N. Y.: Frederick A. Stokes Co., 1927. 142 pp.

The Strong City. London: Burns, Oates & Washbourne, Ltd. [1928]. 12 pp.

Ballads and Poems. Edinburgh and London: W. Blackwood & Sons, 1928. viii, 423 pp.

The Torch-Bearers. Volume III: The Last Voyage. Edinburgh and London: W. Blackwood & Sons, 1930. 229 pp.

The Torch-Bearers. A Trilogy. London: Sheed & Ward, 1937. 422 pp.

If Judgment Comes. N. Y.: Frederick A. Stokes Co., 1941. 46 pp.

Shadows on the Down and Other Poems. N. Y.: Frederick A. Stokes Co., 1941. [ix], 110 pp.

B. SELECTED REFERENCES

Davison, Edward, *Some Modern Poets* (N. Y., 1928), pp. 199-218.

Jerrold, Walter. *Alfred Noyes.* [Modern Writers Series.] London: Harold Shaylor, Ltd., 1930. 252 pp.

JAMES STEPHENS

A. POETICAL WORKS

Insurrections. Dublin: Maunsel & Co., Ltd., 1909. 55 pp. (Also N. Y.: The Macmillan Co., 1909.)

The Lonely God and Other Poems. N. Y.: The Macmillan Co., 1909. 27 pp.

The Hill of Vision. Dublin: Maunsel & Co., Ltd., 1912. viii, 131 pp. (Also N. Y.: The Macmillan Co., 1912.)

Five New Poems. London: Printed by A. T. Stevens for Flying Fame, 1913. 20 pp.

The Adventures of Seumas Beg. The Rocky Road to Dublin. London: Macmillan & Co., Ltd., 1915. vii, 86 pp.

The Rocky Road to Dublin. The Adventures of Seumas Beg. N. Y.: The Macmillan Co., 1915. 94 pp.

Songs from the Clay. London: Macmillan & Co., Ltd., 1915. 106 pp. (Also N. Y.: The Macmillan Co., 1915.)

Green Branches. Dublin: Maunsel & Co., Ltd., 1916. [19 pp.] (Also N. Y.: The Macmillan Co., 1916. [40 pp.])

Reincarnations. London: Macmillan & Co., Ltd., 1918. viii, 66 pp. (Also N. Y.: The Macmillan Co., 1918, 76 pp.)

A Poetry Recital. London: Macmillan & Co., Ltd., 1925. vi, 36 pp. (Also N. Y.: The Macmillan Co., 1925. 41 pp.)

Collected Poems. London: Macmillan & Co., Ltd., 1926. xxii, 260 pp. (Also N. Y.: The Macmillan Co., 1926.)

The Outcast. [Ariel Poems, No. 22.] London: Faber & Faber, Ltd., 1929. [11 pp.]

Theme and Variations. N. Y.: Fountain Press, 1930. [viii], 31 pp. (Also London: G. Toulmin & Sons, Ltd., 1930. 32 pp.)

Strict Joy. London: Macmillan & Co., Ltd., 1931. v, 57 pp. (Also N. Y.: The Macmillan Co., 1931.) (Includes *Theme and Variations.*)

Kings and the Moon. London: Macmillan & Co., 1938. vi, 83 pp. (Also N. Y.: The Macmillan Co., 1938. 68 pp.)

B. SELECTED REFERENCES

BOYD, ERNEST, *Portraits: Real and Imaginary* (N. Y., 1924), pp. 246-55.

DAVISON, EDWARD, *Some Modern Poets* (N. Y., 1928), pp. 175-97.

MOORE, GEORGE, *Hail and Farewell* [Vol. 3—*Vale* (N. Y., 1914), pp. 251-53.] (Account of Russell's discovery of Stephens.)

[RUSSELL, GEORGE W.], *Imaginations and Reveries* (N. Y., 1916), pp. 34-45.

SIEGFRIED SASSOON

A. POETICAL WORKS

Twelve Sonnets. [Privately printed, 1911.]

Hyacinth. [Privately printed, 1912.]

Melodies. [Privately printed, 1912.]

An Ode for Music. [Privately printed, 1912.]

Apollo in Doelyrium. [Privately printed, 1913.]

Discoveries. [Privately printed, 1915.]

Morning Glory. [Privately printed, 1916.]

The Old Huntsman and Other Poems. London: William Heinemann, 1917. ix, 109 pp. (Also N. Y.: E. P. Dutton & Co., 1918.)

Counter-Attack and Other Poems. London: William Heinemann, 1918. [64 pp.] (Also N. Y.: E. P. Dutton & Co., 1918.)

The War Poems of Siegfried Sassoon. London: William Heinemann, Ltd., 1919. 95 pp.

Picture-Show. Cambridge: [privately printed, 1919. 38 pp.] (200 copies).

Picture-Show. London: William Heinemann, 1919. 56 pp. (Also N. Y.: E. P. Dutton & Co., [1920].)

Selected Poems. London: William Heinemann, 1925. vii, 75 pp.

Satirical Poems. London: William Heinemann, 1926. 61 pp. (Also N. Y.: Viking Press, 1926. New ed., with five poems added, London: William Heinemann, 1933. 69 pp.)

Nativity. Designs by Paul Nash. [Ariel Poems, No. 7.] London: Faber & Gwyer, Ltd. [1927. 8 pp.]

The Heart's Journey. N. Y.: Crosby Gaige; London: William Heinemann, Ltd., 1927. 30 pp.

To My Mother. [Ariel Poems, No. 14.] London: Faber & Gwyer, Ltd. [1928. 4 pp.]

In Sicily. [Ariel Poems, No. 27.] London: Faber & Faber, Ltd., 1930. [12 pp.]

To the Red Rose. [Ariel Poems, No. 34.] London: Faber & Faber, Ltd., 1931. [12 pp.]

Poems by Pinchbeck Lyre [pseud.]. London: Gerald Duckworth & Co., Ltd., 1931. 22 pp.

Prehistoric Burials. [Borzoi Chapbooks, No. 1.] N. Y.: Alfred A. Knopf, Inc., 1932. 3 pp.

The Road to Ruin. London: Faber & Faber, Ltd., 1933. 23 pp.

Vigils. [Bristol: privately printed, 1934. Engraved on copper and printed from plates. 50 pp.] (Also London: William Heinemann, Ltd., 1935. 35 pp.)

Rhymed Ruminations. London: Faber & Faber, Ltd., 1940. 52 pp. (Issued in a limited private ed., 1939.)

Poems Newly Selected, 1916-1935. London: Faber & Faber, Ltd., 1940. 78 pp.

B. SELECTED REFERENCES

BLUNDEN, EDMUND, "Siegfried Sassoon's Poetry," *London Mercury*, XX (June, 1929), 156-67.

DARTON, F. J. HARVEY, *From Surtees to Sassoon* (London, 1931), pp. 81-121.

SASSOON, SIEGFRIED, *The Old Century and Seven More Years*. London: Faber & Faber, Ltd., 1938. 293 pp. (Autobiography.) (Also N. Y.: The Viking Press.)

SWINNERTON, FRANK, *An Autobiography* (N. Y., 1936), pp. 306-8.

CECIL DAY LEWIS

A. POETICAL WORKS

Country Comets. London: Martin Hopkinson & Co., Ltd., 1928. 35 pp.

Transitional Poem. London: Hogarth Press, 1929. 72 pp.

From Feathers to Iron. London: Hogarth Press, 1931. 56 pp.

Magnetic Mountain. London: Hogarth Press, 1933. 55 pp.

Collected Poems: 1929-1933. London: Hogarth Press, 1935. 156 pp. (Also N. Y.: Random House, 1935. 256 pp. [Includes "A Hope for Poetry"—an enlightening essay on Auden, Lewis himself, and their group.])

Time to Dance and Other Poems. London: Hogarth Press, 1935. 64 pp.

Noah and the Waters. [Play.] London: Hogarth Press, 1936. 59 pp.

Overtures to Death and Other Poems. London: J. Cape, 1938. 62 pp.

Selected Poems. London: Hogarth Press, 1940. 80 pp.

Poems in Wartime. London: J. Cape, 1941.

B. SELECTED REFERENCES

KUNITZ, STANLEY J., "Between Two Worlds," *Poetry*, XLVII (Dec., 1935), 158-62.

SOUTHWORTH, JAMES G., "Cecil Day Lewis," *Sewanee Rev.*, XLV (Oct.-Dec., 1937), 469-84.

W. H. AUDEN

A. POETICAL WORKS

Poems. London: Faber & Faber, Ltd., 1930. 79 pp. (2nd ed., 1933, 89 pp.)

The Orators. An English Study. London: Faber & Faber, Ltd., 1932. 116 pp.

The Dance of Death. London: Faber & Faber, Ltd., 1933. [38] pp.

Poems. N. Y.: Random House, 1934. 218 pp.

[with Christopher Isherwood] *The Dog beneath the Skin.* [Play.] London: Faber & Faber, Ltd., 1935. 180 pp.

[with Christopher Isherwood] *Ascent of F 6.* [Play.] London: Faber & Faber, Ltd., 1936. 123 pp.

Look, Stranger! London: Faber & Faber, Ltd., 1936. 68 pp. (Published in the U. S. as *On This Island.* N. Y.: Random House, 1937.)

Spain. London: Faber & Faber, Ltd., 1937. 12 pp.

[with Louis MacNeice] *Letters from Iceland.* London: Faber & Faber, Ltd., 1937. 268 pp.

Selected Poems. London: Faber & Faber, Ltd., 1938. 128 pp.

[with Christopher Isherwood] *On the Frontier.* [Play.] Faber & Faber, Ltd., 1938. 123 pp.

[with Christopher Isherwood] *Journey to a War.* London: Faber & Faber, Ltd., 1939. 301 pp. (Also N. Y.: Random House, 1939.)

Another Time. London: Faber & Faber, Ltd., 1940. 114 pp. (Also N. Y.: Random House, 1940. 114 pp.)

Some Poems. London: Faber & Faber, Ltd., 1940. 80 pp.

The Double Man. N. Y.: Random House, 1941. 189 pp. (Published in England as *New Year Letter.* London: Faber & Faber, Ltd., 1941. 192 pp.)

B. SELECTED REFERENCES

Cowley, Malcolm, "Auden and Spender," *New Republic*, LXXX (Sept. 26, 1934), 189-90.

Flint, F. Cudworth, "New Leaders in English Poetry," Va. Quar. *Rev.*, XIV (Autumn, 1938), 502-19.

Lewis, C. Day, "A Hope for Poetry" in *Collected Poems 1929-1933.* N. Y.: Random House, 1935. pp. 157-256.

Spender, Stephen, "The Importance of W. H. Auden," *London Mercury*, XXXIX (April, 1939), 613-19.

LOUIS MacNEICE

A. POETICAL WORKS

Blind Fireworks. London: Victor Gollancz, Ltd., 1929. 80 pp.

Poems. London: Faber & Faber, Ltd., 1935. 115 pp.

The Earth Compels. London: Faber & Faber, Ltd., 1938. 64 pp.

Autumn Journal. A Poem. London: Faber & Faber, Ltd., 1939. 96 pp.

The Last Ditch. Dublin: Cuala Press, 1940. 34 pp.

Selected Poems. London: Faber & Faber, Ltd., 1940. 80 pp.

Poems: 1925-1940. N. Y.: Random House, 1940. 326 pp.

Plant and Phantom. London: Faber & Faber, Ltd., 1941. 86 pp.

B. SELECTED REFERENCES

SCHWARTZ, DELMORE, "Adroitly Naive," *Poetry*, XLVIII (May, 1936), 115-18.

SYMONS, JULIAN, "Louis MacNeice: The Artist as Everyman," *Poetry*, LVI (May, 1940), 86-95.

WILSON, T. C., "One of the Best," *Poetry*, LI (March, 1938), 339-44.

STEPHEN SPENDER

A. POETICAL WORKS

Poems. London: Faber & Faber, Ltd., 1933. 57 pp. (Second ed., revised and enlarged, 1934. 69 pp.) (Also N. Y.: Random House, 1934. 68 pp.)

Vienna. London: Faber & Faber, Ltd., 1934. 43 pp.

Trial of a Judge. [Play.] London: Faber & Faber, Ltd., 1938. 115 pp.

The Still Centre. London: Faber & Faber, Ltd., 1939. 107 pp.

Selected Poems. London: Faber & Faber, Ltd., 1940. 80 pp.

Ruins and Visions. London: Faber & Faber, Ltd., 1942. 84 pp.

B. SELECTED REFERENCES

COWLEY, MALCOLM, "Auden and Spender," *New Republic*, LXXX (Sept. 26, 1934), 189-90.

FLINT, F. CUDWORTH, "New Leaders in English Poetry," *Va. Quar. Rev.* (Autumn, 1938), 502-19.

SOUTHWORTH, JAMES GRANVILLE, "Stephen Spender," *Sewanee Rev.*, XLV (July-Sept., 1937), 272-84.

The American Poets

EDGAR LEE MASTERS

A. POETICAL WORKS

A Book of Verses. Chicago: Way & Williams, 1898. 207 pp.

Maximilian. A Five-Act Drama in Verse. Boston: Richard G. Badger, 1902. 154 pp.

Blood of the Prophets. By Dexter Wallace [pseud.]. Chicago: The Rooks Press, 1905. 112 pp.

Songs and Sonnets. By Webster Ford [pseud.]. Chicago: The Rooks Press, 1910. 90 pp.

Songs and Sonnets. Second Series. By Webster Ford [pseud.]. Chicago: The Rooks Press, 1912. 85 pp.

Spoon River Anthology. N. Y.: The Macmillan Co., 1915. (Another edition, with further poems, N. Y.: The Macmillan Co., 1916.) 306 pp.

Songs and Satires. N. Y.: The Macmillan Co., 1916. [x] 172 pp.

The Great Valley. N. Y.: The Macmillan Co., 1916. ix, 280 pp.

Toward the Gulf. N. Y.: The Macmillan Co., 1918, xvi, 292 pp.

Starved Rock. N. Y.: The Macmillan Co., 1919, viii, 171 pp.

Domesday Book. N. Y.: The Macmillan Co., 1920. [x] 396 pp.

The Open Sea. N. Y.: The Macmillan Co., 1921. [viii] 302 pp.

The New Spoon River. N. Y.: Boni & Liveright, 1924. 368 pp.

Selected Poems. N. Y.: The Macmillan Co., 1925. 411 pp.

Lee. A Dramatic Poem. N. Y.: The Macmillan Co., 1926. [x] 139 pp.

Jack Kelso. A Dramatic Poem. N. Y.: D. Appleton & Co., 1928. 264 pp.

The Fate of the Jury. N. Y.: D. Appleton & Co., 1929. 173 pp.

Gettysburg, Manila, Acoma. N. Y.: Horace Liveright, Inc., 1930. 219 pp.

Lichee Nuts. N. Y.: Horace Liveright, Inc., 1930. 137 pp.

Godbey. A Dramatic Poem. N. Y.: Dodd, Mead & Co., 1931. 253 pp. (347 copies.)

The Serpent in the Wilderness. N. Y.: Sheldon Dick [1933]. 91 pp. (400 copies.)

Dramatic Duologues. N. Y.: Samuel French, 1934. 95 pp.

Richmond. A Dramatic Poem. N. Y.: Samuel French, 1934. 55 pp.

Invisible Landscapes. N. Y.: The Macmillan Company, 1935. 163 pp.

The Golden Fleece of California. Weston, Vermont: Countryman Press [1936]. 79 pp. (550 copies.)

Poems of People. N. Y.: Appleton-Century Co., Inc., 1936. viii, 198 pp.

The New World. N. Y.: Appleton-Century Co., Inc., 1937. 272 pp.

More People. N. Y.: Appleton-Century Co., Inc., 1939. [xii] 192 pp.

Illinois Poems. Prairie City, Ill.: James A. Decker, 1941. 66 pp.

Along the Illinois. Prairie City, Ill.: James A. Decker, 1942. 85 pp.

B. SELECTED REFERENCES

HANSEN, HARRY, *Midwest Portraits* (N. Y., 1923), pp. 227-28; 243-51.

MASTERS, EDGAR LEE. *Across Spoon River: An Autobiography.* N. Y.: Farrar & Rinehart, [1936]. 426 pp.

MONROE, HARRIET, *Poets and Their Art* (N. Y., 1926), pp. 46-55.

E. A. ROBINSON

A. POETICAL WORKS

The Torrent and the Night Before. By Edwin Arlington Robinson, Gardiner, Maine, 1889-1896. [Cambridge: Riverside Press.] Printed for the Author, 1896. 44 pp.

The Children of the Night. A Book of Poems. Boston: R. G. Badger & Co., 1897. 121 pp.

Captain Craig. A Book of Poems. Boston: Houghton Mifflin, 1902. 171 pp. (Also London: Gay & Bird, 1903.)

The Town down the River. A Book of Poems. N. Y.: Charles Scribner's Sons, 1910. 129 pp.

The Man against the Sky. A Book of Poems. N. Y.: The Macmillan Co., 1916. 149 pp. (Also London: Macmillan & Co., Ltd., 1916.)

MUNSON, GORHAM B. *Robert Frost. A Study in Sensibility and Good Sense.* [The Murray Hill Biographies.] N. Y.: George H. Doran Co., [1927]. 135 pp.

THOMPSON, LAWRANCE. *Fire and Ice: The Art and Thought of Robert Frost.* N. Y.: Henry Holt & Co., 1942. 241 pp.

THORNTON, RICHARD, ed. *Recognition of Robert Frost.* N. Y.: Henry Holt & Co., 1937. 321 pp.

CARL SANDBURG

A. POETICAL WORKS

In Reckless Ecstasy. [Pamphlet. Galesburg: Asgard Press, 1904.]

Chicago Poems. N. Y.: Henry Holt & Co., 1916. 183 pp.

Cornhuskers. N. Y.: Henry Holt & Co., 1918. 147 pp.

Smoke and Steel. N. Y.: Harcourt, Brace & Co., 1920. 268 pp. (Also London: J. Cape, 1922.)

Slabs of the Sunburnt West. N. Y.: Harcourt, Brace & Co. [1922]. 76 pp.

Selected Poems of Carl Sandburg. Edited by Rebecca West. London: J. Cape, 1926. 287 pp. (Also N. Y.: Harcourt, Brace & Co., [1926].)

Carl Sandburg. [Pamphlet Poets.] N. Y.: Simon & Schuster [1926]. 30 pp.

Good Morning, America. N. Y.: Harcourt, Brace & Co., 1928. 251 pp.

Early Moon. N. Y.: Harcourt, Brace & Co., 1930. 136 pp.

The People, Yes. N. Y.: Harcourt, Brace & Co., 1936. 286 pp.

B. SELECTED REFERENCES

DETZER, KARL. *Carl Sandburg: A Study in Personality and Background.* N. Y.: Harcourt, Brace & Co., 1941. 210 pp.

HANSEN, HARRY, *Midwest Portraits. A Book of Memories and Friendships* (N. Y., 1923), pp. 17-92.

WEIRICK, BRUCE, *From Whitman to Sandburg in American Poetry* (N. Y., 1924), pp. 210-20.

WHIPPLE, T. K., *Spokesmen* (N. Y., 1928), pp. 161-84.

Merlin. A Poem. N. Y.: The Macmillan Co., 1917. 168 pp.

Lancelot. A Poem. N. Y.: Thomas Seltzer, 1920. 184 pp. (Also published, 1919, N. Y.: Poetry Book Shop.)

The Three Taverns. A Book of Poems. N. Y.: The Macmillan Co., 1920. 120 pp.

Collected Poems. N. Y.: The Macmillan Co., 1921. 591 pp. (Also London: Cecil Palmer, 1922. Another edition, in five volumes, N. Y.: The Macmillan Co., 1927.)

Avon's Harvest. N. Y.: The Macmillan Co., 1921. 65 pp. (Also London: Macmillan & Co., Ltd., 1921.)

Roman Bartholow. N. Y.: The Macmillan Co., 1923. 191 pp. (Also London: Cecil Palmer, 1923.)

The Man Who Died Twice. N. Y.: The Macmillan Co., 1924. 79 pp. (Also London: Cecil Palmer, 1924.)

Dionysus in Doubt. A Book of Poems. N. Y.: The Macmillan Co., 1925. 117 pp.

Tristram. N. Y.: The Macmillan Co., 1927. 210 pp.

Sonnets (1889-1927). N. Y.: The Macmillan Co., 1928. 89 pp.

Cavender's House. N. Y.: The Macmillan Co., 1929. 103 pp.

Modred: A Fragment. New Haven: E. B. Hackett, 1929. [20 pp.]

The Glory of the Nightingales. N. Y.: The Macmillan Co., 1930. 83 pp.

Matthias at the Door. N. Y.: The Macmillan Co., 1931. 99 pp.

Nicodemus. A Book of Poems. N. Y.: The Macmillan Co., 1932. 90 pp.

Talifer. N. Y.: The Macmillan Co., 1933. 98 pp.

Amaranth. N. Y.: The Macmillan Co., 1934. 105 pp.

King Jasper. N. Y.: The Macmillan Co., 1935. 110 pp.

B. SELECTED REFERENCES

CESTRE, CHARLES. *An Introduction to Edwin Arlington Robinson.* N. Y.: The Macmillan Co., 1930. 230 pp.

HAGEDORN, HERMANN. *Edwin Arlington Robinson. A Biography.* N. Y.: The Macmillan Co., 1938. 402 pp.

HOGAN, C. B. *A Bibliography of Edwin Arlington Robinson.* New Haven: Yale University Press, 1936. 221 pp.

KAPLAN, E. *Philosophy in the Poetry of Edwin Arlington Robinson.* N. Y.: Columbia University Press, 1940. 162 pp.

LIPPINCOTT, LILLIAN. *A Bibliography of the Writings and Criticism of Edwin Arlington Robinson.* Boston: F. W. Faxon Co., 1937. 86 pp.

MORRIS, LLOYD. *The Poetry of Edwin Arlington Robinson. An Essay in Appreciation.* With a Bibliography by W. Van R. Whitall. N. Y.: George H. Doran Co., [1923]. 116 pp.

REDMAN, BEN RAY. *Edwin Arlington Robinson.* [Modern American Writers. VI.] N. Y.: Robert M. McBride & Co., 1926 [97 pp.]

RICHARDS [MRS.], L. E. *E. A. R.* Cambridge: Harvard University Press, 1936. 61 pp. (Concerning his childhood and youth.)

ROBINSON, EDWIN ARLINGTON, "The First Seven Years," *The Colophon,* Vol. One, Part IV, 1930 [pages unnumbered but circ. pp. 50-58].

TORRENCE, RIDGELY. *Selected Letters of Edwin Arlington Robinson.* N. Y.: The Macmillan Co., 1940. 191 pp.

VAN DOREN, CARL. *Edwin Arlington Robinson.* N. Y.: Literary Guild of America, 1927. 93 pp.

AMY LOWELL

A. POETICAL WORKS

A Dome of Many-Coloured Glass. Boston: Houghton Mifflin, 1912. 139 pp. (Also London: Constable & Co., Ltd., 1913.)

Sword Blades and Poppy Seed. N. Y.: The Macmillan Co., 1914. 246 pp. (Also London: Macmillan & Co., Ltd., 1914.)

Men, Women and Ghosts. N. Y.: The Macmillan Co., 1916. 363 pp. (Also London: Macmillan & Co., Ltd., 1916.)

Can Grande's Castle. N. Y.: The Macmillan Co., 1918. 232 pp. (Also Oxford: Blackwell, 1920.)

Pictures of the Floating World. N. Y.: The Macmillan Co., 1919. 257 pp.

Fir-Flower Tablets. Poems Translated from the Chinese by Florence Ayscough. English Version by Amy Lowell. Boston: Houghton Mifflin, 1921. 227 pp.

Legends. Boston: Houghton Mifflin, 1921. 259 pp.

A Critical Fable . . . [Published anonymously.] Boston: Houghton Mifflin, 1922. 99 pp.

What's O'Clock? Boston: Houghton Mifflin, 1925. 240 pp. (Also London: Jonathan Cape, 1926.)

East Wind. Boston: Houghton Mifflin, 1926. 240 pp.

Ballads for Sale. Boston: Houghton Mifflin, 1927. 311 pp.

Selected Poems of Amy Lowell. Edited by John Livingston Lowes. Boston: Houghton Mifflin, 1928. 240 pp.

B. SELECTED REFERENCES

DAMON, S. FOSTER. *Amy Lowell. A Chronicle, with Extracts from Her Correspondence.* Boston: Houghton Mifflin, 1935. 773 pp.

HUGHES, GLENN, *Imagism and the Imagists* (Stanford University, 1931), pp. 197-224.

LOWES, JOHN LIVINGSTON, *Dict. Am. Biog.,* Vol. XI, pp. 453-55.

WOOD, CLEMENT. *Amy Lowell.* N. Y.: Harold Vinal, 1926. 185 pp.

ROBERT FROST

A. POETICAL WORKS

A Boy's Will. London: David Nutt, 1913. 63 pp. (Also N. Y.: Henry Holt & Co., 1915.)

North of Boston. London: David Nutt, 1914. 144 pp. (Also N. Y.: Henry Holt & Co., 1915.)

Mountain Interval. N. Y.: Henry Holt & Co. [1916]. 99 pp.

New Hampshire. A Poem with Notes and Grace Notes by Robert Frost. With Woodcuts by J. J. Lankes, N. Y.: Henry Holt & Co., 1923. 113 pp. (Also London: Grant Richards, 1924.)

Selected Poems. N. Y.: Henry Holt & Co., 1923. 143 pp. (Also London: William Heinemann, 1923.)

West-Running Brook. N. Y.: Henry Holt & Co. [1928]. 64 pp.

Collected Poems. N. Y.: Henry Holt & Co., 1930. 349 pp. (Another edition, 1939. 436 pp.)

A Lone Striker. [Borzoi Chapbooks, No. 8.] N. Y.: Alfred A. Knopf, 1933.

A Further Range. N. Y.: Henry Holt & Co., [1936]. 102 pp.

From Snow to Snow. N. Y.: Henry Holt & Co., 1936. 20 pp.

A Witness Tree. N. Y.: Henry Holt & Co., [1942]. 91 pp.

B. SELECTED REFERENCES

CLYMER, W. B. S. & GREEN, C. R. *Robert Frost: A Bibliography.* Amherst, Mass.: Jones Lib., Inc., 1937. 158 pp.

Merlin. A Poem. N. Y.: The Macmillan Co., 1917. 168 pp.

Lancelot. A Poem. N. Y.: Thomas Seltzer, 1920. 184 pp. (Also published, 1919, N. Y.: Poetry Book Shop.)

The Three Taverns. A Book of Poems. N. Y.: The Macmillan Co., 1920. 120 pp.

Collected Poems. N. Y.: The Macmillan Co., 1921. 591 pp. (Also London: Cecil Palmer, 1922. Another edition, in five volumes, N. Y.: The Macmillan Co., 1927.)

Avon's Harvest. N. Y.: The Macmillan Co., 1921. 65 pp. (Also London: Macmillan & Co., Ltd., 1921.)

Roman Bartholow. N. Y.: The Macmillan Co., 1923. 191 pp. (Also London: Cecil Palmer, 1923.)

The Man Who Died Twice. N. Y.: The Macmillan Co., 1924. 79 pp. (Also London: Cecil Palmer, 1924.)

Dionysus in Doubt. A Book of Poems. N. Y.: The Macmillan Co., 1925. 117 pp.

Tristram. N. Y.: The Macmillan Co., 1927. 210 pp.

Sonnets (1889-1927). N. Y.: The Macmillan Co., 1928. 89 pp.

Cavender's House. N. Y.: The Macmillan Co., 1929. 103 pp.

Modred: A Fragment. New Haven: E. B. Hackett, 1929. [20 pp.]

The Glory of the Nightingales. N. Y.: The Macmillan Co., 1930. 83 pp.

Matthias at the Door. N. Y.: The Macmillan Co., 1931. 99 pp.

Nicodemus. A Book of Poems. N. Y.: The Macmillan Co., 1932. 90 pp.

Talifer. N. Y.: The Macmillan Co., 1933. 98 pp.

Amaranth. N. Y.: The Macmillan Co., 1934. 105 pp.

King Jasper. N. Y.: The Macmillan Co., 1935. 110 pp.

B. SELECTED REFERENCES

CESTRE, CHARLES. *An Introduction to Edwin Arlington Robinson.* N. Y.: The Macmillan Co., 1930. 230 pp.

HAGEDORN, HERMANN. *Edwin Arlington Robinson. A Biography.* N. Y.: The Macmillan Co., 1938. 402 pp.

HOGAN, C. B. *A Bibliography of Edwin Arlington Robinson.* New Haven: Yale University Press, 1936. 221 pp.

KAPLAN, E. *Philosophy in the Poetry of Edwin Arlington Robinson.* N. Y.: Columbia University Press, 1940. 162 pp.

LIPPINCOTT, LILLIAN. *A Bibliography of the Writings and Criticism of Edwin Arlington Robinson.* Boston: F. W. Faxon Co., 1937. 86 pp.

MORRIS, LLOYD. *The Poetry of Edwin Arlington Robinson. An Essay in Appreciation.* With a Bibliography by W. Van R. Whitall. N. Y.: George H. Doran Co., [1923]. 116 pp.

REDMAN, BEN RAY. *Edwin Arlington Robinson.* [Modern American Writers. VI.] N. Y.: Robert M. McBride & Co., 1926 [97 pp.]

RICHARDS [MRS.], L. E. *E. A. R.* Cambridge: Harvard University Press, 1936. 61 pp. (Concerning his childhood and youth.)

ROBINSON, EDWIN ARLINGTON, "The First Seven Years," *The Colophon,* Vol. One, Part IV, 1930 [pages unnumbered but circ. pp. 50-58].

TORRENCE, RIDGELY. *Selected Letters of Edwin Arlington Robinson.* N. Y.: The Macmillan Co., 1940. 191 pp.

VAN DOREN, CARL. *Edwin Arlington Robinson.* N. Y.: Literary Guild of America, 1927. 93 pp.

AMY LOWELL

A. POETICAL WORKS

A Dome of Many-Coloured Glass. Boston: Houghton Mifflin, 1912. 139 pp. (Also London: Constable & Co., Ltd., 1913.)

Sword Blades and Poppy Seed. N. Y.: The Macmillan Co., 1914. 246 pp. (Also London: Macmillan & Co., Ltd., 1914.)

Men, Women and Ghosts. N. Y.: The Macmillan Co., 1916. 363 pp. (Also London: Macmillan & Co., Ltd., 1916.)

Can Grande's Castle. N. Y.: The Macmillan Co., 1918. 232 pp. (Also Oxford: Blackwell, 1920.)

Pictures of the Floating World. N. Y.: The Macmillan Co., 1919. 257 pp.

Fir-Flower Tablets. Poems Translated from the Chinese by Florence Ayscough. English Version by Amy Lowell. Boston: Houghton Mifflin, 1921. 227 pp.

Legends. Boston: Houghton Mifflin, 1921. 259 pp.

A Critical Fable . . . [Published anonymously.] Boston: Houghton Mifflin, 1922. 99 pp.

What's O'Clock? Boston: Houghton Mifflin, 1925. 240 pp. (Also London: Jonathan Cape, 1926.)

East Wind. Boston: Houghton Mifflin, 1926. 240 pp.

Ballads for Sale. Boston: Houghton Mifflin, 1927. 311 pp.

Selected Poems of Amy Lowell. Edited by John Livingston Lowes. Boston: Houghton Mifflin, 1928. 240 pp.

B. SELECTED REFERENCES

DAMON, S. FOSTER. *Amy Lowell. A Chronicle, with Extracts from Her Correspondence.* Boston: Houghton Mifflin, 1935. 773 pp.

HUGHES, GLENN, *Imagism and the Imagists* (Stanford University, 1931), pp. 197-224.

LOWES, JOHN LIVINGSTON, *Dict. Am. Biog.*, Vol. XI, pp. 453-55.

WOOD, CLEMENT. *Amy Lowell.* N. Y.: Harold Vinal, 1926. 185 pp.

ROBERT FROST

A. POETICAL WORKS

A Boy's Will. London: David Nutt, 1913. 63 pp. (Also N. Y.: Henry Holt & Co., 1915.)

North of Boston. London: David Nutt, 1914. 144 pp. (Also N. Y.: Henry Holt & Co., 1915.)

Mountain Interval. N. Y.: Henry Holt & Co. [1916]. 99 pp.

New Hampshire. A Poem with Notes and Grace Notes by Robert Frost. With Woodcuts by J. J. Lankes, N. Y.: Henry Holt & Co., 1923. 113 pp. (Also London: Grant Richards, 1924.)

Selected Poems. N. Y.: Henry Holt & Co., 1923. 143 pp. (Also London: William Heinemann, 1923.)

West-Running Brook. N. Y.: Henry Holt & Co. [1928]. 64 pp.

Collected Poems. N. Y.: Henry Holt & Co., 1930. 349 pp. (Another edition, 1939. 436 pp.)

A Lone Striker. [Borzoi Chapbooks, No. 8.] N. Y.: Alfred A. Knopf, 1933.

A Further Range. N. Y.: Henry Holt & Co., [1936]. 102 pp.

From Snow to Snow. N. Y.: Henry Holt & Co., 1936. 20 pp.

A Witness Tree. N. Y.: Henry Holt & Co., [1942]. 91 pp.

B. SELECTED REFERENCES

CLYMER, W. B. S. & GREEN, C. R. *Robert Frost: A Bibliography.* Amherst, Mass.: Jones Lib., Inc., 1937. 158 pp.

MUNSON, GORHAM B. *Robert Frost. A Study in Sensibility and Good Sense.* [The Murray Hill Biographies.] N. Y.: George H. Doran Co., [1927]. 135 pp.

THOMPSON, LAWRANCE. *Fire and Ice: The Art and Thought of Robert Frost.* N. Y.: Henry Holt & Co., 1942. 241 pp.

THORNTON, RICHARD, ed. *Recognition of Robert Frost.* N. Y.: Henry Holt & Co., 1937. 321 pp.

CARL SANDBURG

A. POETICAL WORKS

In Reckless Ecstasy. [Pamphlet. Galesburg: Asgard Press, 1904.]

Chicago Poems. N. Y.: Henry Holt & Co., 1916. 183 pp.

Cornhuskers. N. Y.: Henry Holt & Co., 1918. 147 pp.

Smoke and Steel. N. Y.: Harcourt, Brace & Co., 1920. 268 pp. (Also London: J. Cape, 1922.)

Slabs of the Sunburnt West. N. Y.: Harcourt, Brace & Co. [1922]. 76 pp.

Selected Poems of Carl Sandburg. Edited by Rebecca West. London: J. Cape, 1926. 287 pp. (Also N. Y.: Harcourt, Brace & Co., [1926].)

Carl Sandburg. [Pamphlet Poets.] N. Y.: Simon & Schuster [1926]. 30 pp.

Good Morning, America. N. Y.: Harcourt, Brace & Co., 1928. 251 pp.

Early Moon. N. Y.: Harcourt, Brace & Co., 1930. 136 pp.

The People, Yes. N. Y.: Harcourt, Brace & Co., 1936. 286 pp.

B. SELECTED REFERENCES

DETZER, KARL. *Carl Sandburg: A Study in Personality and Background.* N. Y.: Harcourt, Brace & Co., 1941. 210 pp.

HANSEN, HARRY, *Midwest Portraits. A Book of Memories and Friendships* (N. Y., 1923), pp. 17-92.

WEIRICK, BRUCE, *From Whitman to Sandburg in American Poetry* (N. Y., 1924), pp. 210-20.

WHIPPLE, T. K., *Spokesmen* (N. Y., 1928), pp. 161-84.

VACHEL LINDSAY

A. POETICAL WORKS

The Tree of Laughing Bells. [Pamphlet. N. Y., 1905.]

God Help Us to Be Brave. [Pamphlet. N. Y., 1908.]

The Last Song of Lucifer. [Pamphlet. N. Y., 1908.]

The Tramp's Excuse and Other Poems. [Springfield, Ill., 1909. 169 pp.]

The Village Magazine. [Privately printed. Springfield, Ill., 1910. 75 pp. (A second number, 1920.)]

Rhymes to Be Traded for Bread. [Privately printed. Springfield, Ill., 1912.]

The Wedding of the Rose and the Lotus. A Poem Written on the Near-Completion of the Panama Canal. . . . Nicholas Vachel Lindsay, Rhymer and Designer, Springfield, Illinois. [1912. 2 pp.]

The Soul of the City Receives the Gift of the Holy Spirit. [Privately printed, Springfield, Ill., 1913. 18 pp.]

General William Booth Enters intc Heaven and Other Poems. N. Y.: M. Kennerley, 1913. 119 pp. (Also London: Chatto & Windus, 1919.)

The Congo and Other Poems. With an Introduction by Harriet Monroe. N. Y.: The Macmillan Co., 1914. 159 pp.

The Chinese Nightingale and Other Poems. N. Y.: The Macmillan Co., 1917. 127 pp.

The Daniel Jazz and Other Poems. London: George Bell & Sons, 1920. 94 pp.

The Golden Whales of California and Other Rhymes in the American Language. N. Y.: The Macmillan Co., 1920. 181 pp.

I Know All This When Gipsy Fiddles Cry. [Pamphlet, San Francisco, 1922.]

Collected Poems. N. Y.: The Macmillan Co., 1923. 390 pp. (Revised and Illustrated Edition, N. Y.: The Macmillan Co., 1925. 464 pp.)

Going-to-the-Sun. N. Y. and London: D. Appleton & Co., 1923. 101 pp.

The Candle in the Cabin. A Weaving together of Script and Singing. N. Y. and London: D. Appleton & Co., 1926. 130 pp.

Going-to-the-Stars. N. Y. and London: D. Appleton & Co., 1926. 102 pp.

Johnny Appleseed and Other Poems. [Children's Classics.] N. Y.: The Macmillan Co., 1928. 144 pp.

Every Soul Is a Circus. N. Y.: The Macmillan Co., 1929. 120 pp.

Selected Poems. With an Introduction by Hazelton Spencer. [Modern Readers' Series.] N. Y.: The Macmillan Co., 1931. 226 pp.

B. SELECTED REFERENCES

GRAHAM, STEPHEN. *Tramping with a Poet in the Rockies.* With Thirty-Eight Emblems by Vernon Hill. N. Y.: D. Appleton & Co., 1922. 279 pp.

LINDSAY, VACHEL. *Adventures while Preaching the Gospel of Beauty.* N. Y.: M. Kennerley, 1914, 186 pp. (Also N. Y.: The Macmillan Co., 1921.)

LINDSAY, VACHEL. *A Handy Guide for Beggars. Especially Those of the Poetic Fraternity. Being Sundry Explorations Made While Afoot and Penniless in Florida, Georgia,* [etc.] [N. Y.]: The Macmillan Co., 1916. 205 pp.

MASTERS, EDGAR LEE. *Vachel Lindsay. A Poet in America.* N. Y.: Charles Scribner's Sons, 1935. 392 pp.

SARA TEASDALE

A. POETICAL WORKS

Sonnets to Duse and Other Poems. Boston: Poet Lore Co., 1907, 44 pp.

Helen of Troy and Other Poems. N. Y. and London: G. P. Putnam's Sons, 1911. 106 pp. (New edition, revised, N. Y.: The Macmillan Co., 1922.)

Rivers to the Sea. N. Y.: The Macmillan Co., 1915. 148 pp.

Love Songs. N. Y.: The Macmillan Co., 1917. 91 pp.

Vignettes of Italy. A Cycle of Nine Songs for High Voice. Music by W. Watts. Boston: Ditson, 1919. 32 pp.

Flame and Shadow. N. Y.: The Macmillan Co., 1920. 144 pp. (Also London: J. Cape, 1924.)

Poems. [*Flame and Shadow, Love Songs, Rivers to the Sea.*] [3 vols.] N. Y.: The Macmillan Co., 1923.

Dark of the Moon. N. Y.: The Macmillan Co., 1926. 92 pp.

Stars To-Night. Verses New and Old for Boys and Girls. N. Y.: The Macmillan Co., 1930. 49 pp.

Country House. [Borzoi Chapbooks, No. 4.] N. Y.: Alfred A. Knopf, 1932.

Strange Victory. N. Y.: The Macmillan Co., 1933. 37 pp.

Collected Poems. N. Y.: The Macmillan Co., 1937. 311 pp.

B. SELECTED REFERENCES

M[ONROE], H[ARRIET], "Sara Teasdale," *Poetry*, XLII (April, 1933), 30-33.

RITTENHOUSE, JESSIE B., "Sara Teasdale," *Bookman*, LXV (May, 1927), 290-95.

T[IETJENS], E[UNICE], "A Singer," *Poetry*, XVII (February, 1921), 272-76.

UNTERMEYER, LOUIS, "Sara Teasdale, 1884-1933," *Sat. Rev. of Lit.*, IX (February 11, 1933), 426.

WILKINSON, MARGUERITE, "Sara Teasdale's Poems," *Forum*, LXV (February, 1921), 229-36.

ELINOR WYLIE

A. POETICAL WORKS

Nets to Catch the Wind. N. Y.: Harcourt, Brace & Co., 1921. 47 pp.

Black Armour. A Book of Poems. N. Y.: Doubleday, Doran & Co., 1923. 77 pp.

Trivial Breath. N. Y.: Alfred A. Knopf, Inc., 1928. 80 pp.

Angels and Earthly Creatures. N. Y.: Alfred A. Knopf, Inc., 1929. 63 pp.

Collected Poems. [With a Foreword by William Rose Benét.] N. Y.: Alfred A. Knopf, Inc., 1932. 318 pp.

B. SELECTED REFERENCES

HOYT, NANCY. *Elinor Wylie. The Portrait of an Unknown Lady.* Indianapolis, Ind.: Bobbs-Merrill Co., 1935. 203 pp.

M[ONROE], H[ARRIET], "Elinor Wylie," *Poetry*, XXX (February, 1929), 266-72.

EZRA POUND

A. POETICAL WORKS

A Lume Spento. Venice, Italy: Antonelli, 1908.

A Quinzaine for This Yule. Being Selected from a Venetian Sketch-Book, "San Trovaso," by Ezra Pound. London: Pollock & Co., 1908. 27 pp.

Personae. London: E. Mathews, 1909. 59 pp.

Exultations. London: E. Mathews, 1909. 51 pp.

Provença. Poems Selected from *Personae, Exultations, and Canzoniere* of Ezra Pound. Boston: Small, Maynard & Co. [1910]. vi, 84 pp.

Canzoni. London: Elkin Mathews, 1911. viii [52] pp.

Ripostes of Ezra Pound. Whereto Are Appended the Complete Poetical Works of T. E. Hulme. With Prefatory Note. London: Stephen Swift & Co., Ltd., 1912. 64 pp. (Also Boston: Small, Maynard & Co., 1913.)

The Sonnets and Ballate of Guido Cavalcanti. With Translation and Introduction by Ezra Pound. Boston: Small, Maynard & Co. [1912]. 119 pp. (Also London: Stephen Swift & Co., 1912.)

Canzoni and Ripostes of Ezra Pound. . . . London: Elkin Mathews, 1913. 51, 63 pp.

Personae and Exultations. London: Elkin Mathews, 1913. 59, 51 pp.

Cathay. . . . [Translations from the Chinese, from notes by Ernest Fenollosa.] London: Elkin Mathews, 1915. 31 pp.

Certain Noble Plays of Japan: From the Manuscripts of Ernest Fenollosa. Chosen and Finished by Ezra Pound, with an Introduction by William Butler Yeats. Churchtown, Dundrum: Cuala Press, 1916. [50 pp.] (Translations in prose and verse.)

Lustra of Ezra Pound. . . . London: Elkin Mathews, 1916. 115 pp.

Lustra of Ezra Pound, with Earlier Poems. N. Y.: Alfred A. Knopf, 1917. 202 pp.

'Noh' or Accomplishment. A Study of the Classical Stage of Japan. By Ernest Fenollosa and Ezra Pound. London: Macmillan & Co., Ltd., 1916. [268 pp.] (Also N. Y.: Alfred A. Knopf, 1917.) (Some verse translations included.)

Quia Pauper Amavi. London: Egoist Press, 1919. 51 pp.

Hugh Selwyn Mauberley. By E. P. London: The Ovid Press, 1920. 28 pp. (200 copies.)

Umbra. The Early Poems of Ezra Pound. . . . London: Elkin Mathews, 1920. 128 pp.

Poems—1918-21. Including Three Portraits and Four Cantos. N. Y.: Boni & Liveright [1921]. 90 pp.

A Draft of XVI Cantos. Paris: Three Mountains Press, 1925.

Personae. The Collected Poems of Ezra Pound . . . N. Y.: Boni & Liveright, 1926. 231 pp.

A Draft of the Cantos 17-27 of Ezra Pound. Initials by Gladys Hynes. London: John Rodker, 1928. 56 pp. (101 copies.)

Selected Poems. Edited with an Introduction by T. S. Eliot. London: Faber & Gwyer, Ltd., 1928, xxxii, 184 pp.

A Draft of XXX Cantos. Paris: Hours Press, 1930. [154] pp. (Also London: Faber & Faber, Ltd., 1933. Also N. Y., Farrar and Rinehart, Inc., n. d.)

Eleven New Cantos, XXXI-XLI. N. Y.: Farrar & Rinehart [1934]. 56 pp.

Homage to Sextus Propertius. London: Faber & Faber, Ltd., 1934. 35 pp.

Fifth Decad of Cantos. N. Y.: Farrar & Rinehart, 1937. 46 pp.

Selection of Poems. London: Faber & Faber, Ltd., 1940. 80 pp.

Cantos LII-LXXI. Norfolk, Conn.: New Directions, 1940. 167 pp.

B. SELECTED REFERENCES

Amdur, Alice, *The Poetry of Ezra Pound.* Cambridge: Harvard University Press, 1936. 106 pp.

Blackmur, R. P., "Masks of Ezra Pound," *Hound and Horn,* VII (March, 1934), 177-213.

[Eliot, T. S.] *Ezra Pound. His Metric and Poetry.* N. Y.: Alfred A. Knopf, 1917. 31 pp.

Hughes, Glenn, *Imagism and the Imagists* (Stanford University, 1931), pp. 224-50.

Kreymborg, Alfred, *Our Singing Strength* (N. Y., 1929), pp. 334-47.

Leavis, F. R., *New Bearings in English Poetry* (London, 1932), pp. 133-158.

JOHN GOULD FLETCHER

A. POETICAL WORKS

Fire and Wine. London: Grant Richards, 1913. 75 pp.

Fool's Gold. London: Max Goschen, Ltd., 1913. 92 pp.

The Dominant City (1911-12). London: Max Goschen, Ltd., 1913. 75 pp.

The Book of Nature. London: Constable & Co., Ltd., 1913. 108 pp.

Visions of the Evening. London: Erskine MacDonald, 1913. 43 pp.

Irradiations—Sand and Spray. Boston: Houghton Mifflin, 1915. [60 pp.] (Also London: Constable & Co., Ltd., 1915.)

Goblins and Pagodas. Boston: Houghton Mifflin, 1916 [99 pp.] (Also London: Constable & Co., Ltd., 1918.)

Japanese Prints. Imagist Poems . . . Boston: Four Seas Co., 1918. 94 pp.

The Tree of Life. London: Chatto & Windus, 1918. 127 pp. (Also N. Y.: The Macmillan Co., 1918.)

Breakers and Granite. N. Y.: The Macmillan Co., 1921. 163 pp.

Preludes and Symphonies. Boston: Houghton Mifflin, 1922. [60, 99 pp.] (A reprint of *Irradiations—Sand and Spray* and of *Goblins and Pagodas.*)

Parables. With Woodcut Frontispiece by John J. A. Murphy. London: K. Paul, Trench, Trubner & Co., 1925. 143 pp.

Branches of Adam. London: Faber & Gwyer, [1926]. 81 pp.

The Black Rock. London: Faber & Gwyer, 1928. 176 pp.

XXIV Elegies. Santa Fe: Writers' Editions [1935]. 87 pp.

Selected Poems. N. Y.: Farrar & Rinehart, 1938. 237 pp.

South Star. N. Y.: The Macmillan Co., 1941. 117 pp.

B. SELECTED REFERENCES

FLETCHER, JOHN GOULD, *Life Is My Song.* N. Y.: Farrar & Rinehart, 1937. 406 pp. (Autobiography.)

HUGHES, GLENN, *Imagism and the Imagists* (Stanford University, 1931), pp. 125-53.

HILDA DOOLITTLE (H. D.)

A. POETICAL WORKS

Sea Garden. London: Constable & Co., Ltd., 1916. 47 pp. (Also Boston: Houghton Mifflin, 1916.)

Hymen. London: Egoist Press; N. Y.: Henry Holt & Co., 1921. [47 pp.]

Heliodora and Other Poems. London: Jonathan Cape; Boston: Houghton Mifflin. [1924]. 127 pp.

Collected Poems of H. D. N. Y.: Boni & Liveright, 1925. 306 pp.

H. D. [Pamphlet Poets.] N. Y.: Simon & Schuster, 1926. 32 pp.

Hippolytus Temporizes. A Play in Three Acts. Boston: Houghton Mifflin, 1927. 139 pp.

Red Roses for Bronze. Boston: Houghton Mifflin Co., 1931. 148 pp. (Also London: Chatto & Windus, 1931.)

B. SELECTED REFERENCES

Blackmur, R. P., "The Lesser Satisfactions," *Poetry*, XLI (November, 1932), 94-100.

Fairclough, H. R., *The Classics and Our Twentieth-Century Poets* (Stanford University, 1927), pp. 31-36.

Hughes, Glenn, *Imagism and the Imagists* (Stanford University, 1931), pp. 109-25.

Monroe, Harriet, *Poets and Their Art* (N. Y., 1926), pp. 92-100.

ROBINSON JEFFERS

A. POETICAL WORKS

Flagons and Apples. Los Angeles: Grafton Pub. Corp., 1912. 46 pp.

Californians. N. Y.: The Macmillan Co., 1916. 217 pp.

Tamar and Other Poems. N. Y.: Peter G. Boyle, 1924. 127 pp.

Roan Stallion, Tamar, and Other Poems. N. Y.: Boni & Liveright, 1925. 253 pp.

The Woman at Point Sur. N. Y.: Boni & Liveright, 1927. 175 pp.

Cawdor and Other Poems. N. Y.: Horace Liveright, Inc., 1928. 160 pp.

Dear Judas and Other Poems. N. Y.: Horace Liveright, Inc., 1929. 129 pp.

Descent to the Dead. N. Y.: Random House, Inc., 1931. 29 pp.

Thurso's Landing and Other Poems. N. Y.: Horace Liveright, Inc., 1932. 147 pp.

Give Your Heart to the Hawks and Other Poems. N. Y.: Random House, Inc., 1933. 199 pp.

Solstice and Other Poems. N. Y.: Random House, Inc., 1935. 151 pp.

Such Counsels You Gave to Me and Other Poems. N. Y.: Random House, Inc., 1937. 129 pp.

The Selected Poetry of Robinson Jeffers. N. Y.: Random House, Inc., 1938. 622 pp.

Two Consolations. With an Excerpt from Una Jeffers' English Journal. San Mateo, Cal.: Quercus Press, 1940. 6 pp.

Be Angry at the Sun. N. Y.: Random House, Inc., 1941. 156 pp.

B. SELECTED REFERENCES

ADAMIC, LOUIS. *Robinson Jeffers. A Portrait.* [University of Washington Chapbooks, No. 27.] Seattle, Washington: University of Washington Bookstore, 1929. 35 pp.

ALBERTS, S. S. *A Bibliography of the Works of Robinson Jeffers.* N. Y.: Random House, Inc., 1933, xvi, 262 pp. (487 copies.)

POWELL, LAWRENCE CLARK. *Robinson Jeffers. The Man and His Work.* Pasadena, Cal.: San Pasqual Press, 1940. 222 pp.

STERLING, GEORGE. *Robinson Jeffers: The Man and the Artist.* N. Y.: Boni & Liveright, 1926. 40 pp.

JOHN CROWE RANSOM

POETICAL WORKS

Poems about God. N. Y.: Henry Holt & Co., 1919. 76 pp.

Chills and Fever. N. Y.: Alfred A. Knopf, Inc., 1924. 95 pp.

Two Gentlemen in Bonds. N. Y.: Alfred A. Knopf, Inc., 1927. 87 pp.

T. S. ELIOT

A. POETICAL WORKS

Prufrock and Other Observations. London: Egoist Press, Inc., 1917. 40 pp.

Poems. N. Y.: Alfred Knopf, Inc., 1920. 63 pp.

Ara Vus Prec. [London]: Ovid Press [1920]. 54 pp.

The Waste Land. N. Y.: Boni & Liveright, 1922. 64 pp. (Also Richmond, Surrey: L. & V. Woolf, 1923. 35 pp.)

Poems, 1909-1925. London: Faber & Gwyer, Ltd., 1926. 98 pp.

Journey of the Magi. [Ariel Poems, No. 8.] London: Faber & Gwyer, Ltd. [1927]. 4 pp.

A Song of Simeon. [Ariel Poems, No. 16.] London: Faber & Gwyer, Ltd. [1928]. 4 pp.

Animula. [Ariel Poems, No. 23.] London: Faber & Faber, Ltd., 1929. [4 pp.]

Ash-Wednesday. London: Faber & Faber, Ltd., 1930. 29 pp. (Also N. Y.: G. P. Putnam's Sons, 1930.)

Marina. [Ariel Poems, No. 29.] London: Faber & Faber, Ltd., 1930. [11 pp.]

Triumphal March. [Ariel Poems, No. 35.] London: Faber & Faber, Ltd., 1931. 4 pp.

Sweeney Agonistes. Fragments of an Aristophanic Melodrama. London: Faber & Faber, Ltd., 1932. 31 pp.

The Rock. A Pageant Play. London: Faber & Faber, Ltd., 1934. 86 pp. (In prose and verse.)

Murder in the Cathedral. N. Y.: Harcourt, Brace & Co., 1935. 87 pp.

Collected Poems: 1909-1935. N.Y.: Harcourt, Brace & Co., 1936. 220 pp.

The Family Reunion. N. Y.: Harcourt, Brace & Co., 1939. 131 pp.

Old Possum's Book of Practical Cats. N. Y.: Harcourt, Brace & Co., 1939. 46 pp.

East Coker. London: Faber & Faber, Ltd., 1940. 15 pp.

Later Poems: 1925-35. London: Faber & Faber, Ltd., 1941. 160 pp.

Burnt Norton. London: Faber & Faber, Ltd., 1941. 16 pp.

B. SELECTED REFERENCES

McGreevy, Thomas. *Thomas Stearns Eliot.* A Study. London: Chatto & Windus, 1931. 71 pp.

Matthiessen, F. O. *The Achievement of T. S. Eliot.* Boston: Houghton Mifflin Co., 1935. xvi [160] pp.

Williamson, George. *The Talent of T. S. Eliot.* [University of Washington Chapbooks, No. 32.] Seattle, Washington: University of Washington Bookstore [1930]. 37 pp.

WILLIAMSON, HUGH ROSS. *The Poetry of T. S. Eliot*. London: Hodder & Stoughton, Ltd., 1932. 187 pp.

WILSON, EDMUND, *Axel's Castle* (N. Y., 1931), pp. 93-132.

CONRAD AIKEN

A. POETICAL WORKS

Earth Triumphant and Other Tales in Verse. N. Y.: The Macmillan Co., 1914, ix, 219 pp.

Turns and Movies and Other Tales in Verse. Boston: Houghton Mifflin, 1916. [91 pp.] (Also London: Constable & Co., 1916.)

The Jig of Forslin. A Symphony. Boston: Four Seas Co., 1916. 127 pp. (Also London: M. Secker, 1921. 99 pp.)

Nocturne of Remembered Spring and Other Poems. Boston: Four Seas Co., 1917. 140 pp. (Also London: M. Secker, 1921. 122 pp.)

The Charnel Rose, Senlin: A Biography, and Other Poems. Boston: Four Seas Co., 1918. 156 pp.

The House of Dust. A Symphony. Boston: Four Seas Co., 1920. 148 pp.

Punch: the Immortal Liar. Documents in His History. N. Y.: Alfred A. Knopf, 1921. 80 pp. (Also London: M. Secker, 1921. 95 pp.)

Priapus and the Pool. Cambridge: Dunster House, 1922 [66 pp.] (425 copies.)

The Pilgrimage of Festus. N. Y.: Alfred A. Knopf, 1923. 75 pp. (Also London: M. Secker, 1924.)

Priapus and the Pool and Other Poems. N. Y.: Boni & Liveright, 1925. 151 pp.

Senlin: a Biography. London: Hogarth Press, 1925. 36 pp.

Conrad Aiken . . . [Pamphlet Poets.] N. Y.: Simon & Schuster [1927]. 31 pp.

Selected Poems. N. Y.: Charles Scribner's Sons, 1929. xiii, 361 pp.

John Deth, a Metaphysical Legend, and Other Poems. N. Y.: Charles Scribner's Sons, 1930. 140 pp.

The Coming forth by Day of Osiris Jones. N. Y.: Charles Scribner's Sons, 1931. 44 pp.

Preludes for Memnon. N. Y.: Charles Scribner's Sons, 1931. 112 pp.

Prelude, a Poem. [Equinox Quartos, No. 4.] N. Y.: Equinox Coöperative Press, 1932. 4 pp.

Landscape West of Eden. London: J. M. Dent & Sons, Ltd. [1934]. 40 pp. (Also N. Y.: Charles Scribner's Sons, 1935.)

Time in the Rock. N. Y.: Charles Scribner's Sons, 1936. xii, 138 pp.

And in the Human Heart. N. Y.: Duell, Sloan & Pearce, Inc., 1940. 87 pp.

B. SELECTED REFERENCES

AIKEN, CONRAD. *Scepticisms. Notes on Contemporary Poetry.* N. Y.: Alfred A. Knopf, 1919, 305 pp. (Of some autobiographical value; incidentally throws light on Aiken's own poetry.)

PETERSON, HOUSTON. *The Melody of Chaos.* N. Y.: Longmans, Green & Co., 1931. 280 pp.

EDNA ST. VINCENT MILLAY

A. POETICAL WORKS

Renascence and Other Poems. N. Y.: Mitchell Kennerley, 1917. 73 pp. (Also N. Y. and London: Harper & Brothers [1917].)

Aria da Capo. A Play in One Act. N. Y.: D. Appleton & Co., 1920. 51 pp. (Also N. Y. and London: Harper & Brothers [1920].)

A Few Figs from Thistles. Poems and Four Sonnets. N. Y.: Frank Shay, 1920. 20 pp. (Also N. Y. and London: Harper & Brothers, 1923.)

The Lamp and the Bell. A Drama in Five Acts. N. Y.: Frank Shay, 1921. 71 pp. (Also N. Y. and London: Harper & Brothers [1923].)

Second April. N. Y.: Mitchell Kennerley, 1921. 112 pp. (Also N. Y. and London: Harper & Brothers [1921].)

Two Slatterns and a King. A Moral Interlude. [Stewart Kidd Modern Plays.] Cincinnati: Stewart Kidd Co. [1921]. 18 pp.

The Ballad of the Harp-Weaver. N. Y.: Frank Shay, 1922. 10 pp.

The Harp-Weaver and Other Poems. N. Y. and London: Harper & Brothers, 1923. 93 pp. (Also London: M. Secker, 1924.)

Poems. London: Martin Secker, 1923. [146 pp.]

Three Plays. [*Two Slatterns and a King, Aria da Capo, The Lamp and the Bell.*] N. Y. and London: Harper & Brothers, 1926. 147 pp. (Also London: J. Cape, 1927.)

Edna St. Vincent Millay. [Pamphlet Poets.] N. Y.: Simon & Schuster, [1927]. 31 pp.

The King's Henchman. A Play in Three Acts. N. Y. and London: Harper & Brothers, 1927. [132 pp.] (Also London: J. Cape, 1927.)

The Buck in the Snow and Other Poems. N. Y. and London: Harper & Brothers, 1928. 69 pp.

Poems. Selected for Young People. N. Y.: Harper & Bros., 1929. 113 pp.

Fatal Interview. Sonnets. N. Y.: Harper & Bros., 1931. 52 pp.

The Princess Marries the Page. A Play in One Act. N. Y.: Harper & Bros., 1932. 50 pp.

Wine from These Grapes. N. Y.: Harper & Bros., 1934. 91 pp.

Conversation at Midnight. N. Y.: Harper & Brothers, 1937. 126 pp.

Huntsman, What Quarry? N. Y.: Harper & Brothers, 1939. 94 pp.

There Are No Islands Any More. N. Y.: Harper & Brothers, 1940. 10 pp.

Make Bright the Arrows. N. Y.: Harper & Brothers, 1940. 65 pp.

Collected Sonnets. N. Y.: Harper & Brothers, 1941. 161 pp.

B. SELECTED REFERENCES

Atkins, Elizabeth. *Edna St. Vincent Milley and Her Times.* Chicago: University of Chicago Press, 1936. 266 pp.

Yost, K. *A Bibliography of the Works of Edna St. Vincent Millay.* N. Y.: Harper & Brothers, 1937. 248 pp.

ARCHIBALD MacLEISH

POETICAL WORKS

Tower of Ivory. New Haven, Conn.: Yale University Press, 1917. 71 pp.

The Happy Marriage and Other Poems. Boston: Houghton Mifflin Co., 1924. 80 pp.

The Pot of Earth. Boston: Houghton Mifflin Co., 1925. 44 pp.

Nobodaddy. A Play. Cambridge: Dunster House Bookshop, 1926. 90 pp.

Streets in the Moon. Boston: Houghton Mifflin Co., 1926. 101 pp.

The Hamlet of A. MacLeish. Boston: Houghton Mifflin Co., 1928. 45 pp.

New Found Land. Boston: Houghton Mifflin Co., 1930. 54 pp.

Before March. [Borzoi Chapbooks, No. 3.] N. Y.: Alfred A. Knopf, 1932. 8 pp.

Conquistador. Boston: Houghton Mifflin Co., 1932. 114 pp.

Frescoes for Mr. Rockefeller's City. [John Day Pamphlets, No. 29.] N. Y.: John Day Co., Inc., 1933. 28 pp.

Poems, 1924-1933. Boston: Houghton Mifflin Co., 1933. 304 pp.

Panic. A Play in Verse. Boston: Houghton Mifflin Co., 1935. 102 pp.

Public Speech. N. Y.: Farrar & Rinehart, Inc., 1936. 32 pp.

The Fall of the City. A Verse Play for Radio. N. Y.: Farrar & Rinehart, Inc., 1937. 33 pp.

Air Raid. A Verse Play for Radio. N. Y.: Farrar & Rinehart, Inc., 1938. 36 pp.

Land of the Free. (Photographs Illustrated by Verse.) N. Y.: Harcourt, Brace & Co., 1938. 93 pp.

America Was Promises. N. Y.: Duell, Sloan & Pearce, 1939. 20 pp.

E. E. CUMMINGS

A. POETICAL WORKS

Tulips and Chimneys. N. Y.: Thomas Seltzer, Inc., 1923. 125 pp.

XLI Poems. N. Y.: Dial Press, 1925. 54 pp.

is 5. N. Y.: Boni & Liveright, Inc., 1926. 115 pp.

W[*viva*]. N. Y.: Liveright Pub. Corp., 1931. 70 pp.

No Thanks. Mt. Vernon, N. Y.: Golden Eagle Press, 1935. 77 pp.

1/20: Poems. London: Stanley Nott, Ltd., 1937. 20 pp.

Collected Poems. N. Y.: Harcourt, Brace & Co., 1938. 332 pp.

Fifty Poems. N. Y.: Duell, Sloan & Pearce, Inc., 1940. 110 pp.

B. SELECTED REFERENCES

HAYAKAWA, S. I., "Is Indeed 5," *Poetry*, LII (August, 1938), 284-92.

LESEMANN, MAURICE, "The Poetry of E. E. Cummings," *Poetry*, XXIX (Dec., 1926), 164-70.

TATE, ALLEN, "Personal Convention," *Poetry*, XXXIX (March, 1932), 332-38.

HORACE GREGORY

POETICAL WORKS

Chelsea Rooming House. N. Y.: Covici, Friede, Inc., 1930. 65 pp.

No Retreat. N. Y.: Harcourt, Brace & Co., Inc., 1933. 51 pp.

A Wreath for Margery. [Poetry Series, Pamphlet 2.] N. Y.: Modern Editions Press, 1933.

Chorus for Survival. N. Y.: Covici, Friede, Inc., 1935. 127 pp.

Poems: 1930-1940. N. Y.: Harcourt, Brace & Co., Inc., 1941. 163 pp.

HART CRANE

A. POETICAL WORKS

White Buildings. With an Introduction by Allen Tate. N. Y.: Boni & Liveright, 1926. 58 pp.

The Bridge. N. Y.: Liveright Pub. Corp., 1930. 82 pp.

Collected Poems. With an Introduction by Waldo Frank. N. Y.: Liveright Pub. Corp., 1933. 179 pp.

B. SELECTED REFERENCES

COWLEY, MALCOLM, "A Preface to Hart Crane," *New Republic*, LXII (Ap. 23, 1930), 276-77.

HORTON, PHILIP, *Hart Crane. The Life of an American Poet*. N. Y.: W. W. Norton & Co., Inc., 1937. 352 pp.

TATE, ALLEN, "Hart Crane and the American Mind," *Poetry*, XL (July, 1932), 210-16.

KENNETH FEARING

A. POETICAL WORKS

Angel Arms. N. Y.: Coward-McCann, Inc., 1929. 64 pp.

Poems. With an Introduction by Edward Dahlberg. N. Y.: Dynamo Press, 1935. 62 pp.

Dead Reckoning. A Book of Poetry. N. Y.: Random House, 1938. 56 pp.

Collected Poems. N. Y.: Random House, 1940. 149 pp.

B. SELECTED REFERENCES

KEES, WELDON, "Fearing's Collected Poems," *Poetry*, LVII (January, 1941), 264-70.

WILSON, T. C., "The Real Thing," *Poetry*, LIV (April, 1939), 26-29.

Indexes

Index of Authors

Index of Titles and First Lines

Titles of poems are set in italic, and first lines in ordinary roman type.